Marketing Associations and Job Postings Online

Ad Council	www.adcouncil.org
Advertising Internships	newsline.byu.edu/comms/internships/advertising.html
Advertising Media Internet Center	www.amic.com
Advertising Research Foundation	www.arfsite.org
American Advertising Federation	www.aaf.org
American Marketing Association	www.ama.org
America's Employers	www.americasemployers.com
America's Job Bank	www.ajb.dni.us
Analytic Recruiting, Inc.	www.analyticrecruiting.com
Best Jobs USA	www.bestjobsusa.com
Business Marketing Association	www.marketing.org
Career Mart	www.careermart.com
Career Mosaic	www.careermosaic.com
CareerWeb	www.cweb.com
College Grad Job Hunter	collegegrad.com
Creative Central	www.creativecentral.com
Direct Marketing Association	www.the-dma.org
Direct Marketing World: Job Center	dm.com/jobcenter/jobs.html
4Work	www.4work.com
Head Hunter	www.headhunter.net
Healthcare Marketing Jobs	www.strategichealthcare.com/jobs.html
Hospitality Sales and Marketing	www.hsmai.org
HotJobs.com	www.hotjobs.com
International Marketing Job Site	www.job-sites.com/intl/injobs.htm
JobNET	www.jobnet.com
JobOptions	www.joboptions.com
JOBTRAK	www.jobtrak.com
JobWeb	www.jobweb.org
Marketing Dreamjobs	www.rosengren.net/marketingjob.htm
MarketingJobs	www.marketingjobs.com
Marketing Jobs and Careers	www.swan.ac.uk/ebms/market/mkjobs.htm
Marketing Jobs for Women	www.womcom.org/marketing
Marketing Research Association	www.mra-net.org
Medical Marketing Association	www.mmanet.org
Monster Board	www.monster.com
National Association of Sales Professionals	www.nasp.org
NationJob	www.nationjob.com/marketing
New York AMA Job Bank	www.nyama.org/mkjobs.htm
Robert Half	www.roberthalf.com
Sales/Marketing Jobs	www.snellingusa.com/salejobs.html
TOPjobs	www.topjobsusa.com
Wall Street Journal Careers	careers.wsj.com

Marketing
BEST PRACTICES

Marketing
BEST PRACTICES

Michael R. Czinkota
Georgetown University

Peter R. Dickson
University of Wisconsin–Madison

Patrick Dunne
Texas Tech University

Abbie Griffin
University of Illinois–Urbana

K. Douglas Hoffman
Colorado State University

Michael D. Hutt
Arizona State University

John H. Lindgren, Jr.
University of Virginia

Robert F. Lusch
University of Oklahoma

Ilkka A. Ronkainen
Georgetown University

Bert Rosenbloom
Drexel University

Jagdish N. Sheth
Emory University

Terence A. Shimp
University of South Carolina

Judy A. Siguaw
Cornell University

Penny M. Simpson
Northwestern State University of Louisiana

Thomas W. Speh
Miami University–Ohio

Joel E. Urbany
University of Notre Dame

THE DRYDEN PRESS
Harcourt College Publishers

Fort Worth Philadelphia San Diego New York Orlando Austin San Antonio
Toronto Montreal London Sydney Tokyo

Publisher: Michael Roche
Acquisitions Editor: Bill Schoof
Executive Marketing Strategist: Lisé Johnson
Development Editor: Tracy Morse
Project Editor: Rebecca Dodson
Production Manager: Lois West
Art Director: Scott Baker
Picture and Literary Rights Editor: Linda Blundell

Cover Design: Bill Brammer Design

ISBN: 0-03-021109-3

Library of Congress Catalog Card Number: 99-74242

Address for Domestic Orders
The Dryden Press, 6277 Sea Harbor Drive, Orlando, FL 32887-6777
800-782-4479

Address for International Orders
International Customer Service
The Dryden Press, 6277 Sea Harbor Drive, Orlando, FL 32887-6777
407-345-3800
(fax) 407-345-4060
(e-mail) hbintl@harcourtbrace.com

Address for Editorial Correspondence
The Dryden Press, 301 Commerce Street, Suite 3700, Fort Worth, TX 76102

Web Site Address
http://www.hbcollege.com

THE DRYDEN PRESS, DRYDEN, and the DP LOGO are registered trademarks of Harcourt College Publishers.

Printed in the United States of America

0 1 2 3 4 5 6 7 8 9   048   9 8 7 6 5 4 3 2 1

The Dryden Press
Harcourt College Publishers

The Dryden Press Series in Marketing

To the students of Marketing—
past, present, and future:

It is our collective wish that this text play some role toward
improving marketing practice throughout the 21st century.

—The *Best Practices* Author Team

PREFACE

NOTES FROM THE *BEST PRACTICES* AUTHOR TEAM

In a market full of traditional and established principles of marketing textbooks, there are at least 16 good reasons to take notice of the intriguing approach taken by *Marketing: Best Practices*. This project combines the expertise of 16 leading marketers into one principles text. Each chapter is penned by an authority from a particular field of marketing. The end result is a principles text that offers a sense of passion and added insight in every chapter that is not found in customary principles of marketing textbooks.

The *Best Practices* author team consists of current Dryden Press textbook authors and selected individuals who are specialists in their respective fields. *Marketing: Best Practices* allowed us as authors to showcase our areas of expertise for the principles market. As a result, *Marketing: Best Practices* covers the latest issues and topics from the field while equipping students with a solid foundation in marketing basics. The *Best Practices* author team and their respective areas of specialization are as follows:

Introduction to Marketing	Peter R. Dickson, *University of Wisconsin–Madison*
The Marketing Environment and Social Responsibility	Peter R. Dickson, *University of Wisconsin–Madison*
International Marketing	Michael R. Czinkota, *Georgetown University*
	Ilkka A. Ronkainen, *Georgetown University*
Marketing Research and Information Systems	Peter R. Dickson, *University of Wisconsin–Madison*
Consumer Behavior	Jagdish N. Sheth, *Emory University*
Business-to-Business Marketing	Michael D. Hutt, *Arizona State University*
	Thomas W. Speh, *Miami University–Ohio*
Market Segmentation and Target Markets	Penny M. Simpson, *Northwestern State University of Louisiana*
Product Decisions and Marketing's Role in New Product Development	Abbie Griffin, *University of Illinois, Urbana–Champaign*
Services Marketing	K. Douglas Hoffman, *Colorado State University*
Marketing Channels and Distribution	Bert Rosenbloom, *Drexel University*
Retailing and Wholesaling	Patrick Dunne, *Texas Tech University* Robert F. Lusch, *University of Oklahoma*
Integrated Marketing Communications: Advertising, Promotions, and Other Tools	Terence A. Shimp, *University of South Carolina*

Personal Selling and Sales Management	Judy A. Siguaw, *Cornell University*
Pricing Strategies and Determination	Joel E. Urbany, *University of Notre Dame*
Marketing on the Internet	John H. Lindgren, Jr., *University of Virginia*

If we may say so ourselves, the *Best Practices* Author Team is an interesting group of individuals. As a group, the team accounts for more than 362 years of teaching experience at 62 universities, earning 39 teaching awards. Writing is this groups' forté—throughout our collective careers, the *Best Practices* author team has published 112 books and more than 942 articles. As a group, we are genuinely excited to be collaborating with one another and to have the opportunity to influence, educate, and challenge students of marketing. As the dedication to the book indicates, we sincerely wish to make an impact on improving the practice of marketing.

NOTES FROM THE PUBLISHER

16 Experts, One Voice

While *Marketing: Best Practices* includes insight from 16 marketing experts, it offers a single, uniform voice. In addition to his chapter on services marketing, Dr. Doug Hoffman served as consulting editor on the project, enabling this innovative text to have the valued expertise of many but the succinct voice of one.

Since the onset of the project, the publisher, the authors, and the editorial and marketing teams have been committed to the highest level of quality possible. And achieving that uncompromising quality required a very thorough writing, editing, and review process.

As a result of these efforts, each chapter is consistent in format and pedagogy, the writing level is uniform, topics are linked throughout the text, and the copy maintains a lively, energetic tone. However, consistency was not achieved at the expense of content or the authors' individual personalities. Each chapter is purposely a true reflection of its author's personal style and individual marketing expertise.

Real-World Emphasis

Students receive "an insider's view" of marketing issues throughout the text, as the authors relate myriad firsthand accounts from their personal experiences in consulting and research. Readers gain additional insight into real-world marketing practice through experiential exercises, leadership applications, time-management training, career development, cases, and much more. The text and package alike have a strong emphasis on careers, giving students insight into the marketing opportunities available after graduation. For example, each chapter features a *Careers in Marketing* box spotlighting successful individuals—former students and personal acquaintances of the authors—in their various career paths. In addition, Dryden's *Discovering Your Marketing Career* CD-ROM is integrated with the video series accompanying the text.

Technologically Focused

A technology focus is integrated throughout the text and package, as well. A unique Chapter 15 is devoted to Marketing on the Internet. In addition, *Marketing Technologies* boxes are featured in each chapter, integrating chapter concepts with Internet applications and exercises. Web addresses of companies highlighted in text examples are included throughout, and Internet exercises are included in the end-of-chapter material. In addition, the text includes its own comprehensive, interactive Web site:

http://www.dryden.com/marketing/principles.html

SUPPORT MATERIALS: A POWERHOUSE PACKAGE

Marketing: Best Practices combines a collection of the strongest names in the market with one of the most innovative and comprehensive packages available. In Dryden tradition, this expansive resource is replete with teaching tools helpful to instructors at all levels of experience, as well as a plethora of insightful, interactive learning tools for students.

Customized Instructor's Manual

Designed to offer support for novice instructors and marketing veterans alike, this comprehensive *Instructor's Manual* includes key term definitions, learning objectives, lecture outlines, answers to critical-thinking questions, answers to the end-of-chapter review questions, teaching notes for the Internet exercises, and answers to the chapter case questions. To ensure quality, each author was individually responsible for the *IM* chapter that corresponds with his or her text material.

Test Bank

Thoroughly reviewed for accuracy, the *Test Bank* includes approximately 3,000 true/false, multiple-choice, short-answer, and essay questions. To ensure the accuracy of quality of the questions, each author was responsible for the *Test Bank* questions for his or her corresponding text chapter. In addition, the *Test Bank* has been reviewed and checked for accuracy by Davis Folsom (University of South Carolina–Aiken), who is also the author of the *Study Guide*. The test questions are tied directly to chapter learning objectives, have corresponding page references, and each question is rated according to its level of difficulty.

Computerized Test Bank

Dryden's newest offering—ExaMaster 99—is a cross-platform program available on CD-ROM that works with the latest versions of Macintosh, Windows, and Windows NT operating systems. ExaMaster 99 includes online testing capabilities, a grade book, and much more.

Comprehensive Study Guide

Designed to enhance student understanding and provide additional practice application of chapter content, this comprehensive learning tool includes chapter outlines, experiential exercises, self-quizzes, matching exercises for key terms and concepts, multiple-choice review questions, Internet application problems, marketing plan exercises, and solutions to study questions. The *Study Guide* was written by Davis Folsom, University of South Carolina–Aiken. Also included for each chapter are Text Maps,™ contributed by Ruth Taylor of Southwest Texas State University.

Full-Color Transparencies

Over 125 full-color overhead transparency acetates have been created from striking figures in the text.

Cutting-Edge Video Package

Twenty videos are provided to give students insight into how real-world companies apply chapter concepts to their own marketing operations. Videos feature such companies as Yahoo!, Andersen Consulting, Tommy Hilfiger, Kmart, and many others. Videos include interviews with top business executives and successful entrepreneurs. Integrated video cases, found at the back of the textbook, create an even stronger link between the video package and the text.

The videos illustrate such themes as quality, customer satisfaction, brand equity, relationship marketing, teamwork, product revitalization, regulation, and ethics. Additionally, many segments conclude with career profiles of key marketing managers and executives, who discuss their career paths, marketing successes, key managerial skills, the role of marketing, as well as offer personal advice to students entering the field. The video career profiles are coordinated with Dryden's *Discovering Your Marketing Career* CD-ROM.

Incredible PowerPoint Instructor and Student CD-ROMs

Created by Jack Lindgren of the University of Virginia, *PowerPoint Instructor* multimedia presentation brings lectures and classroom discussions to life. Organized by chapter, this extremely user-friendly program enables instructors to custom create their own multimedia classroom presentations, using overhead transparencies, figures, tables, graphs, ads, and more from the text, *as well as video segments and additional material from outside sources.*

Instructors can use the approximate 75 to 125 slides per chapter as is, or expand and modify each chapter's program for individual classes. The software is available in two formats: PowerPoint 95 and PowerPoint 97. The PowerPoint 97 version allows instructors to simply click on links to move from the PowerPoint presentation to Web sites.

The *Student CD-ROM* is an interactive, multimedia supplement. It puts chapter concepts and issues into action, driving home text topics with its full-color ads, figures, graphs, and other text material, video clips, and outside material. In addition, a skeletal marketing plan is included.

Marketing Simulation Game

This innovative Windows-based computer simulation by Robert Schaffer (California Polytechnic State University) offers a traditional simulation game with some new twists. The underlying model is based on the digital camera industry and will help students develop their marketing skills within the framework of an evolving product life cycle. Large classes can play *The Marketing Game* in solitaire mode, with each student competing against computer-generated opponents. This option greatly reduces classroom game management problems and allows instructors to provide their students with a computer simulation experience that they would otherwise be unable to implement. Because of its link to the Internet, there also is an option to allow competitive play between *teams of students at different universities.*

Discovering Your Marketing Career CD

This expanded version of Eric Sandburg's popular Marketing Career Design Software enables students to explore marketing career opportunities based on their own personal interests and skills. Along with the traditional software's features—self-assessment tools, résumé and letter-writing assistance—this newly expanded CD adds videos, interviews with marketing professionals, and an interactive student study component integrated with chapter material.

In addition, a comprehensive study program and tutorial written in Windows allows students to learn key words and concepts and test their knowledge of each chapter through matching quizzes, true/false tests, and multiple-choice tests. A glossary, chapter outlines, and chapter summaries are included as well. This unique CD-ROM program reinforces text material, provides practical application of chapter concepts, and gives students a real-world taste of actual careers and career paths in today's market.

Best Practices Web Site

Developed by Eric Sandburg, this innovative Web site (**http://www.dryden.com/marketing/principles.html**) is an incredible resource for instructors and students alike. The *Best Practices* Web site gives students hands-on experience using the Internet as a marketing tool. For example, through the online exercises, students can review chapter material and explore the vast resources available online, while a reading room section links users to business journals, daily newspapers, magazines, and marketing publications across the country and around the world.

An online case library includes an extra collection of cases of varying lengths and levels. In addition, the site links instructors to a wealth of teaching resources, bibliographies of articles related to text material, ideas on incorporating the Internet into the classroom, and much more. The resources and Internet-based interactive exercises are organized by topic.

AUTHOR TEAM ACKNOWLEDGEMENTS

Marketing: Best Practices greatly benefited from the quality of reviews provided by numerous colleagues representing a variety of academic institutions. In particular, the *Best Practices* author team is very grateful to the following colleagues for giving their time and insightful direction:

Tim Aurand	*Northern Illinois University*
Arni Authorsson	*College of St. Francis*
Mike Barone	*Iowa State University*
Mark Bennion	*Bowling Green University*
Edward Bond	*Bradley University*
Bill Carner	*University of Texas–Austin*

Sean Dwyer	*Louisiana Tech University*
Dave Fallin	*Kansas State University*
Dwayne Gremler	*University of Idaho*
Steve Grove	*Clemson University*
Braxton Hinchey	*University of Massachusetts–Lowell*
Earl Honeycutt	*Old Dominion University*
Ina Midkiff	*Austin Community College*
Terry Paul	*Ohio State University*
Tom Pritchett	*Kennesaw State University*
Glen Reicken	*East Tennessee State University*
Alan Sawyer	*University of Florida*
Don Schreiber	*Baylor University*
Jane Sojka	*Ohio University*
Ruth Taylor	*Southwest Texas State University*
Joyce Young	*Indiana State University*

Jagdish Sheth would also especially like to thank Dr. Balaji Krishnan, University of Memphis, for the invaluable support provided in the preparation of early versions of the "Consumer Behavior" chapter and related support materials.

We would also like to thank the good folks at The Dryden Press, many of whom we have had the pleasure of knowing for many years through our other text projects. Special thanks to Lisé Johnson, Executive Marketing Strategist, and Bill Schoof, Senior Acquisitions Editor, for initiating the project and navigating it through the parent company of Harcourt College Publishers. Bill and Lisé, thank you for generating and maintaining the level of enthusiasm associated with this project throughout the entire process.

We would especially like to thank Tracy Morse who acted as Senior Developmental Editor. Tracy, words are inadequate to express our gratitude for your monumental efforts in coordinating an author team of 16 academics. It is often said that leading academics is a lot like attempting to herd a bunch of cats. Tracy can now attest to that fact. Thank you, Tracy!

Additional thanks are extended to Rebecca Dodson, Project Editor; Lois West, Production Manager; Scott Baker, Art Director; Bill Brammer, Designer; Mark Humphries, Photographer; and Marcia Masenda, Marketing Assistant for putting the project together… no small task! A number of other good people focused on putting together the *Instructor's Manual, Test Bank, Study Guide,* and *Video Cases.* We would like to thank Dona Hightower, Martin Meyers, Davis Folsom, Ruth Taylor, Ken Lawrence, and Reshma Shah for their support and dedication to the project.

We would also like to thank the Dryden sales force for supporting this unique project and stirring up the worldwide principles of marketing market. We truly appreciate your efforts in bringing this package to the marketplace and offer our assistance in support of your efforts.

This project has generated a great deal of interest in the academic and publishing communities. We thank the parent company of Harcourt College Publishers for wholeheartedly and enthusiastically accepting and supporting the project.

Finally, each of us would like to thank our families, friends, and colleagues for their support. Writing a text is a time-consuming experience that often takes us away from those who mean the most in our lives. Thank you for your understanding, patience, and encouragement.

CONTENTS IN BRIEF

TABLE OF CONTENTS

PART TWO
Understanding the Market 101

PART THREE
Product 247

PART SIX
Pricing 497

PART SEVEN
The Future of Marketing

Part I

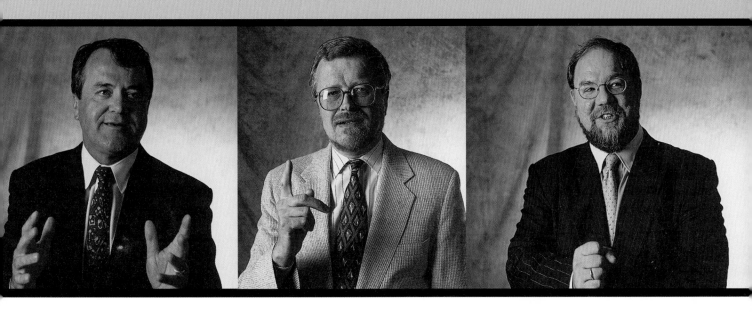

Introduction—
Marketing
Environment

Chapter I

Introduction to Marketing

Peter R. Dickson
University of
Wisconsin–Madison

Arthur C. Nielsen Jr., Chair of Marketing Research, University of Wisconsin-Madison. Dr. Dickson earned his Ph.D. at the University of Florida and his undergraduate degrees, at the University of Otago, New Zealand. He has served on the editorial board of several publications, including *Journal of Business Research*, *Journal of Marketing*, and *Marketing Letters*. He is the author of *Marketing Management*, published by The Dryden Press.
Dr. Dickson helped found the Business School at the University of Waikato where he taught for seven years. After receiving a Fulbright-Hays Bicentennial scholarship and completing his Ph.D. at the University of Florida, he taught for 14 years at The Ohio State University where he became the Crane Professor of Strategic Marketing and an adjunct professor of Industrial Design.

In its most basic form, marketing is about identifying customer needs and developing products that satisfy those needs. Customer needs constantly change with each new generation. In the United States, the Baby Boomers and Generation Xers have made their mark on society, and business has responded to their needs and wants by developing a multitude of product selections. Ladies and gentlemen, it is time to meet the next generation—Generation Y.[1]

Who Is Generation Y?

Generation Y members (also referred to as the "Millenium Generation" and "Echo Boomers") are the offspring of Baby Boomers, and were born between 1979 and 1994. The impact of Generation Y on marketing and business in general is undeniable. The mere size of Generation Y is awe inspiring. Generation Y (60 million) is more than three times the size of Generation X (17 million) and rivals the size of the Baby Boom generation (72 million). More important to marketers is that Generation Y will soon rival Baby Boomers in buying clout. Clearly, Generation Y is unlike any generation marketers have experienced before. (See Cool Stuff! on page 4.) For instance, one in three Ys is *not* Caucasian; one in four lives in a single-parent household; and three of four have working mothers. In contrast to previous generations, Gen Ys have considerable financial responsibility (one in nine high school students today have their own credit cards) and they are heavily involved in family purchases. Gen Ys are also Internet savvy, many have been "clicking away" since nursery school.

Marketing's Challenge

The excitement and challenges faced by marketers involves developing new products and repositioning existing products that will appeal to new generations of customers. Many of the brands now favored by Generation Y such as *Mudd, Paris Blues, In Vitro, Cement,* and *What's Over?* are unrecognizable to Baby Boomers and Gen Xers. However, some established brands such as *Tommy Hilfiger, Volkswagen, Lee, Mountain Dew,* and *Arizona Jeans* have successfully tapped into this emerging market. Other established brands that were huge successes with previous generations such as *Nike, Pepsico,* and *Levi Strauss* are struggling to adapt to the changes occurring in the marketplace.

Adapting to changes in the marketplace is the essence of successful marketing firms. Firms that fail to adapt are overcome by competition and customer feelings of indifference towards the firm's products. Successful firms scan the environment for changing customer needs and then develop effective marketing strategies to provide customers what they want, when and where they want it, and at a price they want to pay for it. The question remains whether the brands of the future that appeal to Generation Y will be new brands to be created by new firms, or existing brands that are able to make the transformation and reinvent themselves as they adapt to changing market conditions. The stakes are high. New firms such as Delia's, a New York cataloger that sells urban fashion to girls between the ages of 12 and 17, can attest to Generation Ys sales and profit potential. Delia's reported sales in the last three quarters of 1998 were in excess of $98 million. In contrast, *Levi Strauss* began a series of layoffs and plant closings in early 1999.

www.parisblues.com

www.delias.com

Learning Objectives

After you have completed this chapter, you should be able to:

1. Develop an appreciation for the historical perspective of how markets have evolved.

2. Appreciate both views of the evolution of marketing.

3. Introduce marketing as an exchange process.

4. Understand the societal implications of marketing.

5. Comprehend marketing as an organizational process.

6. Introduce the fundamentals of marketing strategy.

Cool Stuff	
According to Boomers	**According to Generation Y**
LEXUS LS400 What to drive when you have your own parking spot. It says you've arrived without the ostentation of a Beemer.	**JEEP WRANGLER** Who cares about gas mileage? It looks great in the high school parking lot.
MAJOR LEAGUE BASEBALL Mark McGwire and the New York Yankees have made the game hot again.	**SKATEBOARD TRIPLE CROWN** Stars compete for glory instead of multiyear contracts.
GAP Those chinos and jeans still look cool. Really.	**DELIA'S** Definitely not your mother's dress catalog.
ER A worthy successor to *Marcus Welby, MD.*	***DAWSON'S CREEK*** High school drama with sizzle.
SUPERBOWL ADS Usually they're more entertaining than the game.	**LILITH FAIR SPONSORSHIP** Supporting the sound of new voices.
HARRISON FORD Tough and fiftysomething. Plus, his action figure is a hot collectible.	**LEONARDO DICAPRIO** Dashing, sensitive, and irresistible to 12-year-olds.
ESTEE LAUDER For the way we ought to look.	**HARD CANDY** For the way we really look.
L.L. BEAN A favorite for decades, but does anyone actually go duck-hunting in those boots?	**THE NORTH FACE** Does anyone actually go mountain climbing in that stuff?
PALM PILOT A Rolodex for your pocket, with a high-tech edge.	**MOTOROLA FLEX PAGERS** Stay in touch anytime, anyplace.
NICK AT NIGHT All our favorite reruns in one convenient place.	**WB NETWORK** Creating new favorites and a new look for prime time television.
POLITICAL ACTIVISM Make yourself heard.	**VOLUNTEERISM** Make yourself useful.
THE BEATLES Rock 'n' roll as the signal artistic achievement of a generation.	**SPICE GIRLS** Rock 'n' roll packaged and marketed to children.
COKE Water + sugar + caffeine. Besides, it's the real thing.	**MOUNTAIN DEW** Water + sugar + more caffeine. Besides, it's an extreme thing.
DAVID LETTERMAN Late-night TV, slightly mellowed with age. Still among the Top Ten reasons to stay awake.	**JENNY McCARTHY** Think Carol Burnett with a bad attitude.
NIKES From Michael to Tiger, no shortage of sports celebs saying Just Do It.	**VANS** No sports celebs allowed. And they're the coolest shoes on skateboards.

Source: *Business Week*, February 15, 1999.

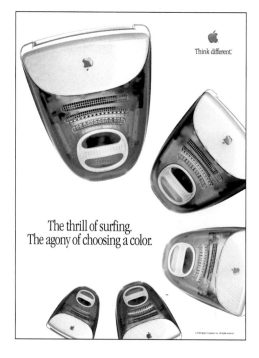

The thrill of surfing.
The agony of choosing a color.

"Think different." Will Apple's Stylish iMac be the computer of choice for Generation Y? Marketers who are able to appeal to youthful Gen Y now, will have a tremendous advantage in the marketplace as the 60 million Yers move into adulthood.

Welcome to *Marketing: Best Practices!* The first three chapters, which comprise Part 1 titled "Introduction—Marketing Environment," provide the fundamental building blocks that lay the foundation for the remainder of the text. Chapter 1 introduces a historical perspective of how *markets* and *marketing* have evolved. In its most basic form, marketing is based on the principle of exchange. Marketers facilitate the exchange process by engaging in a variety of marketing activities that have profound societal and organizational implications.

HOW MARKETS EVOLVED

To understand why marketing is such a fascinating economic and sociological activity, we have to first understand the fundamental reason why *markets* developed. Markets exist because we get better at doing things the more we do them **(labor specialization)** and we get less interested in consuming things the more we consume them **(consumption satiation)**. Put labor specialization and consumption satiation together in any society of humans and *markets* and *marketing* will be spontaneously created. Let us walk slowly through the logic of this theory of spontaneous economic combustion.

Labor specialization is the process of increasing and improving production process skills in a specific industry through specialization.

Consumption satiation means that more consumption over time of one product leads to less interest in the consumption of another unit of the same product.

The Theory of Spontaneous Economic Combustion

Throughout history, tribes of humans have flourished in very different geographical locations. Each location provided very different access to raw materials (for example, mangos, turtles, wheat, water buffalo, potatoes, walrus blubber, iron ore, gold, salt). Making the best of what they had on hand, different tribes survived and flourished by becoming skilled at hunting, gathering, growing, and processing what was on hand. How did they become so skilled? They did so through labor specialization.

Labor Specialization
Labor specialization is based on the principle that we get better at doing things the more we do them. As people specialize in a particular activity, they learn to get better, more efficient, and more skilled at that particular activity. Of course there are setbacks to learning, and some individuals are more motivated to learn than others. As a general principle, however, the benefits of labor specialization were established and made famous by Adam Smith in the 1700s. His consulting report to the British government on how to compete in the global marketplace was later published in book form as *The Wealth of Nations.**

Yet, the principles Adam Smith wrote about some 200 years ago are still relevant today. Think about your own early work experiences. Even when working as a dishwasher or when mowing neighborhood lawns as a kid to earn spending money, you learned over time how to do the job faster and better. Your hand–eye coordination required to perform tasks improved, but you also thought of better or easier ways of accomplishing the tasks at hand. The same learning process makes a brain surgeon better, a runner faster, and a golf professional more accurate. Management scientists and economists have also observed that the same learning occurs at the organizational level. This learning process, by doing and thinking creatively, has been studied by economists who analyze it in terms of **learning curves.**[2] In general, as a company's experience increases, the cost of production decreases.

Learning curves track the decreasing cost of production and distribution of products or services over time as a result of learning by doing, innovation, and imitation.

Consumption Satiation
The other necessary ingredient to generate spontaneous economic combustion is consumption satiation. It is based on the idea that the more we consume the same product over time, the less interested we are in consuming another unit of that same product.

---

*The Wealth of Nations is available as part of the Great Minds Series from Prometheus Books.

Marginal utility
is the want-satisfying power of the next unit of the same product that is consumed.

Hence, the marginal utility of consuming another unit is less than the marginal utility of the unit preceding it. For example, the marginal utility of a customer's third bowl of Ben & Jerry's ice cream is less than the marginal utility of the second bowl, which is less than the marginal utility of the first bowl. The bottom line is that humans get satiated even when consuming the products they enjoy the most.

As a result of consumption satiation, opportunities exist in the marketplace for new products that not only satisfy unmet customer needs, but also provide customers with alternate means of satisfying needs currently being met by existing products. Consequently, spontaneous economic combustion occurs due to customer needs and wants for a variety of products, and the impracticality and inefficiency of each individual inventing and making distinct products for their personal use. Hence, labor specialization and consumer satiation are the major forces behind the development of markets and the field of marketing itself.

THE EVOLUTION OF MARKETING

The Traditional Viewpoint

Most introductory marketing textbooks present the historical and philosophical development of marketing in terms of eras. The most frequently noted eras include the ***production era,*** the ***sales era,*** the ***marketing era,*** and the ***relationship marketing era.*** (See Figure 1.1.)

Production Era
The ***production era*** was based on the philosophical attitude that good products would sell themselves. Perhaps the most famous line from the Kevin Costner movie *Field of Dreams* typifies the prevailing beliefs of the production era—"If we build it, they will come." The production era is said to be characterized by companies that focused on developing mass production skills in the belief that if good products were made affordable and widely available, the consuming public would beat a pathway to the doors of the manufacturers of these products. Henry Ford's Model-T automobile and the development of the production line assembly plant are often noted as prime examples of the production era. Throughout the production era, marketing played a secondary role to production.

How many times did you see the *Lion King*? Some very young children have seen it 50 or more times on home video. This illustrates that consumption satiation can vary greatly across consumers.

Figure 1.1   The Evolution of Marketing

1. Production Era
Business philosophy
focusing on
manufacturing efficiency.

2. Sales Era
Business philosophy
focusing on selling
existing products.

3. Marketing Era
Business philosophy
focusing on customer
needs and wants.

**4. Relationship
Marketing Era**
Business philosophy
focusing on suppliers
and keeping existing
customers.

Sales Era

The realities of the production era were piles of unsold inventory because the product did not sell itself. Customers do not always want the best product on the market. If they did, they would all be wearing Rolex watches and driving Mercedes Benz automobiles, or something similar to that effect. The prevailing philosophy of the *sales era* was to find customers for inventories that went unsold. Advertising campaigns were developed to convince customers to buy products that they otherwise would not have purchased. In essence, during the sales era, companies were trying to sell what they produced as opposed to producing what they could sell. Marketing continued to play a secondary role during the sales era to other functional areas such as engineering, production, and finance. Throughout the sales era, the head of the marketing department was frequently given the title sales manager.

Marketing Era

Based on the knowledge gained by the mistakes made during the production and sales eras, business organizations began to appreciate the value of market information prior to making plans for production. As a result, the *marketing era* is characterized by the importance placed on identifying and satisfying customer needs and wants prior to producing the product. The rationale being that the company would produce what the customer wanted, and the customer would then purchase the product. During the marketing era, marketing moved to the forefront of business strategy, and satisfying customer needs became the responsibility of everyone in the organization regardless of whether employees were engineers, production specialists, financial analysts, or sales personnel.

Relationship Marketing Era

The driving philosophical approach of the ***relationship marketing era*** is to reinforce and broaden the scope of the customer-oriented focus of the marketing era. Traditionally, businesses have focused on **conquest marketing** activities, which emphasized the sale itself rather than the parties to the sale. In contrast, the relationship marketing era recognizes the value and profit potential of ***customer retention***—creating trading relationships by providing reasons to keep existing customers coming back. The relationship marketing era is also characterized by a broadening of the definition of customers to include suppliers. Hence, the guiding emphasis is to develop long-term, mutually satisfying relationships with the firm's customers and suppliers.

Conquest marketing
is the process of recruiting new customers as opposed to keeping existing customers.

An Alternative to the Traditional Viewpoint

The traditional viewpoint described above portrays distinct stages that businesses moved through during specific time periods. The production era is said to have occurred prior to 1925, the sales era occurred between 1925 and the early 1950s, the marketing era took place over the next 30 years, and the relationship marketing era began in the 1990s. The problem with this view is that it does not fit the facts.

The alternative viewpoint proposes that inventing and marketing products that customers need and want and then supplying them has been fundamental to the development of free market economies from prehistory on. The history of global trade and economic development has been about bringing new attractive products, such as chocolate or spices, to market and creating long-term trading relationships between countries, companies, and wealthy customers.[3] Economies that were very good at such relationship marketing flourished and came to dominate other economies. There never was a production era or a sales era. In reality, what there have been are companies that become too production oriented or too sales oriented, at the expense of listening to the voice of the customer. Eventually, these companies are forced by the competition (with more of a marketing orientation) to become more customer oriented, or they are driven out of the market.

What then has been the real history of the development of market economies and marketing? It is the history of the development of well over 10,000 product-markets each with its own unique evolutionary story.[4] It is therefore very hard to make generalizations about the evolution of markets and marketing that hold across all or most of these markets.

Exchange
is an activity in which two or more parties give something of value to each other to satisfy perceived needs.

MARKETING AS AN EXCHANGE PROCESS

Marketing is based on the principle of **exchange.** Marketing as an exchange process is clearly stated in the most accepted definition of marketing provided by the American Marketing Association:

> Marketing is the process of planning and executing the conception, pricing, promotion, and distribution of ideas, goods, and services to create *exchanges* that satisfy individual and organizational goals.[5]

To illustrate the fundamentals of exchange, consider the following scenario. The grower of beef would rather exchange a steak for a watermelon because he is tired of eating steak and it costs him a lot less to produce an additional steak than grow a watermelon. The grower of watermelons also would like to exchange one of her watermelons for a steak because she is sick of eating watermelons and it costs her a lot less to produce a watermelon than a steak. Therefore, if they meet, an exchange is likely to occur between the beef farmer and the watermelon grower.

Marketing exchanges exist because they are beneficial to both parties. They are beneficial because of the principles of labor specialization and consumption satiation. Comparative advantage in the cost of producing various goods has long been understood to underlay the benefits of trading. But labor specialization and production comparative advantage do not, by and of themselves, lead to production surpluses that create trade and markets. The satiation principle is also necessary. In other words, if the more the farmer ate of steak, the more he liked it and wanted more to eat, then he would be very happy growing more beef at an ever lower cost and eating more beef. In essence, the farmer would have an ever-increasing interest in eating his cattle, rather than exchanging them for other products in the marketplace.

Marketing facilitates the exchange process by performing a variety of activities that benefit consumers, producers, and resellers alike. Marketing activities include:

▼ Buying: Marketers buy assortments of products from many different manufacturers that are made available to customers under one roof.

▼ Selling: By making a variety of products available under one roof, marketers sell to numerous customers in a single location, thereby, alleviating the need for individual customers to deal with individual manufacturers for each and every product they desire to purchase.

▼ Transporting: Marketers facilitate the transportation of products by providing the products customers want, where and when they want them.

▼ Storing: Marketers store products so that customers do not have to (e.g., grocery store), and so that manufacturers do not have to keep everything that they produce in their own inventories until the product is sold.

▼ Financing: Marketers provide special paying arrangements (e.g., 90 days same as cash) and leasing agreements that enable more customers access to the products they desire to purchase. In addition, by purchasing the product from the manufacturer before it is sold to the customer, funds are provided to the manufacturer that enable it to produce additional products.

▼ Risk taking: By purchasing products from manufacturers before they are sold to customers, marketers assume the risk that the product will actually sell in the marketplace.

▼ Standardization and grading: Marketers play a role in standardizing and grading the quality and quantity of products made available to customers (e.g., eggs, beef, etc.).

▼ Obtaining market information: Marketers collect information about buyers and suppliers to increase the efficiency and effectiveness of the exchange process.

MARKETING AS A SOCIETAL PROCESS

Marketing activities facilitate the flow of products from producers to customers. In doing so, marketing can have profound societal implications. In historical times, marketing activities raised the quality of life and survival potential of tribes trading with each other. For example, one tribe (A) simply did not have the raw material (clay) available where they lived to make the products they desired (pottery). If a neighboring tribe (B) had pottery, the immediate solution was to send war parties to take it by force. But many warriors were hurt or killed in the raids, and much of the treasured pottery was broken. Left in those raids were stone arrowheads made by the warriors of tribe A and much desired by tribe B. At some point, individuals from the two tribes learned to exchange the coveted items—establishing *trade*. Once trading practices and markets were invented, they took

on a life of their own and have evolved in many different ways. In the process, trading has replaced raiding as the best way of existing in the world.

Marketing systems are closely related to political and economic systems. In fact, we do not have to look far to find examples of where ineffective marketing systems have contributed to the overthrow of governments, such as the fall of communism in eastern Europe. In contrast, the development of effective marketing systems has the potential to raise the standards of living for an entire country's population to new heights.

Marketing as a societal process is evident in China. From about 500 to 1500 A.D., China was the world's economic and technological superpower. But it was slow to develop global trading routes and accept the flood of technological innovation that was a large part of the European renaissance, reformation, enlightenment, and industrial revolution that energized Western Europe over the next 500 years. China fell behind in large part because it saw itself as the center of the world with little need to trade with the rest of the world. In fact, for several hundred years no one in China was allowed to own an ocean-going boat because such boats might bring home unwanted new products. The leader-ship of China believed that their way was the right way of doing things. An inventor risked death for challenging the all-powerful authority of the state. The same sort of crushing of market innovation and imitation occurred under the communist regimes from 1950 to 1980.

www.economist.com

Only now is China reemerging as an economic power. It is radically changing the landscape of thousands of global product markets. The reason why China's renaissance will be so important over the next 50 years is quite simple. It is a huge economy, comprising a quarter of the world's population, whose GNP has been expanding at a rate of 8–9 percent over the last 20 years. The influential business magazine, *The Economist,* has estimated that even at a lower, and more sustainable, rate of expansion of 6 percent over the next 30 years, the Chinese economy will become twice the size of the current United States economy.[6] In no other part of the world will such a dramatic change in economic supply and demand occur. However, many other emerging economies in Asia and South America will also expand. Marketing managers must be at the forefront of understanding the impact of these rapid economic developments on specific markets. Chapter 3 is dedicated to international marketing for this very reason.

Ultimately, effective marketing systems can lead to increased international trade and economic development, which increases the country's tax base. These benefits can be quickly translated into better education and health care systems for all citizens. Truly, the benefits of effective marketing go far beyond the grass roots marketing objectives of providing customers what they want, when they want it, and at a price they want to pay for it at the local supermarket.

MARKETING AS AN ORGANIZATIONAL PROCESS

The Marketing Concept

LEARNING
OBJECTIVE
LO5

As an organizational process, marketing strategy was originally based on the ***marketing concept.*** The marketing concept is based on three fundamental principles:[7]

1. The organization exists to identify and to satisfy the needs of its customers.

2. Satisfying customer needs is accomplished through an integrative effort throughout the organization.

3. The organizational focus should be on long-term as opposed to short-term success.

The marketing concept has its roots in customer orientation founded on the philosophy that production and selling efforts must be based on understanding and serving customer needs and wants. The marketing concept puts companies and managers on notice that neither production, nor sales, nor customers exist in a vacuum: They exist in a competitive marketplace that is becoming more competitive. It is this competitiveness that really drives the marketing concept.

The Strategic Marketing Concept

During the business boom of the 1960s and 1970s, the marketplace became increasingly crowded with companies serving the same groups of customers.[8] This problem is evident in countries such as the United States, which protect and promote strong competition in markets. To combat this competitive threat, the marketing concept has evolved into the *strategic marketing concept* defined as the corporation's mission to seek a sustainable competitive advantage by meeting customer needs.

According to an old business adage, "The sales department isn't the whole company, but the whole company had better be the sales department." For today's business environment this needs to be altered to read, "Not everyone in this company is a marketing manager, but everyone here is in marketing management." Everyone within the company must understand and appreciate the fundamentals of competitive decision making.

The strategic marketing concept is the guiding philosophy that directs a firm's overall marketing strategy. Marketing strategy answers the goal-oriented questions of: (1) where the firm wants to go; (2) how to get there; and (3) how to maintain a competitive advantage. Developing marketing strategy can be very exciting and rewarding. Marketing strategy is the firm's game plan that ultimately deals with such issues as corporate survival and growth. Much of the remainder of this text discusses strategic issues in depth, but before we can move on, we must begin by discussing the fundamentals of marketing strategy.

The Fundamentals of Marketing Strategy

Markets consist of *market segments*—homogeneous groups of customers who have similar wants and needs. For example, the soft drink market consists of a regular cola segment, a diet cola segment, and a caffeine-free segment among others. Many firms lack the resources to efficiently and effectively appeal to every segment in a market; therefore, they often choose to focus on specific segments called *target markets.*

In its most effective form, marketing strategy develops a *marketing mix* that is specifically tailored to meet the needs of each of its intended target markets. The marketing mix assists the firm in developing a **positioning** strategy. For example, Pepsi's positioning strategy is to be thought of as a product targeted to "the younger generation." Similarly, Dr Pepper is positioned to those who want to be considered "individuals" or "original," and Mountain Dew is positioned as the drink of "active Generation Xers." These various positioning strategies are evident in Figure 1.2. The marketing mix is purposely and strategically developed to support the product's positioning strategy.

A firm's marketing mix represents the controllable elements of the firm's marketing strategy. It consists of developing strategies in four decision areas: *product, pricing, distribution,* and *promotion.* (See Figure 1.3.) Frequently, distribution decisions are also referred to as "place decisions," and the marketing mix is then called the *Four Ps.* Now we will take a brief look at each of the marketing mix elements. An in-depth discussion on each of the elements is provided in later chapters.

Product Decisions

Product decisions encompass a wide array of issues such as new product development, branding, packaging, labeling, and the strategic management of products throughout their life cycle. These issues are discussed in detail in Chapter 8.

Products provide **form utility** to customers. However, we would like you to think of products as more than just tangible goods. Throughout this text, unless otherwise specifically stated, the term *product* refers to *goods* (e.g., appliances, automobiles, clothing),

LEARNING OBJECTIVE LO6

Positioning
refers to how a product is perceived by customers in the marketplace relative to the competition.

www.pepsico.com
www.drpepper.com

Form utility
is achieved by the conversion of raw and component materials into finished products that are desired by the marketplace.

Figure 1.2 Positioning Strategies

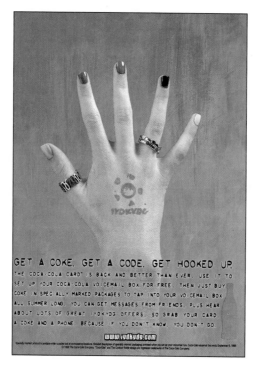

The target market and product positioning strategy on the left is very different from an alternative form of the same brand on the right.

Figure 1.3 A Marketing Strategy Framework

services (e.g., legal, health care, and financial), *people* (e.g., political candidates, religious leaders, students looking for their first job), *places* (e.g., tourism destinations, shopping centers, countries seeking economic development) and *ideas* (e.g., HIV protection, Mothers Against Drunk Driving, and anti-drug campaigns). Similarly, the term **customer** includes both **business users** and **household consumers. Business users** resell products (e.g., wholesalers and retailers), use products as component parts (e.g., windshield wipers utilized in new vehicle production), or use products in their daily business operations (e.g., janitorial supplies, paper, ink cartridges). Household consumers simply refers to the consuming public.

Traditionally, marketing has focused on the exchange of goods with little or no discussion concerning the modification of marketing strategy that is required to market effectively to the other product and customer definitions described above. However, some differences do exist and marketing strategy must be adjusted to compensate for these differences. For example, Chapter 5 is dedicated to household consumers, Chapter 6 examines business-to-business marketing, and Chapter 9 focuses specifically on the marketing of services.

Pricing Decisions

Pricing decisons should satisfy multiple objectives. At the very least, a firm's pricing strategy should:

1. support a product's marketing strategy,

2. achieve the financial goals of the organization, and

3. fit the realities of the marketplace environment.

Despite decades of study by economists and market researchers, price setting is still often determined by a best-guess decision that is quickly revised when the guess turns out to be wrong. For example, when the great packaged-goods manufacturer and marketer Procter & Gamble first marketed Pampers, it priced diapers at 10 cents apiece. The product bombed, because mothers perceived disposable diapers to cost more than buying and washing cloth diapers. The convenience advantage of disposable diapers did not compensate for their higher cost. P&G returned to the drawing board and developed a new design for its product and package. It cut material costs and lowered production time, thereby, decreasing production costs. P&G relaunched the product at a price of six cents per unit, and Pampers became a great success and hugely profitable.

www.pg.com

Distribution (Place) Decisions

Distribution decisions reflect the marketer's ability to create time, place, and possession utilities for customers. *Time utility* and *place utility* reflect the marketer's ability to provide products *when* and *where* customers would like to purchase them. *Possession utility* facilitates the transfer of ownership of the product from the producer to the customer through **marketing channels.** A typical marketing channel would consist of the following *channel members:* the manufacturer who produces the product and sells it to a wholesaler, the wholesaler who resells the product to a retailer, and the retailer who sells the product to the final consumer.

Marketing channels
are the networks of organizations that move a product from the producer to its intended market.

The importance of distribution's role in the marketing mix cannot be overstated. By far the greatest achievement of the ancient Romans was the construction of 50,000 miles of highways, some of which are still used today. By comparison there are 42,000 miles of federal highways in the United States. These Roman roads were the first interstate highways in the world, and contributed greatly to the *Pax Romana,* the peace that Rome brought to the Mediteranian world for several hundred years. The Romans did so by reducing the cost of trading, which increased the likely returns, and therefore increased trading.

Similarly, the history of the development of markets and marketing in the United States is best understood by thinking about it in terms of two periods—the period before the railway and the period from 1840–1900 when the railway network came to dominate trade and commerce in the United States. Before the railway, markets were local and economies were local. A few luxury goods made their way across the country, but even the wealthiest had to wait months for items to arrive at their front door. As the tentacles of the railway lines raced out across the country, the economy changed. Goods could travel thousands of miles, rather than tens of miles, in a few days. Markets went from local to regional almost overnight. Eventually, isolated markets became mass markets through the web of the railway system. Mass markets provided the incentive for producers to manufacture on a larger scale, which led to great innovation and advances in manufacturing.[9] These innovations led to even lower costs of manufacturing, which, combined with still lower distribution costs, led to even lower prices and further market growth.

Yet even as the railway network dominated the United States economy, the new road network was evolving. Road transportation really took off with the construction of the interstate highway system in the 1950s. Air transportation's network of hubs and spokes rapidly developed during the 1970s as a result of deregulation. Companies such as FedEx and UPS continue to thrive on this once innovative distribution system. Marketing is about learning to harness new and improved transportation and distribution networks, as illustrated in the UPS ad featured in Figure 1.4. Marketing has evolved into management of geographical distribution networks that are evolving through technological innovation.

Promotion Decisions
Promotion decisions communicate the firm's marketing strategy to customers and channel members who assist in the product's distribution to the market. Every firm has choices to make as to how to communicate with the market. Communication is accomplished through managing the firm's ***promotion mix.*** Elements of this mix include advertising, personal selling, publicity, and sales promotion. Each element has its advantages and disadvantages as will be discussed in Chapters 12 and 13.

Promotion elements that are used simultaneously are termed ***integrated marketing communications.*** For example, when the Disney/Pixar movie *A Bug's Life* was released into theatres, it was frequently advertised on television. In addition, sales promotions such as the "Find Flik and Win Instantly" game that was printed on cans of Dr Pepper also promoted the movie, and fast food restaurants included *A Bug's Life* toys in their children's meals. Integrated marketing communications support one another and reinforce the customer's awareness of the product being promoted.

Ultimately, promotion is a form of communication. The evolution of communication technology has been a major force in the development of human relations, and has greatly reduced the costs of buyers and sellers communicating with each other. For thousands of years trading and communication required personal travel by land and sea. It was very slow, dangerous, and costly. The Roman's greatly sped up and improved the transportation of both goods and information. The Roman highway system allowed couriers to travel faster and even led to the invention of billboards (first used by roadside inns), which were the first forms of advertising. The irony was that the Roman highway system was a strategic defense initiative, built to move troops around the empire. It worked so well that the roads were converted to a peaceful purpose increasing communication and trading between people.

If you have grown up with cable television where you can watch what is happening anywhere in the world as if you are actually there, then it is hard to appreciate how isolated people were 200 years ago. They could not communicate easily with anyone more than 50 miles away. Today we can use the Internet to trade with anyone in the world in real time, most likely in the emerging language of world trade, which is English.

This split-second communication with anyone, anywhere, has come about through the invention and creation of a whole series of communication technologies and networks. The invention of printing created advertising flyers as well as making the Bible available for ordinary folks to read. But it was the invention of the telegraph and telephone that

Figure 1.4   Technological Innovations for Today's Distribution Networks Must "Move at the Speed of Business" to Succeed

created a huge step forward in placing orders, explaining how to use and repair products, and reporting on when the order was dispatched or where it got held up. It created two-way communication between buyer and seller that took minutes or hours rather than days or weeks. This greatly reduced order-delivery cycle time (both its average time and its variance in time taken), which greatly increased the amount and efficiency of trading. Notice that both the telegraph and telephone networks were basically primitive Internet networks.

Radio and television transmission networks further enabled buyers and sellers to communicate as never before. These communication technologies led to the tremendous growth of advertising that has become a separate profession. Marketing success is about learning to master ever new and improved one-way and two-way communication technologies. It has evolved into management of communication networks that themselves are evolving through technological innovation. Mastering the use of the Internet in marketing is today's exciting challenge and why Chapter 15 is dedicated to marketing on the Internet.

The Future of Electronic Shopping

The Internet has already become the backbone of commercial communication between businesses, involving trillions of dollars of trading around the world each year. It will ultimately kill business-to-business snail mail. The less certain question is how big will home electronic shopping become? In 1995 forecasts of such sales ranged from $5–$300 billion by the year 2000. In early 1999 the 2000 estimate looks more like $20–$40 billion. Experts predict that Internet business will take over traditional marketing and selling channels for many products. The Internet market reduces prices by cutting selling and marketing costs and provides more quality information to buyers than traditional markets.

The stock market is a case in point. At the start of 1999 5 million Americans were buying and selling stocks on the Internet and the number is increasing by 15,000 a week. They are attracted by services such as Etrade.com (see advertisement) that offer low trading fees and a great deal of information about companies. This is virtually the same information that traditional brokers access to give expensive advice to clients (advice that often also favors the stocks that the brokerage house is pushing). But are these shoppers behaving the way that the marketing experts expected? Are these Internet shoppers carefully appraising the long-term prospects of the companies whose stock they are buying? Not always, maybe not at all. Most of the shoppers may be following the tips on the message boards and chase the stocks that are in high demand. Some examples of their buying tactics are:

> "My philosophy is to buy high and sell higher and not be afraid to take risks. I use no research tools or software, I just surf the message boards and look for volume."

> "My philosophy is don't marry your stocks and, above all, take your profits and run … I pay no attention to P/Es. They don't matter."

The traditional way of assessing a stock is to use its price to earnings ratio. Traditionally the P/E for the stock market has been around 15–20. In the late 1990s it shot up to around 30, and for some internet stocks it is infinite because the company has yet to generate any earnings. The traditional safe way of creating a nest egg is to invest for the long-haul. That way you weather the short-term runs up and down, and gain through the long-term trend in stock prices. According to *The Economist* (January 30, 1999, p.17):

> "The casino capitalists who spend 7 or 8 hours a day at their PCs trading Internet shares appear to be stark, staring mad."

Questions

1. What sort of irrational consumer behavior may Internet shopping create? How does it create such behavior?

2. What effect can it have on market dynamics?

3. What long-term effect may it have on Internet shopping?

References: Joseph Alba et al., "Interactive Home Shopping: Consumer, Retailer, and Manufacturer Incentives to Participate in Electronic Marketplaces," *Journal of Marketing*, 61, July 1997, 38–53; Mathew Schifrin and Om Malik, "Amateur Hour on Wall Street," *Forbes*, January 25, 1999, 82–85; "Why Internet Shares Will Fall," *The Economist*, January 30, 1999.

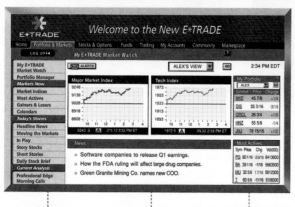

The Marketing Environment

Businesses do not operate in a vacuum. Decisions must be made in response to changes in the firm's internal (micro) and external (macro) environment. The firm's *microenvironment* consists of the influences of the organization's own objectives and resources. Objectives provide direction for marketing decisions while resources pose constraints on activities to be undertaken. Hence, marketers must be mindful of corporate resource availability and corporate objectives when making decisions.

External forces constantly change the *macroenvironment* in which the firm operates. The macroenvironment consists of the competitive environment, the legal/political environment, the sociocultural environment, the economic environment, and the technological environment. Although firms may attempt to influence these outside forces, they are primarily uncontrollable. Successful firms track changes in the macroenviroment via *environmental scanning.* Environmental scanning identifies important trends in the environment and then considers the potential impact of these changes on the firm's existing marketing strategy.

Successful firms regularly modify their marketing mix decisions to adapt to the changing environment. However, success sometimes breeds complacency. For instance, 12 of the 14 companies described as "The Excellent American Companies of 1982" in the classic book, *In Search of Excellence,* soon stumbled because they failed to adapt to changes in the marketing environment.[10] Between 1973 and 1988, the great marketing company Procter & Gamble lost an estimated quarter of a billion dollars while conducting business in Japan. The company's marketing strategy did not fit consumer values, perceptions, and behavior; it did not fit the distribution realities; it did not respond to public policy environmental concerns; and it underestimated the competition. The bottom line is that the product and the marketing strategy failed to fit the environment.

Some environmental changes present future market opportunities while others present threats. Consider the impact of macroenvironmental forces on the true stories of these two entreprenuers:

> Leo, a former merchant marine, owned a pawn shop in Burgaw, North Carolina. One night Leo was awakened from a dream and carved a new product idea from a bar of soap with his pocket knife. His new product idea was a collapsible folding stock for hunting rifles. Leo advertised the prototype of his new product in *Soldier of Fortune* and *Guns and Ammo* magazines. The new product was a hit, and shortly Leo received thousands of dollars of orders, before the first stock was ever produced.

> Leo's success attracted the interest of competitors. Soon the Chinese were exporting folding stocks to the U.S. and cutting into Leo's profits. The U.S. government took notice of the Chinese business activities and was not pleased that this new product would allow for the concealment of firearms. In time, collapsible folding stocks were banned, and Leo was looking for new business opportunities.

Leo's story provides a good example of how competitors and the legal/political environment threatened his livelihood. In contrast, changes in the macroenvironment often present new business opportunities as well:

> While attending the University of North Carolina at Wilmington as an undergraduate business student, Jimmy Thomas came across a belt he had purchased in Mexico a year earlier. The belt was made from a colorful cloth material that is commonly found in Mexico. The belt no longer fit Jimmy, but he thought it might make an interesting collar for his dog. To make a long story short, Jimmy is now part owner of a company called Color Pet that markets upscale pet products to domestic and international markets.

Much of Color Pet's success has been driven by changes in the social-cultural and economic environments. Consumer segments of pet owners exist that are willing to spend top dollar for pet products that distinguish their pets. A thriving economic environment provides the discretionary income available to purchase such products, and attitudes of pet owners who seek out unique apparel for their pets have flourished as well.

Stories such as Leo's and Jimmy's illustrate the critical point of this discussion—marketers need to understand changes in the marketing environment to be able to make good business decisions. As the marketing environment changes, marketers must adjust their marketing mixes to remain effective in the new market arena. Consider the changes that marketing firms have already made as they adjust their marketing strategies to appeal to Generation Y.

Marketing Strategy in Action

www.leejeans.com

As discussed in the opening vignette of this chapter, Generation Y will present a number of challenges and opportunities for marketers for the foreseeable future.[11] Generation Y is different, and the marketing successes thus far with this generation are keying into these differences. Although some of Gen Y's choices are driven by fads and rebelliousness, many of the other differences are much more subtle. Given the young age of this generation at this point in time, most of the industries that have made changes are in the fashion, entertainment, and toy markets. For instance, the popular Generation X hit MTV's *House of Style* has been reformulated to appeal to Generation Y. The show, which originally featured celebrity fashion and lifestyles, has switched to more practical information such as buying a prom dress and decorating a bedroom. Lee Apparel recently modified its marketing mix by introducing a line of oversized, multipocketed pants called *Pipes* targeted to 10- to 14-year-old boys. Lee then modified its promotion strategy by spending its marketing budget on the Internet (see Figure 1.5), outdoor posters, and skateboard magazines. According to the president of the Lee brand, "As a brand, you need to go where they [Gen Y] are, not just pick a fashion statement, put it on TV, and wait for them to come to you."[12]

Generation Y has been bombarded by more advertisements and exposed to more brands than any generation that has preceded it. As a result, they have "tuned out" traditional media channels and are often indifferent about brands that their parents love. Marketers have had to discover new methods to communicate with this market. Universal Studios, Coca-Cola, and McDonald's are currently using "street teams" of young adults that hang out in clubs, parks, and malls to talk about trends and emerging issues. Other marketers are using "wild-postings," which are ad posters that are tacked up on street corners, telephone poles, and construction sites. The whole idea is that to appeal to Generation Y, marketers want this group to stumble into their brands in unexpected places. It also helps if the company can get customers to talk about the brand among themselves. For example, the success of Mountain Dew is generally attributed to the "buzz" surrounding the product that it's loaded with caffeine—a claim never mentioned in any of Mountain Dew's promotional materials.

The content of promotions is also being modified. Generation Y appears to respond to humor, irony, and the brutal truth. The Mountain Dew commercials are a good example. Many of the new commercials that are aimed at this generation are oblique in that they do not talk about product attributes and benefits. For instance, Volkswagen's latest marketing campaign does not inform customers about gas mileage, horsepower, or warranty information. What it does feature is a nonmainstream "edge." The discarded chair ad featuring the Golf and the in-sync musical tempo of the Passat advertisement have enabled Volkswagen to maintain its appeal with the last three generations. The Baby Boomers loved the VW Beetle, Gen Xers made the Jetta hip, and now the Golf and the Passat have been noted by Gen Ys as two of their favorites.

So far, the marketing success stories pertaining to Generation Y have one view in common. Marketing to this generation is not about teen marketing, it's about recognizing that Generation Y is a generation that is coming of age. In a few years, they will be buying their

Figure 1.5 Pipe Jeans Home Page

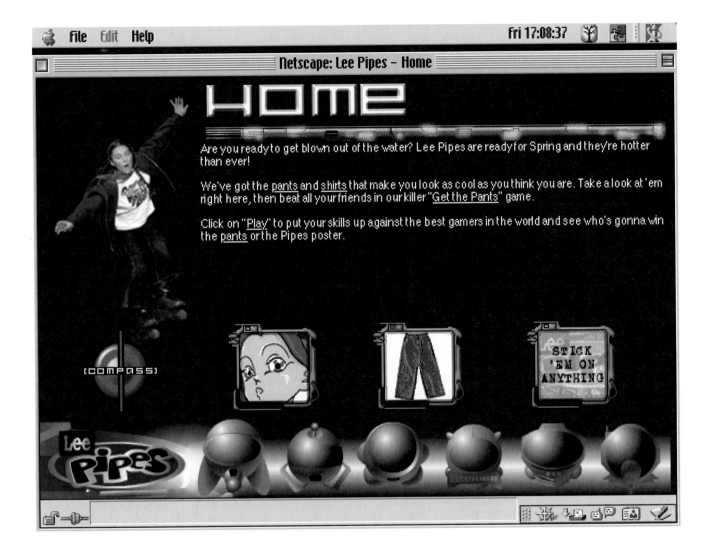

first cars, moving into their first homes, and requiring a multitude of financial and other services. Recognizing the potential of this market, General Motors Corporation is currently putting together a task force to investigate the needs of this emerging group. Car clinics are held where Gen Ys from teenagers to sixth graders voice their opinions about current car styles and future needs. The motivation for General Motors and other automobile companies to identify with this new generation is understandable—between 1999 and the year 2010, 4 million new drivers each year will be looking for new forms of transportation.

Ultimately, marketing strategy is deciding what to make and how to distribute what is made. This requires developing and mastering an understanding of customer and competitor behavior and a host of market trends. These topics are covered in Chapters 4, 5, and 6. It also requires great, unbiased insight into the current and potential operational strengths of the business. Marketing strategy is about a firm developing decision-making and planning processes that adapt the firm to changing market conditions. The Marketing Planning Appendix at the end of the text provides an in-depth discussion of the formal planning processes for marketing decisions.

CAREERS IN MARKETING

Marketing is hot in many organizations. Research conducted by an international executive recruiting company suggests that the best route to becoming a corporate CEO is to pursue a marketing career. Financial expertise has fallen out of favor, and about three out of every eight CEOs come from a marketing background.

It often comes as a surprise to many students who view marketing solely as a career for those interested in sales and advertising, but marketing expertise is heavily sought after for a wide variety of career opportunities such as:

▼ Marketing, Advertising, and Public-Relations Managers

▼ Sales Representatives

▼ Advertising Specialists

▼ Public-Relations Specialists

▼ Purchasing Agents and Managers

▼ Market Research Analysts

▼ Wholesale and Retail Buyers and Merchandise Managers

▼ Logistics: Material Receiving, Scheduling, Dispatching, and Distributing Occupations

The Careers Appendix at the end of the text presents an overview of marketing careers, suggestions for résumé development, and tips for interviewing. In addition, the text has been packaged with "Discovering Your Marketing Career." This CD enables students to explore marketing career opportunities based on their own personal interests and skills.

Chapter Summary

Markets came into being and the field of marketing developed due to spontaneous economic combustion. The two essential ingredients for spontaneous economic combustion are labor specialization and consumption satiation. In essence, markets and marketing exist due to customer needs and wants for a variety of products, and the impracticality and inefficiency of each individual developing distinct products for their personal use.

Traditionalists believe that marketing evolved during eras spanning specific periods of time. These eras included the production era—where it was thought that the "best" product on the market would sell itself; the sales era—where companies were attempting to sell what they produced, as opposed to producing what they could sell; the marketing era—where production was based on the principle of identifying and satisfying customer needs; and the relationship marketing era—which recognizes the value of customer retention and views suppliers as well as consumers as customers. In contrast, an alternative view is presented that believes that these eras never existed. The alternative view believes simply that some companies are more production-oriented than others, some are more sales-oriented than others, and some are more marketing-oriented than others. Competition drives a company's orientation. As competitive pressures increase, companies that adopt a marketing perspective substantially enhance their ability to compete and thrive in the future.

Marketing is based on the principle of exchange and facilitates the exchange process by performing a variety of activities such as buying, selling, transporting, storing, financing, risk taking, standardization, grading, and obtaining market information. Ultimately, the completion of these marketing activities facilitates the flow of products from producers to customers. In doing so, marketing can have profound societal implications and is often closely related to political and economic systems. Ineffective marketing systems have contributed to the fall of governments, while effective marketing systems lead to the creation of value and capital that can benefit all citizens.

As an organizational process, marketing develops a marketing mix consisting of product, place, promotion, and pricing decisions specifically tailored to meet the needs of intended target markets. The marketing mix elements are controllable and assist firms in developing positioning strategies that differentiate their products from competitive offerings. Since businesses do not operate in a vacuum, successful firms regularly modify their marketing mix decisions to adapt to the changing internal and external environment. Macroenvironmental forces include competitive, legal/political, sociocultural, economic, and technological influences. The microenvironment is comprised of organizational objectives and resources.

The marketing profession faces some very large challenges and opportunities over the next 20 years—within the span of your careers in business. Marketing to Generation Y and China are just two of these challenges. This text and its collection of authors are dedicated to providing you with an understanding of these issues and the "best practices" currently in place to face the challenges of an ever-changing marketplace. We hope that you find *Marketing: Best Practices* thought-provoking and that it increases your interest in what the field of marketing has to offer in terms of careers and practical business strategy.

Key Terms

Labor specialization is the process of increasing and improving production process skills in a specific industry through specialization.

Consumption satiation means that more consumption over time of one product leads to less interest in the consumption of another unit of the same product.

Learning curves track the decreasing cost of production and distribution of products or services over time as a result of learning by doing, innovation, and imitation.

Marginal utility is the want-satisfying power of the next unit of the same product that is consumed.

Conquest marketing is the process of recruiting new customers as opposed to keeping existing customers.

Exchange is an activity in which two or more parties give something of value to each other to satisfy perceived needs.

Positioning refers to how a product is perceived by customers in the marketplace relative to the competition.

Form utility is achieved by the conversion of raw and component materials into finished products that are desired by the marketplace.

Marketing channels are the networks of organizations that move a product from the producer to its intended market.

Additional Key Terms and Concepts

Production era

Marketing era

Customer retention

Strategic marketing concept

Target markets

Four Ps

Customer

Household consumers

Place utility

Channel members

Integrated marketing communications

Microenvironment

Sales era

Relationship marketing era

Marketing concept

Market segments

Marketing mix

Product

Business users

Time utility

Possession utility

Promotion mix

Macroenvironment

Environmental scanning

Questions for Discussion

1. What is wrong with the statement, "Trade came about because of labor specialization"?

2. What are historically considered the four marketing eras? Discuss the different characteristics of each era.

3. For thousands of years a market was a marketplace, a physical place where buyers and sellers gathered to trade goods and services. Why is it so difficult to define what a market is today?

4. While R.D., a frequent flyer, is waiting in line at the gate for an American Airlines flight, he is paged. The ticket agent invites him to sit in an empty seat in first class. What type of focus or approach to business does American have toward business if this is a deliberate program? How have computers and Internet communication helped in creating such a program? What other invention does this program depend on?

5. Marketing is based on what principle? Explain this principle.

6. Marketing is often described as a societal process. Discuss how marketing as a societal process is relevant to China.

7. Discuss how Generation Y is different from previous generations. How are these differences impacting marketing strategy?

8. In many organizations the marketing function is in a separate department from the sales organization. Some say it came about through organization politics: Senior management set up a separate marketing department to create more senior executives. Yet today, many sales managers have degrees in marketing. Answer the following questions in light of today's marketing environment.
   a. If the cost of developing and supporting a large sales force makes up a large part of a firm's marketing effort and expense, why isn't sales integrated with marketing or vice versa?
   b. If the two functions remain separate, what is likely to determine whether the organization is sales-driven or market-driven?
   c. Which group is more likely to have the stronger relationship-marketing orientation?
   d. How does Internet communication between buyers and sellers impact the integration question?
   e. What is the continued separation of marketing from sales an example of?

9. Discuss the significance of the marketing environment to marketing strategy.

10. The Careers Appendix at the end of the text discusses tips for interviewing and résumé development. Summarize the key points of this discussion.

Internet Questions

1. Generation Y will have grown up using the Internet in school and at home as if it is second nature. Why is it so important for marketing executives to understand the Internet buying behavior of Generation Y in the next few years compared to understanding the Internet buying behavior of Generation X's or the baby boomers?

2. By 2010 shopping will very likely benefit from the invention and marketing of a very useful new product. You will have price search engine software ("pengine" for short) that comes with your notepad that will search for the lowest price within your

requested delivery time of the book that you want. The search can be undertaken while you are asleep or doing other tasks on your computer. The software will identify the best deals, and all you have to do is click the mouse and the book is ordered, paid for by credit card, and on its way to you that day. How will this change the marketing strategy of Internet marketing companies? Is the price search engine software likely to be sold by Microsoft, Netscape, or Yahoo!?

3. Internet marketers may come and go. Some of the new companies may become huge, others may disappear as did some of the first PC companies. But there are some companies in the added value chain that are surely going to benefit greatly from the growth of Internet shopping and grow a lot larger and more profitable. Who are they?

Endnotes

[1]Ellen Neuborne and Kathleen Kerwin, "Generation Y," *Business Week,* February 15, 1999, pp. 80–88.

[2]See Frank J. Andress, "The Learning Curve as a Production Tool," *Harvard Business Review* (January–February 1954), pp. 16–19; Kenneth Arrow, "The Economic Implications of Learning by Doing," *Review of Economic Studies* (April 1962), pp. 166–170; Winfred B. Hirschmann, "Profit from the Learning Curve," *Harvard Business Review* (January–February 1964), pp. 125–139; George S. Day and David B. Montgomery, "Diagnosing the Experience Curve," *Journal of Marketing,* 47 (Spring 1983), pp. 44–58.

[3]David S. Landes, *The Wealth and Poverty of Nations* (New York: W.W. Norton & Company, 1988); Joel Mokyr, *The Lever of Riches* (Oxford: Oxford University Press, 1990).

[4]A superb history of the development of the global market for clocks and watches is presented in David S. Landes, *Revolution in Time* (Cambridge, MA: Harvard University Press, 1983).

[5]Peter D. Bennet, ed., *Dictionary of Marketing Terms* (Chicago: American Marketing Association, 1988), p. 54.

[6]Joseph S. Nye Jr., "As China Rises, Must Others Bow?" *The Economist,* June 27, 1998, pp. 23–25.

[7]Adapted from William O. Bearden, Thomas N. Ingram, and Raymond W. LaForge, *Marketing,* 2d ed. (Boston: Irwin McGraw-Hill, 1998), p. 8.

[8]Adapted from Peter R. Dickson, *Marketing Management* (Fort Worth: The Dryden Press, 1994), pp. 4–5.

[9]Alfred D. Chandler, Jr., *The Visible Hand* (Cambridge, MA: Harvard University Press, 1977).

[10]Ellen Neuborne and Kathleen Kerwin, "Generation Y," *Business Week,* February 15, 1999, pp. 80–88.

[11]Ibid, p. 86.

[12]Ibid.

[13]Source: Jennifer Lach, "Reading Your Mind, Reaching Your Wallet," *American Demographics,* November 1998, pp. 39–42.

Amazon.com[13]

At the end of 1998 Amazon.com announced it had fourth quarter sales of $250 million, but it had yet to earn a dime of profit. The reason is that most of its sales are of books and music CDs that do not earn high margins, and it continues to invest in an extensive advertising campaign that gives it very high prominence on America Online (that reaches 15 million households) and in other media. It also is spending heavily on developing book warehouses and distribution centers. Meanwhile, Barnes & Noble (www.barnesandnoble.com) purchased Ingram, the major wholesale distributor of books to bookstores across the United States. It also purchased a major distributor of books in Europe.

Both companies are attempting to develop long-term relationships with their customers by using what is called *collaborative filtering software*. This software interacts with the customer at the point of purchase selection and suggests the customer consider other books or music albums. It does this by comparing the history of a customer's purchases with thousands of other customer histories and then recommending as incremental purchases books selected by other customers with similar interests and tastes. The recommendations become more targeted and fine-tuned as the company learns more about the customer, which increases the likelihood of a further sale. It also creates a Web site shopping experience that is unique for each shopper—no two shoppers experience the exact same interchange.

Before answering the following questions, please visit Amazon.com and barnes-andnoble.com. Compare the feel of their sites and compare their prices.

Discussion Questions

1. What long-term advantage over Barnes & Noble is Amazon.com creating by spending so much more on its America Online advertising?

2. Which user interface has the better feel? What are the best features of each?

3. How different are their prices? Did Amazon.com make a strategic mistake by not buying Ingram itself? What effect may it have on the long-term success of Amazon.com?

4. What should Barnes & Noble do to make its current stores more competitive with electronic book shopping? Think about the competitive advantages of shopping for a book at a current Barnes & Noble store.

5. What is the use of collaborative filtering software an example of? How does it compare with a friendly sales clerk you get to know?

Chapter 2

**Peter R. Dickson,
University of
Wisconsin–Madison**

Arthur C. Nielsen Jr., Chair of Marketing Research, University of Wisconsin-Madison

Dr. Dickson has written some 60 articles on consumer research, market segmentation, pricing, decision marketing biases, competitive thinking, and marketing planning. His current research is on process learning, competitive dynamics, relationship theory, and marketing planning best practices.

The Marketing Environment & Social Responsibility

I s it fair if companies insert messages such as "Drink Coke" and "Eat Popcorn" into single frames of a motion picture, and through such *subliminal messages* (messages we cannot detect) lead movie goers like sheep to the theatre's concession counter? Such behavior would seem to be very unethical. Vance Packard used this marketing practice as the central premise of a book called *The Hidden Persuaders,* that took modern marketing practices to task for their unethical behavior and lack of social responsibility. The book sold millions of copies. This sweeping condemnation of marketing was picked up uncritically by the popular press and mass media, and led several states to pass laws against subliminal persuasion. This manifesto of the manipulative sneakiness used by big business and the capitalist system, is still being taught in high school classrooms.

There is but one small problem. It has absolutely no basis in fact. When challenged, Packard and his publisher were never able to document where and when such practices occurred, and cognitive psychologists, in search of fame and fortune, have not been able to create such effects in controlled experiments.[1] Vance Packard and his publisher made millions by promoting a lie. The image of all-powerful marketing tactics manipulating a vulnerable and gullible customer was indelibly burned into the folklore of American culture. Was that fair and socially responsible? Vance Packard becomes a folk hero, and modern marketing, despite all the wonderful products that it has brought to the modern world, is vilified. The fact is that the vast majority of marketing practices are socially responsible, aimed at honestly and competitively serving customers. Indeed, the concept of serving, respecting and satisfying customers, in a long-term relationship, is central to most marketing practices. Of course, as with any profession, there are the bad eggs. For example, there are the jackals who prey on the elderly, sometimes charging thousands of dollars for inspecting and repairing a chimney that "was about to burn the house down," or suckering them into ridiculous get-rich schemes and stealing all of their savings.

And very occasionally a whole industry goes bad, as we have witnessed with the tobacco manufacturers. Thirty years ago their own scientists were informing them that tobacco was addictive and caused lung cancer and other fatal illnesses. But that did not stop the industry from publicly challenging and dismissing every published study that came to the same conclusion. The industry fought against the health warnings on tobacco packaging, and then, 10 years later, used the presence of these warnings as an excuse for not being liable to consumers. Why? Because consumers had been warned on the packaging that smoking was not good for their health. The CEOs of the industry testified under oath at congressional hearings that tobacco was not addictive, when they knew it to be so. Officials swore that they never targeted children with their marketing campaigns, such as Joe Camel. Yet, independent market research revealed that 90 percent of children 8 to 13 years old could recognize Joe Camel.[2] Court documents obtained from these company's own research and marketing departments revealed that children had been targeted. The World Heath Organization estimates that 200–300 million children, and young people under the age of 20 today, will eventually be killed by tobacco.

The American tobacco companies are now starting to have to pay for their actions, but are they apologetic? Some are, but most are not. They have worked hard with their bought politicians to torpedo controlling legislation, and are spending their marketing budgets

(Continued)

Learning Objectives

After you have completed this chapter, you should be able to:

1. Discuss the six components of the marketing environment and their impact on marketing strategy.

2. Name and discuss the three dimensions of marketing's social responsibility.

3. Understand the real issues behind the belief that marketing creates unneeded and unwanted products. Realize the bases for these and other criticisms of distribution and advertising.

4. Develop an understanding of the possible unintended consequences of too much marketing.

5. Understand that the most important ethic in marketing is honesty—honesty with customers, honesty between colleagues, and honesty with yourself.

6. Explain the principles of ethics and the difficulties encountered in creating a code of ethics for global trading.

7. Appreciate the challenges involved in cause-related marketing campaigns.

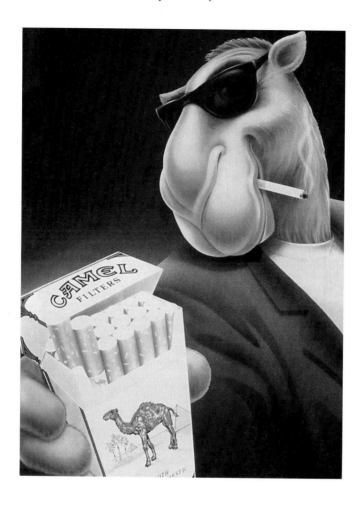

Despite industry claims of not targeting children, market research has revealed that 90 percent of children 8 to 13 years old recognize Joe Camel.

expanding overseas sales. It is hard to understand how a whole industry could go so bad. Perhaps they slipped so slowly into the slime, they did not notice where they ended up. Maybe they were very ill advised by their lawyers. Whatever the reason, the lesson is chilling.

As a profession, marketing can try to counter these negative images with stories about socially responsible companies that are working to save the environment. But such stories are unlikely to significantly impact the impression of the popular press, or influence those people who already view marketing practices in a very negative light. Members of the marketing profession must therefore be ever vigilant that they are behaving responsibly. They must be willing to pull the plug on bad schemes, and blow the whistle on those who disgrace the discipline. Further, they must be responsive to the media and the general public, and be able to counter some of the currently popular, yet perhaps unreasonable, criticisms of marketing. ▪

In Chapter 1, we learned how successful firms adapt to changes in the marketing environment by adjusting one or more of their marketing mix elements (product, place, promotion, and price). Chapter 2 focuses on the marketing environment and social responsibility. Changes in the internal and external marketing environment often produce both challenges and opportunities. Firms that are successful in the long term respond to these challenges and opportunities in a socially responsive manner. Failure to do so often leads to government regulation, public scrutiny, and ultimately the demise of the firm in question.

THE MARKETING ENVIRONMENT

As introduced in Chapter 1, marketing strategy takes into account changes in the firm's internal (micro) and external (macro) environment. By identifying current changes and trends in the environment, a marketer can attempt to predict future changes, and how these changes may affect the effectiveness of the company's marketing programs. New opportunities for the company may be identified in the process. In contrast, potential threats may be identified, averted, and turned into opportunities.

In general, a firm's marketing environment is comprised of six components. First, the firm's internal marketing environment (the *microenvironment*) consists of the firm's own objectives and resources. The external environment (the *macroenvironment*) consists of the competitive environment, the legal/political environment, the sociocultural environment, the economic environment, and the technological environment.

Figure 2.1 provides a framework that incorporates these six environmental forces. The model illustrates that these forces impinge on and influence all elements of the marketing mix.

The Internal Marketing Environment

Objectives and Resources

Top-level corporate executives formulate annual and long-term objectives that affect marketing decision-making.[3] For example, a corporate objective to increase profits by 15 percent over the previous year has implications for current marketing actions. Objectives are critical to any company's success. Without objectives, a company has no direction. If no objectives are set, a company will waste a great amount of time, money, and effort in pursuing what may prove to be unprofitable or unrealistic strategies. A company must know where it is going if it is to be successful. A firm needs an overall set of objectives to guide its efforts. Every functional area in the company (e.g., operations, finance, marketing) also has it own objectives, but their goals must fit into or be guided by the company's overall objectives. It is imperative that the entire company works together towards the same goals. Hence, marketing strategy is influenced by, and is even to some extent constrained by, overall corporate objectives.

Similarly, marketing strategy is also constrained by available resources. A firm's resources includes finances, technological and production capabilities, managerial talent, and so on. Resource constraints prevent marketing managers from pursuing every available opportunity. For example, financial restrictions can prevent a firm from running a prime-time television campaign for a new product introduction. But it may be able to afford a national radio campaign instead. Or a firm's current production line may not be equipped to package a trial size of an existing product. New equipment may be needed, but perhaps finances won't allow it at this time. If a firm is fully aware of its limitations, strategies can be developed and opportunities pursued that *are* within the company's limits.

The External Marketing Environment

Competitive Environment

Competitiveness is how effective and efficient a firm is, relative to its rivals, at serving customers.[4] *Effectiveness* has to deal with the quality of products, market share, and

Figure 2.1   Environmental Forces in Marketing

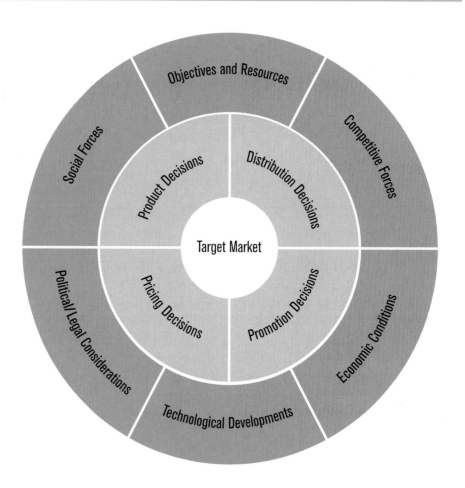

profitability, while *efficiency* has to do with response speed and low costs. Both effectiveness and efficiency ultimately depend on the strength of the firm's competitive drive and its decision-making skills.

Businesses are constantly exhorted by almost everyone—government agencies, associates oversees, and industry insiders, among others—to become more competitive. But becoming more competitive is like losing weight or converting fat to muscle. It is easy to talk about it, but not that easy to do. The task is almost impossible if it is not based on a thorough competitive analysis (see Chapter 4). The analysis should start with a general overview of the competitive structure and dynamics of the market. This includes market share analysis, a review of the history of the market, and a search for emerging competitors that threatens to drive existing firms and their products into extinction. The analysis should then zoom in on major rivals and their likely behavior.

It is surprising how often companies, even the best-run companies, take their eyes off the competition. Throughout the late 1970s and early 1980s, the DEC Vax computer architecture made major inroads in the mid-range computer market previously dominated by IBM. It took until 1986 for IBM to set up a task force (with its own war room) to really respond to DEC. By then, it was too late; the new unforeseen competitive threat was from networkable PCs.

One problem with talking about competitiveness is that we sometimes have very ambivalent attitudes toward it. We admire competitiveness in sport, but often disparage it in the classroom. Executives often use up all their energy fiercely competing among themselves for promotions. In other cases, management can sometimes become so fixated on the competition that it loses sight of what is happening with its customers. A competitive orientation involves understanding the competition and gaining an advantage from exploiting its weaknesses. It does not mean attacking the competition at every opportunity, no matter what the cost.

When monitoring the competitive environment, these key points should be remembered:

▼ Competition is a dynamic concept. Analyzing changes in market share is more important than who has what market share at any point in time.

▼ The threat of new competition depends on many types of barriers that block newcomers from entering the market. For example, the new automaker Samsung will have to spend at least $5 billion to make a ripple in the automobile market.

▼ Many markets that were once separate are now merging to create head-to-head competition.

▼ New competitive threats may emerge from new technologies.

▼ The strengths and weaknesses of existing competitors should be identified by studying their specific skills and competencies, from buying to after-sale service, throughout the order-delivery cycle.

▼ Competition is more intense because today's customers are more informed. Today's products are better and provide more information than ever before.

▼ Globalization means that there will be a lot more competition. Competition is no longer limited to local, regional, or national companies; international competitors now contend for customer dollars in almost every product category.

Legal/Political Environment

The legal and political environment poses another external force for the marketer. It is the job of the government to establish the rules and regulations to which businesses must conform. These rules and regulations affect each element in the marketing mix. Marketers must therefore be aware of and conform to all laws affecting their business.

As individual citizens, our behavior is constrained by the law and by our individual views of right and wrong.[5] It is no different for firms and marketing decision makers that compete in domestic and international markets. Marketplaces are full of rules. Many are written into law, some are stated in professional codes of ethics, and others are stated in company rules of good conduct. This section does not list all of the possible laws and ethics that might apply to a marketing decision. Instead, it asks you to think about some of the legal issues that affect marketers, in order to lay a foundation or framework for your understanding of marketing law. Such considerations may seldom be specifically stated in actual written marketing plans or decisions, but they are important.

Despite the fact that the U.S. marketplace is one of the most open and free in the world, federal, state, and local laws and agencies impose numerous constraints. The great surge of consumerism that occurred in the 1960s resulted in several new agencies, including the Product Safety Commission, and numerous new laws. More regulation means more restrictions, and more crusading regulators means higher legal expenses and the risk of a company losing its reputation if a case is tried in the press. The Library of Congress has calculated that the annual cost of completing, filing, and handling an estimated 15,000 different government forms is $40 billion, well over the national expenditure for *all* research and development. Clearly, some of this paperwork is worth the cost, but much is not.

While the legal/political environment can frustrate initiative, in general it is positive for business. For example, in the United States, many of the laws that affect marketing practice are in place to encourage competition and protect consumers (see Table 2.1).

The point is that marketers can be just as shortsighted about changes in the legal/political environment as they can about changing customer needs and technological innovations. A hostile attitude toward the legal/political environment that is generalized into a hostile

Table 2.1 Sampling of Major Laws That Affect Marketing	
Acts	**Prohibitions**
Major Laws That Protect Consumers	
Child Protection Act of 1966	Prohibits the sales of hazardous toys.
Fair Packaging and Labeling Act of 1967	Requires certain information be listed on all labels and packages, including product identification, manufacturer or distributor mailing address, and the quantity of contents.
Consumer Credit Protection Act of 1968	Requires the full disclosure of annual interest rates on loans and credit purchases.
National Environmental Policy Act of 1970	Established the Environmental Protection Agency to deal with organizations that create pollution.
Consumer Product Safety Act of 1972	Created the Consumer Product Safety Commission and empowered it to specify safety standards for consumer products.
Nutritional Labeling and Education Act of 1990	Prohibits exaggerated health claims and requires all processed foods to provide nutritional information.
Americans with Disabilities Act (ADA) of 1991	Protects the rights of people with disabilities; prohibits discrimination against the disabled (illegal in public accommodations, transportation, and telecommunications).
Brady Law of 1993	Imposes a five-day waiting period and a background check before a customer can take possession of a purchased gun.
Laws That Encourage Competition	
Sherman Antitrust Act of 1890	Prohibits restraint of trade and monopolization; delineates a competitive marketing system as a national policy.
Clayton Act of 1914	Strengthens the Sherman Act by restricting such practices as race discrimination, exclusive dealing, tying contracts, and interlocking boards of directors where the effect may be to substantially lessen competition or tend to create a monopoly.
Federal Trade Commission Act of 1914	Prohibits unfair methods of competition; establishes the Federal Trade Commission, an administrative agency that investigates business practices and enforces the FTC Act.
Robinson-Patman Act of 1936	Prohibits price discrimination in sales to wholesalers, retailers, or other producers. Also prohibits selling at unreasonably low prices to eliminate competition.
Miller-Tydings Resale Price Maintenance Act of 1937	Exempts interstate fair trade contracts from compliance with antitrust requirements.
Wheeler-Lea Act of 1938	Amended the FTC Act to further outlaw unfair practices and give the FTC jurisdiction over false and misleading advertising.
Celler-Kefauver Antimerger Act of 1950	Amended the Clayton Act to include major asset purchases that decrease competition in an industry.
American Automobile Labeling Act of 1992	Requires a vehicle's manufacturer to provide a label informing consumers of where the vehicle was assembled and where its components originated.
North American Free Trade Agreement (NAFTA) of 1993	International trade agreement existing between Canada, Mexico, and the United States. Encourages trade by removing tariffs and other trade barriers among these three countries.

attitude toward public policy is unreasonable, and if it encourages a marketing strategy that willfully frustrates the letter or intent of the law, it can be disastrous. For example, Toys 'R' Us lost market share after the Federal Trade Commission pressed charges that the toy giant was violating antitrust regulations.[6] Bill Gates and Microsoft are facing similar backlash affects as the government pursues its antitrust campaign against the computer software monolith.

www.toysrus.com

Sociocultural Environment

Changes in the sociocultural environment reflect the reshaping of the world's population in terms of numbers, characteristics, behavior, and growth projections. Consider the following changes in the socioeconomic environment and their corresponding marketing implications.[7]

▼ When Social Security began in 1936, the normal retirement age was 65. Given today's life expectancy, the corresponding retirement age would currently be 79.

▼ The number of individuals in the labor force disabled with hemorrhoids last year was almost exactly equal to the number of people who were killed by falling hot iron in steel mills in 1910.

▼ Southern Europe is committing collective suicide with a birthrate of less than one child per woman of reproductive age.

▼ In Italy there are about 60 million people; by the end of the next century there will only be 20 million Italians.

▼ The population growth rate of third-world countries is triple that of industrialized nations.

▼ In the U.S., the 50-and-over age group controls 77 percent of the nation's assets, plus more than half of the nation's discretionary income.

▼ In 1950, 70 percent of U.S. households were traditional (i.e., Dad went off to work and Mom stayed home with the kids). In 1987, just 17 percent of families were traditional.

The sociocultural environment includes changes in population growth. In 1960, 3 billion people inhabited the planet; in 1984 this number increased to 5 billion; by 2025, the world population is expected to exceed 8 billion.[8] The sociocultural environment also includes age categories within populations. The median age of Americans is increasing. In 1970, the median age was 28, in 1980, it was 30, and in 1990, 33. It is expected to rise to 36 by the year 2000.[9] Nearly 55 million U.S. citizens are over age 55, representing approximately 21 percent of the total population. This group alone accounts for over $7 trillion of the country's wealth. Some major advertisers who have recognized the importance of marketing to this segment have begun using seniors in cross-generational ads.

Customer attitudes and behavior also impact the sociocultural environment and the way marketers perceive the market. Even marketing vocabulary is changing, as seen in Table 2.2. As changes in the sociocultural environment occur, so do customer needs and wants, and so should marketer's attempts at fulfilling customer requests. For example, consider these statistics about today's women.

▼ 70 percent of women between the ages of 25 and 54 are in the labor force.[10]

▼ Women head nearly 1 in 3 of all households compared with 1 in 7 in 1950.[11]

▼ A larger share of women are remaining single into their 30s because of disenchantment with marriage and more educational and employment opportunities.[12]

Marketers must consider the changing roles of women both in marketing their products and in reaching target markets. A traditional medium like daytime television is no longer

Table 2.2   We're Not Just Yuppies Anymore

In the 1980s, Yuppies, the nickname for young, upwardly mobile, urban professionals, represented a market frequently targeted by marketers. In the 1990s, markets have changed and become increasingly fragmented. The new terms below describe some of the changes that have taken place in the sociocultural environment.

SKIPPIES	School kids with purchasing power
MOBYS	Mother older, baby younger (Reflects the trend that women are waiting until they are older to start a family.)
DINKS	Double income families, no kids
DEWKS	Dual earner families, with kids
PUPPIES	Poor urban professionals
GUPPIES	Gay urban professionals
WOOFS	Well-off older folks

an effective medium for reaching working women. Direct mail, magazines, and radio are proving to be more effective in reaching this group.

Cultural and age diversity, between and within countries, also impacts the sociocultural environment. Marketers are now targeting the specific needs of ethnic markets such as African Americans, Asians, and Latinos. This change in marketing strategy reflects the growing purchasing power of ethnic groups, their increasing rate of population growth relative to the slower growth rate of Caucasian populations, and cultural differences in how different groups purchase and use products. By the year 2010, minorities will represent one-third of the U.S. population.[13] Marketers are also gearing many of their efforts toward reaching the student market (see Figure 2.2). The increased focus on this market is partly due to the sheer numbers in the Gen X and Gen Y market segments, but is due also to corporate desires to establish name recognition and potential brand loyalty for the future.

The Americanization of world culture through science, entertainment, and business has helped to reduce the cultural differences, particularly among countries with highly educated populations.[14] This opens up the possibility for global segmentation and positioning, where segmentation spreads across rather than within cultures. In short, cultures no longer follow national, political, or cultural borders as much as they did even 50 years ago.

However, through and beyond the year 2000, many countries will still vary in their consumer wealth, buying power, price elasticity, experience with the product category, and competitive behavior. Consequently, relatively few products can be positioned exactly the same way across the global marketplace. Those that *can* normally have a strong symbolic or intangible image that transcends cultural, technological, and economic differences (for example, Coca-Cola has such an image).

Figure 2.2 Levi's Adjusts Its Marketing Strategy to Tap into the Changing Psyche of Its Customers

THE MODEL: **A premed student at New York University**
"We wanted people who are not defined by what they do but by what they are. We chose her because she looks like a Levi's type. She's young. She has her own point of view. She's sexy, but in an understated way. She's not trying too hard. She's definitely got something about her."

THE CLOTHES: **Levi's cargo pants, her own T-shirt, zip-up sweatshirt, combat boots, and accessories**
"It's important that she wore what she wanted. We're not trying to create a Levi's uniform; that wouldn't be very 'real.' We didn't use a professional stylist or a hairdresser; that wouldn't be real."

THE SETTING: **Manhattan's East Village**
"We picked New York City because it's the best reflection of today's youth life. We drove around the grittiest parts of the city. The people in the background [of this image] give it a street feel; it's obviously not staged in a studio."

THE STATEMENT: **"Music is my female soul"**
"It's hard for people to believe, but the [language] came totally from the kids; there was no prompting.... We liked the music theme [in this statement] because we do a lot to promote original music; we see music as being *the* voice of the young people."

THE TAG LINE: **"What's true"**
"The challenge with youth marketing these days is not to dictate to kids. This [line] is both a statement and a question. Is what we're saying true? Or is it a declaration? It works because it's provocative and ambiguous."

The Economic Environment

Marketers must also monitor changes in the economic environment.[15] More specifically, the economic environment includes factors such as the purchasing power of markets, per capita expenditures, employment rates, and the cost of capital that may be necessary to produce products. The mere size of markets is not enough to make a market profitable. Customers within those markets must have, in addition to the *willingness* to purchase products, the *ability* to purchase (purchasing power) as well. For example, although there are 3 billion people in Asia, half of them are under age 25 and do not possess much purchasing power. However, many of these countries have a growing middle class that outnumbers the middle classes of industrialized countries. India, for example, has a middle class of approximately 250 million consumers. Marketers such as Coca-Cola, Frito-Lay, Kentucky Fried Chicken, Motorola, and Walt Disney have recently started operations in India, which they consider to be one of the largest untapped markets in the world.

Today, it is more apparent than ever that, with the growth and reliance on international marketing, the economies of individual countries are linked into a global economy. One only needs to observe the daily fluctuations of U.S. stock markets as they reflect the trials and tribulations of Asian and Latin markets (and vice versa) to realize the connection between markets. Interest rates in one country can affect the world currency markets, which ultimately can affect the price and subsequent sales of products worldwide.

Perhaps the most significant change in industrialized economies has been the phenomenal growth in service industries. How pervasive is the service economy? Recently, Union Bank of Switzerland offered a cost of living rating service in various worldwide sectors using the "Big Mac Scale"—the percentage of weekly wages needed to buy a Big Mac! In economic terms, the service sector now accounts for 58 percent of the worldwide gross national product (GNP). In 1980, service business worldwide was valued at $350 billion and accounted for 20 percent of all world trade, whereas by 1992 that figure nearly tripled to $1,000 billion. All developed countries now have large service sectors, and Japan and Germany in particular have service economies at least as developed as that of the United States. Many service firms now operate internationally, and exports of services are also increasing. The United States remains the world's leading service exporter. Given that the U.S. balance of payments deficit in manufactured goods is nearly $130 billion a year, the $50 billion trade surplus in services is obviously vital to the U.S. economy.

Technological Environment

Successful firms must also monitor changes in the technological environment. Technology is advancing at an incredible rate.[16] For example, new sites on the World Wide Web are being developed at the rate of one per minute. Over 97 percent of large businesses report that they have Internet sites, and approximately 450,000 businesses are expected to engage in some form of electronic commerce by the year 2000. This represents a threefold increase over 1997. E-commerce is revolutionary. It has caught on faster with customers than the shopping centers of the 1950s, the discount stores of the 1960s, and the category killers like Home Depot and Circuit City of the 1980s (see Table 2.3).

Christmas 1998 was America's first Internet-driven Christmas. Americans spent $4 billion dollars in the fourth quarter of 1998 online, and $10 billion dollars for the year, more than tripling online sales from the year before. Big winners for the holiday season included Amazon.com and eToys. In the fourth quarter of 1998, Amazon.com sold enough CDs, videos, and gifts that if the packages were placed end to end, they would stretch more than 100 miles. eToys, which had 3.4 million visitors during the holiday season, shipped 95 percent of its customer orders within 24 hours of receipt. Compared to the category killer Toys 'R' Us, which had recently launched its new online service, eToys carried double the inventory and conducted nearly three times as much business. According to eToys' founder, CEO, and Harvard graduate Toby Lenk, "We just kicked butt!" The potential for e-commerce is immense. The $10 billion of online sales in 1998 represents less than 1 percent of total U.S. retail sales.

www.etoys.com

Table 2.3	Miles and Miles of Virtual Aisles	
Category of Goods Sold Online	**1998 Revenues** *Estimated in Millions*	**Growth Rate** *From 1997*
Computer hardware and software	$4,650	230%
Travel	$1,600	250%
Books, music, and entertainment	$1,300	290%
Auctions	$500	N.A.*
Gifts	$500	340%
Household goods	$500	210%
Apparel	$300	150%
Food and wine	$200	40%
Automobiles	$70	60%
Toys	$40	310%

*Not available.

Source: Patricia Sellers, "Inside the First E-Christmas," *Fortune*, v. 139, no. 2 (Feb. 1, 1999), p. 71.

Technological advances typically influence marketing practice in two ways. First, as technology advances, it enables firms to develop new products and compete in new markets.[17] In many markets today, the new competitors are often established companies with new technology that has expanded the boundaries of their traditional market. For example, in 1974, Federal Express launched its overnight letter and package delivery service, which is now a $5 billion-plus market. Beyond its direct competition, such as the U.S. Postal Service, Federal Express faced threats from several other technologies. Western Union, the original telegraph company, launched an easylink electronic mail service that would also converse with Telex, the long-established conventional business-to-business electronic mail system. Easylink failed, but the really serious threats were posed by the fax machine, and the integration of telephone and computer systems that enabled organizations and individuals to create and operate their own electronic mail services. MCI is now attempting to foster such networks.

Technological advances also assist marketers in improving how business is conducted on a day-to-day basis. Examples of these advances are discussed throughout this text. For instance, UPS handles more than 3 billion packages and 5.5 percent of the United States GDP annually.[18] Jim Kelley, the CEO of UPS, attributes much of his firm's success to technology:

> We have 12 mainframes capable of computing 5 billion bits of information every second. We have 90,000 PCs, 80,000 hand-held computers to record driver deliveries, the nation's largest private cellular network and the world's largest DB-2 data base designed for package tracking and other customer shipping information. To give you an idea of how valuable information [technology] has become to our company, the database actually has more storage capacity than the repositories of the U.S. Census Bureau.

SOCIAL RESPONSIBILITY

Marketing's First Social Responsibility: Efficiency and Effectiveness

As marketers respond to changes in the marketing environment, they must do so in a manner that is socially responsible to ensure corporate survival and growth. Marketing's first responsibility to society is to advance life, liberty, and the general happiness through the creation of markets, product innovations, and trading innovations that increase the effi-

www.federalexpress.com

www.ups.com

LEARNING **OBJECTIVE** LO2

ciency and effectiveness of the economic process. In short, the first responsibility of marketers is to keep learning to do their job ever more efficiently and effectively. This makes markets more competitive, makes our lives as workers and customers more productive, and wastes less of the scarce resources that need to be preserved for future generations.

Many people believe that marketing is not fulfilling its first **social responsibility** very well. They believe a lot of products that are marketed are not needed, and a lot of marketing effort, particularly advertising, is not needed. In the following sections, we address such criticisms.

Too Many New Unneeded Products Are Marketed That Fail

Although it is almost impossible to assess what percentage of new products succeed, it has been estimated that about half of the resources spent on developing and marketing new products is spent on failures.[19] It is very probable that better marketing research and marketing planning could increase the success rate, but it must always be appreciated that success often comes as a result of lessons learned through failures. Babe Ruth hit more home runs than any baseball player in history, and he also struck out more times than any baseball player in history. In other words, new product development and marketing is always risky, and the price of occasional success is frequent failure. Each year tens of thousands of new products fail. But do you think, before the fact, that the marketers of these products believed they would be unwanted and unneeded? Did they intend to waste all of their money and effort in such ways? Presumably not. Such wastage of money, blood, sweat, and tears is an argument for *better marketing, not less marketing.* But even the best marketing efforts often fall short. Companies can misunderstand customer preferences, fail to anticipate competitors lowering prices, or miss the clues that foreshadow the unveiling of a product even better than their own. The responsibility of marketers is to keep learning how to improve their market research, new product development, and marketing processes. Whether the science and art of marketing is getting better as fast as it could is perhaps an open question.

Too Many Unneeded Products Are Marketed That Succeed

The role of research and development in marketing is to invent, design, manufacture, and market new products that customers prefer over their currently used products. That is part of the natural evolution of markets where ever-better products replace inferior alternatives. Who would argue against the marketing of better painkillers, cancer treatments, and safer, more fuel-efficient cars? There are several reasonable and rational answers to the criticism that other successful products are just not needed, and are a waste of earth's dwindling resources and poor people's meager earnings.

The first answer is that care must be taken in making judgments for other people as to whether they should need or want a particular product. The individual freedom to pursue life, liberty, and happiness is one of the most noble principles and "rights" of the age of enlightenment that started in the 18th century. Millions of men and women have given their lives to defend this "right" and extend it to peoples who have not possessed such freedom. *Freedom and free choice* does not simply mean the right to choose the political leadership of a society. It is freedom to pursue a desired education, freedom to pursue a vocation and career in a free labor market, and freedom to spend one's earnings and savings as one chooses. If we believe in such freedoms, then we must allow the expression of this freedom in other people's choices of products. It is a slippery slope to criticize disposable diapers as a waste of trees that could be better used in producing books on enlightened thinking. It ends in a managed economy where the powerful elite prescribes what is good and what is bad for everyone else. Again and again such a system of top-down dictatorship, no matter how well meaning, has been tested and has failed—most recently in communist economies. In the United States, its citizens live with the fact that every supermarket has a full aisle of pet foods containing hundreds of choices. Is it wrong that many families spend more on their pets than on donations to feed starving children in other parts of the world? Perhaps. Do these same families have the right to choose to spend their

Social responsiblity
is the collection of marketing philosophies, policies, procedures, and actions intended primarily to enhance society's welfare.

LEARNING **OBJECTIVE** LO3

Built-in obsolescence

is the design of a product with features that the company knows will soon be superceded, thus making the model obsolete.

www.gateway.com

money this way and to respond more positively to pet food marketing campaigns than charities' marketing campaigns? Yes, they have this right, and it is a right that many have died for.

An extension of this criticism is that marketing encourages **built-in obsolescence** by coming out with new, "improved" models too often (e.g., Microsoft 98). But consumers do not need to buy the new model and they often do not. Women do not always buy into the latest spring or fall fashions. If consumers are concerned about the rapid obsolescence of their purchase, they often postpone their purchase. Such a concern also creates a marketing opportunity for an enterprising seller to introduce an innovative leasing scheme that enables consumers to easily trade-in and upgrade to the latest technology. This is precisely what Gateway Computer has done with its "Your:) ware." If this leasing solution proves that obsolescence is a real concern to PC buyers, then all sellers will offer similar leasing programs and the obsolescence concern will be addressed (see Figure 2.3).

Sometimes products are criticized for being too shoddy, with built-in components that fail too quickly. The answer to this is that quality always wins out when it is desired. The big three domestic automobile manufacturers learned this lesson the hard way in the 1980s. Should they have learned this lesson at the expense of their customers and share-

Figure 2.3

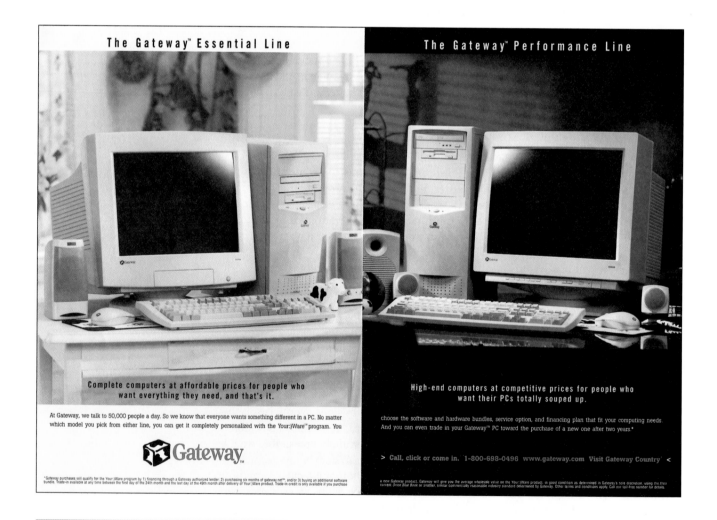

Gateway was the first major home PC manufacturer to offer purchase leases that allow customers to trade in their home PCs for an updated and advanced system.

Marketing Technologies

What to Do with Old Technology?

About 15 million computers will be sent to the landfill in the United States in 1999, and this number will increase by at least 10 percent each year. While this represents a small portion of the total solid waste stream (less than one-half of one percent), computers contain a variety of hazardous materials that can adversely impact the environment. For instance, monitors and televisions that contain cathode ray tubes (CRTs) possess significant amounts of lead—an element that can damage the nervous system, especially in children. The U.S. Environmental Protection Agency reported that 24 percent of all lead in the municipal waste stream is attributable to CRTs. Other computer components that contain hazardous materials include mercury switches, cadmium batteries, and lead solder.

As a result of the rapid obsolescence of computers and worries about their environmental impact, governments around the world are crafting regulation to keep electronic equipment out of landfills. The Commonwealth of Massachusetts began banning businesses and households July 1, 1999, from putting CRTs into its landfills. European countries are also pursuing far-reaching "Take Back" legislation that requires manufacturers to bear the full cost and responsibility of unwanted electronic equipment disposal.

Driven by this environmental concern and government regulation, a whole new industry of electronic recycling has emerged. The largest such firm is Aurora Electronics of California. In 1995 it posted revenues of $95 million: $52 million from the resale of spare computer parts and $43 million from recycling and refurbishing. Envirocycle of Pennsylvania recycled over 500,000 monitors in 1996 and its full service demanufacturing operation is growing at more than 40 percent each year. Additionally, hundreds of small firms have been formed in recent years around the world to refurbish, demanufacture, and recycle electronic waste. These companies succeed by regularly forming strategic alliances with the original equipment manufacturers (OEMs) to process their surplus inventory, warranty returns, and off-spec products, and by offering full service asset management disposition to businesses and municipalities that generate electronic waste.

Electronic asset recovery programs excel in the marketplace for two reasons. First, they satisfy the growing demand by consumers for more environmentally friendly products. Second, they provide services that result in cost savings and avoided liability claims to OEMs (original equipment manufacturers) and other waste generators. These issues propelled Xerox to institute its own asset recovery and remanufacturing program. "The switch to asset recovery was not done primarily because of environmental considerations, although we realized that would be a benefit," notes Jack Azar, manager of environmental design and resource conservation for Xerox. "We saw competitive advantage coming from this program." From 1991–1995, Xerox reaped $200 million in raw material and parts savings, and reduced its landfill and potential liability costs by more than $450,000 annually. These cost savings are shared with the customers.

Electronics recycling firms are finding treasure in other people's electronic trash. By responding to a market demand created by the growth of a "waste" product, new government regulations, consumers' environmental concerns, and operational cost reduction projects at OEMs, these businesses are able to earn a profit while providing a beneficial service to the environment.

Questions

1. How is the rapid reduction in the price of PCs and the increase in performance affecting the dumping and recycling of old PC systems?

2. What other products are likely to pose a major recycling problem in the future?

---

holders? No, but such behavior always catches up with companies in free markets. The reputation of the offending firm is hurt for years, sometimes decades. On the other hand, many critics of the modern market economy complain that product parts last too long, and that manufacturers should be required to dispose of their products at the customer's request and recycle the materials. The free market answer to this criticism is the creation of a new service market where firms compete to dispose of and recycle such products.

Market Distribution Systems Are Inefficient

There has been a long tradition of criticizing the inefficiency of distribution systems. It has its roots in the complaints of farmers who, for example, calculate that they are paid only 20 cents for the corn that is finally sold by the supermarkets as cornflakes for $2 or more. Does this seem fair? Who is making all the profits in the added-value process from the farm to the breakfast table, and how much "added value" are they really adding?

It is hard not to have sympathy for the farmer, particularly if you come from a farming heritage. But to ask whether each player in the chain deserves its margins, and to try to calculate some efficiency measure, is to ask the wrong question. The truth is a great deal of innovation and learning has occurred in physical distribution in the United States over the last 30 years. So much so that the percentage of the gross domestic product spent on the cost of physical distribution (order processing, transportation, and inventory storage) has dropped from 12 percent to about 8 percent. At the same time, the reliability and quality of these services has greatly increased. This came about because deregulation of the transportation and communication industries in the late 1970s led to an incredible burst of competition and innovation that reduced the cost of their services and increased their quality. The cost of distribution has also benefited from stable and low interest rates and fuel costs. No other major sector has increased its efficiency, as measured by its reduced share of GDP, by anything like physical distribution's 50 percent improvement. It puts the increased costs of health care and education to shame. No other country has as efficient a physical distribution system as the United States. Has enough innovation occurred in physical distribution to make it "efficient"? Again, this is a silly question because it cannot be answered. What is clear is that competitive forces are forcing supermarkets, mass merchandisers, and department stores to adopt the new technologies of distribution. If they do not, then fierce competitors who are trendsetters in innovation of new efficient distribution processes such as Wal-Mart and Home Depot will drive them out of business.

The current distribution system will last only as long as a more competitive system is not invented and developed. The current system replaced the earlier system, that replaced the earlier system, that replaced the earlier system. As long as we see this occurring in distribution, we know that distribution is becoming more efficient. We see this occurring everywhere: Cars are being marketed by super-dealerships; vacations are being booked using travel agents identified by Web searches; books are being purchased through online stores on the Web. We see an increase in mail-order catalog sales. We saw Kmart replace Sears as *the* mass merchandiser, and now Wal-Mart has replaced Kmart. But stores such as Meijer and Target are now challenging Wal-Mart. We see major new airports being built, major container ports being expanded, and trains stacking containers two high.

Of course some intermediaries will stubbornly remain inefficient relative to best practices, and they can be viewed as betraying the first social responsibility of marketing, which is to strive to improve and become ever more efficient. They are a blight on marketing, just as doctors who refuse to improve their practices and teachers who refuse to improve their teaching are a blight on their profession. But how long will the inefficient distributor survive before competition eats their lunch? Not as long as the inefficient doctor or teacher who is protected from competition. If marketing is socially irresponsible because it does not try hard enough to improve the efficiency of its distribution systems, then the medical and teaching professions presumably face much greater condemnation because their comparative improvement in performance over the last 30 years to some has seemed pitiful. The reason is also clear—doctors and teachers have too little competition to force better customer service at lower cost.

A Lot of Advertising Is Wasteful Expenditure

Perhaps what is underlying a lot of the criticism of marketing is identified with mass advertising, and mass advertising is inherently inefficient in reaching interested customers. This inefficiency leads to a lot of people being exposed to advertising of products or brands that they are not the least interested in, and hence is viewed as intrusive and wasteful, even alien to their values.[20]

For example, let us consider a typical flight of six 30-second television commercials. Even if the advertiser has targeted a program that has a high percentage of its target customers as viewers, it is unlikely that more than 20 percent of the viewing audience are *potential buyers:* They are current satisfied users of the brand, or open to switching to the brand. What percentage of the viewing audience will be interested in three or more of the advertisements in the flight of six commercials? The answer is less than 10 percent. No wonder so many people say that television advertising, junk mail, and telephone marketing is a waste of money and intrudes on their privacy. It is because advertising and marketing is very **inefficient in its targeting** of interested audiences, not because it is efficient, skilled, and manipulative.

www.wal-mart.com
www.homedepot.com

www.meijer.com
www.target.com

Inefficient targeting
results when advertising and distribution reaches too broad an audience, most of whom are not interested in the product.

In fact the phrase "being turned off" by advertising may not be simply a phrase that describes a negative attitude. It may actually describe the psychological mechanism that customers in a "high consumption" materialistic society develop, from an early age, to cope with the irrelevance and inefficiency of advertising and sales pitches. It is entirely possible that we learn to develop attention mechanisms that allow us to tune out advertising, just as we tune out of so many other stimuli that are competing for our attention day in and day out.

How do advertisers cope with the increased tuning out of customers? They increase their efforts to try to get us to tune in, through more powerful attention-grabbing mechanisms. This explains why television advertisements have become ever more expensive and elaborate productions, crafted to gain and keep our attention, often by using popular celebrities or zany humor. It also explains why direct marketing has developed more devious ways of getting us to open the mail—a common ruse is to disguise the mail as coming from a friend or from the IRS! But it is also likely that we are not fooled for long. We develop ever more powerful and selective tuning out mechanisms to cope with these increasingly attention-grabbing mechanisms. Thus, the cost of creating advertising that gains our attention is spiraling upward with little or no long-term increase in its effectiveness. And it is not just that mass advertising is becoming more expensive. A greater percentage of the money is being spent on gaining our attention than on explaining why the product is better than other alternative products.

A development that may save the image and cost efficiency of advertising is the development of very specialized digital TV channels and specialized electronic and print magazines. If this results in a much better overlap of the product target market and the audience, the average ratings of advertising would become more positive. If the overlap were strong enough that an average of 50 percent of the viewing audience would be interested in any particular advertisement, then this would result in two-thirds of the audience reporting interest in three or more of the ads in a flight of six 30-second commercials. The audience would also learn to pay more attention to such advertising because it is of interest. In short, the answer to the criticism of advertising's social value is better targeting of interested audiences, which requires the invention of communication channels that are better targeted to the "interested" audience.

Marketers have a social responsibility to keep learning to undertake their functions more effectively, but there is more to this responsibility than increased efficiency and effectiveness. Marketers have to learn to consider the full consequences of their collective actions. Making marketing practices ever more efficient and effective is of no help if it leads to the destruction of resources that are vital to humankind or to a corruption of values that are considered fundamental to a civil society.

Supply-Side Market Failure

In a free market, the individual activities of sellers can have an accumulative effect that is often not intended, and can lead to harmful effects on others or society at large. This is called the **tragedy of the commons** because it was first described in the context of the common grazing area (sort of equivalent to the modern public park) that villages in England used to make available for local residents to graze their sheep. To each village household it did not seem unreasonable to increase its small flock of sheep. But across a hundred villagers this pursuit of individual self-interest led to such severe over-grazing that all of the grass on the commons died. Now no one was able to graze their sheep on the commons, and everyone's sheep starved and died. Modern examples of "the tragedy of the commons" are everywhere. The world's fish resources are running out because fishermen have used modern technology to increase their fishing capabilities, and each individual fisherman does not believe that his individual behavior will ruin fishing for everyone. But when accumulated, such behavior has led to such a destruction of supply that many varieties of fish have fallen below a sustainable breeding population. This is a prime example of **supply-side market failure.** The incremental self-interested behavior of millions of

Tragedy of the commons
is the name given to the process where individuals, pursuing their own self-interest, overuse a common good to such an extent that the common good is destroyed.

Supply-side market failure
results when the individual activities of suppliers inadvertently lead to destructive effects on the overall supply.

Table 2.4 Earth's Three Socioecological Classes		
Overconsumers **1.1 Billion** **> US $7,500 per capita** **(cars, meat, disposables)**	**Sustainers** **3.3 Billion** **US $7,500 per capita** **(living lightly)**	**Marginals** **1.1 Billion** **< US $700 per capita** **(absolute deprivation)**
Travel by car and air	Travel by bicycle and public surface transport	Travel by foot, maybe donkey
Eat high-fat, high-calorie, meat-based diets	Eat healthy diets of grains, vegetables, and some meat	Eat nutritionally inadequate diets
Drink bottled water and soft drinks	Drink clean water, plus some tea and coffee	Drink contaminated water
Use throwaway products and discard substantial waste	Use unpackaged goods and durables and recycle wastes	Use local biomass and produce negligible wastes
Live in spacious, climate-controlled, single-family residences	Live in modest, naturally-ventilated residences with extended/multiple families	Live in rudimentary shelters or in the open; usually lack secure tenure
Maintain image-conscious wardrobe	Wear functional clothing	Wear secondhand clothing or scraps

Source: Based on Alan Durning, *How Much Is Enough,* Worldwatch Institute, 1993.

businesses and consumers around the world is threatening the very supply of trees, fresh water, and fresh air.

But how do you tell a family in China not to burn coal to heat their house, or a utility not to burn coal to generate electricity, when families and utilities in Europe and America have done so for hundreds of years, creating much of the ozone problem? It is not easy. Table 2.4 presents earth's three *socioecological* classes. As the economies of China, India, and other countries experience very rapid growth over the next 20 years, a billion "sustainers" will become "overconsumers" and the stresses on the earth's environment resources will be tremendous. Markets will have to be regulated, and marketers will have to obey these regulations. If the abilities and resources of marketing are spent on fighting (or finding ways around) regulation, then we will face a "tragedy of the commons" of global proportions. The responsibility of marketers is to promote conservation, recycling, and product innovations that save energy, air, water, trees, fish, and other scarce resources (see Figure 2.4). They can be helped by government programs and policies that encourage sellers to market more earth-friendly products. Such efforts make everyone more environmentally conscious, and consciousness raising is what is needed. It is everyone's responsibility to save the supply of scarce resources for the hundreds of generations of our descendants.

Not all is doom and gloom. Between 1980 and 1995 water use in the United States dropped by 9 percent even with a population growth of 16 percent.[21] Using innovative recycling programs, industry water use has dropped by 35 percent. Water use for farm irrigation has dropped by 11 percent primarily because farmers have switched from rotary sprayers (that waste a lot of water) to underground systems that water the roots. Household use has stayed steady, but innovations such as the short-flush toilet are making a difference. The answer to gloom and doom is the marketing of clever new innovations.

Demand-Side Market Failure

The self-destructive accumulation problem in free markets is not only occurring on the supply side. It also occurs on the demand side in some interesting ways, resulting in **demand-side market failure.** Over the last two decades in the United States, market research tools such as focus groups and political polling have been used to target voter concerns and issues. But instead of being used to guide the creation of innovative new programs and policies, the resulting customer insights have often been used to create negative advertising that attacks the values and character of political opponents. Today voters get most of their information about candidates running for election from TV ads, and yet more than 90 percent of adults believe that the claims made in these ads are mostly (or at least

Demand-side market failure is the cumulative effect of the marketing practices of many thousands of advertising campaigns that has a residual negative impact on the values of buyers and the demand for various products (e.g., voting).

Figure 2.4   Ford Motor Company Promoting Their Recycling Efforts

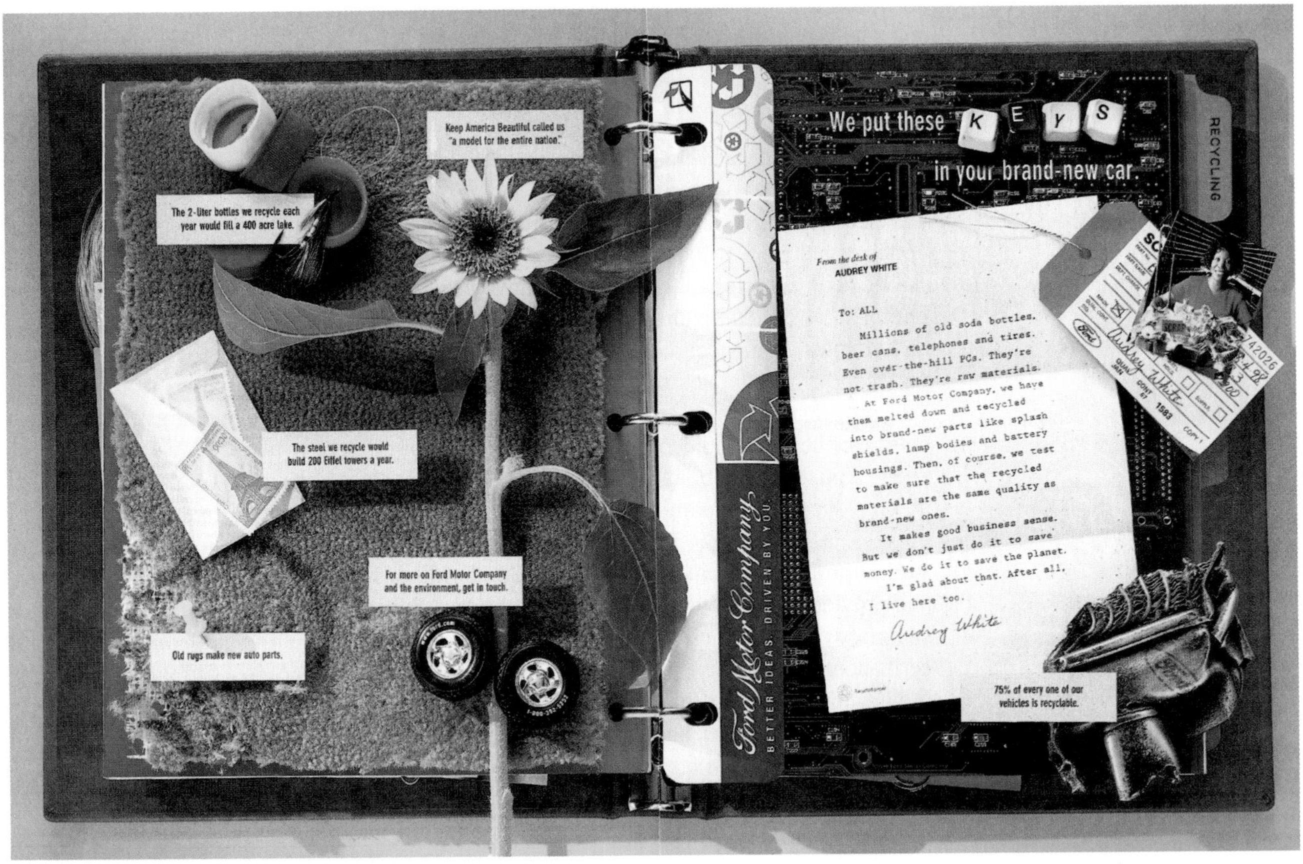

partially) not true.[22] The result has been to greatly reduce voters' respect for politicians and the electoral process: "I'm so sick of these ads . . . because nine out of 10 are negative," is a typical response. Such turn-off has reduced participation in the fundamental democratic process. The participative democracy market is in danger of failing because of the marketing practices of candidates and political parties.

More generally, the cumulative effect of the marketing practices of many thousands of advertising campaigns has been claimed to have a residual negative impact on the values of certain groups. This surfaces in T-shirts worn by women that say "There are 9 supermodels and 3 billion other women on this earth." The point, which is immediately understandable to tens of millions of women and men, is that the extensive use of these supermodels in advertising sets impossible standards for girls to aspire to in their appearances. The result is low self-esteem and self-confidence. A quite reasonable reaction is for women to be turned off by fashion and "lookism," and to turn to other self-esteem boosting activities. Demand is again being killed by the accumulated impact of advertising. The problem is that marketers have found that using supermodels sells. Consumers, both men and women, respond to such marketing—we find such models very appealing. If this were not true, then marketers would not spend billions of dollars on marketing campaigns using such models. Should we then limit the opportunities of people to make a living off their beauty? Should we limit the ability of advertisers to use beauty to sell, because it makes ordinary folks feel more ordinary? Again, this is a slippery-slope question. What if great writers, painters, composers, athletes, and heroes inspire us, enrich our dreams, and lift the human spirit, but they also make our own achievements seem very ordinary? Should their works be banned? This at least raises an issue of whether critics of marketing apply the same ethical standards and codes to marketing as they do to other fields of human achievement and activity. It brings us to the second major social responsibility of marketing.

Marketing's Second Social Responsibility: Ethical Codes of Behavior

The second major social responsibility of marketing is to consistently abide to ethical codes of behavior. Most companies do live up to this responsibility. Despite the well-publicized exceptions that the media have used to help create an image that business is unethical, many companies in the United States today are moral enterprises, led by men and women of impeccable character. The moral rudder of most enterprises is under the very solid control of senior executives, particularly the chief executive officer and senior vice presidents of sales and marketing, who lead by example and encourage a corporate culture of honesty and decency. Such enterprises often have written codes of ethics. It has been estimated that about 60 percent of U.S. companies have written codes of ethics that all employees agree to abide by. They are commonly accepted as a "given" across all employees.[23] Some larger companies have appointed an ethics officer, or ombudsperson, to further promote ethical behavior. These individuals help executives in tough decisions, and provide a safe haven (and source of support) for whistle blowers. Table 2.5 presents a summary of the business conduct guidelines of IBM and P&G. The guidelines reflect concern about treating customers (and everyone in the marketplace) in a fair and decent way, but also expresses more general concerns—such as respecting the intellectual property rights of others, caring about the environment, and encouraging community service. Notice that the IBM code focuses more on trading ethics, while the P&G code is a more general social contract.

Figure 2.5 summarizes the content of some two hundred company ethics statements. United States companies are more concerned about intellectual property rights (such as

Table 2.5 Business Conduct Guidelines for IBM and Guides for P&G	
IBM	**P&G**
Do not make misrepresentations to anyone you deal with.	To provide customers with superior benefits.
Do not use IBM's size unfairly to intimidate or threaten.	To listen and respond to customer opinions.
Treat all buyers and sellers equitably.	To ensure products are safe for intended use and anticipate accidental misuse.
Do not engage in reciprocal dealing.	To strive for fair and open business relationships with suppliers and retailers.
Do not disparage competitors.	To help business partners improve performance.
Do not prematurely disclose an unannounced offering.	To reject illegal or deceptive activities anywhere in the world.
Do no further selling after competitor has the firm offer.	To safeguard the environment.
Keep contact with the competition minimal.	To encourage employees to participate in community activities.
Do not illegally use confidential information.	To be a good neighbor in communities in which business is done.
Do not steal or obtain information by willful deceit.	To provide employees a safe workplace.
Do not violate patents or copyrights.	To show concern for the well-being of all employees.
Do not give or accept bribes, gifts, or entertainment that might be seen as creating an obligation.	To create opportunities for employee achievement, creativity, and personal reward.
	To provide a fair annual return to the owners.
	To build for the future to maintain growth.

Sources: Gene R. Laczniak and Patrick E. Murphy, *Marketing Ethics* (Lexington, MA: Lexington Books, 1985), 117–23; and Jan Willem Bol, Charles T. Crespy, James M. Stearns, and John R. Walton, *The Integration of Ethics into the Marketing Curriculum* (Needham Heights, MA: Ginn Press, 1991), p. 27.

Figure 2.5   Issues Addressed by Company Ethics Statements

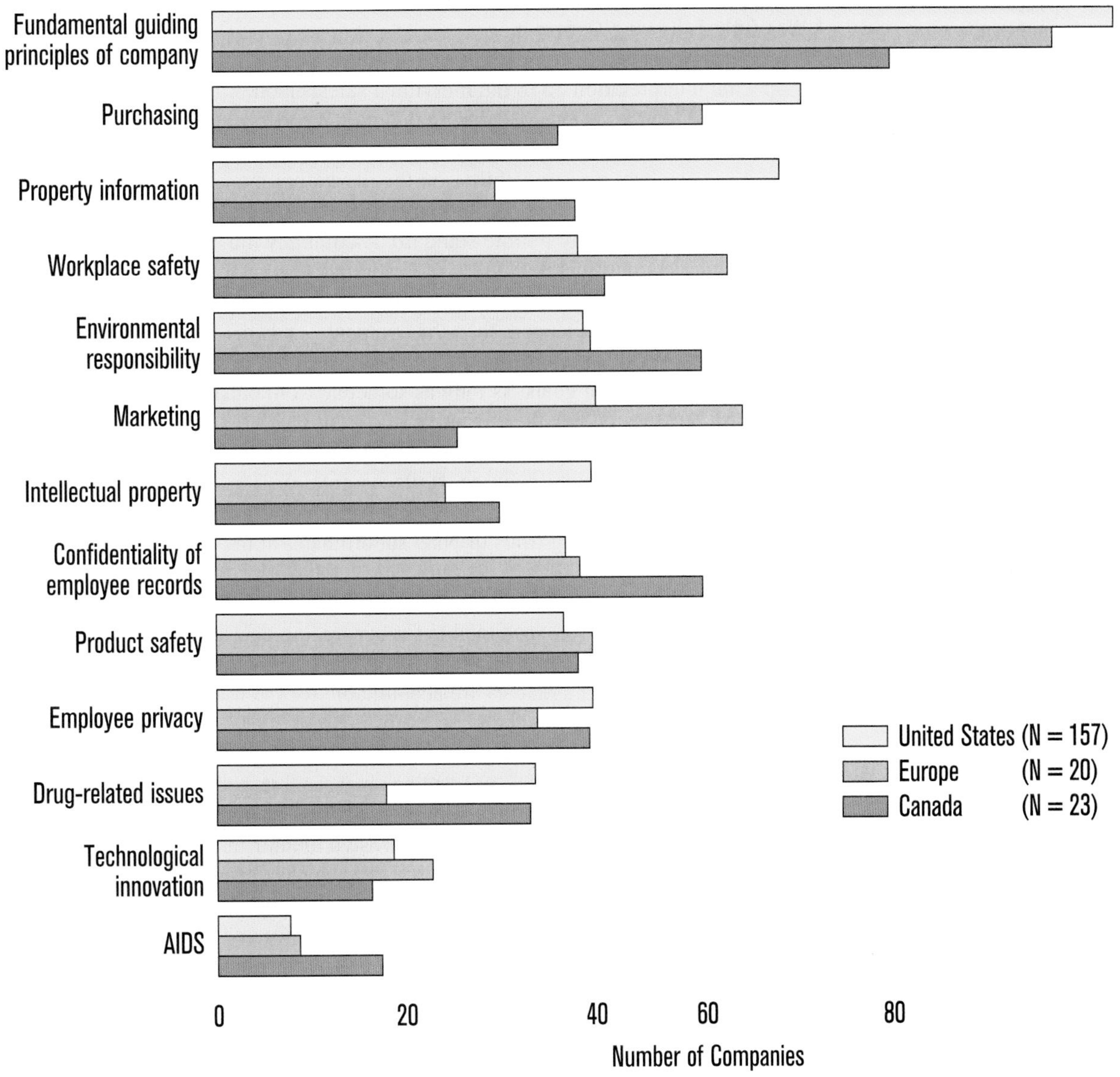

It seems that companies are more concerned that their purchasing is ethical than that their marketing is ethical. In comparison, U.S. firms are more frequently concerned about proprietary information, Canadian firms are more frequently concerned about environmental responsibility, and European firms are more frequently concerned about workplace safety.

Source: Reproduced with permission from Ronald E. Berenheim, *Corporate Ethics Practices* (New York: The Conference Board, 1992).

not stealing patents, copyrighted material, and confidential information) and about ethical purchasing practices. Does this mean that some companies are more concerned about making sure that their buyers do not take bribes and indulge in other unethical behavior, and less concerned about the ethical behavior of their own marketing practices (such as offering bribes)? Whatever your opinion, this figure reminds us that ethical trading requires both the seller and the buyer to behave ethically. European companies seem to address purchasing and marketing ethical issues in about the same proportion. Canadian companies are somewhat more concerned about environmental issues, suggesting that concern over the environment is a more important part of the "social contract" and culture in Canada.

I Was Only Following Orders

As was seen in Table 2.5, company codes of ethics are often stated in general terms, leaving specific interpretation up to the individual salesperson or marketing executive. However, ethical dilemmas often arise during the implementation of marketing strategy. When this happens, decisions must be made without an opportunity to consult superiors. Such situations throw heavy responsibility on the marketing manager, product manager, and sales force. This ethical stress on the marketing executive can be greatly heightened by the presence of a company double standard. A company must make clear what action it will take against unethical behavior, and establish credibility by following through. It must walk the talk. If actions are taken only when a company's unethical behavior is discovered and publicly challenged, then the company sends the worst signals to its marketing executives. What it says is that the company does not really mind what an executive does to achieve financial goals, as long as someone from outside does not find out. If the misconduct becomes public, the executive in question will take the fall, and the company will deny any knowledge of his actions. Unfortunately, many marketing decision makers face this conflict to varying degrees. It places great demand on their personal code of ethics. It also greatly undermines their respect for senior executives.

The famous Nuremberg trials of Nazi subordinates at the end of World War II established a new principle of ethical accountability. All of the evil could not be blamed on Hitler, nor was the excuse "If I did not obey orders, then I would have been punished," found acceptable. We are all accountable for our trading decisions and behavior. Subordinates are responsible for their own behavior, even if following orders or under the threat of dismissal. Advertising agencies are accountable for the honesty of the messages they create for their clients. Ignorance is no excuse. No one gets an easy way out. To take a stand may put a promotion, a business contract, a trading relationship, or even a job at risk. To not take a stand is to sell out one's values, self-respect, and soul. To pass the responsibility on to senior executives may be construed as weakness, or worse, setting up the boss. When orders and ethics collide, a trusted mentor in the organization can be invaluable. That is why ethics ombudsmen and women have been created.

The American Marketing Association also has developed a code of ethics (see Figure 2.6) that marketing professionals can turn to for guidance and direction. The emphasis is on ethical trading behavior, and approximately half of the points mentioned are associated with honesty and disclosure. The code can help bolster an executive's belief that the stand that he is taking is ethical and socially responsible. However, the American Marketing Association, unlike some other "professional" organizations, is not in a position to provide legal support to its members who face a conflict between their personal ethics and what they are being asked to do. This places a great deal of responsibility on the individual marketing executive. Exercising this responsibility requires a much deeper understanding of what is prescribed as right and wrong. It requires an understanding of where such values and rules originate, and the issues and moral philosophy that underlie personal and organizational ethics.

Theories of Marketing Ethics

It is no accident that both primitive and advanced civilizations have ethical and moral codes that constrain group and individual behavior and attempt to maintain the social fabric of the culture. The enlightenment of a civilization is often measured by its underlying ethics. When ethical codes break down, societies cease to function and ultimately collapse from within (for example, the decline and fall of the Roman Empire, the collapse of communist systems) or under external pressures (for example, the defeat of the Third Reich in World War II).

The great philosophers of the "enlightenment," Jean-Jacques Rousseau and Thomas Hobbes, argued that society needs a set of ethical rules, a morality accepted by all, called

Figure 2.6   American Marketing Association Code of Ethics

American Marketing Association Code of Ethics

Members of the American Marketing Association are committed to ethical professional conduct. They have joined together in subscribing to this Code of Ethics embracing the following topics:

Responsibilities of the Marketer
Marketers must accept responsibility for the consequences of their activities and make every effort to ensure that their decisions, recommendations, and actions function to identify, serve, and satisfy all relevant publics: customers, organizations, and society.

Marketers' Professional Conduct must be guided by:
1. The basic rule of professional ethics: not knowingly to do harm
2. The adherence to all applicable laws and regulations
3. The accurate representation of their education, training, and experience
4. The active support, practice, and promotion of this Code of Ethics

Honesty and Fairness
Marketers shall uphold and advance the integrity, honor, and dignity of the marketing profession by:
1. Being honest in serving consumers, clients, employees, suppliers, distributors, and the public
2. Not knowingly participate in conflict of interest without prior notice to all parties involved
3. Establishing equitable fee schedules including the payment or receipt of usual, customary, and/or legal compensation for marketing exchanges

Rights and Duties of Parties in the Marketing Exchange Process
Participants in the marketing exchange process should be able to expect that
1. Products and services offered are safe and fit their intended uses
2. Communications about offered products and services are not deceptive
3. All parties intend to discharge their obligations, financial and otherwise, in good faith
4. Appropriate internal methods exist for equitable adjustment and/or redress of grievances concerning purchases

It is understood that the above would include, but is not limited to, th following responsibilities of the marketer:

In the area of product development and management:

Disclosure of all substantial risks associated with product or service usage
Identification of any product component substitution that might materially change the product or impact on the buyer's purchase decision
Identification of extra cost-added features

In the area of promotions:
Avoidance of false and misleading advertising
Rejection of high-pressure manipulations, or misleading sales tactics
Avoidance of sales promotions that use deception or manipulation

In the area of distribution:
Not manipulating the availability of a product for the purpose of exploitation
Not using coercion in the marketing channel
Not exerting undue influence over the reseller's choice to handle a product

In the area of pricing:
Not engaging in price fixing
Not practicing predatory pricing
Disclosing the full price associated with any purchase

In the area of marketing research:
Prohibiting selling or fundraising under the guise of conducting research
Maintaining research integrity by avoiding misrepresentation and omission of pertinent research data
Treating outside clients and suppliers fairly

Organizational Relationships
Marketers should be aware of how their behavior may influence or impact the behavior of others in organizational relationships. They should not demand, encourage, or apply coercion to obtain unethical behavior in their relationships with others, such as employees, suppliers, or customers.

1. Apply confidentiality and anonymity in professional relationships with regard to privileged information
2. Meet their obligations and responsibilities in contracts and mutual agreements in a timely manner
3. Avoid taking the work of others, in whole, or in part, and representing this work as their own or directly benefiting from it without compensation or consent of the originator or owner
4. Avoid manipulation to take advantage of situations to maximize personal welfare in a way that unfairly deprives or damages the organization or others

Any AMA member found to be in violation of any provision of this Code of Ethics may have his or her Association membership suspended or revoked.

a *social contract,* for it to function effectively. If you want to be part of society, you obey the rules. If entrepreneurs and firms wish to trade in a society and profit from such trade, then they have a social and moral obligation to accept the general ethical rules of the society, and not undermine them with unacceptable trading practices. So what are some of these rules?

Choose to Do the Most Good for the Most People. The famous philosophers, David Hume, Jeremy Bentham, and John Stuart Mill, developed the principle of utility. The ***principle of utility*** is that "ethical behavior" is the behavior that produces the most good for the most people in a specific situation. At first brush, this sounds like a very good rule. But in practice this ethical principle is hard to apply. First, how does one calculate the most good for the most people? How do you total up all of the good and bad? Can you measure *good* by adding up all the positive outcomes and then subtracting all the negative outcomes? For example, is it allowable to have 1 out of 10,000,000 consumers die from the side effects of a new drug, if the drug is twice as effective at relieving the headache pain for the other 9,999,999 users?

And how do you keep your perspective and independence in making such judgments? How do people avoid underemphasizing what is good for others and overemphasizing what is good for themselves? How does a decision maker avoid overweighing the benefit that he or she is likely to receive personally? In our personal lives we have all experienced how hard it is to separate one's desires and goals from the judgement of what is right. Furthermore, no less than Adam Smith pointed out that pursuing your own self-interest over the interests of others promotes the overall good. This sounds like ethical permission to overemphasize the good you will receive over the good and bad outcomes for others.

The utility principle can be twisted into some interesting interpretations. It can lead an otherwise ethical company to decide that it must sink to the lowest ethical standards among a group of competitors. "If we were to be more ethical," a company might argue, "we, as a good guy, might go out of business, and what good would be gained from that? It is in the interest of our employees, our customers, and society (that is, the total good) that we, who are basically an ethical firm, stay in business even if it means that we have to stoop to the unethical practices of our rivals." This kind of thinking can become moral quicksand. It can mean being dragged down to the ethics of the most desperate competitor. How common is this dilemma? It is as common as the occurrence of paying off government officials in many markets around the world, which is still quite common. It is as common as competing against companies that have lower costs because they are not using scrubbers or other technology to reduce global pollution, again another very common event.

Another harsh reality is that the more desperate the company or personal situation, the lower the applied ethical standards will be, and the more the decision maker will be fixated with how his or her company will benefit. Again, the rationalization is that behaving unethically is for the total good, and that the means justifies the ends, which are saving the jobs of employees, etc. Sometimes it seems that only successful companies and executives can afford a conscience. In economic terms marketing ethics is called a ***normal good*** because demand for it increases as the income of a company increases.

What If Everyone Did It? Immanuel Kant's famous categorical imperative offers an alternative to the utility principle. The ***categorical imperative*** asks whether the proposed action would be right if everyone did it. What would happen to the social fabric? This view of ethics asks us to think about the social destructiveness of trading practices that, if only we do it, seem hardly serious violations. For example, consider the trading practice of including puffery (exaggerated claims) in advertising. If only done occasionally it does not seem so serious, but if everyone did it all the time then advertising would lose its integrity, its credibility, and end up destroying the usefulness of a major marketing tool. It would also greatly reduce the efficiency of markets, because markets rely on advertising to transmit information to everyone about prices, availability, new innovations, and quality. What would happen if the one million plus companies in the United States each made several hundred unsolicited phone calls each evening? Would that be socially responsible and fair? What would happen if you were constantly on the receiving end of such ethics? At a global marketing level, many companies lobby their government to erect trade barriers to protect them from foreign competitors. But what happens if all countries were to erect such barriers? It would kill global trade, and the world would be plunged into a depression such as occurred in the 1930s.

This approach takes most of the situation or context out of the ethical evaluation and, in that sense, is more explicit than the utilitarian principle. It also has elements of "do unto others what you would have them do unto you." But the categorical imperative still requires the decision maker to see the universal wrong or evil in the act if everyone did it, including doing it to them. Immoral or amoral individuals, caring nothing for society, may answer that, yes, it would be fine for society, and that others are welcome to act in the same way toward them. Both situational ethics and the categorical imperative still require a basic set of values. Whose responsibility is it to instill such values in marketing decision makers?

Where Do Our Basic Values Come From?

Basic decency and morality are taught on or across a father or mother's knee, with grandmothers, grandfathers, uncles, aunts, or other surrogate parents helping out. If not taught by extended family members, such basic values are taught to us as children by teachers, coaches, and through organizations such as the YMCA, Boy Scouts, and Girl Scouts. Finally, ethical teachings are provided to us at our church, synagogue, mosque, or other sources of our spiritual and religious beliefs. But what if, somehow as adults, some of us seem to have missed these lessons. Some say it is way too late to teach adults about the basic ethics of honesty, decency, and consideration for others. Others seem to expect companies to take on this impossible task for their employees. But is that really the firm's responsibility? Are parents, schools, and the world's great religions becoming lax in living up to their side of the social contract to teach children decency, honesty, and consideration for others?

One of the distinguishing characteristics of different civilizations, countries, societies, and tribes is their dominant religion. It often has great impact. For example, the **predominant religion** of the United States is Christianity. The Judeo-Christian creed, along with "enlightenment thinking" has greatly influenced the Constitution, common law, and the system of justice in the United States. Thus, it can be argued that marketers in the United States fulfill the social contract by adopting a code of marketing ethics based on Judeo-Christian religious beliefs that have defined our society's law and morality.

But what happens to those who believe in some other religion's ethical code? It is to be expected in a free society that a believer of another religion will apply his or her religious ethics to all situations, including marketing decision making. This exercise of different religious beliefs and values increases the variability in ethics that we are likely to observe in the marketplace. One economic reason we should use the "predominant religion" values as the common core for our society's ethics, even if we are not followers of that religion, is that the universal acceptance of its code enables us to anticipate the likely behavior of other parties in the market. This anticipation leads to an increase in trust, and a sense of confidence and control that the market is orderly and fair, and thus reduces the costs of doing business. Notice that this creates a fundamental ethical dilemma: a trade-off between freedom of religion, beliefs in different ethical codes, and the efficiency of the market. An example of this problem has occurred in diamond trading around the world. For years, a fundamental sect of Jews dominated the global trading of these precious gems. The ethical behavior of these diamond traders in their trading between themselves was very high for centuries. A trader's word was his bond. But now the sect's religious ethics do not have the same hold on some younger generations of traders, and new traders from Russia and Asia have entered the market. The result is that there is much less trust in the diamond-trading business than there used to be, and this has increased the risk and cost of diamond trading.

www.ymca.com

Situational ethics
is that societal condition where "right" and "wrong" are determined by the specific situation, rather than by universal moral principles.

www.lizclaiborne.com

If the clearly dominant and underlying religious creed in a society or amongst a group of specialized traders is not to be used as the foundation for a generally accepted code of business ethics, then what should be used? It would be extraordinarily difficult to argue that some other religious or moral philosophy should be substituted. More generally, a serious and unresolved **situational ethics** problem often occurs in global marketing.

No international code of business ethics exists, because each society's ethics vary—some slightly and others greatly. Fortunately, most of the world's major religions and cultures share common norms and ethics, and would answer the questions on an ethical checklist similarly. But in some countries bribery, kickbacks, and dishonesty in advertising, selling, and dealing are much more acceptable than in others. How should American firms behave in such markets? If they do not tolerate such standard practices, they risk not doing business, and further, may be hated for arrogantly imposing their values where they are not wanted. For example, should American garment manufacturers be concerned about the working conditions in the offshore factories that produce many of their clothing lines? Liz Claiborne makes unscheduled visits to its suppliers to ensure they meet the company's standards, and attempts to work with those suppliers that provide the best working conditions. Presumably, other companies are less particular, only caring about price and output quality. But just how much American companies should be held responsible for the human rights abuses of their suppliers is unclear, particularly if caring puts the American company at a competitive cost disadvantage.

The quick and easy answer, "When in Rome, do as the Romans do," is no real answer for at least two reasons. First, international business is carried out in two places at once, for example, between a seller in New York and a buyer in Rome. What is the social contract in this situation? Is it determined by the accepted norms of the American or the Italian trading partner's political economy? Second, this philosophy suggests abandoning one's own "moral compass," and replacing it with the ethical standards of your trading partner—not a comfortable or natural position to be in. With the increase in global marketing comes a pressing need to adopt an international code of ethics. Unethical behavior will always exist, but it can be defined the same way and condemned by every society. Even if this occurs some time in the future, international marketing decision makers still will have to reconcile their personal moral compass with situational issues and trade-offs among interest groups and stakeholders they are paid to serve. All of the above issues make it very difficult to prescribe answers to the ethical questions and dilemmas that surround marketing and trading practices.

Recognizing Ethical Issues

The set of general questions in Table 2.6 can be asked by the decision maker or decision-making team seeking to develop its own ethical standards. Although most questions are self-explanatory, others need some brief justification or raise issues worth exploring.[24] It seems that the least society should require of marketing executives is that they ask such questions. Sometimes not asking a question can be as wrong as asking and giving a poor answer. For example, not considering the safety of a toy being marketed seems to be as irresponsible as considering the safety, and deciding to sell the toy anyway. The effects are the same. One of the most common situations where marketing executives suffer a lapse of ethics is when they have to make a quick decision and are preoccupied with other concerns. The ethical sufficiency of the decision is simply not examined.

Ethical vigilance
means paying constant attention to whether one's actions are "right" or "wrong," and if ethically "wrong" asking why you are behaving in that manner.

Ethical vigilance means, in practice, asking hard questions. It is important to confront excuses and reasons for violating personal ethics. Avoiding or shelving the answers to such questions is no solution. Decision makers who ask why they do or do not behave in certain ways are more honest with themselves about their true intentions. This is the essence of executive responsibility, and it also can be the first step down the path of change. Such questions lead people to recognize that most of us have at least two codes of ethics: (1) the set we espouse and want others to apply in their behavior toward us, and (2) the code of ethics that, for whatever rationalizations, we actually live up to. The more we recognize the differences between them, the closer we come to under-

Table 2.6   A Personal Ethics Checklist for Marketers

☐ Am I violating the law? If yes, why?
☐ Are the values and ethics that I am applying in business lower than those I use to guide my personal life? If yes, why?
☐ Am I doing to others as I would have them do to me? If not, why not?
☐ Would it be wrong if everyone did what I propose to do? Why?
☐ Am I willfully risking the life and limb of consumers and others by my actions? If yes, why?
☐ Am I willfully exploiting or putting at risk children, the elderly, the illiterate, the mentally incompetent, the naive, the poor, or the environment? If yes, why?
☐ Am I keeping my promises? If not, why not?
☐ Am I telling the truth, all the truth? If not, why not?
☐ Am I exploiting a confidence or a trust? If yes, why?
☐ Am I misrepresenting my true intentions to others? If yes, why?
☐ Am I loyal to those who have been loyal to me? If not, why not?
☐ Have I set up others to take responsibility for any negative consequences of my actions? If yes, why?
☐ Am I prepared to redress wrongs and fairly compensate for damages? If not, why not?
☐ Are my values and ethics as expressed in my strategy offensive to certain groups? If yes, why?
☐ Am I being as efficient in my use of scarce resources as I can be? If not, why not?

This set of questions can be used as the basis for a team's or an individual's mental model to perceive and recognize an ethical issue associated with a proposed goal, strategy, program, or tactic.

standing how easy it is to talk about ethics in black and white, while practicing them in shades of gray.

The list of questions shown in Table 2.6 is organized in approximate order of importance, and by the nature of the ethical or moral principles involved. The first question in the table is the first and last question the ethical minimalist will ask. The second question addresses the application of a double standard and the basis for such a double standard. The third question addresses the extent to which marketers apply the Golden Rule: "Do unto others as you will have them do unto you." A prominent British chief executive officer has suggested that a better way of posing the question is to look at oneself and ask, "What would I think of someone who has my business ethics or took the action that I propose to take?"[25]

Marketing's Third Social Responsibility: Cause-Related Marketing

The third important dimension of marketing's social responsibility is to encourage its use in the promotion of worthy public causes. Today's marketers have come to recognize, as has been confirmed in a recent Roper poll, that in many markets a company's media expression of social responsibility influences consumer behavior more than advertising.[26] You do well by doing good; for example, see Allstate Insurance's stand on drunk driving in Figure 2.7. It also helps if your do-gooding can be associated with your product. Clothing designer Ralph Lauren donated $13 million to restore the 184-year-old "old faithful" American flag that flew in the rockets' red glare and inspired the National Anthem. Kimberly Clark sells disposable diapers and builds children's parks and playgrounds. McDonald's works with environment groups to increase its recycling. Some companies are starting up their own nonprofit organizations, and these are not simply cynical efforts to buy public relations. They are mostly initiatives suggested by their workforce and welcomed by management, who recognize that they will build company morale and are a positive expression of a company's ethics (for another example, see Figure 2.8). They are a way of expressing what should be done by a socially responsible organization rather than what should not be done.

Cause-related marketing are those activities that governments, public service organizations, companies, and individuals undertake in an effort to encourage target customer

www.kimberly-clark.com

**Figure 2.7   Allstate and Mothers Against Drunk Driving Team Up
to Promote Safe and Sober Driving**

participation in socially redeeming programs. These efforts are usually delivered through educational campaigns and provide free or low-priced services at convenient times and places. The following are examples of cause-related marketing:

1. How should future societies deal with the issue of using inexpensive genetic testing to reduce genetic disabilities? Genetic disabilities create very high medical care costs that are carried by everyone participating in health insurance pools, and great anguish to families, not to speak of the misery of those afflicted with such disabilities. Education campaigns might inform and persuade individuals to take the tests, and might then target those with the flagged genetic markers with further education about the value of choosing not to have children. Marketing campaigns would be more proactive, setting up testing sites at convenient times and locations, providing professional counseling on test results, and as an alternative, offering special adoption priority programs coupled with voluntary sterilization.[27]

Figure 2.8   Chevron's "People Do" Program Is Committed to Preserve and Protect Our Natural Environment

2. Advertising campaigns sponsored by public service organizations and liquor companies are undertaken around holiday seasons to discourage drinking and driving. Over the years these campaigns have become more targeted at the friends of problem drinkers, suggesting appropriate behaviors such as taking the keys away from those at risk and creating a designated driver in a group. Market research found that targeting the problem drinker had no effect. What sort of products might be invented to support such communication campaigns? Some communities have sponsored free taxi services and encouraged bars to offer more recreational activities such as providing pool tables and dancing to reduce the amount of liquor consumption in an evening. Other "social marketers" have encouraged the invention of devices that can be installed in problem drinkers' vehicles that require a "breath test" to start the engine.

The challenge for social marketing is coming up with alternative products that can be marketed to those at risk. Some suggestions, based on experts' extended study of the problem, are designed to lessen the evil, but are still considered too controversial. Examples of such products are providing free less-addictive drugs or clean needles for drug addicts,

Careers in Marketing

The Case of Development Organizations

Rosemary aced her graduate degree in marketing, but what motivated her was not money but idealism. This led her to work for a not-for-profit nongovernmental organization (NGO) in New York that worked closely with the United Nations. The mission of this organization was to promote information, communications, and networking with the objective of women's advancement worldwide and achieving equality between men and women in all spheres of activity, using the analytic and policy frameworks developed under international agreements.

Rosemary worked for a specific project, which marketed information pertaining to the involvement of women as decision makers and beneficiaries in development programs, addressing a wide range of issues, ranging from Women's Human Rights to Women in Science and Information Technology, from Women's Roles in Culture and Religion to Gender Analysis in Economics and Macro Policies. The project distributed books and literature on such topics not only from established publishers in "developed" countries, but also from indigenous publishers and grassroots activist groups in developing countries. While the job was poorly paid, it was fascinating and opened up new horizons for Rosemary. She traveled to many international conferences and book fairs to locate publishers and target audiences for the literature, making connections with networks of small groups and publishers worldwide. After several years working for this organization, Rosemary was hired by the United Nations Development Program (UNDP) to work on information management around its gender programs in over 130 different countries, and to liaise with related initiatives of other UN agencies and nongovernmental organizations.

Pursuing cause-related marketing careers poses a number of formidable challenges. "Not-for-profit" organizations, especially those focused on economic and social development in developing countries, often vary widely in staff competencies, geographic and subject focus, and organizational structures and incentives. Nongovernmental organizations are typically small, focus on a single or few issues, and offer low pay but attract highly motivated staff with specific skills. UN agencies, on the other hand, are extremely large, bureaucratic, and address a whole slew of development topics. Since all these organizations tend to work together for common causes through continuous networking and partnership building, they offer ample scope for application of marketing concepts and skills. However, there is less competitive pressure to innovate and learn new improved ways of doing things than there is in profit-driven organizations, and efficiency and effectiveness often have to be sacrificed to address the needs or interests of specific constituencies. On the other hand, helping marketing human rights, health care, and environmental protection can be so much more rewarding than marketing toothpaste. Indeed, many retired marketing executives continue to work on causes that they feel deeply about.

The Internet is also revolutionizing cause marketing. Cause marketing depends on small groups working together, and the Internet enables communication as never before. It is also able to provide a great deal more information literally at the fingertips of not-for-profit organizations and people out in the field. Finally, despite the naysayers, young people today, and particularly college students, are giving more of their time to working on charitable causes than they ever have before. The idealism of younger generations and their comfort level and skill with new technology suggests that cause marketing has an exciting future.

and free birth control pills or abortions to teenagers. Marketing such products to reduce the problem is often argued to promote or encourage, rather than reduce the socially undesirable behavior. The problem is that the critics do not have good alternative solutions, or their solutions are draconian new laws and punishment. On the other hand, there have been many successful social marketing programs that can be used as benchmarks of best practice for marketing professionals interested in using their talents for good causes. The above box is an example of one such case.

The National High Blood Pressure Education Program (NHBPEP)[28]

When the NHBPEP started in 1972, about 60 million Americans had blood pressure over 140/90 or were taking hypertensive medication. Less than 30 percent of the public knew that high blood pressure greatly increases the risks of strokes and heart disease. The initial goal of the campaign was to raise awareness of the risks, and get tens of millions who were at risk to have their blood pressure checked. A social marketing consulting company coordinated a national advertising/education campaign that involved sponsored television advertising, public service announcements, publicity events, posters, and magazine and newspaper advertising. A partnership with over 40 public health organizations and charitable foundations was created. These organizations acted as channels of distribution for the campaign materials and for staging blood pressure monitoring events. The service was *brought to* as many people at risk as possible rather than just trying to persuade people to visit a doctor.

After 10 years, over 70 percent of the public knew about the link to specific diseases, and 92 percent understood that, in general, high blood pressure cannot be cured and a hypertensive person must always stay on a treatment program. By 1985, over 90 percent of the population knew what their blood pressure was, but half of the hypertensives had still not taken any action to treat their chronic condition. At this time the goal of this social marketing campaign shifted from general public awareness to a focus on those who had done nothing about it. Again, an education campaign was launched directed at doctors and nurses in contact with those at risk, supported by a targeted campaign mainly directed at the loved ones of those at risk and getting them to use their influence. By 1991, 73 percent of hypertensives were under medical treatment. Of this group, over 80 percent dieted and exercised. In the late 1990s, the focus has become targeted on African-American males over the age of 45 who have a high incidence of hypertension, and who live in the southeastern United States where the incidence of strokes amongst hypertensives is 10 percent higher than in any other region.

Chapter Summary

Marketing strategy takes into account changes in the firm's internal (micro) and external (macro) environments. By identifying current changes and trends in the environment, a marketer can attempt to predict future changes and how these changes should influence the firm's marketing strategy. The firm's marketing environment is comprised of six components. The microenvironment consists of the firm's own objectives and resources. The macroenvironment consists of the competitive environment, the legal/political environment, the sociocultural environment, the economic environment, and the technological environment.

As marketers respond to the marketing environment, they must do so in a manner that reflects their concern for the welfare of others. This has been called the social contract by philosophers. A "free market" does not mean suppliers and customers are free to do what they like. Competition forces sellers to serve the interests of customers. But ethical behavior, particularly honesty, is required to make the market work efficiently and to keep it free and open. Marketers must therefore respond to the almost universal ethical codes involved in trading: to be honest and not conspire to cheat and steal.

But their decisions as to what to offer the marketplace and how to offer it also have an impact on the prevailing values and ethics of a society. Some products and marketing practices are ethically questionable. This heavy responsibility cannot be simply shrugged off. The enlightened leadership that marketing planners are expected to display is most put to the test when they are faced with ethical dilemmas created by conflicts of interests among customers, employees, and owners. How they choose to resolve such dilemmas tells them a lot about themselves.

A lot of the criticisms of marketing that are popular amongst modern socialists simply have no basis in fact—reflecting the ideological prejudices of the critics. The collapse of the corrupt and hopelessly inefficient communist systems has not muted the shrillness of capitalist market's critics. It has also not increased their insights. But the world faces several potential "tragedy of the commons" effects—clean air, fresh water, trees, fish, democracy, and young women's self-esteem and happiness with themselves.

This chapter was full of "on the other hand" statements reflecting the complexity of the issues associated with the ethics and social responsibility of marketing, in an attempt to present a balanced view of modern marketing's social responsibility at its best and at its worst. It also posed a lot of questions rather than offering a lot of answers. This is because there are a lot of questions that have to be confronted by marketers, and there are not a lot of definitive answers. Like any marketing skill, the skill of behaving ethically and socially responsibly develops with practice—the practice of asking the right questions, answering them honestly, and resolving dilemmas by balancing interests.

Key Terms

Social responsiblity is the collection of marketing philosophies, policies, procedures, and actions intended primarily to enhance society's welfare.

Built-in obsolescence is the design of a product with features that the company knows will soon be superceded, thus making the model obsolete.

Inefficient targeting results when advertising and distribution reaches too broad an audience, most of whom are not interested in the product.

Tragedy of the commons is the name given to the process where individuals, pursuing their own self-interest, overuse a common good to such an extent that the common good is destroyed.

Supply-side market failure results when the individual activities of a supplier inadvertently lead to destructive effects on the overall supply.

Demand-side market failure is the cumulative effect of the marketing practices of many thousands of advertising campaigns that has a residual negative impact on the values of buyers and the demand for various products (e.g., voting).

Situational ethics is that societal condition where "right" and "wrong" are determined by the specific situation, rather than by universal moral principles.

Ethical vigilance means paying constant attention to whether one's actions are "right" or "wrong," and if ethically "wrong" asking why you are behaving in that manner.

Additional Key Terms and Concepts

Microenvironment	Macroenvironment
Competitiveness	Effectiveness
Efficiency	Freedom and free choice
Social contract	Principle of utility
Normal good	Categorical imperative
Predominant religion	Cause-related marketing

Questions for Discussion

1. Why must a firm's microenvironment and macroenvironment both be considered when formulating marketing strategy?

2. A competitor's disgruntled employee has just mailed you plans for what looks like a promising new product. Should you throw the plans away? Send them to your R&D people for analysis? Notify your competitor about what is going on? Call the FBI?

3. All-terrain vehicles were involved in 1,500 deaths and 400,000 serious injuries during the 1980s—20 percent of these affecting children 12 and under. The automobile industry stopped selling the three-wheel version and notified dealers to instruct buyers that the vehicles should not be driven by children under 16. However, many dealers have ignored the direction. The industry view is that because state laws allow children to use the vehicle, it is the parents' responsibility to supervise their children's use. Should the product be banned?

4. In the late 1970s, credit card interest rates rose to between 18 and 20 percent because of inflation. Through the 1980s, many credit card interest rates remained at around 18 to 20 percent, long after inflation had cooled and the cost of money had dropped to under 10 percent. Many banks have argued that the cost of servicing credit card debt is high, but some banks charge only 13 percent on their cards. The merchant is charged a fee (2 to 5 percent) for each purchase made on a card. This covers the cost of the transaction and some of the risk of card theft and bad debt. Is still charging 18 to 20 percent ethical?

5. Increasingly, prescription drugs are being marketed directly to consumers, as if they were soap powder. How might such marketing be socially responsible? How might it be socially irresponsible?

6. A supermarket serving a low-income African-American market charges higher prices for its staples (such as bread and milk) than do supermarkets in the suburbs. Consumer groups have complained that this practice exploits the poor. The store argues that suburban shoppers buy more profitable luxuries, allowing suburban stores to lower their prices on staples. The store's management also can prove that there is a greater incidence of shoplifting and vandalism in its store, resulting in hardly any profit, even at the higher prices. Should the store lower its prices? Should it simply close down, if it would lose money by lowering its prices? What other creative options does the store have?

7. A Save the Children Fund (SCF) ad features little Pedro with the sad eyes and Joanne Woodward saying, "Imagine, the cost of a cup of coffee, 52 cents a day, can help save a child." But SCF has not been in the business of directly sponsoring children for many years. It is involved in community development work, such as building playgrounds and providing start-up loans for small businesses. The problem is that community development does not pull cash donations the way that little Pedro does. Only about 35 percent of the funds raised are actually spent on charitable projects—the rest is spent on marketing and overhead.[29] Was SCF's behavior ethical? Should SCF be held to a higher or lower standard than would be applied to a for-profit organization?

8. You are in a foreign country where bribing government officials and businesspeople is essential to do business, and bribery is not outlawed as it is in the United States. Officials from the country approach you, saying that there are many buyers for your products and you could make good profits in their country. Would you do business and pay the bribes? Would you hide the practice, hoping that no one in the United States would find out? Would you pay a distributor in the country a set fee to take care of everything for you, pretending not to know what taking care of everything means?

9. A major U.S. bank in Chicago has been approached by an oil sheik who wishes to make a major investment in its New Ventures Mutual Fund that has been brilliantly managed by a 35-year-old female executive. The bank is very keen to make the sale, but the sheik will only do business with men. Normally, the female mutual-funds manager would travel to meet such a client. Should the bank send her anyway? What if a major commission is involved in making the sale? Would it make any difference if the sheik was visiting the United States and refused to meet the female executive?

10. In February the audiences for the major network's programs are measured, and these ratings are used to compute audience size, and what advertisers will be charged for

advertisements placed within these programs. It is called "Sweeps Week," and all of the networks advertise fresh new episodes to boost their audiences. Before and after sweeps week, the networks present reruns of previous shows or episodes, sometimes quite out of sequence. How ethical is the sweeps-week practices of the networks? How should audience measurement be undertaken?

Internet Questions

1. Pornography is one of the biggest businesses on the Web, and naturally attracts the interest of children. Banning such sites is very difficult because it would require enforceable international laws and would not be popular. The most sensible solution is for parents and teachers to monitor the sites that children visit. A survey undertaken by *Family PC* found that 71 percent of parents say they monitor their children's use of the Internet, but only 26 percent say they use either built-in or commercial filtering or monitoring software. Imagine you have an easy-to-use monitoring software and operating system that operates on any PC and that tracks the sites that your PC visits. It could be sold on a disk for $3 per unit in bulk to a distributor. How might you use several nonprofit organizations to distribute this product to families with young children for under $10? The alliance has to be consistent with the goals of the organization and would earn them badly needed income. It also has to avoid unnecessary controversy.

2. A major social responsibility of marketing is try to make trading more efficient. One way the Internet can do this is to create inexpensive auction markets that bring buyers and sellers together at low cost to exchange goods. Which of the following auction sites is easiest and least expensive to use: <u>www.auctionuniverse.com</u>, <u>www.buycollectibles.com</u>, <u>www.collectoronline.com</u>, <u>www.ebay.com</u>, <u>www.icollector.com</u>? What sorts of product markets are likely to be made more efficient by such Internet trading sites?

3. A problem with the Internet is that it is very good at spreading rumors very fast. For example, a recent rumor started by a "Nancy Markle" accused the artificial sweetner, aspartame, of causing Alzheimer's, birth defects, brain cancer, diabetes, Gulf War syndrome, lupus, multiple sclerosis, and seizures.[30] The site <u>urbanlegends.miningco.com</u> presents many other socially irresponsible slanders on the products we use. Reliable health sites such as <u>mayohealth.org</u>, <u>www.medhelp.org</u>, <u>www.oncolink.org</u>, <u>cancernet.nci.nih.gov</u>, and <u>navigator.tufts.edu</u> give excellent information on nutrition and illnesses. They are obviously required to back up their advice and information with credible scientific research. How can the spread of false or unsubstantiated health claims that create great fear and distress be controlled on the Web? What long-term effect might such rumor mongering have on Internet use?

Endnotes

[1]For a review of the lack of evidence, see Timothy E. Moore, "Subliminal Advertising: What You See Is What You Get," *Journal of Marketing* 46 (Spring 1982): pp. 38–47. For an interesting discussion of how the media persists in believing in subliminal messages in advertising and music, see John R. Vokey and J. Don Read, "Subliminal Messages: Between the Devil and the Media," *American Psychologist* (November 1985): pp. 1231–1239.

[2]Richard W. Pollay, et al., "The Last Straw? Cigarette Advertising and Realized Market Shares Among Youths and Adults, 1979–1993," *Journal of Marketing* 60 (April): pp. 1–16.

[3]This section adopted from John H. Lindgren, Jr. and Terence A. Shimp, *Marketing: An Interactive Learning System* (Fort Worth, TX: The Dryden Press, 1996), pp. 35–37.

[4]This section adopted from Peter Dickson, *Marketing Management* (Fort Worth, TX: The Dryden Press, 1994), p. 126.

[5]This section adopted from Peter Dickson, *Marketing Management* (Fort Worth, TX: The Dryden Press, 1994), pp. 188–189.

[6]Kate Fitzgerald, "Antitrust Case Threatens the Image of Toys 'R' Us," *Advertising Age* (May 27, 1996): p. 6.

[7]This section developed from a variety of sources including Brent Schlender, "Peter Drucker Takes the Long View," *Fortune* 138, no. 6 (September 28, 1998): pp. 162–173. K. Douglas Hoffman, class note archives developed over the years.

[8]This section adopted from John H. Lindgren, Jr. and Terence A. Shimp, *Marketing: An Interactive Learning System* (Fort Worth, TX: The Dryden Press, 1996), p. 57.

[9]This section adopted from John H. Lindgren, Jr. and Terence A. Shimp, *Marketing: An Interactive Learning System* (Fort Worth, TX: The Dryden Press, 1996), p. 58.

[10]Susan E. Shank, "Women and the Labor Market: The Link Grows Stronger," *Monthly Labor Review,* 111 (March 1988): pp. 3–8.

[11]Daphne Spain and Suzanne M. Bianchi, "How Women Have Changed," *American Demographics* (May 1983): pp. 18–25.

[12]Ibid.

[13]This section adopted from John H. Lindgren, Jr. and Terence A. Shimp, *Marketing: An Interactive Learning System* (Fort Worth, TX: The Dryden Press, 1996), p. 60.

[14]This section adopted from Peter Dickson, *Marketing Management* (Fort Worth, TX: The Dryden Press, 1994), p. 277.

[15]This section was adapted from John Ward Anderson, "Thundering Herd," *The Courier-Journal* (Louisville, KY), January 2, 1994, p. A8; John E. G. Bateson and K. Douglas Hoffman, *Managing Services Marketing* (Fort Worth, TX: The Dryden Press, 1999), pp. XI, 6.

[16]This section was developed from: Evan I. Schwartz, *Webonomics: Nine Essential Principles for Growing Your Business on the World Wide Web* (New York, NY: Broadway Books, 1997), p. 1; Patricia Sellers, "Inside the First E-Christmas," *Fortune* 139, no. 2 (February 1, 1999): pp. 70–73.

[17]This section adopted from Peter Dickson, *Marketing Management* (Fort Worth, TX: The Dryden Press, 1994), p. 135.

[18]Jim Kelly, "From Lip Service to Real Service: Reversing America's Downward Service Spiral," *Vital Speeches of the Day* 64, no. 10 (1998): p. 302.

[19]Booz-Allen & Hamilton, *New Product Management for the 1980s* (New York: Booz-Allen & Hamilton Inc., 1982).

[20] Steven H. Star, "Marketing and its Discontents," *Harvard Business Review* (November–December, 1989): pp. 148–154.

[21]See "Turning off the Tap," *The Economist* (November 14, 1998): p. 29.

[22]From the results of a survey of 511 Wisconsin adults surveyed two weeks before the 1998 elections, reported in the *Wisconsin State Journal* (Saturday October 31, 1998): p. 1.

[23]"Good Grief," *The Economist* (April 8, 1995): p. 57.

[24]Some of the questions are based on the thinking of Gene R. Laczniak, "Framework for Analyzing Marketing Ethics," *Journal of Macromarketing* (Spring 1983): pp. 7–18; and William David Ross, *The Right and the Good* (Oxford: Clarendon Press, 1930).

[25]Sir Adrian Cadbury, "Ethical Managers Make Their Own Rules," *Harvard Business Review* 87, no. 5 (September/October 1987): pp. 69–75.

[26]Claudia Gaines, "Next Step in Cause Marketing: Business Start Own Nonprofits," *Marketing News* (October 12, 1998): p. 4.

[27]See Michael L. Rothschild, "Promises, Carrots, and Sticks: A Conceptual Framework for the Management of Public Health and Social Issue Behaviors," *Journal of Marketing*, forthcoming (1999), for an excellent review of contemporary social marketing issues and practices.

[28]The following examples are drawn from Alan R. Andreasen, *Marketing Social Change* (San Fancisco: Jossey-Bass Publishers, 1995).

[29]See Richard Behar, "SCF's Little Secret," *Forbes* (April 21, 1986): pp. 106–107.

[30]See Christine Gorman, "A Web of Deceit," *Time* (February 9, 1999): p. 76.

[31]Philip, P. McGuigan, "Stakes Are High in Battle to Bar Internet Gambling," *The National Law Journal,* November 3, 1997, p. B8.

Gambling and the Internet

One in $10 of all the money spent in the United States on recreation is spent on gambling—about $47 billion a year in total. Gambling is very big business. Las Vegas is booming, and Indian tribes are building casinos around the country. As a form of "compensation" for the theft of their tribal lands in the 1800s, small regional tribes have become rich off their "right" to run casinos. According to surveys by respected market research firms, over 90 percent of adult Americans find casino gambling quite acceptable, particularly those local residents who benefit from the employment and entertainment that casinos create.[31] The typical casino gambler has a slightly higher income than the national norm, but otherwise is very average.

Why then is there so much objection to gambling on the Internet? Such gambling would require prepayment off a credit card that would make it difficult for children to participate. It is not even that clear that children would find gambling more attractive than video games. Providing the gambling Web sites were audited by government agencies for the fairness and integrity of their games, as casinos are now, the risk of widespread corruption and fraud would be very low. Thirty-six states run their own lotteries, so it is hard for state legislators to object to Web-based gambling on moral grounds. Why then has the National Association of Attorney Generals created a special committee to draw up federal regulation to make Internet gambling illegal? Why has the state of Nevada already passed legislation banning Internet gambling? The reason seems simple. Internet gambling would pose a long-term serious competitive threat to existing gambling products marketed by casino companies and by state governments. It is banned to restrict competition. How long will such a ban last?

Legitimate and respectable Internet gambling companies operating from the Caribbean, or from other countries, that allow such businesses and regulate them appropriately, cannot be prevented from offering the excitement of their gaming sites to Americans, and for that matter the rest of the world. Further, there is no way that governments anywhere can stop their citizens from using their credit cards to purchase such entertainment. When this happens, the major casino companies and their software suppliers will be more than ready to enter the market, and the federal and state regulations will fade into the sunset.

Discussion Questions

1. Surveys show that people believe casinos should be responsible for offering programs to help problem casino gamblers. What unique problems exist in requiring Internet gambling services to be responsible for offering programs for problem Internet gamblers?

2. Do you think those who are attempting to restrict gambling on the Internet are behaving ethically?

3. Do you think gambling on the Internet is an unethical product? Is it more or less ethical than the purveying of pornography on the Web? Is it more or less ethical than the selling of violent video games on the Web?

Chapter 3

International Marketing

Michael R. Czinkota, Georgetown University

Dr. Czinkota has earned his doctorate degree in logistics and international business from The Ohio State University. He has received honorary degrees from Universidad Pontificia Madre y Maestra in the Dominican Republic and Universidad del Pacifico in Lima, Peru. Dr. Czinkota is a former U.S. deputy assistant secretary of commerce, former head of the U.S. delegation to the OECD Industry Committee in Paris, and a member of the Board of Governors of the Academy of Marketing Science. He is also a former board member and vice president of the American Marketing Association.

He has authored *International Marketing 5/e, International Business 5/e,* and *Global Business 2/e,* all from the Dryden Press.

By the 21st century, Campbell Soup wants half of company revenues to come from outside domestic markets. This is an ambitious goal, since only a quarter have come from foreign sales in the 1990s. Adding to the challenge is the fact that prepared food may be one of the toughest products to sell overseas. It is not as universal or easily marketed as soap or soft drinks, given regional taste preferences. Italians, not surprisingly, shy away from canned pasta, and while an average Pole consumes five bowls of soup a week, 98 percent of Polish soups are homemade.

Campbell has managed to overcome some cultural obstacles in selected countries. To shake the powdered-soup domination in Argentina, it markets its Sopa de Campbell as "The Real Soup," stressing its list of fresh ingredients on the label. In Poland, Campbell advertises to working Polish mothers looking for convenience. Says Lee Andrews, Campbell's new-product manager in Warsaw: "We can't shove a can in their faces and replace Mom."

However, in many regions, Campbell is trying to cook more like her. This means creating new products that appeal to distinctly regional tastes. The approach has been to use test kitchens and taste testing with consumers. Results have included fiery cream of poblano soup in Mexico as well as watercress and duck-gizzard soup for China. The cream of pumpkin has become Australia's top-selling canned soup.

Asia has traditionally accounted for only 2 percent of Campbell's worldwide sales, but the region—China, in particular—is being targeted as the area with the strongest growth potential. New markets are entered gingerly. Campbell typically launches a basic meat or chicken broth, which consumers can doctor with meats, vegetables, and spices. Later, more sophisticated soups are brought on line. In China, the real competition comes from homemade soup, which comprises over 99 percent of all consumption. With this in mind, Campbell's prices have been kept at an attractive level and the product promoted on convenience. While many of the products, such as corn-and-chicken soup, have been developed in the company's Hong Kong kitchens, some U.S. standbys, such as cream of mushroom, have been selling well, possibly to the segment of westernized Chinese.

Local ingredients may count, but Campbell draws the line on some Asian favorites. Dog soup is out, as is shark's fin, since most species are endangered. For most other options, including snake, for example, the company keeps an open mind.

Furthermore, Campbell is also finding that ethnic foods are growing in popularity around the world. With its emphasis on vegetables, Asian cuisine benefits from a healthy image in Europe and North America. This means that some new products being presently developed for the Asian consumer may become global favorites in no time.[1]

Learning Objectives

After you have completed this chapter, you should be able to:

1. Understand the importance of international marketing.

2. Appreciate the opportunities and challenges offered by international marketing.

3. Recognize the effect of the global environment on international marketing activities.

4. Understand the process of market selection.

5. Recognize the process of gradual internationalization.

6. Aappreciate the different forms of market entry.

7. Comprehend the international adjustment of the marketing mix.

8. Understand the steps necessary for the implementation of an international marketing strategy.

Ilkka A. Ronkainen, Georgetown University

Dr. Ronkainen has earned his doctorate and master's degrees from the University of South Carolina and an additional master's degree from the Helsinki School of Economics. He has served on the review board of the *Journal of Business Research, International Marketing Review,* and the *Journal of International Business Studies.* He is a former North American coordinator for the European Marketing Academy and also a former board member of the Washington International Trade Association.

Dr. Ronkainen serves as a docent of international marketing at the Helsinki School of Economics. He has served as a consultant to IBM, the Rank Organization, and the Organization of American States. In addition, he maintains close ties with a number of Finnish companies and their internationalization and educational efforts.

www.campbellssoup.com

LO1

International marketing is the process of planning and conducting transactions across national borders to create exchanges that satisfy the objectives of individuals and organizations.

International marketing takes place all around us every day, has a major effect on our lives, and offers new opportunities and challenges. International marketing is necessary because economic isolationism has become impossible. Failure to participate in the global marketplace assures firms and nations of declining economic capability and consumers of a decrease in their standard of living. Successful international marketing, however, holds the promise of higher profits, an improved quality of life, a better society, and perhaps, due to increased linkages between people, even a more peaceful world.

The objective of this chapter is twofold. First, we discuss the opportunities and challenges that face marketers as they expand into international markets. This chapter is presented early in this text as recognition of the importance of international marketing in today's business world. Secondly, this chapter provides a glimpse of "marketing strategy in action." Thus far, Chapters 1 and 2 have provided the fundamental building blocks of marketing strategy. This chapter illustrates the importance of modifying marketing strategy to meet the needs of new markets.

WHAT INTERNATIONAL MARKETING IS

International marketing is the process of planning and conducting transactions across national borders to create exchanges that satisfy the objectives of individuals and organizations. International marketing has forms ranging from export-import trade to licensing, franchising, joint ventures, wholly owned subsidiaries, and management contracts.

As this definition indicates, international marketing retains the basic marketing tenets of "satisfaction" and "exchange." The fact that a transaction takes place "across national borders" causes the international marketer to be subject to new sets of macro environmental factors, to different constraints, and quite frequently to conflicts resulting from different laws, cultures, and societies. The basic principles of marketing strategy still apply, but their implementation, complexity, and intensity may vary substantially. It is in the international marketing field that one can observe most closely the role of marketing as a societal process and as an instrument for the development of socially responsive business strategy. One look at the emerging market economies of central Europe shows some of the many new challenges that confront international marketers. How does the marketing concept fit into these societies? How should distribution systems be organized? How can one get the price mechanism to work? Similarly, in the international areas of social responsibility and ethics, the international marketer is faced with a multicultural environment with differing expectations and often inconsistent legal systems when it comes to monitoring environmental pollution, maintaining safe working conditions, copying technology, or paying bribes.[2] The capability to master these challenges successfully affords a company the potential for new opportunities and high rewards.

The definition also focuses on international transactions. Marketing internationally is an activity that needs to be aggressively pursued. Those who do not actively participate in the transactions are still subject to the changing influences of international marketing. The international marketer is part of the exchange, recognizes the changing nature of transactions, adjusts to a constantly moving target, and reacts to shifts in the business environment. This need for adjustment, for comprehending change, and, in spite of it all, for successfully carrying out transactions, highlights the fact that international marketing is as much art as science.

To achieve success in the art of international marketing, it is necessary to be firmly grounded in its scientific aspects. Only then will consumers, policymakers, and business executives be able to incorporate international marketing considerations into their thinking and planning, and make decisions based on the answers to such questions as these:

1. How will my product fit into the international market?

2. What marketing adjustments are or will be necessary?

3. What threats from global competition should I expect?

4. How can I work with these threats to turn them into opportunities?

The integration of international dimensions into each decision made by individuals and by firms can make international markets a source of growth, profit, and needs satisfaction, and can also lead to a higher quality of life.

OPPORTUNITIES AND CHALLENGES IN INTERNATIONAL MARKETING

To prosper in a world of abrupt changes, of newly emerging forces and dangers, and of unforeseen influences from abroad, firms need to prepare themselves and develop active responses. New strategies need to be envisioned, new plans need to be made, and the way of doing business needs to be changed. To remain players in the world economy, governments, firms, and individuals need to respond aggressively with innovation, process improvements, and creativity.[3]

The growth of international marketing activities offers increased opportunities. By integrating knowledge from around the globe, an international firm can build and strengthen its competitive position. Firms that heavily depend on long production runs

LEARNING OBJECTIVE LO2

can expand their activities far beyond their domestic markets and benefit from reaching many more customers. Market saturation can be avoided by lengthening or rejuvenating product life cycles in other countries. Plants can be shifted from one country to another, and suppliers can be found on every continent as illustrated in Figure 3.1. Cooperative

Figure 3.1   The Global Components of a Big Mac in Ukraine

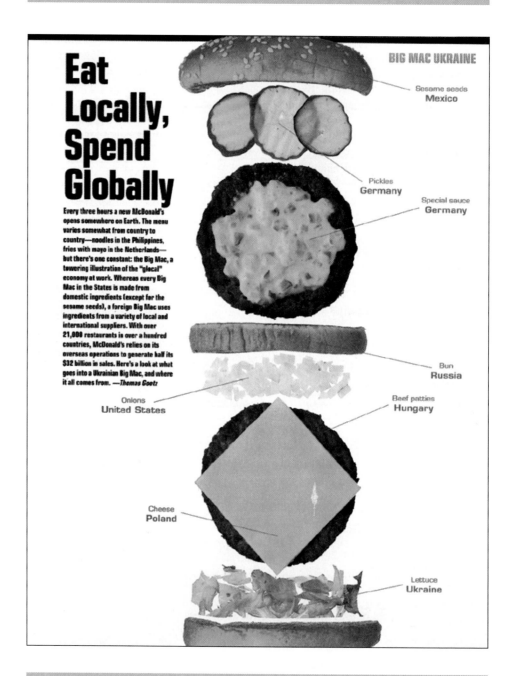

Michael R. Czinkota, Ilkka A. Ronkainen, Michael H. Moffett, *International Business,* 5th edition (Fort Worth: Harcourt Brace College Publishers, 1998), 9.

Table 3.1	Multinational Corporations with the Largest Proportion of Nondomestic Employees (1995)			
		Workforce		Foreign as % of Total
Company	Country	Foreign	Total	
Nestlé	Switzerland	203,100	209,800	97%
Phillips Electronics	Netherlands	200,000	244,400	82
Unilever	Netherlands	187,000	294,000	64
Ford	U.S.	180,000	332,700	54
IBM	U.S.	130,655	256,207	51
Volkswagen	Germany	103,000	253,000	40
Matsushita Electric	Japan	98,639	254,059	38
Siemens	Germany	153,000	403,800	38
General Motors	U.S.	270,000	756,000	36
PepsiCo	U.S.	128,054	423,000	30
General Electric	U.S.	59,000	222,000	27
Fiat	Italy	66,712	287,957	23
Daimler-Benz	Germany	82,160	366,736	22
AT&T	U.S.	47,000	227,000	21

Source: United Nations Conference on Trade and Development.

www.unctad.org

agreements can be formed that enable all parties to bring their major strengths to the table and emerge with better products than they could produce on their own. In addition, research has found that firms that export grow faster, are more productive, and, equally important, have employees who tend to earn more.[4] At the same time, international marketing enables customers all over the world to find greater varieties of products at lower prices and to improve their lifestyles and comfort.

International opportunities require careful exploration. What is needed is an awareness of global developments, an understanding of their meaning, and a development of the capability to adjust to change. Firms must adapt to their international markets if they are to be successful.

Many firms do not participate in the global market. Often, managers believe that international marketing should only be carried out by large multinational corporations. It is true that there are some very large players from many countries active in the world market, as Table 3.1 shows. But smaller firms are major players, too. For example, 50 percent of German exports are created by firms with 19 or fewer employees.[5]

Those firms and industries that do not participate in the world market have to recognize that in today's trade environment, isolation has become impossible. Even if not by choice, most firms and individuals are affected directly or indirectly by economic and political developments that occur in the international marketplace. Those firms that refuse to participate are relegated to react to the global marketplace, and therefore are unprepared for harsh competition from abroad.

THE INTERNATIONAL MARKETING ENVIRONMENT

International environmental forces will have similar, but most likely more powerful, impacts on the development of international marketing strategies when compared to purely domestic ones. Not only are these international environments different from the domestic ones, but they usually differ considerably between individual country markets as well. Key international environments are the cultural, socioeconomic, and legal/political environments.

LEARNING OBJECTIVE LO3

www.whirlpool.com

Change agent
is a person or institution that facilitates change in a firm or in a host country.

Degree of individualism
is the extent to which individual interests prevail over group interests.

Level of equality
is the extent to which less powerful members accept that power is distributed unequally.

Uncertainty avoidance
is the extent to which people feel threatened by ambiguous situations and have created beliefs and institutions to try to avoid these feelings.

Material achievement
is the extent to which the dominant values in society are success, money, and things.

www.3m.com

Cultural Environment

The challenge for the marketing manager is how to handle the differences in languages (both spoken and nonverbal), values and attitudes, and subsequent behavior at two levels: first, as they relate to customer behavior, and second, with regard to their impact on the implementation of marketing programs within individual markets and across markets. After conducting market research throughout Europe, Whirlpool entered the fastest growing appliance market for microwaves with a product clearly targeted at the Euroconsumer, but one that offered various product features with different appeal in different countries.[6]

The international marketer is a **change agent** trying to impress on a local consumer the need to adopt a new product. The propensity to change will be a function of (1) customers' cultural lifestyles in terms of how deeply held their traditional beliefs and attitudes are, and also which elements of culture are dominant, (2) the power of opinion leaders and change agents themselves, and (3) communication about new concepts from sources ranging from reference groups and government to commercial media.[7]

It has been argued that differences in cultural lifestyle can be accounted for by four dimensions of culture.[8] These dimensions consist of the **degree of individualism** in a culture (as compared to submitting to group decision making); the **level of equality** in a society (e.g., the presence of class differences and possessions); **uncertainty avoidance** (e.g., need for formal rules and regulations, risk taking); and attitudes toward **material achievement.** For example, Northern Europe features very high individualism, high equality, low uncertainty avoidance, and low focus on material achievement. For a marketing manager, this means there will be relatively low resistance to new products, strong consumer desire for novelty and variety, and high consumer regard for environmentally friendly and socially conscious solutions.[9] Similar analyses can and should be performed for markets and regions targeted for marketing action.

To foster cultural sensitivity and acceptance of new ways of doing things within the organization, management must institute internal training programs. These programs may include (1) culture-specific information (e.g., data in the form of videopacks or culturegrams covering other countries), (2) general cultural information (e.g., values, practices, and assumptions in countries other than one's own), as well as (3) self-specific information that involves finding out one's own cultural paradigm, including values, assumptions, and perceptions about others.[10]

These cultural dimensions can be looked at not only as a challenge but also as an opportunity to make the marketer's efforts more effective not only in one market but throughout the world. For example, when 3M's designers in Singapore discovered consumers wanted to use 3M's Nomad household floormats in their cars, the designers spread the word to their counterparts in Malaysia and Thailand. Today, the specially made car mats with easy-to-clean vinyl loops are best sellers across Southeast Asia.[11]

MAKING CULTURE WORK FOR YOU

Thousands of European and U.S. companies have entered or expanded their operations in the fastest-growing region in the world—Asia. In the 1990s, the region outpaced the growth of the world's 24 leading industrial economies by more than six times. A total of 400 million Asian consumers have disposable incomes at least equal to the rich-world average.

Few companies have had as much experience—or success—as the 3M company. The maker of everything from heart-lung machines to Scotch tape, the company's revenues for 1996 from international sales reached $7.6 billion (54 percent of total), with $900 million coming from the Asia-Pacific. At the root of the company's success are certain rules that allow it both to adjust to and exploit cultural differences.

▼ **Embrace Local Culture**—3M's new plant near Bangkok, Thailand, is one example of how the company embraces local culture. A gleaming Buddhist shrine, wreathed in flowers, pays homage to the spirits Thais believe took care of the land prior to the plant's arrival. Showing sensitivity to local customs helps sales and builds employee morale, officials say. It helps the company understand the market and keeps it from inadvertently alienating people.

▼ **Employ Locals to Gain Cultural Knowledge**—The best way to understand a market is to have grown up in it. Of the 7,500 3M employees in Asia, fewer than 10 are Americans. The rest are locals who know the customs and buying habits of their compatriots. 3M also makes grants of up to $50,000 available to its Asian employees to study product innovations, making them equals with their U.S. counterparts.

▼ **Build Relationships**—3M executives started preparing for the Chinese market soon after President Nixon's historic visit in 1972. For 10 years, company officials visited Beijing and invited Chinese leaders to 3M headquarters in St. Paul, Minnesota, building contacts and trust along the way. Such efforts paid off when, in 1984, the government made 3M the first wholly owned foreign venture on Chinese soil, 3Mers call the process FIDO ("first in defeats other"), a credo built on patience and long-term perspective.

▼ **Adapt Products to Local Markets**—Examples of how 3M adapts it products read like insightful lessons on culture. In the early 1990s, sales of 3M's famous Scotchbrite cleaning pads were languishing. Company technicians interviewed maids and housewives to determine why. The answer: Fillipinos traditionally scrub floors by pushing a rough coconut shell around with their feet. 3M responded by making the pads brown and shaping them like the foot. In China, a big seller for 3M is a composite to fill tooth cavities. In the United States, dentists pack a soft material into the hole and blast it with a special beam of light, making it hard as enamel in five seconds. But in the People's Republic, dentists cannot afford the light. The solution is an air-drying composite that does the same thing in two minutes: it takes a little longer but is far less expensive.

▼ **Help Employees Understand You**—At any given time, more than 30 Asian technicians are in the United States, where they learn the latest product advances while gaining new insights into how the company works. At the same time, they are able to contribute by infusing their insight into company plans and operations.

▼ **Coordinate by Region**—When designers in Singapore discovered that consumers wanted to use 3M's Nomad household floor mats in their cars, they spread the word to their counterparts in Malaysia and Thailand. Today, the specially made car mats are big sellers across Southeast Asia. The company encourages its product managers from different Asian countries to hold regular meetings and share insights and strategies. The goal is to come up with regional programs and "Asianize" a product more quickly.[12]

Socioeconomic Environment

The main socioeconomic variables of concern to the international marketer relate to population and its various characteristics, such as age distribution, income, and infrastructure. The global economy has witnessed unprecedented growth and change in the 1990s. The industrialized world is aging dramatically, resulting in a dramatic expansion for consumer products. Japan, whose baby boom ended in 1950, well before that of the United States (in 1964), will see its 40–50 age bracket actually shrink, while its 50–60 age bracket will soar. The newly-industrialized countries, such as Taiwan and Singapore, are also beginning to age as a function of health standards and economic development. They should, therefore, emerge as strong markets for products traditionally consumed by working-age people. Only 69 percent of Taiwan's population had TV sets in 1980, for instance, but by the mid-1990s it had reached 99 percent. Sales of other consumer goods can be expected to follow this trend in the NICs (nonindustrialized countries). In most developing countries, the population is expected to rise in all age groups. A key factor in consumer markets has always been the number of women in the paid workforce. Women who work outside the home create a demand for labor-saving devices, packaged and prepared foods, and household services. Working women typically have smaller households and greater disposable income. Infrastructure will also determine market opportunity for marketers. The huge installed base of personal computers in the United States, compared with a smaller number in Japan, suggests that the United States will remain a much larger market for software, while Japan should become a major market for computers. China has one computer per 6,000 people, while the number in the United States is one for every three.[13]

A significant factor influencing international marketing is economic integration. This relates to an increasing tendency among nation states to cooperate in using their respective resources more effectively, and to provide larger markets for their member-country companies. The forms these efforts have taken vary from bilateral trade agreements (such as between Chile and Canada) to free-trade areas (such as NAFTA), to common markets (such as MERCOSUR), and to economic unions (such as the European Union). Membership in such agreements provides marketers opportunity by lowering barriers and increasing access to new markets; lack of membership may hinder such endeavors. For example, U.S. telecommunications marketers have lost deals in Chile to their Canadian counterparts due to an 11 percent tariff Americans have to pay, but which Canadians are exempted from as a result of the bilateral trade treaty between Chile and Canada. Overall, in the more advanced stages of economic integration, marketing environments are being standardized in terms of regulations and even currencies (in the EU by 1999 and in the MERCOSUR early in the 21st century). This makes marketers' operations easier, but at the same time competitively more challenging.

Legal and Political Environment

Legal and political factors often play a critical role in international marketing activities. Even the best business plans can go awry as a result of unexpected legal or political influences, and the failure to anticipate these factors can be the undoing of an otherwise successful business venture.

Of course, a single international legal and political environment does not exist. The business executive must be aware of legal and political factors on a variety of levels. For example, although it is useful to understand the complexities of the host country legal system, such knowledge does not protect against a home country imposed export embargo.

Many laws and regulations, not designed specifically to address international marketing issues, can have a major impact on a firm's opportunities abroad. Minimum wage legislation, for example, affects the international competitive position of a firm using production processes that are highly labor intensive. Other legal and regulatory measures, however, are clearly aimed at international marketing activities. Some may be designed to assist firms in their international efforts, others may protect the international marketer from adverse activity in another country. For example, the U.S. government is quite concerned about the lack of safeguards of **intellectual property rights** in China. Counterfeiting results in inferior products being sold under fake logos, which damages the reputation of the company. It also reduces the chances that an innovative firm can recoup its investment in research and development through the sale of newly spawned products.

Countries differ in their laws as well as in their use of these laws. For example, the United States has developed into an increasingly litigious society, in which institutions and individuals are quick to take a case to court. As a result, court battles are often protracted and costly, and simply the threat of a court case can reduce marketing opportunities. In contrast, Japan's legal tradition tends to minimize the role of the law and lawyers.

From an international business perspective, the two major legal systems worldwide can be categorized into common law and code law. **Common law** is based on tradition

www.nafta.org
www.mercosur.com

Intellectual property rights
is the protection provided by patents, copyrights, and trademarks.

Common law
is law based on tradition and depending less on written statutes and codes than on precedent and custom.

and depends less on written statutes and codes than on precedent and custom. Common law originated in England and is the system of law found today in the United States.

On the other hand, code law is based on a comprehensive set of written statutes. Countries with code law try to spell out all possible legal rules explicitly. Code law is based on Roman law and is found in the majority of the nations of the world. In general, countries with the code law system have much more rigid laws than those with the common law system. In the latter, courts adopt precedents and customs to fit the cases, allowing the marketer a better idea of the basic judgment likely to be rendered in new situations.

Although wide in theory, the differences between code law and common law, and their impact on the international marketer, are not always as broad in practice. For example, many common law countries, including the United States, have adopted commercial codes to govern the conduct of business.

Host countries may adopt a number of laws that affect a company's ability to market. There can be laws affecting the entry of goods, such as tariffs and quotas. Also in this category are antidumping laws, which prohibit below-cost sales of products, and laws that require export and import licensing. In addition, many countries have health and safety standards that may, by design or by accident, restrict the entry of foreign goods.

Other laws may be designed to protect domestic industries. For example, the Chinese government has prohibited foreign investment for projects that are not in line with national economic development and projects under the unified state plan. Barred project areas include developing and printing of color films; production of cigarettes, liquors, foods, and drinks targeted at the home markets; and assembly lines of computers, refrigerators, washing machines, watches, and sewing machines.[14]

Very specific legislation may also exist to regulate where a firm can advertise or what constitutes deceptive advertising. Many countries prohibit specific claims by marketers comparing their product to that of the competition and restrict the use of promotional devices. Some countries regulate the names of companies or the foreign language content of a product's label.

International law plays an important role in the conduct of international business. Although no enforceable body of international law exists, certain treaties and agreements, respected by a number of countries, profoundly influence international business operations. As an example, the World Trade Organization (WTO) defines internationally acceptable economic practices for its member nations. Although it does not directly affect individual firms, it does influence them indirectly by providing a more stable and predictable international market environment.

INTERNATIONAL MARKET SELECTION

The process of target market selection involves narrowing down potential country markets to a feasible number of countries and market segments within them. Rather than try to appeal to everyone, marketers utilize their resources best by (1) identifying potential markets for entry and (2) expanding selectively over time to those markets deemed attractive.

Identification and Screening

A four-stage process for screening and analyzing markets internationally is presented in Figure 3.2. It begins with general criteria and ends with product-specific analyses.

The preliminary screening process must rely chiefly on existing data for country-specific factors as well as product- and industry-specific dimensions. Country-specific factors typically include those that indicate the market's overall buying power: for example, population, gross national product in total and per capita, and total exports and imports. Product-specific factors narrow the analysis to the marketer's operations. A company such as Motorola, manufacturing for the automobile aftermarket, is interested in the number of

Code law
is law based on a comprehensive set of written statutes.

Antidumping laws
are laws designed to help domestic industries that are injured by unfair competition from abroad due to imports being sold at less than fair value.

www.wto.org

World Trade Organization (WTO)
is the institution that administers international trade and investment accords. It supplanted GATT in 1995.

Marketing Technologies

The Latin Web of Information

For marketers interested in Latin America, the growth of the Internet has provided a wealth of market research tools at their fingertips. Although the rapid expansion of global Web sites has received much publicity, there are also many lesser-known region-specific databases and timely information sources on the Web. Companies and governments alike have found that the Web is a valuable yet inexpensive way to provide updated information to a wide and geographically diverse audience.

A Mexican government program provides one example of such timeliness. When Mexico announced a new program for financing development, it was able to give instant access to an extensive report on the program at the same time that the announcement appeared in media reports. Marketers had immediate access to primary-source information that otherwise would have been difficult and time-consuming to acquire.

However, the swift growth and dynamic nature of Internet-based information sources has magnified the fundamental challenge facing market researchers using the Web: the Internet has little structure to organize its abundance of information, and it has no filter to determine the quality of information. As a result, researchers need explicit knowledge of the information they are seeking, the sources for that information, and their Web addresses before starting their task. Language skills are also a plus; as with many region-specific Web sites are printed in the local language, Latin American Web sites often bury a lot of the English-language material under pages of Spanish or Portuguese. Nevertheless, the following sites give an indication of the quality of information available to researchers:

▼ **Official Economic Statistical Agencies.** All of the basic details about Latin economies can now be found quickly over the Web. Inflation, unemployment, industrial production, and similar indicators may even be available on the Web before they are published in the press.

Argentina's Instituto Nacional de Estadistica y Censos (www.indec.mecon.ar) and Brazil's Instituto de Geografia e Estatistica (www.ibge.gov.br) offer extensive historical demographic and economic data.

▼ **Central Banks and Regulatory Agencies.** These sites provide recent data both on financial indicators, such as foreign exchange movements, as well as developments in the different sectors of the economy. Most central banks and regulatory agencies offer downloadable material and economic and statistical analyses.

▼ **Stock Exchanges.** All major Latin American exchanges are now on-line, providing same-day information on trading. Many provide daily bulletins with company announcements.

▼ **Company Web sites.** One study concluded that 30 percent of the major Latin American companies now have Web sites. Although they vary in depth and quality, many contain production, export, and services information, as well as press releases. For example, Garoto, one of the three greatest chocolate makers of the Southern Hemisphere, includes in its site (www.garoto.com.br) useful corporate information about its operations in its domestic market in Brazil and its expanding operations worldwide (it opened a sales office in the United States in 1998).

Question

1. Among the downloadable reports through Brazil's statistical agency, IBGE, is the *National Household Sample Survey 1997*. Suggest how these data can be used in establishing the market potential for various household goods.

Source: Christopher Tilley and Mary Gwynn, "The Internet Advantage," *Latin Finance* 89 (September 1997): 57–59.

www.indec.mecon.ar
www.ibge.gov.br
www.garoto.com.br

Market potential
is the level of sales that might be available to all marketers in an industry in a given market.

passenger cars, trucks, and buses in use. The statistical analyses must be accompanied by qualitative assessments of the impact of cultural elements and the overall climate for foreign firms and products. Internally, the marketer must decide on the strategic fit of a market as well. In some cases, an individual market may not be attractive in its own right but may have some other significance, such as being the home market of the most demanding customers (thereby aiding in product development) or being the home market of a significant competitor (presenting a preemptive rationale for entry). Furthermore, the time dimension will have to be incorporated into the analysis. An insignificant market may turn into an emerging market, and those with a foothold may reap the benefits.

Total **market potential** is the sales, in physical units or in monetary terms, that might be available to all marketers in an industry. The marketing manager needs to assess the size of existing markets and forecast their future growth. Two general approaches are used. Analytical techniques based on the use of existing data include using indexes to measure potential through proxy variables that have been shown (by research or by intuition) to correlate closely with the demand of a product. For example, an index for consumer goods might involve population, disposable personal income, and retail sales in the

Figure 3.2 The Screening Process in Target Market Choice

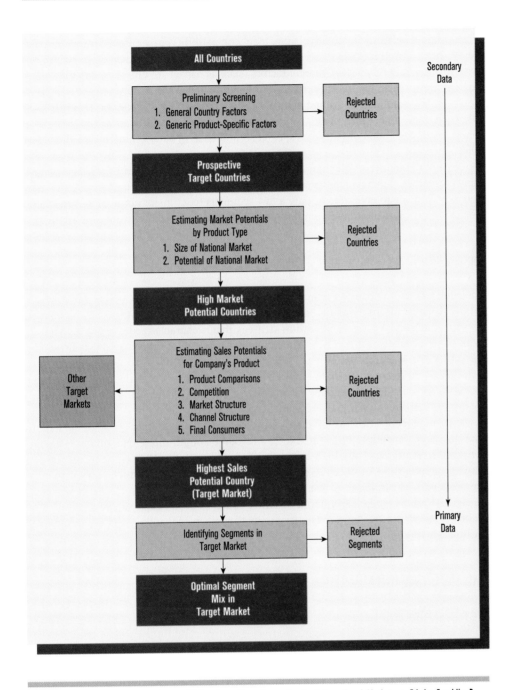

Source: Reprinted by permission of the publisher from *Entry Strategies for International Markets*, p. 56, by Franklin R. Root (Lexington, MA: Lexington Books, D.C. Heath & Co., Copyright 1994, D.C. Heath & Co.).

market concerned. In addition to quantitative techniques, marketers also use various survey techniques. These are especially useful when marketing new technologies. A survey of end-user interest and responses may provide a relatively clear picture of the possibilities in a new market. A second commonly used approach to assess the size of existing markets is estimating by analogy—where demand patterns in one market are expected to repeat themselves in other markets as function of indicators such as disposable income.

Even when the international marketer has gained an understanding of overall demand conditions, the potential of the marketer's own efforts may not be known. **Sales potential** is the share of the market potential that the marketer can reasonably expect to gain over the long term. To arrive at an estimate, the marketer needs to collect data on perceptions of the product (as far as its relative advantage, compatibility, ease of use, trialability, and the extent to which it lends itself to word-of-mouth communication), competition (its strength and likely responses), market factors (such as barriers to entry), channel structure (such as access and support of intermediaries), and final consumers (their ability and willingness to buy something new and nonlocal). The marketer's questions can never be fully answered until the commitment has been made to enter the market and operations have commenced. The mode of entry has special significance in determining the final level of sales potential.

Within the markets selected, final consumers and business users will vary in their wants, resources, geographical locations, attitudes, and buying practices. Initially, the decision may be made to enter one or only a few segments (e.g., major coastal cities in China; the government market, or the premium-priced segment) and later expand to others.

Concentration versus Diversification Strategies

Choosing a market expansion policy involves the allocation of effort among various markets. The major alternatives include a **concentration strategy** that focuses on a small number of markets, or a **diversification strategy** that is characterized by growth in a relatively large number of markets.[15] The decision to concentrate or diversify is driven by market factors (e.g., market growth, sales stability, competitive lead time, and extent of restraints), marketing-mix related factors (i.e., the extent to which the same mix can be used across borders), and company factors (e.g., resources available and the level of direct control the marketer wants to exert on local operations).

Either concentration or diversification is applicable to market segments or to mass markets, depending on the marketer's resource commitment. One option is a dual-concentration strategy, in which efforts are focused on a specific segment in a limited number of countries. Another is a dual-diversification strategy, in which entry is to most segments in most available markets. The first is likely for small firms or firms that market specialized products to clearly defined markets, such as ocean-capable sailing boats. The second is typical for the large consumer-products companies that have sufficient resources for broad coverage.

THE INTERNATIONALIZATION PROCESS

The Role of Management

LEARNING OBJECTIVE LO5

The type and quality of a firm's management are key to whether and how a firm will enter the international marketplace. Management dynamism and commitment are crucial in the first steps toward international operations.[16] Conversely, the managers of firms that are unsuccessful or inactive internationally usually exhibit a lack of determination or devotion to international marketing. The issue of **managerial commitment** is a critical one because foreign market penetration requires a vast amount of market development activity, sensitivity toward foreign environments, research, and innovation. Regardless of what the firm produces or where it does business internationally, managerial commitment is crucial for enduring occasional setbacks and failures.[17]

Initiating international marketing activities takes the firm in an entirely new direction, quite different from adding a product line or hiring a few more people. Going international means that a fundamental strategic change is taking place. The first step in developing international commitment is to become aware of international marketing opportunities. Management may then decide to enter the international marketplace on a limited basis and evaluate the results of the initial activities. An international business orientation develops over time.

Motivations to Go Abroad

A variety of motivations can push and pull individuals and firms along the international path. An overview of the major motivations that have been found to make firms go international is provided in Table 3.2. Proactive motivations represent firm-initiated strategic change. Reactive motivations describe actions that result in a firm's response and adaptation to changes imposed by the outside environment. In other words, firms with proactive motivations go international because they want to; those with reactive motivations do so because they have to.

Proactive Motivations

Profits are the major proactive motivation for international marketing. Management may perceive international sales as a potential source of higher profit margins or of more added-on profits. Of course, the profitability perceived when planning to go international is often quite different from the profitability actually obtained. In international start-up operations, initial profitability may be quite low, particularly since unexpected influences, such as shifts in exchange rates, can change the profit picture substantially.[18]

Unique products or a technological advantage can be another major stimulus. A firm may produce products that are not widely available from international competitors. Special knowledge about foreign customers or market situations may be another proactive stimulus. Such knowledge may result from particular insights by a firm, special contacts an individual may have, in-depth research, or simply from being in the right place at the right time (for example, recognizing a good business situation during a vacation trip). Tax benefits can also play a major motivating role. Many governments use preferential tax treatment to encourage exports. In the United States, for example, a tax mechanism called foreign sales corporation (FSC) provides firms with certain tax deferrals and makes international business activities more profitable.

A final major proactive motivation involves economies of scale. International activities may enable the firm to increase its output and therefore ride more rapidly on the learning curve. The Boston Consulting Group has shown that the doubling of output can reduce production costs up to 30 percent. Increased production for international markets can therefore help to reduce the cost of production for domestic sales and make the firm more competitive domestically as well.[19]

www.bcg.com

Reactive Motivations

Here firms respond to environmental changes and pressures rather than attempt to blaze new trails. Competitive pressures are one example. A company may fear losing domestic

Table 3.2 Major Motivations to Internationalize Small and Medium-Sized Firms	
Proactive	**Reactive**
Profit advantage	Competitive pressures
Unique products	Overproduction
Technological advantage	Declining domestic sales
Exclusive information	Excess capacity
Tax benefit	Saturated domestic markets
Economies of scale	Proximity to customers and ports

Source: Michael R. Czinkota, Ilkka A. Ronkainen, Michael H. Moffett, *International Business*, 5th edition (Fort Worth: Harcourt Brace College Publishers, 1998), 368.

market share to competing firms that benefit from the economies of scale gained through international marketing activities.

Overproduction can result in international activities. During downturns in the domestic business cycle, foreign markets have historically provided an ideal outlet for excess inventories. International expansion motivated by overproduction usually does not represent full commitment by management, but rather a safety-valve activity. As soon as domestic demand returns to previous levels, international activities are curtailed or even terminated.

Declining domestic sales or a saturated domestic market have a similar motivating effect. Firms may attempt to prolong the product life cycle by expanding the market. Excess capacity can also be a powerful motivator. If equipment for production is not fully utilized, firms may see expansion abroad as an ideal way to achieve broader distribution of fixed costs.

Physical and psychological closeness to the international market can often play a major role in the international marketing activities of the firm. For example, a firm established near a border may not even perceive itself as going abroad if it does business in the neighboring country. Except for some firms close to the Canadian or Mexican border, however, this factor is much less prevalent in the United States than in many other nations. Most European firms automatically go abroad simply because their neighbors are so close.

In general, firms that are most successful in international markets tend to be motivated by proactive—that is, firm internal—factors. Proactive firms are also frequently more service oriented than reactive firms. Further, proactive firms are more marketing-strategy oriented than reactive firms, which have as their major concern operational issues.

ALTERNATIVE ENTRY STRATEGIES

The key entry strategies used by the majority of firms to initiate international business activities are indirect exporting and importing, direct exporting and importing, licensing, and franchising.[20] Once firms are established in the international market, other modes of expansion are used, such as direct foreign investment, joint ventures, and contract manufacturing.

Indirect Exporting and Importing

Indirect involvement means that the firm participates in international marketing through an **international intermediary** and does not deal directly with foreign customers or firms. While such indirect activities represent a form of international market entry, they are unlikely to result in growing management commitment to international markets or increased capabilities in serving them.

Many firms are indirect exporters and importers without their knowledge. As an example, merchandise can be sold to a domestic firm that in turn sells it abroad. This is most frequently the case when smaller suppliers deliver products to large multinational corporations, which use them as input to their international sales. Foreign buyers may purchase products locally and send them to their home country. At the same time, many firms that perceive themselves as buying domestically may in reality buy imported products. They may have long-standing relations with a domestic supplier who, because of cost and competitive pressures, has begun to source products from abroad rather than produce them domestically. In this case, the buying firm has become an indirect importer.

Direct Exporting and Importing

Firms that opt to export or import directly have more opportunities ahead of them. They learn more quickly the competitive advantages of their products and can therefore expand more rapidly. They also have the ability to control their international activities better and

International intermediaries

are marketing institutions that facilitate the movement of goods and services between the originator and customer.

can forge relationships with their trading partners, which can lead to further international growth and success.

However, these firms are faced with obstacles that those who indirectly access international markets avoid. These hurdles include identifying and targeting foreign suppliers and/or customers and finding retail space, processes that can be very costly and time-consuming. Some firms are overcoming such barriers through the use of intermediaries or "storeless" distribution networks (such as mail-order catalogs and Web sites on the Internet).

International Intermediaries

Both direct and indirect importers and exporters frequently make use of intermediaries who can assist with troublesome yet important details such as documentation, financing, and transportation. Intermediaries also can identify foreign suppliers and customers and help the firm with long- or short-term market penetration efforts. Two major types of international intermediaries are export management companies and trading companies.

Export management companies (EMCs) specialize in performing international business services as commission representatives or as distributors. EMCs have two primary forms of operation: They take title to goods and operate internationally on their own account, or they perform services as agents. They often serve a variety of clients, thus their mode of operation may vary from client to client and from transaction to transaction. An EMC may act as an agent for one client and as a distributor for another. It may even act as both for the same client on different occasions.

When working as an **agent,** the EMC is primarily responsible for developing foreign business and sales strategies and establishing contacts abroad. Because the EMC does not share in the profits from a sale, it depends heavily on a high sales volume, on which it charges commission. EMCs that have specific expertise in selecting markets because of language capabilities, previous exposure, or specialized contacts appear to be the ones most successful and useful in aiding client firms in their international marketing efforts.

When operating as a **distributor,** the EMC purchases products from the domestic firm, takes title, and assumes the trading risk. Selling in its own name, it has the opportunity to reap greater profits than when acting as an agent. The potential for greater profit is appropriate, because the EMC has drastically reduced the risk for the domestic firm while increasing its own risk. The domestic firm selling to the EMC is in the comfortable position of having sold its merchandise without having to deal with the complexities of the international market, but it is less likely to gather much international expertise.

A second major intermediary is the **trading company.** Today, the most famous trading companies are the **sogoshosha** of Japan. Names such as Mitsubishi, Mitsui, and C. Itoh have become household words around the world. A trading company engages in a wider variety of activities than an EMC. It can purchase products, act as a distributor abroad, or offer services. It can provide information on distribution costs, handle domestic and international distribution and transportation, book space on ocean or air carriers, and handle shipping contracts.

Licensing

Under a **licensing agreement,** one firm permits another to use its intellectual property for compensation designated as **royalty.** The recipient firm is the licensee. The property licensed might include patents, trademarks, copyrights, technology, technical know-how, or specific business skills. For example, a firm that has developed a bag-in-the-box packaging process for milk can permit other firms abroad to use the same process. Licensing therefore amounts to exporting intangibles.

Licensing has intuitive appeal to many would-be international managers. As an entry strategy, it requires neither capital investment nor detailed involvement with foreign

www.mitsui.com

Export Management Companies (EMCs) are firms that specialize in performing international services as commissioned representatives or as distributors.

Agent is a marketing intermediary who does not take title to the products but develops marketing strategy and establishes contacts abroad.

Distributor is a marketing intermediary who purchases products from the domestic firm and assumes the trading risk.

Trading company is a marketing intermediary that undertakes exporting, importing, countertrading, investing, and manufacturing.

Sogoshosha are the trading companies of Japan including firms such as Sumitomo, Mitsubishi, and Mitsui.

Licensing agreement is an arrangement in which one firm permits another to use its intellectual property in exchange for compensation, typically a royalty.

Royalty is the compensation paid by one firm to another under licensing and franchising agreements.

Franchising is one way to expand into international markets. An example is this Dunkin' Donuts franchise in Thailand.

Expropriation

is a government takeover of a company's operations frequently at a level lower than the value of the assets.

Franchising

is a form of licensing that grants a wholesaler or a retailer exclusive rights to sell a product or a service in a specified area.

customers. By generating royalty income, licensing provides an opportunity to earn income from research and development investments already made. After initial costs, the licensor can reap benefits until the end of the license contract period. Licensing also reduces the risk of **expropriation** because the licensee is a local company that can provide leverage against government action. Licensing also may provide a means by which foreign markets can be tested without major involvement of capital or management time.

Licensing is not without disadvantages. It is a very limited form of foreign market participation and does not guarantee a basis for future expansion. Quite the opposite may take place. In exchange for the royalty, the licensor may create its own competitor not only in the market for which the agreement was made but in third-country markets as well.

Franchising is the granting of the right by a parent company (the franchisor) to another independent entity (the franchisee) to do business in a prescribed manner. The right can take the form of selling the franchisor's products; using its name, production, and marketing techniques; or using its general business approach.[21] The major forms of franchising are manufacturer–retailer systems (such as car dealerships), manufacturer–wholesaler systems (such as soft drink companies), and service firm–retailer systems (such as lodging services and fast-food outlets).

To be successful in international franchising, the firm must be able to offer unique products or unique selling propositions. With its uniqueness, a franchisee must offer a high degree of standardization. In most cases, standardization does not require 100 percent uniformity, but rather, international recognizability. Concurrent with this recognizability, the franchisor can and should adapt to local circumstances. Food franchisors, for example, will vary the products and product lines offered depending on local market conditions and tastes. The need to do so, however, has to be researched. TGI Friday's assumed that Korean customers would expect to see kimchi (a kind of pickled cabbage that is a staple in Korean restaurants) on TGIF menus as well. They quickly found out that customers in American restaurants want only American food.[22]

Foreign Direct Investment

All types of firms, large or small, can carry out global market expansion through foreign direct investment or management contracts, and they are doing so at an increasing pace. Key to the decision to invest abroad is the existence of specific advantages that outweigh the disadvantages and risks of operating so far from home. Since foreign direct investment often requires substantial capital and a firm's ability to absorb risk, the most visible players in the area are large **multinational corporations,** which are defined by the United Nations as "enterprises which own or control production or service facilities outside the country in which they are based."[23] They come from a wide variety of countries, depend heavily on their international sales, and in terms of sales generate revenues that exceed the GNPs of many nations.

Many of the large multinationals operate in well over 100 countries. For some, their original home market accounts for only a fraction of their sales. For example, Nestlé's sales in Switzerland are only 2 percent of total sales. Through their investment, multinational corporations create economic vitality and jobs in their host countries. For example, in the United States, foreign-owned firms provide jobs for 4.9 million Americans and pay higher wages than do average U.S. owned firms.[24]

Reasons for Foreign Direct Investment

Marketing considerations and the corporate desire for growth are major causes of **foreign direct investment.** Today's competitive demands require firms to operate simultaneously in the "triad" of the United States, Western Europe, and Japan. Corporations therefore need to seek wider market access in order to maintain and increase their sales. This objective can be achieved most quickly through the acquisition of foreign firms. Through such expansion, the corporation also gains ownership advantages consisting of political know-how and expertise.

Foreign direct investment permits corporations to circumvent current barriers to trade and operate abroad as a domestic firm, unaffected by duties, tariffs, or other import restrictions. Further, local buyers may wish to buy from sources that they perceive to be reliable in their supply, which means buying from local producers. Another incentive is the cost factor, with corporations attempting to obtain low-cost resources and ensure their sources of supply. Finally, once the decision is made to invest internationally, the investment climate plays a major role. Corporations will seek to invest in those geographic areas where their investment is most protected and has the best chance to flourish. Often, government incentives also play a role in guiding the investment location of firms.

As large multinational firms move abroad, they are quite interested in maintaining their established business relationships with other firms. Therefore, they frequently encourage their suppliers to follow them and continue to supply them from a foreign location. As illustrated in Figure 3.3, many Japanese automakers have urged their suppliers in Japan to begin production in the United States in order for the new U.S. plants to have access to their products. As a result, a few direct investments can gradually form an important investment preference for subsequent investment flows.

A Perspective on Foreign Direct Investors

All foreign direct investors, and particularly multinational corporations, are viewed with a mixture of awe and dismay. Governments and individuals praise them for bringing capital, economic activity, and employment, as investors are seen as key transferers of technology and managerial skills. Through these transfers, competition, market choice, and competitiveness are enhanced.

At the same time, the dependence on multinational corporations is seen negatively by many. International direct investors are accused of actually draining resources from their host countries. By employing the best and the brightest, they are said to deprive domestic firms of talent, thus causing a brain drain. Once they have hired locals, multinational firms are accused of not promoting them high enough and of imposing many new rules on

Multinational corporations are companies that have production operations in at least one country in addition to their domestic base.

www.nestle.com

Foreign direct investment is an international entry strategy that is achieved through the acquisition of foreign firms.

| Figure 3.3 | Japanese Products Can Drive the U.S. Economy |

The 2.2 liter DOHC Camry engine. Made in Georgetown, Kentucky.

IT ALSO DRIVES THE ECONOMY.

AT TOYOTA, we're continuing our commitment to | engines per year. It's part of Toyota's $5 billion invest-

building in America. In fact, at our manufacturing | ment in American manufacturing, an investment that's

plant in Kentucky, we're producing nearly 250,000 | driving more than 16,000 direct jobs across America.

INVESTING IN THE THINGS WE ALL CARE ABOUT. **TOYOTA**

For more information about Toyota in America write Toyota Motor Corporate Services, 9 West 57th Street, Suite 4900-D15, New York, NY 10019.

their employees abroad. By bringing in foreign technology, they are either viewed as discouraging local technology development or as perhaps transferring only outmoded knowledge. By increasing competition, they are declared the enemy of domestic firms. There are concerns about foreign investors' economic and political loyalty toward their host government. And, of course, their sheer size, which sometimes exceeds the financial assets that the government controls, makes foreign investors suspect. Clearly, a love–hate relationship exists between governments and the foreign direct investor. As the firm's size and investment volume grow, the benefits it brings to the economy increase. At the same time, the dependence of the economy on the firm increases as well.

Types of Ownership
A corporation has a wide variety of ownership choices, ranging from 100 percent ownership to a minority interest. The different levels of ownership will result in varying degrees of flexibility for the corporation, a changing ability to control business plans and strategy,

and differences in the level of risk assumed. Often, the ownership decision is either a strategic response to corporate capabilities and needs or a necessary result of government regulations.

Full Ownership Full ownership may be a desirable, but not a necessary, prerequisite for international success. At other times, it may be a necessity, particularly when strong linkages exist within the corporation. Interdependencies between and among local operations and headquarters may be so strong that anything short of total coordination will result in a benefit to the firm as a whole that is less than acceptable. This may be the case if centralized product design, pricing, or advertising is needed. Yet, increasingly, the international environment is growing hostile to full ownership by multinational firms. Many governments exert political pressure to obtain national control of foreign operations. Ownership options are limited either through outright legal restrictions or through measures designed to make foreign ownership less attractive—such as **profit repatriation limitations.** The international marketer is therefore frequently faced with the choice either of abiding by existing restraints and accepting a reduction in control or losing the opportunity to operate in the country.

Joint Ventures **Joint ventures** are a collaboration of two or more organizations for more than a transitory period.[25] The participating partners share assets, risks, and profits. Equality of partners is not necessary. The partners' contributions to the joint venture can also vary widely and may consist of capital, technology, know-how, sales organizations, or plant and equipment. Joint ventures can help overcome existing market access restrictions and open up or maintain market opportunities that otherwise would not be available. If a corporation can identify a partner with a common goal, joint ventures may represent the most viable vehicle for international expansion. Joint ventures are valuable when the pooling of resources results in a better outcome for each partner than if each attempted to carry out its activities individually. This is particularly the case when each partner has a specialized advantage in areas that benefit the joint venture. For example, a firm may have new technology available, yet lack sufficient capital to carry out foreign direct investment on its own. By joining forces with a partner, the technology can be used more quickly and market penetration is easier. Similarly, one of the partners may have a distribution system

Profit repatriation limitations
are restrictions set up by host governments in terms of a company's ability to pay dividends from their operations back to their home base.

Joint ventures
result from the participation of two or more companies in an enterprise in which each party contributes assets, owns the new entity to some degree, and shares risk.

Foreign direct investment creates jobs. The United States benefits from additional employment opportunities provided by foreign investments in production facilities such as the Toyota–GM plant in California.

already established or have better access to local suppliers, either of which permits a greater volume of sales in a shorter period of time. Greater experience with the culture and environment of the local partner may enable the joint venture to be more aware of cultural sensitivities and to benefit from greater insights into changing market conditions and needs.

Joint ventures also permit better relationships with local organizations—government, local authorities, or labor unions. Particularly if the local partner can bring political influence to the undertaking, the new venture may be eligible for tax incentives, grants, and government support and may be less vulnerable to political risk. Negotiations for certifications or licenses may be easier because authorities may not perceive themselves as dealing with a foreign firm.

Problem areas in joint ventures, as in all partnerships, involve implementing the concept and maintaining the relationship. Seven out of ten joint ventures have been found to fall short of expectations and/or are disbanded.[26] The reasons typically relate to conflicts of interest, problems with disclosure of sensitive information, and disagreement over how profits are to be shared. In some cases, managers dispatched to the joint venture by the partners may feel differing degrees of loyalty to the venture and its partners. Reconciling such conflicts of loyalty is one of the greatest human resource challenges for joint ventures.[27]

Strategic alliances
are informal or formal arrangements between two or more companies with a common business objective.

Strategic Alliances Strategic alliances are informal or formal arrangements between two or more companies with a common business objective. They are more than the traditional customer–vendor relationship but less than an outright acquisition. The great advantage of such alliances is their ongoing flexibility since their formation, although stable at any given point in time, is subject to adjustment and change in response to environmental shifts.[28] In essence, strategic alliances are networks of companies that collaborate in the achievement of a given project or objective. However, partners for one project may well be fierce competitors in another situation.

Companies must carefully evaluate the effects of entering such a coalition. The most successful alliances are those that match the complementary strengths of partners to satisfy a joint objective. Often the partners have different product, geographic, or functional strengths, which the alliance can build on in order to achieve success with a new strategy or in a new market. Figure 3.4 shows how some firms have combined their individual strengths to achieve their joint objective. In light of growing international competition and the rising cost of technology, strategic alliances are likely to continue their growth in the future.

Contractual Arrangements Firms have found contractual arrangements to be a useful alternative or complement to other international options, since they permit the international use of corporate resources and can also be an acceptable response to government ownership restrictions.

Complementary marketing
is a contractual arrangement where participating parties carry out different but complementary activities.

Outsourcing
is using another firm for the manufacture of needed components or products or delivery of a service.

Contract manufacturing
is using another firm for the manufacture of goods so that the marketer may concentrate on the research and development as well as marketing aspects of the operation.

One form such an arrangement may take is that of **complementary marketing**, where the contracting parties carry out different activities. For example, Nestlé and General Mills have an agreement whereby Honey Nut Cheerios and Golden Grahams are made in General Mill's U.S. plants, shipped in bulk to Europe for packaging at a Nestlé plant, and are then marketed in France, Spain, and Portugal by Nestlé.[29] Other contractual arrangements exist for **outsourcing** where a firm enters into long-term arrangements with its suppliers. For example, General Motors buys cars and components from South Korea's Daewoo, and Siemens buys computers from Fujitsu. As corporations look for ways to grow and focus simultaneously on their competitive advantage, outsourcing has becomes a powerful new tool for achieving these goals. Firms increasingly also develop arrangements for **contract manufacturing** that allow the corporation to separate the physical production of goods from the research, development, and marketing stages, especially if the latter are the core competencies of the firm. Such contracting has become particularly popular in the footwear and garment industries. For example, Nike, the footwear company based in Beaverton, Oregon, has 100 percent of its footwear produced by subcontractors,

Figure 3.4 Complementary Strengths Create Value

Partner *Strength...*	+ Partner *Strength...*	= Joint Objective
Pepsico *marketing clout for canned beverages*	**Lipton** *recognized tea brand and customer franchise*	*To sell canned iced tea beverages jointly*
Coca-Cola *marketing clout for canned beverages*	**Nestlé** *recognized tea brand and customer franchise*	*To sell canned iced tea beverages jointly*
KFC *established brand and store format, and operations skills*	**Mitsubishi** *real estate and site-selection skills in Japan*	*To establish a KFC chain in Japan*
Siemens *presence in range of telecommunications markets worldwide and cable-manufacturing technology*	**Corning** *technological strength in optical fibers and glass*	*To create a fiber-optic-cable business*
Ericsson *technological strength in public telecommunications networks*	**Hewlett-Packard** *computers, software, and access to electronics-channels*	*To create and market network management systems*

Sources: Joel Bleeke and David Ernst, "Is Your Strategic Alliance Really a Sale?" *Harvard Business Review* 73 (January–February 1995): 97–105; and Melanie Weils, "Coca-Cola Proclaims Nestea Time for CAA," *Advertising Age,* January 30, 1995, 2. See also www.pepsico.com, www.lipton.com, www.cocacola.com, www.nestle.com, www.kfc.com, www.siecor.com, www.ericsson.com, and www.hp.com

most of them outside the United States. Nike's own people focus on the services part of the production process, including design, product development, marketing, and distribution.[30]

www.generalmills.com
www.nike.com

A COMPREHENSIVE VIEW OF INTERNATIONAL EXPANSION

The central driver of internationalization is the level of managerial commitment. This commitment will grow gradually from an awareness of international potential to the adaptation of an international strategic direction. It will be influenced by the information, experience, and perception of management, which in turn is shaped by motivations and concerns of the firm.

Management's commitment and its view of the capabilities of the firm will then trigger various international marketing activities, which can range from indirect exporting and importing to a more direct involvement in the global market. Eventually, the firm may expand further through foreign direct investment measures such as joint ventures or strategic alliances. All of the developments, processes, and factors involved in the overall process of going international are linked to each other. A comprehensive view of these linkages is presented schematically in Figure 3.5.

Adjusting the Marketing Mix

The choice of target markets and entry modes has to be accompanied by decisions relating to the marketing mix and the degree to which its elements should be standardized or localized. Three basic alternatives in approaching international markets are available:

▼ Make no special provisions for the international marketplace but, rather, identify potential target markets and then choose products that can easily be marketed with little or no modification (**standardized approach**).

LEARNING OBJECTIVE LO7

Standardized approach
is the aproach to international marketing in which products are marketed with little or no modification.

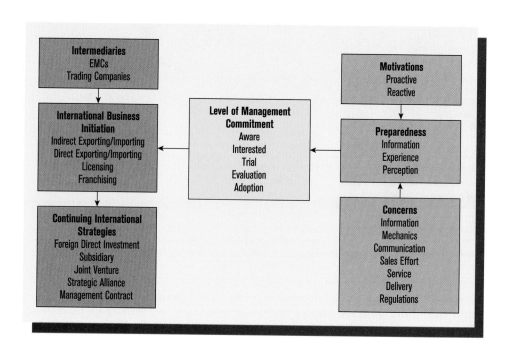

Figure 3.5 A Comprehensive Model of International Entry and Expansion

Multi-domestic approach
is the approach to international marketing in which local conditions are adapted to in each and every target market.

Globalization approach
is the approach to international marketing in which differences are incorporated into a regional or global strategy that will allow for differences in implementation.

▼ Adapt to local conditions in each and every target market (**the multi-domestic approach**).

▼ Incorporate differences into a regional or global strategy that will allow for local differences in implementation (**globalization approach**).

Ideally, the marketing manager should "think globally and act locally," not by focusing on the extremes of full standardization or full localization, but rather on exploiting good ideas, strategies, and products on a wider regional basis.

Macroenvironmental Influences

Typically, as stated in Chapter 1, macroenvironmental influences often mandate a variety of marketing-mix adjustments (see Figure 3.6). Among them, government regulations present the most stringent requirements. Some regulations may serve no purpose other than a political one, such as protection of domestic industry or response to constituent pressure. Because of the sovereignty of nations, marketers need to comply, but can influence the situation by lobbying, directly or through their industry associations, for an issue to be raised during trade negotiations. Government regulations may be spelled out, but marketers need to be vigilant in terms of changes and exceptions.

Standards often present the marketing manager with a set of adaptation challenges. For example, France requires the use of the French language in any offer, presentation, or advertisement whether written or spoken; in instructions for use; in specification or guarantee terms; as well as on invoices and receipts. This includes Websites as well. Increasingly, quality standards may be imposed on marketers especially in business marketing. The EU has chosen ISO 9000 as a basis to harmonize varying technical norms of its member states, thereby making it also necessary for all marketers interested in the EU to comply.[31] Increasing environmental concern is leading some governments to require marketers to take responsibility for their packaging waste, thereby resulting in attempts to redesign products

Figure 3.6   Factors Affecting Marketing-Mix Adjustments

Regional, Country, or Local Characteristics	Product Characteristics	Company Considerations
Government regulations	Product constituents	Profitability
Customer characteristics, expectations, and preferences	Brand	Market opportunity
Purchase patterns	Positioning	Policies
Stage of economic development	Packaging	
Competitive offerings	Country of origin	
Climate and geography		

Source: Adapted from V. Yorio, *Adapting Products for Export* (New York: The Conference Board, 1983): p. 7.

www.toyota.com

and their packaging, reducing the waste generated, recycling it, and reusing it. At the Geneva auto show in 1998, Toyota introduced a concept car that is predominantly recyclable.

Product Decisions

While there are arguments for an increasing amount of product standardization from an economies of scale perspective, international marketing managers will have to balance these considerations against factors that may call for adaptation. These factors can be categorized into three groups: (1) regional, country, or local characteristics, (2) product characteristics, and (3) company considerations. With some of these factors, the marketing manager has no choice but to make the adaptations. For example, Murray Ohio Manufacturing has had to make its lawnmowers quieter for the European market because of the noise standards imposed by the European Union.[32] In some cases, the choice is based on customer preferences (e.g., Chrysler making available, in 1996 for the first time, right-hand drive vehicles for the Japanese market).

Design Considerations Climate and geography of international markets can have an impact on product design. For example, the marketing of chocolate products is challenging in hot climates and has led three companies to take different approaches to their marketing-mix adaptation. Nestlé's solution was to produce a slightly different Kit Kat wafer for Asia with reduced fat content to raise the chocolate's melting point. Cadbury Schweppes has its own display cases in the retail outlets to reject the heat and humidity, while Toblerone has confined its distribution to air-conditioned outlets.

The international marketer must also make sure products do not contain ingredients or features that might be in violation of legal requirements or religious or social customs. In Islamic countries, for example, animal fats have to be replaced by ingredients such as vegetable shortening.

Branding Considerations The use of standardization in branding is strongest in culturally similar markets; for U.S. marketers this means Canada and the United Kingdom. Standardization of product and brand do not necessarily move hand in hand; a global or regional brand may well have local features (such as Ford's Escort), or a highly standardized product may have local brand names (e.g., Snuggle, Cajoline, Kuschelweich, Mimosin, and Yumos). While the same brand name may be used, additional dimensions may have to be considered. Chinese consumers expect more in terms of how the names are spelled, written, and styled, and whether they are considered lucky. Chee-tos are marketed in China under the Chinese name *qi duo* (roughly pronounced "chee-do") that translates as "Many Surprises." Segmentation decisions will affect branding as well.[33] At Whirlpool, the Whirlpool brand name will be used as the global brand name to serve the broad middle market segment, while regional and local brands will cover the others. Throughout Europe, the Bauknecht brand is targeted at the upper end of the market seeking a reputable

Coca - Cola
可口可乐
(Tasty and happy)

Pepsi - Cola
百事可乐
(Hundred happy things)

Sharp
声宝
(Treasure of sound)

In Europe and the Americas, brand names such as Coca-Cola and Sharp have no meaning in themselves, and few are even aware of the origins of the name. But to Chinese-speaking consumers, brand names include an additional dimension: *meaning*. Coca-Cola means "tasty and happy," Pepsi-Cola means "hundred happy things," and Sharp stands for "treasure of sound."

Sources: "The Puff, the Magic, the Dragon," *The Washington Post*, September 2, 1994, B1, B3; "Big Names Draw Fine Line on Logo Imagery," *South China Morning Post*, July 7, 1993, 3.

German brand. Ignis and Laden are positioned as price-value brands—Ignis Europe-wide, Laden in France.[34]

Packaging Considerations With packaging, marketers will have to worry about the protective, promotional, and user convenience dimensions of the function. Packaging will have to vary as a function of the transportation mode, transit conditions, as well as transit time. Promotional features take into consideration regulations and customer preferences, while package sizes take into account purchase patterns and market conditions.

Labeling Considerations Country-of-origin has considerable influence on the quality perceptions of a product. For example, when Canon changed its supply of copiers to the Russian market from their Japanese production facilities to their newly-opened China plant, sales slumped and Canon's dealers started importing Canon copiers from around the world that displayed the "made in Japan" label. This **gray marketing** of its copiers forced Canon to switch its procurement for Russia back to the Japanese source.

Promotion Decisions

Positioning Considerations The most important category of adaptations is based on local behavior, tastes, attitudes, and traditions—all reflecting the marketer's need to gain customer's approval. The product itself may not change at all, only its positioning may need to be adjusted. For example, Coca-Cola launched Diet Coke in Japan by changing its name to Coke Light and shifted the promotion theme from "weight loss" to "figure maintenance."Japanese women do not like to admit that they are dieting by drinking something clearly labeled *diet*. Examples of such adjustments are provided in Figure 3.7. While the ads share common graphic elements, two separate approaches in adjustment are evident. The top set of advertisements from the United States and Saudi Arabia are an example of a relatively standard approach given the similarity in target audiences (i.e., the business traveler) and in the competitive conditions in the markets. The second set features ads for Latin America and German-speaking Europe. While the Latin advertisement stresses comfort, the German version focuses on results. While most of Marriott's ads have the theme ("When you're comfortable, you can do anything") translated into the local language, the German version keeps the original English-language theme.

Copy Considerations While positioning strategy tends to be decided on a broader basis, the actual copy of the advertisement by market may well have to be adjusted. American Express, for example, with its "places you want to go, people you want to be" campaign wanted to give traveling card holders the same campaign they see at home but one that would also look like a domestic effort to locals. This was achieved by having all spots around the world follow the same formula: merchants expound on their business philosophies, then talk about the card. Featured were, among many, British designer and retailer Sir Terence Conran, Japanese innkeepers Koin and Emiko Horibe, and Toys "R" Us founder Charles Lazarus.[35]

Similarly, ads for cosmetic products marketed in countries such as Saudi Arabia have to take into account local moral standards. While a global creative approach can be used, it may have to be adjusted. For example, Guy Laroche's ad for Drakkar Noir shows a man's hand clutching the perfume bottle and a woman's hand seizing his bare forearm. This version used around the world was adjusted for Saudi Arabia to show the man's arm clothed in a dark suit sleeve, and the woman's hand merely brushing his hand.[36]

Distribution Decisions

While distribution decisions continue to be mostly tactical and made on a market-by-market basis, marketing managers have to be aware of the changes in the distribution function as well. Distribution formats are crossing borders, especially to newly emerging markets. While supermarkets accounted for only 8 percent of consumer nondurable sales in Thailand in 1990, the figure today approaches 45 percent. The other trend is that intermedi-

www.canon.com

Gray marketing

is the marketing of authentic, legally trademarked goods through unauthorized channels.

www.cocacola.com

www.americanexpress.com

Figure 3.7   Global Advertising Approaches

www.marriott.com

Source: Courtesy of Marriott International.

aries themselves have embarked on globalization efforts either independently or through strategic alliances. Entities such as Toys 'R Us from the United States, Galeries Lafayette from France, Marks & Spencer from the United Kingdom, and Takashimaya and Isetan from Japan have expanded worldwide.[37]

Some markets may require unique approaches to developing global products. At Gillette, timing is the only concession to local taste. Developing markets, such as China, Eastern Europe, and Latin America, are first introduced to the older, cheaper products before the latest, state-of-the-art versions are sold. In a world economy where most of the growth is in developing markets, the global product's inevitable premium pricing may keep them out of the hands of the average consumer. As a result, Procter & Gamble figures out what consumers in various countries can afford and then develops products accordingly. In Brazil, the company launched a diaper called Pampers Uni, a less-expensive version of its mainstream product. The strategy is to create price tiers, hooking customers early and then encouraging them to trade up as their incomes and desire for better products grow.[38]

www.pg.com

The monitoring of competitors' approaches—determining what has to be done to meet and beat them—is critical. In many markets, the international marketer is competing with local manufacturers and must overcome traditional purchasing relationships or face large multinational marketers that have considerable resources to commit. BNN, a marketer of interactive data-processing equipment and support services, is facing such competitors as Siemens and Philips and will have to prove not only that its products are competitive in price and quality but also that the company will honor its commitments and provide the necessary after-sales service.[39] This may mean that the marketer has to establish a sales office and employ its own personnel in selected target markets rather than being able to rely on independent distributors as is done at home.

Pricing Decisions

International competitiveness in price is a challenge for the marketing manager in two broad ways. First, exported products are threatened by price escalation—the combined effect of costs incurred in modifying products to the international marketplace, operational costs in exports (such as shipping), and market-entry costs (such as tariffs and taxes). Second, marketers may also face unfavorable foreign-exchange rates. The marketing manager has two options in making sure prices remain competitive: either to absorb the price increases, especially when customers are felt to be price elastic, or pass-through, which means that the customer bears the added costs but is still willing to buy the product due to its other attractive features. With the advent in 1999 of the *euro,* the common European Union currency, foreign-currency fluctuations will no longer present a challenge to marketers from the 11 member countries that have elected to utilize the common currency.

Company Decisions

Before launching a product or a program in the international marketplace, marketing managers need to consider organizational capabilities as well as the level of the endeavor needed to succeed. The issue of adaptation often climaxes in the question "Is it worth it?" The answer depends on the company's ability to control costs, correctly estimate market potential, and finally, secure profitability in the long term.

IMPLEMENTING MARKETING PROGRAMS WORLDWIDE

With world markets rapidly converging and merging, marketers have to make sure that their organizations are capable of taking advantage of the resulting opportunities. The necessary actions will relate to management processes, organization structure, and corporate culture, all of which should ensure the successful implementation of marketing programs both across borders and within individual markets.

The new realities of the global marketplace require, by design, a balance between sensitivity to local needs and deployment of technologies and concepts across borders. This means that neither headquarters nor country managers can alone call the shots. If decisions are not made in coordinated fashion, or if standard procedures are forced upon country operations, local resistance in the form of the not-invented-here syndrome may lead to the demise of potentially attractive innovation. Resistance may stem from opposition to any idea originating from the outside, from lack of involvement in strategy development, or from valid concerns about the applicability of a concept to that particular market. Without local commitment, no global marketing effort can survive.

Management Process

In the multi-domestic approach, marketing managers at the country level had very little incentive to exchange ideas or coordinate activities with their counterparts. Globalization, however, requires transfer of information both between the headquarters and country organizations and within the country organizations themselves. By facilitating the flow of information and sharing best practices from around the world, whether through regular meetings or use of corporate intranets, ideas are exchanged and organizational values are strengthened.[40] IBM, for example, has a Worldwide Opportunity Council that sponsors fellowships for employees to listen to business cases from around the world and to develop global platforms and solutions. At Levi Strauss, as with most successful global marketers, marketing personnel are supported through electronic networking capabilities, and are encouraged to adopt ideas from other markets. Headquarters exercises its control only when necessary, for example, in protecting brand identity, image, and quality.

Part of this global marketing readiness is personnel exchange. Many companies encourage (or even require) marketing managers to gain experience abroad during the early

www.ibm.com
www.levi.com

Advances in telecommunications allow staff in different countries to talk together and share pictures and data on their computer screens. In the state-of-the-art video conference center at Hoffmann-LaRoche's U.S. headquarters in Nutley, N.J., scientists discuss research goals and results with Roche colleagues in Basel, Switzerland.

Careers in Marketing

Looking for Work? Try the World!

In growing numbers, students in U.S. universities are looking to go abroad. Traveling, studying, and working abroad traditionally has been a way to gain new experiences both for life and a future career. Business schools across the country report 15–30 percent of the student body studying abroad during their four years and increasing numbers planning to work abroad after graduation. For example, at Duke, 9.2 percent of 1993 graduating seniors said they planned to work abroad, in contrast to 3.2 percent only a year earlier.

In Buenos Aires, Martin Porcel, spokesman for the American Chamber of Commerce in Argentina, receives up to 10 resumés per month. Some 19 Americans arrive in Hong Kong every day to take up jobs. Throughout the 1990s, the Japanese government's Japan Exchange and Teaching Program, which offers one-year contracts to foreigners to work with local municipalities or as assistant language teachers, has attracted 4,000 applications, a four-fold increase over the figure of the 1980s. This whole phenomenon even has its own magazine, *Transitions Abroad*, targeted at U.S. college students who want to work overseas.

Young people venturing abroad is a function of both entrepreneurial zeal and the squeezed domestic job market. One observer says that the 20-somethings are frustrated by the logjam caused by baby boomers, so many of whom are ahead of them in management jobs and will not retire for another 20 years.

Students should think globally even if they cannot find the perfect opportunities at home. Their skills might be out into more efficient use in places like Mexico, Thailand, or Russia. One professor tells students asking for job advice to "learn Spanish and go to Mexico," and not only to look in the *New York Times* for a job, but to include *The Economist* as well. Worldwide career searches and paths are going to be more commonplace in the future rather than isolated experiences. Three areas are attracting the majority of U.S. graduates: the Pacific Rim, including Tokyo and Hong Kong, as well as China and Vietnam; Latin America, especially Mexico; as well as Eastern and Central Europe. This interest and need for talent is visible in the on-campus recruiting for non-U.S. posts by companies such as Procter & Gamble.

Some have argued against this type of brain drain. William Glavin, former vice chairman of Xerox and now the president of Babson College, says, "It is not a brain drain but an enhancement of the brain power of the United States." The new expatriates are receiving—and will return with—invaluable training they cannot get at home. "A major problem in corporate America is a lack of global management knowledge and ability to vision things across national borders and across regions." The dean of the Haas School of Business at the University of California, Berkeley, William Hasler, finds the outflux of young business people "very positive, because most of them will end up working for U.S. companies and will be able to make those companies more successful and globalized." Even those who may not return will benefit U.S. businesses by providing advice to their employers on how to deal most productively in the United States.

James Firestone is 27 and works in Moscow. He says, "Here the work is like being a doctor in an emergency room—everything is critical." What could be next for Firestone? "Jakarta, maybe. I hear that's a pretty interesting place."

Source: Paul Gray, "Looking for Work? Try the World," *Time*, September 19, 1994, 44.

or middle levels of their careers. The more experience people have in working with others from different regions and ethnic backgrounds, the better a company's global philosophy, strategy, and actions will be integrated locally.

The role of headquarters staff should be that of coordination and leveraging the resources of the corporation worldwide. This may mean activities focused on combining good ideas that come from different parts of the organization to be fed into global planning. Many companies employ world-class advertising and market research staffs whose role should be to consult country organizations in upgrading their technical skills and getting them to focus their attention not only to local issues but also on those with global impact.

Globalization calls for a substantial degree of centralization in marketing decision making, far beyond that in the multi-domestic approach. Once a strategy has been jointly developed, headquarters may want to permit local managers to develop their own programs within specified decision-making boundaries. These programs could then be subject to headquarters' approval, rather than forcing local managers to adhere strictly to the formulated strategy. For tactical elements of the marketing mix, such as choice of distribution channels or sales promotional tools, decisions should be left to the country managers. Colgate Palmolive allows local units to use their own ads, but only if they can beat the global "benchmark" version. With a properly managed approval process, effective control can be exerted without unduly dampening country managers' creativity and initiative.

www.colgate.com

Organization Structure

Various organizational structures have emerged to support global marketing efforts. Some companies have established global or regional product managers and their support groups at headquarters. Their task is to develop long-term strategies for product categories on a worldwide basis and to act as the support system for the country organizations. This matrix structure focused on customers, which has replaced the traditional country-by-country approach, is considered more effective in today's global marketplace by companies that have adopted it.

Whenever a product group has global potential, firms such as Procter & Gamble, 3M, and Henkel create strategic-planning units to work on the programs. These units, such as 3M's EMATs (European Marketing Action Teams), consist of members from the country organizations that will market the products, managers from both global and regional headquarters, as well as technical specialists.

Local marketing organizations are absorbing new roles as markets scan the world for ideas that can cross borders. The consensus among marketers is that many more countries, in addition to the strategic leaders, are now capable of developing products and solutions that can be applied on a worldwide basis. This realization has given birth to centers of excellence. Ford's centers of excellence have been established with two key goals in mind: to avoid duplicating efforts and to capitalize on the expertise of specialists on a worldwide basis. Located in several countries, the centers will work on key components for cars. One will, for example, work on certain kinds of engines, while another may engineer and develop common platforms. Designers in each market will then style the exteriors and passenger compartments to appeal to local tastes.

Chapter Summary

International marketing offers new complexities, challenges, and opportunities to the firm. Managers need to understand and cope with a new set of macroenvironmental variables. These consist of varying cultural dimensions, different socioeconomic levels, and divergent and sometimes even conflicting legal and political approaches.

In investigating global market opportunities, the firm must first identify and screen markets internationally based on general country factors and firm-specific criteria. After identifying specific desirable markets, management must then choose between a concentrated or diversified expansion approach to these markets.

The initiation of internationalization depends very heavily on managerial commitment to the international strategy and on the firm's motivation for going international. Initial modes of entry are typically exporting or importing, and licensing and franchising and are often assisted by intermediaries. Over time and with growing experience, firms then expand through direct foreign investment, joint ventures, or contract manufacturing.

As a next step, the firm needs to adjust its marketing mix in order to be responsive to differences in market, product, or company characteristics. Finally, managerial processes as well as the organizational structure need to be reviewed and adjusted in order to enable the worldwide implementation of marketing programs.

Key Terms

International marketing is the process of planning and conducting transactions across national borders to create exchanges that satisfy the objectives of individuals and organizations.

Change agent is a person or institution that facilitates change in a firm or in a host country.

Degree of ndividualism is the extent to which individual interests prevail over group interests.

Level of equality is the extent to which less powerful members accept that power is distributed unequally.

Uncertainty avoidance is the extent to which people feel threatened by ambiguous situations and have created beliefs and institutions to try to avoid these feelings.

Material achievement is the extent to which the dominant values in society are success, money, and things.

Intellectual property rights is the protection provided by patents, copyrights, and trademarks.

Common law is law based on tradition and depending less on written statutes and codes than on precedent and custom.

Code law is law based on a comprehensive set of written statutes.

Antidumping laws are laws designed to help domestic industries that are injured by unfair competition from abroad due to imports being sold at less than fair value.

World Trade Organization (WTO) is the institution that administers international trade and investment accords. It supplanted GATT in 1995.

Market potential is the level of sales that might be available to all marketers in an industry in a given market.

Sales potential is the share of the market potential that a particular marketer may hope to gain over the long term.

Concentration strategy is the market development strategy that involves focusing on a smaller number of markets.

Diversification strategy is the market development strategy that involves expansion to a relatively large number of markets.

Managerial commitment is the desire and drive on the part of management to act on an idea and support it in the long run.

International intermediaries are marketing institutions that facilitate the movement of goods and services between the originator and customer.

Export Management Companies (EMCs) are firms that specialize in performing international services as commissioned representatives or as distributors.

Agent is a marketing intermediary who does not take title to the products but develops marketing strategy and establishes contacts abroad.

Distributor is a marketing intermediary who purchases products from the domestic firm and assumes the trading risk.

Trading company is a marketing intermediary that undertakes exporting, importing, countertrading, investing, and manufacturing.

Sogoshosha are the trading companies of Japan including firms such as Sumitomo, Mitsubishi, and Mitsui.

Licensing agreement is an arrangement in which one firm permits another to use its intellectual property in exchange for compensation, typically a royalty.

Royalty is the compensation paid by one firm to another under licensing and franchising agreements.

Expropriation is a government takeover of a company's operations frequently at a level lower than the value of the assets.

Franchising is a form of licensing that grants a wholesaler or a retailer exclusive rights to sell a product or a service in a specified area.

Multinational corporations are companies that have production operations in at least one country in addition to their domestic base.

Foreign direct investment is an international entry strategy that is achieved through the acquisition of foreign firms.

Profit repatriation limitations are restrictions set up by host governments in terms of a company's ability to pay dividends from their operations back to their home base.

Joint ventures result from the participation of two or more companies in an enterprise in which each party contributes assets, owns the new entity to some degree, and shares risk.

Strategic alliances are informal or formal arrangements between two or more companies with a common business objective.

Complementary marketing is a contractual arrangement where participating parties carry out different but complementary activities.

Outsourcing is using another firm for the manufacture of needed components or products or delivery of a service.

Contract manufacturing is using another firm for the manufacture of goods so that the marketer may concentrate on the research and development as well as marketing aspects of the operation.

Standardized approach is the approach to international marketing in which products are marketed with little or no modification.

Multi-domestic approach is the approach to international marketing in which local conditions are adapted to in each and every target market.

Globalization approach is the approach to international marketing in which differences are incorporated into a regional or global strategy that will allow for differences in implementation.

Gray marketing is the marketing of authentic, legally trademarked goods through unauthorized channels.

Questions for Discussion

1. What are the principal differences between domestic and international marketing?

2. Is it beneficial for nations to become more dependent on each other?

3. Discuss the different effects that code law and common law can have on the international marketer.

4. Why is management commitment so important to export success?

5. What determines the mode of market entry of a firm?

6. What is the purpose of export intermediaries?

7. Suggest criteria on which international marketing managers can base their market choice.

8. Why are more marketers forming alliances with other companies to achieve their goals?

9. If there is a love–hate relationship between governments and foreign investors, what marketing approaches can be taken to present the investor as a contributor to its host country?

10. With more companies adopting global or regional marketing strategies, how can the participation of country-level marketers be ensured in the implementation of those strategies?

Internet Questions

1. Various companies, such as Wyndham International, are available to prepare and train international marketers for the cultural challenge. Using Wyndham's Web site (www.wyndham.com), assess their role in helping the international marketer.

2. Compare and contrast international marketers' home pages for presentation and content; for example, Coca-Cola (at www.coca-cola.com) and its Japanese version (cocacola.co.jp), as well as Ford Motor Company throughout the world (www.ford.com).

3. Benetton, the Italian manufacturer of sportswear, has been in the center of controversy ever since its "United Colors of Benetton" campaign was launched to symbolize its commitment to "racial and multicultural harmony." Using Benetton's Web site and its gallery of advertising (www.benetton.com), assess whether shock and publicity value fit a global image campaign.

Endnotes

[1]"Souping Up Campbell's," *Business Week* (November 3, 1997): 70–72; Linda Grant, "Stirring It Up at Campbell," *Fortune* (May 13, 1996): pp. 80–86; "Ethnic Food Whets Appetites in Europe, Enticing Producers to Add Foreign Fare," *The Wall Street Journal,* November 1, 1993, p. B5A; "Hmm, Could Use a Little More Snake," *Business Week* (March 15, 1993): 53; and "Canned and Delivered," *Business China* (November 16, 1992): p. 12. http://www.campbellsoup.com

[2]Robert W. Armstrong and Jill Sweeney, "Industrial Type, Culture, Mode of Entry, and Perceptions of International Marketing Ethics Problems: A Cross-Culture Comparison," *Journal of Business Ethics* 13, 1944: pp. 775–785.

[3]Peter R. Dickson and Michael R. Czinkota, "How the U.S. Can Be Number One Again: Resurrecting the Industrial Policy Debate," *The Columbia Journal of World Business* 31, 3 (Fall 1996): pp. 76–87.

[4]J. David Richardson and Karin Rindal, *Why Exports Matter: More!* Washington, DC: Institute for International Economics and The Manufacturing Institute (February 1996), p. 9.

[5]Cognetics, Cambridge, MA, 1993.

[6]Warren Stugatch, "Make Way for the Euroconsumer," *World Trade,* February 1993, pp. 46–50.

[7]Jagdish N. Sheth and S. Prakash Sethi, "A Theory of Cross-Cultural Buying Behavior," in *Consumer and Industrial Buying Behavior,* eds. Arch G. Woodside, Jagdish N. Sheth, and Peter D. Bennett (New York: Elsevier North-Holland, 1977): pp. 369–386.

[8]Geert Hofstede, *Culture's Consequences: International Differences in Work-Related Values* (Beverly Hills, CA: Sage Publications, 1984).

[9]Sudhir H. Kale, "Grouping Euroconsumers: A Culture-Based Clustering Approach," *Journal of International Marketing* 3 (number 3, 1995): pp. 35–48.

[10]W. Chan Kim and R. A. Mauborgne, "Cross-Cultural Strategies," *Journal of Business Strategy* 7 (Spring 1987): pp. 28–37.

[11]John R. Engen, "Far Eastern Front," *World Trade,* December 1994, pp. 20–24.

[12]John R. Engen, "Far Eastern Front," *World Trade,* (December 1994): pp. 20–24; "A Survey of Asia," *The Economist* (October 30, 1993). www.3m.com

[13]"Consumers in the 1990s: Older, Richer, More Numerous," *Business International,* April 1, 1991, pp. 113–116.

[14]*1991 National Trade Estimate Report on Foreign Trade Barriers* (Washington, D.C.: U.S. Government Printing Office, 1991), p. 50.

[15]Igal Ayal and Jehiel Zif, "Marketing Expansion Strategies in Multinational Marketing," *Journal of Marketing* 43 (Spring 1979): pp. 84–94.

[16]Warren J. Bilkey and George Tesar, "The Export Behavior of Smaller Sized Wisconsin Manufacturing Firms," *Journal of International Business Studies* 8 (Spring–Summer 1977); pp. 93–98.

[17]Finn Wiedersheim-Paul, H. C. Olson, and L. S. Welch, "Pre-Export Activity: The First Step in Internationalization," *Journal of International Business Studies* 9 (Spring–Summer 1978): pp. 47–58.

[18]George Tesar and Jesse S. Tarleton, "Comparison of Wisconsin and Virginia Small and Medium-Sized Exporters: Aggressive and Passive Exporters," in *Export Management,* eds. Michael R. Czinkota and George Tesar (New York: Praeger, 1982), pp. 85–112.

[19] Anthony C. Koh and James Chow, "An Empirical Investigation of the Variations in Success Factors in Exporting by Country Characteristics," *Midwest Review of International Business Research,* ed. Tom Sharkey, Vol. VII (Toledo, 1993).

[20]S. Tamer Cavusgil, "Preparing for Export Marketing," *International Trade Forum 2* (1993): pp. 16–30.

[21]Donald W. Hackett, "The International Expansion of U.S. Franchise Systems," in *Multinational Product Management,* eds. Warren J. Keegan and Charles S. Mayer (Chicago: American Marketing Association, 1979), pp. 61–81.

[22]Wallace Doolin, "Taking Your Business on the Road," *The Wall Street Journal,* July 25, 1994, p. A14.

[23]United Nations, *Multinational Corporations in World Development* (New York: United Nations, 1973), p. 23.

[24]U.S. Department of Commerce, Bureau of Economic Analysis, *Survey of Current Business,* July 1996, p. 113.

[25]W. G Friedman and G. Kalmanoff, *Joint International Business Ventures* (New York: Columbia University Press, 1961).

[26]Yankelovich, Skelly and White, Inc., *Collaborative Ventures: A Pragmatic Approach to Business Expansion in the Eighties* (New York: Coopers and Lybrand, 1984), p. 10.

[27]Oded Shenkar and Shmuel Ellis, "Death of the 'Organization Man': Temporal Relations in Strategic Alliances," *The International Executive,* 37, 6, November/December 1995: pp. 537–553.

[28]John Hageddoorn, "A Note on International Market Leaders and Networks of Strategic Technology Partnering," *Strategic Management Journal* 16 (1995): pp. 241–250.

[29]Richard Gibson, "Cereal Venture Is Planning Honey of a Battle in Europe," *The Wall Street Journal,* November 14, 1990, pp. B1, B8.

[30]Dori Jones Yang, Michael Oneal, Charles Hoots, and Robert Neff, "Can Nike Just Do It?" *Business Week,* April 18, 1994, pp. 86–90.

[31]"ISO 9000: International Update," *Export Today* 11 (November/December 1995): pp. 63–64.

[32]Stephen C. Messner, "Adapting Products to Western Europe," *Export Today* 10 (March/April 1994): pp. 16–18.

[33]"The Puff, the Magic, the Dragon," *The Washington Post,* September 2, 1994, pp. B1, B3.

[34]"Teach Me Shopping," *The Economist,* December 18, 1993, pp. 64–65.

[35]"Don't Leave Home Without It, Wherever You Live," *Business Week,* February 21, 1994, pp. 76–77.

[36]Michael Field, "Fragrance Marketers Sniff Out Rich Aroma," *Advertising Age,* January 30, 1986, p. 10.

[37]Rahul Jacob, "The Big Rise," *Fortune,* May 30, 1994, pp. 74–90.

[38]"Divide and Conquer," *Export Today* 5 (February 1989): p. 10.

[39]Ilkka A. Ronkainen and Ivan Menezes, "Implementing Global Marketing Strategy," *International Marketing Review* 13 (number 3, 1996): pp. 56–63.

[40]Ingo Theuerkaut, David Ernst, and Amir Mahini, "Think Local, Organize . . . ?" *International Marketing Review* 13 (number 3, 1996): pp. 7–12.

[41]Source: This case was written by Michael R. Czinkota based on the following sources: Mark Clayton, "Minnesota Chopstick Maker Finds Japanese Eager to Import His Quality Waribashi," *Christian Science Monitor,* October 16, 1987, 11; Roger Worthington, "Improbable Chopstick Capital of the World," *Chicago Tribune,* June 5, 1988, 39; Mark Gill, "The Great American Chopstick Master," *American Way,* August 1, 1987, 34, 78–79; "Perpich of Croatia," *Economics,* April 20, 1991, 27; interview with Ian J. Ward, President, Lakewood Forest Products.

Lakewood Forest Products[41]

Since the 1970s, the United States has had a merchandise trade deficit with the rest of the world. Up to 1982, this deficit mattered little because it was relatively small. As of 1983, however, the trade deficit increased rapidly and became, due to its size and future implications, an issue of major national concern. Suddenly, trade moved to the forefront of national debate. Concurrently, a debate ensued on the issue of the international competitiveness of U.S. firms. The onerous question here was whether U.S. firms could and would achieve sufficient improvements in areas such as productivity, quality, and price to remain successful international marketing players in the long term.

The U.S.-Japanese trade relation took on particular significance because it was between those two countries that the largest bilateral trade deficit existed. In spite of trade negotiations, market-opening measures, trade legislation, and other governmental efforts, it was clear that the impetus for a reversal of the deficit through more U.S. exports to Japan had to come from the private sector. Therefore, the activities of any U.S. firm that appeared successful in penetrating the Japanese market were widely hailed. One company whose effort to market in Japan aroused particular interest was Lakewood Forest Products in Hibbing, Minnesota.

COMPANY BACKGROUND

In 1983, Ian J. Ward was an export merchant in difficulty. Throughout the 1970s, his company, Ward, Bedas Canadian Ltd., had successfully sold Canadian lumber and salmon to countries in the Persian Gulf. Over time, the company had opened four offices worldwide. However, when the Iran–Iraq war erupted, most of Ward's long-term trading relationships disappeared within a matter of months. In addition, the international lumber market began to collapse. As a result, Ward, Bedas Canadian Ltd. went into a survivalist mode and sent employees all over the world to look for new markets and business opportunities. Late that year, the company received an interesting order. A firm in Korea urgently needed to purchase lumber for the production of chopsticks.

Learning about the Chopstick Market

In discussing the wood deal with the Koreans, Ward learned that in the production of good chopsticks, more than 60 percent of the wood fiber is wasted. Given the high transportation cost involved, the large degree of wasted materials, and his need for new business, Ward decided to explore the Korean and Japanese chopstick industry in more detail.

He quickly determined that chopstick making in the Far East is a fragmented industry, working with old technology and suffering from a lack of natural resources. In Asia, chopsticks are produced in very small quantities, often by family organizations. Even the largest of the 450 chopstick factories in Japan turns out only 5 million chopsticks a month. This compares with an overall market size of 130 million pairs of disposable chopsticks a day. In addition, chopsticks represent a growing market. With increased wealth in Asia, people eat out more often and therefore have a greater demand for disposable chopsticks. The fear of communicable diseases has greatly reduced the utilization of reusable chopsticks. Renewable plastic chopsticks have been attacked by many groups as too newfangled and as causing future ecological problems.

From his research, Ward concluded that a competitive niche existed in the world chopstick market. He believed that if he could use low-cost raw materials and ensure that the labor-cost component would remain small, he could successfully compete in the world market.

The Founding of Lakewood Forest Products

In exploring opportunities afforded by the newly identified international marketing niche for chopsticks, Ward set four criteria for plant location:

1. Access to suitable raw materials.

2. Proximity of other wood product users who could make use of the 60 percent waste for their production purposes.

3. Proximity to a port that would facilitate shipment to the Far East.

4. Availability of labor.

In addition, Ward was aware of the importance of product quality. Because people use chopsticks on a daily basis and are accustomed to products that are visually inspected one by one, he would have to live up to high quality expectations in order to compete successfully. Chopsticks could not be bowed or misshapen, have blemishes in the wood, or splinter.

To implement his plan, Ward needed financing. Private lenders were skeptical and slow to provide funds. This skepticism resulted from the unusual direction of Ward's proposal. Far Eastern companies have generally held the cost advantage in a variety of industries, especially those as labor-intensive as chopstick manufacturing. U.S. companies rarely have an advantage in producing low-cost items. Further, only a very small domestic market exists for chopsticks.

However, Ward found that the state of Minnesota was willing to participate in his new venture. Since the decline of the mining industry, regional unemployment had been rising rapidly in the state. In 1983, unemployment in Minnesota's Iron Range peaked at 22 percent. Therefore, state and local officials were eager to attract new industries that would be independent of mining activities. Of particular help was the enthusiasm of Governor Rudy Perpich. The governor had been boosting Minnesota business on the international scene by traveling abroad and receiving many foreign visitors. He was excited about Ward's plans, which called for the creation of over 100 new jobs within a year.

Hibbing, Minnesota, turned out to be an ideal location for Ward's project. The area had an abundance of aspen wood, which, because it grows in clay soil, tends to be unmarred. The fact that Hibbing was the hometown of the governor also did not hurt. In addition, Hibbing boasted an excellent labor pool, and both the city and the state were willing to make loans totaling $500,000. Further, the Iron Range Resources Rehabilitation Board was willing to sell $3.4 million in industrial revenue bonds for the project. Together with jobs and training wage subsidies, enterprise zone credits, and tax increment financing benefits, the initial public support of the project added up to about 30 percent of its start-up costs. The potential benefit of the new venture to the region was quite clear. When Lakewood Forest Products advertised its first 30 jobs, more than 3,000 people showed up to apply.

THE PRODUCTION AND SALE OF CHOPSTICKS

Ward insisted that in order to truly penetrate the international market, he would need to keep his labor cost low. As a result, he decided to automate as much of the production as possible. However, no equipment was readily available to produce chopsticks because no one had automated the process before.

After much searching, Ward identified a European equipment manufacturer that produced machinery for making popsicle sticks. He purchased equipment from this Danish firm in order to better carry out the sorting and finishing processes. However, because aspen wood was quite different from the wood the machine was designed for, as was the final product, substantial design adjustments had to be made. Sophisticated equipment was also purchased to strip the bark from the wood and peel it into long, thin sheets. Finally, a computer vision system was acquired to detect defects in the chopsticks. This system rejected over 20 percent of the production, and yet some of the chopsticks that passed inspection were splintering. However, Ward firmly believed that further fine-tuning of the equipment and training of the new workforce would gradually take care of the problem.

Given this fully automated process, Lakewood Forest Products was able to develop capacity for up to 7 million chopsticks a day. With a unit manufacturing cost of $0.03 per pair and an anticipated unit selling price of $0.057, Ward expected to earn a pretax profit of $4.7 million in 1988.

Due to intense marketing efforts in Japan and the fact that Japanese customers were struggling to obtain sufficient supplies of disposable chopsticks, Ward was able to presell the first five years of production quite quickly. By late 1987, Lakewood Forest Products was ready to enter the international market. With an ample supply of raw materials and an almost totally automated plant, Lakewood was positioned as the world's largest and least labor-intensive manufacturer of chopsticks. The first shipment of 6 containers with a load of 12 million pairs of chopsticks was sent to Japan in October 1987.

Discussion Questions

1. Is Lakewood Forest Products ready for exports? Using the export-readiness framework developed by the U.S. Department of Commerce and available through various sites such as www.tradeport.org (from "Trade Expert" go to "Getting Started" and finally to "Assess Your Export Readiness"), determine whether Lakewood's commitment, resources, and product warrant the action they have undertaken.

2. What are the environmental factors that are working for and against Lakewood Forest Products both at home in the United States and in the target market, Japan?

3. New-product success is a function of trial and repurchase. How do Lakewood's chances look along these two dimensions?

Part 2

Understanding the Market

Chapter 4

Marketing Research and Information Systems

**Peter R. Dickson,
University of
Wisconsin–Madison**

Arthur C. Nielsen Jr. Chair of Marketing Research, University of Wisconsin-
Madison. Dr. Dickson helped found
the Business School at the University
of Waikato where he taught for seven
years. After receiving a Fulbright-Hays
Bicentennial scholarship and completing his Ph.D. at the University of Florida, he taught for 14 years at The Ohio
State University where he became the
Crane Professor of Strategic Marketing
and an adjunct professor of Industrial
Design.

Dr. Dickson has won several awards
for his teaching and research, including the Journal of Marketing Maynard Award. He has participated in
the start up of several companies and
has consulted with numerous other
organizations.

SLIPPERY PROFITS

In the mid-1980s R.G. Barry, the manufacturer of over half of the slippers sold in the United States, faced an unusual problem for such a dominant player—low profitability. Having gone public recently, the Board was asking questions. Although headquartered in Columbus, Ohio, most of the manufacturing was being undertaken in Mexico so manufacturing cost was not the problem. The question that senior management confronted was whether its prices were too low.

Recently, Isotoner, the glove manufacturer, had entered the slipper market with a line of attractive silk and velvet ballerina slippers targeted to the younger generation. They were priced at between $10–$15, some $5 above R. G. Barry's standard best-selling traditional Dearfoam slipper, and had grabbed about 20 percent of market sales.

The slipper market is very seasonal with well over 60 percent of sales made through department and discount stores in the gift-giving season, mostly between Thanksgiving and Christmas. The CEO of R. G. Barry decided to undertake a pricing experiment, but insisted that it would have to be undertaken during the peak selling season. The Lazarus Department store chain, at that time also headquartered in Columbus, agreed to cooperate, and two very similar stores were chosen as sites for the experiment. Over four weeks the prices of all models of R. G. Barry slippers were set at normal, raised, returned to normal, and raised again over each of the four weeks. The price sensitivity of shoppers was measured and tested in three different ways:

1. Did sales volume, adjusted for total store sales, decrease when prices on slippers normally priced below $10 were raised 50 cents and slippers normally priced $10 or more were raised by $1?

2. Did sales volume on items that were the lower-priced items in each line of slippers increase when prices were raised? A signal of price sensitivity is when consumers shift to lower-priced items in a product line, when all of the prices in the product-line are raised.

3. Does the number of shoppers who buy, compared to the number of shoppers who are observed to check the price of the slipper, decrease when prices are raised? This measure was called the purchase-inspection percentage (PI%) and measured the shoppers observed reaction to price at the point of purchase. A lower PI% when prices were raised would indicate that shoppers were being turned off by the price of the slipper.

A temporary employment service was hired to supply observers who posed as inventory checkers and restockers, but whose job was to observe when shoppers checked price at the point of purchase. Store clerks were asked to keep the shelves stocked to make sure that no stock-outs occurred. Each Sunday night during the study, all of the inventory was changed because it was easier to replace the inventory than change the price tags. As with any field experiment, things could be expected to go wrong and they did. A vicious winter storm closed down one of the stores for two days, and Lazarus decided to run two unexpected chainwide sales because of slow Christmas sales. These unexpected events made it extremely important to adjust for total store sales and to focus on the second and third measures of price sensitivity.

(Continued)

Learning Objectives

After you have completed this chapter, you should be able to:

1. Understand the most commonly used market research methods to explain changing consumer, competitor, and channel behavior.

2. Explain the basic market research process.

3. Describe a number of methods of studying consumers.

4. Understand how new technology such as scanners and the Web is revolutionizing market research.

5. Question the validity of survey research.

6. Know where to start looking for secondary data.

7. Evaluate current and potential competitors.

8. Understand the importance of studying the history of a market.

9. Understand the principles of channel research.

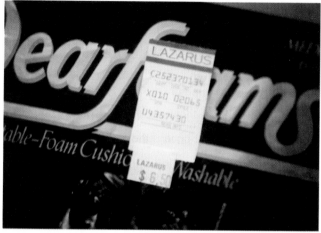

The conclusion of the study was that the price increases had no impact on the sales of about 90 percent of R. G. Barry's line of slippers. In particular, its line of ballerina slippers competing against Isotoner could be raised by $1 in price. The only slippers that showed any evidence of price sensitivity were Yak boot slippers that were already high priced at $18. In the following year, R. G. Barry raised its prices and its profit-to-sales ratio did increase. However, it also experienced a decline in sales. The experimental study serendipitously observed that too much shelf space in the department store slipper section was given over to poor-selling slipper styles and colors. While this problem was reported to the company and to Lazarus, apparently this problem was not solved and continued to hurt category sales. Isotoner also continued to out-design R. G. Barry and take market share away. The problem for R. G. Barry was not just its prices, it was also the attractiveness of its slippers. ▥

THE COMPETITIVE IMPORTANCE OF MARKET RESEARCH

Firms that are able to adjust their marketing strategies to reflect changes in domestic and international markets more quickly than competitors are able to sustain a competitive advantage. Often the key to this advantage lies within the firm's ability to collect, organize, and act upon information that is gathered through market research and information systems.

www.shell.com

The competitive importance of market research and analysis can be observed in Shell Oil's study of 30 companies that had survived in business for more than 75 years.[1] What impressed the Shell planners was the ability of these companies to learn about their changing marketplaces. Successful companies developed a shared way of thinking about consumers, competitors, distributors, and themselves. The cross-functional management teams in these companies were able to change their thinking about the marketplace faster than their competition. Such fast insight and learning also gave them more time to innovate, imitate, and avoid crisis management. Companies with such superior decision-making skills have a strategic competitive advantage over their rivals. Such skills start with a clear understanding about what market intelligence the firm needs to gather.

From a sociological perspective, a market is a mix of many diverse players, each with its own distinct interests and behavior. Successful marketing decision-making teams do not think exclusively about how consumers will react to a new product or business tactic. They think about how the different important "players" in the marketplace will react to the firm's change in business strategy. It is like a game—you have to anticipate how the different players will react to your move. Some will welcome your moves, others will be indifferent to them, and yet others will contest your moves. A market typically contains four types of players: consumers, competitors, distribution channel members, and regulators—those that monitor the marketplace. Each of these groups can be further subdivided into segments, types, and individual entities. Consequently, it is generally recommended that the study of the market be divided into four topics: consumer research, competitor research, channel research, and public-policy research.

Surprisingly, little is known about what market information decision makers actually use when thinking about the market. Two studies have been undertaken in 1980 and 1990 of the contents of the typical market analyses in the annual marketing plans of divisions of very large U.S. companies.[2] About three-quarters of the plans describe a customer segment analysis in detail, and about half analyze the competition in detail. More noteworthy is that despite all of the advances in information technology during the 1980s, the market analyses in the 1990 plans were no more thorough than they were in 1980. If anything, they were less thorough—particularly those analyzing the competition. Figure 4.1 reveals

Figure 4.1 Market Research Analysis Presented in Marketing Plans

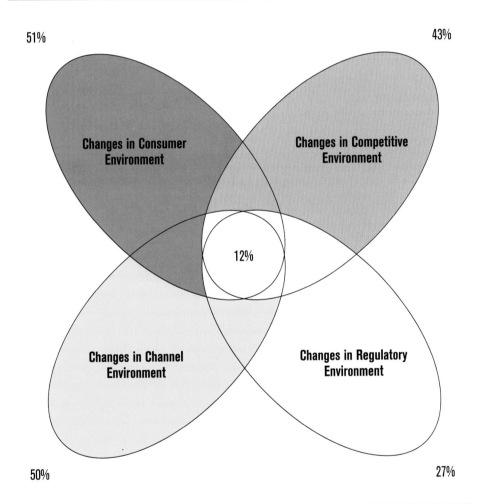

The percentages indicate the proportion of firms in the 1990 Conference Board study that include such information in their typical marketing plans. Changes in consumer environment include both a consumer needs analysis and a segmentation analysis. Changes in competitive environment include both a market share analysis and an analysis of individual competitor behavior. Changes in channel environment were only considered for companies that used distributors/dealers/retailers.
Source: Adapted from Howard Sutton, *The Marketing Plan* (New York: The Conference Board, 1990).

what percentage of the firms' plans in the 1990 study presented detailed market research about customers, competition, channels, and regulatory environment. Only 12 percent contained such enlightened insights. It is to be hoped that the decision makers in the other 88 percent of these large firms are briefed about such changes during their informal decision-making sessions by market researchers; otherwise, a great deal of market decision-making is less informed than it could be. It is clear that even the biggest firms might benefit from rethinking how they use their market research and what they learn from such analyses.[3] In the following sections, we highlight the different techniques that are used to research consumers, competitors, and distribution channels. How firms research the regulatory and policy environment is beyond the scope of this chapter that already takes a much broader view of market research than most introductory marketing texts.

CONSUMER RESEARCH

For many, market research means research that focuses on final consumers and users of the product or service. Such research can take many and varied forms but should always start with first-hand observational research by decision makers. A firm that does not require its marketing decision-makers to be involved in some form of direct observational

---

Figure 4.2   The Basic Market Research Process

1. Problem recognition:
Basic questions are what happened and why?
What is happening?
Should we do it?

2. Meet and define problem and determine how to solve it:
When is the answer needed? Limits research method that is used.
How valuable is the answer to us? Limits research method that is used.
How valuable is high accuracy? Limits research method that is used.

3. Search secondary data sources and own databases:
Has it happened elsewhere? Check archives.
Call outside experts for answers.
How can syndicated research suppliers help?
Does any published research on the problem exist? Search the Internet.
Meet and review answers. *Stop if answers are satisfactory.*

4. Undertake quick-and-dirty primary research:
Conduct an electronic voice-mail survey of the sales force.
Call on or fax customers/distributors.
Run focus groups. Meet and review answers. *Stop if answers are satisfactory.*

5. Undertake thorough primary research:
Select sampling frame (random-sample national panel provided by market research firm).
Choose survey technique (personal visit, mall intercept, telephone, mail). Design questionnaire.

6. Analyze information:
Review descriptive statistics (such as percentages, means, standard deviations).
Conduct relationship analyses (such as cross-tabs, Chi-square, correlational analyses, structural equations modeling, logit, ANOVA, MANOVA, Conjoint).

7. Present findings:
Offer progress briefings on important findings.
Report the presentation.
Archive findings and data under problem/topic key words.

This figure presents the conventional approach to research. Firms often undertake steps 1 through 4. If they require more formal primary research, they will likely hire a market research firm that will take a month or more to do the study at a cost of $10,000–$30,000, sometimes a lot more.

Marketing Technologies

A Dumb Study of a Smart Product or Smart Study of a Dumb Product?

In the fall of 1997 Henry Mundt, a vice-president of MasterCard, said, "What we're doing today is launching a revolution. It will start here today and expand across the U.S." What he was referring to was the start of a major test market of plastic money, consumer smart cards containing a computer microchip that can store cash. What actually started was an example of how not to undertake a test market. Smart cards are being very successfully used on military bases and college campuses where they are used for a multitude of product and service purchases. The four sponsors of the market test in Manhattan were Master-Card, Visa, Chase Manhattan, and Citibank. Sixty thousand residents were issued the card, but during the year less than $20 was purchased in total on each card. On November 3, 1998 the plug was pulled on the whole test.

What went wrong with the test and could it have been anticipated? First of all, unlike the bookstores, video stores, snack bars, restaurants, bars, and laundromats on or around campuses, getting the merchants in Manhattan to participate was a real problem for two understandable reasons. First, the test involved two different technologies, requiring each merchant to install two smart-card readers on top of their credit/debit card readers. Second, the smart-card readers were unreliable. The result was that as the merchants discovered the smart cards were not catching on with consumers, they literally pulled the cords on their smart-card readers. By the end of the test, the number of participating merchants had shrunk from 600 to 200. As the number of merchants accepting the card shrunk, consumers stopped carrying the smart card. But even at the beginning, the smart card offered very little benefit over and above the credit and debit cards that consumers already carry. Midtrial survey research of users discovered that consumers wanted to use the cards to ride the subways and for phone calls but could do neither.

The major sponsors should have undertaken survey research beforehand that would have established that there was no demand for the smart card that was tested. Several focus groups with merchants would have established that requiring merchants to use two readers, both of which were unreliable, was a really dumb idea. It might even be asked whether this experiment was ever needed. Smart cards have been very successful in Europe and Asia, but there they store much more than money. They are used to store medical histories and for security clearance. In short, the U.S. is not on the cutting edge of this high technology. It can and should learn from the use of the product in foreign markets. Instead, it undertook a market test that made four otherwise great companies look like they have no understanding or skill at undertaking market research.

Source: Marcia Stepanek, "What Smart Cards Couldn't Figure Out," *Business Week*, November 30, 1998, 142.

research can hardly claim that it is customer oriented. The excuse that executives are too busy doing other more important things simply says that the leadership of the firm is more focused on other issues than understanding its customers.

Figure 4.2 presents the conventional consumer research process. It indicates that consumer research often proceeds incrementally. The least costly source of answers to the perceived problem should be first searched. Major studies are only undertaken if satisfactory answers cannot be found from secondary sources, by studying other markets, or if the issue is of great importance and a precise answer is required.

Many marketers are starting to question this conventional problem-oriented market research process. In today's world of rapidly changing supply and demand, the conventional consumer research process, with its problem-solving emphasis, is being challenged by a process that emphasizes the continuous observation and tracking of consumer behavior. The reason is simple. Once a significant problem is detected, whose full understanding and solution requires extensive study, it is too late to respond effectively. Continuous tracking detects a problem almost immediately, allowing more time for an effective response.

Qualitative Observation Research

Having cross-functional team members visit customers has emerged as one of the most important market research activities a firm can adopt. Talking directly to customers seems so obvious, yet some firms have lost themselves in sophisticated, arm's-length consumer research. The problem with survey research is that too many steps and interpretative judgments separate the consumer and the decision-maker. The vivid impact of listening to the

Voice of the customer

is the expression of the preferences, opinions, and motivations of the customer that needs to be listened to by managers.

www.fisherprice.com

Hands-on consumer research

is conducted by direct observation by managers of the way current customers use specific products and brands. The opposite is arm's-length research which is undertaken by external suppliers.

Motivational research

is a research method directed at discovering the conscious or subconscious reasons that motivate a person's behavior.

www.panasonic.com
www.sony.com

www.marriott.com

customers' own words, of seeing how they use a product in their homes, in their offices, or on their production lines, is lost if the customers are not visited at the point of use. Consequently, the importance of customers' concerns has less impact on decision making: "Visits allow the **voice of the customer** to be heard, and they make this voice audible throughout the organization."[4]

Companies are often very creative in the ways that they observe customers. Fisher-Price, the toy manufacturer, has a special play laboratory and a waiting list of several years for kids to participate in their new product testing, which is observed through one-way mirrors. Other toy manufacturers spend a lot of time visiting day-care facilities and watching how children play with toys. Day-care employees, who are "professional" observers, are great sources of ideas for product improvements. In general, there are millions of salespeople whose business it is to observe consumers and shoppers, who are great sources of information.

Japanese firms such as Panasonic and Sony have for several decades used **hands-on consumer research** that focuses on the way current customers use specific products and brands.[5] For example, one appliance manufacturer took hundreds of photos of actual Japanese kitchens, and concluded from the photos that the major problem that manufacturers have to address when designing new appliances is the tremendous shortage of space in many kitchens. This observation might not have been made had executives not visited the homes in person and taken the photographs. Such photos should be displayed on the walls of the room where the team meets. They are a constant reminder of the customers' usage situation that can be "revisited" by simply looking up from the meeting table.

Other market researchers encourage consumers to take photos that describe how they use the product and then tell the story about the photo. This encourages consumers to reveal the deeper meaning and significance of the product in their lives. But this in-depth technique, called **motivational research,** can sometimes be taken too far. It can lead management to attribute too much meaning and consumer involvement with a product or a brand because the rich and fanciful stories of a minority of consumers are highlighted in the research reports to management. An example is the research done in the 1950s that concluded that baking a cake was a surrogate for having a baby!

A major camera company used observational research in a clever way to improve the design of its camera line. Research and development engineers searched through thousands of prints being processed at one-hour processing labs and counted the most common problems with the photos, such as poor focus adjustment, poor lighting, incorrect film speed, and double exposures because the film was not wound forward. From the situations that were captured in the photo, they could observe when and where these problems occurred and improve the design of future cameras.

Customer Visits in Business-to-Business Marketing

The customer visit is particularly crucial for business-to-business marketing because a few key customers often account for 80 percent of the firm's business. Marketing's responsibility in such markets is to make sure that everyone interacts with customers instead of simply passing on secondhand information about customers. DuPont's customer-oriented culture goes beyond its cross-functional teams by staying in close contact with its customers; its *"Adopt a Customer"* program encourages manufacturing process workers to visit a customer once a month and represent the customer's needs on the factory floor.[6]

Marketing executives should also have firsthand experience of being a customer of competitor's products. For example, a team of Marriott executives spent six months on the road staying in economy hotels, learning about competitors' strengths and weaknesses. The result was the $500 million launch of its Fairfield Inn chain that immediately achieved an occupancy rate ten points higher than the industry average.[7] Japanese companies have been known to send up-and-coming executives to the United States for several years to do nothing but travel around and study the market for their products firsthand. The importance of creating a company culture that encourages direct contact with the customer explains why the chief executive officer of United Airlines spends time at the ticket counter, and why senior executives at 3M spend several days a month visiting customers, and not just big accounts. Some process guidelines for such visits are listed here:

www.ual.com
www.3m.com

▼ Have customer visits arranged by the sales force: cooperation between factory engineers and the sales force is crucial. No one likes someone else in a company doing anything behind his or her back, particularly a sales rep whose commissions depend on customer trust and goodwill.

▼ Visit 10 to 20 randomly chosen customers, as well as important customers who are leaders in adopting new technology: This reduces the impact of an extreme, atypical opinion in later decisions.

▼ Only use jargon if the customer uses the same jargon. Listen carefully and note the way customers talk about the product. This gives you clues about the benefits they seek, how they think about the benefits, what problems they confront, and how to design the product to gain a competitive advantage. Rather than asking the customer to adopt your jargon, you should be adopting the customer's words and metaphors. This is how a team changes its thinking about the customer and related decisions. Do not talk in front of customers using jargon that makes them feel like you are foreign tourists.

▼ Learn to listen and observe; do not treat the visit as a sales call. This is something the sales rep will find hard to accept. Do not engage in disparaging the competition when the customer praises them. Instead, be open to ideas that can be quickly imitated.

▼ Define your research objectives in advance, and use a discussion guide based on these objectives. Write a report on the visit that addresses the research objectives. Report separately on the serendipitous (unexpected) information. "Report" means informing key people within your organization about what you saw or heard.

▼ Observe the product in use in every usage situation. Particularly, note and photograph how an innovative customer has adapted your product, package, or service to improve its performance in a particular usage situation. This may suggest a promising new design feature to better service a market niche.

▼ If possible, have two or three members of the team make the visit together. The time spent talking while traveling before and after the visit is invaluable. Shared expectations, perceptions, and insights are best when made close to the customer visit. Members of the team also discover what they did not see or hear and thus learn from each other how to become better observers and listeners.

Focus Group Research

Next to observation and in-depth discussions with consumers, the most common way of undertaking consumer research is to use a *focus group.* A focus group is a carefully recruited group of six to twelve people who participate in a freewheeling, one- to two-hour discussion that focuses on a particular subject, such as product usage, shopping habits, warrantee experiences, what to do about health care, and so on. In recent years, it has been found that smaller focus groups are often more effective because individuals are more talkative, and they can be conducted in more casual locations, such as hotel suites. Young marketing executives often spend 1–2 weeks a year criss-crossing the country doing 3–4 focus groups a day. In more formal focus groups, a skilled, trained conversationalist called a *moderator* often conducts the session to encourage conversation and debate, and members of the cross-functional decision team watch the discussion through a one-way mirror or on closed-circuit television.

Focus groups can be used successfully by following these process suggestions:

▼ The random calling and screening of participants based on their product usage experience and target **demographics,** such as age and education, can be expensive, sometimes nearly $1,000 to find 30 to 50 willing participants. Consider spending more to create a longer list of willing, qualified participants that can be drawn from at fairly short notice. This will greatly speed up the process of running future focus groups. Take care to check how frequently they have participated in focus groups—avoid professional participants.

▼ Expect to pay at least $50 per participant to cover travel expenses and two to three hours of his or her time. Professionals such as doctors and architects may expect to be paid several hundred dollars for participating.

▼ Find a good moderator who can relate to your target group, and develop a long-term relationship with the moderator. Do not conduct focus groups yourself unless you have had professional training and you can remain emotionally detached from the subject.

▼ Encourage the cross-functional team and senior management to watch the focus group. The focused attention and discussion that ensues has an immediacy that will have a long-term impact on decision making. It also enables questions to be passed to the moderator during a break.

▼ Continue to run focus groups until no new, important insights are learned from the last focus group that is run. This often means only three or four focus groups need to be run.

▼ The concept of focus groups has been taken a step further in new product development where experts are recruited to participate.

While focus groups are great at surfacing issues, problems, and the range of services and features desired, they are seldom completely representative of the thoughts and opinions of the firm's total target market. Typically, focus groups are followed up with more formal survey research of a representative sample of the target market.

Electronic Observational Research[8]

In the mid-1970s consumer-packaged-goods companies and grocery retailers settled on a system of bar codes called the **Universal Product Code (UPC)** that is now on almost all items. These bar codes are read by scanners at the checkout and have greatly increased the efficiency and speed of checkout processes. Now the UPC and the **European Article Numbering (EAN)** systems are used in drug stores, mass merchandisers, and libraries in North America and Europe and are expected to be used worldwide in almost all product categories in the next 20 years.

A very important side-benefit of this technology is that it allows companies to observe what is purchased. This data about grocery store sales is now purchased by two major market research companies, A. C. Nielsen and IRI, who combine all of the individual retailers' data into massive syndicated databases that can report on sales of tens of thousands of grocery items in over 70 metro-markets. The top 100 packaged-goods companies spend an average of about $5 million dollars a year each buying this market research information. What they get is the reports plus a team of Nielsen or IRI researchers, who spend all of their time working with their clients analyzing what is happening on a

---

Demographics

are measures such as age, gender, race, occupation, and income that are often used as a basis for selecting focus group members and market segments.

Universal Product Code (UPC)

is a bar code on a product's package that provides information read by optical scanners.

European Article Number (EAN)

The European version of the Universal Product Code that is located on a product's package that provides information read by optical scanners.

Supermarket checkout scanners are singularly responsible for the initial development and acceptance of UPC codes. By allowing for easier inventory control, customer traffic flow, and price adjustments, scanners revolutionized the grocery industry. The collection and analysis of the data from scanners allows the development of market research reports that have a greater depth of detail, cover larger geographic areas, and are more time-sensitive than previously available.

week-to-week basis in product categories of interest to the packaged goods company. For example, Quaker Oats spends about $4 million a year just studying the supplement drink category created by its Gatorade brand, which generates over $1 billion in sales each year. Ultimately, almost all consumer retail sales will be tracked by such syndicated services that already make up about 20 percent of all spending on market research.

Both IRI and A. C. Nielsen also collect other information that they combine with their scanner data. For example, the IRI BehaviorScan service that operates in over a dozen markets uses a device that attaches to a household's TV sets and controls which TV advertisements are shown in the household. This allows IRI to undertake field experiments that track the impact of advertising campaigns. The purchase behavior of a randomly chosen sample of households from the IRI household panel is compared against a random sample of households that is not exposed to the advertising campaign (the **control sample**). Hundreds of such field experiments have revealed that TV advertising campaigns are usually only effective for new products and do very little for established brands. A. C. Nielsen has household panels that track the total purchases of the household and its exposure to all sorts of marketing campaigns carried by TV, radio, magazines, newspapers, the Internet, and direct mailings. Such panel behavior can then be combined with **geodemographic information** to make predictions about the behavior of households in different parts of a city or a county—called **census blocks.** Geodemographic analysis is based on two premises. The first is that any two people who live in the same neighborhood are more likely to share similar lifestyles and demographic characteristics than any two people who live far apart. The second is that a number of market research firms have used **cluster analysis** on household census data that has enabled them to "label" neighborhoods by their demographics and lifestyles. These names can be quite colorful such as "Blue Blood Estates," "Pools and Patios," "Shot-guns and Pickups," and "Family Ties." Table 4.1 lists ways that geodemographic market research has been used in marketing. Information from A.C. Nielsen panels combined with geodemograhic analysis enable companies to better pinpoint what types of households are heavy buyers of certain product categories and specific brands.

www.QuakerOats.com
www.gatorade.com

Control sample
is that part of a sample group that is left unchanged and receives no special treatment, and serves as a basis of comparison to allow analysis of the results of an experiment.

Geodemographic information
allows identification of customer segments based on geographical location and demographic information.

Census blocks
are geographical areas made up of several city blocks or part of a rural county identified as such by the Census Bureau.

Cluster analysis
is the geographic grouping and labeling of individuals based on their buying behavior, demographics, and lifestyles.

Decision Support Systems

A *decision support system (DSS)* is a set of computer software programs built into a user-friendly interface package, such as Windows, that helps a manager make marketing mix decisions. It enables a user to answer state-of-the-market questions, undertake market forecasts, and create simulations showing what might happen if tactics were changed. Behind the interactive, user-friendly icons, frameworks, prompts, and pull-down guide screens are major online market and accounting databases full of millions of observations of individual consumer behavior provided by companies such as A. C. Nielsen and IRI, but also

Table 4.1	Applications of Geodemography
Application	**Description**
Repositioning	A geodemographic system was used to determine if changing the title of a national magazine from *Apartment Life* to *Metropolitan Home* along with upscaling its format would induce a shift in readership. Subscriptions before and after the change were classified by geodemographic segment to track subscriber trends.
Recruiting	Branches of the U.S. Armed Forces classify their recruits by geodemographic segment in order to determine where to locate recruiting centers and to decide what media and appeals work well to attract young men and women into the military.
Locating	A national chain of boutiques analyzed its clientele by geodemographic segment in order to determine the type of shopping center in which to locate to maximize store traffic. Supplemental analyses were used to select within-center locations and a store format.
Linking Research and Strategy	A household appliance manufacturer interested in coordinating distribution and media coverage for a new product linked each positive response from a national telephone survey to the respondent's geodemographic segment. Program results focused the manufacturer's new product roll-out, media selection, and distribution decisions.
Qualifying Lists	Direct marketers classify current clientele by geodemographic segment. A marketer then identifies segments that contain particularly high concentrations of those clients exhibiting superior purchase volumes. The marketer then identifies new lists that target these geodemographic segments.
Fund-Raising	Organizations seeking funds to support medical research, literacy programs, or other causes classify previous givers by geodemographic segment. Mailing lists and telephone contact lists with high concentrations of sympathetic segments are used to expand the program's donor base.

Transaction-Based Information System (TBIS) is a system that captures and analyzes all of the transactions between a firm and its customers.

Electronic data interchange (EDI) is the computer-to-computer exchange of invoices, orders, and other business documents.

generated from a company's own records of customer trading exchanges. These databases are "mined" for insights by powerful spreadsheets, statistical programs, and mathematical models. Some companies use these systems to target individual customers with special promotions through direct marketing (see Figure 4.3).

Similarly, **Transaction-Based Information Systems (TBISs)** link, communicate, and process all of the transactions with a firm's distributors/customers. The TBIS has evolved out of the **electronic data interchange (EDI)** among businesses. Examples are McKesson's ECONOMIST system for its drugstore customers, and American Airline's Sabre reservation system for its travel agents. Transaction-based information systems are having a dramatic effect on channel and business-to-business customer relationships. By speeding up transaction communication and increasing the monitoring and control of sales and orders, TBISs have greatly reduced the working capital tied up in inventory and the risks of obsolete inventory. Beyond saving billions of dollars a year by reducing warehousing and inventory costs, they have enabled retailers and manufacturers to become much more responsive to market demand because a TBIS provides the manufacturer with online information about what is "hot" and what is not. This "observational market research" can immediately be used to change manufacturing schedules and the procurement of supplies.

Consumer Survey Research

Survey research involves the sampling and surveying of a population of consumers using a carefully prepared set of questions. Surveys of individuals or households are normally taken to study and categorize the variation in buyer values, lifestyles, product usage, benefits sought, and beliefs about product performance (see Chapter 5, "Consumer Behavior"). This categorization process helps marketers segment consumers into subgroups that share similar preferences and behavior. Table 4.2 compares the major survey research approaches. Unfortunately, low response rates are becoming a growing problem. The cooperation of households has been worn thin by too much telemarketing (sometimes unethi-

Figure 4.3   Database Mining and Direct Marketing

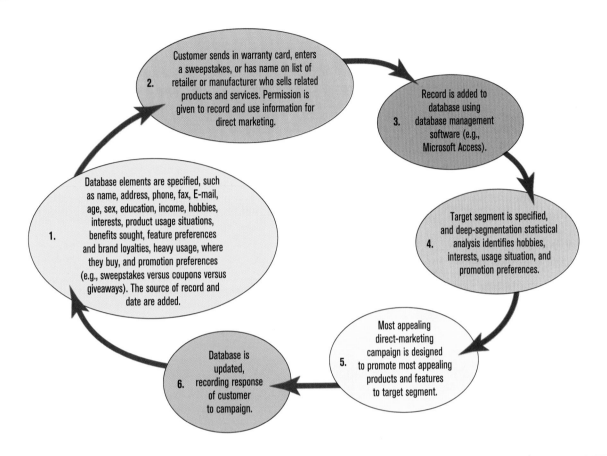

Direct-database marketing is a tool for direct communication with target customers of a special product and promotion offer that has a high chance of appealing to customers. It combines the fundamentals of deep market segmentation with modern database technology and the implementation of microcommunication promotions offered to thousands of hot prospects, rather than millions of mostly indifferent customers. As the database records the history of interactions with each customer, customer segmentation can go beyond a deep understanding of heavy users and identify the sort of marketing interactions and trading relationships that groups of customers wish to have with the company.

cally disguised as survey research), political polling, and market research. CASRO, the Council of American Survey Research Organizations, estimates that about one-third of households now refuse to participate in telephone surveys because of inconvenience or a suspicion that the call is really selling under the guise of research (called **sugging**), which has now been made illegal by the Federal Trade Commission.

These days survey research is mostly used to track customer satisfaction. In a competitive market, customer loyalty and satisfaction are leading indicators of future sales. If they begin to decrease, then it is likely future sales also will decrease. Therefore, in an effort to avoid losing customer sales, marketers are increasingly conducting surveys of customer satisfaction.[9] Table 4.3 presents an example of such an analysis. It categorizes customers by their past loyalty. A slip in satisfaction from a company's most loyal customers is much more serious than a decline in satisfaction among customers who never have been very loyal. The most rigorous customer satisfaction index (CSI) counts the percentage of "happy" customers in a satisfaction survey. Happy customers say (1) they are completely satisfied, (2) they would definitely recommend the product to friends, and (3) they definitely plan to continue to be loyal customers. Experts recommend multiple-item scales

Sugging
refers to an illegal survey(s) conducted under the guise of research but with the intent of selling.

		Table 4.2 Major Survey Research Methods			
Criteria	**Direct/Cold Mailing**	**Mail Panels**	**Telephone**	**Personal In-Home**	**Mall Intercept**
Complexity and versatility	Not much	Not much	Substantial, but complex or lengthy scales difficult to use	Highly flexible	Most flexible
Quantity of data	Substantial	Substantial	Short, lasting typically between 15 and 30 minutes	Greatest quantity	Limited to 25 minutes or less
Sample control	Little	Substantial, but representativeness may be a question	Good, but nonlisted households can be a problem	In theory, provides greatest controls	Can be problematic; sample representativeness may be questionable
Quality of data	Better for sensitive or embarrassing questions; however, no interviewer is present to clarify what is being asked		Positive side, interviewer can clear up any ambiguities; negative side, may lead to socially accepted answers	The chance of cheating arises	Unnatural testing environment can lead to bias
Response rates	In general, low, as low as 10%	70%–80%	60%–80%	Greater than 80%	As high as 80%
Speed	Several weeks; completion time will increase with follow-up mailings	Several weeks with no follow-up mailings, longer with follow-up mailings	Large studies can be completed in 3 to 4 weeks	Faster than mail but typically slower than telephone surveys	Large studies can be completed in a few days
Cost	Inexpensive; as low as $2.50 per completed interview	Lowest	Not as low as mail; depends on incidence rate and length of questionnaire	Can be relatively expensive, but considerable variability	Less expensive than in-home but higher than telephone; again, length and incidence rates will determine cost
Uses	Executive, industrial, medical, and readership studies	All areas of marketing research, particularly useful in low-incidence categories	Particularly effective in studies that require national samples	Still prevalent in product testing and other studies that require visual cues or product prototypes	Pervasive-concept tests, name tests, package tests, copy tests

Reliability

means the consistency of data. It is often tested by reexamining customer opinions using the same survey on a different occasion, or by another method of measurement.

Validity

in customer survey results refers to their accuracy in measuring what they are intended to measure.

that track satisfaction. Using multiple measures of customer satisfaction increases the **reliability** of the answers.

Such survey questions have to be carefully designed to avoid "leading" customers. For example, if a question starts with an explanation of how a company has recently spent $50 million on training its employees to be more friendly and responsive, then answers are likely to overstate customer satisfaction because the respondents' answers have been led. In general, the **validity** of survey research results depends on:

1. Whether the consumers being surveyed have been drawn from the population of interest. Most companies do not seek to survey a sample drawn from the entire adult population of a country: they are interested in a particular group who are buyers of the product category. The question that needs to be asked is: "Is the sample drawn from the target consumers of interest?"

2. Whether the responding sample has been randomly drawn from the target population of interest. If it has not been randomly drawn, then a biased sample may produce results that do not reflect the opinions and behavior of the population of interest. For example, a telephone sample excludes unlisted numbers and undersamples those who are seldom at home. When there are high refusal rates in a telephone survey, the sample may be further biased, reflecting only the opinions of consumers who are cooperative and who have the greatest interest in the topic. The question that needs to be asked is: "Does the responding sample reflect the opinions and behavior of the target consumers of interest?"

Table 4.3   Customer Satisfaction by Past Loyalty

	Current Satisfaction				
Past Loyalty	**Completely Satisfied**	**Somewhat Satisfied**	**Neutral**	**Dissatisfied**	**% of Sales**
Firm friends	7%	3%	0%	0%	10%
Core loyal	10	5	5	5	25
Loyal switchers	10	10	10	10	40
Buy-on-price customers	0	5	10	10	25
Overall	27%	23%	25%	25%	100%

Just looking at the overall result, the situation looks rather grim. An analysis of the past loyalty figures, however, provides a little more assurance and explanation. Fortunately, the customers who are most loyal are generally still satisfied. The firm should be somewhat concerned with the 20% of core loyal customers who are currently dissatisfied. The customers who buy on price have a tendency to be less satisfied because they have not developed a continuous cooperative relationship, and they always will be dissatisfied if they think they could have gotten a better deal.

3. Whether the questions are fair and can be answered by the respondent. Questions can be leading, confusing and hard to follow, or simply unanswerable because the respondent cannot remember their behavior. To avoid such problems, experts in question design should be consulted and the questions should be pretested. The

question that needs to be asked is: "Do the questions measure the true opinions and behavior of the respondent?"

4. Whether the report is clear and factual including all of the answers. Sometimes results that will not be popular with management are suppressed or are not highlighted. The question that needs to be asked is: "Do the results and report fairly reflect what has been learned from the study?"

Even top business schools are not above trying to destroy the objectivity of consumer survey research. The annual rankings of business schools, such as undertaken by *Business Week,* has become big business. When a school's ranking jumps, so do its applications. This has led some otherwise very respectable business schools to ask their graduates who are surveyed by such rating services to rate the school very high on customer satisfaction questions—because it increases the reputation of the school and their degree.

A useful follow-up question in satisfaction survey research is to ask the **open-ended question,** "How can we improve?" These answers can then be used to increase the quality of the product and reduce dissatisfaction. For example, for several years United Parcel Service (UPS) asked customers questions about their satisfaction with the speed and reliability of their shipping service. But when they asked the more general question about how the service could be improved, they discovered customers wanted more face-to-face contact with the UPS drivers; they wanted a person to front the service whom they could get to know, ask for advice on shipping, and personally approach with problems and emergencies. As a result, the company is now giving its 62,000 drivers an additional 30 minutes a day to spend time with customers, and a small commission on any leads they generate.[10] In 1994, the program cost about $6 million in extra drivers' hours and commissions but has generated tens of millions in additional revenue.

A common sense approach should always be adopted in undertaking survey research. For example, before a firm undertakes regular surveys of customer satisfaction, it should develop a program to monitor customer dissatisfaction. Unsolicited consumer complaints send red-alert signals about problems with product design or after-sales service. Tracking service requests is another way of identifying customer dissatisfaction. The downtown Chicago Marriott hotel discovered that two-thirds of its guest calls to housekeeping were for an iron and ironing board. Instead of replacing the black-and-white televisions in the bathrooms of concierge-level guest rooms (housekeeping had received no calls requesting color televisions in the bathroom), the hotel spent $20,000 putting irons and ironing boards in all guest rooms.[11]

Open-ended questions

allow respondents to determine the direction of the answer without being led by the question. They also prevent "yes" or "no" answers.

Secondary Data Analysis

The U.S. Census Bureau, the biggest market research organization in the world, compiles masses of information about household trends. Almost every public library has the Bureau's reports, and it has offices in large cities with specialists whose job is to help businesspeople find out what they need to know. Data from any published source is called *secondary data* because, in a sense, it is secondhand information. *American Demographics* magazine also presents analyses of census data, in addition to other analyses on population trends and changes in values, habits, hobbies, and entertainment. The Government Printing Office (Washington, D.C. 20402) has a subject bibliography index, which lists free government publications on some three hundred subjects. The Library of Congress (202–707–5000) also specializes in helping people find information. The U.S. government also produces 3- to 30-page annual industry reports on more than 300 industries that cover both national and global trends in supply and competition. These U.S. Industrial Outlook reports provide references for further information, and the names and phone numbers of the government researchers who prepared the report. Other important government publications are Statistical Abstract of the United States and the transcripts of industry

Careers in Marketing

From "On Wisconsin" to "Advance Australia Fare"

While Sara loved to travel since her teenage years, she never dreamed that she'd one day be working in destinational marketing. Sara initially completed a Bachelor's Degree in Business Management and Marketing in 1985. During her studies, she was able to gain an internship in Turkey and work part-time as a sales representative for a major truck leasing company. These positions gave a practical view of business to the academic work Sara was undertaking.

Following graduation, Sara worked for a major computer company as a sales representative covering southeastern Wisconsin. While the position was challenging in that weekly sales quotas had to be achieved, the product category was not complex and provided limited opportunities for development. After achieving her first promotion in the company to Account Manager, Sara began looking for a position that provided more challenges. While the position did not provide the long-term career options that Sara had envisioned, the position did solidify her interest in marketing research. As a sales representative, customers were continually making suggestions on product enhancements or voicing complaints with various product attributes, and there did not seem to be formal mechanisms for collecting and encoding this information within the company.

Sara left this position to again head overseas and she worked as a university lecturer. While this position represented a significant deviation from Sara's main career aspirations, in this position Sara developed her communication and presentation skills. However, after three years, the time had come to get back into the main game. Because the Marketing Research industry had progressed so significantly with the development of inexpensive personal computer systems and statistical software packages for data analysis, Sara decided to update her skills and knowledge by completing a Master's Degree in Marketing Research.

Following graduation and moving back to Australia, Sara accepted a position with one of Australia's larger research suppliers (A.G.B. McNair—subsequently purchased by A.C. Nielsen). Sara started as a Senior Researcher with the company working with a variety of clients on research projects ranging from small qualitative studies of a few focus groups to large national household surveys. Working for a large research supplier, Sara honed and refined her research skills. In accepting the position with A.G.B McNair, one of the main considerations was the caliber of other staff working within the organization. The company had established a reputation for doing sound reliable quantitative research. A number of the research directors had been recruited from the Australian Bureau of Statistics and had advanced research skills particularly in the areas of research design and sampling methods. Working alongside these individuals on major projects enabled Sara to operationalize her academic knowledge successfully.

As is frequently the case, clients often recruit individuals from their research suppliers. Sara was asked to apply for a position within one of her clients research unit. While the initial position offered represented a lateral move, the career advancement opportunities in both marketing research and marketing were significant. Furthermore, when working with a research supplier one develops excellent research skills but is never able to become an expert in one subject area. Working on the client side provided Sara an opportunity to develop expertise in one subject area—and in an area of personal interest—TRAVEL!

Sara started working as a market analyst with the Northern Territory Tourist Commission responsible for the analysis of data from the Northern Territory Travel Monitor Surveys. Within six months, Sara was promoted to Manager of the Research Unit and from there to the Commission's Senior Management Team as Deputy GM-Marketing. While Sara is still involved with the research unit, her current role is primarily managerial in focus.

---

studies undertaken by the Federal Trade Commission, Justice Department, and U.S. International Trade Commission. The best free source of advice on obtaining secondary information is your local library.

Calling and asking for secondary information from an expert in government or industry is an important market intelligence skill. Some general contact process rules are listed here:

▼ The hard part is the introduction. You should politely and cheerfully introduce yourself, give your name and the name of the person who recommended you call, and state the purpose of your call. Credible compliments go a long way.

▼ Initially, ask specific, easy questions. Be open, enthusiastic, optimistic, humble, courteous, and grateful.

▼ Use a list of questions, but do not sound as if you are following a list. An apparent lack of structure encourages spontaneous insights and allows for bond-forming casual discussions of other icebreaking topics such as sports, world events, children, or hobbies.

▼ Send a thank-you note (you may wish to call again), and offer to return the favor.

▼ Be persistent. Keep generating leads. Calling a cooperative expert is by far the best $10 value for the money in market research and analysis. It may take ten such calls before you find the "true" expert who is willing to share her or his expertise.[12]

The trade associations, trade journals, and trade newsletters associated with a particular industry can be located through a local library or by consulting the *Directory of Directories,* the *Encyclopedia of Associations,* the *Encyclopedia of Business Information Sources,* and the *Nelson Directory.*

The World Wide Web has revolutionized the use of secondary data in market research because of its marvelous ability to search for relevant information at almost no, or at least very low, cost. Examples of important data sources on the Web are the Census Bureau site at www.census.gov and STAT-USA, another comprehensive source of government statistics that focuses on trade and economic information at www.stat.usa.gov. Examples of sites that provide search engines that will search for key words, phrases, and topics about consumer behavior are www.yahoo.com, www.altavista.digital.com, and www.lycos.com.

www.census.gov

www.stat-usa.gov

www.yahoo.com

www.altavista.digital.com

www.lycos.com

COMPETITOR RESEARCH

The first question almost every company asks in its decision-making process is who are the major players in the market; that is, who has what share of market sales? *Market share* is measured as a percentage of total industry sales over a specified time period. But first the meaning of "the market" must be decided. Clearly, problems exist in defining the "market." A company's market share can change dramatically depending on whether the market is defined as global, a particular export market, the U.S. market, a region of the United States, a city, or a segment of users or usage. The scope of the market is normally specified by a realistic assessment of company resources and by company growth objectives. Often, the market is defined by the way market researchers are able to collect sales and market-share information. This information is often supplied by government agencies, trade associations, or market research firms that survey all of the firms in a market.

Some of the different types of markets a product competes in are illustrated in Figure 4.4. The closest and most immediate competition comes from rivals' products targeted at the same segment that share similar, specific design features (e.g., a 12-ounce can of diet cola). The next level of product category competition comes from products that share some similar features (e.g., soft drinks). More general competition comes from products that satisfy a core benefit (e.g., thirst-quenching or pick-me-up drinks). The most distant competition is for consumers' discretionary spending. At this level, a new car may compete against a new deck for the house or an overseas trip.

The historical problem with research into competition has been too much focus on measuring the number of current competitors, the concentration of market share (the combined market share of the largest three competitors), and the current balance-sheet assets of major competitors. The emphasis needs to be placed on market dynamics, such as who is introducing new manufacturing, distribution, and product development processes into the market. Competitive insight comes from explaining such drivers of success in the market, and not from knowing who has the largest market share. The acid test for such insight is whether an executive wants to know what company has the largest market share *(static thought)* or what company has experienced the largest change in market share *(dynamic thought).* Does the firm study the history of change in the industry to identify the trends in changing supply to further identify which paths the market will take in the future (i.e., production and distribution technological paths)? A dynamic analysis is thus able to identify what and who are the drivers of change in the market.

Competitor research efforts are misspent on working out to the last share point (1 percent of market share) what the market share is, because defining the exact bounds of the market is seldom that precise. Such efforts are better spent on finding out which estab-

Figure 4.4   Examples of Levels of Competition

Target
Segment
Competition:
Diet Colas

Product
Category
Competition:
Soft
Drinks

Core
Benefit
Competition:
Beverages

Budget
Competition:
Food and
Entertainment

Diet-Rite Cola · Diet Pepsi · Diet Coke · Regular Colas · Diet Lemon Limes · Lemon Limes · Fruit Flavored Colas · Beer · Juices · Coffee · Bottled Water · Ice Cream · Wine · Fast Food · Video Rentals · Baseball Cards

Most managers just consider their segment or product category competition and are sometimes blindsided by the success of less direct competition (e.g., bottled water and iced tea's effect on diet cola sales).

lished competitor or new start-up is using radical new product or process technology to increase customer satisfaction and reduce costs. The history of technology suggests that small start-up companies often revolutionize a market.[13] For example, the typewriter was invented by Christopher Sholes, working in Milwaukee as a civil servant, and not for a printing or publishing company. The electric typewriter was developed and enhanced by IBM, and not by Remington or Underwood, the market leaders in manual typewriters. In turn, it was Wang and Apple, rather than IBM, that developed the computer word

www.ibm.com
www.wang.com
www.apple.com

processing and desktop publishing market. Amazon.com was started by a Wall Street analyst in 1994 working out of his home.

The change in market share over time is a vital indicator of the competitive environment. However, market share is not the only measures of competitiveness. The following measures are often used as leading indicators of a likely change in future sales and profits.

1. *Mind share:* The percentage of customers who name the brand when asked to name the first brand that comes to mind when they think about buying a particular type of product. This indicates the consumer's top-of-mind brand awareness and preferences. How is it changing among different segments?

2. *Voice share:* The percentage of media space or time a brand has of the total media share for that industry, often measured simply as dollars spent on advertising. This is likely to lead to a change in mind share (but not always, if the messages are weak). How and why is it changing?

3. *Research and development (R&D share):* A company's expenditure as a percentage of the total industry R&D expenditure. This is a long-term predictor of new product developments, improvements in quality, cost reductions, and, hence, market share. It is an important measure of future competitiveness in many high-technology markets. How is it changing, and what is it being spent on?

Researching the History of the Market

www.duracell.com

A study of the recent history of the product market identifies the marketing mix and product dimensions on which sellers have competed most strongly to serve the interests of the resellers and consumers. In some markets, this competition may have resulted in a price war. In others, sellers have competed with each other to improve product and service quality. Often, a technological improvement made by an innovator forces every competitor to respond. This occurred when Duracell introduced the alkaline battery. All of its competitors were forced to match the new technology. The history of the product market is seldom recorded. It is often carried around in the heads of experienced executives, and the invaluable insights they can provide are lost when they retire.

An industry often has standard marketing tactics and rules that are universally adopted. Examples are certain formulas for cost-plus pricing and spending a certain percentage of the previous year's sales on advertising in the next year. Sales force commissions and incentives are also often standardized in an industry. These rules of doing business make the market more predictable and stable. If the market "learns" and has moved toward more efficient ways of making and marketing its products, then these rules and processes should reflect such learning, and hence make sense. Knowing how and why standard industry practices and decision rules came about enables a firm to better understand whether the rules are based on continuous market learning or whether they have simply become "established" practice to keep from rocking the boat.[14] If they are based on market learning then a competitor can better understand what works and what does not in the marketplace and why. However, if the rules are based on old-fashioned agreements to restrain competition, then violating them represents an opportunity for the aggressive firm.

Michael Porter's pioneering text, *Competitive Strategy,* changed the way many companies think about their competition.[15] Porter identified five forces that shape competition: current competitors, the threat of new entrants, the threat of new substitutes, the bargaining power of distributors (or business-to-business customers), and the bargaining power of suppliers. This structure can be reduced further to include simply current competitors and potential competitors and substitutes. The way distributors and suppliers behave determines the threat posed by immediate and potential competition. Distributors and suppliers are therefore not separate competitive elements but moderators or amplifiers of competition (see Figure 4.5). Generally, suppliers and distributors are used to gain

Figure 4.5   Current and Potential Competition

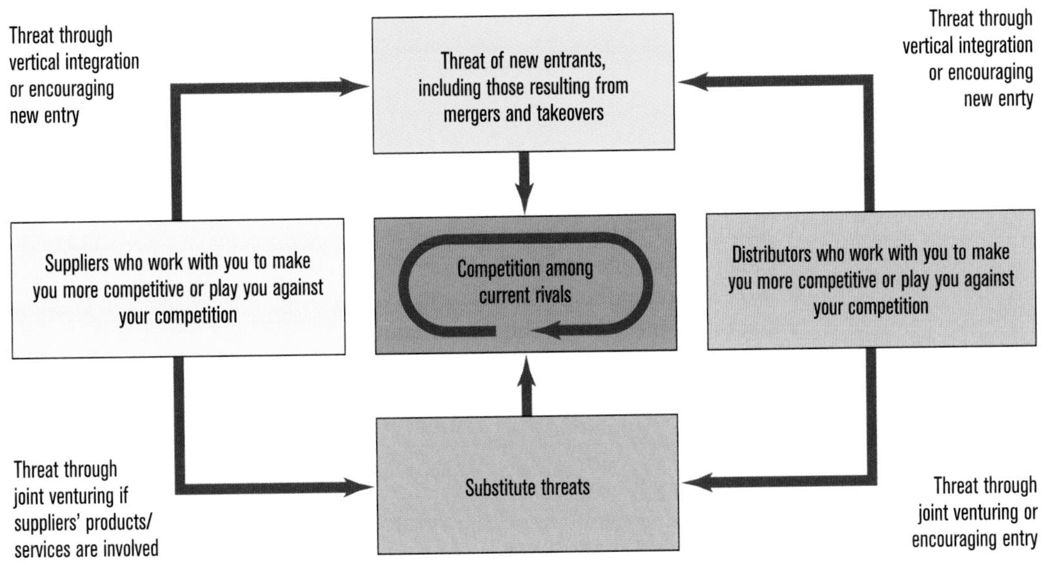

Competition occurs among current rivals. Distributors and suppliers can help or hinder a firm's efforts to become more competitive. Sometimes, they even encourage a new entrant or the development of a new substitute. They seldom, if ever, discourage such entry or the development of a new technological substitute. However, distributors and suppliers are not competitors. In fact, the trading relationship a firm has with a supplier or distributor is a cooperative effort that competes with other trading relationships in the market.

competitive advantage and should be seen in this light. That is why distributor and channel research should be undertaken separately from competitor research. It is true that at times distributors and suppliers have to be directly considered in a competitive analysis, but only when they threaten to become a new direct competitor. A company must be on its guard against new entrants and from others up and down the supply chain. This concern is best addressed in competitive research by asking and answering the questions presented in Table 4.4.

Auditing Current Competitors

For most companies it is not possible to put all current competitors under the microscope and undertake an in-depth analysis of their competitive strengths and weaknesses. However, particular competitors are always worthy of such attention, either because they are attacking with a new product or because a firm has decided, in a previous plan, to attack them. The isolation of "aggressors" or "targets" usually requires a preliminary analysis that identifies from which rivals you are gaining business and to which competitors you are losing business. This is the way you identify your immediate current competition, which may or may not be using similar technology.[16] For example, many major U.S. cities now only have one daily newspaper, yet such monopolies have not created super profits for the publisher. The reason is simple. Although other major newspapers may have died, competition for advertising has increased from the suburban weeklies, direct marketing, and other media. Television, radio, and local magazines also have become more competitive with their news and features. The mistake the newspaper publishers made was not identifying these competitors early on when they could have taken counter measures.[17]

Table 4.4   New Competitive-Threats Audit

The skill in identifying potential new competition is to ask a series of questions that narrows in on the most likely competitor and its situation.

New Technology—Converging Markets Threat

▼ What price changes in other technology markets appear to influence our sales? Is this effort changing?
▼ Which new technology or service is starting to be considered as a substitute for our product or service by consumers? Is this occurring in any particular usage situation or by any particular group of buyers? Are our existing channels encouraging such substitution?
▼ What is our closest new technological or service competition?
▼ Who is the major mover and shaker in this new industry?
▼ What appears to be its current objective and strategy?
▼ What is its growth rate?
▼ What has been its effect on our sales?
▼ What further threat does it pose?
▼ What constraints does it face?

Channel Integration Threat

▼ Which supplier is most likely to become a downstream direct competitor in the near future? Why? How would it do it? Is there any evidence of this occurring?
▼ Which customers are most likely to become upstream, do-it-themselves competitors in the near future? Why? How would they do it? Does any evidence of such plans exist?

Competitor Takeover—Merger Threat

▼ Which mergers, takeovers, or trading coalitions among competitors or from inside pose the greatest threat to our position? What evidence exists that this is likely to occur?

The initial investment in time, effort, and expense necessary to audit competitors may be very high (amounting to several weeks or even months of an executive's or consultant's time), but it should be treated as an investment. The results will produce a report that can be built on from year to year with constantly expanding details and insights. This file then becomes part of the collective memory of your organization to be passed on to successive managers.

Table 4.5 presents a competitor analysis template that a company can use as a basis for developing its own unique competitor analysis form. The competitive strategy guru Michael Porter has argued that competitive advantage in product quality and costs can come from one or more of the following stages in the added-value chain:[18]

1. Inbound logistics processes

2. Operations processes

3. Outbound logistics processes

4. Marketing and sales processes

5. Service processes

The implication is that a rival's competitive standing at all stages of the added-value chain from inbound logistics to after-sales service must be studied. The analysis form presented in Table 4.5 addresses characteristics of these processes. This analysis should involve at least three types of information. The first type of information is a rating of the rival's performance compared or "benchmarked" against the very best in the industry. The second type of information is the direction this performance is moving (improving indicated by an up-arrow and declining indicated by a down-arrow beside the rating). The

Table 4.5   A Competitor Analysis Template

Competitor _____   Analyst _____   Date _____

SUMMARY OF COMPETITOR'S POSITION

▼ Goals and major competitive strategy   _____
▼ Current success story   _____
▼ Current mistakes   _____
▼ Competitive advantages/disadvantages   _____

BENCHMARKING ANALYSIS*

Financial Position
Cash flow, cost structure, access to capital, profits   _____

Market Position
Major geographical markets, target segments   _____

Product Position
Raw material, manufacturing, design quality, features   _____
Brand strength and image with target markets   _____

Price Position
How much above/below average, types of promotions   _____

Inbound Logistics Process
Sources of supply, purchasing skills, inventory flow   _____

Production Processes
Production capacity, adaptability, efficiency, quality, costs   _____
Labor adaptability, skill, and loyalty   _____

Outbound Logistics Processes
Order-delivery time, inventory flow, special services   _____

Trade Relations Processes
Major channels used, channel relationships   _____

Advertising and Promotion Processes
Message themes, media usage, campaign schedules   _____

Sales Force Processes
Sales force management, morale, training, incentives   _____
Use of technology, service quality, and efficiency   _____

*Comparative benchmarking rating, direction of change, what processes, technology, people are driving its performance improvement.

third type of information should be a detailed explanation as to what is unique and interesting about the rival's behavior or product, or at least the name and e-mail of someone who can provide such detail. This brings us to the question of how competitor research is undertaken. It is seldom gathered through James Bond methods of industrial espionage, using sources of doubtful reputation. Interestingly, the great market research company A.C. Nielsen started up in business in 1923, doing competitive market research for machinery manufacturers. It was not until 1928 that it started to undertake consumer research. Table 4.6 reports on the most useful sources of competitor information and the most useful type of information. The following is a nice description of how many firms make sense of the information they gather about competitors:

We gather about 10 people in a room, twice a month, in long (think-tank) sessions—anything from three hours to a couple of days. The sessions have no formal structure. We examine and massage the latest competitor and industry information to determine where things are going and what we should be doing. There are a lot of people in the business unit who know something about a competitor. But it's almost like the three blind men and the elephant: Each one examines a small part of the whole. When you put them all together in a

	Table 4.6	**Competitor Intelligence**		

Most Useful Source of Information
(by type of market)

Percent Distribution

	Total	**Industrial Products**	**Consumer Products**	**Both Consumer and Industrial**
Sales force	27%	35%	18%	23%
Publications, databases	16	13	15	22
Customers	14	13	11	17
Marketing research, tracking services	9	3	24	9
Financial reports	5	7	3	1
Distributors	3	4	1	1
Employees (unspecified)	2	2	6	—
Analysis of products	2	1	3	3
Other	8	6	8	13
No answer	14	16	11	11
	100%	100%	100%	100%
Number of responding companies	308	158	72	78

Most Useful Type of Information
(by type of market)

Percent Distribution

	Total	**Industrial Products**	**Consumer Products**	**Both Consumer and Industrial**
Pricing	23%	26%	20%	19%
Strategy	19	20	15	22
Sales data	13	11	18	12
New products, product mix	11	13	8	10
Advertising/marketing activities	7	3	19	4
Costs	6	8	3	5
Key customers/markets	3	3	6	1
Research and development	2	2	1	3
Management style	2	1	3	1
Other	4	4	—	8
No answer	10	9	7	15
	100%	100%	100%	100%
Number of responding companies	308	158	72	78

Source: Howard Sutton, *Competitive Intelligence* (New York: The Conference Board, 1988).

room, they are amazed about how much they know. That coalesces into one or two sheets of paper presenting all we know about a competitor's strengths and weaknesses, and our judgments with respect to a competitor's strategies and measures of success. That is the beginning of a competitor file.[19]

CHANNEL RESEARCH

The first professional market researcher, Charles Parlin, started in business in 1911 doing distribution channel research and not consumer research. He studied the distribution channels for agricultural instruments and then for textiles. Interest in researching channels of distribution has greatly increased in the 1990s for at least two reasons. The first is that

Table 4.7   Channel Change Audit

▼ **Who are the latest new entrants in the reseller market?**
What is their competitive advantage?
Which existing resellers are being most affected?
How has it affected us?

▼ **What new trading coalitions among resellers are occurring?**
What will be their competitive advantage?
How will it affect us?

▼ **What changes in order-processing technology are now occurring?**
What impact will they have on the way business is done?
What competitive advantage do they provide?

▼ **What changes in transportation technology are now occurring?**
What impact will they have on the way business is done?
What competitive advantage do they provide?

▼ **What changes in warehousing technology are now occurring?**
What impact will they have on the way business is done?
What competitive advantage do they provide?

▼ **What changes in payment technology are now occurring?**
What impact will they have on the way business is done?
What competitive advantage do they provide?

retailing has become much more competitive because the market is becoming over-stored. Management Horizons, a retailing consulting company, estimates that in the 1990s the amount of retailing square footage increased from about 15 square-feet for every person in the U.S. to 20 square-feet. By comparison, for every person in the United Kingdom, it is estimated there is only two square-feet of retail space per person. There is so much available retail space competing for consumer dollars that rivalry between retailers has become ferocious. The second reason for undertaking distribution market research is that in the next few years Web direct-marketing is predicted by many to gain 10–20 percent of sales in some product categories such as computer software, computer hardware, recorded music, books, videos, and air travel. How are traditional distribution channels going to respond to this threat?

The suggested procedure for learning about distribution channels is to first address a number of questions about general changes and then to zero in on a detailed audit of some key resellers (sometimes called trade customers). Table 4.7 lists several questions that address the impact on the distribution channel of (1) changes in technology, (2) new entrants, (3) changes in established channel relations, and (4) changes in the way existing channel members do business. The recorded music market provides an excellent example of how such changes impact product marketing.

In the 1950s and early 1960s, record retailers allowed consumers to play new records in the store. This was an important way of exposing a new artist or title to the public because the enthusiasts and opinion leaders did most of this in-store sampling. But as popular music took off with rock 'n'roll, and the spending power of the Baby Boomers increased, chain stores opened record bars that did not provide the sound booths for sampling but undercut the record stores in prices. Consumers would often listen to the music in the record store and buy at the chain store. To compete, the record stores dropped the sound booths but offered a generous return policy. Eventually, even the return policy was also dropped.

As a result of the termination of in-store sampling, popular radio stations became critical in marketing records. But radio was also going through a transition. Increased competition was forcing the stations into Top 20 or Top 40 formats where the hit-parade music was played continuously at the expense of the new artists and songs. This program format kept the audiences and advertisers happy, but it forced the recording companies to buy airtime in order to advertise their new releases (where previously such exposure was free). This increased the cost of launching a new release, thus giving a major competitive advantage to the larger recording studios and distributors. MTV pulled the recording industry out of the doldrums in the early 1980s, but this new promotion channel also forced the studios into a whole new marketing activity—video production. The music video component has become an important new competitive element in selling compact discs and tapes and a further entrance barrier for new competition. But Web marketing is again revolutionizing the distribution of music. It is possible that individual musicians will be able to make their own digital recordings and distribute them directly from their own Web site to consumers who pay a small fee to download the music onto their home computer that is also their home sound system. What effect will this have on the traditional music distribution system? The role of distribution research is to answer this question as quickly as possible.

Researching Individual Trade Customers

Once the general channel change audit has been undertaken, important trade customers will have been identified for further study. Clearly, not all of these resellers can be studied, and some good managerial judgment is needed to make sure greater attention is paid to the major players and innovators. When a manufacturer's sales force uses an account management approach for its major retail trade accounts, it should be relatively easy to complete audits of such trade customers. However, care must be taken that day-to-day operating relations do not drive the evaluations of those who are in constant contact with representatives of suppliers and resellers. The reseller audits require the auditor to stand back, to assess the changes that have occurred over the past trading year, and explain some of the basic reasons for predicting longer-term changes.

The reseller audit in Table 4.8 starts with a summary evaluation that can also be used as a short-form audit when the product team does not have the time or interest to fully evaluate particular resellers. A paragraph can be written to provide responses to the concerns listed. The evaluation can be updated on a regular basis (normally annually), so the

Table 4.8   Individual Distributor Audit

Company Name: _____   **Date:** _____

Summary Evaluation	**Competitive Selling Effort**
▼ Image and reputation	▼ Quality of locations
▼ Geographical markets/customer segments served	▼ Quality of advertising
▼ Major strength, unique value, and importance of this reseller	▼ Quality of premises
▼ Major weakness and failure of reseller	▼ Quality of sales staff
▼ Special personal relations with distributor	▼ Sales staff knowledge of our products
Detailed Evaluation	▼ Inventory management
Trading Performance	▼ Extent we are treated as a preferred supplier
▼ Annual sales	▼ Special marketing efforts and cooperation
▼ Annual sales of our products	*Purchasing Behavior*
▼ Contribution earned from sales to this reseller	▼ Recent ordering history
▼ Average stock-turn of our products	▼ Volume deals/discounts sought and given
▼ Past average stock-turn of our products	▼ Other allowances and considerations sought and given:
▼ Profit performance	Freight
	Cooperative advertising
	Promotions
	Returns
	Push money and sales contests
	Special credit terms

major investment is in preparing the initial evaluation. The detailed evaluation questions have been categorized into those dealing with the reseller's trading performance, marketing position, competitive effort, and purchasing behavior. Understanding what is going right or wrong in a channel relationship almost always involves taking information and putting it together like a jigsaw puzzle. That is why it is important to add depth to the audit by answering as many questions as possible, using facts, good judgment, and best guesses. Trying to understand the reasons for a channel member's change in performance or behavior often means tracing back from its buying behavior, through trading and operating indicators, to its competitive effort and market position. Distribution market research also must forecast distributors' future competitive strengths and weaknesses.

Chapter Summary

Market research and analysis is a very large topic covering many topics and techniques. This explains why there are many advanced courses in marketing research that can be taken at the undergraduate and graduate level. There are even specialized master's degrees in marketing research and analysis offered by centers of marketing research at universities such as the University of Wisconsin–Madison and the University of Georgia. It also explains why so much market research is contracted out by companies to research suppliers who, like advertising agencies, are specialists in their profession.

Some people might argue that market research is only "research" when it involves complex scientific method and analysis borrowed from the social sciences and economics. But such research often costs tens of thousands of dollars, sometimes millions of dollars. In reality, how many firms undertake such research? Several hundred huge packaged-goods and service companies spend millions of dollars a year on market research, employing highly skilled researchers. A few thousand companies spend hundreds of thousands a year on marketing research, mainly using smaller market research firms whom they work with over many years. What sort of market research do the remaining hundreds of thousands of businesses undertake? Their managers spend a lot of time observing customers, competitors, and distributors first hand. They are increasingly using secondary sources of information they obtain from the business press, government sources, or from Web searches. The reason why this chapter emphasized simple methods such as observing customers, competitors and distributors is because these are the methods that all firms should use, and these are the only research methods that most firms actually use.

Over the last 100 years, a lot has been learned about how to practice market research, and some of that learning is presented in this chapter. The first general lesson that has been learned is that market research is about helping to improve managers' intuitive understanding of the behavior of customers, competitors, and distributors.

A second general lesson is that a firm should first gather, analyze, and discuss all the information that managers have already on hand from their own information systems, from their sales force, from secondary information, and from their own personal observation. As explained in Figure 4.2, a particular market research project needs to be defined in terms of the crucial questions that need to be answered. Ways of quickly and cheaply answering these questions need to be pursued, and then a cost/benefit decision has to be made as to whether to pursue more expensive research. In the chapter opener, millions of dollars were at stake in the decision by R.G. Barry to raise it slipper prices. For about $40,000 the company was able to assure itself and its retail customers that it could raise its prices with little loss in sales. The research also provided other valuable information about product design and merchandising practices.

A third general lesson is that market research methods are evolving as new technologies are being used. Fifty years ago, computers did not exist and all analyses had to be undertaken mechanically or by hand. Today, a PC can do sophisticated quantitative and qualitative analyses that were unheard of 30 years ago. Twenty years ago scanner technology was invented and with it the ability to track company and competitor sales through specific distribution channels. Today, companies that specialize in Web-based market research are being invented. These companies may greatly increase the quality and decrease the cost of market research in the near future.

A fifth and final lesson is that research needs to be reported in ways that make it easy for decision-makers to understand what is going on. From the results of the Conference Board study presented in Figure 4.1, there is much room for improvement even amongst the biggest and best companies in the world. This is best achieved by developing digital files on consumer, competitor, and distributor behavior that can be readily consulted and analyzed for changing patterns. Companies with superior market research and analysis skills are able to change their thinking about the marketplace faster than their competition. Such fast insight and learning gives them more time to innovate, imitate, and avoid crisis management. A company with such superior decision-making skills has a clear competitive advantage over its rivals.

Key Terms

Voice of the customer is the expression of the preferences, opinions, and motivations of the customer that need to be listened to by managers.

Hands-on consumer research is conducted by direct observation by managers of the way current customers use specific products and brands. The opposite is arm's-length research which is undertaken by external suppliers.

Motivational research is a research method directed at discovering the conscious or subconscious reasons that motivate a person's behavior.

Demographics are measures such as age, gender, race, occupation, and income that are often used as a basis for selecting focus group members and market segments.

Universal Product Code (UPC) is a bar code on a product's package that provides information read by optical scanners.

European Article Numbering (EAN) The European version of the Universal Product Code that is located on a product's package that provides information read by optical scanners.

Control sample is that part of a sample group that is left unchanged and receives no special treatment, and serves as a basis of comparison to allow analysis of the results of an experiment.

Geodemographic information allows identification of customer segments based on geographical location and demographic information.

Census blocks are geographical areas made up of several city blocks or part of a rural county identified as such by the Census Bureau.

Cluster analysis is the geographic grouping and labeling of individuals based on their buying behavior, demographics, and lifestyles.

Transaction-Based Information System (TBIS) is a system that captures and analyzes all of the transactions between a firm and its customers.

Electronic data interchange (EDI) is the computer-to-computer exchange of invoices, orders, and other business documents.

Sugging refers to an illegal survey(s) conducted under the guise of research but with the intent of selling.

Reliability means the consistency of data. It is often tested by reexamining customer opinions using the same survey on a different occasion, or by another method of measurement.

Validity in customer survey results refers to their accuracy in measuring what they are intended to measure.

Open-ended questions allow respondents to determine the direction of the answer without being led by the question. They also prevent "yes" or "no" answers.

Additional Key Terms and Concepts

Adopt a Customer

Moderator

Secondary data

Static thought

Mind share

R&D share

Focus group

Decision support systems (DSS)

Market share

Dynamic thought

Voice share

Questions for Discussion

1. In the mid 1980s, Pepsi overtook Coke in supermarket sales with its highly successful "Take the Pepsi Challenge" marketing campaign. The challenge was to choose which cola you preferred in a blind taste test. A blind taste test is when you do not know what brand you are testing. Coke's response was to search for a new flavor that beat Pepsi in blind taste tests. After 200,000 taste tests, it settled on New Coke, a sweeter, smoother flavor that beat Pepsi and Old Coke in the blind taste tests. The result was a marketing disaster. In 1985 New Coke replaced Classic Coke on the shelves, and tens of thousands of angry Coke customers called Coke to complain. Coca-Cola brought back Classic Coke along side New Coke and insisted that it had not made a mistake. Five years later, New Coke was dead. What mistake did Coca-Cola make in the market research it undertook? (Hint: Did it not do enough research or did it do the wrong sort of research?)

2. Imagine that you were part of the cross-functional team developing the Depend's adult disposable diaper. Several members of the team seem to have a problem understanding consumer complaints about the existing product in the market. What market intelligence-gathering activity might you suggest to raise their understanding?

3. When researching customer needs, would it be better for a product designer to visit customers personally or to read a survey research report on customer needs, beliefs, and behaviors? What biases are inherent in each approach that might lead to misunderstanding consumer behavior?

4. How would a company that combines a bar with a laundry service use geodemographic analysis?

5. In the recent case brought against Microsoft charging that it monopolizes the PC software market, Microsoft claimed that 80 percent of software developers are happy with the situation as it is. This result was based on a yes/no question that followed a 350 word statement describing all of the advantages of the current situation and none of the disadvantages. The Dean of the MIT Business School defended the question saying that he saw nothing wrong with it. What is wrong with such a question?

6. Table 4.6 presents information about the usefulness of competitive intelligence and the most useful sources of competitive intelligence. Why is price information more important than strategy information? List several reasons. What do the results of the most useful sources tell us about how we should set up an intelligence-gathering operation?

7. The State Department is in charge of over a hundred U.S. Embassies and Consulates scattered around the globe. How is the U.S. diplomatic service and State Department likely to change if the predominant conflict between countries in the 21st century will be economic rather than ideological?

8. "To outguess them, [General George] Washington sought the best strategic advice and had no pride of ownership. The excellence and not the origin of the plan was decisive with him. He learned by listening well, or by observing and reflecting. During the greater part of the struggle, he had to be his own chief intelligence officer, and he did so with considerable success. Always he tried to learn what was not happening as well as what was, and he frequently undertook the careful analysis, in person, of conflicting intelligence reports."[20] If General George Washington could, with his "now you see it, now you don't" army, win a war and a nation's freedom against the world's superpower of the time by doing this, why is it that a CEO of a modern corporation does not lead in a similar way?

Internet Questions

1. The PC revolution has led to executives doing a lot of their own typing, letter writing, and report writing themselves rather than relying on an executive assistant or secretary to do the work. The Internet provides a huge source of information about markets, countries, consumers, products, and technologies that can be searched using key words very easily. School children learn from a very early age today how to search the Internet for research projects. How will this change the demand for market researchers and market analysts in the future? How will their jobs change?

2. An infamous bank robber, when asked why he robbed banks, said because that is where the money is. Some have argued that a similar but much more legal principle applies to Internet marketing. Those with wealth, who are prime targets for marketers, are online wired. The rich of the world are online, the poor are not and never will be. Starting wherever you wish, search Web sites so that you can participate in a class discussion of the following two questions:
   a. Are the world's rich, those with the top 10 percent of incomes, already connected to the Internet wherever they live in the world? Are the wealthy in India, Africa, China, Russia, and South America already connected to the Web? If they are, what impact will this have on the marketing of premium brands to the world's wealthy? (Hint: Start searching U.S. government or Internet company sites.)
   b. Which group of very wealthy Americans has the Internet and Internet shopping hardly penetrated yet? How will this change in the future?

3. The table on page 131 presents a number of examples of different types of questions that can be used to learn about Internet usage. Please identify any problems with the measures (such as ambiguous, hard to answer, shows bias).

Endnotes

[1]Arie P. DeGeus, "Planning as Learning," *Harvard Business Review,* March/April 1988, pp. 70–74.

[2]Peter R. Dickson and Rosemary Kalapurakal, "The Theory and Reality of Environment Analysis in the Marketing Plan," Working Paper, College of Business, Ohio State University, 1991.

[3]See George S. Day and Prakash Nedungadi, "Managerial Representations of Competitive Advantage," *Journal of Marketing* 58 (April 1994): pp. 31–44; George S. Day, *Learning about Markets* (Cambridge, MA: Marketing Science Institute, 1991): pp. 91–117; and Jeffrey Pfeffer and Gerald R. Salancik, *The External Control of Organizations: A Resource Dependence Perspective* (New York: Harper, 1978).

Types of Questions

Dichotomous Questions

Have you ever browsed the Internet?   Yes   No

Open-Ended Questions

Microsoft has been prosecuted for unfair business practices, such as trying to drive competitors out of business. What is your opinion of Microsoft's browser?

_____
_____
_____
_____
_____
_____

"The most important consideration for me in choosing a browser is . . ."

_____
_____
_____
_____
_____

Multiple-Choice Questions

Which one of the following products have you purchased from a Web site:

Books   Software   Music CDs   Airline tickets
Clothing   X-rated material   Stocks   Computers and peripherals

Intention-to-Buy Scale

How likely is it that next Christmas Holiday Season you will buy a gift for a family member or a friend from a Web site:

Definitely will buy   Probably will buy   Maybe will buy   Not certain   Probably will not buy   Definitely will not buy

Rating Scales

Amazon.com's Web site is:

Excellent   Very good   Good   Fair   Poor

On a scale of 1 to 10, where 10 is excellent and 1 is a dog, how would you rate the Amazon.com Web site? _____

Semantic Differential Scale

Amazon.com's Web site is:

Easy to use ____:____:____:____:____:____:____ Hard to use
Fun   ____:____:____:____:____:____:____ Boring
Modern   ____:____:____:____:____:____:____ Old-fashioned
Friendly   ____:____:____:____:____:____:____ Unfriendly
Laid back   ____:____:____:____:____:____:____ Pushy
Soft sell   ____:____:____:____:____:____:____ Hard sell
Helpful   ____:____:____:____:____:____:____ Unhelpful
Cluttered   ____:____:____:____:____:____:____ Uncluttered

Importance Scale

How important is it for you to pay a price in Web shopping that is less than regular retail?

Extremely important   Very important   Somewhat important   Not very important   Not important at all

Likert Scales

"Amazon.com is very easy to learn to use compared with other shopping sites."

Strongly disagree   Disagree   Somewhat disagree   Neither agree nor disagree   Somewhat agree   Agree   Strongly agree

"You learn more about products when you Web shop than when you shop in a regular store."

Strongly disagree   Disagree   Somewhat disagree   Neither agree nor disagree   Somewhat agree   Agree   Strongly agree

[4]Edward F. McQuarrie and Shelby H. McIntyre, "The Customer Visit: An Emerging Practice in Business-to-Business Marketing," working paper (Cambridge, MA: Marketing Science Institute, 1992), pp. 92–114.

[5]Johny K. Johannson and Ikujiro Nonaka, "Market Research the Japanese Way," *Harvard Business Review,* May/June 1987, pp. 16–22; Lance Ealey and Leif Soderberg, "How Honda Cures Design Amnesia," *The McKinsey Quarterly,* Spring 1990, pp. 3–14; and Kenichi Ohmae, *The Borderless World* (New York: Harper Business, 1990).

[6]B. Dumaine, "Creating a New Company Culture," *Fortune,* January 15, 1990, pp. 127–31.

[7]B. Dumaine, "Corporate Spies Snoop to Conquer," *Fortune,* November 7, 1988, pp. 68–76.

[8]Much of the material in this section is drawn from the following book written by David J. Curry, which is an excellent review of the new high tech use of scanner data: *The New Marketing Research Systems* (New York: John Wiley & Sons, 1993).

[9]Robert A. Westbrook, "A Rating Scale for Measuring Product/Service Satisfaction," *Journal of Marketing,* 44 (Fall 1980): pp. 68–72; and Richard L. Oliver and John E. Swan, "Consumer Perceptions of Interpersonal Equity and Satisfaction in Transactions: A Field Survey Approach," *Journal of Marketing* 53 (April 1989): pp. 21–35.

[10]David Greising, "Quality: How to Make It Pay," *Business Week,* August 8, 1995, pp. 54–59.

[11]The bad news is that it took the hotel 15 years to discover the ironing problem! See Leonard L. Berry, "Improving America's Service," *Marketing Management* 1, no. 3 (1992): pp. 29–37.

[12]This list is based in part on advice from "The Art of Obtaining Information," Washington Researchers, Washington, D.C.

[13]James M. Utterback, *Mastering the Dynamics of Innovation* (Cambridge, MA: Harvard Business School Press, 1994).

[14]Gloria P. Thomas and Gary F. Soldow, "A Rules-Based Approach to Competitive Interaction," *Journal of Marketing* 52 (April 1988): pp. 63–74.

[15]Michael E. Porter, *Competitive Strategy* (New York: The Free Press, 1980).

[16]Thomas W. Dunfee, Louis Stern, and Frederick D. Sturdivant, "Bounding Markets in Merger Cases: Identifying Relevant Competitors," Northwestern University *Law Review* 78 (November 1983): pp. 733–73.

[17]Subrata N. Chakravarty and Carolyn Torcellini, "Citizen Kane Meets Adam Smith," *Forbes,* February 20, 1989, pp. 82–85.

[18]Michael E. Porter, *Competitive Advantage* (New York: The Free Press, 1985).

[19]Howard Sutton, *Competitive Intelligence* (New York: The Conference Board, 1988), pp. 31, 37.

[20]Richard Harwell, *Washington* (New York: Collier Books, 1992), pp. 511–12.

Online Marketing Research

Computers have been used to tabulate surveys and analyze relationships between responses since the late 1960s. They have greatly reduced the cost of survey research while greatly increasing its quality. As computers became increasingly accessible, the field of multivariate statistical analysis flourished. The next great advancement occurred in the 1970s with the birth of computer-assisted telephone interviewing (CATI), which allowed for survey automation. These systems prompted telephone interviewers with the questions to be asked, and provided immediate data capture as a respondent's answers were recorded. Data analysis could be undertaken as soon as the last interview in the sample was completed.

However, it took the computer revolution until the mid-1990s for it to have its most dramatic and potentially revolutionary impact on survey research. In September 1995 America Online (AOL) and a prominent research firm called The M/A/R/C Group launched a joint venture called Digital Marketing Services (DMS). The goal was to activate the online medium for conducting marketing research. As development options were considered, a revelation occurred: why not put a front-end on the CATI software and allow respondents to enter their answers to questions directly? In many research applications, respondents are asked to fill out paper surveys. This self-administered surveying could be taken to a new level, characterized by a scientifically controlled computer experience. A new method of surveying was born.

This partnership opens the doors to millions of AOL subscribers as potential respondents via an area called Opinion Place, only two clicks away from the AOL Welcome Screen. As of 1999, AOL accounts for 60–70 percent of all household Internet traffic, and the composition of its members looks more "mainstream America" than the entire Internet population. Given this tremendous volume of potential respondents, The M/A/R/C Group opened access to some of its traditional competitors in the best interests of growing the online research business. Within the first two years of their existence, DMS had completed hundreds of surveys and over 1 million interviews.

The team of researchers at DMS had to solve some interesting problems in creating this business. How do you encourage online users to participate in 15-minute surveys? You create AOL Rewards, a frequent-flyer program for AOL subscribers, where points are earned for participating in surveys, as well as for buying products from merchants' AOL Web sites. The points can be redeemed for products from DMS' online catalog, but the vast majority of participants use their points to pay for their monthly AOL service fee.

In 1999 Opinion Place attracted hundreds of thousands of respondents per week, and participation is growing. But doesn't this violate the random sampling requirement of good survey research? DMS handles this by pre-qualifying whether a respondent is in the target population to be sampled. Upon entry to Opinion Place, a survey is randomly selected for a respondent, who is then put to the test of qualification. If they are qualified, they are sent into the survey. If they fail the qualification for the pre-selected survey, they are sent to a randomly chosen survey from those for which they qualified. Respondents do not select which survey they would "like" to respond to (which would create a serious self-selection bias). Instead, they are selected into a sample by their responses to the screening questions. Client companies have found that a major advantage to this approach is the ability to reach very specialized target populations, given AOL's wide reach across millions of consumers.

Major companies are finding that online market research increases the quality of survey data, reduces the data collection time, and reduces the cost of the study: it is a win-win-win. It enables companies to do survey research they could never do before: low costs lead to more studies, and iterative research to refine ideas. Companies are using previously difficult (or impossible) techniques such as including colored graphics, photos, and multimedia stimuli. JCPenney tested 60 styles of women's swimsuits in a survey, allowing complex branching and asking of different follow-up questions depending on earlier answers (very difficult to handle with mail surveys). A study can take only days from start to finish, with all study materials sent to and from a client via e-mail. In fact, a major packaged-goods manufacturer works with DMS to get feedback on concepts from thousands of consumers in less than 24 hours. They take the iterative approach to idea refinement, learning from each study. The velocity of this volume of information is unattainable in other research methods.

Finally, DMS claims that it charges 30–50 percent less for an equivalent survey undertaken in a mall or by mail. Proponents of online survey research point out that this capability is less than five years old, and that it will have its greatest impact in the area of global market research. Companies are increasingly interested in the preferences and behavior of the emerging economic elite in countries such as China, where they can contact those who are highly educated, high tech, and wired. Companies as diverse as Coca-Cola, Avon, the Discovery Channel, Hewlett-Packard, Hickory Farms, Kodak, Sprint, Starbucks, and Warner Bros. are using DMS' services and the services of others offering online marketing research. For example, IntelliQuest specializes in doing online product development research for PC hardware and software companies.

The main argument against online marketing research is that participants are not representative of the entire population of U.S. households. For example, AOL's Opinion Place respondents are younger, more highly educated, and somewhat more affluent than the average U.S. adult. They appear more likely to buy brands, try new products, and influence the purchase decision of others. But the questions companies must ask themselves remain: does the sample validly represent the desired marketing target? Can any method attract a sample representative of the U.S. population? Maybe the critics of online research (who are mostly research companies using telephone, mail, or mall intercept methods) are encountering their own problems as new technologies and changing attitudes impede interviews. What type of target customers are most easily reached by online market research? What target customers are not able to be reached by online market research? What are the greatest advantages of online market research?

Discussion Questions

1. What types of target customers are most easily reached by online market research? What target customers are not able to be reached by online market research?

2. What are the greatest advantages of online market research?

3. Almost all orders between retailers and manufacturers and between businesses will be done on the Internet within 10 years. What invaluable market research information will this generate to complement online market research?

Chapter 5

Consumer Behavior

Jagdish N. Sheth,
Emory University

Charles H. Kellstadt Professor of Marketing in the Goizueta Business School and founder of the Center for Relationship Marketing, Emory University. Dr. Sheth is also the author of *Customer Behavior: Consumer Behavior and Beyond* from The Dryden Press.

Dr. Sheth earned his Ph.D. and MBA from the University of Pittsburgh. He is a Distinguished Fellow of both the International Engineering Consortium and the Academy of Marketing Science. He has won numerous awards, including the P.D. Converse Award from the American Marketing Association, the 1989 Outstanding Marketing Educator Award from the Academy of Marketing Science, and the Viktor Mataja Medal from the Austrian Research Society in Vienna, Austria. He has served as past president of the American Psy-

I t is 4 o'clock on a cold winter morning. Consumers from all corners of Boston leave on their pilgrimage a few miles away. Also joining them are several out-of-towners, who came into town the previous evening and stayed with friends, relatives, or in hotels. They came just to join this consumer pilgrimage. The destination: Filene's Basement, an off-price clothing store. A store so famous that it attracts 15,000 to 20,000 shoppers per day. A Boston landmark, which is also a tourist attraction. On this particular day, the store is holding a special event—the Bridal Gown Sales, an event held four times a year, to clear unsold inventory. Filene's carries gowns that are regularly priced from $1,000 to $8,000. Today, they are marked down to $249—one and all.

The store will open at 8 A.M., but consumers start lining up at 5 A.M. to get a good place in line. As soon as the doors open, the crowd instantly turns into a frenzied mob, rushing in, running down the stairs to the basement store. There on racks are wedding gowns, thousands of them. Shoppers grab them by the dozen, with-

out regard to size or style. A thousand gowns disappear in less than one minute. The shopping teams hold on to the gowns, hoarding their inventory while someone—bride-to-be—tries them on one by one. Rather than wait for the fitting rooms to become available, the hopefuls don't mind undressing in the aisles, "public stripping" in plain view of bystanders. They try one on and then another. The gowns they discard are quickly grabbed by others waiting and hovering around the shopping teams. Media have described this event as "a magical event, a mystery tour, a lovable, thrilling hole in the ground, as transforming and madcap as Alice's entry into Wonderland."

By the end of the day, many lucky "Alices" will have walked away with the gown of their dreams. Many of them are soon-to-be-brides. But the lure of merchandise is such that others—with no wedding plans in the immediate future—also come seeking and purchasing the dress of their dreams—just in case! Filene's Basement—an extraordinary oasis of market value consumers seek; consumers—***brides, brides-to-be, and brides-wannabe alike.***[1]

chological Association's Consumer Psychology Division and also the Association for Consumer Research.

Prior to his present position, Dr. Sheth was the Robert E. Brooker Professor of Marketing at the University of Southern California and the founder of the Center for Telecommunications Management; the Walter H. Stellner Distinguished Professor of Marketing at the University of Illinois, and on the faculty of Columbia University, as well as the Massachusetts Institute of Technology. He has published more than 200 articles and research papers.

Dr. Sheth has worked for numerous industries and companies in the United States, Europe, and Asia, both as an advisor and as a seminar leader.

Learning Objectives

After you have completed this chapter, you should be able to:

1. Describe the three different roles of the consumer.

2. Differentiate between *needs* and *wants.*

3. Appreciate the differences between *seeing* and *perceiving*, and how this difference influences marketing efforts.

4. Understand the theories of *how people learn.*

5. Comprehend the facets of motivation, including Maslow's needs hierarchy and Reisman's social character theory.

6. Understand the process of consumer decision making.

7. Recognize the issues that generate conflict in family decision making and the tactics available for resolution of these conflicts.

DOMAIN OF CONSUMER BEHAVIOR

Consumer behavior

is the mental and physical activity undertaken by household and business consumers that result in decisions and actions to pay for, purchase, and use products.

Consumer behavior is the mental and physical activities undertaken by household and business customers that result in decisions and actions to pay for, purchase, and use products.[2] Our definition of consumer behavior includes a variety of activities and a number of roles that people hold as consumers. In addition to the actual purchaser (buyer), our definition of consumer includes payers as consumers and users as consumers. For example, a child may be the user but not the buyer or the payer, or in gift giving where the buyer and the payer are not the users. Figure 5.1 below illustrates consumer's behavior, as we will shortly explain.

Consumer behavior deals with the buying behavior of consumers for both goods and services. However, since there is a separate chapter on services marketing (Chapter 9) in this textbook, in this chapter we focus mainly on consumer's behavior as it may relate to goods. Similarly, though our definition of consumer behavior includes business customers, the focus in this chapter will be on household consumers since the behavior of business customers is covered in Chapter 6.

IMPORTANCE OF THE THREE ROLES

Needs

are unsatisfactory conditions of the consumer that lead him or her to actions that will make the conditions better.

Wants

are desires to obtain more satisfaction than is absolutely necessary to improve unsatisfactory conditions.

In identifying and satisfying consumer **needs** and **wants,** it is important to recognize the value of each consumer role. Ignore one of them and you lose the consumer. First and foremost, the ***user role*** is important in the very design of the product. The features of the product have to be the ones that the user is seeking and that will best meet the user's need or want. As seen in Figure 5.2, a pet is a good example of a user.

The other two roles are equally important. The ***payer role*** is critical, in that if the price or other financial considerations do not satisfy the payer, the user simply cannot buy the product. Without the payer, no sale will ever occur. The mushrooming of consumer credit card companies is testimony to this fact. Today, financing and leasing for consumers is a booming business. Affordability to the payer constrains marketplace transactions more than any other factor.

Finally, the ***buyer role*** is also important. The buyer's task is to find the merchandise and find a way to order or acquire it. If the buyer's access to the product is constrained, the buyer will simply not buy the product, and thus, the user will not have the product

---

Figure 5.1   Customers: Types, Roles, and Behaviors

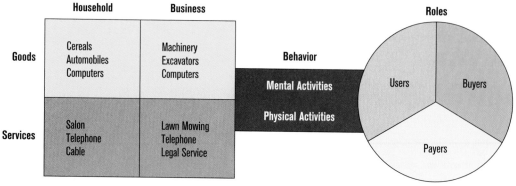

Figure 5.2   The User Is Neither a Payer nor a Buyer

available for use. For example, if the store is open only on weekdays and not on weekends, it will result in access problems. Also, if the product is not on the store shelf, it creates access problems.

To understand consumer behavior, we need to understand about consumers needs and wants, their perceptions, how they learn, their motivations and emotions, how they form attitudes, and how they make purchase decisions. This chapter will address each of these issues. In the following section, we will discuss the differences between consumers' needs and wants, as well as the factors that influence needs and wants.

CONSUMER NEEDS AND WANTS

To understand consumer behavior, we need to understand how consumers' perceive, learn, and make decisions to satisfy their needs and wants. In this section we will discuss the differences between consumers' needs and wants, as well as the factors that influence them.

It is important to understand what the needs and wants of users, payers, and buyers are. It is the needs and wants of consumers that marketers have to satisfy. A *need* is an unsatisfactory condition of the consumer that leads him or her to an action that will make the condition better. A *want* is a desire to obtain more satisfaction than is absolutely necessary to improve an unsatisfactory condition. The difference between a need and a want is that need arousal is driven by discomfort in a person's physical and psychological conditions, while wants occur when humans desire to take their physical and psychological conditions beyond the state of minimal comfort. Thus, food satisfies a need, and gourmet food additionally satisfies a want. Just any car satisfies a need for transportation from point A to point B, whereas a Miata, Porsche, or Lexus, in addition, satisfies a want to get the excitement of performance, or gain prestige among one's peers, or project the right self-image to significant others. Only when needs are satisfied do wants surface.

Needs and wants also differ because the factors that cause them are different. Consumer needs are determined by the *physical characteristics of the individual* and *the environment.* In contrast, consumer wants are determined by the *socioeconomic context of the individual* and *the environment.* This is represented in Figure 5.3.

Determination of Needs

Three physical characteristics of the individual person determine needs: *genetics, biogenics,* and *psychogenics.*

The science of **genetics** is a branch of science that deals with the heredity and chemical/biological characteristics of organisms. Recently, there has been an explosive growth in research and knowledge in this field. People in different parts of the world have different clusters of gene types, and their food and beverage habits and needs differ accordingly.

Another determinant of needs consists of the biological characteristics that people possess at birth, such as gender, race, and the age. The study of these characteristics is called **biogenics.** Biogenic characteristics create obvious differences in the needs of men and women, young and old, and whites and non-whites. Many consumption decisions are

www.lexus.com

Genetics

is a branch of science that deals with the heredity and chemical/biological characteristics of organisms.

Biogenics

is the study of the biological characteristics that people possess at birth, such as gender, race, and age.

Figure 5.3 Determinants of Customer Needs and Wants

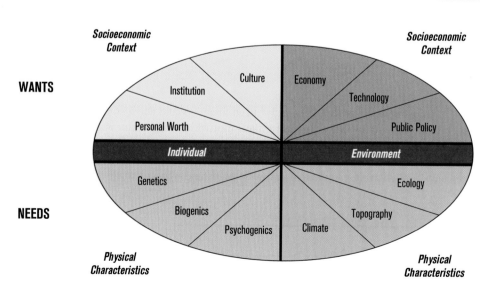

attempts to satisfy biogenic needs, such as drives of hunger, thirst, and sleep. For example, as people age beyond 50 years, they begin having difficulty falling asleep.

The third individual characteristic that affects needs is psychogenics—which refers to individual states and traits induced by a person's brain functioning. These states are represented by such entities as moods, emotions, perceptions, cognition, and experiences stored in the brain. Thus, mood swings and emotional states necessitate the consumption of certain products. For example, the need for social conversation and interaction, need for affection, need to succeed, need to feel in control, need for recreation, and need to express oneself are all psychogenic needs. Although these are not traditionally considered needs, their deprivation causes near traumatic discomfort on the person both physically and mentally. Thus, it is reasonable to classify these psychogenic effects as needs to the extent that their minimal satisfaction is imperative rather than discretionary.

Consumers often buy products to satisfy a need based on their mood or emotions, such as buying a greeting card, jewelry, perfume, or patriotically buying only nationally-produced products.

Three physical characteristics of the environment also affect consumer needs: climate, topography, and ecology.

Climate includes conditions such as temperature, altitude, and rainfall, which affect consumers' need for food, clothing, and shelter. For example, needs for clothing are different in cold climates versus those in warmer climates. As the marketplace continues to expand globally, and countries ship products around the world, packaging becomes more critical if there are significant climate differences.

The *topography* of a geographic area refers to the physical condition of the location on earth, the spatial profile of the territory (e.g., mountains or plains), and the presence of bodies of water (e.g., river, ocean, etc.). For example, consumers living in the mountains will need hiking boots, four-wheel-drive vehicles, and a whole range of other products. On the other hand, individuals living near water will be more likely to own boats and water skis.

The third physical characteristic of the environment that influences consumer needs is *ecology,* which includes the quality of air, the ozone layer, and the food chain. Ozone pollution at ground level (due to smog) affects the quality of the air we breathe, resulting in ozone alerts that keep individuals with heart or breathing conditions indoors on those days. Similarly, pollen in the atmosphere at the onset of spring or fall affects a large portion of people who suffer from cough and cold allergies. Both of these ecological concerns can affect individuals' activity levels and need for medication.

Determination of Wants

People's wants are determined by two factors: the personal context and the environmental context surrounding the consumers. The personal context consists of three dimensions: personal worth, institutional relationships, and cultural surroundings.

Personal worth refers to the financial resources available to a consumer. These comprise a person's income, assets, inheritance, and borrowing power. These resources influence wants by giving the consumer the purchasing power to buy products that would satisfy more than the basic, physical needs. Thus, rather than merely buying a car, a person with economic resources is able to buy a luxury car with higher driving thrill and greater social prestige.

The *institutional relationships* context refers to the groups and organizations a person belongs to. The institutional context includes the workplace, religious and educational institutions, family and friends, and peer groups. All of these serve as settings that can shape our wants as users, payers, and buyers. The workplace may require a uniform particular style of clothing or a particular type of footwear. For example, the Southern Baptist church influenced the buying activities of many of its members when it advised its members to boycott the Walt Disney company when the American Broadcasting

Psychogenics
refers to the study of individual states and traits induced by a person's brain functioning.

Personal worth
refers to the financial resources available to a consumer. These comprise a person's income, assets, inheritance, and borrowing power.

Institutional context
refers to the groups and organizations a person belongs to. The institutional context includes the workplace, religious and educational institutions, family and friends, and peer groups.

www.disney.go.com
www.abc.com

Corporation (ABC), a television network owned by Disney, did not drop the series of a lesbian star.

The third dimension affecting wants comes from the consumers' **cultural surroundings context.** Culture's influence on consumers is pervasive, for culture shapes everything we do, desire, or become. For example, in some cultures, people are valued for who they are, rather than for what they possess. Consumers in these cultures are less likely to seek the conspicuous consumption of goods. Similarly, some cultures value age (for age is supposed to give wisdom), while others value youth. Consumers from the former culture are less likely to want anti-aging products (such as plastic surgery), compared with consumers from the latter culture.

The environmental context also consists of three dimensions: *economy, technology,* and *public policy.*

Economy refers to economic development and business cycles in a nation's economy. The economic level of a nation, the level of inflation, unemployment rate, and wage and income growth, all have an impact on consumers. For example, high inflation can impact a consumer's decision not to purchase a house because interest rates may be too high, or it may influence a business company to postpone capital budget spending if the money is to be borrowed at a high interest rate.

The environmental influence of **technology** on consumers' wants is manifested in many ways. Technology consists of the man-made inventions and devices used to sustain, facilitate, and enhance human life and activities. With respect to infrastructure, some countries have better technology deployment, such as the transportation, energy, telecommunications, or educational systems. The proposed national information superhighway will similarly influence business consumers' wants for new communications services. For example, the electronic commerce is dramatically changing the way business consumers order products and process payments.

The final influence within the environmental context is **public policy,** especially as it relates to market behavior. Public policy refers to governmental laws and regulations that control human behavior. For example, in Saudi Arabia and Kuwait, public policies have been enacted to create a dress code for women. Likewise, in Singapore and Malaysia very strong policy initiatives have been instituted to make drug usage a crime punishable by death in most cases. Most business practices such as product safety and reliability, advertising and promotion, and pricing practices are regulated by public policy.

PERCEPTION

Perception
is the process by which an individual selects, organizes, and interprets the information received from the environment.

The objective reality of a product matters little; what matters is the consumer's **perception** of a product or a brand. The sometimes dramatic difference between perception and reality is illustrated in Figure 5.4. Perception is the process by which an individual selects, organizes, and interprets the information he or she receives from the environment. Marketers want to understand the sources of consumer perceptions and to influence them. For example, cereals are sometimes produced darker in color to make them appear more masculine, while mouthwashes are colored green or blue to connote a clean, fresh feeling.

The perceptual process in consumer behavior, illustrated in Figure 5.5, consists of three steps: sensation, organization, and interpretation.

1. *Sensation*—attending to an object or an event in the environment with one or more of the five senses: seeing, hearing, smelling, touching, and tasting. Examples include the sensation of an aircraft taking off or feeling the texture and taste of a hot, juicy hamburger at a particular restaurant.

2. *Organization*—categorizing by matching the sensed stimulus with similar object categories in one's memory. In the example of eating a hamburger, organization

Figure 5.4   Confronting the Problem of Customer (Mis)Perception Head On

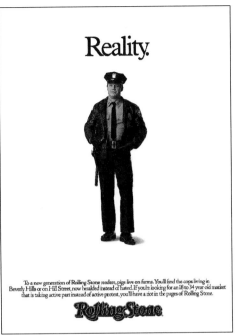

Figure 5.5   Stages in Customer Perception

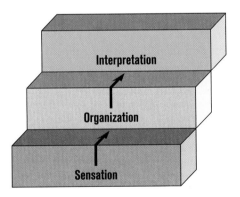

occurs as the consumer identifies all the ingredients and classifies the hamburger as a specific type similar to or different from the ones he or she has eaten before.

3. *Interpretation*—attaching meaning to the stimulus, forming a "ruling" as to whether it is an object you like, and of what value it would be to you, the perceiver. In the

hamburger example, interpretation occurs when the consumer judges whether the hamburger tastes good and whether you like it more or less than those eaten before.

www.tacobell.com

Taco Bell restaurants, for example, currently feature a bright purple and green motif in their interiors, replacing a somewhat lackluster look of the past. When they made this change a few years ago, the new colors were so significantly different from before, that most customers inevitably sensed the change. Moreover, given the prior associations most people have had with bright, neon colors, customers readily interpreted the new motifs to signify youthfulness and an upbeat ambience.

Factors that Shape Perception

Perception is not merely a matter of objectively absorbing the stimuli present in the environment. There are three factors that shape consumer perceptions: the characteristics of the stimulus, the context of the stimulus, and the characteristics of the perceiver (consumer).

> **Stimulus Characteristics**—The nature of the information from the environment.
>
> **Context**—The setting in which the information is received; this includes social, cultural, and organizational contexts.
>
> **Consumer Characteristics**—Personal knowledge and experiences, including the consumer's expertise on the relevant topic and prior experience with similar stimuli.

Stimulus Characteristics

People will perceive a stimulus differently depending on its *stimulus characteristics.* For example, you might respond differently to a salesperson depending on whether he is wearing pinstripes or a plaid jacket. When evaluating stimulus characteristics, marketers need to consider both their sensory characteristics and informational content. A characteristic is *"sensory"* if it stimulates any of the five senses. Strong sensory characteristics include bright colors, loud noises, and strong aromas. These strong characteristics tend to attract more attention (and thus are perceived more strongly) than weak sensory characteristics. The other characteristic of a stimulus that shapes perception is its *informational content.* Assuming that through its sensory characteristics, an advertisement has caught the customer's attention, achieved sensation, or sense perception; next, how consumers come to perceive the advertised brand depends on the information in the advertisement. Informational content moves the perceptual process beyond sensation, toward organization and interpretation.

Context

Context
is the setting in which the information is received; this includes social, cultural, and organizational contexts.

In perceiving a stimulus with a given set of characteristics, consumers will also be influenced by the **context** of the stimulus.[3] Say a restaurant waiter presents a polite but impersonal demeanor. A waiter with this style could be deemed unfriendly in a low- to mid-price, mass-market restaurant such as Denny's—a restaurant chain in the United Sates. The same mannerism in an upscale European restaurant may be perceived, on the other hand, as respectful (not getting too personal).

Consumer Characteristics

Finally, perceptions are influenced by *consumer characteristics*—personal knowledge and experiences, including their expertise on the relevant topic and prior experience with similar stimuli. Such prior knowledge and feelings become expectations—prior beliefs about what something will possess or offer. Expectations influence perception in that we often end up seeing what we expect to see. This is called *confirmatory bias.* There are also other biases that occur in the perceptual process of consumers.

Biases in the Perceptual Process

To cope with the barrage of marketing communications (and other information in everyday life), consumers become "selective." They screen out some of the "noise" by employing three selective processes: selective exposure, selective attention, and selective interpretation.

Selective Exposure

Of the more than 3,000 marketing communications that a typical consumer is potentially exposed during a typical week, only a small number achieve actual exposure. Consumers *seek out* some advertisements, some shelf displays, some salespersons or other sources of information, while *avoiding* others, depending on their needs and interests of the moment. For example, think about how many times you have visited the same mall and how many stores here you have never even set foot in. In these and other ways, consumers choose to selectively expose themselves to market communications.

Selective Attention

Even if an advertisement or a product display manages to come face-to-face with a consumer, the consumer may still choose to ignore it if it does not relate to his or her interests. Initially, a person's attention is impelled by the stimulus characteristics of contrast and vividness. Beyond, the initial attention, however, a person's further processing of a stimulus advertisement or display depends on the personal interest the featured product arouses.

Selective Interpretation

Consumers also interpret the content and message of marketing communications selectively. People generally view a political message or a political candidate, for example, positively or negatively, based on their political affiliation. Similarly, after an important purchase, consumers seek communication that will reassure them about the wisdom of their selection. Consumers also distort negative information that might threaten their ego. This phenomenon is called ***perceptual distortion*** and refers to information being interpreted by a person in a manner that makes it more consistent with his or her personal beliefs than it objectively is.

Perceptual Threshold

The perception process has been described as consisting of sensation, organization, and interpretation. Of these, sensation is the most important; if it fails, then the marketing stimulus is rendered totally inconsequential. But not every stimulus gets sensed. Imagine sitting in your classroom. You have been here before—every week this semester. Now take a look around the room. Are the lights today somewhat dimmer than before? No? Are you absolutely sure? What if the university authorities decided to lower the lights just a tad in all the campus buildings? That small decrease in light illumination can save the university a bundle, and you wouldn't even notice it. You don't notice this change because it is below your ***perceptual threshold,*** the minimum level or magnitude at which a stimulus begins to be sensed. A related concept is the ***just noticeable difference.*** This refers to the magnitude of change necessary for the change to be noticed. Some years ago, M&M/Mars successfully reduced the size of its candy bars by keeping the size change small.

www.m-ms.com

www.mars.com

LEARNING

Learning is a change in the content of long-term memory. As humans, we learn because what we learn helps us respond better to our environment. Thus, a child who accidentally puts his hand on a hot electric bulb learns never again to touch anything resembling that

Learning
is a change in the content of long-term memory. As humans, we learn because what we learn helps us respond better to our environment.

Careers in Marketing

Why Study Consumer Behavior?

As we begin the next century, understanding the consumer will be the key to business success. It is the first step toward meeting the challenges of the exciting world of business. The study of consumer behavior provides the basic knowledge necessary for successful business decisions.

Studying and understanding consumer behavior opens several avenues for a student embarking on a career in the field of marketing. A person with a good understanding of consumer behavior understands the underlying reasons as to why consumers are loyal to a brand. Having knowledge about the psychology and sociology of consumers helps the *Brand Manager* in preparing strategies for his/her business. Thus, studying consumer behavior can lead to a career in brand management.

Similarly, understanding the psychology of consumers can help one to secure a position as an *Account Executive* in an advertising agency. Knowing how consumers will react to certain types of cues should help determine the advertising strategy for different brands in different industries.

If a student has strong quantitative and analytical skills, a course in consumer behavior will be useful in conjunction with marketing research courses in securing a market research analyst position. As a *market research analyst* who understands consumer behavior, one is able to provide a deeper insight into what the numbers mean. This helps provide better recommendations to top management.

Some students become very fascinated by the field of consumer behavior and pursue a masters and even a doctorate in this field. They thus work at developing the knowledge in the field and further our understanding of consumers.

---

object again. A consumer who gets trapped into buying a substandard product from a mail-order firm on nonreturnable terms of purchase learns never again to buy anything from that firm. Thus, human learning is directed at *acquiring a potential for future adaptive behavior.*

Mechanisms of Learning

As consumers, we face a marketplace environment of a multitude of product choices; we learn to adapt and respond to this environment. There are four different mechanisms of learning: cognitive learning, classical conditioning, instrumental conditioning, and modeling.

Cognitive Learning

When people talk about learning, they often are thinking of *cognitive learning,* or acquiring new information from written or oral communication. When we acquire information about something, whether incidentally and passively or deliberately and actively, we learn. Much of our learning about products comes this way.

Cognitive learning occurs on two levels: rote memorization and problem solving. With *rote memorization,* we rehearse the information until it gets firmly lodged in our long-term memory. This can occur actively (memorizing a phone number) or passively (from repeated exposure to a stimuli). A great deal of advertising aims simply to create a rote memory of the brand name by repeated presentation. *Problem solving,* on the other hand, is a type of cognitive learning that occurs when the consumer is actively processing information (weighing it, discounting some, combining and integrating disparate pieces of information) to reach certain judgments. We often go through the problem solving process when making purchasing decisions.

Classical Conditioning

Pavlov's experiment with his dog is very famous. Ivan Pavlov, a Russian psychologist, studied human learning processes by experimenting on animals. Pavlov harnessed a dog, gave him some meat powder, and observed that the dog salivated. This salivation is an inherited reflex. Next, he rang a bell just before giving the meat powder, repeating this sequence several times. Then he merely rang the bell without giving any meat powder. The dog, however, still salivated. The dog was said to have been *conditioned* to salivate to the bell ringing. It had learned a salivating response to the bell.

It should be noted that the salivating response to the meat powder itself did not have to be learned, since it already existed as an instinctual response. Rather, the transfer (i.e., conditioning) of this response to a previously neutral stimulus (the bell) what constitutes "learning." In this experiment, the meat powder is called an unconditioned stimulus, and the bell is called the conditioned stimulus. ***Unconditioned stimulus*** refers to a stimulus toward which a consumer already has a pre-existing specific response, so the response to it does not have to be conditioned. ***Conditioned stimulus*** is a stimulus to which the consumer either does not have a response, or has a pre-existing response that needs modification, so a new response needs to be conditioned.[4] ***Classical conditioning*** is the process in which a person learns an association between two stimuli due to their constant appearance as a pair. Because of this constant pairing, consumers tend to attribute to the previously unknown stimulus whatever they think or feel about the paired other stimulus.

Classical conditioning is pervasive in our daily lives. Marketers use this principle in pairing their brand with a likable celebrity. The celebrity's personality, by classical conditioning, rubs onto the product itself. Thus, CK perfume is more "youthful" because of the teenage models used in the brand's advertising. Similarly, while Coca-Cola used "Mean" Joe Greene to convey its "real-thing" image, Pepsi has used Michael Jackson and Michael J. Fox to promote its "New Generation" image.

Instrumental Conditioning

The third learning mechanism is ***instrumental conditioning,*** whereby we learn to respond in certain ways because they are rewarding; that is, a response is *instrumental* to obtaining a reward. We frequent a particular restaurant because we always find the food there satisfying. We visit the same barber because the haircut is always perfect. Marketers use this learning mechanism through instrumental conditioning when they make the product its own intrinsic reward. But when a brand becomes a *parity* brand with no intrinsically superior rewards compared to its competing brands, marketers offer extrinsic rewards—coupons, sweepstakes, or rebates—to attract consumer patronage. The best examples of instrumental conditioning learning are the frequent-flier programs that accumulate mileage toward future free-flight rewards.

Modeling

The fourth mechanism of learning is ***modeling,*** whereby we learn by observing others. Children learn much of their social behavior by observing the elders around them. Some psychologists have found that we imitate the behavior of those whom we see rewarded, because we expect to be rewarded ourselves by adopting that behavior, either by the person we model or by others who admire that person.

We may model our behavior based on persons superior in the age hierarchy (as is common in eastern countries like Japan and India) or grade hierarchy (as in Western countries like the U.S.). We may also model our behavior based on social status, or people who are superior in intelligence.

MOTIVATION

Motivation is what moves people—the driving force for all human behavior. More formally, it is defined as the state of drive or arousal that impels behavior toward a goal-object. Thus, motivation has two components: (1) drive or arousal and (2) goal-object. A *drive* is an internal state of tension that produces actions purported to reduce that tension. A *goal-object* is something in the external world whose acquisition will reduce the tension. Arousal or drive provides the energy to act; the goal-object provides the direction for one to channel that energy. As an analogy, the arousal or drive is akin to "stepping on the

www.cocacola.com
www.pepsi.com

Motivation
is the state of drive or arousal that impels behavior toward a goal-object.

accelerator pedal" in an automobile, while the goal-object is analogous to the steering of the vehicle. Having one without the other is not productive.

Facets of Motivation

Whatever the direction of motivation, it manifests in five facets: needs, emotions, involvement, psychographics, and attitudes. Needs are gaps between the desired and the current state, and lend themselves more readily to cognitive consciousness and appraisal. Emotions and moods are self-governed feelings and engender more personal experience. Involvement is a measure of a person's attachment to or interest in a product, activity, or service and can direct the degree of motivation. Psychographics combines psychological and behavioral characteristics of individuals that drive their motivations. Attitudes are learned predispositions that often affect consumers' motivations.

Consumer Needs

The concept of needs and wants described earlier is closely aligned to the concept of motivation. There is a nearly infinite number of possible needs a human could possess. To make sense of them, psychologists and consumer researchers have suggested various categories of needs. Among the most relevant to marketers is Maslow's needs hierarchy.

Maslow's Hierarchy of Needs

According to psychologist Abraham Maslow, human needs and wants are arranged in a hierarchy. Higher level needs are dormant until lower level needs are satisfied. As shown in Figure 5.6, Maslow's hierarchy of needs consists of (from lowest to highest):

1. Physiological needs

2. Safety and security needs

3. Belongingness and love needs

4. Esteem and ego needs

5. Need for self-actualization[5]

A person "progresses" to higher-level needs if the lower-level needs are satisfied; he or she "regresses" back to lower-level needs should these needs become unsatisfied again. Maslow does not distinguish between needs and wants, but most contemporary books on marketing do. According to this distinction, only the first two levels—physiological and safety—are "needs," while the last three levels are "wants."

Examples of Maslow's needs abound. Physiological needs lead consumers to strive for, purchase, and use food, clothing, and shelter. For all humans, these needs are paramount. For many, such as those below the poverty line, these needs remain perpetually less than adequately met so that they never rise to higher-level needs.

At the next level, safety and security concerns are what is responsible for many people's fear of flying, for example, and the motivation for buying insurance against various uncertainties of life. Personal safety is a motive as old as survival itself—early man developed arrows and spears to kill predatory animals that threatened his survival. In marketing terms, automobile safety is becoming a major concern, reflected in the renewed emphasis on safety features by almost all carmakers. For example, Volvo appeals to the concern for this need in all their advertisements with their slogan—"Drive Safely."

Social motives of belongingness and love are evident when consumers want to buy products that are well regarded by others, so that the use of those products brings the user

www.volvo.com

Figure 5.6 Maslow's Needs Hierarchy

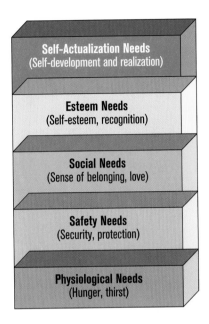

their peers' approval, affection, and a sense of belonging. Many products, such as greeting cards, flowers, and other kinds of gifts, are bought specifically to promote relationships between individuals. Marketers, such as those employed by greeting card manufacturers, have been credited with promoting Mother's Day, Father's Day, Boss's Day, Secretary's Day, Mother-in-Law's Day, and the like. In these cases, the marketers are hoping to cash in on consumers' needs to conform and belong.

Next, we all work hard to gain success in our individual sphere of activity and to acquire the qualities others consider desirable and virtuous, so that we may win our own and others' esteem. We also buy products we deem fitting of our esteem. Beyond impressing others, we even buy and give gifts to ourselves because we feel we "we deserve it."

Finally, once these physiological, safety, social, and esteem needs are satisfied, people begin to explore and extend the bounds of their potential—seeking self-actualization. This self-actualization motive is what is behind a person engaging in self-improvement activities, such as taking an adult education course or tenaciously pursuing a skill towards perfection. The U.S. Army's slogan "Be All You Can Be" is a call to a person's need for self-actualization. The Marine Corps advertisement shown in Figure 5.7 conveys the same message.

www.army.mil

Consumer Emotions

Needs and emotions are closely related. Similar to needs, emotions are also capable of energizing the person toward relevant goal-objects. Felt deprivations of desired goal-objects (which engender the drive) are experienced in consciousness as negative emotion. The attainment of goal-objects (which causes the drive to subside) is experienced in consciousness as positive emotion. We all seek positive emotional experiences and avoid negative emotional experiences. Much of the consumption or use of products is driven by and immersed in emotion.

Figure 5.7   A Call to Need for Self-Actualization

As humans, we are creatures of emotion. Emotions lace our lives and guide everyday actions. We cuddle a baby because we feel affection and love for it. We swear at a rude driver who cuts in front of us because we feel anger and frustration. Although we have all experienced emotion, it is not easy to define because that emotion is a complex set of processes occurring simultaneously. Emotions are awareness of the occurrence of some physiological arousal, followed by a behavioral response, combined along with the appraised meaning of both. Thus, emotions have three components: physiological, cognitive, and behavioral.[6]

Let's say you are going about your day. Suddenly a stimulus appears before you (e.g., the shadow of some intruder in the dark). Instantly and automatically, your nervous system is aroused: that is, you feel a tremor in the visceral system; you perspire. This is the physiological component, and because it occurs by reflex, almost automatically, it is called "autonomic" arousal. Then follows cognitive interpretation or "meaning analysis"—what does the stimulus mean: For example, is the intruder a friend or a foe? This is the cognitive component. Depending on the cognitive appraisal and the meaning you make of the initial stimulus, there can be further autonomic arousal (or reduced arousal, when the nervous system is "calming down"). If the intruder is a friend, your arousal calms down; if a foe, you experience more arousal. Almost instantaneously, you act out a behavioral response. Thus, you flee if the intruder is a foe and approach if the person is a friend.

Consumer Moods

Do you recall the last time you really enjoyed shopping? Maybe you were in a bookstore such as Border's, and some especially mellow music was playing. You relaxed and lingered on, browsing through the books on the "new release" shelves. Maybe you ended up buying four books that day. That is the power of positive mood! This is the same reason many online storefronts have audio files attached such that when you visit their Web site, you hear music playing in the background.

Moods are simply emotions felt less intensely; they are also short-lived. They are easy to induce, and they appear and disappear in consciousness frequently and readily. They are pervasive in that we are always in some kind of mood—happy mood or sad mood, pensive mood or "brain dead" mood, irritated or pleased, amused or bored. Moods affect our behavior of the moment in general and our response to the marketing activities to which we might be exposed at the time. For this reason, moods are important for marketers to understand.

Moods are induced both by external stimuli as well as internally by autistic thinking—that is, recalling some past incident or fantasizing about some event. Among the marketing stimuli that can induce positive or negative moods are:

▼ The ambiance of the store,

▼ The demeanor of the salesperson,

▼ The sensory features of the product, and

▼ The tone and manner of advertising.

Mood states have consequences in terms of the favorable or unfavorable consumer response to marketer efforts. We would simply not buy from salespersons who put us in an unpleasant mood—for example, by not indicating that they appreciate our business. Research studies indicate that consumers linger longer in positive mood environments, recall those advertisements more that had created positive moods, and feel more positive toward brands based on advertising that creates feelings of warmth.[7]

Emotions and moods drive a host of consumption behaviors. While detergents, microwave ovens, and insurance policies are purchased and used for some utilitarian/functional end-states, other such goods—such as perfumes, colognes, and bubble baths—and activities—such as sports, theater, and going to the movies—and so on, are used or engaged in purely for the emotional or hedonic values they provide. *Hedonic consumption* refers to the use of products for the sake of intrinsic enjoyment rather than to solve some problem in the physical environment. More specifically, hedonism refers to sensory pleasure. Many products such as those mentioned above are bought based on the emotional appeal they represent or the mood of the consumer at the time of purchase.

Involvement

Involvement is a general term that can be defined as the degree of personal relevance of a product to a consumer—how important or *central* it is to his lifestyle. Some consumers who are interested in hunting may be involved with a decision to purchase guns. Others who have pets, but are not interested in hunting, may be involved in decisions regarding pet foods rather than with guns. Furthermore, involvement is a matter of degree—how relevant or how central a product is. We can expand the definition of involvement to refer, beyond relevance, to the degree to which a consumer finds a product of interest. While table salt and golf clubs are both relevant to consumers, it is quite likely that

www.borders.com/

Involvement

is the degree of personal relevance of a product to a consumer.

they would be more involved (interested) in a decision concerning golf clubs rather than table salt.

Involvement, defined as the degree of interest, can be viewed as having two forms: enduring involvement and situational involvement. ***Enduring involvement*** is the degree of interest a consumer feels about a product on an ongoing basis. In contrast, ***situational involvement*** is the degree of interest in a specific situation or on a specific occasion, such as when buying a product or when consuming something in the presence of an important client or friend. Consumers typically are not very interested in dishwashers. But when a dishwasher breaks down and has to be replaced, they get very involved in the decision to buy a dishwasher. However, this involvement is temporary and ceases to exist once the problem is solved. Hence, this would be situational involvement. Some consumers are interested in knowing more about computers, irrespective of whether they are purchasing one or not. This kind of involvement does not depend on the situation but is enduring in nature. The extreme form of enduring involvement is *deep involvement.*

Psychographics

Psychographics
are characteristics of individuals that describe them in terms of their psychological and behavioral makeup.

The fourth facet of motivation is psychographics. **Psychographics** are characteristics of individuals that describe them in terms of their psychological and behavioral makeup—how people occupy themselves (in terms of behavior) and what psychological factors underlie that activity pattern. People's need to seek affiliation or peer approval may make them engage in going to theaters or playing golf. Theater-going or playing golf thus becomes part of their psychographics. This psychographic in turn drives them to buy golf equipment or do whatever is needed to implement that particular psychographic; it thus becomes motivational. Psychographics have three components: values, self-concept, and lifestyles.

Values

Values
are end-states of life, the goals one lives for.

When you think about what is important to you in life, you are thinking about your values. **Values** are end-states of life, the goals one lives for. Psychologist Milton Rokeach has identified two groups of these: terminal and instrumental. **Terminal values** are the goals we seek in life (e.g., peace and happiness), whereas **instrumental values** are the means or behavioral standards by which we pursue these goals (e.g., honesty).

Terminal values
are the goals we seek in life.

Consumer researchers felt a need for values more directly relevant to everyday consumer behavior. For this purpose, consumer researches Lynn Kahle and his associates developed a List of Values (LOV), consisting of nine terminal values:

Instrumental values
are the means or behavioral standards by which we pursue our goals.

1. Self-respect.
2. Self-fulfillment.
3. Security.
4. Sense of belonging.
5. Excitement.
6. Sense of accomplishment.
7. Fun and enjoyment.
8. Being well respected.
9. Warm relationships with others.[8]

Marketing often links product attributes to customer values. One of the basic tenets of marketing has been that consumers don't buy goods or services; rather, they buy benefits. Thus, when consumers buy an automobile, they are not buying simply 5,000 pounds of sheet metal; they are buying transportation. When they want a car with ergonomic seats, the shape and construction of the seats have no use to them if they did not make their body feel comfortable. A car that can accelerate from 0 to 60 miles per hour in 7 seconds versus 10 seconds has no meaning if it does not translate into greater driving thrill.

But we need not stop here. We can ask, "Why is it important to consumers to experience a greater driving thrill, to have their bodies sit comfortably, or to have transportation?" The possible answers would be to overcome the physical distance barrier, or to escape to a more desirable place, to master the machine, and to get a sense of using material tools for bodily comfort. Ultimately, then, the product features make sense only because they serve some fundamental needs (as in Maslow's hierarchy) or values (as in "List of Values"). Identifying the connections between product features on the one hand, and consumers' fundamental needs and values on the other, is important if marketers are to design features that would offer value to consumers.

Self-Concept

Everyone has a self-image—who he or she is. This is called self-concept. Furthermore, the self-concept includes an idea of what the person currently is and what he or she would like to become. These two concepts are respectively called *actual self* and *ideal self.*

Self-concepts influence a person's consumption deeply, for people live their self-concepts in large measure by what they consume. For example, some business students who in their senior years begin to think of themselves as businesspersons, begin to dress like one, retiring their baseball caps and sneakers. According to one report, many Generation X youth, now past their teen years, have begun to nurture a self-concept of being a "grown-up, responsible person," and consequently, they are flocking to tattoo parlors to take off their body tattoos—the same tattoos that they had proudly sported as badges of rebellion.

Individuals have their self-concepts as individuals in general, of course. But they also have a self-concept of themselves, which varies, in part, according to the consumer role they play. The three consumer roles we described earlier were that of users, payers, and buyers. In the role of user, an individual could have the self-concept of a very discerning connoisseur, user, or a very involved user. The payer could think of himself as having the self-concept of being thrifty, financially prudent, or personifying the attitude that "money is no object to me." Finally, the buyer could have the self-concept of being a convenience seeker, or a service seeker, or being a very time-conscious individual.

Self-concept
refers to a person's self-image.

Lifestyle

Along with what we think of ourselves and what we value, psychographics describes us in terms of lifestyles, or the way we live. *Lifestyle* is determined by (a) a consumer's personal characteristics, namely, genetics, race, gender, age, and personality; (b) his or her personal context, namely, culture, institutions, reference groups, and personal worth; and (c) needs and emotions. These three sets of factors together influence the pattern of our activities—how we spend time and money.

Values and Lifestyles (VALS)

One of the most used psychographic profiling schemes is called *VALS* (Values and Lifestyle). Developed by SRI International, Inc., its first version (VALS 1) divides the entire U.S. population into nine groups, based on the identities they seek and implement via marketplace behaviors. According to SRI, "People pursue and acquire products and experiences that provide satisfaction and give shape, substance, and character to their identities."[9] Although this scheme has been replaced by an eight-segment classification (called VALS 2), the original scheme, introduced in 1978, is important to understand. The scheme used two dimensions for its conceptual foundation: (1) Maslow's hierarchy (as we have discussed earlier in this chapter)—the theory that people rise from physiological, to safety, to social belonging, to self-esteem, to self-actualization motivations; and (2) *Riesman's Social Character Theory*—that people are either inner-directed or outer-directed, deriving their code of conduct respectively from themselves or from others. Inner-directed

www.future.sri.com

persons are more independent-minded, whereas outer-directed persons are concerned with the opinions of others.

At the bottom of the VALS hierarchy are *Survivors* and *Sustainers,* who are, respectively, the elderly poor and unemployed youth. *Belongers* is the next group, the largest of the nine groups and comprising middle-aged, middle-class, outer-directed Americans. Along with the Belongers, the two other outer-directed groups are called *Emulators* and *Achievers.* Achievers are the most affluent, successful professionals and businesspeople. In contrast, Emulators don't have as much money or success, but try to emulate the lifestyles of achievers. On the other side are three inner-directed segments, *"I-am-me's," Experientials,* and *Societally Conscious.* "I-am-me's" are teenagers with rebellion against the established ways as their principal motto. Experientials are big on experiencing all the sensory and recreational experiences life has to offer—mountaineering, skiing, sports, travel, and so on. The Societally Conscious are concerned about and work for larger, societal issues such as the environment, world peace, and racial harmony. Finally, the group at the top is the *Integrateds,* a small group that has gained material well-being and success in the material world and is at the same time working for larger issues or in jobs that give some intrinsic meaning to life rather than merely fame and wealth.

Attitude

Attitudes
are learned predispositions to respond to an object or class of objects in a consistently favorable or unfavorbale way.

Gordon Allport, the psychologist, writes that "**attitudes** are learned predispositions to respond to an object or class of objects in a consistently favorable or unfavorable way."[10] This definition has several implications:

▼ Attitudes are learned. That is, they get formed on the basis of some experience with or without information about the object.

▼ Attitudes are predispositions. As such they reside in the mind.

▼ Attitudes cause consistent response. They precede and produce behavior.

Therefore, attitudes can be used to predict behavior. If we know that your attitude toward a candidate in some election is positive, then we could reasonably predict that you are likely to vote for that candidate. Marketers therefore measure attitudes before launching new products. Alternatively, behavior can be used to infer the underlying attitudes. In everyday life, we observe somebody's behavior toward us and use that observation to infer whether that person likes us; we then use that inferred attitude to predict how the person will behave toward us in the future. Marketers, too, often use this logic. When consumers buy a product, this purchase behavior is used to infer a favorable attitude toward the related product class, which is in turn deemed to be an indicator of the potential purchase of an item in the related product class.

Attitudes, then, are our evaluations of objects—people, places, brands, products, organizations, and so on. People evaluate in terms of their goodness, likability, or desirability. Consumers may hold attitudes toward salespeople in general (for example, "Salespeople are basically all hucksters"), or about specific companies (such as, "Company X is a company that makes good electronic appliances but not good computers").

CONSUMER DECISION MAKING

Many psychological concepts and processes involved in consumer behavior have been described thus far. They include consumers' needs and wants, perception, learning, motivation, and attitude formation. Consumers use all or some of these processes when they make decisions to buy (or not buy) a product. Household purchase decisions are sometimes

Got a negative attitude toward milk—that, somehow, it is not for the adult you are? Look again. In this campaign by the National Fluid Milk Processor Promotion Board, the milk mustache has appeared on the lips of such celebrities as Danny DeVito, Conan O'Brien, Bob Costas, Martha Stewart, Pete Sampras, Jennifer Aniston, Larry King, Dennis Rodman, and even Bill Clinton and Bob Dole. Shown here is Mark McGwire, sporting the now famous milk mustache.

made by individuals in households; at other times, they are made collectively by groups of people, including spouses and children. There are similarities and differences in these decision processes. The individual consumer decision making is described next, and this is followed by household decision making.

Individual Consumer Decision Making

We had earlier discussed three different roles that consumers adopt in the decision-making scenario—buyer, payer, and user. In each of these roles, consumers constantly face choices—how much to spend, what alternative to acquire, and where to purchase it from. These choices call for consumers to make decisions. Typically, these decisions include *whether* to purchase, *what* to purchase, *when* to purchase, from *whom* to purchase, and *how* to pay for it. Consumers have finite resources by way of money and time, and hence they have to constantly weigh the possibility of either postponing or forsaking the purchase of a product. You may have to scrap a vacation plan because you have to study for a test (lack of time), or postpone buying a Lexus until you have landed your dream job (lack of money). Thus, we constantly make decisions about *whether* to purchase and *what* to purchase at the product level.

An important consumer behavior at this category level decision is ***mental budgeting***—how the budget consumers set for a product category guides their subsequent behavior as a consumer. The payer plays the most important role in case of mental budgeting, as the user is constrained by what the payer has budgeted and whether the product

Figure 5.8   Coustomer Decision Making Process

is within the budget. This occurs even when the same consumer is playing both the payer and user roles.

Following the choice at the product level, the consumer makes another "what to purchase" decision—a choice among brands. Thus, illustratively, if a "product category level" decision is made—namely, "take the vacation"—the next decision is which brand to purchase (e.g., which travel destination to select, and how to get there, and so on).

The process of consumer decision making consists of the steps shown in Figure 5.8.

Step 1: Problem Recognition

The decision-making process begins with a consumer recognizing a problem to be solved or a need to be satisfied. The consumer notices, for example, that he or she is hungry and needs to get some food; that the light bulb in the patio has blown out and needs replacement; that the roof has begun to leak and needs repairing. As these examples illustrate, a consumer "problem" is not necessarily a physical problem such as a hungry stomach. Rather a *consumer problem* is any state of deprivation, discomfort, or wanting (whether physical or psychological) felt by a person. **Problem recognition** is a realization by the consumer that he or she needs to buy something to get back to the normal state of comfort.

Problem recognition can occur due to either an internal stimulus or an external stimulus. **Internal stimuli** are perceived states of discomfort—physical or psychological (e.g., hunger or boredom, respectively). **External stimuli** are informational cues from the marketplace that lead the consumer to realize the problem (see Figure 5.9). Thus, an advertisement about multivitamins can serve as a purchase reminder, or the smell of coffee coming from a restaurant coffee house can serve as external stimulus to arouse the recognition of a need.

Problem recognition can occur for each consumer role. A VCR was not considered a need until one was made available. There was no obvious problem that the VCR solved. However, once it was available, consumers could use it to view programs that they had missed, and the need to be able to watch a program at one's convenience was recognized. Hence, though the need had existed, it was not recognized till the advent of the VCR. The same is true for a product such as Post-it® Notes. These products serve the latent needs of the consumer in the user role.

Consumers typically had to go to a pizza parlor to buy their pizza before home-delivery was made available. The convenience of being able to order the pizza from home is a solution to buying a pizza. This serves the needs of a consumer in the role of a buyer. For the payer, the availability of leasing automobiles has improved affordability. Also, availability of credit makes many consumers realize the need to buy a new car or furniture.

To see the variety of problems consumer recognize, we can classify them along two dimensions: familiar versus novel, and vivid versus latent (see Figure 5.10). *Familiar problems* generally occur due to what is commonly called "stock depletion"—for example, a hungry stomach or a worn-out tire. *Novel problems* arise generally with life events that mark passage from one stage to another. Examples include a new job, a marriage, or even a child going to the next school grade.

Problem recognition

is a consumer's realization that he or she needs to buy something to get back to the normal state of comfort.

Internal stimuli

are perceived states of discomfort—physical or psychologoical.

External stimuli

are informational cues from the marketplace that lead a consumer to identify a problem.

Figure 5.9   How Marketers Help Customers' Problem Recognition

Figure 5.10   Four Situations for Problem Recognition

	Vivid	Latent
Familiar	Stock depletion	Educational marketing
Novel	Life stage change	New product technology

Vivid problems such as a just emptied cereal box or the arrival of the "back-to-school" month are easily recognized. A *latent problem* is not immediately obvious and needs shaping either by self-reflection, or more likely by an external agent such as a salesperson. Hence, the recognition of latent problems (whether familiar or novel) generally requires an educational marketing effort (e.g., counseling by a salesperson about the need for a life-insurance policy). Similarly, novel problems which are latent, like the need for caller ID service or a microwave oven before their advent, are solved typically with the availability of a new product due to technology.

Step 2: Information Search

Once the need has been recognized, consumers search for information about various alternative ways of solving the problem. That search rarely includes every brand in existence. Rather, as shown in Figure 5.11, consumers consider only a select subset of brands, organized as follows:

▼ The *awareness set* consists of brands a consumer is aware of.

▼ An *evoked set* consists of the brands in a product category that the consumer remembers at the time of decision making.

▼ Of the brands in the evoked set, not all are deemed to fit your needs. Those considered unfit are eliminated right away. The remaining brands are termed the *consideration set*—the brands a consumer will consider buying.

Initially, consumers seek information about the consideration set of brands, which is a subset of evoked sets. New information can bring in additional brands into the awareness, evoked, and consideration sets. Three elements characterize the information search phase of the decision process: (1) sources of information, (2) search strategies, and (3) amount of search.

Sources of Information Sources of information may be categorized into marketer or nonmarketer. Marketer sources are those that come from the marketer of the product itself. These consist of advertising, salespersons, product literature and brochures, and in-store displays. One of the latest marketer sources is the Internet—more and more companies have set up a home page on the Internet—a site that consumers can visit at their convenience.

Figure 5.11   Awareness, Evoked, and Consideration Sets

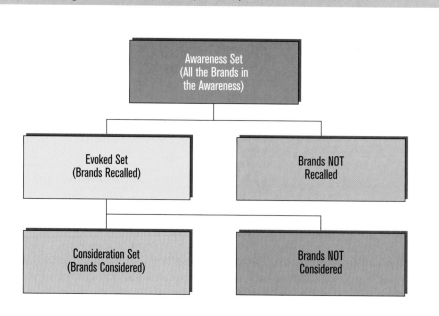

Marketing Technologies

Dell Continues Its Success on the Web

The World Wide Web (WWW) is like the wild-west of the past, where there are not many rules and nobody knows what it takes to succeed. Even as we observe more companies jumping on the bandwagon of a Web presence, many people have started questioning the rationale behind the move. The question that is often asked is, "How does it affect the bottom line?" There are two approaches to this question. First, companies can decide to use the Net as a customer support tool leading to cost savings that help the company. Alternately, companies can decide to use the Web as a tool to generate revenue. The first seems to be an easier option than the second. However, those who are able to generate revenue on the Web have a distinct advantage over the competition.

While most companies are trying to put together a successful business model for the Web, Dell is selling PCs valued at $5 million per day. At the turn of the century, Scott Eckert, the director of Dell Online, expects to obtain 50 percent of their sales online. Given Dell's track record it is not too ambitious a plan. This begs the question: *What has Dell done right that others have not?*

Unlike most companies that try to sell on the Web, Dell focuses primarily on providing customers with information. A visit to *www.dell.com* should satisfy a buyer's curiosity about technical terms associated with computers. Dell provides information that any novice would feel like asking, but is afraid to ask. Their attitude is "what is good for the customers, is good for the company." They have customized their Web site with specific versions of the sites for nearly forty countries with the appropriate currency. They also have separate links for novices vis-à-vis experienced customers. The focus thus is on the customer and adding value to his/her experience.

Providing extensive information in the form of a "knowledge center" consisting of frequently asked questions (FAQs), computer components, and software

has helped Dell shift most of the customer queries to the Web. They had a Web site visit for every call they received a year back. Now the ratio is approximately 3.5 visits to the Web site for every call that they receive. This cost saving exercise has been very successful.

From a revenue generation standpoint, it has been found that Web customers typically end up buying a higher priced PC with more high-end features than those ordering through the phone. These customers who use the WWW seem to visit the Web site many more times and, using the knowledge on display, talk themselves into buying a higher-end PC.

To answer the question, "What has Dell done right that others have not?" one has to understand the adjustments they have made on the Web. Their focus has been on making it easier to do business (thus providing value), reducing the cost of doing business for Dell and their customers, and enhancing their relationship with customers. Their ultimate goal is to create a "frictionless" environment.

Questions

1. Is the Internet going to cause sales increases? Will people buy more expensive items just because they are buying on the net as opposed to traditional marketing channels?

2. If you were assigned the task of redesigning the Dell Web site, what are the issues you would address?

3. Study two other companies that have succeeded in revenue generation on the Web and compare them with two companies that focus on using the Web as a cost-saving tool only.

Nonmarketer sources are those that are independent of the marketer's control. They include *personal sources* and *independent sources.* Since these sources have no personal interest in biasing the information (unlike marketer sources), they are deemed to be more credible. Friends and other acquaintances with past experience and/or greater knowledge of the product category are sought and valued for their advice as personal sources. There are several organizations that evaluate offerings within certain product categories and can serve as independent sources of information. One such organization is *Consumer Reports,* which publishes a monthly magazine and offers a subscription information service on the Internet.

Search Strategies The choice of information sources depends partly on the consumer's search strategy. A *search strategy* is the pattern of information acquisition consumers use to solve their decision problems. Since information acquisition has costs in terms of time, physical effort, and mental effort, consumers weigh the costs against the likely gains from information acquisition. This comparison helps them decide how much information they will acquire and from what sources.

Based on the amount of search deemed necessary, consumer decision strategies may be routine, limited, or extended problem-solving strategies.[11] **Routine problem solving**

www.consumerreports.com

Routine problem solving
occurs when no new information is considered.

Extended problem solving
occurs when the search is extensive and deliberation prolonged.

Limited problem solving
occurs when the consumer invests some limited time and energy in search and evaluating alternative solutions.

is a strategy in which no new information is considered. This strategy is used for purchase problems that have occurred and have been solved previously. It is akin to purchasing out of habit. Information search in this case is minimal. **Extended problem solving** occurs when the search is extensive and deliberation is prolonged. This strategy becomes necessary for purchases never made before, or made long ago, or where costs risks of wrong choices are high. For example, purchasing life insurance or an automobile would entail extended problem solving. Finally, **limited problem solving** is a strategy wherein the consumer invests some limited amount of time and energy in both the search and the subsequent evaluation of alternative solutions. Consumers adopt this strategy when purchases are nontrivial, the risk is limited, and the product is not complex or technical in terms of its features. There is some familiarity with the product class, but a desire for variety (e.g., buying a new dress) or unavailability of previous solutions (e.g., out of stock of your usual brand) necessitates some amount of search.

The description so far seems to imply that consumers prefer systematic search strategies, which consist of a comprehensive search and evaluation of alternatives. However, consumers may also use a contrasting search strategy, termed heuristics. *Heuristics* are quick rules of thumb and shortcuts used to make decisions. Heuristics can be implemented in a variety of ways:

▼ Broad inferences are quickly drawn from partial information (e.g., price may be used to judge quality).

▼ Past experiences are considered adequate.

▼ Others' judgments are sought and summarily adopted as final choice.

▼ Brand names are heavily relied on to the exclusion of seeking further attribute information.

Although these strategies are not systematic, they are also not irrational. They are rational to their users in terms of the cost versus benefit trade-offs they perceive.

Determinants of the Amount of Search Imagine you are in the market for a CD player or a pair of shoes. How much information will you seek? How much effort will you put in processing this information? Actually, this depends on several factors. These factors include perceived risk, involvement, prior experience and expertise, time pressure, and information overload.

The *perceived risk* is the degree of loss (i.e., amount at stake) in the event that a wrong choice is made. There are five types of risks:

1. *Performance risk*—The product may not perform well or not as well as some other alternatives.

2. *Social risk*—Reference group members and significant others may not like it.

3. *Psychological risk*—The product may not reflect oneself.

4. *Financial risk*—The alternative may be overpriced; there may exist a better purchase.

5. *Obsolescence risk*—The alternative may be replaced by newer substitutes.

The financial risk is of most concern to the payer, whereas other risks are of concern to the user. The greater the perceived risk, the greater the likelihood that the purchase will be postponed, or in any case, the search and deliberation will be extensive.

The consumer's degree of involvement with a purchase is another significant determinant of the amount of energy spent in the information search. As discussed earlier, *involvement* is defined as the perceived importance of the product. We purchase and consume hundreds of products in our lives, but we are not equally involved in all of them. We take some for granted, not even noticing unless something wrong happens. There are other products we consider very important in our lives, which we consume with full consciousness and which we purchase with great care. Involvement in this context may be classified as purchase-decision involvement and enduring involvement. **Purchase-decision involvement** is the degree of concern and caring that consumers bring to bear on the purchase decision. For example, we sometimes spend 30 minutes or more to purchase a greeting card that costs only $2. There are other products that we may have an ongoing interest in. This is termed as *enduring involvement.* Many consumers have an enduring involvement in products such as music CDs, automobiles, and computers.

Consumers have familiarity and expertise as a result of prior information acquisition and prior personal experience. The relationship between prior experience and external information search is generally inverse; with increasing prior experience, less external search occurs. Prior experience also implies that the purchase problem is solved in the routine problem-solving mode, as happens with most of the day-to-day purchases of staple items. However, even with high prior experience, routine problem solving may not be considered a desirable strategy if: (a) the experience with the prior purchase was not positive; (b) technology has changed to render the prior experience obsolete; (c) the goal is to build an assortment rather than replace prior purchase; (d) the purchase is infrequent; or (e) the product is a high-risk purchase.

Prior experience refers to the history of purchase, record of consumption, and information obtained with respect to that product. In contrast, *expertise* refers to the understanding of the attributes in a product class, and knowledge about how various alternatives stack up on these attributes. When a consumer judges prior experience to be inadequate for the impending purchase and decides that new information search will be useful, expertise comes into play in determining how much search will be undertaken.

One of the most conspicuous characteristics of the consumer in the 1990s is *time pressure.* Time has become and is becoming more and more scarce, due to: (a) both spouses working, (b) some consumers being employed in more than one job; (c) many consumers re-enrolling in school to acquire new skills necessary for a more complex employment market; and (d) new leisure activities enabled by technology. Some have called the "always on the go" consumer the "harassed decision maker." Time pressure is making consumers look for more convenience in shopping. In addition, time-pressed consumers are likely to cut short their information search, comparison shopping, and decision-making time.[12]

There are times when helpful salespeople in their zeal overload us with information. *Information overload* occurs when exposed to too much information—so much so that you are unable to process it to make a decision. There are a number of studies that have been conducted that indicate that consumers experience discomfort when they are overloaded with information. Also, they tend to avoid information when they are exposed to too much of it. Hence, it follows that consumers tend to be selective in their acquisition of information, and because of this selectivity, they may not always make the best decisions.

Step 3: Alternative Evaluation

Now that the consumer has all the information, how does he or she use that information to arrive at the choice? Consumers select one of the several alternatives (brands, dealers, and so on) available to them. These specific processes and steps used in making the choice are referred to by researchers as "choice models." There are two broad categories of choice models: compensatory and noncompensatory.[13]

Compensatory Models In the *compensatory model,* the consumer arrives at a choice by considering all of the attributes for a product, and mentally trading off the alternative's perceived weakness on one or more attributes for its perceived strength on other attributes. A consumer may go about making this calculation in two ways. One method of arriving at a choice is simply to add the number of positive attributes and subtract the number of negative attributes each alternative has, and then choose the one that has the most positive

Purchase-decision involvement
is the degree of concern and caring that consumers bring to bear on the purchase decision.

and fewest negative attributes. While sometimes consumers do make decisions based on a simple numerical count of pluses and minuses, often the individual does not consider each plus or minus equally significant. Some considerations are clearly more important than others, and every minus may or may not cancel a plus on some other feature. Hence, the simple method described above may lead to arbitrary decisions.

A second and more systematic approach is to weigh every attribute for each alternative in terms of its relative importance. To implement this approach, the decision-maker also estimates the degree to which the alternative possesses each positive and negative attribute. This can be done on a numerical scale of, say 0 to 10, where 10 means a perfect performance on that attribute. The score on the scale is then multiplied by the relative importance of the attribute. The sum of these products for each alternative provides a total score for that alternative. This model is called compensatory because a shortfall on one attribute may be compensated by a good rating on another attribute.

Noncompensatory Models

While there are several *noncompensatory models* that have been identified, four are considered the most common and useful. These are called conjunctive, disjunctive, lexicographic, and elimination by aspects.[14] In the *conjunctive model,* the consumer begins by setting the *minimum cutoffs on all important attributes.* Each alternative is then examined on each attribute, and any alternative that meets the minimum cut-offs on all attributes can potentially be chosen. If an alternative fails the cut-off, even on one attribute, it is dropped from further consideration. If all the alternatives fail to meet the cut-off levels, then the consumer may revise his or her minimum cut-off levels or use another decision model. On the other hand, if more than one alternative meets all the minimum cut-off levels, the consumer might resort to another decision model, to further eliminate alternatives until only one survives the process.

The *disjunctive model* entails *trade-offs between aspects of choice alternatives.* Sometimes the consumer is willing to trade off one feature for another. For example, a homebuyer might say that the house he or she would be willing to consider buying should have either five bedrooms or, if it has only four bedrooms, a finished basement. Although similar trade-offs are made in the compensatory model, there are differences. First, the disjunctive model considers the sheer presence or absence of attributes, rather than the degree or amount in which these attributes are present. Second, in the compensatory model, the attributes traded off need not serve the same purpose, while in the disjunctive model they tend to.

Another model consumers use to make a choice is termed the *lexicographic model.* In this model, attributes of *alternatives are ranked in terms of importance.* Consumers examine all alternatives on the most important criterion and identify the one with the highest level on that criterion. If more than one alternative remains in the choice set, then they consider the second most important criterion, and examine the remaining alternatives with respect to that criterion. The process continues until only one alternative remains.

The *elimination by aspects model* is similar to the lexicographic model but with one important difference. The consumer *rates the attributes in the order of importance and, in addition, defines cut-off values.* He or she then examines all alternatives, first on the most important attribute, admitting for further consideration only those that satisfy the minimum cut-off level on this most important attribute. If more than one alternative meets the requirement, then the consumer goes to the next step, appraising the remaining alternatives on the second attribute, delineating those that meet the minimum cut-off level on this attribute, and so on.

It has been found that consumers may use any of these choice models independently or use a combination of the choice models discussed thus far. For some of the more important decisions, a consumer might first use a noncompensatory model and then, to further identify the choice, use a compensatory model. The noncompensatory model could be used to eliminate choices and narrow down the set of alternatives for closer compar-

Figure 5.12   Customer Behavior at the Purchase Step

isons. In the second stage, termed "alternative selection stage," the smaller set of alternatives is further examined. The objective of the first stage is thus to identify the acceptable alternatives, whereas the second stage is meant to identify the best, among all acceptable alternatives.

Step 4: Purchase

Once the consumer has evaluated the alternatives, he or she makes the purchase. This appears to be a straightforward action, but even here consumer behavior at times becomes intriguing. To understand this behavior, let us break down this action step into three substeps as shown in Figure 5.12.

The first substep occurs when the consumer identifies the most preferred alternative, based on the alternative evaluation process described earlier. The next substep is to form a purchase intent—a determination that one would buy that product. It is the act of giving self-instruction, like, "The next time I am in the market, I am going to buy it"; it is to make a mental note, to put it on the "to do" list, so to speak. The final substep is implementing the purchase. This entails arranging the terms of the transaction, seeking and obtaining the transfer of title or ownership from the seller, paying for the product, and receiving possession of the product commitment from the seller. While the three steps described here are automatic in the case of groceries, they become important in the case of purchases such as automobiles or homes. In case of rare artifacts, purchase implementation, including finding the seller, may be a long, drawn-out process.

Sometimes the consumer purchase implementation process may be derailed due to a deviation from the identified choice. Several conditions might account for this. First, the preferred brand may be out of stock, thus forcing the consumer to buy a brand different from the one identified. Second, new in-store information may reopen the evaluation process. Third, financing terms may render a purchase infeasible, forcing the consumer either to abandon the purchase altogether, or to substitute the purchase with a lower-level model or another brand available on preferred terms.

Step 5: Post-Purchase Experience

The consumer's decision process does not end with the purchase. Rather, the experience of buying and using the product provides information that the consumer will use in future decision making. In some cases, the consumer will be pleased with the experience and will buy the same product from the same supplier again. In other cases, the consumer will be disappointed and may even return or exchange the product. In general, the postpurchase process includes four steps: decision confirmation, experience evaluation, satisfaction or dissatisfaction, and future response (exit, voice, or loyalty).

After a consumer makes an important choice decision, he or she experiences an intense need to confirm the wisdom of that decision. The flip side is that he or she wants to avoid the disconfirmation. One of the processes that occurs at this stage is ***cognitive dissonance:*** a postpurchase doubt the buyer experiences about the wisdom of the choice. Methods of reducing dissonance and confirming the soundness of one's decision are seeking further positive information about the chosen alternative and avoiding negative information about the chosen alternative.

Following purchase, the product is actually consumed. Marketers need to know whether purchasers consume the product routinely without much thought, or if they are consciously evaluating it. This depends on the level of enduring involvement in the product and the finality of the preference that caused this purchase. Also, consumers buy some products on a trial basis, without making their preference final yet. These products, even if not of enduring involvement, are the ones that the consumer is likely to be using with an eye to appraisal. Often, when consumers receive free samples, they are not necessarily in an evaluative mode; therefore, they use them routinely, without consciously trying to register the product performance.

Whether or not they actively evaluate a product during product use or consumption, users do experience the usage outcome. This outcome is characterized as satisfaction or dissatisfaction. Measuring overall satisfaction/dissatisfaction is easy, as consumer researchers do so frequently. What is more challenging is to understand *why* consumers feel the way they do. Research indicates that consumers do not evaluate the performance of a product on an absolute basis, but compare it to the expected performance. Thus, if the product fulfills prepurchase expectations, then satisfaction results. On the other hand, if the prepurchase expectations are not met, dissatisfaction results. This makes intuitive sense in our everyday experience.

Following the experience of satisfaction or dissatisfaction, consumers have three possible responses: exit, voice, or loyalty. If consumers are dissatisfied with their experience with a brand, they may decide never again to buy the brand. This places them back to the start of the decision process the next time the problem recognition arises. Some dissatisfied consumers may complain, and then decide either to give the brand or marketer another chance, or simply to exit. Following the complaint, negative word-of-mouth is less likely, and repatronage more likely, if the complaint is successfully redressed. If the complaint is not successfully redressed, the negative word-of-mouth might in fact be further intensified beyond what it would have been had the consumer not made the complaint in the first place. Research has found that consumer complaints may actually be good for marketers—complainers care enough to complain. Noncomplainers simply walk out, taking their patronage to a competitor.

The third response is, of course, loyalty. Consumer loyalty means the consumer buys the same brand repeatedly. It is reasonable to assume that loyal consumers are more likely to be satisfied, however the converse is not necessarily true as some researchers have found that not all satisfied consumers are loyal. Some consumers will still exhibit a switching behavior despite being satisfied with the current brand.

Household Decision Making

Households are the basic unit of buying and consumption in a society. A *household* is a consumption unit of one or more persons identified by a common location with a common address. While a number of consumer decisions are no doubt made by individuals for their personal consumption (e.g., buying food during office lunch hour), the more significant decisions are made by individuals jointly with other members of their household, and for joint use by the members of the household.

Household decisions are important to study as they are likely to be different from those of the individual decision making process. The critical difference is that while in the case of the individual it is quite likely that all three roles—that of buyer, user, and payer—are more likely to merge in one person, in the case of the household it is possible to separate the three roles. The separation of the three roles makes household buying behavior somewhat complicated to track and influence. Moreover, these role allocations are dy-

Figure 5.13   Consumption as Common Ground

Common consumption in the family socializes children by developing preferences.

namic. They vary from time to time, from one product to another, and from one family type to another. For a purchase to be made, the household must reach a form of consensus. This atmosphere is depicted in Figure 5.13.

Steps in Family Buying Decisions

If you think back to a recent marketplace decision made in your family, you might recall that various members undertook various activities, en route to the final decision. Based on research and observations, scholars have identified and described the family buying process as consisting of the following steps:[15]

1. Initiation of the purchase decision.

2. Gathering and sharing of information.

3. Evaluating and deciding.

Years ago, a typical U.S. household would have been described as a nuclear family, consisting of a husband, wife, and 2.5 children. In 1970, married couples with children comprised 41 percent of all households in the United States. By 1998, such households had declined to 23.4 percent. In their place the proportion of single-parent households rose from 6 percent in 1970 to 11.70 percent in 1998.[16] Today's households display much more diversity.

4. Shopping and buying.

5. Conflict management.

The first four steps are self-explanatory and are similar in interpretation to those described in the case of the individual consumer. The fifth step is particularly important in the context of family decision making and will be discussed in detail later in this section. Although the meaning of the first four steps is self-evident and their basic operation similar to that in individual decision-making, the actual dynamics are more involved. Different members of the family play different roles in the decision process. Thus, one member might initiate the purchase decision by making a product request. Another member of the family might collect information. A third member might evaluate and decide. Yet another member might make the actual product purchase. Finally, someone must take the responsibility of resolving any differences of preference and conflicts that may arise. Such conflicts not only arise before the decision is made, but may continue, or may arise anew, after the purchase. The interspousal or intrafamily influence can vary from step to step.

Children's Influence in Family Decision Making In 1997, U.S. children controlled or influenced about $120 billion in spending and enjoyed a personal income of $46 billion from allowances, gifts, and part-time jobs.[17] Children's influence increases with age. Children influence household buying in three ways. First, children influence household purchases by having individualistic preferences for products paid for and bought by parents. Second, children in their teen years begin to have their own money and become their own payers and buyers of items of self-use. Third, children influence their parents' choice of products that are meant for shared consumption (e.g., family vacation) or even products used by parents only, by exerting expertise influence (e.g., high-tech products or latest fashions in clothes).

Children's influence on family decision making also differs based on the nature of the parents. If the parents are authoritarian, children's influence on decision making is lowest. In cases where the parents are neglectful, there is not much communication between the children and the parents. Hence, the children may not be able to influence the purchase of products that the parents use. However, if they have a source of income and parents are neglectful, the children are fairly autonomous in decisions to purchase products for their own use. In cases where parents are democratic, the children share influence with other members of the household. If the parents are permissive, children exercise relative autonomy regarding products for which they are the principal or sole user, exercising both the buyer and the decision-maker role.

Conflict in Family Decisions

Family decision making may give rise to conflict, whether the consumer roles are distributed among family members or shared by family members. Conflict among distributed roles arises when the user, payer, and buyer roles are played by different family members, and different alternatives satisfy each. Conflict also arises due to shared roles, when a single role is shared by multiple family members, and their goals diverge. For example, in the case of a family car, the husband may be interested in the high-performance of a turbo engine car, while the wife may want a minivan that is safe and roomy for small children in the family.

Inevitable conflicts arise if there is disagreement between family members either on goals or on perceptions. The nature of the conflict will differ according to whether there is a disagreement in one or both of these areas.

Four strategies of conflict resolution have been suggested by scholars: problem solving, persuasion, bargaining, and politicking. ***Problem solving*** entails members trying to gather more information or add new alternatives. When motives/goals are congruent and only perceptions differ, obtaining and sharing information often suffices to resolve conflicts. ***Persuasion*** requires educating about the goal hierarchy; the wife might argue how a safe and large car is in the best interest of the whole family since the car is needed to transport children. ***Bargaining*** entails trading favors (husband gets to buy the house of his choice as long as the car that is being bought is one that the wife prefers). When goals and evaluations are so divergent that even bargaining is infeasible, ***politicking*** is resorted to. Here, members form coalitions and subgroups within the family and by so doing simply impose their will on the minority coalition. (It is not unusual for parents to find themselves a part of the minority coalition).

Chapter Summary

In this chapter, you learned that a consumer is a person who is party to a transaction with the marketer. Consumer behavior consists of the mental and physical activities undertaken by consumers. The three roles a consumer plays are those of a user, the payer, and the buyer.

The first section in the chapter described the needs and wants of consumers—whether as users, payers, or buyers. A need was defined as an unsatisfactory condition of the consumer that leads him or her to an action that will satisfy or fulfill that condition. A want was defined as a desire to obtain more satisfaction than is absolutely necessary to improve an unsatisfactory condition. Needs are determined by the physical characteristics of the consumer (genetics, biogenics, and psychogenics) and by the physical characteristics of the environment (climate, topography, and ecology). Wants are determined by the personal context (culture, institutions and groups, and personal worth), and environmental context (economy, technology, and public policy).

In the next section, we discussed some of the underlying processes consumers use to make product and brand choices: perception, learning, motivation, and attitude formation. In the perceptual process, we identified the influence of the characteristics of the stimulus (or incoming information), the context, and consumers themselves. Next, we described three biases in the perception process: selective exposure, selective attention, and selective interpretation.

In discussing the consumer as a learner, we described four models of learning: cognitive learning, classical conditioning, instrumental conditioning, and modeling. Classical conditioning occurs when a preexisting consumer response to a stimulus is transferred to another product that the stimulus is constantly paired with. Instrumental conditioning occurs when consumers learn to engage in a behavior repeatedly because the behavior is rewarding. Cognitive learning occurs when consumers obtain new information. Modeling occurs by observing other consumers whose behavior we find worth imitating.

Next, we dealt with consumer motivations—why consumers buy, pay for, and use specific products. This topic was organized in terms of needs, emotions, and psychographics.

Needs are felt deprivations of desired states. In this context, we discussed Maslow's hierarchy of needs. Human emotions also play a significant role in motivating human behavior. One specific topic in our discussion of emotions and moods was hedonic consumption and the related phenomenon of "product use involvement." Psychographics describe consumers' profile of needs, emotions, and resulting behaviors, and as such explain much of consumer behavior. Psychographics include self-concept, personal values, and lifestyles. We discussed, in depth, one type of psychographics—namely the VALS (Values and Life Styles). This was followed by our discussion on attitude. Attitudes are described as consumers' likes and dislikes toward various products and their predispositions to respond to them (approach or avoid them).

Based on these processes, we studied consumer decision making. This is a five-step process: problem recognition → information search → alternative evaluation → purchase → post-purchase experience. The consumer decision problem begins with problem recognition. Problem recognition occurs due to an internal cue that comes from one's motives being in a state of unfulfillment, or from external stimuli evoking these motives. A typology of problems was suggested—namely, familiar-latent, familiar-vivid, novel-latent, and novel-vivid. Once problem recognition occurs, the consumer either (a) relies on prior knowledge and previously learned solutions, or (b) searchers for new solutions through new information acquisition and its evaluation and integration. In the information search stage, there are several determinants of information search, including perceived risk, involvement, prior experience, expertise, and time pressure.

Evaluations of alternatives entail use of compensatory (trade off) and noncompensatory (nontrade-off) decision models. The latter include conjunctive, disjunctive, lexicographic, and elimination-by-aspects models. The outcome of these evaluation processes is the identification of a preferred brand and the formation of purchase intent. Such purchase intent is then implemented by the actual purchase act, but it was suggested that the purchase act does not always occur as planned. Sometimes, substantial delays occur in purchase implementation, and other times, the brand actually bought is different from the one planned, because of stockouts or new information at the time of purchase. In the post-purchase phase, the processes of decision confirmation, satisfaction/dissatisfaction, exit, complaining, and loyalty responses were discussed.

Consumers make purchase decisions as individuals and as members of households. Household decisions are complex because the user, payer, and buyer roles are distributed among different individuals. Next, children's influence in family buying decisions was described. Children influence parental choices of products, both in products the children use, as well as those used by parents only.

Thus, in this chapter we have defined consumer behavior, discussed various processes involved in consumer behavior, and described how these psychological processes are related to consumer decision making—both as individuals as well as members of a household unit.

Key Terms

Consumer behavior is the mental and physical activity undertaken by household and business consumers that result in decisions and actions to pay for, purchase, and use products.

Needs are unsatisfactory conditions of the consumer that lead him or her to an action that will make the condition better.

Wants are desires to obtain more satisfaction than is absolutely necessary to improve an unsatisfactory conditions.

Genetics is a branch of science that deals with the heredity and chemical/biological characteristics of organisms.

Biogenics is the study of the biological characteristics that people possess at birth, such as gender, race, and the age.

Psychogenics refers to the study of individual states and traits induced by a person's brain functioning.

Personal worth refers to the financial resources available to a consumer. These comprise a person's income, assets, inheritance, and borrowing power.

Institutional context refers to the groups and organizations a person belongs to. The institutional context includes the workplace, religious and educational institutions, family and friends, and peer groups.

Perception is the process by which an individual selects, organizes, and interprets the information received from the environment.

Context is the setting in which the information is received; this includes social, cultural, and organizational contexts

Learning is a change in the content of long-term memory. As humans, we learn because what we learn helps us respond better to our environment.

Motivation is the state of drive or arousal that impels behavior toward a goal-object.

Involvement is the degree of personal relevance of a product to a consumer.

Psychographics are characteristics of individuals that describe them in terms of their psychological and behavioral makeup.

Values are end-states of life, the goals one lives for.

Terminal values are the goals we seek in life.

Instrumental values are the means or behavioral standards by which we pursue our goals.

Self-concept refers to a person's self-image.

Attitudes are learned predispositions to respond to an object or class of objects in a consistently favorable or unfavorable way.

Problem recognition is a consumer's realization that he or she needs to buy something to get back to the normal state of comfort.

Internal stimuli are perceived states of discomfort—physical or psychological.

External stimuli are informational cues from the marketplace that lead the consumer to identify a problem.

Routine problem solving occurs when no new information is considered.

Extended problem solving occurs when the search is extensive and deliberation prolonged.

Limited problem solving occurs when the consumer invests some limited time and energy in search and evaluating alternative solutions.

Purchase-decision involvement is the degree of concern and caring that consumers bring to bear on the purchase decision.

Additional Key Terms and Concepts

User role
Buyer role
Topography
Institutional relationships
Economy
Public policy
Organization
Stimulus characteristics
Confirmatory bias
Perceptual threshold
Cognitive learning
Problem solving
Conditioned stimulus
Instrumental conditioning
Moods

Payer role
Climate
Ecology
Cultural surroundings context
Technology
Sensation
Interpretation
Consumer characteristics
Perceptual distortion
Just noticeable difference
Rote memorization
Unconditioned stimulus
Classical conditioning
Modeling
Hedonic consumption

Enduring involvement

Situational involvement

Actual self

Ideal self

Lifestyle

VALS

Riesman's Social Character Theory

Mental budgeting

Consumer problem

Familiar problems

Novel problems

Vivid problems

Latent problems

Awareness set

Evoked set

Consideration set

Personal sources

Independent sources

Search strategy

Heuristics

Perceived risk

Performance risk

Social risk

Psychological risk

Financial risk

Obsolescence risk

Involvement

Prior experience

Expertise

Time pressure

Information overload

Compensatory model

Noncompensatory model

Conjunctive model

Disjunctive model

Lexicographic model

Elimination by aspects model

Cognitive dissonance

Household

Problem solving

Persuasion

Bargaining

Politicking

Questions for Discussion

1. When users lack the buying power to make a purchase, they often look to others to buy and pay for the products they need. Give one example of a household user who depends on others to play the payer and buyer roles.

2. How do needs differ from wants? How are needs and wants determined?

3. Why does classical conditioning work better for unknown brands than for known brands? What characteristics would you use to select a celebrity to pair with your brand? Or to be a spokesperson for your company?

4. What is Maslow's hierarchy of needs and how is this hierarchy helpful to marketers in gaining a better understanding of consumer needs and wants?

5. What is VALS and VALS2? Why is an understanding of these two concepts so important to consumer researchers?

6. Discuss factors that influence the amount of search an individual consumer will undertake during the Information Search step of the Consumer Decision Making process.

7. What is meant by search strategies? Explain systematic versus heuristic search strategies. What factors influence the extent of search a consumer would engage in?

8. Contrast individual consumer decision making with family buying decisions.

9. Marketing is criticized by some for targeting children with specifically tailored advertising. From a marketer's viewpoint, why does targeting children make sense?

10. Suggest strategies for resolving conflicts associated with family buying decisions.

Internet Questions

1. Choose a consumer product. Go to Yahoo! (www.yahoo.com) and search for the product. Visit three Web sites that carry information about this product. For each of the three sites, answer the following questions:
   a) How useful is the site for making a purchase decision in this product category?
   b) Is this site promoting the product category or promoting a specific brand? What customer values does the site offer different customers?
   c) Does the site make any reference to the different roles that customers assume (user, payer, buyer)?
   d) How effective is this site in communicating its message to customers? Is it believable?

2. The Web offers a number of different sources of information about consumers. Among them is the site at www.marketingtools.com
   a) Visit the site.
   b) Based on your assessment of the information at this site and others like it, do you believe that the development of the Internet has defined a new subculture of customers? Who are they? Describe their characteristics.
   c) What market values do they share? How do these customers differ from the larger population?
   d) How should companies market to this new subculture (or set of new subcultures), keeping customer behavior principles in mind?

3. In 1978, the research and consulting firm, SRI International, developed a psychographic segmentation system called VALS, which stands for values and lifestyles. VALS, and the thinking behind it, is described in this chapter.
   a) Go to SRI's home page (www.future.sri.com) and link to the VALS2 service.
   b) Complete the survey on this page to place yourself into a VALS segment.
   c) Do you agree with the results? Why or why not? What values and lifestyle issues are dominant for you as a customer?
   d) How do companies use the VALS information to infer customer behavior?

Endnotes

[1] "Bridal Wave Sweeps Store," *Chicago Tribune,* November 8, 1994. Patrick Collins, "Charge of the White Brigade," *Sunday Standard Times,* January 15, 1995, Vol. 87, no.4, E1-E2, New Bedford, Massachusetts.

[2] Ibid.

[3] Adapted from Jagdish N. Sheth, Banwari Mittal, and Bruce I. Newman, *Customer Behavior: Consumer Behavior and Beyond* (The Dryden Press, 1999).

[4] Abhijit Biswas and Edward A. Blair, "Contextual Effects of Reference Prices in Retail Advertising," *Journal of Marketing* 55 (July 1991), pp. 1–12.

[5] For a fuller description of the Pavlov experiments, see Leland C. Swenson, *Theories of Learning: Tradition Perspectives/Contemporary Developments* (Belmont, CA: Wadsworth Publishing Company, 1980), pp. 13–30.

[6] Abraham H. Maslow, "A Theory of Human Motivation," *Psychological Review* 50 (July 1943), pp. 370–96; also, Abraham H. Maslow, *Motivation and Personality* (New York: Harper & Row, 1970).

[7]Edward J. Murray, *Motivation and Emotion* (Englewood Cliffs, NJ: Prentice Hall, 1964).

[8]Lynn R. Kahle, Sharon E. Beatty, and Pamela Homer, "Alternative Measurement Approaches to Consumer Values: The List of Values (LOV) and Values and Life Style (VALS)," *Journal of Consumer Research* 13 (December 1986), pp. 405–409; Sharon Beatty, Lynn R. Kahle, Pamela Homer, and Shekhar Misra, "Alternative Measurement Approaches to Consumer Values: The List of Values and the Rokeach Value Survey," *Psychology & Marketing* 2 (Fall 1985), pp. 181–200.

[9]Rajeev Batra and Douglas M. Stayman, "The Role of Mood in Advertising Effectiveness," *Journal of Consumer Research* 17, no. 2 (September 1990), pp.203–14.

[10]VALS description on the Internet, at www.futures.sri.com.

[11]Gordon W. Allport, "Attitudes," in C.A. Muchinson, ed., *A Handbook of Social Psychology* (Worcester, MA: Clark University Press, 1935), pp. 798–844.

[12]John A. Howard and Jagdish N. Sheth, *The Theory of Buyer Behavior* (New York: John Wiley & Sons, 1961).

[13]Peter L. Wright, "The Harassed Decision Marker: Time Pressure, Distractions, and the Use of Evidence," *Journal of Applied Psychology* 59 (October) pp. 555–61.

[14]For a fuller discussion of these and other models, see James R. Bettman, *An Information Processing Theory of Consumer Choice* (Reading, MA: Addison-Wesley, 1979), pp. 173–228.

[15]Hillel J. Einhorn (1970), "Use of Nonlinear, Noncompensatory Models in Decision Making," *Psychological Bulletin* 73, pp. 221–30.

[16]Jagdish N. Sheth, "Models of Buyer Behavior: Conceptual, Quantitative, and Empirical," in *A Theory of Family Buying Decisions* (New York: Harper & Row), pp. 17–33.

[17]Based on U.S. government census estimates, obtained from the Internet Web site www.census.gov/population/socdemo/hh-fam/98ppla.txt.

[18]Lisa Reilly Cullen (1997), "Ride the Echo Boom to Stock Profits," *Money* 26, July, pp. 98–104.

[19]Based on Elizabeth Jensen, "Wireless Carriers Try New Hook to Win Consumers," *The Wall Street Journal,* March 4, 1998, p. B4.

Prepaid Wireless: Protecting the Payer from the User[19]

Of the 452 messages your roommate will take for you this year, how many of them will you actually get?

Suppose you were a college student and you were to hear a pitch in a TV ad for a company selling its wireless phone service. Would you find this pitch appealing? You might if you have a lot of friends calling you while you are away from your room, and if you are paranoid about not missing a message some caller may have left for you. The above message was actually used recently by Bell Atlantic Corp.'s wireless phone service division, called Mobile, in the Washington D.C. area.

Early users of wireless service included affluent consumers and businessmen. But after a decade of promoting to these groups, the wireless companies are now casting their net wider. Wireless service is now being promoted to ordinary men and women as an emergency aid (e.g., stranded on the highway with a flat tire or stuck in traffic on the way to an important social appointment). The current group that companies are trying to court is students. Historically, students have been the least attractive target, because their financial means are limited. But now companies are realizing that the wireless phone naturally appeals to the youth. This was humorously epitomized in the movie *Clueless,* where two high-school girls constantly talked with each other on their wireless phones until they would actually bump into each other, still connected by wireless!

But the *Clueless* girls were rich; most students are not. Enter wireless services with a twist; prepaid wireless. "Worriless Wireless" is how a TV ad by Omnipoint Corp.—another provider of wireless phone service—promotes its prepaid wireless service. It goes on to say, "You control what you spend on your wireless calls—because you pay for them in advance."

According to a Yankee group report, in 1997 there were about 580,000 subscribers to prepaid wireless services in the United States, which is a small fraction of the 54 million wireless subscribers; by the year 2000, their number is supposed to grow to 1.9 million and by 2002, 2.7 million. Correspondingly, prepaid wireless revenues are expected to grow from $400 million in 1997 to $1.5 billion in 2000 and $2.2 billion by 2002.

The market share leaders in prepaid service are not recent upstarts, but established phone companies. Omnipoint Corp. and PrimeCO Personal Communications LP are two pioneers in promoting prepaid service; for each, as many as 50 percent of the total subscribers are prepaid consumers.

Who buys prepaid? Initially, these were people who could not pass a credit check, accounting for some 30 to 40 percent of all wireless subscribers. Now, prepaid wireless is being offered as an insurance against getting bills one would find hard to pay. It is a check on overspending.

Prepaid doesn't come cheap. Vendors get lower sales commissions, and subscribers don't get subsidized phones. No one is certain about the longevity of consumers of prepaid service. Is this a trend likely to grow? How long can one keep consumers who are not tied down by a long-term contract? Will these consumer stay brand loyal? These are the questions that wireless companies face. Correctly gauging consumer interest in both wireless service and in prepaid cards would be crucial to companies as they pursue new markets for prepaid wireless.

Discussion Questions

1. The case is subtitled, "Protecting the Payer from the User." Is that subtitle apt? Briefly explain.

2. Why are students and youth a natural target for wireless? Why does wireless appeal to them?

3. What other consumer groups might find the prepaid wireless useful?

4. Some companies fear that due to a lack of a long-term contract, prepaid consumers would not be loyal to the company. Discuss this statement. Is this fear real? What can companies do to increase consumer loyalty?

Chapter 6

Business-to-Business Marketing

Michael D. Hutt, Arizona State University

Michael D. Hutt (Ph.D., Michigan State University) is the Earl and Gladys Davis Distinguished Professor of Marketing at Arizona State University. He has also held faculty positions at Miami University (Ohio) and the University of Vermont.

Dr. Hutt's teaching and research interests are concentrated in the areas of business-to-business marketing and strategic marketing. His current research centers on the cross-functional role that marketing managers assume in the formation of strategy. Dr. Hutt's research has been published in the *Journal of Marketing, Journal of Marketing Research, Sloan Management Review, Journal of Retailing, Journal of the Academy of Marketing Science,* and other scholarly journals. He is the co-author of *Business Marketing Management* (The Dryden Press), now in its sixth edi-

The J. M. Smucker Company is the nation's leading producer of branded preserves, jams, jellies, and other fruit spread products and ice cream toppings. Almost everyone knows that "with a name like Smucker's, it has to be good!" What most people don't know is that the J. M. Smucker Company also serves the business-to-business market, supplying a variety of processed fruit and topping products to manufacturers of yogurt and dessert items. In fact, the industrial products area is one of

the fastest growing segments of the firm's business, contributing over $100 million in annual sales.[1]

Marketing strawberry preserves to household consumers differs significantly from marketing a filling mix to an organization that produces yogurt or dessert items. The business marketer emphasizes personal selling, rather than advertising, to reach potential buyers. The Smucker salesperson begins by contacting the purchasing manager at a food manufacturer and then spends a great deal of time with various members of the new product development team. Special attention is given to isolating the special needs of the organization and to identifying the **key buying influentials**—those who will have power in the buying process.

Armed with product specifications (for example, desired taste, color, calories), the salesperson returns to the R&D department at Smucker to develop samples. Several months may pass before a mixture meets the approval of a group of buying influentials at the food manufacturer. Next, attention turns to price, and the salesperson's contact point shifts to the purchasing department. Because large quantities (truckloads or drums rather than jars) are involved, a few cents per pound can be significant to both parties. Quality and service are also vitally important. Once an order is placed, the product is shipped directly from the Smucker warehouse to the manufacturer's plant. The salesperson follows

(Continued)

Key buying influentials are those individuals in the buying organization who have the power to influence the buying decision.

tion, and of *Macro Marketing* (John Wiley & Sons).

Thomas W. Speh, Miami University, Ohio
James E. Rees Distinguished Professor of Marketing and Director of the Warehousing Research Center, Miami University, Ohio.

Dr. Speh earned his Ph.D. from Michigan State University. He is the recipient of several awards, including the Beta Gamma Sigma Distinguished Faculty award from Miami University's School of Business and the Effective Educator award from the Miami University Alumni Association. He is the past president of the Warehousing Education and Research Council and also the past president of the Council of Logistics Management.

Prior to his tenure at Miami University, Dr. Speh taught at the University of Alabama and Michigan State University.

Learning Objectives

After you have completed this chapter, you should be able to:

1. Understand the major types of customers that comprise the business market.

2. Understand the basic similarities and differences between household consumer and business-to-business markets.

3. Recognize the importance of close buyer-seller relationships in the business market.

4. Explain the decision process that organizational buyers apply as they confront different buying situations.

5. Understand the environmental, organizational, group, and individual factors that influence the buying decisions of organizations.

6. Explain how organizational buyers evaluate the performance of business marketers.

up frequently with the purchasing agent, the plant manager, and other executives. Product movement and delivery information is openly shared, and close working relationships develop between managers at Smucker's and key decision makers in the buying organization.

This chapter explores the unique characteristics of the business market and the special opportunities and challenges that it presents for marketers. What are the different types of customers that comprise the business market? What are the distinguishing features of business markets? What types of buying decisions do business (organizational) buyers make? Who participates in the buying process? What factors influence the buying behavior of organizations? ■

THE SIZE AND SCOPE OF THE BUSINESS MARKET

www.gm.com

Business marketers serve the largest market of all: the dollar volume of goods and services purchased in the business market significantly exceeds that of the household consumer market. In the business market, a single customer can account for an enormous level of purchasing activity. For example, the General Motors purchasing department spends more than $70 billion annually on goods and services—more than the gross domestic product for countries such as Ireland or Greece.[2] Indeed, the business market consists of millions of organizations—large or small, public or private, profit or not-for-profit—that collectively buy trillions of dollars of goods and services.

The **business market** consists of all organizations that buy products for use as component parts for the production of other products, as operational supplies (e.g., paper clips, pencils, janitorial supplies, etc.), or for resale. The factors that distinguish business marketing from household consumer marketing are the nature of the customer and how that customer uses the product. In business marketing, the customers are organizations: commercial enterprises, governments, and institutions (see Figure 6.1). Commercial enterprises (businesses) buy products to form or facilitate the production process or as components for other goods and services. Government agencies and institutions (for example, hospitals) buy goods to maintain and deliver services to their own market: the public.

Business market
consists of all organizations that buy goods and services for use in the production of other products and services or for resale.

Types of Customers

www.pg.com

The vast business market is characterized by tremendous diversity. Many goods commonly viewed as household consumer products generate significant demand in the business market. For example, cooking oil is a common grocery item that also enjoys a huge market in the business marketing arena. In fact, estimates place the total business-market usage of cooking oil at somewhere close to 400 million gallons annually. Firms, such as Procter & Gamble, that have established brands of cooking oil displayed on supermarket shelves for final consumers, also serve the business market. Why? Cooking oil is bought by *commercial firms*—manufacturers of food products (frozen foods, breaded fish, and so forth), fast-food restaurant chains, airline meal-preparation contractors, hotel restaurant operators, and business firms that furnish food for their employees; *institutions*—schools, hospitals, and universities (educational institutions, including schools, colleges and universities, sell more than $17 billion of food annually, whereas health-care institutions exceed $23 billion in annual food sales); and *governments*—federal, state, and local (the U.S. Army is the single largest food-service organization in the world, and various officer and NCO clubs serve nearly $1 billion in food each year). Beyond the borders of the United States, international customers, such as food manufacturers, restaurant chains, and

Figure 6.1 Selected Types of Organizational Buyers

Commercial Customers	Institutional Customers	Governmental Customers
Manufacturers	Schools, colleges, universities	Federal government General Services Administration Defense Supply Agency
Construction companies Service firms	Health-care organizations Libraries	State Government Local government Counties Townships
Transportation companies Selected professional groups Wholesalers Retailers	Foundations Art galleries Clinics	

health-care units, also represent a sizable market. The magnitude of the food-service market and its importance to manufacturers of cooking oil is illustrated by its annual sales volume: over $300 billion![3]

Requirements for product quality are as diverse as the types of buyers in the food-service market. For a small, elegant restaurant, how long the cooking oil lasts and its effect on the taste of the food will be critical factors, so the highest-quality oil will be purchased. A school district will be responsive to cost and concentrate on finding the lowest-priced oil. The Marriott Corporation, which operates a major in-flight meal-preparation business for the airlines, will pay close attention to product availability (that is, the reliability of delivery service) as well as the cost and quality. Each of the three types of business market customers—commercial firms, institutions, and governments—have unique characteristics and special needs that must be understood by the business marketer.

www.hostmarriott.com

Commercial Enterprises as Customers

Commercial enterprises include manufacturers, construction companies, service firms (for example, hotels), transportation companies (for example, the airlines), selected professional groups (for example, dentists), and resellers. *Resellers* include wholesalers and retailers. *Wholesalers* are businesses that purchase products to sell to organizational users and retailers. In turn, *retailers* are businesses that sell to consumers. A detailed discussion of wholesalers and retailers is provided in Chapter 11.

Commercial enterprises are the sector of the business market represented by manufacturers, construction companies, service firms, transportation companies, professional groups, and resellers that purchase goods and services.

A Concentration of Customers
Manufacturers are the most important commercial customers, spending more than $1.5 trillion on materials each year. A startling fact about manufacturers is that there are so few of them. There are approximately 387,000 manufacturing firms in the United States. And though only 10 percent of these manufacturers employ more than 100 workers each, this handful of firms ships more than 75 percent of all products manufactured in the United States.[4] Because of this concentration, the business marketer normally serves *far fewer but far larger* customers than a consumer-product marketer. For example, Intel sells microprocessors to a few manufacturers, like Dell and Compaq, who, in turn, target millions of potential computer buyers. In addition to concentration by size, business markets are geographically concentrated. More than one-half of the manufacturers are concentrated in eight states: California, New York, Ohio, Illinois, Michigan, Texas, Pennsylvania, and New Jersey.

www.dell.com

www.compaq.com

Significant Buying Power

Every firm, regardless of its organizational characteristics, must procure the materials, supplies, equipment, and services necessary to operate the business successfully. On average, more than half of every dollar earned from sales of manufactured products is spent on materials, supplies, and equipment needed to produce the goods. The 100 largest industrial firms (from a purchasing standpoint) annually spend almost $900 billion on a wide array of goods and services.[5] The magnitude of expenditures by large corporations is staggering—in one year, Chrysler spent $2.1 billion on car seats alone, Intel doled out $960 million on production equipment, and Black & Decker spent $100 million on batteries. When an automobile producer sells a new car to a dealer for $18,000, the firm has already spent more than $9,000 to buy the steel, tires, glass, paint, fabric, aluminum, and electrical components to build that car. [6]

www.blackanddecker.com

The Purchasing Function

Rarely do individual departments within a corporation do their own buying. Procurement is usually administered by an individual whose title is manager of purchasing or director of purchasing. The purchasing manager is responsible for administering the purchasing process and managing relationships with suppliers. The day-to-day purchasing function is carried out by buyers, each of whom is responsible for a specific group of products (for example, personal computers or office supplies). Organizing the purchasing function in this way permits buyers to acquire a high level of expertise on a limited number of items. The salesperson works closely with buyers and develops relationships with personnel from other departments who may influence purchase decisions.

Purchasing on the Internet Like consumers who are shopping on the Internet, purchasing managers are able to scan the Web to find new suppliers, communicate with current suppliers, or place an order. While providing a rich base of information, purchasing over the Internet is also very efficient: it is estimated that purchase orders processed over the Internet cost only $5, compared to the current average purchase order cost of $100.[7] General Electric is representative of many companies that are using the Internet for a variety of purchasing activities.[8] Within a few years, GE expects to purchase 50 percent of its requirements through the Internet.

Governmental Units as Customers

Governmental units comprise the sector of the business market represented by federal, state, and local governmental units that purchase goods and services.

Federal (1), state (50), and local (87,000) **governmental units** generate the greatest volume of purchases of any customer category in the United States. Collectively, these units spend over $1.3 trillion in goods and services each year—the federal government accounts for $500 billion and states and local government contribute the rest.[9] Governmental units purchase from virtually every category of goods and services—office supplies, personal computers, furniture, food, health care, and military equipment. Business marketing firms, large and small, serve the government market. In fact, 25 percent of the purchase contracts at the federal level are with small firms.[10]

Government Buying

The government uses two general purchasing strategies: formal advertising (also known as open bid) or negotiated contract. *Formal advertising* means the government will solicit bids from appropriate suppliers. This strategy is followed when the product is standardized and the specifications are straightforward (for example, 20-pound bond paper or a personal computer with certain defined characteristics). Contracts are generally awarded to the lowest bidder; however, the government agency may select the next-to-lowest bidder if it can document that the lowest bidder would not responsibly fulfill the contract.

Figure 6.2   Boeing's Space Shuttle Home Page

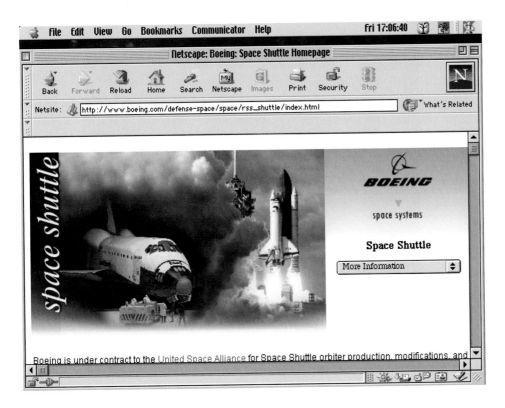

A **negotiated contract** is used by the government to purchase goods and services that cannot be differentiated on the basis of price alone (such as complex scientific equipment or R&D projects) or when there are few potential suppliers. There may be some competition because the contracting office can conduct negotiations with competing suppliers simultaneously. The purchasing decision for the government is much like that of the large corporation. Which is the best possible product at the lowest price, and will the product be delivered on time? Figure 6.2, Boeing's Space Shuttle Home Page, describes complex and sophisticated government contracts.

Institutions as Customers

Institutional customers comprise the third sector of the business market. Institutional buyers make up a sizable market—total expenditures on public elementary and secondary schools alone exceed $400 billion, and national health expenditures exceed $850 billion.[11] Schools and health-care organizations make up a sizable component of the institutional market, which also includes colleges and universities, libraries, foundations, art galleries, and clinics. On one hand, institutional purchasers are similar to governments in that the purchasing process is often constrained by political considerations and dictated by law. In fact, many institutions are administered by government units—schools, for example. On the other hand, other institutions are privately operated and managed like corporations; they may even have a broader range of purchase requirements than their large corporate counterparts. Like the commercial enterprise, institutions are ever cognizant of the value of efficient purchasing.

Institutional customers comprise the sector of the business market represented by health-care organizations, colleges and universities, libraries, foundations, art galleries, and clinics that purchase goods and services.

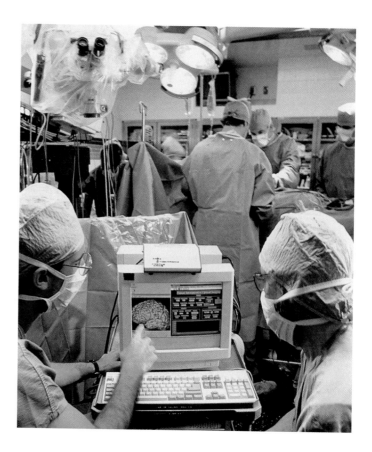

Health-Care Organizations: A Large and Thriving Sector of the Business Market

Institutional Buying

Many institutions are staffed with professionals—doctors, professors, researchers, and others. In most cases, depending on size, the institution will employ a purchasing agent and, in large institutions, a sizable purchasing department. Business marketing and sales personnel, in formulating their marketing and personal selling approaches, must understand the needs of the full range of participants in the buying process. Often, the salesperson must carefully cultivate the professional staff in terms of product benefits and service while developing a delivery timetable, maintenance contract, and price schedule to satisfy the purchasing department.

International Customers A complete picture of the business market must include a horizon that stretches beyond the boundaries of the United States. As introduced in Chapter 3, the demand for many industrial goods and services is growing more rapidly in many foreign countries than in the United States. Countries like Germany, Japan, Korea, and Brazil offer large and growing markets for many business marketers. Countless small firms and many large ones—such as General Electric (GE), 3M, Intel, Boeing, Dow Chemical, Lucent Technologies, and Motorola—derive a significant portion of their sales and profits from international markets. For example, Motorola is helping China leapfrog one stage of industrial evolution for which Western nations have invested billions of dollars—the need to tie every home and business together with copper wire. Motorola's pagers and cell phones provide valuable solutions to customers in an unwired world, and the firm's sales in China and Hong Kong exceed $3 billion annually.[12]

Different Buying Procedures

The process of purchasing, including the formal procedures, negotiations, and personnel, may show marked differences from one country to another. To illustrate, decision making is often a slow and deliberate group process in many Asian countries. Frequently, these buyers will go to extraordinary lengths to avoid individual action on any decision and will work to achieve a group consensus. In this type of decision-making climate, patience and a low-pressure selling approach are the keys to success. Although similarities exist in the business marketing process across countries, the marketing strategy must be targeted to the culture, product usage, and buying procedures of the international buyers.

Classifying Business Customers

Marketers can gain valuable strategy insights by identifying the needs and requirements of different types of commercial enterprises or business customers. The *North American Industrial Classification System (NAICS)* organizes business activity into meaningful economic sectors and identifies groups of business firms that use similar production processes.[13] The NAICS is a result of the North American Free Trade Agreement (NAFTA); it provides for standardization among Canada, Mexico, and the United States in the way that economic data are reported. Every plant or business establishment is assigned a code that reflects the primary product produced at that location. The new system, which includes traditional industries while incorporating new and emerging technology industries, replaces the Standard Industrial Classification (SIC) system that was used for decades.

Figure 6.3 illustrates the building blocks of the system. Observe that the first two digits identify the economic sector and as more digits are added, the classification becomes finer. For example, all business establishments that create, disseminate, or provide the means to distribute information are included in the Information sector: NAICS Code 51. Nineteen other economic sectors are included in the system. More specifically, U.S. establishments that produce paging equipment are assigned an NAICS Code of 513321. The six-digit codes are customized for industry subdivisions in individual countries, but at the five-digit level they are standardized across the three countries.

Using the Classification System

If a manager understands the needs and requirements of a few firms within a classification category, requirements can be projected for other firms that share that category. Each group

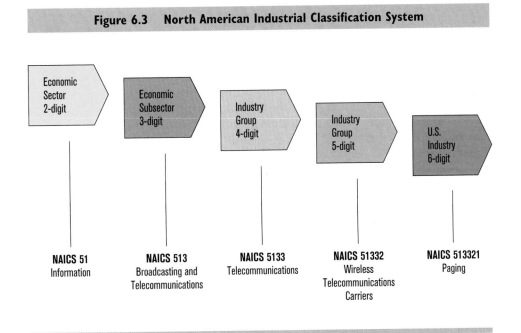

Figure 6.3   North American Industrial Classification System

| Economic Sector 2-digit | Economic Subsector 3-digit | Industry Group 4-digit | Industry Group 5-digit | U.S. Industry 6-digit |

NAICS 51
Information

NAICS 513
Broadcasting and Telecommunications

NAICS 5133
Telecommunications

NAICS 51332
Wireless Telecommunications Carriers

NAICS 513321
Paging

should be relatively homogeneous in terms of raw materials required, component parts used, and manufacturing processes employed. The NAICS provides a valuable tool for identifying new customers and for targeting profitable segments of business buyers.

CHARACTERISTICS OF BUSINESS MARKETS

The basic task of management cuts across both household consumer marketing and business marketing. Marketers serving both sectors succeed by implementing the strategic marketing concept—understanding the needs of customers and by satisfying those needs more effectively than competitors. However, business markets differ from consumer markets in several ways.

Derived Demand

Derived demand refers to the direct link between the demand for an industrial product and the demand for consumer products: *the demand for industrial products is derived from the ultimate demand for consumer products.* Consider the materials and components that are used in a Harley-Davidson motorcycle. Some of the components are manufactured by Harley-Davidson, but the finished product reflects the efforts of over 200 suppliers or business marketers who deal directly with the firm. In purchasing a Harley-Davidson motorcycle, the customer is stimulating the demand for a diverse array of products manufactured by business marketing firms—such as tires, electrical components, coil springs, aluminum castings, and other items.

Fluctuating Demand

Because demand is derived, the business marketer must carefully monitor demand patterns and changing buying preferences in the household consumer market, often on a worldwide basis. For example, a decline in mortgage rates can spark an increase in new home construction and a corresponding increase in appliance sales. Retailers generally respond by increasing their stock of inventory. As appliance producers, like Maytag, increase the rate of production to meet the demand, business marketers that supply these manufacturers with items such as motors, timers, or paint experience a surge in sales. A downturn in the economy creates the opposite result. This explains why the demand for many industrial products tends to *fluctuate* more than the demand for consumer products.

Stimulating Demand

Some business marketers must not only monitor final consumer markets, but also develop a marketing program that reaches the ultimate consumer directly. Aluminum producers use television and magazine ads to point out the convenience and recycling opportunities that aluminum containers offer to the consumer—the ultimate consumer influences aluminum demand by purchasing soft drinks in aluminum, rather than plastic, containers. Over 4 billion pounds of aluminum are used annually in the production of beverage containers. Similarly, Boeing promotes the convenience of air travel in a media campaign targeted to the consumer market to create a favorable environment for longer-term demand for its planes; DuPont advertises to ultimate consumers to stimulate the sales of carpeting, which incorporates their product.

Close Buyer-Seller Relationships

Relationships in the business market are often close and enduring. Rather than providing the end result, a sale in the business market signals the beginning of a relationship. By convincing a chain of sporting-goods stores to use its computers, IBM initiates a potential

Careers in Marketing

A Point Man at IBM

Brad Bochart is a client executive with IBM in southern California and is responsible for 19 large customer accounts that operate within the financial services industry (for example, banks, investment companies). He joined IBM in January 1997 after receiving a B.S. degree in marketing from Arizona State University. Brad's training at IBM involved two components: (1) six months of courses on topics such as business etiquette, territory management, business finance, and negotiation and sales skills; and (2) six months of training to learn more about his assigned industry-financial services.

As a Client Executive, it is my job to build market share within this Industry, develop key strategic relationships with the CEOs and key managers on their staff, as well as to continuously learn about their business and industry. Ultimately, the goal is to produce long-term partnerships with each of these accounts. I am the point-man for IBM for each of my clients and it is my job to understand their business strate-

gies and the IT tactics that they are using to support these strategies. Once this understanding is achieved, I then bring together the IBM resources that will directly support their IT and business strategies. Along with this, I must develop key internal relationships with various IBM consultants, product specialists, and business partners with the objective of using these relations to provide solutions to my customers and strengthen IBM's position across each account.

What I enjoy the most is the responsibility and authority that the job provides. I also enjoy the opportunity to call on and talk with the various CEOs who lead the organizations that I serve. To date, I have had the opportunity to golf with 5 different CEOs. I take great pleasure in understanding their businesses as well as how they are run. Most of all, I enjoy listening: how they think, how they run their day-to-day schedules, how they deal with critical issues, or how they balance their personal and professional lives. Lastly, I enjoy my colleagues at IBM and I enjoy representing the IBM Company.

Source: Interview with Brad Bochart, October 5, 1998.

long-term business relationship. More than ringing up a sale, IBM creates a customer! To maintain that relationship, the business marketer must develop an intimate knowledge of the customer's operations and contribute unique value to the customer's business. **Relationship marketing** centers on all marketing activities directed toward establishing, developing, and maintaining successful exchanges with customers.[14] Managing relationships is the heart of business marketing.

The search for improved quality and superior performance have spawned a significant shift in the purchasing practices of automakers such as Chrysler and Honda, as well as those of other leading-edge firms like Compaq and Motorola. To develop profitable relationships with business customers, business marketers must be attuned to these changes. Rather than relying on competitive bidding and dealing at arms-length with a large number of suppliers, a new approach to purchasing has been adopted in many industries. This approach is characterized by:[15]

www.ibm.com

▼ Longer-term and closer relationships with *fewer* suppliers (for example, over the past decade, the number of suppliers used by Motorola, Xerox, and Ford have been reduced by 60 percent or more).

▼ Closer interactions among *multiple* functions—manufacturing, engineering, and logistics as well as sales and purchasing—on both the buying and selling sides (for example, through computer links with its suppliers, Motorola can change specifications and delivery schedules).

Long-term relationships are built on trust and demonstrated performance. Such relationships require open lines of communication between multiple layers of the buying and selling organizations. Long-term relationships also require delivering on promises. One purchasing executive observed that once a supplier is selected, "that supplier will have the business forever" as long as quality, cost, technology, and delivery requirements are met.[16]

Figure 6.4   The Supply Chain

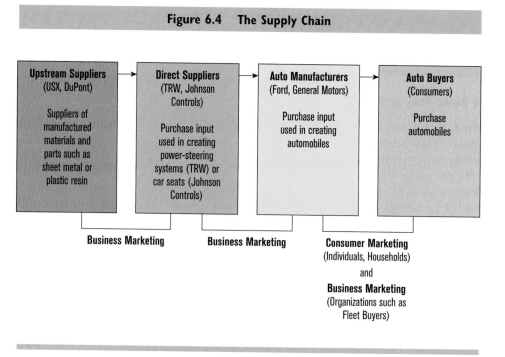

Supply-Chain Management

Figure 6.4 further illuminates the importance of a relationship perspective in business marketing by considering the chain of suppliers involved in the creation of an automobile. Consider Honda and Ford. At its Marysville, Ohio, auto assembly plant, Honda spends more than $5 billion annually for materials and components from some 300 North American suppliers.[17] These expenditures by the 300-member purchasing staff at Honda of America represent 80 percent of the firm's annual sales. Similarly, Ford relies on a vast supplier network, including firms such as TRW and Johnson Controls, to contribute half of the more than 10,000 parts of a typical Ford car. The relationships between these auto producers and their suppliers fall squarely into the business marketing domain. Similarly, business marketers such as TRW rely on a whole host of others farther back on the supply chain for raw materials, components, and other support. Each organization in this chain is involved in the creation of a product, marketing processes (including delivery), and support and service after the sale. In performing these value-creating activities, each also affects the quality level of the Honda Accord or Ford Taurus.

Supply-chain management is a technique for linking a manufacturer's operations with those of all of its strategic suppliers and its key intermediaries and customers to enhance efficiency and effectiveness. A buyer, like Honda, following a supply-chain management strategy, will reach several tiers back in the supply chain to assist second, third, and fourth-tier suppliers in meeting cost, quality, and delivery requirements. The goal of a supply-chain strategy is to improve the speed, precision, and efficiency of manufacturing and delivery through strong supplier relationships.[18] This goal is achieved through information sharing, joint planning, shared technology, and shared benefits. If the business marketer can become a valued partner in a customer's supply chain, the rewards are substantial: a long-term profitable relationship where the supplier is viewed as an extension of the customer's company. To achieve these results, the business marketer must demonstrate the ability to meet the precise quality, delivery, service, and information requirements of the customer. Figure 6.5 highlights Rockwell's position in BMW's supply chain.

www.ford.com

Figure 6.5 Rockwell Highlights Its Position in BMW's Supply Chain

Just-in-Time Systems

A strategy of purchasing, production, and inventory practiced in many manufacturing firms is referred to as *just-in-time* or *JIT*. The essence of the concept is to deliver defect-free parts and materials to the production process just at the moment they are needed. Consider Dell Computer Corporation's JIT system.[19] Most of Dell's suppliers have warehouses near the firm's manufacturing plants. When Dell receives an order for a personal computer, it transmits the requirements to suppliers who pick the proper parts and pack them in reusable bins. Following a continuous loop between suppliers and Dell, trucks deliver the carefully sorted parts to the computer maker's plant for final assembly. The goals of JIT are to minimize inventory costs, improve product quality, maximize production efficiency, and provide optimal levels of customer service. To illustrate, JIT practices have allowed Dell to provide prompt service to its rapidly-growing base of customers—a PC is shipped three days after the order is received.

JIT systems are built on trust, demonstrated performance, and a close supplier-customer relationship. To illustrate, Owens-Illinois is the primary supplier of glass containers to the J.M. Smucker Company, the jam and jelly manufacturer. To reduce container inventory costs, Smucker's maintains only enough glass containers to run the production line for a few hours. Production managers at Smucker's have learned that they can count on Owens-Illinois for deliveries that permit a seamless production process. Such consistent delivery performance to Smucker's standards has created a long-standing customer for Owens-Illinois.

THE ORGANIZATIONAL BUYING PROCESS

Organizational buying behavior is a process rather than an isolated act. Tracing the history of a procurement decision in an organization uncovers critical decision points and evolving information requirements. In fact, organizational buying involves several stages, each of which yields a decision. Figure 6.6 lists the major stages in the organizational buying process.

Stage 1. Problem Recognition

www.pillsbury.com

Similar to the consumer decision-making process discussed in Chapter 5, the business-to-business purchasing process begins when someone in the organization recognizes a problem that can be solved or an opportunity that can be captured by acquiring a specific product. Problem recognition can be triggered by internal or external forces. Internally, a firm, like Pillsbury, may need new high-speed production equipment to support a new product launch. Or a purchasing manager may be unhappy with the product quality, price, or service of a supplier of packaging materials. Externally, a salesperson can precipitate the need for a product by demonstrating opportunities for improving the organization's performance. Likewise, business marketers also use advertising to alert cus-

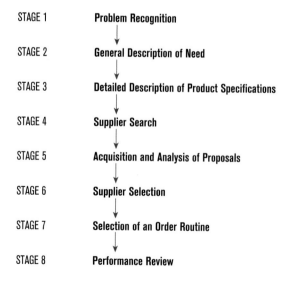

Figure 6.6   Major Stages of the Organizational Buying Process

STAGE 1	**Problem Recognition**
STAGE 2	**General Description of Need**
STAGE 3	**Detailed Description of Product Specifications**
STAGE 4	**Supplier Search**
STAGE 5	**Acquisition and Analysis of Proposals**
STAGE 6	**Supplier Selection**
STAGE 7	**Selection of an Order Routine**
STAGE 8	**Performance Review**

Figure 6.7 An Ad Offering a Total Solution for Organizational Buyers

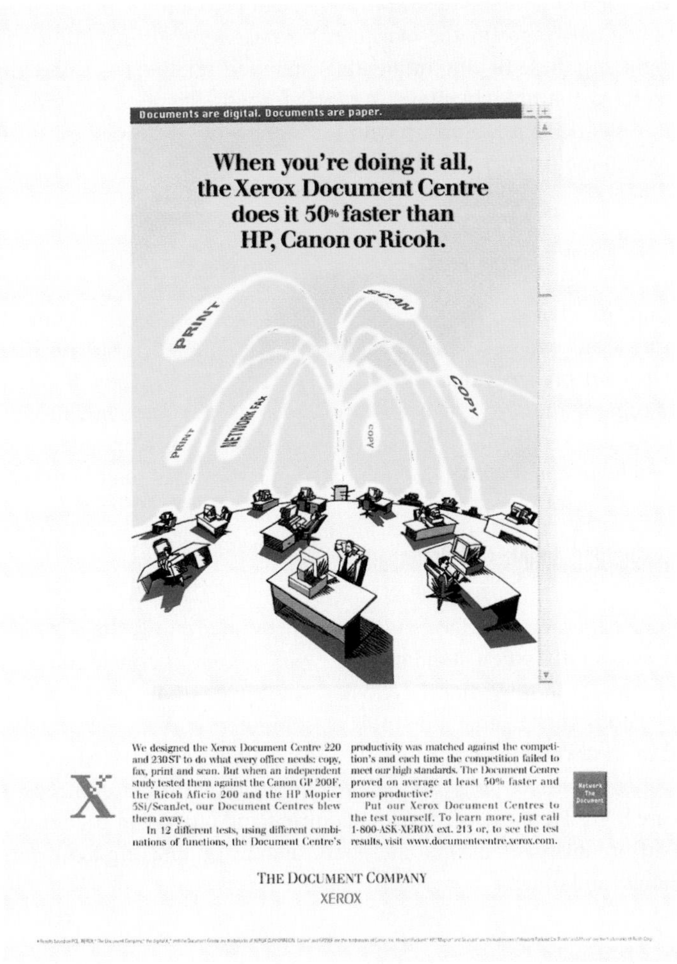
Documents are digital. Documents are paper.
When you're doing it all, the Xerox Document Centre does it 50% faster than HP, Canon or Ricoh.
PRINT
SCAN
COPY
NETWORK FAX
PRINT
COPY
We designed the Xerox Document Centre 220 and 230ST to do what every office needs: copy, fax, print and scan. But when an independent study tested them against the Canon GP 200F, the Ricoh Aficio 200 and the HP Mopier 5Si/ScanJet, our Document Centres blew them away.
In 12 different tests, using different combinations of functions, the Document Centre's productivity was matched against the competition's and each time the competition failed to meet our high standards. The Document Centre proved on average at least 50% faster and more productive.*
Put our Xerox Document Centres to the test yourself. To learn more, just call 1-800-ASK-XEROX ext. 213 or, to see the test results, visit www.documentcentre.xerox.com.
Network The Document
THE DOCUMENT COMPANY
XEROX

SOURCE: Courtesy, Xerox Corporation.

tomers to problems and demonstrate how a particular product may provide a solution (see Figure 6.7).

Stage 2. General Description of Need

Organizational members must determine specifically how the problem can be solved. Here the focus is on the general characteristics and quantity of the needed item. These decisions are generally made within the department where the need originally emerged. For example, members of the production department would determine the characteristics needed in a high-speed packaging system. For technical products, performance specifications are also prepared by the department that will use the product. The development of performance specifications has a critical impact on the final choice of a product and a supplier. The decisions made in the early stages of the process inevitably limit and shape the decision making in the later stages of the process. The salesperson is a vital source of information to organizational buyers throughout the purchasing process.

Stage 3. Product Specifications

An extension of the second stage, Stage 3 involves a detailed and precise technical description of the needed item—a description that can be readily communicated to others. This can be a critical stage for the marketer because key buying influentials enter the process. Recognizing these buying influentials and their relative roles and importance can give the marketer a distinct advantage. A marketer who triggers the initial need has the benefit of a close working relationship with key organizational members throughout these formative stages in the procurement process.

Stage 4. Supplier Search

Once the organization has defined the product that will satisfy its requirements, the search turns to this question: which of the many possible suppliers can be considered potential candidates? The intensity of evaluation varies by organization and by the particular buying situation. The organization invests more time and energy in the evaluation process when the proposed product has a strong bearing on organizational performance. (How organizational buyers evaluate potential vendors is treated in more detail later in the chapter.)

Stage 5. Acquisition and Analysis of Proposals

When the information needs of the buying organization are low, Stages 4 and 5 occur simultaneously, especially when standardized items are under consideration. In this case, the buying organization may merely check a catalog or update price information. For more complex goods such as machine tools or computer workstations, many months may be consumed in the exchange of proposals and counterproposals. Stage 5 emerges as a distinct component of the buying process only when the information needs of the buying organization are high. Here the process of acquiring and analyzing proposals may involve a number of different organizational members such as purchasing managers, engineers, users, consultants, and others.

Stage 6. Supplier Selection

Alternative proposals are analyzed, one or more of the offers is accepted, and the others are rejected. Negotiations concerning the terms of the transaction may continue with the selected suppliers.

Stage 7. Selection of an Order Routine

After surviving the review process and being selected as a source of supply, a marketer faces further tests. The using department (for example, production) will not view its problem as resolved until the specified product is available for its use. Concerning the order routine, a purchase order is forwarded to the vendor, status reports are forwarded to the using department, and inventory levels are planned. So, in this stage, purchasing guidelines are established for the item that detail technical specifications, quantity needed, expected time of delivery, and warranties.

Stage 8. Performance Review

Did the purchased item solve the original problem? This is the final stage in the purchasing process. The performance review may lead the purchasing manager to continue, modify, or cancel the agreement. A review critical of the chosen supplier and supportive of rejected alternatives can lead members of the decision-making unit to reexamine their position. If the product fails to meet the needs of the using department, vendors screened earlier in the procurement process may be given further consideration. To retain a new customer, the marketer must ensure that the needs of the buying organization have been completely satisfied. Failure to follow through at this critical stage leaves the marketer vulnerable.

The flow of stages in this model of the procurement process may not progress sequentially, and may vary with the complexity of the purchasing situation. For example, some of the stages are compressed or bypassed when organizations are making routine buying decisions. However, the model provides important insights into the organizational buying process. Certain stages may be completed concurrently; the process may be discontinued by a change in the external environment or in upper-management thinking. The organizational buying process is shaped by a host of internal and external forces such as changes in economic or competitive conditions or a basic shift in organizational priorities.

BUYING SITUATIONS ANALYZED

The same product may elicit markedly different purchasing patterns in various organizations with various levels of experience and information. Therefore attention should center on buying situations rather than on products. Three types of buying situations have been identified: (1) new task, (2) modified rebuy, and (3) straight rebuy.[20]

New Task

In the **new-task buying situation,** the problem or need is perceived by organizational decision makers as totally different from previous experiences. Therefore, decision makers must explore many alternative ways of solving the problem, and then search for appropriate suppliers. To illustrate, a large health insurance company placed a $600,000 order for workstation furniture. The long-term impact on the work environment shaped the six-month decision process and involved the active participation of personnel from several departments.[21] New task buying decisions can be of extreme importance to the firm—strategically and financially.

When confronting a new-task buying situation, organizational buyers operate in a stage of *extended problem solving.*[22] The buying influentials and decision makers lack well-defined criteria for comparing alternative products and suppliers, but they also lack strong predispositions toward a particular solution. In the consumer market, this is the same type of problem solving an individual or household might follow in buying a first home.

New-task buying situation
is a purchase situation that results in an extensive search for information and a lengthy decision process.

Strategy Guidelines
The business marketer confronting a new-task buying situation can gain a differential advantage by participating actively in the initial stages of the procurement process. The marketer should gather information on the problems facing the buying organization, isolate specific requirements, and offer proposals to meet the requirements. Ideas that lead to new products often originate not with the marketer but with the customer.

Marketers who are presently supplying other items to the organization ("in" suppliers) have an edge over other firms; they can see problems unfolding and are familiar with the "personality" and behavior patterns of the organization. The successful business marketer carefully monitors the changing needs of organizations and is prepared to respond to the needs of new-task buyers.

Straight Rebuy

When there is a continuing or recurring requirement, buyers have substantial experience in dealing with the need, and they require little or no new information. Evaluation of new

Straight rebuy

is routine reordering from the same supplier of a product that has been purchased in the past.

alternative solutions is unnecessary and unlikely to yield appreciable improvements. Therefore, the organization is likely to undertake a straight rebuy.

Routine problem solving is the decision process organizational buyers employ in the straight rebuy. Organizational buyers have well-developed choice criteria to apply to the purchase decision. The criteria have been refined over time and the buyers have developed predispositions toward the offerings of one or a few carefully screened suppliers. This process is termed *routine problem solving.* In the consumer market, this is the same type of problem solving that a shopper might use in selecting 30 items in 20 minutes during a weekly trip to the supermarket.

Strategy Guidelines

The purchasing department handles straight rebuy situations by routinely selecting a supplier from a list (formal or informal) of acceptable vendors and then placing an order. The marketing task appropriate in this situation depends on whether the marketer is an "in" supplier (on the list) or an "out" supplier (not among the chosen few). An "in" supplier must reinforce the buyer-seller relationship, meet the buying organization's expectations, and be alert and responsive to the changing needs of the organization.

The "out" supplier faces a number of obstacles and must convince the organization that significant benefits can be derived from breaking the routine. This can be difficult because organizational buyers perceive risk in shifting from the known to the unknown. The organizational spotlight shines directly on them if an untested supplier falters. Testing, evaluations, and approvals may be viewed by buyers as costly, time-consuming, and unnecessary.

The marketing effort of the "out" supplier rests on an understanding of the basic buying needs of the organization: information gathering is essential. The marketer must convince organizational buyers that their purchasing requirements have changed or that the requirements should be interpreted differently. The objective is to persuade decision makers to reexamine alternative solutions and to revise the preferred list to include the new supplier.

Modified Rebuy

Modified rebuy

is a purchase where the buyers have experience in satisfying the need, but feel the situation warrants reevaluation of a limited set of alternatives before making a decision.

In the modified rebuy situation, organizational decision makers feel that significant benefits may be derived from a reevaluation of alternatives. Several factors may trigger such a reassessment. Internal forces include the search for quality improvements or cost reductions. A marketer offering cost, quality, or service improvements can trigger the reassessment. The modified rebuy situation is most likely to occur when the firm is displeased with the performance of present suppliers (for example, poor delivery service).

Limited problem solving best describes the decision-making process for the modified rebuy. Decision makers have well-defined criteria, but they are uncertain about which suppliers can best fit their needs. In the consumer market, college students buying their *second* computer might follow a limited problem solving approach.

Strategy Guidelines

In a modified rebuy, the direction of the marketing effort depends on whether the marketer is an "in" or an "out" supplier. An "in" supplier should make every effort to understand and satisfy the procurement need and to move decision makers into a straight rebuy. The buying organization perceives potential payoffs from a reexamination of alternatives. The "in" supplier should ask why, and act immediately to remedy any customer problems. The marketer may be out of touch with the buying organization's requirements.

The goal of the "out" supplier should be to hold the organization in modified rebuy status long enough for the buyer to evaluate an alternative offering. Knowing the factors that led decision makers to reexamine alternatives could be pivotal. A particularly effec-

Marketing Technologies

Purchasing Managers Are Wired

Purchasing managers have made the Internet a key addition to the toolkit that they use every day at work. David Herzberg, a purchasing manager at Lucent Technologies, explains: "The Net provides a lot of good financial data and other information on prospective suppliers. It offers access to analysts' reports, credit ratings, and news articles that can also be useful for evaluating suppliers." Like most Internet users, buyers locate valuable information on potential suppliers by using leading search engines such as Yahoo, Alta Vista, and Lycos. Some of the most popular Web sites among purchasing professionals are the Thomas Register (www.thomasregister.com), a directory of 155,000 suppliers; Dunn and Bradstreet (www.dnb.com), a publisher of financial reports and credit ratings of firms; and the Bureau of Labor Statistics (www.bls.gov), a provider of key government, economic, and industry data. While providing a valuable source of information, buy-

ers emphasize that the Internet does not eliminate the need for a thorough evaluation of all new suppliers. A purchasing executive aptly noted: "The Net is just one tool in your sourcing (buying) toolbox. It's not a magic bullet."

Questions

1. In visiting the Web site of a business marketing firm (i.e., a potential supplier), what particular information would a professional buyer look for?

2. Describe the features and characteristics of a business marketer's Web site that might spark the interest of purchasing managers and motivate them to learn more about the firm and its offerings.

Source: Tim Minahan, "Buyers Make Net Part of Sourcing Toolkit," *Purchasing* (18 June 1998), pp. S4–S21.

---

tive strategy for an "out" supplier is to offer performance guarantees as part of the proposal.[23] To illustrate, the following guarantee prompted International Circuit Technology, a manufacturer of printed circuit boards, to change to a new supplier for plating chemicals: "Your plating costs will be no more than x cents per square foot or we will make up the difference."[24] Pleased with the performance results, International Circuit Technology now routinely reorders from this new supplier.

MAJOR INFLUENCES ON ORGANIZATIONAL BUYERS

As illustrated in Figure 6.8, the buying decisions of organizations are influenced by environmental factors (for example, the growth rate of the economy), organizational factors (for example, the size of the buying organization), group factors (for example, patterns of influence in the buying center), and individual factors (for example, personal preferences).

Environmental Forces

A projected change in business conditions, a technological development, or a new piece of legislation can drastically alter organizational buying plans. Among the types of environmental forces that shape organizational buying behavior are economic, political, legal, and technological influences. Collectively, such environmental influences define the boundaries within which buyer-seller relationships develop in the business market. Particular attention will be given to selected economic and technological forces that influence buying decisions.

Economic Influences

Because of the derived nature of industrial demand, the marketer must also be sensitive to the strength of demand in the ultimate consumer market. The demand for many industrial products fluctuates more widely than the general economy. Firms that operate on a global scale must be sensitive to the economic conditions that prevail across regions. For

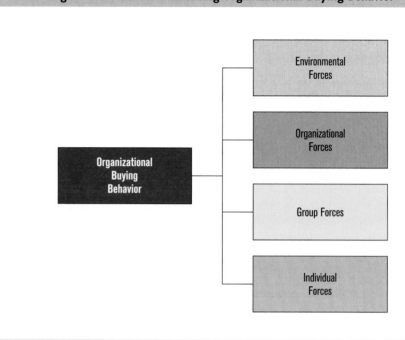

Figure 6.8 **Forces Influencing Organizational Buying Behavior**

example, as the U.S. economy moves out of a recession, the European economy may continue to sputter. A wealth of political and economic forces dictate the vitality and growth of an economy.

The economic environment influences an organization's ability and, to a degree, its willingness to buy. However, shifts in general economic conditions do not affect all sectors of the market evenly. For example, a rise in interest rates may damage the housing industry (including lumber, cement, and insulation) but may have minimal effects on industries such as paper, hospital supplies, office products, and soft drinks. Marketers that serve broad sectors of the business market must be particularly sensitive to the differential impact of selective economic shifts on buying behavior.

Technological Influences

The rate of technological change in an industry influences the composition of the decision-making unit in the buying organization. As the pace of technological change increases, the importance of the purchasing manager in the buying process declines. Technical and engineering personnel tend to be more important to organizational buying processes in which the rate of technological change is great. Recent research also suggests that buyers who perceive the pace of technological change to be more rapid will (1) conduct more intense search efforts and (2) spend less time on their overall search processes.[25] Why? "In cost–benefit terms, a fast pace of change implies that distinct benefits are associated with search effort, yet costs are associated with prolonging the process" because the acquired information is "time sensitive."[26]

Organizational Forces

An understanding of the buying organization is based on the strategic priorities of the firm, the role that purchasing occupies in the executive hierarchy, and the competitive challenges that the firm confronts.

To Boost Productivity: Organizations Are Large Information Technology Buyers

Strategic Priorities

Organizational buying decisions are made to facilitate organizational activities and to support the firm's mission and strategies. A business marketer who understands the strategic priorities and concerns that occupy key decision makers is better equipped to respond to customer needs. For example, IBM centers attention on how its information technology and assorted services can improve the efficiency of a retailer's operations or advance the customer service levels of a hotel chain. Alternatively, a supplier to Hewlett-Packard will strike a responsive chord with executives by offering a new component part that will increase the performance or lower the cost of its ink-jet printers. To provide such customer solutions, the business marketer requires an intimate understanding of the opportunities and threats that the customer confronts. Figure 6.9 presents an ad that features a solution provided for an organizational buyer.

www.hp.com

www.motorola.com

Strategic Role of Purchasing

In many firms, purchasing strategy is becoming more closely tied to corporate strategy. To illustrate, purchasing executives at Motorola have a clear understanding of the firm's objectives, markets, and competitive strategies. As purchasing assumes a more strategic role in the firm, the business marketer must understand the competitive realities of the customer's business and develop a **value proposition** unique to the customer. For example, Motorola's Paging Products Group is keenly interested in working with suppliers who can contribute technology or component parts that enhance the value of the firm's product for customers and that strengthen its competitive position.

Value proposition
is a program of tangible goods, services, ideas, and solutions that a business marketer offers to advance the performance goals of the customer organization.

Organizational Positioning of Purchasing

An organization that centralizes procurement decisions will approach purchasing differently than will a company where purchasing decisions are made at individual user locations. When purchasing is centralized, a separate organizational unit is given authority for purchases at a regional, divisional, or headquarters level. For example, Mead Corporation's centralized purchasing function directs the purchase of common materials used by Mead plants across the United States. Boeing, AT&T, 3M, Hewlett-Packard, and Xerox are among other corporations that emphasize centralized procurement. A marketer who is sensitive to organizational influences can more accurately map the decision-making process, isolate buying influentials, identify important buying criteria, and target marketing strategy for both centralized as well as decentralized organizations.[27]

**Figure 6.9 Organizational Buyers Seek Solutions:
US Web Ad Featuring One Provided for Harley Davidson**

Source: Courtesy, US WEB Corporation.

Group Forces: The Buying Center

Buying decisions typically involve not one but several members of the organization, whether the decisions are made by commercial enterprises, institutions, or governmental organizations. The decision-making unit of a buying organization is called the ***buying center.*** The buying center consists of those individuals who participate in the purchasing decision and who share the goals and risks arising from the decision.[28] The size of the buying center varies, but an average buying center will include more than four persons per purchase; the number of people involved in all stages of one purchase may be as many as twenty.[29]

The composition of the buying center may change from one purchasing situation to another and is not prescribed by the organizational chart. A buying group evolves during the purchasing process in response to the information requirements of the specific purchase situation. Because organizational buying is a *process* rather than an isolated act, different individuals are important to the process at different times.[30] A design engineer may exert significant influence early in the purchasing process when product specifications are

Table 6.1   The Involvement of Buying Center Participants at Different Stages of the Procurement Process

Buying Center Participants	Stages of Procurement Process for a Medical Equipment Purchase			
	Identification of Need	Establishment of Objectives	Identification and Evaluation of Buying Alternatives	Selection of Suppliers
Physicians	High	High	High	High
Nursing	Low	High	High	Low
Administration	Moderate	Moderate	Moderate	High
Engineering	Low	Moderate	Moderate	Low
Purchasing	Low	Low	Low	Moderate

being established; others may assume a more dominant role in later phases. Again, the composition of the buying center evolves during the purchasing process, varies from firm to firm, and varies from one purchasing situation to another. To be successful, the business marketer must identify the organizational members who comprise the buying center and understand each participant's *relative influence* and the *evaluative criteria* that are important to each member in reaching a decision.

Isolating the Buying Situation

Defining the buying situation and determining whether the firm is in the early or later stages of the procurement decision-making process are important first steps in defining the buying center. The buying center for a new-task buying situation in the not-for-profit market is presented in Table 6.1. The product, intensive-care monitoring systems, is a complex and costly purchase. Buying center members are drawn from five functional areas, each participating to varying degrees in the decision process. Moreover, each buying center member emphasizes different evaluation criteria. Administration and purchasing are concerned with price and cost issues, while physicians are concerned with product quality and service. A marketer who concentrated exclusively on the purchasing function would be overlooking key buying influentials.

Salespeople who frequently encounter new-task buying situations generally observe that:

> The buying center is large, slow to decide, uncertain about its needs and the appropriateness of the possible solutions, more concerned about finding a good solution than getting a low price or assured supply, more willing to entertain proposals from "out" suppliers and less willing to favor "in" suppliers, more influenced by technical personnel, [and] less influenced by purchasing agents.[31]

By contrast, salespeople facing more routine purchase situations (that is, straight and modified rebuys) frequently observe buying centers that are "small, quick to decide, confident in their appraisals of the problem and possible solutions, concerned about price and supply, satisfied with 'in' suppliers, and more influenced by purchasing agents."[32]

Buying Center Roles

Members of the buying center assume different roles throughout the purchasing process: users, influencers, buyers, deciders, and gatekeepers.[33] As the name implies, *users* are the personnel who will be using the product in question. Users may have anywhere from inconsequential to extremely important influence on the purchase decision. In some cases, the users initiate the purchase action by requesting the product. They may even develop the product specifications.

Consider Clark Equipment Company—a firm that manufactures forklift trucks for the business market.[34] They found that equipment operators (users) assume an important role in the buying decision. *Users* spend a considerable part of their work day operating the equipment and often receive financial incentives that are tied to their performance. This means that driver comfort and equipment reliability (minimal equipment downtime) are central to the buying decision. In designing a new line of forklifts, Clark Equipment is giving an unprecedented level of attention to driver comfort, reduced engine noise level, and product reliability.

Gatekeepers control information to be reviewed by other members of the buying center. The control of information may be accomplished by disseminating printed information, such as advertisements, or by controlling which salesperson will speak to which individuals in the buying center. To illustrate, the purchasing agent or an administrative assistant might perform this screening role by opening the gate to the buying center for some sales personnel and closing it to others.

Influencers affect the purchasing decision by supplying information for the evaluation of alternatives or by setting buying specifications. Typically, those in technical departments, such as engineering, quality control, and R&D, are significant influences on the purchase decision. Sometimes, individuals outside the buying organization can assume this role. For high-tech purchases, technical consultants often assume an influential role in the decision process and broaden the set of alternatives being considered.[35]

Deciders are the individuals who actually make the buying decision, whether or not they have the formal authority to do so. The identity of the decider is the most difficult role to determine: *buyers* may have formal authority to buy, but the president of the firm may actually make the decision. A decider could be a design engineer who develops a set of specifications that only one vendor can meet.

The *buyer* has formal authority to select a supplier and implement all procedures connected with securing the product. The power of the buyer is often usurped by more powerful members of the organization. The buyer's role is often assumed by the purchasing agent, who executes the administrative functions associated with a purchase order.

One person could assume all roles in a purchase situation or separate individuals could assume different buying roles. To illustrate, as users, personnel from marketing, accounting, purchasing, and production may all have a stake in which information technology system is selected.

Identifying Buying Influentials

Multiple buying influences and group forces are critical in organizational buying decisions. A central challenge for the business marketer is to identify the patterns of influence within the buying center. Except for repetitive buying situations, key influencers are frequently located outside the purchasing department. However, research provides some valuable clues for identifying powerful buying center members.[36] To illustrate, organizational members tend to assume an active and influential role in the buying center when they:

▼ Have an important personal stake in the decision.

▼ Possess expert knowledge concerning the choice at hand.

▼ Have direct access to top management.

▼ Are central to the flow of decision-related information.

Individual Forces

Individuals, not organizations, make buying decisions. Each member of the buying center has a unique personality, a particular set of learned experiences, a specified organizational function, and a perception of how best to achieve both personal and organizational goals.[37] Organizational members are influenced by both rational and emotional motives when choosing among competing offerings. ***Rational motives*** are usually economic, such as price, quality, and service. ***Emotional motives*** include such human factors as the desire for status within the organization, for salary increases, and for increased job security. A marketer concentrating exclusively on rational motives has an incomplete picture of the organizational buyer.

Differing Evaluative Criteria

Evaluative criteria are specifications that organizational buyers use to compare alternative goods and services; however, these may conflict. Organizational product users generally value prompt delivery and efficient servicing; engineering values product quality, standardization, and testing; and purchasing assigns importance to cost savings and delivery reliability.[38] Product perceptions and evaluation criteria differ among organizational decision makers as a result of differences in educational backgrounds, source and type of information exposure, interpretation and retention of relevant information, and level of satisfaction with past purchases.[39] Engineers have an educational background different from that of plant managers or purchasing agents; they are exposed to different journals, attend different conferences, and possess different professional goals and values. A sales presentation that is effective with purchasing may be entirely off the mark with engineering.

HOW ORGANIZATIONAL BUYERS EVALUATE POTENTIAL SUPPLIERS

The business marketer must understand how organizational buyers measure value and evaluate supplier performance. To develop profitable relationships with organizational customers, the value offerings developed by the business marketer must be based on skills and resources that provide value *as perceived by customers.*

Measuring Value

The accurate measurement of value is crucial to the purchasing function. The principles and tools of **value analysis** aid the professional buyer in approaching this task. For example, ideas from suppliers enable Chrysler to reduce costs by $1 billion annually. When Allied Signal reduced the complexity of its antilock braking systems, Chrysler's annual costs were cut by $744,000![40] Note that rather straightforward design and manufacturing alternatives can produce spectacular cost savings. Value is achieved when the proper function is secured for the proper cost. Because functions can be accomplished in a number of different ways, the most cost-efficient way of fully accomplishing a function establishes its value.

Value analysis
is a method of weighing the comparative value of materials, components, and manufacturing processes from the standpoint of their purpose, relative merit, and cost in order to uncover ways of improving products, lowering costs, or both.

Evaluating Supplier Performance

Once a contract is awarded to a supplier, the evaluation process takes a different form. Actual performance must be evaluated. Buyers rate supplier performance in assessing the quality of past decisions, in making future vendor selections, and as a negotiating tool to gain leverage in buyer-seller relationships. The ***weighted-point plan*** is a supplier rating system that is widely used by organizational buyers.

The Weighted-Point Plan

In the weighted-point plan, the buying organization weights each performance factor according to its relative importance. Quality might be given a weight of 40; service, 30; and price, 30. This system alerts the business marketer to the nature and importance of the evaluative criteria used by a particular organization. The marketer's total offering can then be adjusted to fit the organization's needs more precisely.

Figure 6.10   How Chrysler Grades Suppliers

SUPPLIER RATING CHART:

Supplier Name: _____   Commodity: _____
Shipping Location: _____   Annual Sales Dollars: _____

Quality 40%	5 Excellent	4 Good	3 Satisfactory	2 Fair	1 Poor	0 N/A
Supplier defect rates _____						
SQA program conformance _____						
Sample approval performance _____						
Responsiveness to quality problems _____						
Overall rating _____						
Delivery 25%						
Avoidance of late or overshipments _____						
Ability to expand production capacity _____						
Engineering sample delivery performance _____						
Response to fluctuating supply demands _____						
Overall delivery rating _____						
Price 25%						
Price competitiveness _____						
Absorption of economic price increases _____						
Submission of cost savings plans _____						
Payment terms _____						
Overall price rating _____						
Technology 10%						
State-of-the-art component technology _____						
Sharing research development capability _____						
Capable and willing to provide circuit design services _____						
Responsiveness to engineering problems _____						
Overall technology rating _____						

Buyer: _____   Date: _____
Comments: _____

Source: Courtesy, Chrysler Corporation.

Observe in Figure 6.10 how Chrysler Corporation "grades" suppliers of electronic components. Under this program, suppliers can be awarded a total of 100 points, including up to 40 points for quality, 25 points for pricing, 25 points for delivery, and 10 points for technical assistance. Note that a number of dimensions are evaluated for each performance factor.

Working with other departments, such as engineering and production control, purchasing calculates a performance score for each supplier. In the pricing area, Chrysler is giving increased attention to the cost savings plans submitted by the supplier.[41] Detailed records are kept of the number of proposals each supplier makes and the dollar savings that they generate. By focusing on continual improvement, suppliers can improve their profitability and increase the amount of sales they generate from Chrysler. Those scoring 91 points or higher make the preferred supplier list. It is important to note that only 300 of Chrysler's 1,000 electronics suppliers achieve this distinction, and they receive more than 80 percent of the firm's $350 million annual budget for electronic components. Suppliers scoring less than 70 points are usually dropped automatically. As this illustration demonstrates, customers in the business market are interested in the total capabilities of a supplier and how these capabilities might assist them in improving *their* competitive position—now and in the future.

Chapter Summary

In business-to-business marketing, the customers are organizations. The business market can be divided into three major sectors: commercial enterprises, governments (federal, state, and local), and institutions. Many business marketers—like Intel, Boeing, and IBM—generate a significant proportion of their sales and profit by serving international customers. Indeed, the demand for many industrial products is growing more rapidly in many foreign countries than in the United States.

Commercial enterprises include manufacturers, construction companies, service firms, transportation companies, selected professional groups, and resellers. Of these, manufacturers account for the largest dollar volume of purchases. Furthermore, although the majority of manufacturing firms are small, buying power is concentrated in the hands of relatively few manufacturers, which are also concentrated geographically. Governmental units also make substantial purchases of products. Two general purchasing strategies are used by government buyers: the formal advertising approach for standardized products and negotiated contracts for unique requirements. Institutional customers, like health-care organizations and universities, comprise the third sector of the business market. Depending on size, the institution will employ a purchasing agent and, in large institutions, a sizable purchasing department.

Business markets differ from household consumer markets in several ways. Because purchases made by business customers are linked to the goods and services that they sell, derived demand is an important, and often volatile, feature in the business market. Business market customers are developing closer relationships with fewer suppliers than they have used in the past, and they expect these suppliers to provide defect-free products at the moment they are needed. These trends place a premium on the relationship marketing and supply chain capabilities of the business marketer.

Knowledge of the process that organizational buyers follow in making purchasing decisions is fundamental to responsive marketing strategy. As a buying organization moves from the problem recognition phase, in which a need is defined, to later phases, in which suppliers are screened and ultimately chosen, the marketer can play an active role. The nature of the buying process followed in a particular situation depends on the organization's level of experience with similar procurement problems. There are three types of buying situations: (1) new task, (2) modified rebuy, and (3) straight rebuy. Each requires a unique problem-solving approach, involves unique buying influentials, and demands a unique marketing response. A wealth of factors—which can be classified as environmental, organizational, group, and individual—influence the buying decisions of an organization. A central challenge for the business marketer is to identify the organizational members who comprise the buying center.

Key Terms

Key buying influentials are those individuals in the buying organization who have the power to influence the buying decision.

Business market consists of all organizations that buy goods and services for use in the production of other products and services or for resale.

Commercial enterprises are the sector of the business market represented by manufacturers, construction companies, service firms, transportation companies, professional groups, and resellers that purchase goods and services.

Governmental units comprise the sector of the business market represented by federal, state, and local governmental units that purchase goods and services.

Institutional customers comprise the sector of the business market represented by health-care organizations, colleges and universities, libraries, foundations, art galleries, and clinics that purchase goods and services.

New-task buying situation is a purchase situation that results in an extensive search for information and a lengthy decision process.

Straight rebuy is routine reordering from the same supplier of a product that has been purchased in the past.

Modified rebuy is a purchase where the buyers have experience in satisfying the need, but feel the situation warrants reevaluation of a limited set of alternatives before making a decision.

Value proposition is a program of goods, services, ideas, and solutions that a business marketer offers to advance the performance goals of the customer organization.

Value analysis is a method of weighing the comparative value of materials, components, and manufacturing processes from the standpoint of their purpose, relative merit, and cost in order to uncover ways of improving products, lowering costs, or both.

Additional Key Terms and Concepts

Resellers	Wholesalers
Retailers	Formal advertising
Negotiated contract	North American Industrial Classification
Derived demand	System (NAICS)
Relationship marketing	Supply-chain management
Just-in-time (JIT)	Extended problem solving
Routine problem solving	Limited problem solving
Buying center	Users
Gatekeepers	Influencers
Deciders	Buyer
Rational motives	Emotional motives
Evaluative criteria	Weighted-point plan

Questions for Discussion

1. Describe the major categories of customers that comprise the business market.

2. Compare and contrast the two general procurement strategies employed by the federal government: (1) formal advertising and (2) negotiated contract.

3. DuPont, one of the largest industrial producers of chemicals and synthetic fibers, spends millions of dollars annually on advertising its products to final consumers. For example, DuPont invested more than one million dollars in a TV advertising blitz that emphasized the comfort of jeans made of DuPont's stretch polyester-cotton blend. Since DuPont does not produce jeans or market them to final consumers, why are large expenditures made on consumer advertising?

4. The goal of a supply-chain strategy is to improve the speed, precision, and efficiency of manufacturing through strong supplier partnerships. Explain.

5. What strategic advantage does the marketer gain by reaching the buying organization at the early rather than the late stages of the purchase decision process?

6. Mike Weber, the purchasing agent for Smith Manufacturing, views the purchase of widgets as a routine buying decision. What factors might lead him to alter this

position? More important, what factors will determine whether a particular supplier, such as Albany Widget, will be considered by Mike?

7. Harley-Davidson, the U.S. motorcycle producer, recently purchased some sophisticated manufacturing equipment to enhance its position in a very competitive market. First, what environmental forces might have been important in spawning this capital investment? Second, which functional units were likely to have been represented in the buying center?

8. Millions of notebook computers are purchased each year by organizations. Identify several evaluative criteria that purchasing managers might use in choosing a particular brand. In your view, which criteria would be most decisive in the buying decision?

9. Describe the weighted point plan and discuss how a purchasing manager at Xerox might use it in evaluating the performance of a supplier of component parts for the firm's high-speed photocopier.

10. Evaluate this statement: Both rational and emotional factors enter into the decisions that organizational buyers make.

Internet Questions

1. PeopleSoft is a high-growth company that seeks to deliver "outrageous customer service." Surveys suggest that nearly all of the firm's customers would recommend PeopleSoft to others. Go to the company's Web site—www.peoplesoft.com—and identify:
   a. The goods and services that they sell.
   b. The types of customers in the business market that they serve.

2. Dell Computer has been wildly successful in selling its products over the Internet to customers of all types, including every category of customers in the business market: commercial enterprises, institutions, and government. Assume that the library at your university is planning the purchase of 25 new desktop computers. Go to www.dell.com and to the Dell Online Store for Higher Education and:
   a. Identify the price and product dimensions of two desktop systems that might meet your university's needs.
   b. Provide a critique of the Web site and consider the degree to which it provided access to the information that a potential buyer might want.

3. Guardian Industries is a leading supplier to the global automotive industry—a key member of the supply chain for auto manufacturers. Visit www.guardian.com and:
   a. Identify the particular types of automotive products that they manufacture.
   b. Discuss the particular capabilities that the firm seems to emphasize in discussing its automotive products.
   c. Explore the factors that an auto manufacturer like Honda might evaluate in comparing Guardian Industries to other suppliers.

Endnotes

[1]J. M. Smucker Annual Report, 1998.

[2]Anne Millen Porter, "Big Spenders: The Top 250," *Purchasing* (6 November 1997), pp. 40–52.

[3]Michael Bartlett, "Restaurants and Institutions' 1996 Annual Forecasts," *Restaurants and Institutions,* (1 January 1996), p. 18.

[4]U.S. Department of Commerce, Bureau of the Census, *Statistical Abstract of the United States, Report #859, Establishments, Employees and Payroll: 1992* (Washington, D.C., 1992).

[5]Porter, "Big Spenders: The Top 250," pp. 40–52.

[6]Michael R. Leenders and Harold E. Fearon, *Purchasing and Supply Management* (Homewood, IL: Richard D. Irwin, Inc., 1997), p. 9.

[7]"Buyers Find Sources on the Internet," *Purchasing* 118 (14 December 1995), p. 82.

[8]Tim Smart, "E-sourcing: A Cheaper Way of Doing Business," *Business Week* (5 August 1996), pp. 82–83.

[9]U.S. Department of Commerce, Bureau of the Census, *Statistical Abstract of the United States:1995* (115th ed.: Washington, D.C., 1995), p. 297.

[10]Stephanie N. Mehta, "Small Firms Are Getting More Government Contracts," *The Wall Street Journal* (27 April 1995), p. B2.

[11]U.S. Department of Commerce, Bureau of the Census, *Statistical Abstract of the United States: 1995,* pp. 109, 150.

[12]Melanie Warner, "Motorola Bets Big on China," *Fortune* 27 (May 1996), pp. 116–124.

[13]U.S. Census Bureau, "1997 Economic Census: What's New?" *The Official Statistics,* www.census.gov.pub.epcd/www.ec97new.html (World Wide Web site; cited 27 September 1996).

[14]Robert M. Morgan and Shelby D. Hunt, "The Commitment-Trust Theory of Relationship Marketing," *Journal of Marketing* 58 (July 1994), pp. 20–38.

[15]Frank V. Cespedes, *Concurrent Marketing: Integrating Products, Sales, and Service* (Boston: Harvard Business School Press, 1995), pp. 14–18.

[16]"Chrysler Pushes Quality Down the Supply Chain," *Purchasing* 118 (13 July 1995), p. 126.

[17]Kevin R. Fitzgerald, "For Superb Supplier Development: Honda Wins!" *Purchasing* 118 (21 September 1995), pp. 32–40.

[18]Rick Mullin, "Managing the Outsourced Enterprise," *Journal of Business Strategy* (July/August 1996), p. 32.

[19]Tim Minahan, "JIT: A Process with Many Faces," *Purchasing* (4 September 1997), pp. 42–48.

[20]Patrick J. Robinson, Charles W. Faris, and Yoram Wind, *Industrial Buying and Creative Marketing* (Boston: Allyn and Bacon, Inc., 1967), Chapter 1; see also, Erin Anderson, Wujin Chu, and Barton Weitz, "Industrial Purchasing: An Empirical Exploration of the Buyclass Framework," *Journal of Marketing* 51 (July 1987), pp. 71–86; and Morry

Ghingold, "Testing the 'Buygrid' Buying Process Model," *Journal of Purchasing and Materials Management* 22 (Winter 1986), pp. 30–36.

[21]The discussion of buying decision approaches in this section is drawn from Michele D. Bunn, "Taxonomy of Buying Decision Approaches," *Journal of Marketing* 57 (January 1993), pp. 38–56.

[22]The levels of decision making discussed in this section are drawn from John A. Howard and Jagdish N. Sheth, *The Theory of Buyer Behavior* (New York: John Wiley and Sons, 1969), Chapter 2.

[23]Christopher P. Puto, Wesley E. Patton III, and Ronald H. King, "Risk Handling Strategies in Industrial Vendor Selection Decisions," *Journal of Marketing* 49 (Winter 1985), pp. 89–98.

[24]Somerby Dowst, "CEO Report: Wanted: Suppliers Adept at Turning Corners," *Purchasing* 101 (29 January, 1987), pp. 71–72.

[25]Allen M. Weiss and Jan B. Heide, "The Nature of Organizational Search in High Technology Markets," *Journal of Marketing Research* 30 (May 1993), pp. 220–233; see also, Jan B. Heide and Allen M. Weiss, "Vendor Consideration and Switching Behavior for Buyers in High-Technology Markets," *Journal of Marketing* 59 (July 1995), pp. 30–43.

[26]Weiss and Heide, "The Nature of Organizational Search," p. 221.

[27]E. Raymond Corey, *The Organizational Context of Industrial Buyer Behavior* (Cambridge, MA: Marketing Science Institute, 1978), pp. 99–112.

[28]For a comprehensive review of buying center research, see Wesley J. Johnston and Jeffrey E. Lewin, "Organizational Buying Behavior: Toward an Integrative Framework," *Journal of Business Research* 35 (January 1996), pp. 1–15; and J. David Lichtenthal, "Group Decision Making in Organizational Buying: A Role Structure Approach," in *Advances in Business Marketing,* vol. 3, ed. Arch G. Woodside (Greenwich, CT: JAI Press, 1988), pp. 119–157.

[29]For example, see Robert D. McWilliams, Earl Naumann, and Stan Scott, "Determining Buying Center Size," *Industrial Marketing Management* 21 (February 1992), pp. 43–49.

[30]Arch G. Woodside, "Conclusions on Mapping How Industry Buys," in *Advances in Business Marketing and Purchasing,* vol. 5, ed. Arch G. Woodside (Greenwich, CT: JAI Press, 1992), pp. 283–300; see also Gary L. Lilien and M. Anthony Wong, "Exploratory Investigation of the Structure of the Buying Center in the Metalworking Industry," *Journal of Marketing Research* 21 (February 1984), pp. 1–11.

[31]Anderson, Chu, and Weitz, "Industrial Purchasing," p. 82.

[32]Ibid.

[33]Frederick E. Webster Jr. and Yoram Wind, *Organizational Buying Behavior* (Englewood Cliffs, NJ: Prentice-Hall, 1972), p. 77. For a review of buying role research, see J. David Lichtenthal, "Group Decision Making in Organizational Buying," pp. 119–157.

[34]B. G. Yovovich, *New Marketing Imperatives: Innovative Strategies for Today's Marketing Challenges* (Englewood Cliffs, NJ: Prentice-Hall, 1995), pp. 4–5.

[35]Philip L. Dawes and Paul G. Patterson, "The Use of Technical Consultancy Services by Firms Making High-Technology Purchasing Decisions," in *Twenty-First Annual Conference of the European Marketing Academy,* ed. Klaus G. Grunert and Dorthe Fuglede (Aarhus, Denmark: The Aarhus School of Business), pp. 261–275.

[36]John R. Ronchetto, Michael D. Hutt, and Peter H. Reingen, "Embedded Influence Patterns in Organizational Buying Systems," *Journal of Marketing* 53 (October 1989), pp. 51–62; see also Ajay Kohli, "Determinants of Influence in Organizational Buying: A Contingency Approach," *Journal of Marketing* 53 (July 1989), pp. 50–65; and Daniel H. McQuiston and Peter R. Dickson, "The Effect of Perceived Personal Consequences on Participation and Influence in Organizational Buying," *Journal of Business Research* 23 (September 1991), pp. 159–177.

[37]McQuiston and Dickson, "The Effect of Perceived Personal Consequences on Participation and Influence in Organizational Buying," pp. 159–177.

[38]Jagdish N. Sheth, "A Model of Industrial Buyer Behavior," *Journal of Marketing* 37 (October 1973), p. 51; see also Sheth, "Organizational Buying Behavior: Past Performance and Future Expectations," *The Journal of Business & Industrial Marketing* 11, no. 3/4 (1996), pp. 7–24.

[39]Sheth, "A Model of Industrial Buyer Behavior," pp. 52–54.

[40]"Chrysler Expects $1 Billion in Cost Reduction from Suppliers," *Purchasing* 119 (11 April 1996), pp. 49–50.

[41]Jeffrey A. Dyer, "How Chrysler Created an American Keiretsu," *Harvard Business Review* 74 (July/August 1996), pp. 52–56; see also, Lisa M. Ellram, "A Structured Method for Applying Purchasing Cost Management Tools," *International Journal of Purchasing and Materials Management* 32 (Winter 1996), pp. 11–19.

S. C. Johnson's Professional Division

S. C. Johnson & Son, Inc. produces a range of well-established consumer products such as PLEDGE™ furniture polish, GLADE™ air fresheners, SHOUT™ laundry soil and stain remover, OFF™ insect repellant, RAID™ insecticides, and WINDEX™ glass cleaner. Each of these brands enjoys a strong position in the market. Through its Professional Division, the firm is also a leading producer of goods and services for commercial, industrial, and institutional building maintenance and sanitation. The products include a complete line of specialty formulated cleaners, floor finishes, disinfectants, furniture polishes, and products for insect and odor control.

The Professional Division serves a diverse array of organizations in the business market such as retailers, health-care organizations, and educational institutions. Customers are served directly by the company's sales force or by a large network of distributors. Organizations follow two alternative approaches to building or store maintenance: the job is performed by its own personnel, or it is "out-sourced" to a building services contractor who regularly brings a trained staff on site to clean the facility.

Maintaining a sparkling and professional appearance is a desired goal in any organization but, for many, a continuing challenge. Consider the heavy store traffic that retailers such as Wal-Mart generate each day or the stream of shoppers who visit a supermarket around the clock. Some retailers spend $100,000 per store each month in cleaning, floor care, and maintenance programs. For large chains with hundreds of stores, this represents a massive expenditure. Included here are the costs of the cleaning products, labor and equipment costs, training expenses, and costs related to regulatory compliance. At a more fundamental level, retail store managers may be even more concerned about other costs—the lost sales that could arise from consumer concerns about cleanliness, food sanitation, or the unsightly appearance of a store. Moreover, there are safety concerns that worry store managers. A slippery floor that causes a shopper to slip and fall may lead to costly legal action against the retailer.

To meet the needs of organizational customers, the Professional Division at S. C. Johnson has developed an array of goods and services. For a particular customer, like a supermarket chain, the salesperson will recommend a particular range of products and employee training programs to meet the unique needs of the retailer. Special dispensing systems (Solutions Centers) have been developed by S. C. Johnson to assist users in pinpointing the proper dilution level of the company's products to meet different floor-care maintenance tasks. The Professional Division also provides ongoing technical support to a customer. Each year, the unit receives over 30,000 calls from customers on issues that range from product selection for particular types of floor surfaces to environmental or safety queries.

Discussion Questions

1. In purchasing cleaning products, which of the following managers might be members of the buying center at a discount retailer, like Wal-Mart or Target: a purchasing executive at the headquarters level, store managers, a merchandising executive, a marketing manager, a maintenance staff supervisor, or maintenance employees? Who would be most influential in the buying decision?

2. Describe how the evaluative criteria employed by the purchasing manager might be different from those that are important to users?

3. Explore how the needs of a health-care organization might differ from the needs of a retailer in purchasing cleaning goods and services. What adjustments in marketing strategy might be pursued by the Professional Division in the health-care sector?

Chapter 7

Market Segmentation and Target Markets

**Penny M. Simpson,
Northwestern State
University of Louisiana**

David D. Morgan Professor and Associate Professor of Marketing

Dr. Simpson has earned her D.B.A. in marketing from Louisiana Tech University, her master's in finance from Louisiana Tech, and her bachelor's in business administraion from the University of Texas at Pan American. She has received the Distinguished Teacher Award, 1998–1999, and was named the David D. Morgan United Teacher Associates Insurance Co. Endowed Professor at Northwestern State University of Louisiana. She serves on the editorial board of *Teaching Business Ethics* and often supplies book reviews for the *Journal of the Academy of Marketing Science*.

Dr. Simpson spent several years

By far, the largest single group of car purchasers are Baby Boomers. This consumer group buys 65 percent of new cars sold and 77 percent of all luxury cars sold. Not surprisingly, then, the success of some car makers may hinge on appealing to this +40 group. To better improve the chances of creating and marketing cars this market will buy, one research firm has carefully studied the values and beliefs of Baby Boomers about themselves and their cars. They identified the following four distinctive categories of Baby Boomer new car purchasers:[1]

▼ **Accessorized Americans**—These Baby Boomers are patriotic and believe they must buy cars made in America. They are most concerned about resale value when buying a car, are the most brand loyal of all segments, and will buy only from trusted dealers. They tend to spend time gathering information and carefully compare values when buying cars. Keeping their cars clean and polished tends to make these car owners feel good. Boomers in this car-buying segment tend to buy Buick, Oldsmobile, Chrysler, and Chevrolet automobiles.

▼ **Stylish Fun**—This +40 segment likes to keep up with automobile trends and considers style to be the most important factor when purchasing a car, although they do like their car to have good acceleration. The Stylish Fun think of their cars as fun and tend to have "love affairs" with their cars. They are likely to own foreign-made cars and tend to pay more for their cars than their budget allows. Typically, members of this segment own luxury Asian and European cars or Jeep/Eagles.

▼ **Reliables**—Reliable consumers tend to view their cars as merely a means of getting from one point to another and consider cost a major factor in purchasing a new car. They want good gas mileage, a good rating from consumer reports publications, and they believe that small Japanese cars are better than their American counterparts. These consumers are most likely to own a Toyota, Volvo, Lexus, Honda, or Saturn car.

▼ **Uninvolved**—Members of this group are much like Reliables because they view a car as just a means of transportation; but, unlike Reliables, they do not gather information about different cars before making their purchase. Uninvolveds do not like to deal with new car dealers and hate to take their car to the dealer for servicing. Neither car safety nor country of origin is important to this group. Uninvolved consumers are likely to own GMC truck/van, Saturn, or Honda vehicles.

What does this information about each segment mean to car manufacturers trying to sell their cars to Baby Boomers? For Honda, it may mean eliminating costly accessories from cars typically purchased by Reliables, and for Buick, it may mean advertising in *People* magazine, often read by Accessorized Americans. To effectively sell a product to a specific group of consumers, a firm must understand the needs and wants of that group then develop a marketing mix that will satisfy their needs.

Learning Objectives

After you have completed this chapter, you should be able to:

1. Understand the concepts: *market, segmentation,* and *target markets* and their importance to marketing.

2. Describe the advantages and disadvantages of target marketing.

3. Identify and explain the steps in the target market selection process.

4. Discuss criteria for segmentation.

5. Illustrate segmentation strategies.

6. Explain the bases for segmentation.

7. Identify sources of information needed for segmentation.

8. Understand how to profile markets.

9. Explain the term *positioning* and several types of positioning strategies.

10. Discuss segmentation of business and international markets.

in the savings and loan industry and has consulted with a number of regional banks. Her consulting activities have focused primarily on small businesses, predominantly banks and media, and marketing those businesses in a changing environment.

The opening vignette illustrates the importance of understanding customers before defining a total marketing mix that will satisfy customer's needs and wants. After all, satisfying customer needs is at the very heart of the marketing concept. The first step to understanding the customer is identifying those customers that might actually buy a specific product. Once prospective customers are known, they can be analyzed in detail to better understand their needs and wants so that a marketing mix that fills those needs can be created. This process of identifying and analyzing prospective customers is key to target marketing, market segmentation, and positioning, and these activities are key to a successful marketing plan. The target marketing process for household consumer markets, for business markets, and for international markets are discussed in this chapter.

MARKETS AND TARGET MARKETING

LEARNING OBJECTIVE LO1

A *market* is any individual, group of individuals, or organizations willing, able, and capable of purchasing a firm's product. For example, if you want to buy a new car one day, you are in the new car market. Before a firm can effectively market its products to you, or to any other member of the market for that matter, it must fully understand your needs and wants from that product. However, the needs and wants from a product are not the same for everyone in a market. For example, you and your mother may both want a new car, so you are both in the new car market; but, chances are good that you each want a different type of car. You may want a small, fast, red sports car while your mother would like a large, safe, dependable, white car that gets good mileage.

Generally different groups of customers will have differing needs from specific products, or *heterogeneous demand,* as illustrated in the opening vignette. In another example, teens may want blue jeans that are stylish, construction workers want jeans that are durable, and older "gray" consumers want jeans that are comfortable. Real differences in product preferences exist. This means that a company wanting to reach these different groups of consumers must divide the market into distinct groups based on these differences, then analyze each group they want to reach in detail, so they can truly understand customer needs and wants from the products they buy.

As introduced in Chapter 1, the separation of markets into distinctive groups based on homogeneous (similar) characteristics is called *market segmentation,*[2] and is critical to reaching consumers who have different needs from a product. Each of the divided markets, or **market segments**, that a company selects to reach with its marketing efforts is a target market. More formally, the specific group of customers toward which a firm directs its market efforts is the firm's *target market.* This process of matching a specialized marketing mix with the needs of a specific market segment is critical to the marketing success of a product and is called *target marketing.* To illustrate, just imagine the likely success (or failure) of cases where market needs do not match the marketing mix: Cadillac and Ensure diet supplement targeting teenage girls in *Teen* magazine, heavy metal music playing in upscale hotel lobbies, or mascara for men advertised in *GQ* magazine.

Market segment
is a group of consumers that are alike based on some characteristic(s).

www.cadillac.com

A firm will not generally want to reach out and try to appeal to *all* members of a total market in the same way, but rather may concentrate on selected groups of customers. Depending on many factors, firms may target any number of market segments, and each segment targeted may be as small as one consumer or as large as the total mass market. These targeting options are explained next.

Mass Market versus the Individual

Defining specific market segments to target with customized marketing mixes can create a distinctive competitive advantage for a company. As the continuum in Figure 7.1 illus-

Figure 7.1   Continuum of Market Segmentation Size

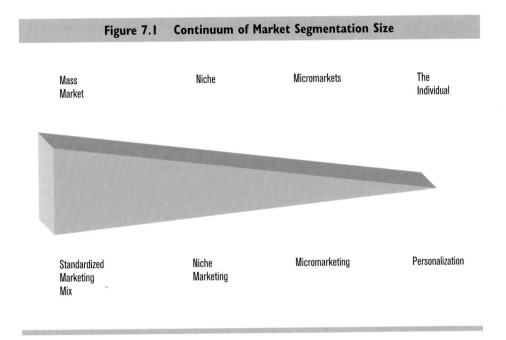

Mass Market   Niche   Micromarkets   The Individual

Standardized Marketing Mix   Niche Marketing   Micromarketing   Personalization

trates, the options for the size of a market segment range from one mass market to one individual, or anywhere in between. For mass markets, the marketing mix is standardized to reach all customers in the same way. The smaller the size of the segments targeted, the more customized or individualized the marketing efforts toward the market can be. A firm choosing the mass market end of the continuum, will choose to make one product and market that product in the same way to everyone who may want it.

Moving toward the middle of the continuum firms may define a relatively small segment, or *niche,* within a large market for targeting, called **niche marketing.** A number of well-known companies illustrate the point: Old Navy and Gadzooks are specialty stores that appeal to teenagers, Estee makes sugar-free food products for diabetics, and Foot Joy makes shoes for golfers. Less well-known is a company called The Rolling Strong Gym. While health clubs appealing to health and fitness enthusiasts have been popular in the past few years, this Richardson, Texas based gym identified a new market segment for targeting—interstate truck drivers. The gym has developed exercise programs for truckers to improve fitness and health, and the program now has the support of the federal government and the trucking industry because physically fit drivers are safer drivers.[3]

Even smaller market segments are known as **micromarkets,** and marketing efforts aimed at these segments are called *micromarketing.* Micromarketing is the process of targeting these small, narrowly defined market segments. A large, upscale retail store, for example, may identify high-income neighborhoods within a city where the store's likely customers live. The retailer can then target those neighborhoods with announcements of special sales or store events.

On the individual consumer end of the continuum, a firm may decide to target individual consumers and individualize and personalize marketing efforts toward each. An example of personalization comes from Levi Strauss who adopted this approach with their Levi's Personal Pair™ and Original Spin™ personalized women's blue jeans. These blue jeans are custom tailored to fit each individual's own size and fit requirements. You can visit Levi Strauss' home page to see how to purchase a unique pair of jeans customized to fit at www.levi.com/originalspin. Other common examples of delivering individual consumers with customized products are common in services: wedding planners, hair stylists, doctors, and even Burger King, who invites customers to "have it your way."

Niche marketing
is the process of targeting a relatively small market segment with a specific, specialized marketing mix.

www.gadzooks.com

Micromarkets
are very small market segments, such as zip code areas or even neighborhoods.

Careers in Marketing

Retirement: The End for Some, the Beginning for One

For most people, retirement signals the end of a career, but for niche marketer David D. Morgan, "retired teachers" meant the beginning of a very successful business endeavor. After graduating from Northwestern State University of Louisiana and gaining eight years of experience in insurance sales, David began selling insurance to a special "niche" market—retired teachers—from the trunk of his car in 1981. As David proudly states, "We work with one group of people who have many things in common." What made this niche strategy especially successful was the exclusive endorsement of his product and company by the Texas Retired Teachers Association. This meant information about his insurance products was mailed to all retired teachers in Texas—140,000 of them—on association letterhead which gave the product instant credibility with association members. In return, membership in the association increased because the retired teachers were required to be a member of the association in order to purchase the association group policy. This strategy worked especially well for both organizations. As David states, "It is really tough selling insurance, or just selling anything. You have to have a way to get in front of people." The Texas Retired Teachers Association provided the means for getting the product in front of interested prospects of the target market.

Did this niche marketing strategy payoff? The company, United Teachers Associates Insurance Co., has greatly expanded and now services new niches, such as government employees in Puerto Rico, and underwrites as well as sells insurance. In 1998, the company was one of the top 30 largest insurance companies with guaranteed renewal premiums, had 140 office employees, 2,000 agents, operations in 47 states and U.S. territories, and assets in excess of $205 million. David advises others interested in this type of success "to do something that you like to do, that's fun, work really hard, and do more than you are being paid to do."

Sources: Interview with David Morgan, October 6, 1998. Earl Golz, "Insurer Finds His 'Niche'," *Austin American Statesman*, July 29, 1997, p. D1–D2.

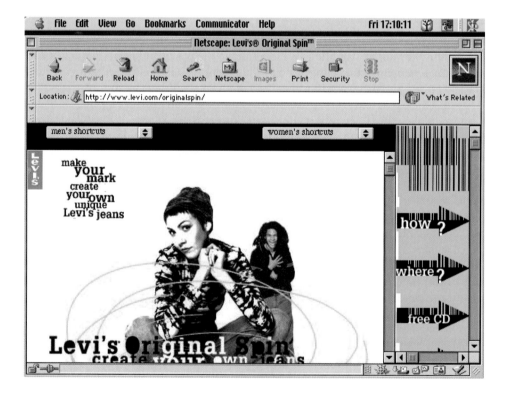

A time-poor society and the increasing popularity of in-home, interactive shopping options, such as the Internet, are leading to greater personalization or customization in markets. Consider the choices. An individual consumer sees a mass media advertisement, wants the product, runs out to a mass merchandiser to buy that product, and returns with a mass-produced version of that product identical to everyone else's. The consumer, on the other hand, sees the product, wants it, connects to the manufacturer's home page on the Internet, requests a customized version of the product, and has that personalized version delivered to his home.

This interactivity, combined with innovative technological capabilities, allows firms to create a complete picture of individual customers based on their individual characteristics and preferences, then customize marketing efforts, especially services and information, to fit individual customer needs. The current trend in targeting markets is clearly toward this individualization and personalization of markets. The day is coming when customers will be able to scan in their own image and "try on" clothing. In fact, Adidas is already testing a digital scanner that measures shoe size.[4] Soon, consumers may even be able to use simple CAD programs to design their own clothes for manufacture.

www.adidas.com

SEGMENTATION AND TARGET MARKETING

Advantages

In general, the process of segmenting markets and targeting them is a widespread practice with numerous advantages. The target market selection process is essential to marketing strategy for the following reasons:[5]

1. Identification of the market allows the company to know who to analyze in their efforts to better understand potential and actual consumers.

2. A detailed analysis and understanding of the market allows a firm to develop and implement a marketing mix tailored to the specific needs of the market. For example, after carefully analyzing the needs of their market, Honda was able to reduce the price of their cars by reducing the number of available options, making the total product better suited to the needs of the car's "reliable" target market.

3. Identification of the market allows a company to assess potential demand for its products. For example, the total market for a principles of marketing textbook can be determined by looking at the number of college students enrolled in college business programs. The textbook publisher can then forecast the percentage of the total market they are likely to acquire, based on some formula or past experience.

4. Knowing the market allows firms to identify competing products in their specific market, and develop responsive competitive positions. Certainly, Burger King and McDonald's recognize that they are direct competitors in the burger market, and each responds to changes in the other's marketing efforts.

5. Targeting market segments with a marketing mix customized for specific market needs increases likelihood of sales effectiveness and cost efficiencies in reaching the market. Foot Joy, for example, could maximize cost efficiencies by advertising its golf shoes in *Golf Digest* instead of in *Teen* or *People* magazine where most of the readers are not golfers.

6. Defining and analyzing a target market allows a firm to position its products to the market based on assessed needs and preferences. For example, Toyota could create a marketing mix that emphasizes an image of dependability, reliability, and good value from their cars, after understanding that these are the characteristics their market segment most desires.

7. Defining a target market allows a firm to identify opportunities. For example, the aging of the 76 million Baby Boomer market suggests the need for products in three major areas: leisure and entertainment, pharmaceuticals and health care, and annuities.[6]

Disadvantages

A number of disadvantages to target marketing have also been identified. These disadvantages center on ethical criticisms of the practice and the possibility of missed opportunities from targeting specific segments. Firms should carefully consider these disadvantages when developing a targeted marketing plan:

1. Targeting multiple markets generally increases marketing costs.

2. Efforts toward personalization and individualization of markets can lead to proliferation of products that becomes overly burdensome and costly to manage.

3. Efforts to overly segment markets into too small niches may be viewed cynically by the targeted individual, and negatively affect consumer response to marketing efforts. After seeing letters to all your friends from Publisher's Clearinghouse, your letter arrives stating that: "Yes, you, Lucky W. Inner, from Muleshoe, Texas, have won $10 million, if. . . ." You may be a little skeptical, or even immune to such personalized tactics, and come to resent companies that engage in the practice. One writer terms this practice "Faux Segmentation" and asks "Who do these guys think they're fooling?"[7]

4. Narrowly segmenting a market to target may actually prevent a product from developing brand loyalty. Ned Anschuetz argues that the only way to build a large, sustainable brand-loyal customer base is to build broad brand popularity. More to the point, he says:

    > "It is very clear, however, that building loyal frequent buyers means broadening brand appeal to more and more different kinds of households rather than narrowing it through segmentation to a small, homogeneous group. One can go further to say that to successfully build a base of loyal frequent buyers a brand must also become broadly popular among category users. This is the opposite of segmentation. It is integration, building brand popularity."[8]

5. Target marketers have been widely criticized for unethical or stereotypical activities.

The most public criticism of segmenting and target marketing comes from minority and consumer groups who claim that the practice of aiming potentially harmful products to disadvantaged or vulnerable markets is highly unethical. Popular examples of such practices include: Camel cigarette's Joe Camel character, which has been accused of targeting children; the widespread practice of using waif-like, extremely thin models in advertisements targeting the identity-seeking, vulnerable teenage-girl market; and beer companies targeting underage college students. The consumer perception of targeting such potentially harmful products, such as cigarettes, alcohol, and lottery tickets, toward vulnerable consumers, such as children, poor, or uneducated consumers, may have negative effects on the marketing firms. Some research evidence suggests that consumer ethical judgment of such practices can lead to consumer behavioral reactions such as negative word-of-mouth and boycotts. In fact, plans for PowerMaster malt liquor and Uptown cigarettes aimed toward African-American males and Dakota cigarettes aimed at pink-collar workers (working class females) were canceled before the products were marketed because of public outcry.

Finally, the process of segmenting and targeting markets is akin to stereotyping and has been criticized for that reason. For decades, women were unrealistically portrayed as submissive to men, domestic, or as sex objects in advertisements, and the +50 market was portrayed by advertisers as doddering old people sitting on a porch and rocking all day. Images such as these further proliferate stereotyping and may alienate potential customers.

These criticisms and potentially negative and positive effects of segmenting and targeting markets are important for firms to consider when developing marketing strategies.

Table 7.1 Summary of Advantages and Disadvantages of Target Marketing	
Advantages	**Disadvantages**
Defines the market for further analysis	Increased costs
Allows creation of a customized marketing mix	Increased number of products
Aids in assessing potential demand	Faux segmentation
Aids identification of competitors	May decrease brand loyalty
Increases sales effectiveness and efficiency	Some practices considered unethical
Aids in positioning products	Proliferates stereotyping
Aids in identifying opportunities	

A summary of these advantages and disadvantages appears in Table 7.1. However, the practice of target marketing is widespread and will likely continue far into the future because firms must understand the needs of their markets and deliver an appropriate marketing mix to succeed. To do this, they must first define their market through the target market selection process.

THE TARGET MARKET SELECTION PROCESS

The process of selecting a potential market, segmenting, analyzing, and profiling the market to better target it with a customized marketing mix is the ***target market selection process.*** This process consists of eight interrelated tasks as seen in Figure 7.2. Although shown as a series of sequential steps, in practice the ordering of tasks varies, with some tasks actually occurring simultaneously or in a completely different order. Moreover, the target market selection process is a continuous, ongoing process because markets are dynamic and constantly changing.[9] Consequently, firms may need to revise their marketing mix based on the segments' changing needs or identify new markets to replace shrinking ones.

Not only is the segmentation process continuous, it may either be *a priori* or *post hoc*. ***A priori*** segmentation occurs when variables for segmenting markets, such as age or income, are selected first, then customers are classified accordingly. For example, a car manufacturer could decide that there are a large number of consumers with incomes greater than $75,000 and develop a car aimed at that group of consumers. ***Post hoc*** segmentation involves the examination of existing customer data, then segmenting it to classify the customers into segments or "clusters" based on similarities of variables.[10] A bank may use post hoc segmentation to analyze its existing customer database and determine which customers have the largest savings and then develop special programs to reach these segments. An example of *post hoc* segmentation for a bank is seen in Figure 7.3. Some evidence suggests that *post hoc* segmentation is more common than *a priori* among businesses, especially small businesses, who actually create and offer a product then examine their customers in efforts to revise and refine their marketing mix.[11]

Identify the Total Market

The first step in the target market selection process is to specifically define the total market of all potential customers for a product category. Purchase patterns of the market and whether the user of the product is the same person as the buyer are a few factors that should be considered when defining the total market.

Who actually buys a product is not always obvious. For decades, men's clothing manufacturers have targeted their marketing efforts toward men. However, a recent survey

Figure 7.2   The Target Marketing Selection Process

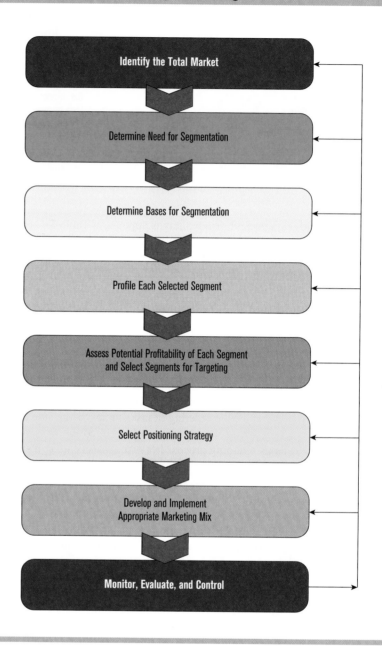

commissioned by the Haggar Clothing Company indicated that women influence the selection of or actually buy 89 percent of all men's clothing purchased in department stores. This finding suggests that the "market" for men's clothing is not men, but rather women. Haggar now intends to direct all of its advertising toward women.[12]

Determine Need for Segmentation

Another important task in the market segmentation process is determining whether the total market needs to be divided into segments for the purpose of targeting with special marketing programs; after all, not all markets need to be segmented. In general, for seg-

Figure 7.3 Segmenting, Profiling, and Responding to Bank Segments

A number of studies have profiled bank customers to allow banks to develop and market specialized programs to meet different customers' needs and to help predict banking behavior. Efforts to segment bank customers by age or income alone have often met with limited success. Using the criteria of segmenting based on similarity of attitudes about goods and services, length of time with the bank, and no appreciable added cost to administer, First Commerce Bank identified the following bank customer segments for targeting purposes, using its existing customer database:

- The Smart Money Segment – This smallest but most profitable segment highly values time and money management improvements and *ease*–ease of understanding, of buying, and of using. Responding to the needs of this market segment, First Commerce redesigned products and services to include: a personal banker, dedicated teller lines, free checks, preferred credit rates, and a statement that includes all accounts on a single statement.

- The Small Business Segment – The small business segment most needs banking services that expedite their business processes. First Commerce answered the needs of businesses by simplifying and speeding up the credit application and financing process, eliminating charges for deposits of large numbers of items, allowing more banking services by phone, ATM and debit cards, providing seminars about business related concerns, and simplifying retirement plans for employees and business owners.

- The Convenience Segment – Members of this segment are generally single account owners and make numerous transactions; they may turn into Smart Money customers one day. First Commerce developed programs to encourage this segment to use alternative delivery systems (ADS) of bank services, such as telephone, ATM, and Internet. These alternative delivery systems help decrease costs associated with numerous transactions and provide more convenient, efficient services for users.

---

mentation to be warranted, there must be differences with respect to customer needs or demands, potential product variations must be cost-effective (profitable), and implemented product differences must be apparent to customers.[13]

For example, the market for sugar is huge. Most kitchens contain sugar; but is there a need to segment markets when selling sugar? Probably not because of the product's homogeneity of demand and little perceived differences in brands. Like the sugar market, the ready-to-eat (RTE) cereals market is huge: an amazing 95 percent of all American households purchase RTEs each year. Should the RTE market be divided into different segments for targeting? Consider this: households with children aged 6 to 17 buy 75 percent more RTE cereal than average, while singles under 35 years old spend 54 percent less than average on RTE cereal. However, these young singles spend 39 percent more than average on granola and natural cereal. Clearly, consumers have different demand preferences for RTE cereals, and they perceive real differences in brands. Some consumers prefer chocolate, rice, and a sweet taste for breakfast, while others prefer cereals that they believe promote good health.

Differences in demand preferences are only one criterion that firms must consider when deciding whether or not to segment a market. There are a total of five criteria for successful segmentation that should be considered along with various strategic and external factors in making the segmentation decision.

Criteria for Successful Segmentation

Once a firm has identified potential market segments, the segments should be analyzed according to five **criteria for successful segmentation** before making the segmentation decision. In general, to successfully segment a market, the market must be:[14]

Criteria for Successful Segmentation
includes target markets that are heterogeneous, measurable, substantial, actionable, and accessible.

▼ Heterogeneous—Clear differences in consumer preferences for the product must exist. If all consumers in the market use the product in the same way and want the same benefits from the product, such as with sugar, there may be no added value from dividing the market into segments for special targeting. Clearly, however, there are consumer differences in consumer preference, or heterogeneity of demand, for ready-to-eat cereals.

▼ Measurable—Difference preferences for the product must be identifiable and capable of being related to measurable variables, such as age, gender, lifestyle, product usage, etc. A number of consumers have larger-than-average feet and require large shoe sizes, such as men's size 20 or women's size 12 shoes. However, identifying these special consumers and associating them with specific variables, such as age, income, or geographic region, is virtually impossible.

▼ Substantial—The proposed market segment must have enough size and purchasing power to be profitable. The benefits of alterations in the marketing mix must exceed the costs incurred for the changes. Obviously, the pet market is substantial, considering that more than half of U. S. households have pets, for a total of 58 million pets, and spend more than $5 billion dollars each year.[15] Segments within the pet market, such as all anaconda snake owners, may not be substantial enough to warrant specialized marketing efforts, however.

▼ Actionable—Companies must be able to respond to difference preferences with an appropriate and profitable marketing mix. Although a marketing mix directed toward consumers with larger than average feet or toward all anaconda snake owners could be developed, the cost of marketing products only to those consumers may far outweigh the benefits derived from the revenue generated.

▼ Accessible—The proposed market segment must be readily accessible and reachable with targeted programs. Consider the problems of reaching homeless consumers with information about discounted food and clothing or of inexpensively reaching only those male consumers who wear a size 20 shoe.

Differentiation
is the process of creating and sustaining a strong, consistent, and unique image about one product in comparison to others.

Strategic Factors

Internally, a firm must consider the appropriate, viable segmentation strategy for reaching segments. Companies might develop one marketing mix strategy that is appropriate for all members of the total market, known as an ***undifferentiated targeting strategy.*** Generally, this strategy is effective when all members of the market have homogenous demand with respect to the product, as the case with sugar. This means that differentiation of the product by brand is difficult because, in general, all consumers derive the same benefits from different brands and there is little perceived differences between brands. Salt, flour, and fresh produce are examples of products where there is virtually no difference in brands or the benefits that consumers derive from those brands.

Where heterogeneity of demand exists, and thus multiple market segments, marketers may adopt either a concentrated strategy or a differentiated strategy. A ***concentrated strategy*** is where only one marketing mix is developed and directed toward a few, or perhaps one profitable market segment. In contrast, a ***differentiated strategy*** exists when a firm develops different marketing mix plans specially tailored for each of two or more market segments. Each of the three types of segmentation strategies a firm might adopt are shown in Figure 7.4 Obviously, marketing costs increase as the number of market segments targeted increase. Considering the substantial costs of differentiated strategies, firms must examine the resource requirements for segmenting in light of available resources.

External Factors

Firms must also consider external factors that may affect the success of segmentation. The stage in the product life cycle, the competition, the product itself, and the market may each affect segmentation strategy. In response to strong competition and flat sales in a slow growth

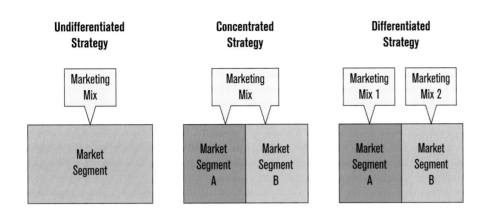

Figure 7.4   Segmentation Strategies

market, Coors Brewing Company implemented a differentiated strategy aiming new marketing efforts for its beer at the African-American and Hispanic markets in the summer of 1998. Together with Asian-Americans, these combined minority markets are expected to account for one-third of the U.S. population by 2010 and almost half by 2040.[16]

www.coors.com

Determine Bases for Segmentation

A number of different variables or descriptors can be used to describe market segments and the data needed for the variables comes from a variety of sources. Specific variables used for segmenting consumer markets and descriptor information sources are discussed in this section.

Segmentation Variables

Segmenting means dividing markets into homogenous, or like, groups based on some related characteristic or trait. Any one, or combination of a number of variables or descriptors of the market, such as astrological sign,[17] and attitudes toward the past[18] can serve as a bases for segmenting markets. The most generally accepted bases for segmenting markets, however, are demographics, geographics, psychographics, benefits sought, situation, and behavior or usage patterns.

   Demographic Segmentation   Age, income, occupation, level of education, race, gender, family life cycle, family size, religion, race, and nationality are demographic characteristics commonly used to segment markets for targeting. Most everyone is familiar with the descriptors associated with these important market segments, such as age, education level, and race.

   Not as commonly known, but perhaps as important as these other segment variables, is the family life cycle. The *family life cycle (FLC)* describes the stages or evolution of the typical consumer, over his or her lifetime. The FLC variable incorporates income and lifestyle to explain differences in expenditure patterns based on family role and transitions between roles.[19] Typically, consumers evolve from bachelor, to married, then to married with children, to no children, to retired, and finally to bachelor again. Quite obviously, consumers' needs for different products vary with each of these stages in the FLC. For example, bachelors buy canned vegetables in single serving sizes and families with babies buy strained vegetables. Retired older persons may "buy" their vegetables by eating out in family-style restaurants. The family life cycle model is presented in Figure 7.5.[20]

Figure 7.5 Family Life Cycle

Bachelor I
Bachelor II
Newlywed
Single Parent (young and middle aged)
Full Nest I (child < 6)
Delayed Full Nest (child < 6)
Full Nest II and III (youngest child ≥ 6)
Childless couple (no children home)
Older Couple
Bachelor III

future.sri.com/vals/
valsindex.html

www.census.gov

www.claritas.com

Geographic Segmentation Geographic regions may be used to segment markets for specialized marketing efforts. Types of products and brands of products purchased vary greatly by regions of the world, country, state, city, or even neighborhood. Certainly snow sleds are common purchases in the northern sections of the United States, while outdoor furniture is popular in the South. Interestingly, one researcher has identified nine distinctively different regions of the U.S., based on individual values called "nations of North America."[21] Regional differences are apparent in more than just values and purchase behavior—in speech and driving behavior, for example. While waiting in stop-and-go traffic, southern women are more likely to apply make-up than women from other regions of the United States, West Coast drivers are more likely to read while driving, and men with higher incomes are more likely to swear.[22]

Generally, geographic segmentation is used in conjunction with other segmentation descriptors. For example, companies may target teenagers in Dallas—which combines *demographics* with *geographics* and is called **geodemographics,** or they may target tennis playing teenagers in New York City—which combines geographics, demographics (age), and psychographics (lifestyle).

Geodemographics is a very commonly used descriptor, and the data for demographically describing a geographic area is widely available from both private and public sources. For example, CACI and SRI Consulting are private providers of descriptor information, and the U.S. Census Bureau serves as a public source of data. A summary of a sample profile from the CACI Web site for Austin, Texas 78701, is shown in Figure 7.6.

Psychographic Segmentation Segmenting markets by social class, lifestyles and psychological characteristics, such as attitudes, interests and opinions (AIO), and values, is increasingly popular and often creates a better picture of market segments than does demographics or geographics. These segmentation bases allow the marketer to truly understand the inner workings of potential consumers before developing a marketing mix aimed at those consumers. For example, a psychographic profile conducted for the automobile industry of the 11 percent of the U.S. population classified as *wealthy* indicates that there are three distinctive groups within the wealthy class, and that each must be targeted differently. Young wealthy individuals are active and are looking for adventure and thrills from driving, while safety and spaciousness are most important for the Baby Boomers. Finally, the eldest group of the wealthy is looking for luxury and utility in their transportation.[23]

Claritas provides other psychographic tools, including the popular PRIZM analysis. PRIZM provides lifestyle segmentation analysis based on 62 distinct clusters throughout the United States. In fact, PRIZM was instrumental in developing the profile of Elvis fans shown in Figure 7.7.

Figure 7.6   Profile of Austin, Texas 78701

"This is the youngest and smallest consumer market, comprising the dormitories and student housing located around universities. Their budget goes to college expenses or an active social life. Top-ranked for take-out fast food, having ATM cards, and making long-distance calls using calling cards, their purchase decisions are based on price. They rank highest for watching sports on TV."

Total Population:	3,871
Male:	60.4%
Female:	39.6%
1998 Median Household Income:	$23,301
1990 Average Rent:	$438

Figure 7.7   Profiling Elvis Fans

Most any market can be profiled for more efficient targeting. Take Elvis fans, for example. Though not a huge market, approximately 700,000 fans pay $15 each to visit his home in Memphis, Tennessee each year. Using information, such as zip codes, from some 7,000 members of Elvis fan clubs across the nation and tying it to Claritas's PRIZM system, Bob Lunn profiled Elvis fans. The profile included a map of the United States showing attitudes toward Elvis by geographic area. For example, the highest concentration of Elvis fans in the nation is in Banks, Georgia, followed closely by Tupelo, Mississippi, Elvis' birthplace. A number of areas around major cities also contain a large number of Elvis fans, such as Washington County, Pennsylvania; Atlanta, Georgia; Austin, Texas; Kansas City, Missouri; and San Diego, California. Despite the fact that typical Elvis fans are white women between the ages of 40 and 50 with no college education, Elvis memorabilia shown on television is sold primarily to women in their 30s and men in their 20s. Lunn's profile also indicated that Elvis lovers typically purchase video cameras, malt liquor, menthol cigarettes, pick-up trucks, Velveeta, *National Enquirer*, frozen dinners, and *Soldier of Fortune*. Get the picture?

Benefits-Sought Segmentation   Markets can also be segmented based on consumer preference for a specific product attribute or characteristic. Nowhere is this more apparent than the toothpaste aisle at your local grocery store. Various toothpastes not only help prevent cavities, they freshen breath, control tartar, contain baking soda or peroxide, provide gum care, are designed for consumers with sensitive teeth problems, and they even whiten teeth. There are even special toothpastes for children that have many of these same attributes including whitening and flavors. Recently, another toothpaste segment was identified: consumers who are concerned about deterioration of tooth enamel. This segment has led to the introduction of Enamelon, which is designed to strengthen tooth enamel. Other examples of product benefits that can serve as a basis for segmentation are: airline systems divided into first, business, and coach classes; restaurant seating in smoking and non smoking sections; and mail delivery via regular service or express mail. Based on preferences for each of these items, customized marketing mixes can be developed.

Most segmentation strategies should include the benefit-sought variable. After all, marketers must understand the benefits their consumers want from a product before an appropriate marketing mix can be tailored to a specific segment. Then, consumers must understand how that product will solve their needs best before they will buy it. Many experts maintain that the benefits sought from a product are more predictive of consumer purchase behavior than any other segmentation variable.[24]

Situation Segmentation   The purchase situation or occasion can also serve as a basis for segmenting markets. Think, for example, about purchasing a meal and what might influence the purchase decision. A meal purchased by a busy student to eat in the ten minutes between classes would likely be much different than a meal purchased for a much anticipated first date, which would be even more different than a meal purchased for a night at home alone watching TV. Each of these situations or purchase occasions represents a different market segment potentially suitable for targeting.

There are five different situational characteristics that may each affect purchase behavior and serve as a descriptor for a market segment. These situational characteristics and examples are:[25]

▼ Physical surroundings—Is the store or salesperson pleasant or offensive?

▼ Social surroundings—Are friends or parents watching the purchase?

▼ Temporal perspective—How much time is there to make the purchase?

> ### Figure 7.8 Opportunities from Databases: The Gerland's Story
>
> Gerland's Food Fair, Inc., based in Houston, Texas, is considered a leader in database marketing in the grocery industry. The company has created a 250,000 household database of its 20-store chain. The data comes from customers themselves. As customers check out, their "Advantage" card is scanned and each purchase is then recorded so the store knows what each customer buys, when they buy it, and how much they buy. The monitoring of individual customer purchases allows the firm to better use their marketing dollars by targeting their loyal shoppers: the ones who shop 2.98 times a week and spend over $35 during each visit. Gerland's has implemented a number of programs aimed at these loyal purchasers. One promotion gave free turkeys to customers who spent $500 during an 11-week period while another promotion continuously rewarded customers who spent $250 with a 5 percent gift over a 13-week period. After these customers spent $1,000, they were given a 10 percent gift certificate.

▼ Task definition—Why is this product being purchased, is it for a gift, and if so, is it a gift for a girlfriend? boyfriend? parent? boss?

▼ Prepurchase attitude—What is the purchaser's mood at the time of purchase, happy or sad?

These situational variables can serve as the basis for a unique marketing mix. For example, in today's time-poor society, marketers can define segments based on the temporal perspective—consumers that are time conscious or time poor—and develop a marketing mix tailored toward them that emphasizes convenience and time savings.

Behavior or Usage Segmentation Loyalty toward a product, the way a product is used, and usage patterns (heavy, medium, or light users) can also serve as a basis for segmenting markets. A major factor to consider here is the *80/20 principle.* This means, in general, that about 20 percent of a firm's customers are responsible for generating 80 percent of the firm's revenue. Firms must pay special attention to developing and maintaining close relations with this "best" 20 percent of their loyal customers. The Gerland's Food Fair example shown in Figure 7.8 illustrates how one company identified their best customers then developed promotions especially for them.

Another example of appealing to the heavy-users segment comes from the classic Miller Lite and its advertising campaign. The beer and its advertising campaign were designed to appeal to heavy beer drinkers who complained of wanting to drink more beer, but often couldn't because they were too full. The advertisements told consumers that Miller Lite tastes great and is less filling, effectively appealing to heavy beer drinkers. The successful campaign lasted over 20 years and resulted in sales as high as 22 percent of all beer sold.[26]

www.millerlite.com

Collect Segmentation Data

LEARNING OBJECTIVE LO7

Information for segmenting markets may be obtained from internal or external sources. Internally, most companies create and retain information about their existing and potential customers in a database. However, to expand their customer base, firms need to get new prospective customers into their database for targeting. This data must be obtained from external sources.

Internal Database Sources

These customer and marketing databases can be tremendous in size: Fleet Financial Group, for example, has a 500 gigabyte marketing database and MCI has about 2.5 terabytes (TB) of sales and marketing data.[27] Examples of customer information often col-

www.mci.com

lected in an internal database are date of birth (age), educational attainment, profession, credit rating, purchases, purchase patterns, and so forth. This information can be sorted and results used to classify customers into segments based on selected attributes or characteristics in a process called data mining.

Data mining is exploring data for patterns and relationships and the practice is becoming increasingly popular. These patterns can be used to target special groups with special programs. For example, American Express could examine the data from all of its customers who purchased an airline ticket using their credit card in the last year. Their ticket purchase patterns—time of day, day of week, destination, frequency of travel, or even class of travel—and purchases made while traveling could be explored to determine patterns or segments. The company could then separate consumers with similar purchase patterns into segments for targeting with special catalogs and direct mail about travel clubs and special products, such as luggage and vacation travel packages. Internal data are readily available to firms and can be extremely valuable in developing customized marketing mixes.

Results from data mining and databases have been used in a number of ways. American Express has helped restaurants identify their frequent, lunch-time-only customers to target with special promotions.[28] AT&T uses their database to send inquiries from the least profitable customers to automated answering systems, while the best customers hear human voices.[29] Federal Express uses its database to segment consumers according to their value and need, matching anticipated customer value with market-segment spending.[30]

www.americanexpress.com
www.at&t.com
www.federalexpress.com

External Data Sources

Databases have been shown to be extremely useful for firms profiling their *existing* customers. In order to grow, however, firms need to expand their customer base. A very useful way of acquiring these prospects is to buy mailing lists. There are a wide variety of types of lists such as magazine or catalog subscribers, associations, voters, and postal residents, and they are available for a myriad of consumer types and interests. For example, *The Lifestyle Market Analyst*™ published by Standard Rate & Data Service contains a section of consumer magazines and direct mail lists sorted by lifestyle. These consumer interest lists include everything imaginable from consumers interested in art, casino gambling, and yachting, to contributors to "Pete Wilson for Governor."

Lists of consumer e-mail addresses by demographic or geographic characteristics can also be obtained by using software that searches the Web with a technique called "spidering." The software allows automated Web site searches for key variables. Possible search variables can include profession, state, city, or even countries. Personalized e-mail can then be sent to the individual names collected.

A large number of private organizations and magazines offer market research data and segmentation profiling. For example, among other publications, CACI Marketing Systems publishes *The Sourcebook of Zip Code Demographics* and *The Sourcebook of County Demographics*, Standard Rate & Data Service publishes *The Lifestyle Market Analyst*, and Simmons Market Research Bureau, Inc., publishes an annual study of media and markets. Magazines such as *American Demographics* and *Sales & Marketing Management* often contain useful data about various types of markets.

Much useful information is available publicly, at no charge. One of the best sources of geodemographic information about market segments is the U.S. Census Bureau. The TIGER/Line Files with LandView Mapping capabilities can be used to access census data and is used by most profiling organizations. The TIGER/Line Files and other U.S. Census data are available online and at any U.S. Federal Repository Library.

Profile Each Selected Segment

Before a marketing program aimed at a specific market segment can be developed, the marketer must truly understand the typical customers in that market—their wants and needs, interests, attitudes, etc. A detailed picture of a market segment is called a *profile.* The profile should paint a clear picture of the typical customer for the company's product

Figure 7.9   Profile of Market Segments Form

	Segment		
	A	**B**	**C**
Size			
Number of consumers			
Growth rate			
Profile			
Demographic characteristics			
Geographic characteristics			
Psychographic characteristics			
Benefits sought			
Product Usage			
Favorite brands			
Quantities consumed			
Occasions of use			
Etc.			
Communications Behavior			
Media used			
Frequency of media usage			
Etc.			
Purchasing Behavior			
Distribution channel preferred			
Outlet preference			
Purchase infrequency			
Price range			
Etc.			

using all applicable segmentation variables discussed previously—demographic, geographic, psychographic, benefits sought, situation, and usage. Although this profile is a *generalized average* of the typical customer in the segment, it will help marketers discover and understand who the potential users of the product are, so that the best marketing mix for that customer can be developed. One way of profiling markets is to use a table such as that shown in Figure 7.9.

A now classic example of profiling comes from Texas and the "Don't Mess with Texas" anti-litter campaign. Research had indicated that the typical deliberate litterer in Texas was a male between the ages of 18 to 34, drove a truck, liked sports, and did not typically respond to appeals to civic duty. The "Don't Mess with Texas" antilitter campaign developed from the profile of this Texas "Bubba" involved using sports celebrities, country music and rock stars in a macho appeal to these Texans' sense of pride in their state. Littering was reduced by an amazing 29 percent within nine months after the campaign began.[31] The success of the campaign comes directly from a true understanding of the "typical litterer" and how to reach him. Another example of a profile, this time of teenagers, is presented in Figure 7.10.

Assess Potential Profitability of Each Segment and Select Segments for Targeting

Forecast Demand

Once segments have been identified and clearly distinguished, profitability of customizing marketing efforts aimed at these segments must be determined. This involves first forecasting demand for the product within each segmented target market. For example, a com-

Figure 7.10   Teens:Can We Really Understand Them?

In 1997 there were about 29 million teenagers who spent, on average, 84 cents of every dollar they got, and they got about $64 each week. Not only do teens spend a lot of money, they influence the expenditures of others—about $58 each week on groceries—for a total exceeding $50 billion each year. They have the most influence on the purchases of sports drinks, breakfast bars, pretzels, tortilla chips, potato chips, sweet snacks, and desserts. Teens also heavily influence purchases of convenience type food items such as frozen foods.

The sheer numbers and purchasing power of teenagers in the United States makes this market attractive to many industries, including the restaurant industry. One research firm compiled a study of the teen market for restaurants and found the following:

- Peer acceptance, spending time with friends, and having fun are high priorities for teens.
- Teens recognize and resent fake attitudes and having others "talk down" to them. They want to be treated politely and with respect by a business.
- Teens value their music, so play "cool" music.
- Teens like to receive special treatment and like to be singled out as with teen-only cards or clubs.
- As for what makes a brand cool in the eyes of teens: 66 percent said quality, 47 percent said, "If it's for people my age," and 39 percent believed advertising made a brand cool.

This information about the teen market may help a new restaurant tailor its marketing mix to better attract those elusive teens.

pany targeting college students in Louisiana would need to determine that there are 19 public colleges and junior colleges and that the total enrollment in these schools in 1995–96 was 159,420 students.[32] If the company expects a 50 percent share of the market, the sales forecast would be 79,710 units.

Firms must consider expected growth and competition in forecasting future sales. A large market share in a small, fast growth market may mean more long-term profits than a small market share in a crowded, stagnate, large market. Think about opening a new fast-food hamburger restaurant under slow growth, highly competitive market conditions with McDonald's as your competitor. Entering 1997, McDonald's owned a 42 percent share of the market and had a restaurant located within four minutes of most consumers.[33] Competitors' actions and other environmental factors that may affect future sales must also be carefully anticipated when forecasting potential demand.

Estimate Costs

The projected cost of developing and implementing specialized marketing efforts must also be determined. In the Louisiana college students example described earlier, the added costs of reaching this market might include: revising the product to meet Louisiana college student needs, changing the price to fit the budgets of these college students, changing distribution channels by offering the product for sale in Louisiana college bookstores, and advertising in Louisiana college newspapers. Finally, the additional costs of the specialized marketing program must be weighed against the estimated revenue to be gained from the market segments and against company objectives and the resources required to generate those revenues.

Select Positioning Strategy

After the target markets have been selected and fully understood, the marketing mix that best suits the target can be developed. Key to developing the appropriate marketing mix is

www.mcdonalds.com

LEARNING OBJECTIVE LO9

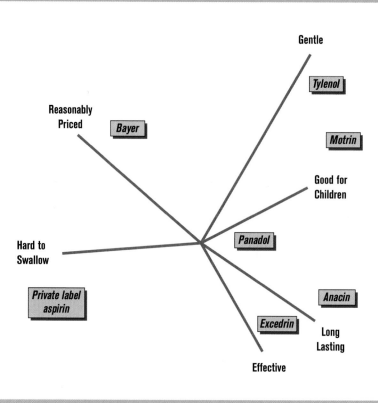

Figure 7.11   Perceptual Map of Pain Relievers

Positioning

is the image that customers have about a product, especially in relation to the product's competitors.

www.pepsiworld.com

www.coke.com

Perceptual mapping

is a commonly used multidimensional scaling method of graphically depicting a product's performance on selected attributes or the "position" of a product against its competitors on selected product traits.

the **positioning** strategy of the product. Creating and sustaining a strong, clear, and consistent customer image of the product in comparison with its competitors is key to *differentiating* the product, which is essential to developing a brand image, that leads to customer loyalty.

The Pepsi-Cola product Mountain Dew knows this firsthand. Sales rose an amazing 13 percent in 1997, placing the brand into the number four position in the carbonated drink market, ahead of Coca-Cola Company's Sprite, now ranked fifth. The success of Mountain Dew in the highly competitive soft drink market is attributed to a consistent, strong image that links teenagers, the major market segment, with outdoors, outrageousness, high energy and the thirst-quenching ability of the drink. Although the messages change to fit the times, Mountain Dew has retained its strong position, packaging, and formula over the last 25 years.[34]

Effective positioning means determining (1) what consumers currently think about the product, especially in relation to competing products, (2) what the marketer wants consumers to think about the product, and (3) which positioning strategy will elevate the consumers' current product image to the desired product image. In other words, where are we now, where do we want to go, and how do we best get there, bearing in mind the product position relative to competitors.

Determining what consumers think of a product often involves market research. A firm may want to survey its potential customers to determine what they think about the product based on several selected criteria, such as color, taste, freshness, etc. Criteria selected should be variables that are important to consumers and can be used to help a firm create a unique advantage or position for a product in the marketplace. A commonly used method for this is **perceptual mapping.** Interested students may want to visit www.surveysite.com/engine/tutormap.htm to view the perceptual mapping tutorial or create their own perceptual map using the demonstration of the Market Visioner™ tool at www.dssresearch.com.

An example of a perceptual map, shown in Figure 7.11, was created from hypothetical data for pain relievers. In this example, consumers rated seven different pain reliever brands

Figure 7.12   Example of Positioning by Price/Quality

according to how they believe each brand performs on the product characteristics: reasonably priced, hard to swallow, gentle, good for children, long lasting, and effectiveness. The perceptual map gives brand manufacturers a clear picture of how their product is perceived to perform on the selected characteristics, how each product performs on the attributes as compared to the competition, and gaps in the market that may need filling. The map of consumer perceptions of product characteristics helps answer the "where are we now" question, and the gaps help provide possible answers to the "where we want to go" question. Figure 7.11 illustrates hypothetical consumer perceptions that Tylenol is the most gentle and competes closely with Motrin, private label brands are the hardest to swallow, and Anacin and Excedrin are the most effective. What would you do if you were the brand manager for Bayer or Panadol?

Not only does the positioning strategy determine "where we want to go," it must also specify "how to get there." Generally, products can be positioned by any one, or combination, of the following ways:

www.tylenol.com

▼ Price/quality. Positioning by price/quality emphasizes the value derived from the product, either in terms of its quality or price or both. Wal-Mart stores are positioned based on every day low pricing (EDLP) and good value, while Neiman Marcus stores offer unique, high quality products for sale. The advertisement for Chrysler Cirrus, shown in Figure 7.12, is another example of positioning by price and quality.

Figure 7.13   Example of Positioning by User

- ▼ Product attributes. The characteristics or attributes of a product may serve as the bases for positioning the product. Some Colgate toothpastes are positioned by their attributes: Colgate Tartar Control Plus Whitening has both an anti-tartar and whitening formula for "clean, white teeth," and Colgate Total toothpaste helps prevent cavities, gingivitis, plaque, and tartar and provides "long lasting fresh breath protection." These toothpastes are clearly positioned in consumers' minds based on product attributes.

- ▼ Product user. The typical user of a product can also be used to position a product. The Marlboro man appeals to the rugged individual, and Revolt blue jeans are positioned to rebellious teenagers, as you can see from the advertisement shown in Figure 7.13.

- ▼ Product usage. Products can be positioned based on the ways in which the product is typically used. For example, the advertisement for Bounce in Figure 7.14 shows different ways in which Bounce fabric softener sheets can be used.

- ▼ Product class. Some products are positioned against another type of product or product class. Figure 7.15 shows Michelob as positioned against the product class

Figure 7.14   Example of Positioning by Product Usage

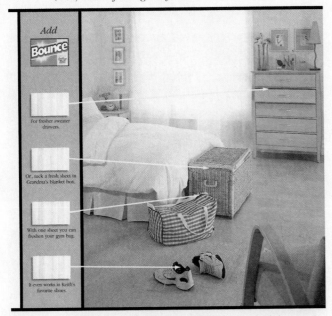

Announcing the most
exciting new use for something you
already have in the house.

(Well, next to finding out your husband can cook.)

Add

For fresher sweater drawers.

Or, tuck a fresh sheet in Grandma's blanket box.

With one sheet you can freshen your gym bag.

It even works in Keith's favorite shoes.

Go ahead and try using Bounce in even more fresh new ways. In fact try it almost anywhere freshness counts.*
Because every new sheet has crisp clean <u>time -released</u> freshness that continues working day after day after day.

Bounce. The freshest ideas are right under your nose.

*Keep out of reach of children and pets. Hang sheets freely or place in an open envelope to avoid direct contact with fabrics.   ®P&G 1997.

"beer." The advertisement implies that Michelob beer is in its own product category. Not only does the Bounce advertisement seen in Figure 7.14 position Bounce by product usage, it also positions the product by product class. The advertised use of Bounce in shoes, dresser drawers, blanket boxes, and gym bags for "time-released freshness" positions the product not against fabric softeners, but against completely different product classes—deodorizers, sachets, and air fresheners.

▼ Competition. Comparing a product to its competition, either directly or indirectly, is another form of product positioning. Burger King and McDonald's often compare their products to each other as do Ragu and Prego spaghetti sauces. Tide claims to "clean better" and Imodium AD is positioned against the "white stuff" and the "pink stuff." Figure 7.16 shows a Samsung camera that "outshoots the competition."

▼ Symbol. Occasionally companies use a symbol or icon to position their product in the minds of consumers. Over time, the symbol can become synonymous with the company or product as with the "Maytag Man," the golden arches of McDonald's

Figure 7.15 Example of Positioning by Product Class

(or Ronald McDonald), the Pillsbury Doughboy, the Jolly Green Giant, and, of course, the Nike swoosh. In each of these cases, most adult consumers have a clear image about the product or company by merely seeing the symbol.

As companies', competitors', and consumers' needs evolve over time, brand positions may also need to change. This process of creating a new image about an existing product in consumers' minds is called **repositioning.** Repositioning involves changing existing attitudes and beliefs about a product, and is much more difficult and more costly than establishing a position for a new product. To illustrate the difficulty in repositioning, imagine Wal-Mart trying to convince you they are a high-priced, prestige store or that Neiman Marcus stores have clothing everyone can afford.

In one advertising campaign aimed at flat sales and a growing designer jeans market, Levi Strauss repositioned its brand of jeans as the brand that designers wore. The advertising campaign involved 20,000 billboards with slogans such as "Calvin wore them," "Tommy wore them," and "Ralph wore them." With this new positioning campaign, the company hopes to reassert Levi's as "America's authentic blue jeans," according to Mark Hogan, director of consumer marketing for Levi's.[35]

Figure 7.16   Example of Positioning by Competition

The Samsung Evoca 115.
It simply outshoots the competition.

Even without its competitive price, the Samsung Evoca 115 is a simply sensational value. Just look at the chart below. Feature for feature you could spend more money, but you can't buy a

better camera than the Evoca 115. Standard features include Switchable Panorama, Message Caption and Quartz Date along with Intelligent Electronics that make the Evoca 115 a snap to use. So if you're looking for a point and shoot zoom camera that outshoots the competition, you simply can't miss with the Samsung Evoca 115. Call 1-800-SNAPSHOT or visit our website at www.simplyamazing.com for product information.

Features	Samsung Evoca 115	Canon Z115	Pentax 115M	Minolta Freedom Supreme	Olympus Stylus Zoom 115
Switchable Panorama	Yes	No	Yes	No	No
Message Caption	Yes	Yes	No	No	No
Multi-Exposure	Yes	No	No	No	No
Continuous Shooting	Yes	Yes	No	Yes	No
Step Zoom	Yes	No	No	No	No

Get a $20 rebate on selected Samsung Cameras. See retailer for details.   SAMSUNG CAMERA

Also in a stagnate market with slow growth, Miller Brewing embarked on a repositioning strategy with its Genuine and Lite beer brands by returning to the old advertising slogan "Miller Time." The purpose of the repositioning strategy was to appeal to the 21-to-30-year-old market, while maintaining their existing beer drinking market. The revised strategy boosted sales revenues by 4.5 percent from 1996 to 1997.[36]

Develop and Implement Appropriate Marketing Mix and Monitor, Evaluate, and Control

The final steps in the target market selection process are to develop and implement a marketing mix matched to the needs of the market segments selected for targeting and evaluating and controlling the plan. After putting the marketing mix into action, indicators of marketing effectiveness, such as sales and consumer perceptions, must be continually monitored and evaluated to determine effectiveness of the marketing mix in meeting desired plan objectives. New segments, new needs, and new opportunities may be identified through continual monitoring of target markets and changes in the mix made accordingly.

SEGMENTING BUSINESS MARKETS

LEARNING OBJECTIVE LO10

Firms that sell products to other businesses rather than household consumers often need to segment their market, depending on heterogeneity of demand. For example, Weyerhaeuser makes wood products, such as particle board. They can sell this product to furniture manufacturers for use in building furniture, or they can sell the product directly to lumber yards for sale to household consumers. Each of these business customers has a different set of needs for the particle board product Weyerhaeuser sells. An understanding of each of the two markets will help Weyerhaeuser tailor an effective marketing mix that will satisfy each customer's needs.

Segmenting the business market can help a firm analyze the market, select the best markets for targeting, and manage marketing programs.[37] While the steps in the target market selection process are essentially the same for business markets as those shown in Figure 7.2, there are three major differences within the steps in segmenting business markets. Those differences include a thorough understanding of the purchase process—which differs greatly from the consumer market—differences in the bases for segmentation, and differences in how the segmentation is implemented. The business-to-business purchase process was discussed in detail in Chapter 6, so the discussion here is limited to segmentation descriptors:[38]

Demographics

The "demographics" components of the business market include the industry, the size and growth potential, and the location of the targeted firm operations. Although some firms sell products to companies in the same industries, as Nike sells shoes to FootLocker or Foot Action, some companies sell products to many different industries. Xerox, for example, sells its copiers to businesses in all industries, ranging from small independent restaurants to multinational heavy equipment manufacturers. By grouping segments into industry type, the selling firm can learn more about the industry to better develop a marketing mix that will to help solve their markets' needs.

Selling firms may need to segment their business markets by company size and tailor their marketing efforts accordingly. For example, Xerox would certainly not devote the same resources to selling a copier to one restaurant in a small town as it would to selling thousands of machines to an international corporation. Finally, location is often a very important descriptor for segmenting business markets. The proximity of the segment to sales offices or manufacturing facilities, or the geographic concentration of the market segment, may substantially affect marketing efforts.

Internet

↑

www.nike.com
www.footlocker.com
www.footaction.com
www.xerox.com

Operating Characteristics

This descriptor is related to the operations of the targeted business and includes company technology, product and brand-user status, and customer capabilities. Obviously, the type and brand of product a customer business uses affects the way in which a selling firm will market the product to that business. Also, a supplying firm may want to approach loyal or heavy product users differently than it approaches infrequent product users. The business customer's technology and capabilities will also affect the types of products that a firm buys and its needs from supplying firms; and so may serve as a segmentation bases. For example, the computer needs of a large multinational firm with their own extensive, in-house computing specialists would differ greatly from those of a small town restaurant. A firm selling computers to these two distinctively different markets would need to tailor the marketing mix to the specific needs of each.

Purchasing Approaches

Factors internal to the buying firm and its purchase process, such as what level in the organization products are purchased, purchasing policies, purchasing criteria, such as speed of delivery, size of order, and nature of the buyer–seller relationship, etc., comprise the various purchasing approaches. A customer firm's purchase process, the policies and criteria for purchasing, and how formalized or centralized the process is, can each affect a customer's special needs. For example, a large fast-food restaurant may purchase products at its main headquarters and disperse those products out to each individual member of the chain, or each store may buy certain products individually. Each of the two purchasing approaches requires different marketing tactics from suppliers. Different type of firms and specific policies for purchasing also require special marketing efforts. Some private firms and governmental agencies often require bids on all purchases over a set dollar figure or require that prices be based on supplier cost.

The stage in the purchase process can also serve as a bases for segmenting business markets. There are three distinctive stages that may each represent a different market segment, regardless of the industry. These stages are First Time Prospects, Novices or new users, and Sophisticates or long-time users.[39] Buyers in each of these buying categories have a different set of needs from the supplying firm, so that marketing mixes customized to the needs of each segment could be developed.

Product Use or Usage Situation

The way in which a product is used in a business and the level of service a customer needs can also determine the marketing efforts required to effectively reach that business market. Weyerhaeuser's sales of particle board to different markets mentioned at the beginning of this section is an example of product use segmentation. Ryan's Family Steakhouse chain has a service technician that visits each site and maintains equipment, such as ice makers, while a single, independent restaurant in a small town may need the seller of the equipment to maintain that equipment. Accordingly, selling firms can devise different marketing plans based on different needs for services from the supplying firm.[40]

Situational Factors

As with consumer market segmentation, a myriad of temporary, situational factors can affect purchasing needs of the business-to-business market. Most obviously, special product uses and special physical distribution requirements such as order size, urgency of delivery, etc. can all affect the purchase process, thus serve as a bases for segmenting the market.

Buyers' Personal Characteristics

Finally, the individual personal characteristics of the participants in the purchase process can influence a buyer's needs. For example, some buyers are afraid to take risks and require a lot of time and information to make the decision, or a buyer could have a brother-in-law that also sells the needed product. In the first case, the supplier may need to develop a marketing mix that provides this type of buyer with testimonials and substantial support about product benefits to reassure the buyer, while in the second case, the supplier may not want to waste valuable resources targeting this buyer.

As with segmenting consumer markets, a combination of these segmentation variables are generally needed to draw a profile of business market segments. Once the potentially profitable segments are profiled, specialized marketing mix programs can be implemented to meet their special needs and the plan can be monitored, evaluated, and controlled.

SEGMENTING GLOBAL MARKETS

Increasingly, companies must reach out to foreign countries to prosper, as opportunities for domestic growth in many industries decline. After all about two-thirds of the world's total purchasing power and 95 percent of the population lives outside the United States.[41] In the restaurant industry, international sales are growing faster than are domestic sales for the industry's top 100 companies.[42] McDonald's alone has over 10,000 restaurants internationally, in over 105 countries with a new store opening, on average, every four hours.[43] Just as in domestic markets, firms must understand who their customers are through market segmentation and match the marketing mix they deliver with the needs of their customers before entering these new global markets.

In general, the target market selection process and the segmentation descriptors are the same for global markets as for household consumer markets. Like domestic consumer markets, global markets can be segmented based on demographics, geographics, psychographics, benefits sought, situation, and usage. A common approach is to segment international markets geographically by country combined with demographics or general lifestyle of the country, although, some research indicates that combining geographics with consumer purchase behavior patterns is preferable.[44] Other variables that are generally considered in defining homogenous demand segments in international markets include economic, legal/political, and cultural factors.

Economic Factors

The stage of industrial development of the country may affect the ability, willingness and capability, and purchase patterns of individuals in the market. For example, consumers in poorer, developing countries spend proportionally more of their incomes on basic consumer goods and services, while more prosperous developing countries spend more on durable goods.

Legal/Political Factors

The political and legal environment of a country may affect the ability of a firm to market to its consumers so that specialized marketing programs must be revised to meet those requirements. For example, the French government requires that marketers get special permission from the Commission Nationale Informatique et Liberté before creating a customer database.[45] The stability and type of government must also be used in defining segments and the way in which products are marketed in countries. The protectionist government in Mexico, for example, has hindered marketing practices in that country.[46]

Cultural Factors

Culture and language can pose real challenges to firms targeting consumers in different countries. Marketers targeting Canadians must consider the fact that both English and French are spoken in Quebec and that a law forbids making offers there in only one language.[47] Cultural and religious factors can also affect consumer needs for goods and services in ways that marketers must consider. The Islamic religion's restrictions on female dress would certainly affect a clothing firm's offerings in Muslim countries, while different colors have different meanings in different countries. For example, white, the symbol for purity in America, is a symbol for death in Asian countries.

Figure 7.17   The Global Consumer

Research has defined profiles of five homogeneous lifestyle segments that apply to consumers worldwide. Those groups are:

- *Rich around the World* – These consumers frequently travel, want quality, and will pay for it; they love new goods and services.

- *Older and Comfortable* – Members of this segment are 55 and older, have plenty of time on their hands and discretionary income to spend, although they are very value-oriented. They look for leisure products and new experiences, they like to buy gifts and to travel.

- *Indulged Kids* – The trend toward one-child families in many developing countries has created families that spend lavishly on things for their children. Typical items purchased by members of this segment include popular clothing, video games, electronics, and compact discs.

- *Emerging Middle Class* – In many developing countries, a growing middle class is now demanding basic goods and services widely available in the U.S., such as household items, consumer electronics, and health and beauty aids. While this segment is value-oriented for these basic products, they will pay premium prices for high quality, high prestige items.

- *Women Employed Outside the House* – In developed and some developing countries, a large percentage of women with families work. These women look for convenience and time-saving products and for services for the family, such as home maintenance and child care.

Despite these differences by country, some market segment lifestyle traits transcend country boundaries in what is know as ***intermarket segmentation.*** A profile of some intermarket "Global Consumers" is shown in Figure 7.17.

As with household consumer markets and business markets, the best market segment profiles are derived from a combination of market descriptors. A summary of these descriptors is shown in Table 7.2. However, firms deciding to target international markets may have difficulty in finding data needed for defining segments. Many countries do not have a standardized, routine census of citizens to provide reliable demographic, such as income, and geodemographic data about potential consumers. Also, data needed for some segmentation descriptors are very difficult or nonexistent to obtain. Finally, an effective target marketing program evaluates potential segments for profitability, then continuously

Table 7.2   Summary of Segmentation Descriptors by Market Type

Consumer Market	Business Market	Global Market Same as Consumer Market, plus:
Demographic	Demographic	Economic
Geographic	Operating characteristics	Legal/political
Psychographic	Buyer's personal characteristics	Cultural
Benefits sought	Purchasing approaches	
Situation	Situation	
Behavior/usage	Product use/usage situation	

Marketing Technologies

Targeting Customers on the Internet: Private Lives or Open Book?

Privacy is now the number one issue relating to the Internet. After all, marketers are using Internet visits to aggressively obtain private consumer Internet behavior information and using that information to target each consumer with specialized marketing efforts. Some of the practices that are causing such concern include:

Cookies—a computer program that allows a site to write information to a visitor's hard drive

Identity theft—taking, using, and possibly selling, personal information, such as name, address, phone number, etc., of site visitors

Internet profiling—keeping track of online behavior—all the sites visited during a session—to determine consumer interests.

Spam—unsolicited junk e-mail.

Search tracking—keeping track of search requests entered at search engines.

The government has threatened to intervene if Web sites don't regulate their own activities to ensure customer privacy. How they may intervene is still unknown, but governmental agencies from the United States, Canada, and Europe have developed general guidelines for fair information practices. For most countries, the guidelines state that Web sites should adhere to the following practices:

1. Notice/awareness—customers should be informed of the Web site's information practices before personal information is collected,

2. Choice/Consent—customers should have a choice about how information about them is used,

3. Access/Participation—customers should be able to access and contest information about them,

4. Integrity/Security—data should be correct and secure, and

5. Enforcement/Redress—there should be a method for enforcement of privacy policies.

One organization, TRUSTe, has already answered the call for self-regulation to protect customer privacy and avoid governmental intervention. The organization has developed a branded, online seal to attach to Web sites of organizations that agree to conform to privacy principles and agree to monitoring and audits by the organization. When you visit a site that has the TRUSTe trustmark, you can feel assured that the site follows most of the guidelines stated above and may be audited for compliance. The Web search engine site Excite is but one of many companies that now display the TRUSTe trustmark. Next time you visit Excite, click on TRUSTe to view their customer information policy.

Questions

1. Do you think that Internet marketers are violating individual customer privacy with their efforts to collect individual customer information? Are Internet marketers violating customer privacy any more or less than non-Internet marketers?

2. Other than self-regulating organizations, such as TRUSTe, can you think of any additional ways that marketers can ensure Internet customers' privacy?

Sources: Sharon Machlis, "Web Sites Rush to Self-Regulate," *Computerworld,* May 11, 1998, p. 2; Bill Machrone, "Trust Me?" *PC Magazine,* June 9, 1998, p. 85; and "Privacy Online: A Report to Congress," Federal Trade Commission, June 1998, at www.ftc.gov/reports/privacy3/toc.htm obtained on October 8, 1998.

monitors the effectiveness of both the marketing mix in meeting customer needs and the environment for opportunities and changes in the market.

Chapter Summary

Successful firms must truly understand the markets they serve and match their marketing mix to the needs of the market, in a process called target marketing. A market is an individual, group of individuals, or organizations willing, able, and capable of purchasing a firm's product. A market may be subdivided into any number of smaller markets, called segments. The number and the size of markets a firm may select for targeting can vary greatly from a mass market to one individual.

The target marketing process is extremely important to businesses because it allows firms to identify and analyze their customers, develop tailored market mixes to meet customer needs, identify market demand, identify competition, increase operating efficiencies, improve product positioning, and identify opportunities. Despite these advantages, there are some disadvantages to target marketing. Most notably, some firms have targeted disadvantaged, poor, or uneducated consumers with illegal or unethical products; others have portrayed some market segments stereotypically and offensively; and in doing so both groups have created cynicism toward target marketing practices. These firms may have actually inhibited brand popularity and loyalty, and wasted money and effort.

Nevertheless, the target marketing process is important and begins with: (1) identifying the total market; (2) determining the need for segmentation based on criteria for segmentation, strategic factors, and external factors; and (3) determining the bases for segmentation using demographic, geographic, psychographic, benefits sought, situation, and behavior (usage) descriptors. The firm must then collect segmentation data. These sources may be internal (from the company's database) or external (from research, other firms, or the government). The target marketing process continues with the following steps: (4) profiling each selected segment; (5) assessing potential profitability of each segment and selecting segments for targeting; (6) selecting the positioning strategy on the basis of price/quality, product attributes, product user, product usage, product class, competition, or symbols; (7) developing and implementing an appropriate marketing mix; and (8) monitoring, evaluating, and controlling the selection process.

Firms that target other businesses can segment their markets using the same process. However, the bases for segmentation for business markets include: demographics, operating characteristics, purchasing approaches, product use or usage situations, situational factors, and buyers' personal characteristics. Targeting global markets also requires the same target market selection process but has slightly different segmentation descriptors. Along with the consumer markets segmentation descriptors, global segments should be profiled using economic, political/legal, and cultural factors.

Key Terms

Market segment is a group of consumers that are alike based on some characteristic(s).

Niche marketing is the process of targeting a relatively small market segment with a specific, specialized marketing mix.

Micromarkets are very small market segments, such as zip code areas or even neighborhoods.

Criteria for Successful Segmentation includes target markets that are heterogeneous, measurable, substantial, actionable, and accessible.

Differentiation is the process of creating and sustaining a strong, consistent, and unique image about one product in comparison to others.

Positioning is the image that customers have about a product, especially in relation to the product's competitors.

Perceptual mapping is a commonly used multidimensional scaling method of graphically depicting a product's performance on selected attributes or the "position" of a product against its competitors on selected product traits.

Additional Key Terms and Concepts

Market

Market segmentation

Target marketing

Micromarketing

A priori

Heterogeneous demand

Target market

Niche

Target market selection process

Post hoc

Undifferentiated targeting strategy
Differentiated strategy
Geodemographics
Data mining
Differentiating
Intermarket segmentation

Concentrated strategy
Family life cycle (FLC)
80/20 principle
Profile
Repositioning

Questions for Discussion

1. StrengthMaker, the maker of a creatine monohydrate product designed to help body builders build muscle mass, is considering targeting high school athletes for its product, even though some people consider the use of creatine risky because it has been associated with pulled muscles and kidney damage. Explain the advantages and disadvantages of this strategy and make a recommendation about targeting the teenage market segment.

2. Using Figure 7.2 as a guideline, select and profile a target market for LitTalk, an audio tape copy of great literature, such as *Great Expectations* and *War and Peace* covered in popular college literature textbooks. Use as many bases of segmentation variables as possible.

3. Since everyone drinks water, explain why you would or would not segment the "water" market if you were selling Naya bottled water. What if you were selling prune juice? Justify your answers using the criteria for successful market segmentation.

4. Which segmentation variable(s) is most important? Why?

5. Find articles in the library that discuss the target market for a particular product, such as Guess jeans or Nike, and profile the market. Include as many of the segmentation bases as possible.

6. Understanding what consumers are looking for in a product, or benefits sought, is an important way of segmenting markets. Ask 10 friends what they most want from their shampoo, then identify possible benefits sought market segments for shampoo.

7. Discuss sources of data for segmenting markets.

8. Find an advertisement that represents positioning based on each of the seven ways discussed in the chapter. Explain each selection.

9. Compare and contrast segmentation for consumer markets, business markets, and international markets.

Internet Questions

1. Profile your home town by visiting the Web site: **census.gov/main/www/access.html.** First click on Map Stats, then click on your home state, and select your county or parish. "Browse Tiger Map of area" to draw a map of your home town area, then access the U.S. Counties General Profile for 1996 to obtain the latest census information about your county. Also access Business Patterns and Economic Profile for your area.

2. Visit www.visa.com and www.mastercard.com. How do these companies target college students? Explain your suggestions for improving their targeting efforts.

3. What is your Internet privacy IQ? Visit www.truste.org and take the TRUSTe Privacy Challenge.

Endnotes

[1]Carol M. Morgan and Doran J. Levy, "Why we kick the tires: going beyond focus groups to learn car buyers motivations," *Brandweek,* September 29, 1997, pp. 24–27.

[2]Peter R. Dickson and James I. Ginter, "Market Segmentation, Product Differentiation, and Marketing Strategy," *Journal of Marketing,* April 1987, pp. 1–10.

[3]"Health Club for Truckers," *Marketing News,* January 5, 1998, p. 1.

[4]David Pescovitz, "The Future of Clothing," *Wired,* at www.wired.com/wired/3.11/departments/reality.check.html on June 17, 1998.

[5]Adapted from Jock Bicker, "Cohorts II: A New Approach to Market Segmentation," *Journal of Consumer Marketing,* Fall–Winter, 1997, pp. 362–380.

[6]N. H. Dover, "Where There's Gray, There's Green," *Marketing News,* June 22, 1998, p. 2.

[7]Kevin Sheridan, "Segs and the Single Card," *Bank Marketing,* August 1997, p. 5.

[8]Ned Anschuetz, "Building Brand Popularity: The Myth of Segmenting to Brand Success," *Journal of Advertising Research,* January/February 1997, pp. 63–7, 65.

[9]Sally Dibb and Lyndon Simkin, "A Program of Implementing Market Segmentation," *Journal of Business & Industrial Marketing,* Winter 1997, pp. 51–66.

[10]Yoram Wind, "Issues and Advances in Segmentation Research," *Journal of Marketing Research,* August 1978, pp. 317–337.

[11]Erwin Daneels, "Market Segmentation: Normative Model Versus Reality," *European Journal of Marketing,* June 1996, pp. 36–42.

[12]Carol Marie Cropper, "Haggar Men's Wear Turns to More Sophisticated Consumers: Women," *The New York Times,* October 6, 1997, p. D12 c3.

[13]Paul E. Green and Abba M. Krieger, "Segmenting Markets With Conjoint Analysis," *Journal of Marketing,* October, 1991, pp. 20–31; Peter R. Dickson and James I. Ginter, "Market Segmentation, Product Differentiation, and Marketing Strategy," *Journal of Marketing,* April 1987, pp. 1–10.

[14]Adapted from Paul E. Green and Abba M. Krieger, "Segmenting Markets with Conjoint Analysis," *Journal of Marketing,* October, 1991, pp. 20–31.

[15]Mary Brophy Marcus, "Target Market: Fido, Fluffy—You," *U. S. News & World Report,* December 1, 1997, p. 57.

[16]Maricris G. Briones, "Coors Turns Up the Heat," *Marketing News,* June 22, 1998, pp. 1, 15.

[17]Vincent-Wayne Mitchell and Sarah Haggett, "Sun-sign Astrology in Market Segmentation and Empirical Investigation," *Journal of Consumer Marketing,* Spring 1997, pp. 113–132.

[18]See Morris B. Holbrook and Robert M. Schindler, "Market Segmentation Based on Age and Attitude Toward the Past: Concepts, Methods, and Findings Concerning Nostalgic Influences on Customer Tastes," *Journal of Business Research,* September 1996, pp. 27–40.

[19]Charles M. Schaninger and William D. Danko, "A Conceptual and Empirical Comparison of Alternative Household Life Cycle Models," *Journal of Consumer Research,* March 1993.

[20]As shown in Charles M. Schaninger and William D. Danko, "A Conceptual and Empirical Comparison of Alternative Household Life Cycle Models," *Journal of Consumer Research,* March 1993.

[21]Lynn R. Kahle, "The Nine Nations of North America and the Value Basis of Geographic Segmentation," *Journal of Marketing,* April 1986.

[22]*Marketing News,* "Drivers' Habits Revealed," June 22, 1998, p. 2.

[23]*Automotive Marketing,* "Profile: The Wealthy," April 3, 1996, pp. 5–28.

[24]Russell I. Haley, "Benefit Segmentation: A Decision-Oriented Research Tool," *Journal of Marketing,* July 1968.

[25]Russell W. Belk, "Situational Variables and Consumer Behavior," *Journal of Marketing,* December 1975.

[26]C. J. Mellor, "Though the Beer Is Lite, Campaign's a Heavyweight," *Back Stage,* January 15, 1988, pp. 1–3.

[27]Craig Stedman, "Marketing Megamarts on the Rise," *Computerworld,* September, 22, 1997, pp. 65–66.

[28]Kate Fitzgerald, "Marketers Capture Prospects Using AmEx 'Closed Loop,'" *Advertising Age,* October 9, 1995, pp. 18–19.

[29]Michael Schrage, "Sticky Times for Customer Service," *Computerworld,* February 23, 1998, p. 25.

[30]Laura Loro, "FedEx Mines Its Database to Drive New Sales," *Business Marketing,* March 1997, pp. 4–6.

[31]*Time,* "Real Men Don't Litter," January 19, 1987, p. 25.

[32]"Statewide Student Profile System, Spring, 1995–96 Master File," available at webserv.regents.state.la.us/sprg9596.html, obtained on May 13, 1998.

[33]Jolie Solomon and John McCormick, "A Really Big Mac: Bruised, Battered and Bashed, McDonald's Deserves a Break—Today," *Newsweek,* November 17, 1997, pp. 56–58.

[34]Louise Kramer, "Mountain Dew Stays True to its Brand Positioning," *Advertising Age,* May 18, 1998, p. 26.

[35]Miles Socha, "Levi's New Ads Play the Name Game," *WWD,* May 5, 1998, p. 16.

[36]Greg W. Prince, "Time and Again: Miller Goes Straight to the Core and Likes the Results," *Beverage World,* February 15, 1998, pp. 32–35.

[37]Benson P. Shapiro and Thomas V. Bonoma, "How to Segment Industrial Markets," *Harvard Business Review,* May/June 1984, pp. 104–110.

[38]Adapted from Benson P. Shapiro and Thomas V. Bonoma, "How to Segment Industrial Markets," *Harvard Business Review,* May/June 1984, pp. 104–110.

[39]Thomas S. Robertson and Howard Barich, "A Successful Approach to Segmenting Industrial Markets," *Planning Review,* November/December 1992, pp. 4–12.

[40]For more detail, see Arun Sharma and Douglas M. Lambert, "Segmentation of Markets Based on Customer Service," *International Journal of Physical Distribution and Logistics Management,* May 1994, pp. 50–58.

[41]Dom Del Prete, "Winning Strategies Lead to Global Marketing Success," *Marketing News,* August 18, 1997, pp. 1–2.

[42]Kimberly D. Lowe, "Going Global; Operating a Restaurant in Familiar Territory Is Tough Enough: Some Companies Raise the Stakes by Going Overseas," *Restaurants & Institutions,* November 1, 1997, pp. 65–70.

[43]Jolie Solomon and John McCormick, "A Really Big Mac: Bruised, Battered and Bashed, McDonald's Deserves a Break—Today," *Newsweek,* November 17, 1997, pp. 56–58; Kimberly D. Lowe, "Going Global; Operating a Restaurant in Familiar Territory Is Tough Enough. Some Companies Raise the Stakes by Going Overseas," *Restaurants & Institutions,* November 1, 1997, pp. 65–70.

[44]Peter G. P. Walters, "Global Market Segmentation: Methodologies and Challenges," *Journal of Marketing Management,* January/April 1997, pp. 165–177.

[45]Hallie Mummert and Lisa Yorgey, "Selling Around the World," *Target Marketing,* January 1995, pp. 28–32.

[46]Ibid.

[47]Ibid.

[48]Sources: "Electronics, Video Game Systems, Household Owns," **www.mediamark.com,** October 10, 1998; Nancy Konish, "Video Game Giants are Neck and Neck for the Profit," *Electronic Design,* September 14, 1998, p. 32A; Terry Lefton, "Looking for a Sonic Boom," *Brandweek,* March 2, 1998, pp. 26–29; "Play N64 In Your Hotel," Game Junkie Online—News, **www.game-junkie.com,** article dated September 8, 1998, obtained on October 13, 1998; John Robinson, Shawn Levin, and Brian Hak, "Computer Time," *American Demographics,* August 1998, pp. 18–23; Robert Scally, "Video Game Market Widens, But Promotionals Hurt Sales," *Discount Store News,* May 25, 1998, p. 19.

Competing in the Future: The Video Games Market[48]

Perhaps no consumer market is more volatile than the video game market because of quickly changing technology and fickle consumer tastes. Despite the volatility, the market can yield tremendous payoffs because of its size and rapid growth. In fact, according to Mediamark Research, about 23.3 percent of all U.S. households own a video game system. In 1997, the U.S. video game market had $6.6 billion in sales, which represented a sales increase of 26 percent over the previous year and a 40 percent increase over the previous year's sales of video game software. These growth rates were expected to continue at about the same rate during 1998, with profits peaking in 1999.

With so many potential sales riding on the line, competition in this market has been fierce. Over the past decade, the market position of the leading players has changed hands dramatically and quickly. In 1993, Nintendo dominated the marketplace with more than an 80 percent share of the total market. In fact, more U. S. consumers had Nintendos in their homes than had personal computers at that time. Then the Sega Genesis, with its highly recognizable "Sonic" hedgehog character, entered the market and gained the affection of hard-core video gamers. Reaching an all time high of more than 50 percent of the market in 1994 and 1995, Sega seriously encroached into Nintendo's market dominance. Also in 1994, the Sony 32-bit PlayStation entered the marketplace. By summer of 1998, Nintendo and Sony were running neck and neck for market dominance, with Sony slightly ahead and Sega not even in the game with less than 1 percent of the total market share.

What accounts for the differences in market share? The early video game market leader, Nintendo, had dominated the market by appealing to the kid market (children under 14 years of age), and by having a strong brand recognition with "the game's the thing" positioning. Sony entered the marketplace with a technologically advanced 32-bit operating system that targeted the 18- to 24-year-old hard-core gamers, adults who had grown up on video games. According to Sony, it would be easier to reach older consumers now and then later go after younger ones, than the other way around—older consumers would resist products tailored for young kids. The primary appeal of the Sony was its 32-bit operating system, over three hundred games available, and the lower price of PlayStation games. Finally, the decline of Sega's market position began with the launch of the Saturn product. With it, Sega abandoned its previous target (slightly-rebellious, hard-core gamers) and its trademark Sonic character, for a younger, unfocused market and no clear-cut brand symbol. Further, Sega's reliance on technology for technology's sake and a limited number of games compatible with its game console led to a poor market performance.

To further complicate market conditions, PC-based games have become increasingly popular. Sales of PC games grew by 20 percent in 1997 with another 20 percent growth rate expected in 1998. The growth is not surprising considering the findings of one 1997 survey. The telephone survey found that about 39 percent of the adult population uses a computer at home for hobbies or enjoyment. Some 69 percent of the 18 to 24 year-olds in that survey reported using computers for hobbies and enjoyment and used their personal computers, on average, four hours per day. Could these young adults be playing video games?

What does the future hold for the volatile video game market? Sega plans to introduce a new platform in September 1999, backed by a $100 million launch, and Nintendo is increasing its number of games available, especially adult-oriented sports games and role-playing games. What's more, Nintendo recently licensed LodgeNet to be the first provider of Nintendo 64 video games in its over 500,000 hotel rooms. Among LodgeNet hotels are such noted names as Sheraton, Ritz-Carlton, Embassy Suites, Holiday Inns, Red Roof Inns, and La Quinta Inns. This licensing agreement should mean that about 35 million hotel guests will have the opportunity to play Nintendo, and purchase an estimated 54 million minutes of Nintendo play time during the summer of 1999 alone. Finally, game developers may be increasing the number of games that can cross over to different platforms and to PCs, and more and more PC games contain online components not available with video game consoles. Newly developing computer technologies, such as the digital videodisc (DVD), may also impact consumer tastes for game platforms.

Discussion Questions

1. Define the target market for Nintendo, Sony, and Sega. How do you think the target market definition has affected each company's past market performance? How do you think it will affect future performance?

2. Discuss the positioning strategy of each of the major companies in the video game market. What changes in positioning would you suggest for any of the three video game companies?

3. Pick one of the three video game manufacturers. Explain how you would define the target market and position the company to prepare for the future. How would you prepare to compete with a growing and technologically advancing PC market?

Part 3

Product

Chapter 8

Product Decisions and Marketing's Role in New Product Development

Abbie Griffin, University of Illinois, Urbana-Champaign

Dr. Griffin earned her Ph.D. in management from the Massachusetts Institute of Technology, her M.B.A. from Harvard University and her B.S. from Purdue University. She is editor of the *Journal of Product Innovation Management,* and serves as director of the Product Development & Management Association. She has received the 1997 Marketing Science Institute Best Paper Award, the 1993 John D.C. Little Best Paper Award, and the 1994 Frank M. Bass Dissertation Paper Award for "Voice of the Customer."

Dr. Griffin teaches product development and business-to-business marketing. Her research interests include measuring and improving new product development processes, obtaining

The Newton personal digital assistant (pda) was conceived by the advanced research group at Apple, evolving out of their development effort to eliminate keyboard entry into computers. The Newton's **core benefit proposition (CBP)** was to capture, organize, and communicate ideas and data, without requiring keyboard entry.[1] The advanced research group and Apple management defined Newton's form and features without first asking how people in the target market captured information now and what unsolved problems remained. Apple found that $800 bought a lot of pens, Post-It Notes™, paper, calendars, and even electronic address books. Newton did not solve people's remaining information-use problems in a cost-effective way. Newton sales were dismal, and the product was ultimately withdrawn from the market.

Contrast Newton's failure to the runaway success of U.S. Robotics' Palm Pilot, another pda. The Palm Pilot's CBP is also to capture, organize, and communicate ideas. However, the Palm Pilot provides value to customers not only by replacing paper or electronic address books and calendars, but also by replacing computer-based time management systems. Individuals are therefore willing to pay the $300–$400 price. The product is so successful that it has spawned a whole host of look-alike competitors.

Why was the Palm Pilot successful while the Newton was a dismal failure? There are three major differences between the Newton and the Palm Pilot, each of which contributed to the Palm Pilot's success. First, the U.S. Robotics team obtained input from potential customers while developing the design. For example, they obtained size and carrying reactions from one of their own employees in the business development group because he wore Brooks Brothers shirts, which have the smallest pockets of any major shirt-maker.

Additionally, the Palm Pilot's buttons that allow users to switch instantly from one application to another, say from the calendar to the to-do list, are arranged according to customer information that was gathered regarding the frequency of use for each application.

Second, the handwriting recognition technology in the Palm Pilot, although less sophisticated than Newton's, works much more effectively. Palm Pilot users must learn a simple, but rather intuitive, alphabet (called "Graffiti") to make written inputs. For example, writing "⌐" with the pen produces a "t". U.S. Robotics created a product from proven technologies that requires users to modify writing behavior to conform to a standard form, but works reliably when they do so.

The third success contributor is the way the Palm Pilot seamlessly integrates with other standard products, including both computers and software. The development team thought through solutions to peripheral details of information management problems, rather than just thinking of the pda as the total answer. The pda itself was one piece in a full system that solved the set of problems surrounding capturing, organizing, and communicating information. The data exchange cradle and desktop software included with the pda create a system that functions effectively, both when a user is in the office and away from the office. Overall, by soliciting customer input to guide the design, using proven technology to deliver the design, and ensuring seamless integration with other already-available products, the Palm Pilot is being accepted by customers in a way the Newton never achieved.

Core Benefit Proposition (CBP)

is the primary benefit or purpose for which a customer buys a product. The CBP may reside in the physical good or service performance, or it may come from augmented dimensions of the product.

www.palm.com

customer inputs to new product development, decreasing time to commercialize products, and management of technology.

Dr. Griffin's professional experience includes consulting in marketing, strategic planning, and technology management to technology dependent firms.

Learning Objectives

After you have completed this chapter, you should be able to:

1. Categorize products by type and develop an understanding of product mix decisions.

2. Discuss the importance of branding, packaging, and labeling decisions.

3. Understand the basic growth strategies utilized by marketing firms.

4. Learn how to evaluate product development success.

5. Identify the three essential activities every firm must successfully undertake to achieve product development success.

6. Discover the range of methods available for understanding customer needs.

7. Describe the processes by which products are developed.

8. Plan how to shepherd products through the organization.

9. Understand the strategic significance of the product life cycle.

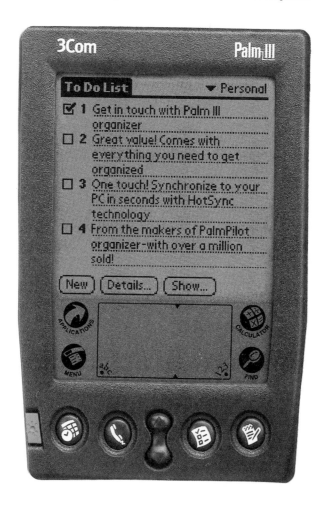

Products

are the set of features, functions, and benefits that customers purchase. Products may consist primarily of tangible (physical) attributes or intangibles, such as those associated with services or some combination of tangible and intangible.

Products are the core of every organization. Whether it be a good, service, person, place, or idea, organizations need a product to offer. In general, products offer customers a bundle of attributes that may include the product itself, its package and brand name, the service that backs up product performance, on-time delivery, courteous and effective customer relations, an adequate warranty, and so on. This chapter discusses the nature of product-related decisions and takes an in-depth examination of the role of marketing in new product development.

TYPES OF PRODUCTS[2]

Consumer Products

In general, products can be classified as either consumer or business-to-business products, depending on *who the buyer is* and *for what purpose the product is being bought.* If a product is purchased by a consumer for his or her own household use, the product is classified as a ***consumer product.*** Consumer products are classified into categories based on how the consumer views and shops for the product. There are four categories of consumer products:

▼ **Convenience Products:** A convenience product is typically an inexpensive item that consumers purchase with little effort. Examples include milk, butter, toothpaste, shampoo, soap, and a variety of other products that are used on a frequent basis.

Consumers spend little time shopping for convenience products. As a result, convenience products are widely distributed to a variety of retail outlets.

▼ **Shopping Products:** Shopping products are more expensive than convenience products, and the decision is more important. The consumer will spend more time searching for information before selecting a particular brand, and compares prices and benefits among brands offering similar characteristics and **features.** Examples include appliances, furniture, perfume and clothing. These products are not as widely distributed as convenience products.

▼ **Specialty Products:** Sometimes consumers desire a particular brand in a product category and are willing to spend a great deal of time to acquire that one particular brand. Substitutes are not an option. The consumer becomes highly involved in the purchase, and the product often reflects the consumer's personality or self-image. A Rolex watch is a classic example of a specialty product. Distribution of specialty products is very limited.

▼ **Unsought Products:** A product that is unknown to the buyer or a known product that is not actively sought is an unsought product. Consumers do not seek out unsought products until they are made aware of or need the products. Examples of unsought products include cemetery plots, medical services, and insurance. Personal selling is often needed to market these products successfully.

Features
are the way that benefits are delivered to customers. Features provide the solution to customer problems.

Business-to-Business Products

Products purchased by organizations to be used in producing other products or in operating their businesses are classified as *business-to-business products.* Business-to-business products are classified into categories based on how the products will be used. There are five categories of business-to-business products.

▼ **Installations:** Products categorized as installations are major capital goods. Usually, installations are customized, expensive, and purchased infrequently. Products such as buildings, laboratories, and major computer systems are all considered installations. The selling process is typically longer, more complex, and more challenging than for all other types of business-to-business products.

▼ **Accessories:** Products that are shorter-lived than installations are classified as accessories. Accessories are usually standardized products that are purchased more frequently than installations. Examples include fax machines, printers, and copiers.

▼ **Raw Materials:** Raw materials are unprocessed products that become part of a company's finished products. For example, farm products such as milk, eggs, corn, wheat, and processed sugar are considered raw materials.

▼ **Component Parts/Materials:** Products that are already processed or need little processing to be ready for assembly within the finished product are component parts/materials. Hamburger patties, buns, ketchup, onions, and pickles are all component parts/materials for both McDonald's and Burger King. Tires, carpeting, and many other products are component parts/materials used in the manufacturing of new automobiles.

▼ **Supplies:** Products that are used in support of business operations but are not part of the finished product are considered supplies. These products are standardized, purchased often, and considered inexpensive compared to installations and accessories. Examples include pens, pencils, paper, paper clips, and Post-It Notes™.

PRODUCT MIX DECISIONS[3]

Few companies are successful by relying on a single product. Most companies manufacture and market a variety of products. All of the products a company markets can be thought of as its ***product mix.*** The mixture of products typically includes various items that are related in terms of the raw materials used to create them or the product end-uses. A group of related items in a company's product portfolio constitutes a ***product line.*** The following example illustrates the number of product mix decisions marketers must make.

The Purex Corporation had a relatively small product mix when it opened its doors. The company primarily manufactured bleach and a few powdered laundry detergents. Over the years, through new product development and acquisitions, Purex extended its product mix (see Figure 8.1) by offering fabric softeners (StaPuff), fabric softener sheets (Toss'n Soft), Brillo Soap Pads, Sweetheart soaps, Sweetheart Dish Liquids, Mildew Stain Removers, and sponge products (Dobie Pads). These products all relate to household cleaning.

The ***product mix width*** is the number of different product lines a company offers. The width of Purex's product mix includes detergents, fabric softeners, cleansers, scour pads, bleach, dish liquids, soaps, ammonia, and bowl cleaners. The ***product mix depth*** refers to the number of brands within each product line. The depth of Purex's detergent product line includes Purex powdered, Purex Liquid with Fabric Softener, Trend Powdered, Trend Liquid, Dutch Powdered, and Dutch Liquid.

Any company limits its growth potential if it chooses to concentrate on a single product line. Companies that offer multiple product lines enjoy numerous benefits:

▼ **Protection against competition:** If a company relies on one product for success, a competitor can enter the market, undercut the price, and steal market share. A company with more than one product line will not be devastated by the effects of a competitor's actions in any one particular area.

▼ **Increase growth and profits:** Companies offer more than one product line to boost market growth and company profits. If a product category is mature with little to no growth, a company may find it difficult to increase its share and profits unless it is willing to spend more to take market share away from a competitor.

▼ **Offset sales fluctuations:** Companies that offer products with seasonal variations find that multiple product lines help to offset these fluctuations in sales.

Figure 8.1   Purex Corporation Product Mix

				Width of the Product Mix					
	Detergents	**Fabric Softeners**	**Cleansers**	**Scour Pads**	**Bleach**	**Dish Liquids**	**Soaps**	**Ammonia**	**Bowl Cleaners**
Depth of Product Lines	Purex Powdered Purex Liquid Purex Liquid with Fabric Softener Trend Powdered Trend Liquid Dutch Liquid	StaPuf Liquid StaPuf Sheets Toss'n Soft	Old Dutch BabO	Brillo Dobie Brillo Lane	Purex	Sweetheart Trend Lemon Trend	Sweetheart	Bo-Peep	SnoBol

▼ **Achieve greater impact:** Multiple product lines allow a company to achieve greater market impact. A company with multiple lines of products often is more important to both consumers and channel members.

▼ **Enable economical resource usage:** Multiple product lines enable the economical use of resources. Spreading operational costs over a series of products enables a manufacturer to reduce the average production and marketing costs for all its products; this results in lower prices to customers.

▼ **Avoid obsolescence:** Companies offering more than one product line avoid becoming obsolete when one product line reaches the end of its life cycle.

BRANDING, PACKAGING, AND LABELING DECISONS[4]

Branding Decisions

Customers handle an enormous amount of information in the course of their daily activities. Consequently, customers develop efficient ways of processing information in order to make decisions. *Brands* are one of the most fundamental pieces of information customers use to simplify choices and reduce purchase risk. Brand names assure customers that they will receive the same quality with their next purchase as they did with their last. Consequently, buyers are willing to pay a premium for quality and assurance. For this reason, branding has become an essential element of product strategy.

Brands serve important communication functions and, in doing so, establish beliefs among customers about the attributes and general image of a product. After a brand has been established, the brand name (letters or numbers used to vocalize the brand), logo (symbols such as McDonald's Golden Arches and Prudential's rock), and trademark (brand name and/or logo that is legally protected) serve to remind and reinforce the beliefs that have been formed. To arrive at this point, the firm must have made good on its promises. The case for a new brand, however, is different. A good brand name, logo, or trademark should have four important characteristics:

1. It should attract attention.

2. It should be memorable.

3. It should help communicate the positioning of the product.

4. It should distinguish the product from competing brands.

Brand Equity

Successful brands develop **brand equity.** The financial value of brand equity is tremendous! For example, Kohlberg Kravis Roberts purchased RJR Nabisco for $25 billion (double its book value); Phillip Morris, Inc., paid $12.9 billion for Kraft (four times book

LEARNING OBJECTIVE LO2

Brand equity
is the marketplace value of a brand based on reputation and goodwill.

Just how important is a good brand name, logo, or trademark? Is it memorable? Do you recognize these?

Figure 8.2	Successful and Unsuccessful Brand Extensions

Successful Brand Extensions to New Product Categories

BIC disposable shavers	BIC disposable lighters
Kodak film	Kodak cameras and batteries
Coleman camping lamps	Coleman stoves, tents, sleeping bags
Winnebago campers	Winnebago tents, sleeping bags
Ivory soap	Ivory shampoo, dishwashing liquid
Woolite detergent	Woolite carpet cleaner
Jell-O gelatin	Jell-O pudding pops
Rubbermaid housewares	Rubbermaid farm food bins
Barbie dolls	Barbie games, furniture, clothes, magazines
Odor-Eater foot pads	Odor-Eater socks
Dr. Scholl's foot pads	Dr. Scholl's shoes, socks, wart remover
Bausch & Lomb optics	Bausch & Lomb contact lenses, sunglasses
Minolta cameras	Minolta copiers
Honda bikes	Honda cars, lawnmowers, rototillers, generators
Fisher-Price toys	Fisher-Price playwear
Lipton tea	Lipton soup mixes

Unsuccessful Brand Extensions to New Product Categories

Jack Daniel's bourbon	Jack Daniel's charcoal briquets
Dunkin' Donuts	Dunkin' Donuts cereal
Jacuzzi baths	Jacuzzi bath toiletries
Harley-Davidson bikes	Harley-Davidson cigarettes
Rubbermaid housewares	Rubbermaid computer tables
Stetson hats	Stetson shirts, umbrellas
Levi jeans	Levi business wear
Certs candy	Certs gum
Mr. Coffee coffeemakers	Mr. Coffee coffee

value) and $5.7 billion for General Foods (over four times book value). Even under the generous notion that the tangible assets of these companies were undervalued by 50 percent, this still means that the reputation and goodwill of their brand names (brand equity) were worth billions.

In addition to the financial value, brand equity also has a very important strategic value. Manufacturers have become increasingly interested in marketing new products under the umbrella of well-established brand names that are already familiar to consumers. Several of these are presented in Figure 8.2. New products marketed under well-established brand names are more likely to be accepted by channel members due to the proven track record of the brand and disenchantment with the risks involved in launching new brands. Strong brand equity is not only used to roll out new products, but it also helps companies break into new markets. For example, in Figure 8.2 we can see where Kodak used its film brand equity to break into the camera market, and Lipton tea used its brand to launch soup mixes. Finally, brand equity can be strategically utilized as an effective barrier to entry, making it difficult for competitors to enter or expand in the market.

Branding Strategies: Individual versus Family Branding

When selecting branding strategies, marketers essentially have two options. The first option is to pursue an ***individual brand name strategy*** where each product in a company's product mix is given a specific brand name. Procter & Gamble and General Mills are often cited as prime examples of companies that employ an individual brand name strategy. The advantage of an individual brand name strategy is that it allows the firm to develop the best brand name possible for every product. In addition, an individual brand name strategy diversifies the firm's risk by not allowing individual product failures to tarnish the reputation and image of all of the company's products. The down side of an individual brand name strategy is that the firm is not taking advantage of the brand equity of existing brands that may facilitate customer acceptance of new products.

The other branding option is to use a *family brand name strategy* where all, or a significant portion, of the company's products are associated with a family brand name. The primary advantage of a family brand name strategy is that it can be used to launch new products. Firms typically extend their family brand names in two ways:

1. The family brand is extended into product categories that are used in the same situation as the original branded product or used by the consumers of the original branded product (e.g., Coke, Diet-Coke, and Caffeine Free-Coke).

2. The family brand is extended to help the company introduce products into new product categories (e.g., Fisher-Price toys introduces Fisher-Price playwear).

Over the years, variations of the family branding strategy have evolved. The three most common include:

▼ Blanket family name for all products: this strategy is followed by General Electric and Heinz.

▼ Separate family names for types of products: this strategy is followed by Sears who markets Kenmore appliances, Craftsman tools, and DieHard batteries.

▼ Family names combined with individual brand names: this strategy is pursued by Kellogg's and is evident in product brands such as Kellogg's Raisin Bran and Kellogg's Corn Flakes.

A strong family brand name will grab the customer's attention and may lead to product trial. It provides a foot in the door. Family branding is most effective when its applied to a product that is complementary in usage to the original branded product. This approach is supported by the successful brand extensions that are presented in Figure 8.2.

www.pg.com
www.generalmills.com

Packaging Decisions

Each year, companies spend more on packaging than on advertising. As markets have matured and competitive differentiation has narrowed, packaging has become a very important component of marketing strategy. Sometimes a firm forgets that it's the packaged product, and not the product alone, that is sold and purchased. A product's package is often its most distinctive marketing effort. Packaging performs a number of essential functions.

▼ **Protection:** A package must protect the product in several different situations: in the manufacturer's warehouse, during shipment to the wholesaler and retailer, in the seller's warehouse, and in transporting the product from the seller's store to the consumer's final point of consumption.

▼ **Identification:** A product's package, particularly one that is distinctive, helps customers identify the product in a crowded marketplace. The classic case of an eye-catching display was the L'Eggs point-of-purchase stand with hundreds of plastic eggs in different colors.

▼ **Information:** The package provides a means of communicating with the customer. A more informed customer gets the very best performance out of a product.

▼ **Packaging to Enhance Usage:** Several very innovative packages have added real convenience to product use. For example, when Beech-Nut apple juice switched from cans to bottles (onto which plastic nipples for babies could be attached), sales quadrupled. Another example involved Cheseborough-Ponds who put nail polish in a special type of felt tip pen. The new packaging helped increase sales by over 20 percent.

▼ **Packaging to Enhance Disposal:** A package that is biodegradable, or made from recycled materials, will appeal to environmentally conscious market segments.

▼ **Packaging to Enhance Channel Acceptance:** New shipping and warehouse technology may require standard package dimensions. *Cubic efficiency* is a term that describes how efficiently a package occupies storage, transportation, and display space. Boxes are more cubic efficient than cans, and cans are more efficient than most bottles. Packaging that suits the needs of channel members is more apt to be adopted over competitive packaging that does not.

Ultimately, effective packaging adds to the value of the product. For instance, opening and resealing, pouring, mixing, processing, and cooking may all be enhanced or made easier by creative packaging. A package also continues to communicate on the kitchen shelf, workshop bench, and, most importantly, during product use. Firms that underestimate the power of the product's packaging are making a major tactical mistake.

Labeling Decisions

A customer can tell a lot about a company by the labels it places on its products. If the label appears to be an afterthought, and contains only what is legally required, then the conclusion is obvious. On the other hand, a customer-oriented label is likely to serve the following functions:

1. Identify the manufacturer, country of origin, and ingredients or materials comprising the product.

2. Report the expiration date and the contents' grading based on a prescribed government standard (as appears on cartons of eggs).

3. Explain how to use the product.

4. Warn about potential misuse.

5. Provide easy-to-understand care instructions.

6. Serve as an important communications link between the user, eventual buyers, and the company.

A quality label signals a quality product. Often the label must also be designed for the market segment. For example, the elderly need labels with large lettering. Furthermore, because many customers toss instructions and packaging away, the only way a customer can reach a manufacturer is through the information provided on the label.

PRODUCT GROWTH OPPORTUNITIES[5]

Established products are the lifeblood for most companies. But a company that depends solely on its current stable of products may be headed for trouble. Aggressive competi-

Figure 8.3 Growth Strategies

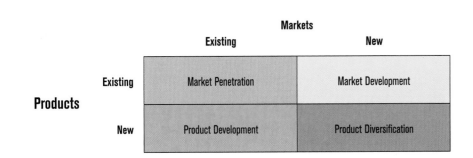

tive activity or a major change in technology can cause a rapid decline in sales even for the most successful product. Growth is fundamental to the long-term success of any organization.

Growth opens up new sales and profit opportunities for the firm while reducing the dependence on existing products for the firm's success. Companies can pursue a number of growth options. Figure 8.3 presents four such options. A firm might attempt to grow its business through **market penetration** by selling more of its *existing products* to *existing markets*. The main objective of this strategy is to convince existing customers to purchase and use more of the firm's product. In other words, the firm is attempting to increase its current market share. Typical market penetration tactics include aggressive promotion campaigns and price discounts. Airlines, soft drink companies, and fast-food chains are examples of firms that actively pursue a market penetration strategy.

Firms that find new uses for existing products are pursuing **market development.** In this scenario, the firm attempts to grow its business by selling more of its *existing products* to *new markets*. Baking soda is the classic example. Although its original use was for baking, it is now marketed as a deodorizer, carpet cleaner and toothpaste among other uses. These new uses have attracted new markets and have increased the overall sales of the product. Other examples include Johnson & Johnson baby shampoo and Tony the Tiger Frosted Flakes that are now being marketed to adults. In addition, the hair growth remedy, Rogaine, that was originally targeted to men is now being targeted to women with thinning hair.

Firms that develop *new products* that they feel will appeal to *existing markets* are pursuing a **product development strategy.** In this scenario, the firm seeks to provide its existing market with a variety of new choices. For example, Procter & Gamble markets Tide, Cheer, and Bold detergents; Wendy's added pita bread sandwiches and salads to its menu; Bacardi, the rum distiller, markets premixed cocktail ingredients such as piña colada and daiquiri mixes; and Disney engages in product expansion in the youth market with the release of each new animated film (e.g., *Mulan*).

The most risky growth option is **product diversification.** Under this option, firms pursue a growth strategy by developing *new products* that appeal to *new markets*. The Chrysler Corporation's introduction of the Neon in 1994 represented a diversification move to appeal to relatively unserved group of Generation Xers. Similarly, the Toyota Motor Corporation recently unveiled the Echo (see Figure 8.4) at the 1999 Detroit auto show that features low emissions and a low price, and is targeted directly at Generation Y (The "Echo" Boom). Product diversification enables a company to be less dependent on any one product or product line.

www.toyota.com

Figure 8.4   Toyota's Echo: A New Product Aimed at the "Echo" Boom

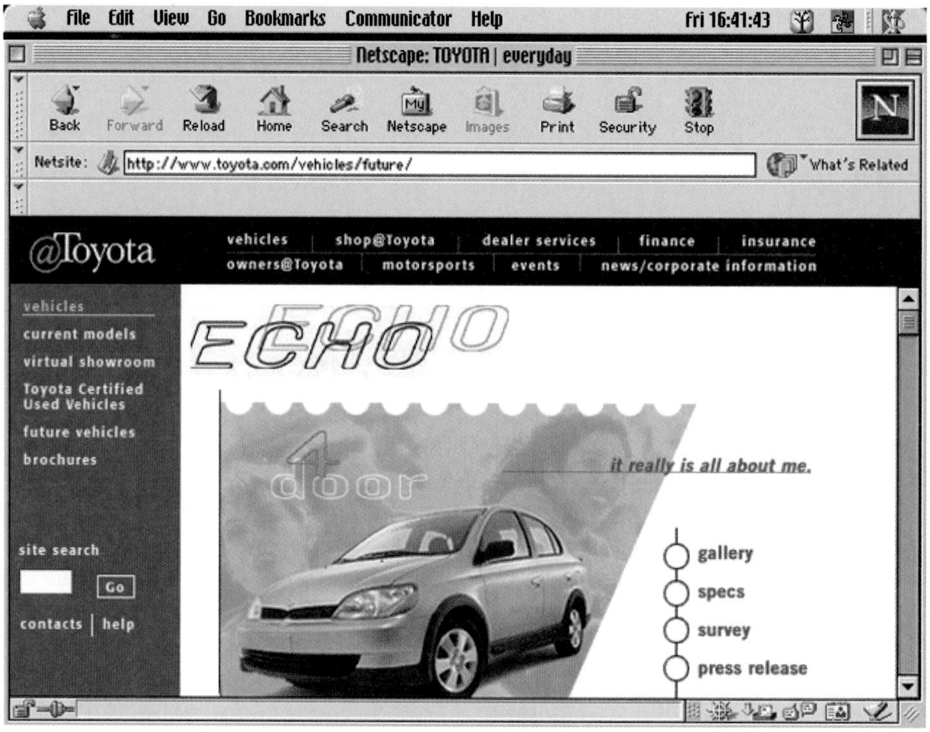

MARKETING'S ROLE IN NEW PRODUCT DEVELOPMENT

Defining Success

LEARNING OBJECTIVE LO4

Developing new products is especially time-consuming, as great care must be taken to ensure the best decisions are made *before* the product reaches channel members and final consumers. This section of the chapter takes a closer look at the process and management of product development. However, before we begin discussing methods for new product development (NPD), we first need to consider what we are actually attempting to achieve by introducing each new product to the market. Quite frankly, new product development success is difficult to define. Whereas most firms' ultimate objective is financial success; different product development projects may have different goals than just financial. The Ford Taurus, for example, while achieving high market share, had the lowest long-run quality of any Ford car or truck in 20 years, and did not break even on recovering development expenses for many years. However, in Ford's eyes, and the eyes of many customers, this product was very successful. How, then, should success be measured?

NPD managers recommend that **NPD project success** be measured using four items spanning three dimensions.[6] One item is a measure of financial success, most frequently the project's *profitability*. A second item assesses technical performance success, often measuring the product's *competitive advantage* from a technical (performance) point of view. The third dimension consists of two measurements that evaluate success from the customer's perspective—most frequently, *market share* and *customer satisfaction*.

Achieving product success along one dimension does not necessarily mean the product will achieve success along another. For example, superior technical performance levels may not lead to market share or customer satisfaction. As the Taurus example shows, a product can even achieve high levels of customer success without achieving profitability, if either development spending or product cost is not controlled. Unfortunately, the perfect product development project, known as the *silver bullet,* which achieves high levels of success on all three dimensions, rarely exists. Firms frequently sacrifice some level of success on one dimension to achieve success on another. For instance, the objective of one project may be to increase customer satisfaction, yet another may be to raise the technical performance bar for the product category. While profits are not necessarily the primary goal of any particular project, the firm does need to generate a profit across the portfolio of products that comprise the firm's product mix.

Requirements for Developing Successful New Products

Product development does not take place just once, but must be repeated over and over for a firm to stay in business over the long run. Once an initial product is developed and introduced to the market, competitors introduce products that improve performance. New technologies also become available over time that allow additional customer problems to be solved that were not addressed by the first generation product. Both events require that firms manage product development as an ongoing spiral, as shown in Figure 8.5. Though some cycles of the spiral may only be small, incremental changes are made in the product. For example, in each of the two years after Ford first introduced the Taurus, they made small changes in a number of components. Some changes were made to reduce costs, and others were to improve quality and performance. In other cycles, more radical changes were made, as when Ford totally redesigned the Taurus for its 1996 reintroduction. The target market for the Taurus remained unchanged, as did its core benefit proposition. However, both the styling and many components and subsystems were updated, some with

Figure 8.5   The NPD Spiral

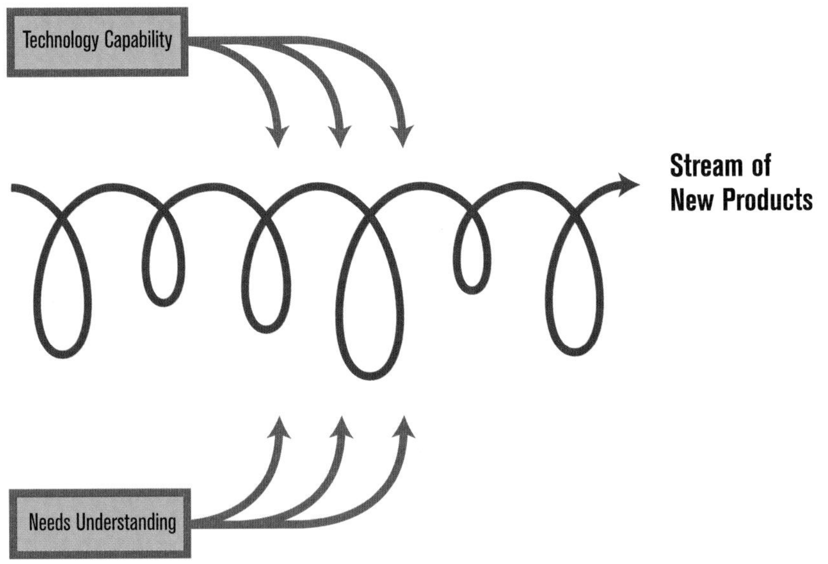

Technology Capability

Stream of
New Products

Needs Understanding

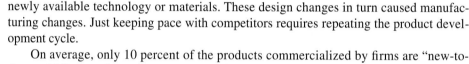

Figure 8.6 The Average Project Portfolio

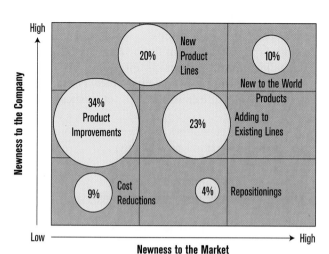

newly available technology or materials. These design changes in turn caused manufacturing changes. Just keeping pace with competitors requires repeating the product development cycle.

On average, only 10 percent of the products commercialized by firms are "new-to-the-world," or products that create an entirely new market. Most of the projects in firm portfolios are improvements to products already on the market or additions to existing lines (brand extensions) and products that are new to the firm, but already manufactured by competitors (new product lines), as shown in Figure 8.6. Fully 70 percent of the projects of the average firm focus on changing or adding to current products.[7]

The objective for marketing professionals and new product development teams, like U.S. Robotics, is to create a series of Palm Pilots for the firm. The key is to be able to do this not just once, but systematically and repeatedly. Actually, successful product development only requires that the firm successfully complete three activities:

▼ Uncover unmet needs and problems.

▼ Develop a **competitively advantaged product.**

▼ Shepherd products through the firm.

These three activities are simple enough in concept. Unfortunately, none of them are easy to complete, and if any one of them is not fully completed the resulting product is unlikely to succeed in the marketplace. Each activity requires that the firm master a different complex set of issues. Each issue must also be addressed across functional lines. Marketing cannot address the issues alone, nor can engineering, nor any other functional area. For example, developing a competitively advantaged product requires: (1) input from customers on unmet needs; (2) input from marketing as to what the competition is doing to address the need; (3) input from manufacturing about what the firm can currently build to satisfy the need; (4) input from engineering as to what additional technologies are available; (5) input from R&D about new ways of potentially addressing the need; and (6) input from finance about the costs and benefits. Excelling at each NPD activity requires cooperation across multiple departments, which is still difficult to achieve in many U.S. corporations.

LEARNING OBJECTIVE LO5

Competitively advantaged product

is a product that solves a set of customer problems better than any competitors' product. This product is made possible due to this firm's unique technical, manufacturing, managerial, or marketing capabilities, which are not easily copied by others.

Unavailability of a technology is not always the reason a feature is not included in a new product. For example, infrared technology, which would allow communication directly from one Palm Pilot to another as in the case of automatically swapping business cards, was already a proven technology when the Palm Pilot was originally introduced. However, the team proactively chose not to include this capability in the first generation product. In their view, it would not provide enough benefit to warrant the increased cost of the product until a large base of users developed. The second generation of the Palm Pilot pda, the Palm III, does include this feature.[8]

Another difficulty is encountered in implementing these activities because product development is not undertaken for just one purpose. Growing the business over time requires a continual process of both repeatedly recommercializing old products to maintain (or grow) the firm's presence in current markets and commercializing new products to expand the firm's market presence. The activities required for sustaining current business through NPD, however, may differ from those needed for expanding market presence.

A product development team working on the next generation product in the Palm Pilot area at U.S. Robotics (now part of 3Com), for example, starts from an already-available base of features, software, and manufacturing assets. All of these must be taken into account in developing a new version so that already-obtained economies are not lost. Their task for the next cycle may be to gather more in-depth information, but in a narrower area of function or use.

A follow-up product development team should be able to focus more on a narrower area of function or use because they already have a great deal of knowledge concerning the needs of all potential customers—both existing and unrealized. *Potential customers* are the population of people or organizations who have the problem your product is trying to solve. If you are the Palm Pilot division of 3Com, your potential customers are people who need to keep their complex lives organized. These people may use many different products to solve their problem. *Existing customers* are one subset of potential customers who already use your firm's products. They are already satisfied enough with your product to purchase it. The product development team gathers further input, usually in narrow areas of function or use, from existing customers to enable refinements for the next generation

www.pert.com

of a product. But it is not until the firm understands the needs of **unrealized customers**—potential customers who are not yet using the firm's product offerings—that the firm can develop products that truly expand its market and go beyond the needs of current customers.

Fulfilling all three of the requirements for successful NPD results in profits, market share, and customer satisfaction. Take the case of Procter & Gamble's Pert+™. The product's core benefit proposition (CBP), to simultaneously clean and condition hair, originally targeted women away from home, either traveling, or those showering after a workout at a health club, for example, because it allowed them to eliminate carrying multiple bottles of products. While other products previously had tried to fulfill this CBP, none had. One firm's failed attempt consisted of supplying both conditioner and shampoo in one bottle, like an oil and vinegar salad dressing. Using it required shaking vigorously to mix the two parts into one consistent fluid. Unfortunately, like oil and vinegar dressings, the first few uses of a new bottle usually contained a lot more of the shampoo than the conditioner, and the last few uses had a higher proportion of conditioner than shampoo. Although the need was well known, achieving cleaning *and* conditioning was as yet an unsolvable technical problem. Indeed, it took researchers at Procter & Gamble nearly 10 years to discover a technical solution—a radically different surfactant system (wetting agent) than had ever been considered. Once the technical problem was solved, the project management system at Procter & Gamble moved the product to market. This very different technology has provided Procter & Gamble with a sustainable competitive advantage and has resulted in a successful new entry in the shampoo category, both in terms of share and profits.

The next sections provide more in-depth understanding of how firms uncover unmet needs, develop competitively advantaged products, and shepherd products through the firm to market.

Uncovering Unmet Needs and Problems

Defining Customer Needs

Customer needs are the problems that a person or firm would like to have solved. They describe what products let you do, not how they let you do it.[9] Customers have general problems they want solved that relate to overall product performance. These needs are readily obvious. For example, people need to "be able to communicate with others when we are not together."

Products deliver the overall solutions to customers' problems. Telephone service solves the problem of communicating with others when we are distant, as long as the other person also has a telephone and you know the phone number (or can get it). Every competitor knows that they must develop a way to transport voices from one location to another. The traditional telephone system's wires deliver the general function of "transporting my voice from here to there." New services may use satellites.

Customers also have very specific needs or details of the overall function that a product must also solve to be truly successful. These detailed needs can be more difficult to learn, because most detailed needs are specific to particular contexts in which the product is used. For example, telephones are used in many different situations. Some of the detailed needs include "let me talk to someone when I'm in the kitchen," ". . . when I'm in the bedroom," ". . . when I'm in the living room," and ". . . when I'm outside sitting on my porch." Features provide the ways in which products function. Wiring multiple rooms in the house for telephone service and installing multiple phones solved these problems. Or one can talk in all of these places (and many more) by purchasing a cordless phone rather than multiple wall phones. Or consider the detailed need of "let multiple people here participate in the conversation." Again, this can be delivered though multiple extensions, or alternatively, by using a speakerphone. Different sets of features are better for each of these detailed needs.

Customer problems are complex, and frequently, different needs conflict. For example, while I want to be able to talk on the phone from any room in the house, my teenager may want to ensure that their conversations are private. Yet, with extensions everywhere in the house, anyone can pick up a phone and listen. Alternative solutions to this problem include installing another phone line or getting the teen his or her own mobile phone. Yet, each of these is rather expensive and is therefore in direct conflict with the need to talk cheaply with others.

As this example shows, no product is perfect. Each product is a compromise, in that it only partially solves a complex set of customer problems. Ultimately, products are sets of features that deliver extremely well against some needs, adequately against others, and do not deliver against others at all. Over time, customers choose products with the set of features that delivers the maximum benefit for them. Because technologies and competitors evolve, customer needs tend to be more stable than product features.

As an example, think about how communications have evolved. Grandmothers separated from grandchildren emigrating west in America in the early 1800s, before the telephone, wanted to talk with their grandchildren then just as much as grandmothers today. Back then, they were limited to exchanging letters rather than speaking with someone distant. Letters have certain disadvantages over talking. Letter conversations take place serially, with long periods of time between responses. Also, nuances of meaning, usually conveyed by tone of voice, are more difficult to convey.

Through telephones, people can talk easily when separated by a great distance, and sometimes even more cheaply than writing. Thus, people have become more likely to pick up a phone to talk to someone rather than take time to write. However, with the Internet, people are moving from verbal (phones) back to written communication by sending e-mail messages. In doing so, customers give up a richer understanding for convenience. For example, I can e-mail someone a message at 3 A.M., when I think of something in the middle of the night, whereas I would be reluctant to phone them unless it was an emergency.

The lessons gleaned from these examples are threefold. First, customer needs are complex. Second, developing successful products requires understanding the *details* of needs. Finally, while needs are rather stable, potential features and technologies change over time. Firms must repeatedly return to the drawing board to understand which new set of compromises customers prefer. Providing product development teams with a rich understanding of complex and detailed customer needs and problems prepares them to select the best technology and feature compromises to continue delivering successful products in the future.

Methods for Understanding Customer Needs

Realistically, customers cannot tell firms exactly what products to develop. Customers are unlikely to have the technical understanding necessary to describe new features or technologies a product should have or forecast what features will best serve those needs in the future. They also cannot provide reliable information about anything with which they are not personally familiar or have experienced. By definition, then, customers are not familiar with a new product the firm may be thinking of developing, and cannot provide reliable information when asked to react to a **concept** or **prototype.**

Does that mean that firms should not try to understand customer needs and problems? Not at all. Customers can indeed provide reliable information about products they have used and situations they have experienced. They will readily talk about problems they have experienced, and potential uses that are relevant to them. They can discuss which products and features they currently use to meet their needs—where these products fall short or where they excel, and why.

Customer needs are often obtained initially through qualitative market research. Qualitative market research is conducted with a small number of customers. Three methods are especially useful for gathering customer needs qualitatively: *becoming* the people with the problems the firm wants to solve, critically *observing* those with the problems of interest, and talking to *(interviewing)* people in depth about their problems. Each method produces slightly different kinds of information. No one technique is sufficient to produce a full understanding of needs. The best results are obtained when a product development team

Concept
is a written description or visual depiction of a new product idea. A concept includes the product's primary features and benefits.

Prototype
is a product *concept* in physical form. A prototype may be a full working model that has been produced by hand or a nonworking physical representation of the final product. It is used to gather customer reaction to the physical form (aesthetics and ergonomics) or to initial operating capability. It is also used in internal performance tests to assure that performance goals have been met.

Marketing Technologies

Information Acceleration: Using Technology to Forecast the Future for Really New Products

One of the more difficult marketing tasks in new product development is forecasting future sales. Accurate forecasts are needed to ensure an adequate return on investment for the project, obtain funding from corporate, and make decisions regarding manufacturing strategy. Early projections frequently are made based on customer "intent to buy" reactions to first one- to two-sentence, text-based concept statements. More refined information may then be obtained from one-page concept statements, which may be accompanied by pictures or additional technical documentation or marketing support materials. Still more accurate information may be obtained from prototypes and pilot production models that allow customers to gain actual experience with the product under development. As the materials presented to customers more realistically, accurately, and completely reproduce the final product and use experience, customers are able to provide more accurate information about their eventual market response to the product, which translates directly to more accurate forecasts of purchase intent.

Forecast accuracy is particularly problematic for really new products, ones that look very different or deliver very different benefits from those currently on the market. Customers find it especially difficult to imagine how they might actually use products that provide new benefits. One new method to provide vastly greater quantities of more realistic information to customers before prototype development is through a multimedia "information accelerator" that combines images, audio, and text stored on videodisk or CD-ROM to provide full-motion, realistic, computer-based simulations of the product and its use. The basis of the system are photo-realistic product simulations that customers can rotate, walk around, and even run demonstrations of how various parts operate. The system also provides access to simulated marketing materials (product brochures, print, and TV advertisements), videotaped word-of-mouth (customer reactions to using the product, mentioning specific features and benefits), shopping visits to virtual stores, and personal selling videos. It allows customers to interact with the materials presented, and choose which information they want to access. Information accelerators provide greater realism at earlier stages of the product development process, and access to larger amounts of information faster, through linking computer-based engineering design and visualization tools with multimedia technologies.

Questions

1. Information acceleration systems are expensive to create, costing as much as $500,000 to develop. List examples of industries and products that might benefit from this level of investment in product forecasting.

2. How might a firm decrease the investment cost for developing information accelerators?

Source: Glen Urban, John R. Hauser, William J. Qualls, Bruce D. Weinberg, Jonathan D. Bohlmann, and Roberta A. Chicos (1997), "Information Acceleration: Validation and Lessons from the Field," *Journal of Marketing Research* 34(1): pp. 143–152.

uses multiple methods to understand people's problems in great detail. Once a full set of needs has been gathered, then a number of different quantitative market research techniques can be used to determine which needs are more important in a projectable manner.

Becoming Customers with Problems An enormous amount of customer needs, knowledge, and understanding can be gained firsthand by putting development team members into situations where they become customers experiencing the problems the firm is trying to solve. This method encourages team members to use your products, and all competitors' products, in "everyday" as well as "extraordinary" situations.

For example, the product development team for a feminine hygiene pad product at one company is known for the extent to which they try to fully understand and identify with customer problems. The entire team—both men and women—personally tests relevant products both from their own firm and the competition. Both male and female team members wear pads underneath armpits and in shoes to test chafing and odor-elimination. They also wear pads in the anatomically appropriate area to simulate normal use. Team members are also sent on expeditions to purchase the product.

This technique applies not just to consumer product firms, but with a bit of creativity is useful for many firms selling business-to-business products. For instance, team members at firms that supply McDonald's with cooking equipment are encouraged to work in the kitchens, both on current equipment and with prototypes in development. McDonald's readily assigns the development people shifts because they hope to get improved products. All kitchen equipment firms of course have test kitchens in which they operate their equipment during development. However, operating a system in a laboratory setting just does not provide the same breadth of operating experience as working in a real McDonald's—crammed in a kitchen full of teenagers, flipping burgers on a Friday night after the local high school football game has ended, requiring that hordes of other teenagers be fed quickly. By working full shifts during different time periods, development personnel learn about shift startup and clean-up, and the effects of different volume levels on operation, breakage, and fatigue. They are exposed to a random day's worth of the strange things that can happen in a kitchen that affect both the operator and the equipment.

Having employees become actively involved customers is the best way, sometimes the only way, to transfer **tacit information** into the product development team. Becoming a routine customer for all the different products in the category may also be the most efficient way to expose development teams to the trade-offs others have made in their products and the effects these decisions have had on product function.

While this technique brings rich data to the product development team, it is only one of several techniques that should be used because it has several inherent problems:

▼ The firm must learn how to transfer one person's experience and tacit knowledge to another.

▼ If experiences are not recorded, retaining personal knowledge becomes a critical issue if organization team members frequently shift jobs or leave the firm.

▼ Project management must take steps to ensure that team members understand that their own needs differ from needs of the "average" customer in unexpected ways.

▼ Being a customer takes time, money, and personal team member effort.

While personally gathering customer information is not possible in all product areas, with a little imagination it is more feasible than many firms currently realize.

Anthropological Excursions: Live with and Critically Observe Customers Product developers who cannot become customers may be able to "live with" their customers, observing and questioning them as they use products to solve problems. Developers of new medical devices for doctors cannot act as doctors and personally test devices in patient situations. However, they can observe operations, even videotape them, and then debrief doctors about what happened and why.

Sometimes observing customers in their natural settings leads directly to new products or features. For example, developers at Chrysler observed that many pick-up truck owners had built holders for 32-ounce drinks into their cabs, so starting in 1995 Ram trucks featured cupholders appropriate for 32-ounce drinks. In other instances, observation only points out a problem. The team must still determine whether the problem is specific to that individual or applies generally across the target market, and if so, develop an appropriate solution. Another Chrysler engineer watched the difficulty his petite wife had wrestling children's car seats around in the family minivan. It took him several years to convince management that his innovative solution—integrating children's car seats into the car's seating system—would solve a major problem for a large number of customers.

Critical observation, rather than just casual viewing, is a major key to obtaining information by watching customers. Critical observation involves questioning *why* people are performing each action rather than just accepting what they are doing. The best results are achieved when team members spend significant time with enough different customers to be exposed to the full breadth of problems people encounter. They must spend enough time observing customers to uncover both "normal" and "abnormal" operating conditions. Using team members from different functions is important because people with different training and expertise "see" and pay attention to different things.

Anthropological excursions identify tacit information and expose team members to customer language. It is also the most effective means for gathering workflow or **process-**

Tacit information

consists of things customers know, but which are difficult or nearly impossible to articulate. This intuitive information, while frequently critical to product success in the marketplace, is the most difficult to provide to the NPD team during product development.

www.chrysler.com

Process-related information is information that provides an understanding of how the product fits into the workflow of the company.

related information. These customer needs are particularly important for firms marketing products to other firms. Products they develop must fit into the workflow of those firms, which means the workflows must be fully understood. Even when questioned in detail, people frequently forget steps in a process or skip over them. Although forgotten in the course of the interviews, these steps may be crucial to product design trade-offs.

Observing and living with customers is not especially efficient. Its problems include:

▼ Anthropological excursions require significant team member time and expense. Events and actions unfold slowly in real time, and there are no shortcuts.

▼ Videotaping or observation, no matter how well designed and intentioned, is intrusive by nature and may change behavior. "Natural" actions may not be captured.

▼ Observations must be interpreted through the filter of team members' own experiences. It is a challenge for the team to turn observed actions into words that reliably capture customer needs.

Being customers and critically observing customers are powerful techniques for gathering rich, detailed data on customer problems. However, they both require significant amounts of time that may not be available in every product development project. These techniques are best used in an ongoing way to continually expand a group's knowledge of customer problems. When time is short, the only means to rapidly gather customer needs is to talk to customers and get them to tell you their problems.

Voice of the Customer (VOC) is an in-depth, one-on-one interviewing process to understand a set of customer needs in great depth.

Talk to Customers to Get Needs Information By talking to customers, NPD teams can gather needs faster and more efficiently than by being or observing customers. A structured, in-depth, probing, one-on-one, situational interview technique called **voice of the customer (VOC)** can uncover both general and very detailed customer needs.[10] This method differs from standard qualitative techniques in the way questions are asked. Rather than asking customers "what do you want" directly, VOC uses indirect questions to discover wants and needs by leading customers through the ways they currently solve particular problems. VOC asks questions about functions rather than about products.

For example, one study asked customers *what* they would use to transport food that they had prepared at home to be consumed at another location, especially if the food would have to be stored for some period of time before consumption. Picnic baskets, coolers, and ice chests most frequently were the items suggested to fulfill this general function. However, asking about *how* they fulfilled the function, rather than about a particular product, yielded information about many different and unexpected products customers would use—including knapsacks, luggage, and grocery store bags with handles—and the reasons *why* they would use them. Detailed probing reveals specific features, drawbacks, and benefits of each product. Most important are questions delving into why various features of the products are good and bad. What problem does each feature solve, and does a particular feature cause any other problems? Probing *why* uncovers needs.

One advantage of interviewing is that many different use situations can be investigated in a short period of time, including a range of both "normal" and "abnormal" situations. Each different use situation provides information about additional dimensions of functional performance. A good way to start an interview is to ask customers to tell about the last time that they found themselves in a particular situation. The food transportation study began, "Please tell me about the most recent time you prepared food in your home, to be shared by you and others, then took the food outside your home and ate it somewhere else later." By asking customers to relate specifics—what they did, why they did what they did, what worked well, and what did not work—both detailed and general customer needs are obtained indirectly.

After customers relate their most recent experiences, they are asked about the specifics of how they would fulfill the function in a series of other potential use situations. These use situations are constructed by the team to attempt to cover all the performance dimen-

Careers in Marketing

Going It Alone in Product Development

Paul Efromson began his career traditionally, as a brand marketing assistant in the product marketing group for cereal products at Post Cereal in General Foods. Marketing assistants provide the analyses that product managers use in devising marketing programs for their brand. In the traditional career path in brand marketing, he then became an assistant product manager for an established brand, gaining responsibility for devising and implementing some marketing tactics. The next step in the brand career path is generally product manager, with responsibilities for all marketing decisions for a brand.

At this point, however, Paul's career deviated from the traditional as he moved into the new product marketing group as a product manager. This group was formed to strengthen the flow of new products into the market. The four associate product managers each became responsible for developing the series of products to be introduced to a particular target market. Paul's segment was the teen market.

Over the next three years, Paul lead initiatives that introduced three new products and introduced improved versions or repositioned three others, resulting in a total sales increase of 6 percent to this market, when the population growth for this segment only grew 2 percent. Through his success in developing new products, Paul was promoted to group product manager and moved back into managing established products.

After the excitement and changes associated with commercializing new products, Paul found managing a group of established products less appealing. However, Post, as with many firms, views assignments in product development as only transitory positions in a marketing manager's career. The marketing ladder continues upward primarily through marketing established brands, not developing new products for the established brand groups.

Because he wanted to stay in new product development, Paul left Post and moved to Dun & Bradstreet, joining a group charged with developing new information products. Paul was again successful, and again, promoted back into a marketing position for established products.

At this point, Paul's career preference was to focus on marketing and managing product development and new products. As he was frustrated that this was only a transitory position in the majority of firms, he opened up his own new product consulting firm. To this day, he consults across a broad industry base, focusing on the issues associated with bringing new products to market.

sions across which customers may expect a product to function. For example, customers were asked about the last time they took food with them:

▼ On a car trip

▼ To the beach

▼ To a football or baseball game

▼ On a romantic picnic

▼ On a bike trip

▼ Hiking or backpacking

▼ Canoeing or fishing

They were also asked to relate the most disastrous and marvelous times they ever took food with them. The set of situations is constructed to vary the different dimensions of expected performance as widely as possible. In the situations above, the amount, types, and temperatures of the food taken varies, the outside temperature varies, and different aesthetics are covered, as is a large range of ease of mobility and transportability. While no customer experiences all situations, the food transporting and storage needs resulting from each situation were fully uncovered by the time 20 to 30 people had been interviewed.

Buried in the stories customers tell about specific use instances are the nuggets of needs. Through indirect questioning, customer needs that relate to technical design aspects can be obtained, even from nontechnical customers. For example, by relating how their car behaves in various driving situations—flooring the accelerator at a stop sign, traveling at city speeds around 35 mph, and traveling at interstate speeds—senior citizens can provide information which determines the gear ratios governing the speeds at which an automatic transmission shifts gears, even though they may have no idea how their transmission works.

While VOC is not difficult, it gathers needs differently than other qualitative market research techniques. It results in a much larger list of very detailed and context- or situation-specific customer needs because the objective is to obtain a level of detail that enables teams to make engineering trade-offs during product development.

There are several keys to successfully obtaining the voice of the customer. First, it is critical to ask about functions (what customers want to do), not features (how it is done). Continually probing about "why" a feature is wanted or works well reveals underlying needs. Only by understanding functional needs can teams make appropriate technology and feature trade-offs in the future. A second key is that VOC only covers reality. If someone has never been on a romantic picnic, they cannot accurately tell you what they would like because they really do not know. Anything they would say is a fantasy. The final key to success is to ask detailed questions about specific use instances. General questions (tell me about going on picnics) produce general needs. General needs are not as useful to the development team in designing products as are details of needs, which are obtained through using specific questions (tell me about the last time you went on a romantic picnic). Customers can provide a tremendous level of detail when asked to relate the story of a specific situation that occurred in the last year.

While voice of the customer provides a large number of details about problems in a verbal form that is directly usable by the team, it also has several drawbacks:

▼ The development team obtains a better understanding of a fuller set of detailed needs if the team interviews customers rather than outsourcing it to a market research group. However, this adds to the set of development team tasks.

▼ Interviewing customers is a nontraditional task for many team members (e.g., engineers, accountants).

▼ Extreme care must be taken to maintain the words of the customer and not translate individual problems into solutions before understanding the full set of customer needs.

▼ Tacit and process-related needs may not be complete.

No one technique easily provides all the customer needs knowledge that product development teams seek. Tacit needs are best conveyed by being a customer. Process-related needs are identified most easily by critically observing customers. In-depth interviewing is the most efficient means to obtain masses of detailed needs, but may not provide the tacit and process-related information. Unfortunately, few projects can afford the time and expense of fully implementing all these processes. Development teams need to understand these processes and use the most appropriate technique(s), given the project's informational requirements, budget, and time frame.

Developing a Competitively Advantaged Product

Developing competitively advantaged products consistently over time is aided by having a strategy for what will be done and a process for how it will be accomplished. Firms with both a new product development strategy and a formal process for doing so demonstrate superior performance in terms of percentage of sales by new products, success rates, and meeting sales and profit objectives.[11] Firms with a strategy but no process, or with a process but no coherent strategy, do not perform as well as those with both.

Product Development Strategy

"If you don't know where you are going, any road will get you there." New product strategy provides the long-term end point for where the firm is going. Effective strategies for product development flow from the overall business strategy for the firm. That is, if the firm's stated strategy is to be a low-cost manufacturer, then an effective new product strategy for the business unit probably is not to develop a continuous stream of technologically leading-edge products. A more effective new product strategy might be to continually improve the cost-effectiveness of the manufacturing processes.

Effective strategies consist of a set of clear, new product goals that derive directly from the overall business strategy. Areas of strategic focus are then selected and prioritized, and a plan of how to attack each area is developed. Areas of strategic focus can be defined in a number of ways, including:

▼ Markets or market segments

▼ Product types or categories (such as by newness categories)

▼ Product lines

▼ Technologies or technology platforms.

A plan of attack defines the way in which the firm will compete in each strategic arena. For example, in the 1980s, Ford Motor Company's plan of attack for the family sedan market was to be the industry design and styling innovator. Thus, successive generations of the Taurus styling have been radically different from other family sedans on the market. However, different plans of attack may be adopted across different strategic arenas of a firm. For example, in the minivan product category, Ford has chosen more of a fast-follower strategy behind Chrysler. Here they have allowed Chrysler to innovate and have chosen to compete using a "second but better" design.

Project Strategy

After the new product development strategy for the business unit is set, a strategy for each individual product development project still must be developed. Each *project strategy* states the specific plan of how this project will proceed and why. An effective project strategy states the reasons the firm is undertaking the project and identifies specific business goals for the product. For example, it outlines whether the firm is undertaking this project to meet a previously unmet customer need, to update performance in a current product, or to counteract share losses from a newly commercialized competitive product. Each project's goals will depend, in part, on why the project is being undertaken. For example, the goal for a performance-improvement project may be increased share or customer satisfaction while maintaining profitability.

The strategy also describes the target market and CBP for the product. The plan describes in detail the firms or individuals who are expected to purchase the new product. Some project teams draw pictures or create collages of people in the target market and hang them on the walls to remind themselves for whom they are developing the products as the project moves forward.

Finally, successful strategies also develop a schedule, establishing key milestones including the planned market introduction date. These are used to help keep the team task focused. It helps managers across the company identify key resources that will be required to achieve success and prepare to supply them. Once the team and management agree on the project purposes, goals, timing, and required resources, it is ready to proceed to development.

A Framework for Managing Product Development: Stage Gate Processes Used in NPD

A formal **product development process,** such as that illustrated in Figure 8.7, outlines the normal way NPD proceeds at the firm. It defines which functions (i.e., marketing or engineering) are responsible for performing what tasks, in what order, and in conjunction with what other tasks and functions. A formalized process institutionalizes learning about what works and does not work, and how interdependent steps must be completed. Projects following a formalized product development process are more successful, and firms that are the best at new product development are more likely to use formalized processes for new product development.[12] Firms without formalized NPD processes depend upon one

Product development process

consists of a clearly defined set of tasks and steps that describes the normal means by which product development proceeds. The process outlines the order and sequence of the tasks and indicates who is responsible for each.

Figure 8.7   NPD Process Tasks and Roadmap

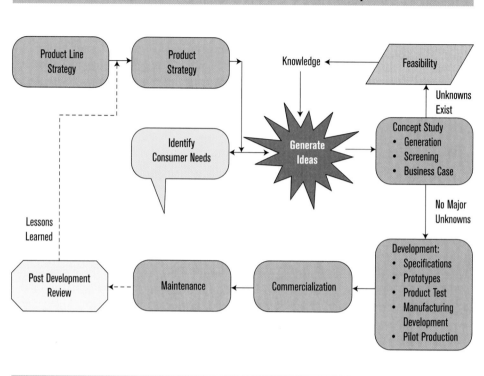

---

or a few product development "craftsmen" who "just know how to do it." If they leave the firm, NPD knowledge leaves with them.

Most firms use a formal **Stage-Gate Process** to organize the tasks for developing new products (Figure 8.8). Stage Gate processes are organized and consistent, and can be understood by and deployed across all those involved in NPD projects at the firm rather easily. Personnel from each function complete tasks that are the function's responsibility for that stage. The process acknowledges that different functions provide a different expertise in each stage, all of which are necessary to successfully complete any stage. Thus, it encourages cross-functional teamwork and problem solving. As the goals for each stage are completed, management reviews progress at a gate meeting, determines whether the criteria necessary to move forward have been met, approves the tasks and resources for the next stage (go), asks for more information (recycle), or stops the project (kill). A well-designed process ensures that senior management participates in the NPD process where there is a significant jump in risk or cost.

Individual firms implement Stage Gate processes differently, personalizing it to meet the needs of their corporation. Table 8.1 shows four actual NPD processes. For example, CalComp uses a 9-stage process that does not include idea generation or post-introduction review. In contrast, the other three firms all use different 7-stage processes. Traditionally, the most common tasks and stages that may be included in the firm's NPD process include the following activities.[13]

Generate and Screen Ideas The objective of this stage is to develop one or more new product ideas that seem "interesting." An interesting idea solves customer problems, fits the strategy and capabilities of the business unit, and presents a profit-making opportunity at reasonable risk, given the size of the profit potential. In this step ideas are first generated, and then screened against a set of criteria to determine which provide the greatest opportunity for the firm. At the end of this stage, a small number of ideas that have

Stage-Gate process
is a common new product development process that divides the repeatable portion of product development into a time-sequenced series of stages, each of which is separated by a management decision gate. In each stage, a team completes a set of tasks that span the functions involved in product development. At the end of each stage, management reviews the results obtained and, based on the team's ability to meet the objectives in that stage, provides the resources to continue to the next stage ("go"), requests additional work ("recycle"), or stops the project ("kill").

Figure 8.8   A Stage Gate Approach to NPD

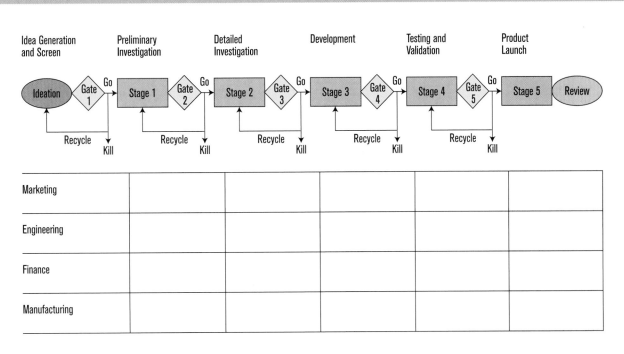

been screened for fit and potential reward will be ready to move forward into the next stage of development.

Ideas come from many sources. Customers may ask directly for a new product or feature. Competitors may introduce a new product that sparks an idea to counteract their effort. Employees frequently have new product ideas they are eager to suggest. Alternatively, creativity sessions can be held specifically to generate new ideas.

Table 8.1	**Stages Used by Firms**			
Stage	**CalComp**	**Xerox**	**Exxon Chemical**	**Keithley Instrument**
Generate ideas		Pre-concept	Idea	Concept
Preliminary investigation	Market requirement Specification Design	Concept	Preliminary assessment	Study
Detailed investigation			Detailed Assessment	Definition
Development	Engineering model Prototype	Design	Development	Design
Test and validate	System verification Manufacturing verification	Demonstration Production	Validation	Prototype Pilot
Launch	Production	Launch	Commercial launch	Introduction
Maintenance	End of life	Maintenance		
Review			Post review	

Sources: Public presentations and brochures.

Frequently the problem is not finding or generating ideas, but gathering ideas from a wide variety of sources into one place where they can be evaluated for potential and fit. Some firms use a database or construct a new product idea bulletin board on their intranet to collect and retain ideas over time.

The objective of idea screening is to evaluate new product ideas rationally and consistently over time, and to maintain the integrity of the process as the membership of the product development team evolves. Initial idea screening is done based on what management already knows, rather than on information specifically developed for this project. Many firms develop a standard set of criteria that managers can use to consistently evaluate ideas. Table 8.2 lists AT&T's idea screening criteria. Other firms numerically rate each idea against objectives, as illustrated in Table 8.3, where a larger number indicates a better rating. Ideas proceed to the next phase based either on their absolute overall rating or their rating relative to the other ideas being considered.

Idea generation and screening can be completed relatively quickly, sometimes in days or hours. The resources required are usually minimal, consisting predominantly of management time, the cost of developing and maintaining an idea database, and the cost of running creativity sessions.

Preliminary Investigation The objective of preliminary investigation is to develop preliminary market assessments, preliminary technical assessments and feasibility, and preliminary financial assessments. This is the up-front "homework" necessary before detailed design can be started. Typically a small, focused, multifunctional core team of marketing and technical specialists using available resources and knowledge performs this

---

Table 8.2   AT&T's Idea Evaluation Criteria

▼ **Do customers care?**
How are customers benefitted?
How many customers benefit?

▼ **Do we care?**
Relevance, potential market share
Will it create shareholder value?

▼ **Can we do it?**
Technology infrastructure
Cost/profits

▼ **Can we stay ahead or match the competition?**

Source: AT&T

Table 8.3   Evaluating Ideas by Rating Them Against Objectives

	Idea 1	Idea 2	Idea 3	Idea 4
Meets customer needs	3	5	3	1
Fits manufacturing capability	1	3	5	1
Fits our strategy	5	3	1	3
Large market size	5	5	1	3
Noncyclical market	3	1	3	1
Fits distribution	5	5	1	1
Sum	**22**	**22**	**14**	**10**

step. At the end of this task, the team will know whether unknowns exist, and thus the project must be routed back through a research step to demonstrate feasibility, or whether the project can proceed to a detailed investigation that builds a business case based on new and more detailed information.

The preliminary market assessment is a quick-and-dirty market study using data that can be quickly assembled to answer several questions: market attractiveness and potential, probable customer acceptance of the concept, and competitive intensity. In the preliminary technical assessment, the task is to identify the key technical risks and how each might be overcome. The firm's technical staff—R&D, engineering, and manufacturing—develop rough initial technical and performance specifications, undertake an initial feasibility study, and pinpoint specific technical risks in both product and manufacturing process design. Regulatory issues and competitor's patent situations are also reviewed. The preliminary financial assessment is an initial check that the project has enough revenue and profit potential to warrant continuation. At this point potential volume, revenue and cost per item, and total development cost are extremely speculative, so these estimates are no more than ballpark estimates.

Because the information used in the analyses is only that which is generally readily available within the firm, preliminary investigation can be completed relatively quickly, within a few weeks. However, completing this step requires inputs from manufacturing, technologists, marketers, and financial analysts. Thus, a lack of support by management, or from any of these functions, can delay completion. Research has repeatedly shown that the quality of the "up-front homework" in preliminary investigation and business case development is strongly associated with increased new product success. A major objective, then, is to obtain functional support for each task in this stage so that high-quality answers are generated.

Detailed Investigation Detailed investigation builds a business case for the project that provides solid enough information to upper management so that they can approve the resources necessary for product development. The business case defines and justifies the project, and details the plan for completing the project. The cross-functional team that develops the business case becomes the core of the team that will take the project through development and into the marketplace. At the end of this stage, management has all the information it needs to make a go/kill decision on the project, and the team will be poised to move rapidly into the more expensive phases of development.

Justification requires completing a market analysis, technical assessment, concept test, competitive analysis, and a detailed financial analysis. The difference between the already completed preliminary investigation and this stage is that detailed investigation requires generating or gathering new information, rather than relying on what we already know. For example, the product is defined based on the combination of a user needs study and a detailed technical assessment. A needs study may use any of the market research techniques covered earlier in this chapter. This information is gathered from potential customers in the target market. It cannot be developed only through internal knowledge. Additional quantitative market research may be done to understand the relative importance of different needs, preferred trade-offs between requirements, and to assess competitive product performance. The development team then translates market inputs into a technically feasible product by determining what aspects of performance delivers each customer need, developing specifications for performance, and assuring feasibility of achieving those specifications. Assuring feasibility may require some laboratory work. The technologists map out the technical solutions to achieving performance and develop the route that will allow them to get that technical solution. Concept manufacturability is investigated simultaneously to ensure that the product is manufacturable.

The market analysis also quantifies market size and growth and analyzes market segments and buyer behavior. A competitive analysis identifies competitors and competing products, including details of product strengths and deficiencies. The team analyzes competitor strategies, position in the market, and performance. These serve as inputs for

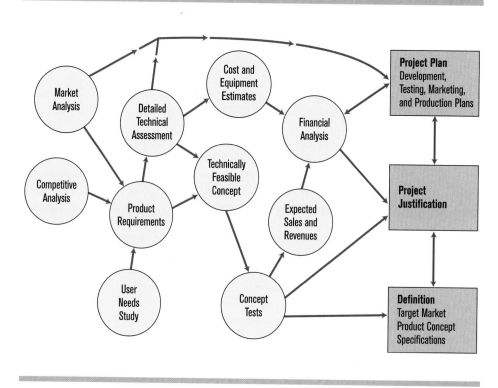

Figure 8.9   Task Interdependencies in Building a Business Case

developing the marketing strategy for product commercialization. The financial analysis includes a cash flow analysis that takes into account the required timing and level of investment. This is possible because we now have a much more detailed definition of the product specifications.

The final component of the business case is the plan of action. This includes a go/kill recommendation and a detailed plan for how physical development, testing, and manufacturing development will proceed. The plan also specifies the intended launch date for the product.

The detailed investigation stage has high levels of interdependency across tasks (see Figure 8.9), and is the first stage that requires significant investment of time, money, and people to provide quality results. The resources required will depend upon the size, complexity, and degree of uniqueness of the project. A firm can expect that even the smallest projects may require a team of three to five individuals (because each function must be represented), working at least half-time over a period of one to four months. Larger, more complex projects, however, may require four to six people working full time for up to six months or even a year. Spending enough time, money, and personnel resources now, in order to produce high quality definitions, justifications, and plans, saves a much larger amount of spending later to fix problems that arise because they were not dealt with in the initial phases of the project.

Development The actual design and physical development of the product takes place in the development stage. The outputs defining the end of this stage are:

▼ A prototype that has been tested in-house for performance and in a limited way with customers for preliminary reaction.

▼ A mapped-out manufacturing process, with critical aspects pilot tested.

▼ A marketing launch plan.

▼ A test and validation plan.

Development is the stage when team size and resource consumption peak. Different parts of the project move forward in parallel, completed by different sub-groups of the team. While some of the tasks can be completed by a function relatively independently, many other tasks still require extensive interaction across functions. At the heart of a successful development stage is a plan that drives the process by organizing the efforts of all of those involved. It includes a chronological listing of tasks by the individual responsible for completing them, and their expected stop and start dates. Successful development projects expect the team members to adhere to the timelines and milestones contained in the charts, and proactively manage the project based on the charts. Project management plans can only be followed when the unknowns have been eliminated from the project prior to development.

Development time increases with the size and complexity of the project. Additionally, the relative newness of the project impacts development time. From studies of new product development covering a broad array of industries, new-to-the-world projects average about three and one-half years to complete, new-to-the-firm projects take just over two years, major revisions of current projects require one and one-half years, line extensions one year, and incremental improvements take about nine months.[14] Team size ranges from two to three people for incremental improvements for relatively simple projects like shampoos or other customer packaged goods, to hundreds, or even thousands, of people when a large and complex new-to-the-firm or new-to-the world project is undertaken. Boeing assembled an entire hierarchy of teams in developing the 777 airplane, with the total staff involved numbering in the thousands.

Testing and Validation This stage provides final validation of the project. The product, production process, and marketing strategy plan are all put through verification tests. The objectives are to provide management with final proof that expectations for the project in terms of performance, volume, and profit will be met, and to eliminate any final bugs in the product, process, or marketing plan. The product typically undergoes customer field trials for performance verification, and test marketing or limited roll-out for testing the marketing plan. Pilot or trial production of the manufacturing process is used to produce the products tested with customers to ensure that the process operates as designed. Finally, based on the results from the field and plant trials, the expected financial outcomes are updated. Results from the field, plant, and financial analyses are presented to management for a final go/kill decision, and to obtain the investment for full market launch.

As with the development stage, the time and effort required in testing and validation varies greatly with the size, complexity, and newness of the project. Field-testing with customers can require as little as a week for a limited test with a few customers to as much as a year for a full test market. The expense can be as little as the cost of producing one or two products, or run as much as 5 percent of the estimated expense of going to market.

Commercialization The final activity in new product development is commercialization, the beginning of full production and commercial selling. Some of the team members on the project may change as the marketing and sales functions ramp up their activities to implement the communications plan, marketing launch plan, and sales plan. Manufacturing may also add people to the team as they deploy production to one or more plants. However, to counterbalance these additions, some of the technical development team may move to a more limited role. While large amounts of money may be spent on advertising and communications at this stage, the project finally starts generating income.

Shepherding Products through the Firm

Even if the firm has uncovered a customer problem and developed a competitively advantaged product that solves the problem, the firm still may not be able to profit from that

effort if they cannot bring the product to market through their own corporate infrastructure. Shepherding products through the firm is done by putting in place appropriate organizational processes. These organizational processes include developing project leaders to manage the NPD process and navigate the politics of the organization.

Leading NPD Projects

NPD projects require a leader who fulfills a number of roles. The leader ensures that the NPD process is followed, that tasks are assigned to those who can complete them, and that those tasks are completed in a timely manner. The leader may help protect the team from external interference and may ensure that necessary resources are available to the team. Generally, the leader represents the team in formal meetings and reviews with management. Leaders can also play other roles including coaching and developing team personnel.

Project leadership can take several forms. Three types that have received considerable attention are project leaders, champions, and more recently, NPD process owners. These leadership types differ in the ways in which they fulfill leadership roles. Studies of NPD projects have found that multiple types of leadership are used during development, with no one type leading to higher performance.

Project leaders, the most-frequently-used leadership type in NPD, are appointed by upper management with formal power and authority to complete the project. They guard the project's objectives, continuously communicate with team members, serve as a translator across different functions, and are the primary management contact point. The project leader manages the efforts of team members from the different functions. In a "lightweight" team, the leader coordinates work through functional liaison representatives but has little influence over the work. In a "heavyweight" team, the leader exerts a strong, direct, integrating influence across all the functions. Shifting to heavyweight teams has been credited with reducing NPD cycle time and increasing development productivity in the automotive industry.[15]

Champions take an inordinate interest in seeing that a particular project is pursued. Champions generally work outside official roles and processes to informally influence others' actions. The role may vary from little more than stimulating awareness of the opportunity to extreme cases where the champion tries to force a project past strongly entrenched internal resistance.[16] The champion's role in new product development has been a topic of discussion for over 30 years, with champion use reported by over 40 percent of firms. While some specific NPD successes may be due to the efforts of a particular champion, using a champion does not raise the probability that any particular project will be a success.[17]

Process owners administer the formal NPD process across business groups within the firm.[18] Process owners build and maintain expertise in the NPD process, including knowledge of all development tools and integration mechanisms. They facilitate NPD process use for all projects in the firm, and in some projects additionally act in leadership roles. Process owners may not be responsible for the success outcome of a project, just for the quality of implementation of the NPD process used. Even though this leadership type is a relatively recent development, about 12 percent of reporting firms claim that process owners lead NPD projects.

Organizing for NPD

Firms use multiple organizational structures to organize for NPD; however, research has not yet found "one best way" to organize for every situation. Different structures appear to be more beneficial, depending upon the uniqueness of the project.

In a *functional NPD structure,* responsibility for NPD resides with a functional manager. For example, assigning NPD responsibility solely to engineering is superior for NPD projects handling routine problems, well-known technologies, stable environments, low product evolution rates, and well-defined markets.[19] Enough knowledge resides in this functional area to enable them to manage the project effectively. Assigning responsibility for a project to marketing may make sense when, for example, the project is a repositioning effort that requires little or no actual physical change to the product. In general, less routine projects developed using functional structures were less successful than those developed in structures that encouraged integration across multiple functions.

A *divisional* or *strategic business unit (SBU) NPD structure* is one in which each division is responsible for commercializing new products for their own markets. These structures are better able to respond to diverse market needs and evolutionary product improvements. Each division or SBU contains all the requisite market information and enough technical information to evolve product performance incrementally, in order to adequately respond to these situations. For example, an evolutionary product improvement like the Palm III could be developed within the pda business unit.

A radical innovation frequently may best be developed in a separate new enterprise division, sometimes called a *venture group structure,* whose sole task is to nurture risky projects. This group is not constrained by the requirement to develop projects to meet the needs of any current group of customers or to use any current technologies. They have the freedom to explore new technologies and markets, because they are not organizationally wedded to an already-operating business area. A separate venture group developed IBM's personal computers in the early 1980s. These products were targeted at a very different market than IBM's traditional markets, and used a different technology development strategy than other divisions had traditionally employed. Separating the group from the rest of the organization was necessary to allow them to do things differently.

Mustering Management Support for NPD

In contrast to the inconsistent success rates of organizational structures, a consistent finding for producing successful new products is tangible and visible top management commitment to NPD. Research has shown that top managers formally control the budgets and plans of NPD groups only loosely, but exert considerably tighter control over them informally in the way they allocate top management attention and contact. The NPD team's goal, then, is to obtain and retain top management commitment to the project through maintaining their attention.

Getting your project favored and approved over others requires managing more than just a rational decision-making process. It requires managing the personalities and politics of the upper managers supporting NPD at your firm to convince them that the value of your project warrants the necessary resources they must provide. The NPD team thus needs to continually communicate with top management about the project. Firms usually have mechanisms for formally communicating with management through gate meetings and design reviews, and during the annual budgeting process. However, communication also needs to occur informally between the team and management. Some strategies include:

▼ Interview specific managers for their view of project expectations or customer needs.

▼ Send out short (one to two paragraphs), weekly e-mail updates.

▼ Invite managers with particular areas of expertise to participate as consultants to the project.

▼ Request management presence in the laboratory as new prototypes are unveiled.

▼ Use one or more managers as subjects in various phases of testing.

▼ Create a weekly or monthly project lunch and invite managers to attend.

▼ Invite managers to after-hours team functions, such as project picnics and parties.

The objectives of some interactions are for the exchange of information, such as informing management about the status of the project, obstacles that are creating roadblocks, and small successes like beating completion time to a milestone. At other times, the objectives of an interaction will be more persuasive in nature. Examples include when the team is interacting to sell the project either to a current sponsor or to a new potential project sponsor, is bargaining for different or additional resources, or is defending the project from criticism from another group within the firm.

MANAGING THE PRODUCT LIFE CYCLE

LEARNING OBJECTIVE LO9

Product life cycle

is the cycle of stages that a product goes through from birth to death: introduction, growth, maturity, and decline.

The product now has been designed, developed, and tested. As product development nears completion, product management is just beginning. The product must now be introduced to the market, and strategies for generating profit over the life of the product must be developed and implemented. Figure 8.10 shows the general pattern of expected sales and profit over the **product life cycle.** *Innovators* and *early adopters,* customers generally willing to take more risk, buy the product shortly after introduction. During growth, product purchase begins to spread to the *early majority* of the mass market, with full penetration and adoption by the *late majority* occurring primarily in the maturity stage. Near the product's decline, only *laggards* are left purchasing the product. Marketing strategy and tactics must be adapted to meet the special opportunities and challenges of each stage of the life cycle as illustrated in Table 8.4.

Introduction Strategies

The introduction stage starts when the new product is presented to the market. Initial sales are slow, as potential customers must go through a learning process about the new product and its benefits before they purchase. Creating customer learning requires heavy expenditures in advertising, selling, sampling, promotion, distribution, and personal selling, all of which contribute to profit losses at this stage. The set of marketing tactics employed must work together to make customers aware of the product and encourage them to try it.

The Individual Adoption Process

Customers go through several distinct stages of learning before purchasing a new product. Ideally, the firm's marketing program helps customers move through these stages, thereby

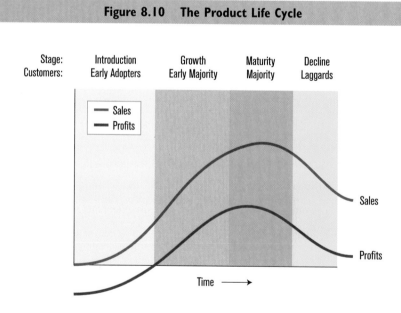

Figure 8.10   The Product Life Cycle

| Stage: | Introduction | Growth | Maturity | Decline |
| Customers: | Early Adopters | Early Majority | Majority | Laggards |

— Sales
— Profits

Sales

Profits

Time ⟶

Table 8.4 Marketing Tactics and Outcomes through the Product Life Cycle				
Outcomes	**Introduction**	**Growth**	**Maturity**	**Decline**
Sales	Low	Fast growth	Slow growth	Decline
Profits	Negligible	Positive	Peak levels	Low or zero
Cash flow	Negative	Moderate	High	Low
Customers	Innovative	Mass market	Mass market	Laggards
Competitors	Few	Growing	Many rivals	Declining number
Tactics	**Introduction**	**Growth**	**Maturity**	**Decline**
Strategic focus	Expanded market	Market penetration	Defend share	Productivity
Expenditures	High	High (declining percentage)	Falling	Low
Emphasis	Product awareness	Brand preference	Brand loyalty	Selective
Distribution	Patchy	Intensive	Intensive	Selective
Price	High	Lowest	Lowest	Rising
Product	Basic	Differentiated	Differentiated	Rationalized

decreasing their risk in purchasing a new product. The stages customers generally go through in the *adoption process* include:

▼ **Awareness:** Realizing that a new product exists.

▼ **Knowledge:** Building an understanding of what the product does, what benefits it provides, and how it works.

▼ **Liking:** Developing positive feelings toward the product.

▼ **Preference:** Coming to prefer this product over any other, if one were to buy.

▼ **Purchase:** Making the decision to buy and acting upon it.

To encourage adoption of a new product, firms use their marketing programs to lead potential customers through each successive stage. Before customers can develop knowledge about what a new product does, they must first have become aware that it exists. Frequently product introductions are accompanied by large initial advertising campaigns designed specifically to create awareness. Only after people develop knowledge about a product can they come to a conclusion as to whether they like it or not. Preference can only develop for products a person likes, which may lead to eventual purchase. The time frame required for new product acceptance varies widely from product to product. Some of the factors that influence this rate of adoption are listed in Figure 8.11.

The elements of the marketing program in the introduction stage of a new product's life cycle are designed to move more innovative customers (early adopters) swiftly through the learning process to purchase. Customers will be slower to adopt products that are more radically innovative, such as microwave ovens when they were first introduced in the 1970s, and products that are expensive, such as the Apple Newton. More innovative and expensive products will require higher marketing effort, especially in the introduction stage.

The Diffusion Process

Broad *product diffusion* into the mass market results from three processes. First, the firm's marketing program induces innovators and early adopters to purchase and try the product, as outlined above. Then, if the design team has developed a product that meets the needs of these customers, they will be satisfied with their purchase and tell other potential customers, generating free "word-of-mouth" product advertising. Finally, positive "word-of-mouth" endorsements work in concert with the firm's marketing program to help provide

Figure 8.11 Factors Influencing the Rate of New Product Adoption

▼ **Relative Advantage:** The greater the relative advantage—lower price, ease of use, savings in time—the faster the adoption process.

▼ **Compatibility:** The greater the compatibility—consistent with values, needs, and experiences of potential users—the faster the adoption process.

▼ **Complexity:** The more difficult a new product is to understand and use, the longer it will take to be adopted.

▼ **Trialability:** The greater the degree that the new product can be used on a trial basis, the faster the adoption process.

▼ **Observability:** The greater the degree to which the results of using a product are visible to others, the faster the adoption process.

less innovative (more imitative) customers, who make up the bulk of most markets, with enough understanding of and confidence in the product to purchase. For a more complete understanding of the profiles of the various types of customers that together create the *market,* see Figure 8.12.

Word-of-mouth approvals from customers reinforce the messages sent by the firm, giving them credibility. Hearing your neighbors rave about their new Palm Pilot and how

Incentives are sometimes offered by marketing departments to induce innovators and early adapters to take a chance on new products.

Figure 8.12   Customer Profiles

▼ **Innovators:** Representing 2.5% of all potential adopters, innovators tend to be younger, higher in social status, more cosmopolitan, and better educated than later adopter groups.

▼ **Early adopters:** Representing 13.5% of all potential adopters, early adopters enjoy the prestige and respect that comes with owning new products, but are less venturesome and more concerned with group norms and values than innovators.

▼ **Early majority:** Representing 34% of all potential adopters, the early majority spends more time deciding whether to try new products and seeks the opinions of the innovators and early adopters.

▼ **Late majority:** Representing 34% of all potential adopters, the late majority is less cosmopolitan and responsive to change than any of the previous groups.

▼ **Laggards:** Representing 16% of all potential adopters, laggards tend to be conservative, older, low income and social status, and suspicious of change.

it changed the way they organize their life is much more powerful for many people than reading about what the product does in a print ad. Of course, if the product does not live up to expectations, negative word-of-mouth will be generated. This will almost certainly guarantee market failure, regardless of the quality of the marketing program used to launch the product. When Apple's Newton routinely failed to recognize the handwriting of early customers, negative word-of-mouth spread rapidly. Some small articles and cartoons were even published in the business press that further contributed to market failure.

Diffusion is only partly under the control of the firm. Diffusion is aided early in the development process by ensuring that the product solves the problems customers want solved, and by getting the details of the product right. Once launched, the firm can speed diffusion by developing a marketing program that maximizes the number of people who become early adopters. More early adopters means that there are more users who can spread positive word-of-mouth endorsements to more potential customers early in the marketing cycle. Finally, the firm can encourage mechanisms to spread word-of-mouth endorsements throughout the target market. For example, Amazon.com allows readers to write and post book reviews that other Amazon.com customers can access. Whatever mechanisms the firm develops must work in concert with the rest of the marketing program surrounding the product launch.

www.apple.com

Growth Strategies

The growth stage of the product life cycle is characterized by rapidly increasing product demand, new competitors entering the market in response, and positive profits for the product varieties that customers decide best meet their needs. The firm's emphasis shifts to building and holding a set of loyal customers and distribution channel members, and sustaining sales growth as long as possible. To do this, they may invest in product improvements and expanding and strengthening distribution channels. Although overall spending increases, profits increase as marketing costs are spread over a larger volume, and per unit manufacturing costs decline due to economies of scale.

Maturity Strategies

Eventually, if the product is good enough, the vast majority of the market becomes regular product purchasers, leaving no new potential customers. The market for the product is saturated. Sales, customers, and competitors begin to level-off and profits reach their peak. The objective of marketing management in this phase is to maximize profits and lengthen this stage of the product life cycle. Typically, profits begin to fall during the later half of the maturity stage as competitors fight for market share and the corresponding price wars begin. However, nonprice strategies exist that may enable firms to sustain profits throughout the maturity stage.

Using the marketing program to maintain customer loyalty and satisfaction are important to maintaining profitability throughout the maturity stage. Airline frequent flyer programs, hotel honored guest programs, and grocery store frequent shopper programs all were developed to maintain customer loyalty and improve profits. The objective is to take the pressure off reducing price to keep customers by using other tactics in the marketing mix.

Several strategies can be used, even in maturity, to attempt to grow the market. For example, the firm can find new users *(market development)* or increase the usage rate per user *(market penetration)*. As mentioned earlier in the chapter, Arm & Hammer baking soda has generated increased usage per household by advertising new uses for baking soda, such as deodorizing the refrigerator and freezer. Johnson & Johnson found new users by positioning their baby shampoos to adults. Another mechanism for growth in the mature stage is to offer significant improvements on a routine basis *(product development)*. Many software firms release new versions of programs with increased features and functions in a very systematic timed release process. Rather than staying with the current version of the software, customers upgrade to get access to new features.

Decline Strategies

Even if new users are found and usage rates are increased, product sales may eventually start a long-term decline, as a substitute product that offers a superior set of benefits displaces the "old" product. Products based on new technologies frequently lead to a current product's demise. For example, 35 years ago nearly every student going to college took with them a typewriter. First the electric typewriter caused the decline of manual typewriter sales. Then word-processing machines started making inroads into electric typewriters. But the real death knell to typewriter sales was dealt by the advent of the PC and easy-to-use word processing programs like *Write, WordPerfect,* and *Word.* A few forms in some offices still require a typewriter. However, the majority of offices and even students depend upon PCs and word-processing programs for producing easily readable written communication.

Reduced sales do not necessarily mean that the firm should exit from the business immediately. The higher a firm's competitive strength in an industry, the longer they will want to stay in the market to reap returns from previous investments. However, the marketing tactics used in this stage will again have to be modified to maintain acceptable profitability levels. Marketing expenses, and promotion expenses in particular, will need to be reduced. IBM divested its typewriter division in the 1990s so that the business could continue operations without being burdened with the large overhead costs associated with IBM's traditional business structures. Products in decline continue to sell, but customer satisfaction (and thus loyalty) and word-of-mouth will become more important generators of sales than marketing campaigns.

Chapter Summary

Products are the lifeblood of every organization whether it is a good, service, person, place, or idea. In general, products can be either classified as consumer or business-to-business products. Consumer products include convenience, shopping, specialty, and unsought products that are characterized based on how the consumer views and shops for the product. Business-to-business products include installations, accessories, raw materials, component parts/materials, and supplies and are classified based on how the products will be used.

Few companies are successful by relying on a single product. Product mix decisions must be made regarding the width and depth of product lines to be marketed. Additional product decisions must be made in the areas of branding, packaging, and labeling. Still more product decisions must be made with regard to the sustaining growth. Established products are the mainstay of most companies. But a company that depends solely on its current stable of products may be headed for trouble. Growth opportunities exist in the form of market penetration, market development, product development, and product diversification strategies.

Marketing's role in successfully accomplishing new product development requires firms to continually:

▼ Understand customer needs and problems.

▼ Match technological capabilities to solving those problems.

▼ Move projects through the corporation and into the market.

Unless all three tasks are performed well, product development is unlikely to be successful.

Understanding customer needs requires performing qualitative market research and making the details available to the development team. No one technique will easily provide a list of *all* the customer needs. Actually being a customer best conveys tacit needs. Process-related needs are identified most easily by critically observing customers. In-depth interviewing is the most efficient means to obtain masses of detailed needs, but may not provide tacit and process-related information. Few projects can afford the time and expense of fully implementing all these processes. Development teams must use the most appropriate customer need generating technique(s), given the informational requirements, budget, and time frame for their project.

Effectively using technological capabilities to solve problems requires implementing a strategy for the NPD program overall, strategies for each project, and a product development process. Commercializing new products consists of repeatable tasks and less repeatable tasks. Firms that use a formalized new product process to help complete the more repeatable tasks in a consistent manner tend to have greater NPD success. Formalized processes are personalized to meet the needs of each firm.

Shepherding products through the firm requires putting in place effective leadership, providing an organizational structure that allows projects to move forward efficiently, and developing mechanisms to maintain management support over the life of the project. Project leaders, champions, and process owners all have been used to lead projects effectively. NPD in firms is organized through two different structures, each providing better ways to organize depending on the "newness to the organization" of the project being developed. No one structure seems to be associated with consistently higher performance. A number of different influence strategies, both formal and informal and affecting both rational and political decision-making processes, are used to obtain and maintain management support for projects.

Once launched, marketing must manage profitability throughout the product life cycle by modifying marketing mix elements to achieve the objectives of different life cycle stages. The objective in the introduction stage is to make potential early adopters aware of the product and persuade them to try it. During growth, the objective is achieving maximum market share. Profitability is the primary objective during both maturity and decline.

Long-term corporate success depends upon executing new product development effectively and efficiently. Managing product development is one of the most complex tasks of the organization, in part, because of the cooperation needed between different departments. Marketing is crucial in achieving successful new product development.

Key Terms[20]

Core Benefit Proposition (CBP) is the primary benefit or purpose for which a customer buys a product. The CBP may reside in the physical good or service performance, or it may come from augmented dimensions of the product.

Products are the set of features, functions, and benefits that customers purchase. Products may consist primarily of tangible (physical) attributes or intangibles, such as those associated with services or some combination of tangible and intangible.

Features are the way that benefits are delivered to customers. Features provide the solution to customer problems.

Brand equity is the marketplace value of a brand based on reputation and goodwill.

Competitively advantaged product is a product that solves a set of customer problems better than any competitors' product. This product is made possible due to this firm's unique technical, manufacturing, managerial, or marketing capabilities, which are not easily copied by others.

Concept is a written description or visual depiction of a new product idea. A concept includes the product's primary features and benefits.

Prototype is a product concept in physical form. A prototype may be a full working model that has been produced by hand or a nonworking physical representation of the final product. It is used to gather customer reaction to the physical form (aesthetics and ergonomics) or to initial operating capability. It is also used in internal performance tests to assure that performance goals have been met.

Tacit information consists of things customers know, but which are difficult or nearly impossible to articulate. This intuitive information, while frequently critical to product success in the marketplace, is the most difficult to provide to the NPD team during product development.

Process-related information is information that provides an understanding of how the product fits into the workflow of the company.

Voice of the Customer (VOC) is an in-depth, one-on-one interviewing process to understand a set of customer needs in great depth.

Product development process consists of a clearly defined set of tasks and steps that describes the normal means by which product development proceeds. The process outlines the order and sequence of the tasks and indicates who is responsible for each.

Stage-Gate process is a common new product development process that divides the repeatable portion of product development into a time-sequenced series of stages, each of which is separated by a management decision gate. In each stage, a team completes a set of tasks that span the functions involved in product development. At the end of each stage, management reviews the results obtained and, based on the team's ability to meet the objectives in that stage, provides the resources to continue to the next stage ("go"), requests additional work ("recycle"), or stops the project ("kill").

Product life cycle is the cycle of stages that a product goes through from birth to death: introduction, growth, maturity, and decline.

Additional Key Terms and Concepts

Consumer products	Business-to-business products
Product mix	Product line
Product mix width	Product mix depth
Brands	Individual brand name strategy
Family brand name strategy	Market penetration
Market development	Product development strategy
Product diversification	NPD project success
Potential customers	Existing customers
Unrealized customers	Customer needs

Anthropological excursions
Project leaders
Process owners
Divisional or Strategic business unit (SBU)
    NPD structure
Early majority
Laggards
Product diffusion

Project strategy
Champions
Functional NPD structure
Venture group structure
Innovators and early adopters
Late majority
Adoption process

Questions for Discussion

1. How do the differences between consumer products and business-to-business products impact the way new product development is managed and organized?

2. What is the weakest aspect in our understanding about how to manage NPD?

3. In which types of NPD projects might a heavyweight project manager not be successful? A champion?

4. Several examples were given in the chapter of products that were successful on one dimension of success, but not on another. What are some other examples, and on what dimensions were they less successful? Why did the companies undertake those?

5. NPD teams always seem to want to include every feature possible in a new product. The restraint shown by the Palm Pilot team in not adding infrared technology to the first-generation product is unusual. What steps can be taken to keep NPD teams from "over-featuring" the product?

6. Why do NPD processes need to be "personalized" for each firm? What are the factors that will contribute to the way in which a firm personalizes the process for their use?

7. What are your options if you just cannot garner management support for a proposed NPD project?

8. Hewlett-Packard started as a firm that developed and sold scientific measurement equipment like oscilloscopes. Over the years they have increased the width of their product mix to include computer equipment and medical equipment. Name three other companies that have increased their product mix width, and name the sets of product lines they sell.

9. Since Procter & Gamble is such a highly-revered company and strong marketer, why do they follow an individual branding strategy rather than take advantage of a family brand name?

10. In what stage of the product life cycle are family sedans? Station wagons? Minivans? If these are all segments of the car market, how is it possible for them to be at different stages of the product life cycle?

Internet Questions

1. Using your favorite search engine, type in the search string "product development." How do you sort through the enormous number of hits obtained to find something useful?

2. Go to the Web site www.pdma.org. This is the Web site for the Product Development & Management Association, a nonprofit association whose mission is to seek out, develop, organize, and disseminate leading-edge information on the theory and practice of product development and product development processes. How does their Web site, and the associated hot-links, help fulfill that mission?

3. Go to www.amazon.com. What is the best-selling book on new product development? What other books have been written by that author?

4. The Internet is changing the way some firms gather customer information. See if you can find a company that is using the Internet to gather customer needs. What evidence on their site suggests that they are using the information gathered to aid in developing new products? What are the benefits of gathering customer needs from the Web? What are the drawbacks? For what kinds of industries might this information be most useful or appropriate to use? Least useful or appropriate?

5. What information about innovation can be obtained from the following Web sites: www.americandemographics.com, www.creativemag.com, www.fastcompany.com, www.idsa.org, www.pachamber.com? How would you use this information in developing a new product?

Endnotes

[1] Markos Kounalakis, *Defying Gravity: The Making of Newton* (Hillsboro, OR: Beyond Words Publishing, 1993).

[2] Adapted from John H. Lindgren, Jr. and Terry Shimp, *Marketing: An Interactive Learning System* (Fort Worth: The Dryden Press, 1996), pp. 227–231.

[3] Ibid., pp. 232–235.

[4] Adapted from Peter R. Dickson, *Marketing Management* (Fort Worth, The Dryden Press, 1994), pp. 310–322.

[5] Adapted from John H. Lindgren, Jr. and Terry Shimp, *Marketing: An Interactive Learning System* (Fort Worth: The Dryden Press, 1996), pp. 262–264.

[6] Abbie Griffin and Albert L. Page (1996), "The PDMA Success Measurement Project: Recommended Measures for Product Development Success and Failure," *Journal of Product Innovation Management* 13(5): 478–496 (November).

[7] Abbie Griffin (1997), "PDMA Research on New Product Development Practices: Updating Trends and Benchmarking Best Practices," *Journal of Product Innovation Management* 14(6): pp. 429–458.

[8] Ed Brown (1998), "How to Read a Palm III," *Fortune* 36 (August 17).

[9] The term "product" refers to both physical goods such as cars and shampoos and to services such as banking, dining, and consulting. Frequently, developing new services

requires developing both a physical good as well as the intangible benefits. For example, a new hotel chain requires developing the physical building, including the room layout, the software and hardware infrastructure to handle reservations and billing, and ancillary physical spaces such as outdoor recreation and parking facilities.

[10]Abbie Griffin and John R. Hauser (1993), "The Voice of the Customer," *Marketing Science,* 12(1): pp. 1–27; Gerald Zaltman and Robin A. Higgie (1993), "Seeing the Voice of the Customer: The Zaltman Elicitation Technique," Working Paper 9-114, Cambridge, MA: Marketing Science Institute.

[11]Robert G. Cooper and Elko Kleinschmidt, "Benchmarking Firm's New Product Performance and Practices," *Engineering Management Review,* 23(3): pp. 112–120; Abbie Griffin (1997), "PDMA Research on New Product Development Practices: Updating Trends and Benchmarking Best Practices," *Journal of Product Innovation Management,* 14(6): pp. 429–458.

[12]Abbie Griffin (1997), "PDMA Research on New Product Development Practices: Updating Trends and Benchmarking Best Practices," *Journal of Product Innovation Management,* 14(6): 429–458.

[13]A fuller explanation of these may be found in Chapters 6 and 8 of Robert G. Cooper, *Winning at New Products,* Second Edition, (Reading, MA: Addison Wesley, 1993).

[14]Abbie Griffin (1997), "PDMA Research on New Product Development Practices: Updating Trends and Benchmarking Best Practices," *Journal of Product Innovation Management,* 14(6): pp. 429–458.

[15]Kim B. Clark and Steven C. Wheelwright, *Managing New Product and Process Development* (New York, NY: The Free Press, 1993).

[16]Milton D. Rosenau, Abbie Griffin, George Castellion, and Ned Anschuetz, editors, *The PDMA Handbook of New Product Development* (New York, NY: John Wiley & Sons, Inc., 1996), p. 519.

[17]Stephen Markham and Abbie Griffin (1998), "The Breakfast of Champions: Associations Between Champions and Product Development Environments, Practices and Performance," *Journal of Product Innovation Management,* 14(6).

[18]Michael E. McGrath, Michael T. Anthony, and Amram R. Shapiro, *Product Development: Success Through Product and Cycle-Time Excellence* (Boston, MA: Butterworth-Heinemann, 1992).

[19]William E. Souder, *Managing New Product Innovations* (Lexington, MA: Lexington Books, 1987).

[20]Many of these definitions used in this chapter are adapted from *The PDMA Handbook of New Product Development,* Milton D. Rosenau, et al., editors, 1996.

Developing a New Degree Offering at Midwestern U.

Sam Stanza, Associate Dean for Teaching at Midwestern University's School of Business, a leading business school in a large city in the Midwest, was contemplating the possibilities for offering an additional degree in business at the school. The Trustees of the University were looking to the business school to provide additional financial contributions to offset large deficits in other departments. They had indicated that he would have free rein to develop any program he could propose, so long as it provided a net positive contribution to the school within the first two years of introduction, and a net positive contribution to the university within the first three years of operation.

The business school currently offered several degree programs. As did all major business schools, it offered a full-time Master's in Business Administration (MBA) to 400 students/class that generally required two years to complete the set of 20 classes. Students competed fiercely to attend this program, which cost $25,000/year in tuition. The MBA program was a world leader for its marketing curriculum, and very highly thought of in finance. Its general management capabilities were not as highly regarded.

The school also offered a part-time MBA program, conferring an identical degree to the full-time program. These students paid the same per-class tuition ($2,500/class), and completed the program in four years. At any point in time about 1,500 part-time students were enrolled in the degree program. These students were drawn primarily from local businesses. Because the curriculum was identical to the full-time program, and the same professors taught in both programs, there was great competition to enter this program as well. The difference between full-time and part-time students lay predominantly in an unwillingness (or inability) to sacrifice two years of full-time salary for the sake of further education.

The business school also offered an Executive MBA (EMBA) degree, which differed significantly from the cachet of an MBA degree. EMBA's were executives who had been out of school for at least 20 years, and whose firms had sent them back to this program on a part-time basis. Each class of the 65 company-sponsored executives attended a full day session each week of the school year—Friday one week, and Saturday the next—for two years. Four one and one-half hour classes were offered each day. Additionally, the students spent two weeks overseas in the summer between the two school years, wrote a summer paper on some aspect of change needed in their firm, and spent spring break of the second year of the program on a U.S. study tour. Tuition (including the study trips) came to $75,000 for the two-year program. Firms sent executives to the program for a number of reasons:

▼ To provide a technical manager with business education.

▼ To indicate within the firm that a manager had top management potential.

▼ To provide a business refresher to a manager changing functional areas (from finance to marketing, for example).

▼ As a reward for service.

While the part-time program was at capacity (this is a class-room and facilities limitation issue due to the evening class schedules), there was capacity within the resources of the full-time program for offering additional daytime classes in terms of both teaching manpower as well as facilities. Dean Stanza considered several concept options that fit into this constraint before narrowing the list to one. Options that did not seem to be as interesting in terms of potential profitability for the effort and risk included:

1. Creating an undergraduate (bachelor's) degree program. This would require an enormous infrastructure much different from that currently in place for the graduate programs currently offered by the school. Payback would require too long a time period to warrant this.

2. Offering a series of management short courses. These would operate in the summer only, when few students attended class. While from a facilities point of view, these would greatly increase the utilization of underutilized space, this would require an enormous amount of time investment as each course would have to be individually developed, with a specific target market identified that could find benefit from the course. Each one- to four-week course would have to be individually marketed to the appropriate target market, creating little marketing synergy across the potential set of courses offered.

The concept most favored at this stage of the development process by Dean Stanza was to offer a one-year (twelve-month) full-time Master's of Management (MM). The focus of the curricula would be to provide a general management master's degree, but with advanced marketing expertise overlaid on top of the general management studies. The program would start in June with classes in business fundamentals. At the end of the summer, students would take the first of two study trips to a consumer marketing power-house. During spring break, students would take a study trip to a business-to-business marketing firm. The target market would be low- to mid-level (10 year out) managers with ultimate top management potential who currently worked in marketing positions or in other functional areas, but with the need to have marketing experience. Dean Stanza believed that 75 percent of the students would be supported by their firms during their matriculation. Tuition for the year would be $35,000, and would include both study trips.

Discussion Questions

1. What procedures might Dean Stanza use to determine if his proposed program would meet the needs of his target market?

2. If the university decides to proceed with this program, list some of the preliminary steps they would have to complete *before* opening the program to students. Discuss the relevance of each of these steps to the ultimate success of the program.

3. If early response to the program proved to be sluggish, what marketing techniques could be used to increase interest and enrollment? What would be the costs and benefits of each technique?

Chapter 9

Services Marketing

**K. Douglas Hoffman,
Colorado State University**

Associate Professor of Marketing, Colorado State University

Dr. Hoffman earned his master's and doctorate degrees from the University of Kentucky and his bachelor's degree from The Ohio State University. He has been formally recognized for teaching excellence and has served as past education coordinator for the Services Marketing Special Interest Group of the American Marketing Association.

Dr. Hoffman has taught such courses as Principles of Marketing, Services Marketing, Retail Management, and Marketing Management. His primary teaching and research passion is in the services marketing area where he launched the first services marketing classes at Mississippi

I t often seems that customers and service providers are in pursuit of different goals. Inevitably, clashes occur that have profound long-term effects on how customers view business organizations and how the service providers view customers in subsequent transactions. It is often a self-perpetuating nightmare. Cynical service providers turn their clientele into "customers from hell" and nightmarish customers return the favor by eventually wearing down even the best service providers. The story of Tina and Tony Apple is typical:[1]

Tina's plan, though hectic, was workable. Show the Garcia property to the Samuelsons at 2 P.M. Stop by the department store at the mall and pick out a pair of shoes for the

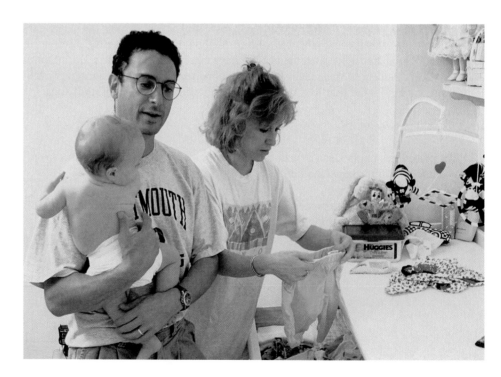

upcoming company party. Swing by the airport and meet Tony's 4:10 flight from Chicago. Drop Tony by the car-repair place. Rescue Correy from daycare. Then hit the dry cleaner, the video store, and the pizza drive-thru en route to a . . . weekend of quiet relaxation. Well, no such luck . . .

. . . the listing agent failed to put out a lockbox at the Garcia property.

. . . the sales assistants at the department store were too busy talking to one another to help any customers.

. . . the airline failed to inform customers that the flight would be 30 minutes late.

. . . Tony's car was nowhere near ready; in fact, the car was still sitting in the same place where it was dropped off the day before.

. . . the daycare center charged Tony and Tina a $50 late fee for picking up Correy a little too late.

. . . the video store was out of "new releases" . . . again.

. . . despite the dry cleaner's sign that read, "In by 8 A.M., Out by 5 P.M." the cleaning was not ready. The shopkeeper offered no apology or discount, but did say that Tony and Tina could pick up their clothes at the fast-food franchise next door later that evening.

. . . finally, the pizza that was ordered was baked with the wrong toppings, and it was cold by the time that our happy couple finally arrived home to begin their "relaxed" weekend.

Learning Objectives

After you have completed this chapter, you should be able to:

1. Understand the changes in the business environment that have led to an increase in the importance of services marketing.

2. Identify the factors that influence the customer's service experience.

3. Discuss concepts of intangibility, inseparability, heterogeneity, and perishability as they relate to service firms.

4. Define and discuss the importance and benefits of customer satisfaction.

5. Discuss the five dimensions of service quality.

6. Define and discuss customer service strategies that facilitate customer retention.

State University, The University of North Carolina at Wilmington, and Colorado State University.

Prior to his academic career, Dr. Hoffman was actively involved in his family-owned golf course business, served as a distribution analyst for Volkswagen of America, and worked as a research analyst for the Parker Hannifin Corp. His current research and consulting activities are primarily in the areas of customer service/satisfaction and services marketing education. Dr Hoffman has co-authored two other Dryden texts: *Essentials of Services Marketing* and *Managing Services Marketing* (both with John E. G. Bateson)

The primary objective of this chapter is to take an in-depth look at the marketing of services. Service businesses are dominating the economies of the industrialized world. Despite the phenomenal growth of service industries, many marketing textbooks continue to emphasize traditional marketing strategies by focusing on tangible goods and conquest marketing strategies (i.e., recruiting new customers). Meanwhile, the business world now demands, in addition to traditional skills, increasing employee competence in customer satisfaction, service quality, and customer service—skills that are essential in sustaining the existing customer base.

THE FUNDAMENTALS OF SERVICES MARKETING

Services are everywhere we turn, whether it is a flight on an airline, a trip to our favorite pizza restaurant, or a shopping excursion to the local mall. Clearly, services include a vast array of businesses ranging from profit to nonprofit services, private to government services, and unskilled to professional services (Table 9.1). Given the pervasiveness of service businesses, it is difficult to understand why only recently services marketing education has become an important component of the educational experience at most colleges and universities. This fact is particularly disturbing when you consider that since 1900, the United States and Great Britain have had more jobs in the service sector than in manufacturing.[2] It was not until the 1970s that services marketing was even considered an academic field.

The distinction between goods and services is not always perfectly clear.[3] In fact, providing an example of a pure good or a pure service is very difficult. In reality, many services contain at least some goods, such as the hamburger at McDonald's or the credit card billing statement from MBNA. Additionally, most goods producing companies offer services. For example, Morton Salt is delivered to grocery stores and stores are billed for the product. Hence, even a product such as simple table salt contains delivery and billing services as part of its total product offering.

The distinction between goods and services is further obscured by firms that conduct business on both sides of the goods/services fence. For example, General Motors, the "goods" manufacturing giant, generates 20 percent of its revenue from its financial and insurance businesses, and the car maker's biggest supplier is Blue Cross–Blue Shield, not a parts supplier as you may have thought. General Electric, the massive manufacturer of products like refrigerators and light bulbs, is another example of a goods producing firm that also participates in the service sector. GE's fastest growing business unit is GE Capital that markets financial services and insurance. GE Capital's annual revenues of $32.7 billion make up 39 percent of GE's overall business.[4]

What Is a Service?

Despite the confusion, the following definitions should provide a sound starting point in developing an understanding of the differences between goods and services.[5] In general, *goods* can be defined as objects, devices, or things, whereas, *services* can be defined as deeds, efforts, or performances. The primary difference between goods and services is the property of tangibility. The *Scale of Market Entities* presented in Figure 9.1 displays a range of products based on their tangibility. According to the Scale of Market Entities, goods are *tangible dominant.* As such, goods possess physical properties that can be felt, tasted, and seen prior to the consumer's purchase decision. For example, when purchasing a car, customers can kick the tires, look at the engine, listen to the stereo, smell that "new car smell," and take the car for a test drive before making the actual purchase.

In contrast to goods, services are *intangible dominant,* and therefore lack physical properties that can be evaluated by customers prior to purchase. As a result, a number of

Table 9.1	Types of Services		
Government Services	**Nonprofit Services**	**For Profit Services**	**Professional Services**
Police and fire protection	Community hospitals	Car rental	Legal
IRS	United Way	Movie theater	Medical
Social Security	American Red Cross	Car wash	Insurance
Social work	Credit unions	Dry cleaning	Financial
Public transportation	Civic organizations	Landscaping	Education
Mail		Taxi service	Architectural
		Airlines	Accounting
		Beautician	Consulting

Figure 9.1   Scale of Market Entities

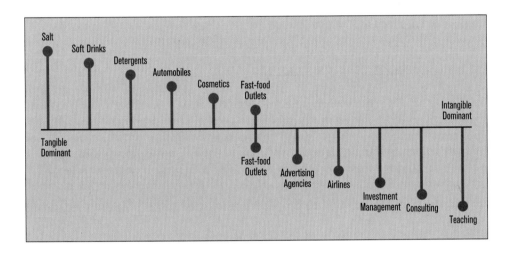

marketing mix challenges arise. For example, how would you (1) advertise a service that no one could see; (2) price a service that had no cost of goods sold; (3) inventory a service that could not be stored; and (4) mass-merchandise a service that needed to be produced by an individual?

THE IMPORTANCE OF SERVICES MARKETING

Substantial changes are taking place in the world's business environment. Due to these changes, a tremendous demand has developed for services marketing knowledge. Practitioners in the service sector have learned very quickly that traditional marketing strategies and traditional managerial models do not always apply to their unique service industries. More specifically, the importance of the study of services marketing has been fueled by (1) tremendous growth in service-sector employment; (2) increasing service-sector contributions to the world economy; (3) the deregulation of many service industries; (4) the service differential advantage; and (5) a revolutionary change in perspective regarding how service firms should manage their companies.

Service Sector Employment

Throughout the world, the shifting of economies from agricultural to industrial to services is evident.[6] Today, manufacturers of goods only employ one out of every six persons in the United States, one out of every five in Great Britain, and one out of three in Germany and Japan. From 1970 to 1993, the U.S. labor force employed by manufacturing fell from 27 percent to 16 percent. Great Britain's labor force experienced a similar move away from manufacturing at a rate of 37 percent to 20 percent. In contrast, labor employed in the service sector has risen to 57 percent in Germany, 62 percent in Japan, 73 percent in Great Britain, and 78 percent in the United States.

The increase in U.S. service sector employment is directly related to new service jobs (see Table 9.2). During the period of 1980 to 1990, 80 percent of all new jobs were developed in service industries. Estimates suggest that 90 percent of all new jobs between 1990 and the year 2000 will also be service-related. Experts project that by the year 2005, only 12 percent of U.S. workers will have manufacturing jobs, and this number is expected to decrease to 10 percent by the year 2020.

The Economic Impact of the Service Sector

Service and service-related industries clearly dominate the U.S. economy and will continue to do so in the foreseeable future.[7] Similarly situated, the economies of other nations once known for their industrial might are also becoming predominantly service economies (see Table 9.3). Countries such as Great Britain, Canada, France, Italy, Japan, and Germany have service economies that make up more than 50 percent of their gross domestic products (GDP).

According to the U.S. Labor Statistics Bureau, the private service sector has increased its contribution to the GDP by more than 300 percent over the past 30 years. As a result,

Table 9.2 New Job Creation
▼ 80% of All New Jobs (1980–1990)
▼ 90% of All New Jobs (1990–2000)
▼ 88% of All Jobs by 2005
▼ 90% of All Jobs by 2020

Source: "The Final Frontier," *The Economist*, February 20, 1993, p. 63.

Table 9.3 Service Sector Employment
▼ 78% in United States
▼ 73% in Great Britain
▼ 62% in Japan
▼ 57% in Germany

Source: "The Final Frontier," *The Economist*, February 20, 1993, p. 63.

Careers in Marketing

Marines, Rock 'N' Roll, and Professional Ice Hockey: What's a Nice Girl Like You Doing in a Place Like This?

Throughout her college experience, Sheila Carter always wanted to break into "event marketing." These days it's a common dream for many students who wish to pursue careers in sports marketing and the marketing of other types of entertainment venues. However, given the number of people that are interested in these types of careers, event marketing is a tough industry to get into.

Sheila broke into the industry through hard work, patience, and a lot of networking. Her first event marketing experience was gained through an internship with, of all places, the Morale, Welfare, and Recreation (MWR) Division of the United States Marine Corps. The MWR division of Camp Lejeune plans and markets programs and events designed to create and maintain a high standard of morale and well-being for more than 6,000 military personnel and their dependents. Upon graduation and with a lot of networking and perseverance, Sheila was eventually hired by the Pace Entertainment Group and worked to promote events at Hardee's Walnut Creek Amphitheater in Raleigh, North Carolina and the Blockbuster Desert Sky Pavilion in Phoenix, Arizona. These jobs allowed Sheila to combine two of the things she loves the most—music and marketing—and allowed her to "rub elbows" with the likes of Jimmy Buffett, Aerosmith, and Natalie Merchant, just to name a few.

Through the experience that Sheila gained while working for the Marines and Pace Entertainment, she has become a sought after commodity. Sheila is now the Marketing Manager for the Carolina Hurricanes NHL Hockey Club and has the task of introducing professional hockey to "southerners" and promoting a new entertainment complex in Raleigh. Sheila has accomplished many goals in the eight short years since graduation, and she has a bright future in front of her.

Source: Interview with Sheila Carter, October 28, 1998.

---

the private service sector now accounts for more than 70 percent of the GDP. In contrast, since 1970, GDP attributed to the manufacturing of goods has fallen from 26 percent to 19 percent. This means that for the first time in U.S. history, the majority of industries in our economy do not *produce* objects, devices, and things; they *perform* deeds and efforts such as "insuring" personal property, "handling" financial investments, and "attending" to consumer health-care needs.

The Impact of Deregulation

Over the past 20 years, an increase in the interest in marketing problems has paralleled the emergence of competition in many parts of the service sector.[8] During the 1980s, deregulation forced many traditional service industries, such as airlines, financial services, telecommunications, and trucking, into the competitive arena for the first time. These industries were forced to be competitive not only with existing firms within their industry, but also with new firms that were permitted to enter the industry due to deregulation. The new firms were leaner, more focused, and extremely competitive.

Faced with excess supply, many of the older established firms engaged in price wars with their new competitors. The consequences were devastating. From 1980 to 1992, the U.S. airline industry declined from 36 to 11 operators. The number of trucking companies that failed during the 1980s was more than the previous 45 years combined, and the number of commercial banks declined by 14 percent. It quickly became apparent that competing on price alone was leading directly to bankruptcy. Services marketing knowledge was needed in nonprice strategy issues such as customer service, customer retention, service differentiation, service quality, image enhancement, and the transformation of public contact personnel into marketing-oriented personnel. Service industries such as the health care industry, which in its not-too-distant past, considered marketing a "dirty word" and beneath the dignity of its personnel, now embrace marketing techniques as means for their firm's survival. However, even in the health-care field, the transformation remains incomplete. If you ask a room full of health-care workers to identify their primary customer, the

**Figure 9.2   Manufacturers of Goods Now Offer Services to Differentiate
Themselves from the Competition**

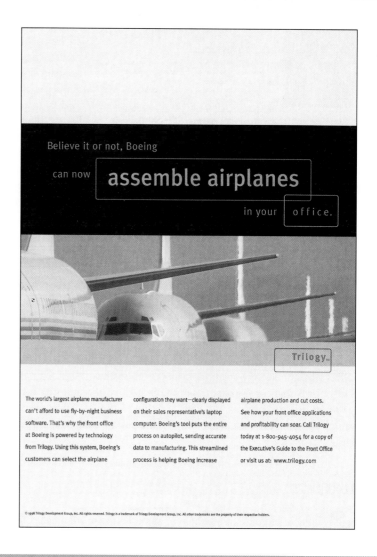

majority of the room will still to this day answer "the physician," or perhaps even more disturbing, "the insurance companies."

The Service Differential Advantage

In the manufacturing of today's consumer and business goods, the goods produced by competitive manufacturers are virtually interchangeable.[9] Consider, for example, the purchases of a personal computer, a sports utility vehicle, and/or a household appliance. The competitive offerings are essentially identical. The service side of the business is where the differentiation between competing companies often lies, and it is the successful command of the service side of the business that often dictates who wins market share in the competitive battlefield.

Marketing Technologies

Mass Customization: The Union of Customer Service and Technology

The industrial management model of making things cheaper by making them the same is losing its last battle. Companies with millions of customers are now making goods and services just for you. You can now build your own computer with Dell, buy a pair of Levi's cut to fit your body, purchase pills with combinations of vitamins, herbs, and minerals that you determine, and design your own radio station (see Internet Exercises). These choices are achieved through mass customization where mass-marketed goods and services are uniquely designed to individual consumers. "Mass customization has two huge advantages over mass production: It is at the service of the customer, and it makes full use of cutting-edge technology."

Customer service and technology go hand-in-hand. New technologies create service opportunities for firms to better serve their customers and to differentiate themselves from the competition. Today's technological improvements that have allowed mass customization to become a reality include: computer controlled factory equipment and industrial robots that permit quick assembly line adjustments, digital printers that permit flexible product packaging, bar-code scanners that track every part of every product, data base systems that store vasts amounts of information about individual consumer tastes; and of course, the Internet which allows firms to move seamlessly from the customer's order form to the factory floor. Computer-assisted communication and coordination between manufacturing and sales representatives, such as that illustrated in Figure 9.2, allow for customization and cost reduction. Technological advances such as these have led to predictions of customers entering into scanning booths that determine their exact 3-D structure. Using these measurements, Levi's will offer the customer a choice of 750 versions of jeans. "Customers can combine any of six colors, three basic cuts, five leg openings, and two types of fly to create the perfect pants." Now, that's service!

Questions

1. How does the customer's experience differ when ordering a computer from a mass customization firm, such as dell.com, as opposed to purchasing a computer at a discount electronics store, such as Circuit City or Best Buy? Which method of purchasing do you prefer? Explain.

2. Does mass customization work for some customers better than others? Explain. How would you segment computer consumers based on their likelihood to prefer mass customization?

Source: "The Customized, Digitized, Have-It-Your-Way Economy," *Fortune*, September 28, 1998, pp. 115–124.

Despite the competitive parity among goods' producers, one study concluded that 42 percent of customers rate the companies they do business with as poor or fair at meeting their needs, and only 8 percent are considered excellent. Consequently, the opportunities for differentiation and adding value to tangible goods are in the intangible areas of reliability, responsiveness, assurance, and commanding an exceptional grasp of knowing and understanding the wants and needs of customers.

Service as a differential advantage is also being used to attract and retain employees. The job market is opening up and competition for attracting and retaining talented employees is becoming fierce. Table 9.4 describes just some of the services that are used as "perks" to increase employee satisfaction and loyalty. The recent cover of *Fortune* shown in Figure 9.3 demonstrates just how much the job market has changed from job candidates begging for jobs to candidates now demanding and obtaining some fairly peculiar job benefits.

Changes in Managerial Philosophy

The Industrial Management Approach

Accompanying the *services revolution* has been a shift in philosophy of how service firms should manage their businesses.[10] Unfortunately, many businesses continue to operate under a management model, the **industrial management approach,** which was originally designed for the manufacturing of industrial goods. Organizations that follow the industrial approach believe that (1) location strategies, sales promotions, and advertising drive sales revenue; and (2) labor and other operating costs should be kept as low as

Table 9.4 Best Perks to Employees of the 100 Best Companies

Perks	Number of Companies	Perks	Number of Companies
Overnight dependent child care	7	Subsidized cafeterias	64
Free lunch (or other meals)	15	On-site ATM or banking service	64
Personal concierge service	15	Personal travel services	68
On-site child care	31	Elder-care resource and referral	73
Dry-cleaning service	40	Casual dress everyday	75
Home-purchasing service	44	Relocation services	83
Adoption aid	60	Child-care resource and referral	83

Figure 9.3 The Changing Face of the Job Market

possible. In sum, the industrial model focuses on revenue and operating costs and ignores (or at least forgets) the role employees play in generating customer satisfaction and sustainable profits.

Followers of the industrial model believe that "it is better to rely on technology, machines, and systems than on human beings."[11] As opposed to valuing front-line employees, the industrial approach places a higher value on upper and middle managers and assumes that only mangers can solve problems. In order to minimize operating costs, full-time, front-line personnel are commonly replaced by part-time personnel. Part-time personnel are paid less and receive few, if any, company benefits. Managerial practices such as this have created a new class of migrant worker in the United States—16 million people now travel from one short-term job to another.

The consequences associated with the industrial model in regard to service organizations have been self-destructive. The industrial model has produced dead-end, front-line jobs, poor pay, superficial training, little opportunity for advancement, and little access to company benefits. Moreover, the industrial approach has led to customer dissatisfaction, flat or declining sales revenue, high employee turnover, and little or no growth in overall service productivity. All in all, many believe that the industrial approach is bad for customers, employees, stockholders, and the standard of living of the countries in which these firms operate.

The Market-Focused Management Approach

In contrast to the industrial management model, proponents of the ***market-focused management approach*** believe that the purpose of the firm is to serve the customer.[12] By following this approach, the service delivery process becomes the focus of the organization and the overall key to successfully differentiating the firm from its competition.

The market-focused management approach recognizes that employee turnover and customer satisfaction are clearly related. Hence, the recruitment and training of front-line personnel is emphasized. Pay is directly tied to performance throughout every level of the organization. Companies that compensate their employees better than competitors often find that as a percentage of sales, their labor costs are actually lower than industry averages. The benefits of superior training and education programs are clear. For example, the turnover rate for employees not participating in training and education programs at Ryder Truck Rental is 41 percent. In comparison, employees who do participate in training programs turn over at a rate of 19 percent.[13] High retention rates reflect well on the image of the company as illustrated in Figure 9.4. Better-trained and better-paid employees provide better service, need less supervision, and are more likely to stay on the job. In turn, their customers are more satisfied, return to make purchases more often, purchase more when they do return, and tell their friends of the positive experience.

www.ryder.com

UNDERSTANDING THE SERVICE EXPERIENCE

All products, be they goods or services, deliver a bundle of benefits to the customer.[14] The ***benefit concept*** is the encapsulation of these benefits in the consumer's mind. For a good such as Tide laundry detergent, the benefit concept for some consumers might simply be cleaning. However, for many other consumers the benefit concept might also include attributes built into the product that go beyond the mere powder or liquid, such as cleanliness, whiteness, and/or being a good mother.

In contrast to goods, services deliver a bundle of benefits through the experience that is created for the consumer. For example, most Tide customers will never see the inside of the manufacturing plant where Tide is produced; they will most likely never interact with the factory workers who produce the detergent or with the management staff that directs the workers; and they will also generally not use Tide in the presence of other customers. In comparison, Taco Bell dine-in customers are physically present in the "factory" where the food is produced; these customers *do* interact with the workers who prepare and serve

Figure 9.4   Bragging Rights Belong to Companies with High Employee Retention Rates

You can tell a lot about a company by the people they KEEP.

where do you want to go today?® **Microsoft®**
www.microsoft.com

the food as well as with the management staff that runs the restaurant. Moreover, Taco Bell customers consume the service in the presence of other customers who may influence one another's service experience. Another excellent example of the bundle of benefits that comprise the service experience is seen in Figure 9.5.

Figure 9.6 illustrates the key factors that create the service experience for the consumer. It is the service experience that creates the bundle of benefits for the consumer. The most profound implication of the service experience is that it demonstrates that consumers are an integral part of the service process. Their participation may be active or passive, but they are always involved in the service delivery process. Factors that influence the customer's service experience include factors that are visible to the customer: the servicescape, service providers, other customers, and the invisible organization and systems.

Figure 9.5   Service Equals Success in the Hotel and Resort Industry

The Servicescape

The *servicescape* refers to the "nonliving" physical evidence that is used to create the service environment (see Table 9.5).[15] The servicescape consists of ambient conditions such as room temperature and music, inanimate objects that assist the firm in completing its tasks such as furnishings and business equipment, and other physical evidence such as signs, symbols, and personal artifacts such as family pictures and personal collections. Physical evidence plays a major role in packaging the service. Due to intangibility, services cannot be evaluated by customers as easily as can goods. Consequently, customers often observe the physical evidence that surround the service in order to base their service performance evaluations. For example, a customer might partially assess the competence and professionalism of their physician by observing the décor, content, and neatness of his or her office. The servicescape extends beyond the physical dimensions of a company's of-

Figure 9.6   Factors Influencing the Service Experience

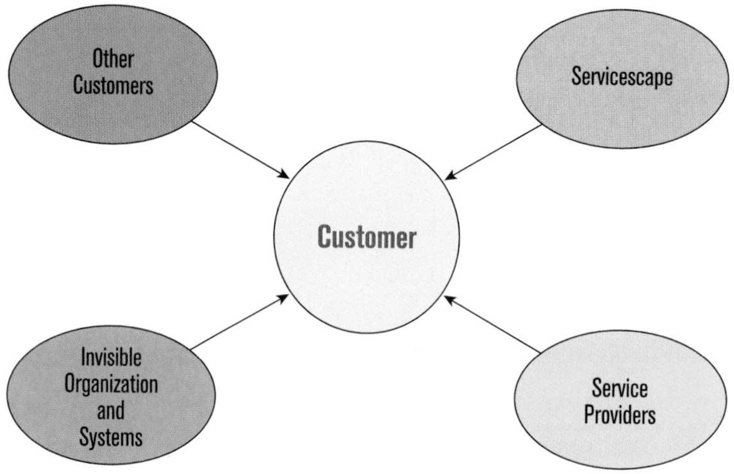

Table 9.5   Servicescape Dimensions

Ambient Conditions	Space/Function	Signs, Symbols, & Artifacts
▼ Temperature	▼ Layout	▼ Signage
▼ Air quality	▼ Equipment	▼ Personal artifacts
▼ Noise	▼ Furnishings	▼ Style or décor
▼ Music		
▼ Odors		

fices. Everything put forward as representative of the company, even the envelope that encloses a business proposal (see Figures 9.7 and 9.8), can affect the impression left in a customer's mind.

The servicescape sends quality cues to customers and influences consumer expectations. For example, customers typically have one set of expectations for restaurants with dimly lit dining rooms, soft music, and linen tablecloths, and a different set of expectations for restaurants with cement floors, picnic tables, and peanut shells strewn about the floor. The servicescape also adds value to the service in terms of image development, which improves consumer perceptions of service while reducing the levels of perceived risk associated with the purchase and levels of cognitive dissonance after the purchase.

The servicescape consists of interior, exterior, and other tangible elements such as the building's architecture, furniture, flooring, lighting, music, odors, wall hangings, countertops, and a variety of other physical evidence that varies according to the service being provided. Since the customer and the employee often share the servicescape during the service encounter, the design of the servicescape must be designed with *both* the needs of the firm's employees and customers in mind.

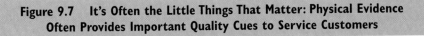

Figure 9.7   It's Often the Little Things That Matter: Physical Evidence
Often Provides Important Quality Cues to Service Customers

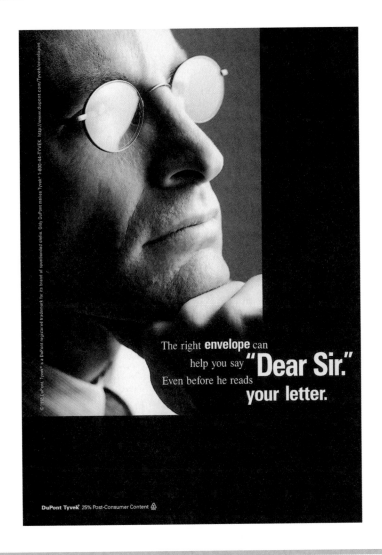

Service Providers

The public faces of a service firm are its *service providers*.[16] Unlike the consumption of goods, the consumption of services often takes place where the service is produced (e.g., hair styling salon, dentist office, restaurant), or where the service is provided at the consumer's residence or workplace (e.g., lawn care, housekeeping, professional massage). Regardless of the service delivery location, interactions between consumers and service providers are commonplace. As a result, the impact of service providers upon the service experience can be dramatic. For example, when asked what irritated them most about service providers, customers have noted seven categories of complaints:[17]

▼ **Apathy:** What comedian George Carlin refers to as DILLIGAD—Do I look like I give a damn?

Figure 9.8   Physical Evidence often Speaks Louder than Words

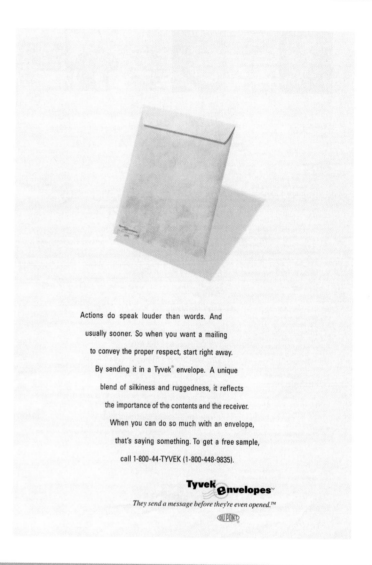

- ▼ **Brush-off:** Attempts to get rid of the customer by dismissing the customer completely . . . the "I want you to go away" syndrome.

- ▼ **Coldness:** Indifferent service providers who could not care less what the customer really wants.

- ▼ **Condescension:** The "you are the client/patient, so you must be stupid" approach.

- ▼ **Robotism:** Where the customers are treated simply as inputs into a system that must be processed.

- ▼ **Rulebook:** Providers who live by the rules of the organization even when those rules do not make good sense. (As this chapter is being written, a young man died in an alleyway outside of a hospital because it was hospital policy not to perform services on anyone who was not physically inside the hospital. A police officer finally carried the young man into the hospital, but it was too late).

▼ **Runaround:** Passing the customer off to another provider, who will simply pass them off to yet another provider.

Other Customers

Other customers can also have a profound impact upon an individual's service experience (Figure 9.9). A wide range of service establishments such as restaurants, hotels, airlines, and physicians' offices serve multiple customers simultaneously. Research has shown that the presence of other customers can enhance or detract from an individual's service experience.[18] The influence of other customers can be active or passive. For instance, examples of other customers actively detracting from one's service experience include unruly customers in a restaurant or a night club, children crying during church service, or patrons carrying on a conversation during a theatrical play. More passive examples would include customers who show up late for appointments, thereby, making each subsequent appointment late for everyone else; an individual who has "big hair" who sits directly in front of another customer at a movie theatre; and being part of a crowd, which as a collective group, increases the waiting time for everyone.

While many of the actions of other customers that enhance or detract from the service experience are difficult to predict or control, service organizations can attempt to manage the behavior of customers so that they may coexist peacefully. Examples include managing

---

Figure 9.9   The Influence of "Other Customers" on the Service Experience

Theater of the Gods

customer waiting times so that customers who arrive earlier than others get first priority, clearly targeting specific age segments to minimize potential conflicts between younger and older generations, and providing separate dining facilities for smoking preferences and child-presence conditions.

The Invisible Organization and Systems

Invisible organization and systems

are the service firm's infrastructure such as rules, regulations, and processes that impact the customer's service experience, but yet are unseen by the customer.

www.ups.com

The invisible component of the service experience, the **invisible organization and systems,** can also have a very profound effect on the consumer's service experience. For example, Jim Kelly, the CEO of UPS, attributes much of the firm's success to the technology the customer seldom sees:

> We have 12 mainframes capable of computing 5 billion bits of information every second. We have 90,000 PCs, 80,000 hand-held computers to record driver deliveries, the nation's largest private cellular network and the world's largest DB-2 database designed for package tracking and other customer shipping information. To give you an idea of how valuable information has become to our company, that database actually has more storage capacity than the repositories of the U.S. Census Bureau.[19]

Indeed, it's often what the customer does not see that makes the difference. UPS handles more than 3 billion packages and 5.5 percent of the United States' GDP annually. Equally impressive is the employment of 338,000 people, a vehicle fleet of more than 157,000 trucks, and an air fleet of more than 500 planes . . . making UPS one the 10 largest airlines in the world![20] The impact of behind-the-scenes technology is not just a significant factor in domestic services as UPS shows in Figure 9.10.

The firm's organization and systems also involve a human component. The behind-the-scenes activities of hiring, training, and rewarding employees is directly related to how well customers are served. Kelly of UPS believes in building trust and teamwork and making employees loyal to the company's mission. UPS spends over $300 million a year on training, paying full-time drivers on average more than $50,000 a year, and surveying its employees for suggestions. The company is virtually 100 percent employee-owned.

UNIQUE DIFFERENCES BETWEEN GOODS AND SERVICES

LEARNING OBJECTIVE LO3

One of the reasons the field of services marketing was slow to grow within the academic community was that many marketing educators felt the marketing of services was not significantly different from the marketing of goods. Markets still needed to be segmented, target markets still needed to be identified, and the marketing mixes that catered to the needs of the firm's intended target market still needed to be developed. However, since those early days, a great deal has been written regarding the specific differences between goods and services and their corresponding marketing implications. The majority of these differences are primarily attributed to four unique characteristics—intangibility, inseparability, heterogeneity, and perishability.[21]

Intangibility

Of the four unique characteristics that distinguish goods from services, *intangibility* is the primary source from which the other three characteristics emerge. As a result of their intangibility, services cannot be seen, felt, tasted, or touched in the same manner that goods can be sensed. For example, compare the differences between purchasing a movie ticket

Figure 9.10   Behind the Scenes Activities Enable UPS to Guarantee On-Time Delivery to Over 200 Countries

and a pair of shoes. The shoes are tangible goods, so the shoes can be objectively evaluated prior to purchase. The customer can pick up the shoes, feel the quality of materials from which they are constructed, view their specific style and color, and actually sample the shoe for comfort and fit. Upon purchasing the pair of shoes, the customer takes the shoes home, and claims the physical possession and ownership of a tangible product.

In comparison, the purchase of a movie ticket buys the customer an experience. Since the "movie experience" is intangible, the movie is subjectively evaluated. For example, prior to purchase, the customer must rely on the judgements of others (e.g., friends, movie critics, etc.) that have previously experienced the service for prepurchase information. Because the information provided by others is based on their own sets of expectations and perceptions, opinions will differ regarding the value of the experience. After the movie is over, the customer returns home with a memory of the experience, and obtains the physical ownership of only a ticket stub. The customer's evaluation of the movie will extend beyond what was seen on the screen, and will include the treatment by service providers, the behavior of other customers, and the condition of the theatre's servicescape.

Inseparability

One of the most intriguing characteristics of the service experience involves the concept of *inseparability.* Inseparability refers to (1) the service provider's physical connection to the service being provided; (2) the customer's involvement in the service production process; and (3) the involvement of other customers in the service production process. Unlike the goods manufacturer, who may seldom see an actual customer while producing the good in a factory, service providers are often in constant contact with their customers, and must construct their service operations with the customer's physical presence in mind. These interactions constitute *critical incidents,* which represent the greatest opportunity for both gains and losses in regard to customer satisfaction and retention. As evidence, a customer recently told the story of his attempt to order a ham and cheese sandwich with mayonnaise from the deli department of a local grocery store. The employee informed him that she could not fulfill his request because the deli was out of mayonnaise—there were dozens of full jars of mayonnaise only two aisles away.

Due to inseparability, employees of service firms need advanced interpersonal skills that allow them to interact with customers more successfully. In addition, since the customer is involved in the service production process and is very aware when the service delivery system fails, employee training is critical. Customers are also keenly aware of when the service delivery system far exceeds common courtesy as shown in Figure 9.11. Companies are wise to seize these opportunities to make a lasting impression. Inseparability also demands that we develop strategies to manage customers so they do not negatively impact one another's service experience. Seating arrangements that separate smokers from nonsmokers and customers with kids from those without are typical examples.

Heterogeneity

Another frequently stressed difference between goods and services is the lack of ability to have total control over service quality before it reaches the consumer. Clearly, the level of service a customer receives often varies from one encounter to the next—even when interacting with the same provider. For example, some McDonald's franchises have helpful and smiling employees, while other franchises employ individuals who act like robots. Not only can this be said for different franchises, but also the same is true within a single franchise on a daily basis because of the mood swings of individuals. Many students who work as wait staff in restaurants readily admit that the quality of interaction between themselves and customers will vary even from table to table.

Unlike goods that are produced by machines, services are primarily produced by individuals, therefore, inconsistency is inevitable. *Heterogeneity* reflects the variability that is inherent in the service delivery process and is a potential problem throughout the service delivery process. For example, service encounters occur in real time—if something goes wrong during the service process, it's generally too late to execute quality control measures before the service reaches the consumer. The waiter who drops a plate of food in a customer's lap creates a service failure that can be neither foreseen nor corrected ahead of time.

Perishability

Perishability also distinguishes goods from services and refers to the trait that services cannot be inventoried. Unlike goods that can be stored and sold at a later date, services that are not sold when they become available cease to exist. For example, hotel rooms that

Figure 9.11   Above and Beyond the Call at Wyndham

go unoccupied for the evening cannot be stored and used at a later date; airline seats that are not sold cannot be inventoried and added on to aircraft during the holiday season when airline seats are scarce; and service providers such as dentists, lawyers, and hairstylists cannot regain the time lost from an empty appointment book.

The inability to inventory creates profound difficulties for marketing services. In a goods manufacturing setting, the ability to create an inventory of the good means that production and consumption of the goods can be separated by time and space. In other words, a good can be produced in one location and transported for sale in another; a good can be produced in January and not released into the channels of distribution until June. Most services, however, are consumed at the point of production.

The existence of inventory also facilitates statistical quality control in goods-producing organizations. A representative sample of the inventory can be easily inspected for variations in quality. In contrast, when you reserve a room at a hotel, you are likely to experience a wide range of factors that may influence your good night's sleep. Finally, the ability to have inventory performs the function of separating the production and marketing departments. In service firms, however, marketing and operations constantly interact with each other and must be in synch to deliver services effectively.

Because of the effects of intangibility, inseparability, heterogeneity, and perishability, marketing plays a very different role in service-oriented organizations than it does in pure goods organizations. This section of the chapter has shown that the different components of the service organization are closely interwoven. The invisible and visible parts of the organization, the contact personnel and the servicescape, the organization and its customers, and, indeed, the customers themselves are all bound together by a complex series of relationships. Consequently, the marketing department must maintain a much closer relationship with the rest of the service organization than is customary in many goods businesses. The concept of operations being responsible for producing the product and marketing being responsible for selling the product cannot work in a service firm.

THE QUEST FOR CUSTOMER SATISFACTION

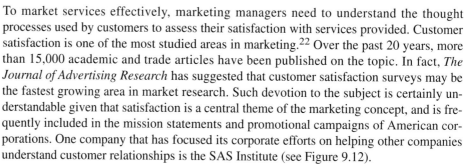

www.asqc.org

To market services effectively, marketing managers need to understand the thought processes used by customers to assess their satisfaction with services provided. Customer satisfaction is one of the most studied areas in marketing.[22] Over the past 20 years, more than 15,000 academic and trade articles have been published on the topic. In fact, *The Journal of Advertising Research* has suggested that customer satisfaction surveys may be the fastest growing area in market research. Such devotion to the subject is certainly understandable given that satisfaction is a central theme of the marketing concept, and is frequently included in the mission statements and promotional campaigns of American corporations. One company that has focused its corporate efforts on helping other companies understand customer relationships is the SAS Institute (see Figure 9.12).

Tracking customer satisfaction in the United States is a highly complex task that has recently been undertaken through the joint efforts of the American Society for Quality Control and the University of Michigan's business school.[23] The two groups have developed the American Customer Satisfaction Index (ACSI), which is based on 3,900 products representing more than two dozen manufacturing and service industries. Companies included in the study are selected based on size and U.S. market share and together represent about 40 percent of the United States's Gross Domestic Product. Government services are also included in the index.

An overview of the best and worst companies included in the ACSI and their satisfaction ratings are presented in Table 9.6. Mercedes-Benz earned top honors, while the IRS brought up the bottom for the fourth straight year in a row (although their performance is improving). McDonald's was the IRS's closest competitor, and American Airlines, who jacked up business fares and stuffed customers into crowded planes, tied with General Public Utilities for the biggest one-year loser award by plummeting 12.7 percent.

Businesses make three common mistakes that lead to lower levels of customer satisfaction. First, many firms continue to view customer service as a cost rather than as an investment. Second, firms tend to forget that customer satisfaction is a constantly rising bar. During the 1980s, automobile consumers demanded technical excellence from manufacturers. Now consumers are looking beyond technical excellence and demanding better ways to purchase and service their vehicles. These are the new battlefields on which fights for future customer satisfaction will be won or lost. The third most common mistake is a firm's inability to link customer satisfaction to its bottom line. Some firms still do not see (or fail to appreciate) the connection.

Perhaps the most disturbing finding of the ACSI results is that the ten companies that are at the top of the list produce goods, while the ten at the bottom, companies such as the Internal Revenue Service, American Airlines, Pizza Hut, and the police, are service organizations. Are service organizations really that bad, or are they evaluated differently than companies that produce goods?

Figure 9.12   SAS Helps Businesses Understand the Revolving Door

Table 9.6   The 1998 Satisfaction Index—Top 10 and Bottom 10

Company or Division	1997 Score	Change from 1996	Company or Division	1997 Score	Change from 1996
1. Mercedes-Benz	87	N.C.	181. Wells Fargo	65	-8.5%
2. H. J. Heinz (food processing)	86	-4.4%	182. Continental Airlines	64	-3.0%
3. Colgate-Palmolive	85	N.C.	183. Northwest Airlines	64	-4.5%
4. H. J. Heinz (pet foods)	85	N.C.	184. Ramada	64	-8.6%
5. Mars	85	-1.2%	185. Pizza Hut	63	-4.5%
6. Maytag	85	2.4%	186. Police	63	6.8%
7. Quaker Oats	85	3.7%	187. American Airlines	62	-12.7%
8. Cadillac	84	-4.5%	188. Unicom	62	-8.8%
9. Hershey Foods	84	-4.5%	189. McDonald's	60	-4.8%
10. Coca-Cola	84	-3.4%	190. Internal Revenue Service	54	8.0%

Source: "Now Are You Satisfied," *Fortune* 137(3), February 16, 1998, pp. 162–164.

In general, products (goods and services) possess three different types of attributes:[24]

▼ **Search attributes**—attributes that can be determined prior to purchase, such as price, fit, feel, color, etc.

▼ **Experience attributes**—attributes that can be evaluated only during and after the production process, such as a meal at a restaurant, the quality of a haircut, etc.

▼ **Credence attributes**—attributes that cannot be evaluated confidently even immediately after receipt of the product, such as guidance from your minister or your financial advisor's retirement investment advice.

Because of the intangible nature of services, it is often difficult for customers to objectively evaluate a service before it is bought. Services thus have very few search attributes. In contrast, goods can be touched, seen, smelled, heard, and in some cases, tasted prior to purchase, and are therefore predominantly characterized by search attributes.

A large proportion of properties possessed by services (e.g., the friendliness of a flight attendant, or the skill level of a landscape designer) can be discovered only during and after the consumption of the service; these are experience attributes. Other properties of services (e.g., how well a car has been repaired by a body shop or how well your doctor performs services) cannot be assessed even after the service is completed, because customers lack the technical or specialized expertise to evaluate these services. These are called credence attributes. As a result, due to the properties of intangibility, inseparability, and the variation in quality provided by service personnel, customer satisfaction tends to be evaluated based on experience and credence attributes. Hence, services are *indeed* evaluated differently than goods, and based on the ACSI statistics, customers *do notice* when the service delivery system has gone awry.

What Is Customer Satisfaction?

Expectancy disconfirmation approach

is an approach that measures customer satisfaction by comparing expectations to perceptions.

The simplest and most powerful method to measure customer satisfaction is the **expectancy disconfirmation approach.**[25] The approach is straightforward. If the perceived service is better than or equal to the expected service, then consumers are satisfied.

Ultimately customer service is achieved through the effective management of customer perceptions and expectations—customer satisfaction can be increased by lowering expectations or by enhancing perceptions. It is crucial to point out that this entire process of comparing expectations to perceptions takes place in the minds of customers. Hence, it is the perceived service that matters, not the actual service. One of the best examples that reinforces this concept involves a high-rise hotel. The hotel was receiving numerous complaints concerning the time guests had to wait for elevator service in the lobby. Realizing that from an operational viewpoint, the speed of the elevators could not be increased, and that attempting to schedule the guest's elevator usage was futile, the hotel's management installed mirrors in the lobby next to the elevator bays. Guest complaints were reduced immediately—the mirrors provided a means for the guest to occupy their waiting time. Guest were observed using the mirror to observe their own appearance and that of others around them. In reality, the speed of the elevators had not changed; however, the customer's perception of time had changed.

It is also feasible to manage expectations in order to produce satisfaction without altering in any way the quality of the actual service delivered. Motel 6, for example, by downplaying its service offering in its cleverly contrived advertising, actually increases consumer satisfaction by lowering customer expectations prior to purchase. The firm's advertising informs consumers of both what to expect and what not to expect: "A good clean room for $19.99 . . . a little more in some places . . . a little less is some others . . . and remember . . . we'll leave the light on for you." Many customers simply do not use services

www.motel6.com

such as swimming pools, health clubs, and full-service restaurants that are associated with higher-priced hotels. Economy-minded hotels, such as Motel 6, are carving out a niche in the market by providing the basics. The result is that customers know exactly what they will get ahead of time and are happy not only with the quality of the service received but also with the cost savings.

The Importance of Customer Satisfaction

The importance of customer satisfaction cannot be overstated. Without customers, the service firm has no reason to exist. Every service business needs to proactively define and measure customer satisfaction. Waiting for customers to complain in order to identify problems in the service delivery system, or gauging the firm's progress in achieving customer satisfaction based on the number of complaints received, is naïve. Consider the following findings gathered by the Technical Assistance Research Program (TARP):[26]

▼ The average business does not hear from 96 percent of its unhappy customers.

▼ For every complaint received, 26 other customers actually have the same problem.

▼ The average person with a problem tells 9 or 10 people. Thirteen percent of disatisfied customers tell more than 20 people.

▼ Customers who have their complaints satisfactorily resolved tell an average of 5 people about the treatment they received.

▼ Complainers are more likely to do business with you again than noncomplainers; 54–70 percent if their problem was resolved at all, and 95 percent if it was handled quickly.

The TARP figures demonstrate that customers do not actively complain to the source of the failure. Instead, consumers voice their dissatisfaction with their feet, by defecting to competitors, and with their mouths, by telling existing and potential future customers exactly how they were mistreated by the offending firm. The impact of dissatisfied customers on future business operations is astounding! Based on the figures, a firm that serves 100 customers per week, and boasts a 90 percent customer satisfaction rating, will be the object of thousands of negative stories by the end of the year. For example, if 10 dissatisfied customers per week tell 10 of their friends of the poor service received, by the end of the year (52 weeks), 5,200 negative word-of-mouth communications have been generated.

The TARP figures are not all bad news. Firms that effectively respond to customer complaints are the objects of positive word-of-mouth communications. Although positive news travels at half the rate of negative news, the positive stories can ultimately translate into customer loyalty and new customers. Businesses should also learn from the TARP figures that complainers are the firm's friends. Complainers are a free source of market information, and the complaints themselves should be viewed as opportunities for the firm to improve its delivery systems, not as a source of irritation. As evidence, the International Customer Service Association found that of customers who had experienced a problem and complained, 54 percent continued to do business with the firm on a long-term basis. In comparison, only 9 percent of customers who experienced problems and did not complain continued to do business with the offending firm.[27] Remember, less than 5 percent of consumers with problems actually complain to companies.[28]

www.icsa.com

The Benefits of Customer Satisfaction

Although some may argue that customers are unreasonable at times (Figure 9.13), little evidence can be found of extravagant consumer expectations.[29] Consequently, satisfying

Figure 9.13	**Is It Always Worthwhile to Keep a Customer?**

Although saving every customer at any cost is a controversial topic and opinions are divided, some experts believe that the customer is no longer worth saving under the following conditions:

▼ The account is no longer profitable.

▼ Conditions specified in the sales contract are no longer being met.

▼ Customers are abusive to the point that it lowers employee morale.

▼ Customer demands are beyond reasonable, and fulfilling those demands would result in poor service for the remaining customer base.

▼ The customer's reputation is so poor that associating with the customer tarnishes the image and reputation of the selling firm.

consumers is not an impossible task. In fact, meeting and exceeding customer expectations may reap several valuable benefits for the firm. Positive word-of-mouth generated from existing customers often translates into more new customers. In addition, satisfied customers often purchase products more frequently and are less likely to be lost to competitors than are dissatisfied customers.

Companies who command high customer satisfaction ratings also seem to have the ability to insulate themselves from competitive pressures—particularly price competition. Customers are often willing to pay more and stay with a firm that meets their needs than to take the risk associated with moving to a lower-priced service offering. Finally, firms that pride themselves on their customer satisfaction efforts generally provide better environments in which to work, and therefore have increased their chances to attract the best and brightest employees. Within these positive work environments, organizational cultures develop where employees are challenged to perform, and rewarded for their efforts. Some companies even use their positive work environments to encourage employee applications (see Figure 9.14). Microsoft, for example, is known for providing a remarkably challenging atmosphere for the "brainy." "Everybody gets stock options, and most professionals hired before 1992 have thus become millionaires, six became billionaires."[30]

In and of themselves, customer satisfaction surveys also provide several worthwhile benefits. Such surveys provide a formal means of customer feedback to the firm, which may identify existing and potential problems. Satisfaction surveys also convey the message to customers that the firm cares about their well-being and values customer input concerning its service delivery process.

Other benefits are directly derived from the results of the satisfaction surveys. Satisfaction results are often utilized in evaluating employee performance for merit and compensation reviews and for sales management purposes, such as the development of sales training programs. Survey results are also useful for comparison purposes to determine how the firm stacks up against the competition. When ratings are favorable, many firms utilize the results in their corporate advertising as in Figure 9.15.

LOOKING TO THE FUTURE: SERVICE QUALITY

Without a doubt, the two concepts of customer satisfaction and service quality are intertwined.[31] Most experts agree that ***customer satisfaction*** is a short-term, transaction-specific measure, whereas ***service quality*** is an attitude formed by a long-term overall evaluation of performance. For example, customer satisfaction evaluations occur after each bank transaction—every time a customer cashes a check. In contrast, service qual-

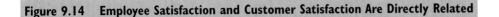

Figure 9.14   Employee Satisfaction and Customer Satisfaction Are Directly Related

ity evaluations are not transaction specific, but reflect an overall impression of all the interactions.

In comparison to a goods manufacturing environment, many difficulties are inherent in implementing and evaluating service quality. In the first place, perceptions of quality tend to rely on a repeated comparison of the customer's expectation about a particular service. If a service, no matter how good, fails to meet a particular customer's expectations, the customer will perceive the service to be of poor quality. Second, unlike goods marketing, where customers evaluate the finished product alone, customers evaluate the service delivery process as well as the final outcome. A customer visiting a hairdresser, for example, will evaluate service not only on the basis of whether he or she likes the haircut, but also on whether the hairdresser was friendly, competent, and well groomed, and whether the tangible components of the servicescape met with the customer's needs.

Service quality offers a way of achieving success among competing services. Particularly, where a small number of firms that offer nearly identical services are competing within a small area, such as banks may do, establishing service quality may be the only

Figure 9.15	Customer Satisfaction Ratings Can Be a Powerful Marketing Tool in Corporate Ad Campaigns

way of differentiating oneself. Service quality differentiation can generate increased market share and ultimately mean the difference between financial success and failure. Firms that excel in delivery service quality do so by concentrating their efforts on five service quality dimensions: tangibles, reliability, responsivness, assurance, and empathy.[32]

The Tangibles Dimension

Because of the absence of a physical product, consumers often rely on the tangible evidence that surrounds the service in forming evaluations. A firm's tangibles consist of a wide variety of objects, such as those that exist within the servicescape, and the appearance of the firm's personnel. Consequently, the ***tangibles dimension*** is two dimensional—one dimension focusing on equipment and facilities, the other focusing on personnel and communications materials. Typical questions pertaining to the tangibles dimension include:

▼ Does the firm have modern looking equipment?

▼ Are the firm's physical facilities visually appealing?

▼ Are employees neat in appearance?

▼ Are the materials associated with the service (such as pamphlets and billing statements) visually appealing? Do customers understand the materials?

The Reliability Dimension

In general, the *reliability dimension* reflects the consistency and dependability of a firm's performance. Does the firm provide the same level of service time after time, or does quality dramatically differ with each encounter? Does the firm keep its promises, bill its customers accurately, keep accurate records, and perform the service correctly the first time? Consumers perceive the reliability dimension to be the most important of the five service quality dimensions and includes such issues as:

▼ When the firm promises to do something, it follows through on that promise.

▼ When customers have problems, employees show a sincere interest in solving them.

▼ Does the firm provide the service right the first time?

▼ Does the firm provide the service at the time it promises to do so?

▼ Are the company's records error-free?

The Responsiveness Dimension

The *responsiveness dimension* reflects the firm's commitment to provide services in a timely manner. As such, the responsiveness dimension reflects the willingness and/or readiness of employees to provide service. Occasionally, customers may encounter a situation in which employees are engaged in their own conversations with one another while ignoring the needs of the customer. Obviously, this is an example of unresponsiveness. Examples of responsiveness include:

▼ Telling customers exactly when services will be performed.

▼ Providing prompt service to customers.

▼ Always being willing to help customers.

▼ Willing to help, even under very busy circumstances.

The Assurance Dimension

The *assurance dimension* of service quality addresses the competence of the firm, the courtesy extended to its customers, and the security of its operations. Competence pertains to the firm's knowledge and skill in performing its service. Courtesy reflects politeness, friendliness, and consideration for the customer's property (e.g., a mechanic who places paper floor mats in a customer's car so as to not soil the car's carpet). In addition to physical danger, the security component of the assurance dimension also reflects financial risk issues (e.g., will my bank fail?) and confidentiality issues (e.g., are my medical records at the school's health center kept private?). Typical assurance dimension issues include:

▼ The behavior of the firm's employees instills confidence in its customers.

▼ Customers feel safe when purchasing from this firm.

▼ Employees are consistently courteous to customers.

▼ The firm's employees have the knowledge to answer customer questions.

The Empathy Dimension

The **empathy dimension** is the ability to experience another's feelings as one's own. Empathetic firms have not lost touch of what it is like to be a customer of their own firm. As such, empathetic firms understand their customer needs and make their services accessible to their customers. In contrast, firms that do not provide their customers individualized attention when requested and that offer operating hours convenient to the firms and not its customers fail to demonstrate empathetic behaviors. Service firms that are empathetic are described as:

▼ Providing customers with individual attention.

▼ Offering operating hours that are convenient to all customers.

▼ Hiring employees who provide customers personal attention.

▼ Operating on a daily basis with the customer's best interest at heart.

▼ Understanding customer's basic needs.

CUSTOMER RETENTION STRATEGIES

Ample evidence suggests that the provision of service quality can deliver repeat purchases as well as new customers.[33] Thus far, the majority of this chapter has focused on the marketing of intangibles. However, there is another aspect of service worth discussing—customer service. **Customer service** refers to the servicing of customers of products, whether the products are services or goods. When lacking, customer service is a sore spot for most of the worlds' customers. When effective, customer service is a primary means of competitive advantage in not only attracting new customers but also and perhaps more importantly in stagnant markets, retaining the firm's existing customers.

The value of retaining existing customers is critical in these days of saturated markets and rising marketing costs. In fact, some experts believe that customer retention has a more powerful effect on profits than market share, economies of scale, and other variables commonly associated with competitive advantage. Studies have indicated that as much as 95 percent of profits come from long-term customers via profits derived from sales, referrals, and reduced operating costs.

Simply stated, **customer retention** refers to focusing the firm's marketing efforts toward the existing customer base. Customer retention is the opposite of **conquest marketing,** which focuses on discounts and markdowns and developing new promotional campaigns that will attract new customers from competitive firms. Two-thirds of customers who defect to competitors do so because they feel that companies are not genuinely concerned for their well-being. In contrast to conquest marketing, firms engaged in customer retention efforts work to satisfy existing customers with the intent of developing long-term relationships between the firm and its current clientele.

Because of the lack of consistent customer service that customers often experience, firms that effectively communicate customer retention as a primary goal are noticed. Consequently, a firm's customer retention efforts should serve to successfully differentiate the firm from its competitors. Methods for retaining customers through the use of effective customer service strategies include maintaining the proper perspective, remembering customers between sales, building trusting relationships, monitoring the service delivery process, focusing on proper installation and training, standing behind the product, providing discretionary effort, and offering service guarantees.

Maintain the Proper Perspective

Managers and employees need to remember that the company exists to meet the needs and wants of its customers. Processing customers like raw materials on an assembly line, or being rude to customers, is incredibly short-sighted. Companies such as U.S. Airways employ slogans such as, "The U in U.S. Air starts with U the passenger." Credos such as this influence customer expectations and reinforce the message to employees exactly where the firm's priorities lie.

Interacting with the public is not an easy task, and, unfortunately, employees occasionally fail to maintain the proper perspective. Different customers may ask the same questions of employees over and over, and not every customer is polite. Maintaining the proper perspective involves a customer-oriented frame of mind and an attitude for service. Employees need to remember that every customer has his or her own personal set of needs, and that the customer's, not the employee's, expectations define performance.

www.usair.com

Remember Customers Between Sales

Contacting customers between sales transactions is a useful approach in building relationships with the firm. The key is in making customer contact sincere and personal. Typical approaches include sending birthday, get-well, and/or anniversary cards; writing personal notes congratulating customers for their personal successes; and keeping in touch with customers concerning past services rendered and offering assistance if necessary. The goal of this tactic is to communicate to customers that the firm genuinely cares for their well-being and values the ongoing relationship.

Build Trusting Relationships

Trust is defined as a firm belief or confidence in the honesty, integrity, and the reliability of another person. In the service environment, three major components of trust are: (1) the service provider's expertise; (2) the service provider's reliability; and (3) the service provider's concern for the customer. Strategies for building trust include:

▼ Protecting confidential information.

▼ Refraining from making disparaging remarks about other customers and competitors.

▼ Telling the customer the truth, even when it hurts.

▼ Providing the customer with full information—the pros and the cons.

▼ Being dependable, courteous, and considerate with customers.

▼ Becoming actively involved in community affairs.

Monitor the Service Delivery Process

After the customer has requested a specific service, monitoring the service delivery process should be a key tactic in the firm's customer retention efforts. Service providers that are able to monitor the service delivery process are able to correct service inadequacies and influence customer perceptions of service quality prior to completion. Obvious examples would involve a restaurant that regularly communicates with its customers throughout their meal, or the owner of the firm who contacts customers about recent purchases. Proactively seeking customer feedback throughout the process builds customer perceptions of trust and facilitates maintaining customers for life.

Focus on Proper Installation and Training

Proper installation of products, and training customers how to use what they have purchased, saves a lot of headaches. Customers should not have to become frustrated over not understanding how to use something or, worse, improperly using the product, which may result in damage and further dissatisfaction. Simply dropping off the product and leaving customers to fend for themselves reinforces the idea that the company is not genuinely concerned for the customer's well-being. It leaves the impression that the company is more interested in short-term profits than in building long-term relationships.

Be There When You Are Needed Most

When a customer returns a product that is in need of service or repair, this is not the time to hide! Every firm should stand behind what it sells, and ensure that every transaction is handled to the customer's satisfaction. Most customers are realistic and understand that nothing lasts forever. Many times customers are simply looking for advice and alternative solutions to problems, and are not looking for someone to blame. Expressing a sincere concern for the customer's situation reinforces the firm's customer retention efforts.

Provide Discretionary Effort

Discretionary effort is behavior beyond the call of duty. It is the Procter & Gamble salesperson who voluntarily bags groceries at the grand opening of a new grocery store. It is the hotel that sends items misplaced by customers to their homes at no charge. It is the oil company that recognizes the special needs of its customers during weather-related disasters. Discretionary effort involves countless personal touches, little things that distinguish a one-time business transaction from an ongoing relationship.

Offer Service Guarantees

One of the most intriguing customer retention strategies to be developed in recent years is the service guarantee.[34] Service guarantees appear to facilitate three worthwhile goals: (1) reinforce customer loyalty; (2) build market share; and (3) force the firm offering the guarantee to improve its overall service quality. The Hampton Inn offers an unconditional guarantee to its customers. "The policy states that any guest who has a problem and is not satisfied by the end of the stay will receive one night's stay at no charge." The guarantee is paid out when the guest settles his account and is not a voucher for a future stay. The impact of the guarantee has been overwhelmingly positive. Employees took notice and re-

www.hamptoninn.com

sponsibility for correcting potential service problems. Moreover, quality standards in the hotel have noticeably changed. During the guarantee's first two years, 7,000 guests representing $350,000 in sales had invoked the guarantee. Of these 7,000 guests, 86 percent said they will return to Hampton Inn, and 45 percent have already done so.

In general, successful guarantees are unrestrictive, stated in specific and clear terms, meaningful and hassle-free when invoked, and quick to be paid out. On the other hand, mistakes to avoid when constructing a guarantee include: (1) promising something that is trivial and normally expected; (2) specifying an inordinate number of conditions as part of the guarantee, and (3) making the guarantee so mild that it is never invoked.

Chapter Summary

In order to provide service excellence, every individual and every department within the business must act in unison to create a *"seamless service"* organization. Creating a seamless organization means providing services without interruption, confusion, or hassle to the customer.[35] Seamless firms manage to simultaneously provide reliable, responsive, competent, and empathetic services, and have the facilities and resources necessary to get the job done. Seamlessness thrives on tightly connected, interrelated parts within the service delivery system. Functionalization and departmentalization kills seamlessness.

Businesses that continue to embrace the industrial management model and cling to functional and departmental mindsets are often besieged by internal conflict as departments compete against one another for resources instead of pulling together to provide exceptional service. Seamlessness is "tooth-to-tail" performance—a term commonly used in the armed forces. The personnel out front in the trenches need to be backed up with coordinated supplies, information resources, personnel reinforcements, and so on. Similarly, the focus of service businesses should be on the service delivery process and the personnel providing customer services. It is the front-line personnel who are the public faces of firm, and it is on the performance of these personnel that customers often solely base their service quality evaluations of the entire firm.

This chapter has focused on the marketing of services. The recent demand for services marketing knowledge has been fueled by increases in service sector employment, the economic impact of the service sector, the deregulation of many service industries, the use of service as a differential advantage, and the differences in managerial philosophy that are needed to lead service operations.

Service consumers purchase a bundle of benefits that are provided by the service experience that is created for consumers. The four primary factors that influence the customer's service experience include service providers, the servicescape, other customers, and the invisible organization and systems.

The major differences between the marketing of goods and services are often attributed to four unique service characteristics: intangibility, inseparability, heterogeneity, and perishability. Of the four unique characteristics that distinguish goods from services, intangibility is the primary source from which the other three characteristics emerge.

A goal for all marketers is to strive for customer satisfaction. Customers typically assess satisfaction by comparing expectations to perceptions. If perceptions meet or exceed expectations, then customers are satisfied. When evaluating services, customers generally evaluate services based on credence and experience attributes, whereas, goods are primarily dominated by search attributes.

Directly related to customer satisfaction is the concept of service quality. Service quality is assessed by the firm's performance on five service quality dimensions: tangibles, reliability, responsiveness, assurance, and empathy. Research has consistently shown that customers place the greatest importance on the reliability dimension.

Ultimately, a primary means for a firm to differentiate itself from competitors is through customer service. Firms that excel at customer service maintain a proper perspective, remember customers between sales transactions, build trusting relationships with customers, monitor the service delivery process, ensure proper product installation and train customers how to use products that they have purchased. Customer service-oriented firms also are available when needed most, provide discretionary effort to assist customers, and may offer service guarantees.

Key Terms

Invisible organization and systems are the service firm's infrastructure such as rules, regulations, and processes that impact the customer's service experience, but yet are unseen by the customer.

Expectancy disconfirmation approach is an approach that measures customer satisfaction by comparing expectations to perceptions.

Additional Key Terms and Concepts

Services	Goods
Scale of market entities	Tangible dominant
Intangible dominant	Industrial management approach
Market-focused management approach	Benefit concept
Servicescape	Service providers
Other customers	Intangibility
Inseparability	Critical incidents
Heterogeneity	Perishability
Customer satisfaction	Service quality
Tangibles dimension	Reliability dimension
Responsiveness dimension	Assurance dimension
Empathy dimension	Customer service
Customer retention	Conquest marketing
Trust	Seamless service

Questions for Discussion

1. Briefly describe the five major reasons services marketing knowledge has become more important to understand in today's business environment.

2. Discuss the differences between the industrial management approach and the market-focused management approach.

3. What is to be learned from the Scale of Market Entities?

4. Define the concepts of intangibility, inseparability, heterogeneity, and perishability.

5. Discuss the factors that influence the service experience. Why is the service experience particularly important for the marketing of intangibles?

6. Define customer satisfaction. How can satisfaction be managed by altering consumer perceptions and expectations? Do consumer perceptions and expectations necessarily reflect reality?

7. What lessons can be learned by the findings reported by the Technical Assistance Research program (TARP)?

8. Discuss how service quality differs from customer satisfaction. Of the five dimensions of service quality, which dimension do customers believe is most important? Why do you think this is so?

9. Discuss the differences between conquest marketing and customer retention.

Internet Questions

1. Visit the Disney home page at www.Disney.com.
 a. What are the components of this Web page? What do you think are the underlying motivations to include these components?
 b. Activate the Disney Careers section. Based on the information provided in the "Events and Auditions" section, compare and contrast the job requirements of a specific job listed to that of a factory worker in a goods manufacturing setting.
 c. The chapter discusses four factors that influence customers' service experiences. Do these same four factors apply to your experience with Web pages? Please explain.

2. Investigate Imagine Radio at www.imagineradio.com.
 a. Is Imagine Radio a form of mass customization? Please explain.
 b. Customize your own radio station. What suggestions would you make for improving the Web site?
 c. From a business standpoint, what's the rationale for offering the Web site? As a radio station, why would you want to be included on the site?

3. Investigate www.mysimon.com.
 a. Discuss the purpose of this Web site. What service does it offer the customer?
 b. How do the sponsors of the Web site make their money?
 c. When would it make sense for a company to sign-up and be listed on the Web site? Under what conditions would it not make much sense? Would these same reasons hold true for customers using the Web site? Please explain.

Endnotes

[1]Jim Kelly, "From Lip Service to Real Service: Reversing America's Downward Service Spiral," *Vital Speeches of the Day* 64(10) 1998, pp. 301–304.

[2]"The Final Frontier," *The Economist* (February 20, 1993), p. 63.

[3]K. Douglas Hoffman and John E. G. Bateson, *Essentials of Services Marketing* (Fort Worth: The Dryden Press, 1997), pp. 4–5.

[4]Geoffrey Brewer, "Selling an Intangible," *Sales & Marketing Management* 150(1) (January 19, 1998), p. 52.

[5]This section adopted from Hoffman and Bateson, *Essentials of Services Marketing* (Fort Worth: The Dryden Press, 1997), p. 6; and G. Lynn Shostack, "Breaking Free from Product Marketing," *Journal of Marketing* (April 1977), p. 77.

[6]"The Final Frontier," *The Economist* (February 20, 1993), p. 63.

[7]Much of this section and the next were adopted from Hoffman and Bateson, *Essentials of Services Marketing* (Fort Worth: The Dryden Press, 1997), pp. 11–13.

[8]Ibid.

[9]Brewer, "Selling an Intangible," pp. 52–58.

[10]Hoffman and Bateson, *Essentials of Services Marketing,* pp. 14–17.

[11]Leonard A. Schlesinger and James L. Heskett, "The Service-Driven Service Company," *Harvard Business Review* (September–October 1991), p. 74.

[12]Ibid., p. 77.

[13]Ibid., p. 76.

[14]This section adopted from Hoffman and Bateson, *Essentials of Services Marketing* (Fort Worth: The Dryden Press, 1997), pp. 7–11; and E. Langeard, J. Bateson, C. Lovelock, and P. Eigler, *Marketing of Services: New Insights from Consumers and Managers,* Report No. 81-104 (Cambridge, MA: Marketing Science Institute, 1981).

[15]Mary Jo Bitner, "Servicescapes: The Impact of Physical Surroundings on Customers and Employees," *Journal of Marketing* 56(2) (April 1992), pp. 57–71.

[16]For more information see Hoffman and Bateson, *Essentials of Services Marketing* pp. 235–250.

[17]Ron Zemke and Kristen Anderson, "Customers from Hell," *Training* (February 1990), pp. 25–29.

[18]Stephen J. Grove and Raymond P. Fisk, "The Impact of Other Customers on Service Experiences: A Critical Incident Examination of 'Getting Along'," *Journal of Retailing* 73(1) (1997), pp. 63–85.

[19]Kelly, "From Lip Service to Real Service: Reversing America's Downward Service Spiral," p. 302.

[20]John Alden, "What in the World Drives UPS?" *International Business,* 11(2) (March/April 1998), pp. 6–7+.

[21]This section adopted from Hoffman and Bateson, *Essentials of Services Marketing* (Fort Worth: The Dryden Press, 1997), pp. 22–45; and Valerie A. Zeithaml, A. Parasuraman, and Leonard L. Berry, "Problems and Strategies in Services Marketing," *Journal of Marketing* 49 (Spring 1985), pp. 33–46.

[22]This section adopted from Hoffman and Bateson, *Essentials of Services Marketing,* pp. 266–294.

[23]*Fortune* (February 16, 1998), pp. 161–170.

[24]Adapted from John E. G. Bateson, *Managing Services Marketing, Text and Readings,* Second Edition, (Fort Worth: The Dryden Press, 1992).

[25]Keith Hunt, "Customer Satisfaction, Dissatisfaction, and Complaining Behavior," *Journal of Social Issues* 47(1) (1991), pp. 109–110.

[26]Karl Albrecht and Ron Zemke, *Service America! Doing Business in the New Economy* (Homewood, IL: Business One Irwin, 1985), p. 6.

[27]Bob Romano and Barbara Sanfilippo, "A Total Approach: Measure Sales and Service," *Texas Banking* 85(8) (1996), pp. 16–17.

[28]Michael Levy and Barton A. Weitz, *Retail Management* (Homewood, IL: Irwin, 1995), p. 506

[29]Leonard L. Berry, A. Parasuraman, and Valerie A. Zeithaml, "Improving Service Quality in America: Lessons Learned," *Academy of Management Executive* 8(2) (1994), p. 36.

[30]Robert Levering and Milton Moskowitz, "The 100 Best Companies to Work For in America," *Fortune* 137(1) (January 12, 1998), p. 84

[31]This section adopted from Hoffman and Bateson, *Essentials of Services Marketing,* pp. 295–321.

[32]A. Parasuraman, Valerie A. Zeithaml, and Leonard L. Berry, "A Conceptual Model of Service Quality and Its Implications for Future Research," *Journal of Marketing* 49 (Fall 1985), pp. 41–50.

[33]This section adopted from Hoffman and Bateson, *Essentials of Services Marketing,* pp. 352–378.

[34]Adapted from Christopher W. L. Hart , Leonard A. Schlesinger, and Don Maher, "Guarantees Come to Professional Service Firms," *Sloan Management Review* (Spring 1992), pp. 19–29.

[35]Benjamin Schneider and David E. Bowen, *Winning the Service Game* (Boston, MA: Harvard Business School Press, 1995), pp. 254–259.

Is This Any Way to Run an Airline?

The following letters are detailed accounts of an actual service encounter and the company's response to the service failures.

July 23, 200X

Dear Customer Service Manager:

Through the Carolina Motor Club, my wife and I booked round-trip first-class and clipper-class seats on the following World Airlines flights on the dates indicated:

> 1 July World Airlines 3072 Charlotte to Kennedy
> 1 July World Airlines 86 Kennedy to Munich
> 21 July World Airlines 87 Munich to Kennedy
> 21 July World Airlines 3073 Kennedy to Charlotte

We additionally booked connecting flights to and from Wilmington and Charlotte on Trans Air flights 263 (on 1 July) and 2208 (on 21 July).

The outbound flights 3072 and 86 seemed pleasant enough, especially since World Airlines had upgraded our clipper class seats on flight 86 to first-class. However, mid-flight on 86 we discovered that we had been food poisoned on flight 3072, apparently by the seafood salad that was served in first-class that day (it seemed warm to us and we hesitated to eat it, but unfortunately did so anyway). My wife was so ill that, trying to get to the restroom to throw up, she passed out cold, hitting her head, and (we discovered a few days later) apparently damaging her back. The flight attendants were very concerned and immediately tried to help her, but there was nothing they could do except help her clean herself up and get the food off her from the food trays she hit. In addition to the nausea and diarrhea, she had a large knot on her head and headaches for several days. Her lower back has been in constant pain ever since. I, too, was very ill for several days. A nice start for a vacation! But it gets worse.

During the long layover between flights at Kennedy, there was a tremendous rainstorm, and our baggage apparently was left out in it—a situation that we discovered when we arrived at our first night's lodging and discovered ALL of our clothing was literally wringing wet. In addition, four art prints we were bringing as gifts for friends were ruined.

The return flights were better only in that we did not get poisoned; instead we did not get fed! Flight 87 out of Munich was apparently short-handed and due to our seating location, the flight attendant who had to do double duty always got to us last. We had to ask for drinks, there were no hot towels left for us, the meals ran out, and we were given no choice but an overdone piece of gray meat with tomato sauce on it—we tasted it, but it was odd tasting and given our experience on flight 3072, we were afraid to eat it.

Flight 87 was delayed in boarding due to the slowness in cleaning the aircraft (according to an announcement made) and also due to the late arrival of the crew. In addition, the flight was further delayed due to a heavy rainstorm, which backed up traffic for takeoff. However, had the flight boarded on time, it would have not lost its takeoff priority and could likely have taken off two hours sooner than it did. We might have been able to make our connection in Charlotte. On board the flight, the plane was the dirtiest and in the most disrepair of any aircraft I have ever flown on—pealing wall coverings, litter on the floor, overhead bins taped shut with duct tape, etc. As a first-class passenger, I asked for some cold beer while we were waiting for the rest of the passengers to board; it was warm. We were quite hungry having not eaten much in the past 12 hours and asked for some peanuts; there were none; the plane had not been stocked. I asked for a pillow and blanket for my wife; there was none. What a great first-class section! There were only three flight attendants for the whole plane, and I felt sorry for the pregnant one who had to do double duty in first-class and the rear cabin. She was very sympathetic to the poor conditions; I don't see how you keep employees when they are treated like that.

Due to the excess delay at Kennedy, flight 87 was very late and we could not make our connection from Charlotte to Wilmington. As it turned out, we would have barely been able to make it if the flight had been on time because World Airlines had changed not only the flight numbers, but also the flight times on the Kennedy–Charlotte leg of our journey—AND WE WERE NEVER NOTIFIED OF THIS CHANGE UNTIL WE ARRIVED AT THE AIRPORT!

I deplaned in Raleigh to try to alert the people meeting us in Wilmington that we would not be in that night; however, it was too late and they had already gone to the airport. The gate attendant at Raleigh assured me that World Airlines would put us up for the night in Charlotte, so I returned to the plane. However, when we arrived in Charlotte, the World Airlines representative refused to take care of us, stating that since we had not booked the Wilmington–Charlotte portion of our trip through World Airlines, "it is not our problem." Furthermore, he tried to wash his hands of it saying we had an "illegal connection" due to the times between flights and that he wouldn't provide lodging and meals. After I pointed out to him at least three times that the connection was not illegal when booked, and World Airlines changed its flight times without notifying us, and further made it clear that not only was I not going to go away, but that there was going to be a lot more said about the matter, he finally capitulated and gave us a voucher.

After traveling for 24 hours, receiving lousy service, poor food, no amenities, it is a real pleasure to run into an argumentative SOB like your agent in Charlotte. He should be fired!!! As first-class passengers, we have been treated like cattle! But, it does not end here.

Upon arriving in Wilmington the next morning, only two of our four bags arrived with us. We had to initiate a baggage trace action. Our missing bags were finally delivered to our house around 3 P.M. on 23 July. And SURPRISE, they were left out in the rain at Kennedy again, and EVERYTHING was so wet that water poured out of the pockets. I poured water out of the hair dryer. All of our paper purchases—maps, guide books, photos, souvenir brochures, etc.—are ruined. I don't know yet if the dryer, radio, electric toothbrush, voltage converters, etc., will work—they are drying out as this is being written. In addition, my brand new bag now has a hole in the bottom of a corner where it was obvious that World Airline baggage handlers dragged it on the tarmac (obviously a water logged duffel bag size piece of luggage is too heavy to lift).

As near as I can figure, we have lost at least a roll of color prints (irreplaceable); approximately $100 in travel guides and tour books, many souvenir booklets, brochures, menus, etc.; $100 in art prints; $50 in damage to luggage; an unknown amount in electronics that may not work; a lot of enjoyment due to pain and suffering resulting from illness and injury (bill for x-rays enclosed); and all sense of humor and patience for such inexcusable treatment by an airline.

If there is to be any compensation for what we have suffered it should be in monetary form. There is no recapturing the lost time and pleasure on the vacation. The art, books, etc., (except for the photos), can be replaced . . . assuming we should make such a trip again. But if we do, you can be assured we would not choose World Airlines.

In closing, I am particularly angry and adamant about this whole fiasco as we wanted this vacation to be special and treated ourselves to the luxury of first-class treatment . . .

which we got everywhere except on World Airlines . . . it is almost unbelievable how poorly we were treated by your airline, almost a perfect negative case study in customer service. I have purposely tried to mention every little nitpicky thing I can recall, because I want you to realize just how totally bad this whole experience has been!

In disgust,

J. Q. Customer

World Airlines' Recovery Strategy

The following are World Airlines' actual responses, which took place nearly two and three months following the customer's letter. The first letter was written by the Claims Manager, and the second letter by the Customer Relations Manager.

September 25, 199x

Dear Mr. and Mrs. Customer:

This letter confirms the settlement agreed upon during our phone conversation just concluded.

Accordingly, we have prepared and enclosed (in duplicate) a General Release for $2,000. Both you and your wife should sign in the presence of a Notary Public, have your signatures notarized, and return the Original to this office, keeping the copy for your records.

As soon as we receive the notarized Release, we will forward our draft for $2000.

Again, our sincerest apologies to Mrs. Customer. It will be most helpful for our Customer Relations staff if you included with the Release, copies of all available travel documents.

Very truly yours,

Manager–Claims
World Airlines

October 12, 199x

Dear Mr. Customer:

Let me begin by apologizing for this delayed response and all of the unfortunate incidents that you described in your letter. Although we try to make our flights as enjoyable as possible, we obviously failed on this occasion.

Our claims manager informs me that you have worked out a potential settlement for the matter regarding the food poisoning. We regret you were not able to enjoy the food service on the other flights on your itinerary because of it. I assure you that such incidents are a rare occurrence and that much time and effort is expended to ensure that our catering is of the finest quality.

Fewer things can be more irritating than faulty baggage handling. Only in an ideal world could we say that baggage will never again be damaged. Still, we are striving to ensure baggage is handled in such a way that if damage should occur, it will be minimized.

Flight disruptions caused by weather conditions can be particularly frustrating since, despite advanced technology, accurate forecasts for resumption of full operations cannot always be obtained as rapidly as one would wish. These disruptions are, of course, beyond the airlines' control. Safety is paramount in such situations and we sincerely regret the inconvenience caused.

We make every reasonable effort to lessen the inconvenience to passengers who are affected by schedule changes. Our practice is, in fact, to advise passengers of such changes when we have a local contact for them and time permits. We also try to obtain satisfactory alternative reservations. We are reviewing our schedule change requirements with all personnel concerned and will take whatever corrective measures are necessary to ensure that a similar problem does not arise in the future.

You made it clear in your letter that the interior of our aircraft was not attractive. We know that aircraft appearance is a reflection of our professionalism. We regret that our airplane did not measure up to your standards since we place great emphasis on cabin maintenance and cleanliness. Please be assured that this particular matter is being investigated by the responsible management, and corrective action will be taken.

As tangible evidence of our concern over your unpleasant trip. I have enclosed two travel vouchers, which may be exchanged for 2 first-class tickets anywhere that World Airlines flies. Once again, please accept our humble apology. We hope for the opportunity to restore your faith in World Airlines by providing you with completely carefree travel.

Sincerely,

Customer Relations Manager
World Airlines

Epilogue

World Airlines filed for bankruptcy 24 months after this incident.

Discussion Questions

1. Identify and classify the customer service failures in this case using the factors that influence the customer's service experience depicted in Figure 9.6.

2. How do the concepts of inseparability and heterogeneity apply to this case?

3. Evaluate the firm's efforts to recover from this customer service disaster.

4. What suggestions would you recommend to the airlines so that this situation does not happen again?

Part 4

Distribution

Chapter 10

Marketing Channels and Distribution

Bert Rosenbloom, Drexel University

Professor of Marketing and Rauth Chair in Electronic Commerce in the LeBow College of Business, Drexel University

Dr. Rosenbloom earned his Ph.D. at Temple University. He is editor of the *Journal of Marketing Channels*. He has served on the editorial boards of several publications including the *Journal of Consumer Marketing, Journal of the Academy of Marketing Science,* and *Journal of International Consumer Marketing.* Dr. Rosenbloom also serves on the ad hoc review boards of the *Journal of Marketing Research, Journal of Marketing,* and *Journal of Retailing.* He is former president of the International Management Development Association and former vice president of the Philadelphia Chapter of the American Marketing Association. Dr. Rosenbloom is a past member of

Marketing channel strategy (place) along with the other three Ps of the marketing mix—product, pricing, promotion—must be developed and then blended together to meet the demands of the organization's target markets. Depending on the particular circumstances involved, marketing channels may play a crucial role in the firm's efforts to compete successfully in the marketplace. Consider, for example, the situation faced by the small boutique beer brewery that produces St. Stan's Ale. The company was founded by Californian Garith Helm after buying a used book entitled *Brew It Yourself* for 10 cents at a garage sale. After trying his hand at brewing the traditional German brown ale de-

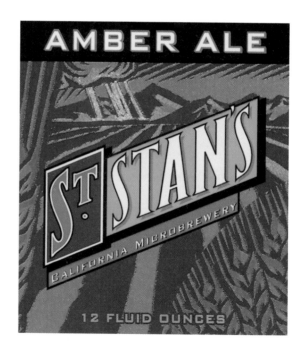

scribed in the book, he found it to be far superior to big name national brands. When the boutique-beer/micro-brewery craze came along in the early 1990s, Garith Helm was eager to cash in on the growing market. He quit his job and went into beer brewing full-time.[1]

The first three Ps of Helm's marketing mix came together quickly: The formula for a superior product already existed, the market would support a premium price, and word-of-mouth advertising took care of much of the promotion as young, affluent consumers talked-up St. Stan's Ale at parties and social gatherings. The fourth P, establishing marketing channels for the ale, was more challenging because Helm had to convince beer wholesalers all over California to carry and aggressively sell the product to retail stores, restaurants, and taverns. A hard slogging effort, coupled with a quality product offering high profit potential, convinced enough beer wholesalers to carry the product so that by 1996, St. Stan's was selling over $300,000 per month throughout California with prospects for distribution into other states on the horizon.

But by 1998, clouds began to appear on that horizon—clouds caused by problems in St. Stan's marketing channels. Anheuser-Busch Co., which controls 44 percent of the beer market and produces the world's leading beer—Budweiser, decided it did not like having competition, even from such little guys as St. Stan's beer. So, Anheuser-Busch initiated a campaign to discourage beer wholesalers from carrying micro-brewery beers. Using its

(Continued)

the Board of Governors of the Academy of Marketing Science.

Dr. Rosenbloom is a leading expert on the management of marketing channels and distribution systems and the author of 10 books and more than 100 articles. His book, *Marketing Channels: A Management View* now in its sixth edition, has been the leading college textbook on marketing channels for over two decades. Another book has been acclaimed in the wholesaling sector for providing the industry with new concepts and analytical methods for increasing productivity in wholesale marketing channels.

Dr. Rosenbloom has consulted for a broad range of industries in manufacturing, wholesaling, retailing, communications, services, and real estate in the United States and abroad. He has won two teaching awards.

Learning Objectives

After you have completed this chapter, you should be able to:

1. Recognize the importance of marketing channels and distribution in the larger field of marketing.

2. Understand the definition of marketing channels in terms of creating time, place, and possession utilities.

3. Discuss the concept of channel structure in terms of the three dimensions of length, intensity, and types of intermediaries.

4. Identify the determinants of channel structure with regard to distribution tasks, economics, and managerial control.

5. Describe the five major flows in marketing channels and the significance of these flows.

6. Realize that marketing channels are not only economic systems, but social systems as well, where power and conflict play a crucial role.

7. Identify and explain the six major areas of channel management and describe the key subsidiary issues associated with any of these areas.

8. Appreciate the role played by marketing channels as the fourth "P" in the marketing mix.

9. Discern the relationship between logistics and the broader field of marketing channels, and appreciate the critical role of logistics in effective and efficient marketing channels.

tremendous marketing channel power, Anheuser-Busch could both reward and punish the beer wholesalers by giving them special discounts on its own products and at least implying that it would stop selling profitable products to those beer wholesalers that continued to sell boutique beers such as St. Stan's. Within a month, five of St. Stan's key beer wholesalers stopped carrying the product and sales decreased by 45 percent. St. Stan's very existence was threatened by this decimation of its marketing channels.

This example points out how important marketing channels can be as a component of the marketing mix and in the overall success of a firm. The struggle to maintain space on distributors' shelves, as exemplified in the case of St. Stan's Ale, is one of the most common challenges in marketing channel management for all kinds of firms, both large and small.[2] In fact, even firms with great strength in products, price, and promotion (the other 3 Ps) may find, as did St. Stan's, that sometimes the greatest challenges they face in managing the marketing mix is in the fourth "P" of marketing channels. ■

www.gap.com

Whether the product is music, an automobile, a bottle of Coca-Cola, a personal computer, a watch, a loaf of bread, or any of the host of other possibilities, somehow this vast array of products must be made available to literally billions of people, as well as millions of industrial firms, businesses, institutions and other organizations all over the world. These millions of products and billions of customers around the globe somehow must be matched up so that customers can get the products they demand when and where they are needed. This may involve a consumer going to a retail store such as the Gap to buy a sweater, ordering a pair of Ray Ban sunglasses over the telephone, or using the Internet to order a book from Amazon.com.[3] In the business-to-business sector, industrial distributors, manufacturer's representatives, and sales agents may be needed to make everything from sophisticated electronic components to paper towels available to organizational customers in a broad spectrum of different industries.[4]

Most customers are unaware of the huge job involved in making such a vast range of products so conveniently available. Indeed, most take it for granted.[5] This virtually limitless array of products can be purchased by simply taking a drive to the mall, picking up the telephone and ordering from a catalog, or clicking the mouse on a PC to buy online.[6] In fact, the availability of so many products from so many sources has become a *given*—a routine fact of everyday life for millions of consumers and organizations. But behind this seemingly routine process is a rather extraordinary combination of businesses, people, and technologies, comprising the marketing channels that have made such effective and efficient distribution possible.[7]

In this chapter we go backstage to examine marketing channels more closely. We take a look at the concept of modern marketing channels—their structure, strategy, design, and management. As we peer behind the scenes to look at marketing channels in this chapter, an important and exciting part of marketing will be revealed.

MARKETING CHANNEL DEFINED

A *marketing channel,* also referred to as a *distribution channel* or *channel of distribution,* is the network of organizations that creates time, place, and possession utilities for consumers and business users.

An example will help to clarify this definition. The new Volkswagen Beetle, inspired by the nostalgia for the Beetles of the 1950s and 60s, is a product that has captured the public's imagination, and so these cars have been in great demand. Though Volkswagen is a German company, the new Beetle is actually manufactured in Mexico. As these cars roll off the assembly line and out the factory door they appear to be totally complete. But are they? Actually, they are complete only to the extent of having *form utility,* which has been provided through the manufacturing process. But as exciting and cute as these cars may be, to be of use to consumers, they must be available when and where customers want them, and arrangements must be made so consumers can actually take possession of the cars through purchasing or leasing. In other words, **time, place, and possession utilities** still need to be added to make these cars complete from the standpoint of meeting customer needs. Clearly, a Beetle sitting on the factory lot in Mexico is of little use to a consumer in San Francisco who wants one to traverse the hilly streets of that city. Marketing channels are what create these other utilities—not just for Volkswagen Beetles but for millions of other products as well.

The creation of time, place, and possession utilities may result from marketing channels that are simple or complex. In the case of the Volkswagen Beetle, the channel is fairly simple. The cars are sold by the manufacturer to retail dealers, who in turn sell the cars to consumers. The cars are transported from the factory to dealer showrooms by independent railroad or truck carriers who charge a fee for their services. Thus, the participants in this marketing channel are the manufacturers, retailers, consumers, and transportation companies. Only the first three, however, are what is referred to as the *sales channel,* which is that part of the channel involved in buying, selling, and transferring title. The rail or trucking firms, which do not buy, sell, or transfer the title to the cars, are part of the *facilitating channel.* Public storage firms, insurance companies, finance companies, market research firms, and several other types of firms also frequently participate as facilitating organizations in various marketing channels.

Some marketing channels are more complex than that used for the Volkswagen Beetle. Beer, for example, which goes from manufacturers to wholesalers to retailers and then to consumers, has an extra organization (the wholesaler) in its sales channel, compared to Volkswagen.[8]

The simplest sales channels go directly from producers to customers, as in the case of Dell Computer Corporation, which sells all of its products directly from its manufacturing plants to customers. Dell's facilitating channel, however, which uses telephone, mail, and the Internet for order placement as well as UPS, Federal Express, and other transportation firms to deliver its computers to customers, is more complex than its sales channel.

Both the sales and facilitating channels are usually needed to create time, place, and possession utilities. But it has become a customary practice in marketing to describe and illustrate marketing channels only in terms of the sales channel, because it is the relationship involving the functions of buying, selling, and transferring of title where most of the strategic marketing issues emerge. Volkswagen, for example, when setting up its sales channel, faced such marketing strategy issues as identifying and selecting the appropriate kinds of dealers to sell the new Beetles, convincing them to carry sufficient numbers of the cars (especially after the cars are no longer as "hot"), motivating the dealers to do an effective job of promoting and selling the cars, as well as making sure that they provide good servicing and warranty support. Moreover, Volkswagen also needed to make provisions for numerous other issues as part of its continuing relationship with independent dealers, such as future inventory levels expected of dealers, training of sales and service people, credit terms, evaluation of dealer performance, and numerous others. In contrast, Volkswagen's efforts to arrange for transportation, storage, insurance, and similar matters, while important, are usually not considered strategic marketing issues.

MARKETING CHANNEL STRUCTURE

The *form* or *shape* that a marketing channel takes to perform the tasks necessary to make products available to consumers is usually referred to as **channel structure.** Firms such as transportation companies, warehousing firms, insurance companies, and the like are

www.vw.com

Time, place, and possession utilities
are conditions that enable consumers and business users to have products available for use when and where they want them.

www.dell.com
www.ups.com
www.federalexpress.com

Channel structure
consists of all of the businesses and institutions (including producers or manufacturers and final customers) who are involved in performing the functions of buying, selling, and transferring title.

usually referred to as ***facilitating agencies,*** because they are not involved in buying, selling, or transferring title and hence, as we mentioned earlier, are not considered to be part of the channel structure.

Marketing channel structure has three basic dimensions:

1. Length of the channel.

2. Intensity at various levels.

3. The types of intermediaries involved.

Length of Channel Structure

Channel length

is the number of levels in a marketing channel.

With regard to **channel length,** marketing channels can range from two levels, where the producer or manufacturer sells directly to consumers (direct distribution), to as many as ten levels, where eight intermediary institutions exist between the producer and consumers. With the exception of Japan, such long channels of distribution are quite rare in industrialized countries. Much more common are channel structure lengths ranging from two levels up to five levels. Figure 10.1 provides an illustration of typical channel structure lengths for consumer products in developed countries.

Many customer-based factors influence the length of the channel structure, such as the size of the customer base, their geographical dispersion, and their particular behavior patterns. The nature of the product, such as its bulk and weight, perishability, value, and technical complexity, can also be very important. For example, technically complex prod-

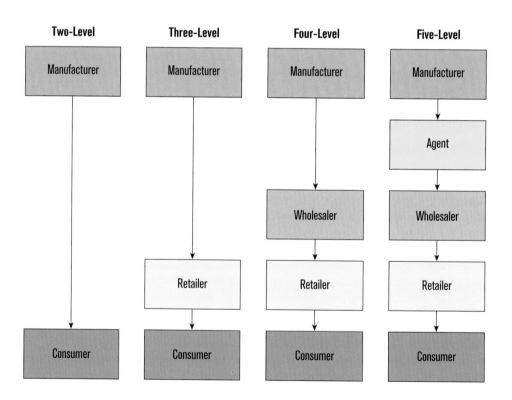

Figure 10.1 Examples of the Length of Dimensions of Marketing Channel Structure for Consumer Products

ucts such as x-ray machines often require short channels because of the high degree of technical support and liaison needed by customers, which may only be available directly from the manufacturer. Moreover, length can also be affected by the size of the manufacturer, its financial capacity, and its desire for control. In general, larger and more well-financed manufacturers have a greater capability to bypass intermediaries and use shorter channel structures.[9] Manufacturers desiring to exercise a high degree of control over the distribution of their products are also more likely to use shorter channel structures because the shorter the channel, the higher the degree of control. We will discuss these issues in greater detail later in this chapter.

Intensity of Channel Structure

Channel intensity is usually described in terms of intensive distribution, selective distribution, or exclusive distribution. *Intensive distribution* means that all possible intermediaries at the particular level of the channel are used. *Selective distribution* means that a smaller number of intermediaries are used, while *exclusive distribution* refers to only one intermediary used at the particular level of the channel to cover a defined territory. The intensity dimension of channel structure can be portrayed as a continuum as shown in Figure 10.2. Although there are many exceptions, in general, intensive distribution is associated with the distribution of convenience goods, selective distribution with shopping goods, and exclusive distribution with specialty goods. Thus, inexpensive Bic pens, Gillette razor blades, and Hallmark greeting cards (convenience goods) tend to be carried by very large number of intermediaries, particularly at the retail level; while home appliances such as Whirlpool refrigerators and apparel such as Levi's jeans (shopping goods) are handled by relatively fewer retailers; and specialty goods such as Rolex watches or Rolls-Royce automobiles are featured by only one dealer in a specified geographical area (territory).

Channel intensity
refers to the number of intermediaries at each level of the marketing channel.

www.bicworld.com
www.gillette.com
www.hallmark.com
www.whirlpool.com
www.snickers.com

Types of Intermediaries in the Channel Structure

This third dimension of channel structure refers to the different kinds of intermediary institutions that can be used at the various levels of the channel. At the retail level, there may be many possibilities for some products. For example, a Snickers candy bar can be sold through many different types of retailers such as candy stores, grocery stores, drugstores, supermarkets, mass merchandisers, discount department stores, and many others. For other products, such as automobiles, the choice is more limited. We should point out, however, that in recent years with the growth of *scrambled merchandising,* where all kinds of products are sold in stores not traditionally associated with those products, the types of stores that sell various products have broadened considerably. Motor oil, for

---

Figure 10.2   Intensity of Channel Structure

Intensive	Selective	Exclusive
All possible intermediaries	Relatively few intermediaries	Just one intermediary

Specialty goods such as Rolex watches are typically offered by only one dealer in a region. Because of the exclusive distribution of this good, Rolex includes a 1-800 phone number in their advertisements to help customers find the nearest official jeweler.

example, is now regularly available in supermarkets, while hardware items are frequently found in drugstores. Consequently, manufacturers today need to be broad-minded when considering the types of intermediaries to use in their channel structures. The conventional wisdom of particular products being distributed only through certain types of wholesalers or retailers may no longer hold.

DETERMINANTS OF CHANNEL STRUCTURE

The structure of marketing channels, in terms of their length, intensity, and types of participating intermediaries, is determined basically by three factors:

1. The distribution tasks that need to be performed.

2. The economics of performing distribution tasks.

3. Management's desire for control of distribution.

Distribution Tasks

Distribution tasks, also often referred to as *marketing functions* or sometimes *channel functions,* have been described by various lists for many years. Such functions as buying,

Marketing Technologies

Music Distribution: From the 78 to the CD to the Net

Hardly anyone except collectors remembers the old 78 records of 50 years ago. Such primitive technology that had been around since the early 20th century has been replaced by LPs, audio tapes, and high-tech CDs. And, of course, the audio equipment has leaped during this period from windup Victrolas to space-age stereo systems.

Yet with all this advancing technology, the distribution of music has remained essentially the same throughout this century: Music has been produced by record companies, who then sold the plastic discs, tapes, or CDs to distributors and retailers, where they were then purchased by consumers. Even today, all six major record manufacturers—EMI, Capitol, Universal, PolyGram, Sony Music, and Warner Music—distribute most of their products via this century-old distribution channel. These giant record companies, when linked with today's huge retailers, combine to dominate the distribution of music to the public. Wal-Mart, for example, which sells more CDs than any other retailer in the world, is so powerful that it can force artists to change lyrics and CD art if Wal-Mart should find them to be offensive.

But as the new millennium dawns, the Internet could drastically change this cozy distribution arrangement between mega-manufacturers and mega-retailers. How? By making the actual physical sale of CDs unnecessary. Instead, music would be distributed electronically by digitally downloading music over the Internet. This is already happening to some extent now, mainly through so-called MP3 sites, many of which are unauthorized. But hundreds of these sites already offer thousands of songs. By downloading onto hard disks and transferring the music to recordable CDs, listeners can put together customized music collections without ever setting foot in a store or even picking up a telephone to order a CD through the mail. With recordable CD players now under $200 and coming down in price, electronic distribution of music via the Internet could profoundly alter existing music channels, from recording artist to final consumer. The big record companies and the massive shelf space offered by their giant retail partners could become irrelevant as artists use their own Web sites to sell their music directly to fans.

So with electronic distribution of music available on the Internet, going to the store to buy a CD could become as outmoded as putting a 78 record on a windup Victrola!

Questions

1. Do you see any problems with direct distribution of music via downloading from the Internet?

2. Would you be willing to purchase most of your music from the Internet rather than buy CDs? Why or why not?

---

selling, risk taking, transportation, storage, order processing, and financing are commonly mentioned. More generalized terms can also be used to describe these tasks, such as *concentration, equalization,* and *dispersion*—whereby the main tasks of marketing channels are grouped together in familial relationships—bringing products together from many manufacturers (concentration), adjusting the quantities to balance supply and demand (equalization), and delivering them to final customers (dispersion). Others describe distribution tasks in terms of a sorting process: *accumulating* products from many producers, *sorting* them to correspond to designated target markets, and *assorting* them into conveniently associated groups to ease the shopping burden of customers. Distribution tasks have also been described in much more detailed terms where specific activities sometimes unique to the particular industry are cited.[10]

Regardless of the particular list of distribution tasks presented, the rationale is the same for all of them: Distribution functions must be performed in order to consummate transactions between buyers and sellers. The reason is that discrepancies exist between buyers and sellers that must be overcome through the performance of distribution tasks. The channel structure the firm chooses to perform these tasks reflects how the tasks are to be allocated to various marketing institutions such as wholesalers, retailers, agents, brokers, or others. The discrepancies between production and consumption can be separated into four basic groups:[11]

1. Discrepancies in quantity.

2. Discrepancies in assortment.

3. Discrepancies in time.

4. Discrepancies in place.

Focus on Discrepancies in Quantity

The quantities in which products are manufactured to achieve low average costs are usually too large for any individual customer to use immediately. Wrigley's chewing gum, for example, produces literally millions of packages of gum each day. Even the most ardent gum chewer could not possibly use that much gum every day! Thus, institutions in the channel structure, such as wholesalers and retailers, provide a buffer to absorb the vast output of manufacturers and provide the smaller quantities desired by individual customers.

Focus on Discrepancies in Assortment

Products are grouped for manufacturing purposes based on efficiencies of production, while customers group products based on convenience of shopping and consuming. In most cases, the production and consumption groupings are not inherently matched. For example, the thousands of items a consumer finds grouped so conveniently together in a supermarket are not, of course, produced by one manufacturer. Hundreds of relatively specialized manufacturers have made those products. The supermarket and many other intermediaries in marketing channels have performed the distribution tasks necessary to regroup this conglomeration of products, thereby overcoming the discrepancy in assortment. This enables particular manufacturers to concentrate on producing a relatively limited range of products, which when combined through marketing channels with the products of many other manufacturers, allows consumers to have wide and convenient assortments of products that greatly simplify shopping and consumption.

Focus on Discrepancies in Time

Most products are not manufactured for immediate consumption or use. Hence, some mechanism must be available to hold products between the time they are produced and needed by final customers. A bottle of Snapple iced tea, a Tommy Hilfiger shirt, or a pair of Rollerblade in-line skates are not desired by consumers at the instant they roll off the production line. So intermediaries in marketing channels, particularly *merchant wholesalers* and *retailers,* who take title to and physically hold goods until they are needed by consumers, are crucial in overcoming this discrepancy in time.

Focus on Discrepancies in Place

The location of manufacturing facilities for products is a function of such factors as raw material availability, labor costs, expertise, historical considerations, and numerous other factors that may have little to do with where the ultimate consumers of those products are located.[12] Thus, the production and consumption of products can literally take place half a world apart from each other. In fact, it is more likely than ever today that the products we buy are made in China, Singapore, Japan, Brazil, India, or some other far away country than in some nearby factory. Channel structures evolve or are consciously designed to connect distant manufacturers and consumers to eliminate place discrepancies.

The Economics of Performing Distribution Tasks

Given that distribution tasks must be performed to overcome the four discrepancies discussed above, the channel structure must be organized to perform the tasks as efficiently as possible. The development of efficient marketing channel structures is based on two principles: specialization or division of labor and transaction efficiency.[13]

Specialization or Division of Labor

The principle of *specialization* or *division of labor* underlies most modern production processes. Each worker in a factory focuses on performing particular manufacturing tasks and thereby develops specialized expertise and skills in performing those tasks. Such specialization results in much greater efficiency and higher output than if each worker were to perform all or most of the tasks necessary to manufacture the product him- or herself.

This 200-year-old principle applies as much to distribution as it does to production. The various intermediaries in marketing channels are analogous to production workers or stations in a factory, but instead of performing production tasks, they are performing distribution tasks. These intermediaries—whether they are wholesalers, retailers, agents, or brokers—develop expertise in distribution that manufacturers would find uneconomical to match. Moreover, many large intermediaries, such as mass merchandisers, enjoy economies of scale and economies of scope which would be impossible for most manufacturers to match. Home Depot, for instance, with over 500 giant warehouse stores enjoys great economies of scale and scope, because it is able to spread its operating costs over a vast quantity and variety of products.

Economies of scale and economies of scope
are obtained by spreading the costs of distribution over a large quantity of products (scale) or over a wide variety of products (scope).

Transaction Efficiency

Transaction efficiency refers to the effort to reduce the number of transactions between producers and consumers. If many producers attempt to deal directly with large numbers of consumers, the number of transactions can be enormous. Paradoxically, by lengthening the channel structure through the addition of intermediaries, the number of transactions can actually be reduced. Consequently, transaction efficiency is increased. This is illustrated in Figure 10.3. As shown in the figure, the number of transactions has been cut in

Figure 10.3   How the Introduction of an Intermediary Reduces the Number of Transactions

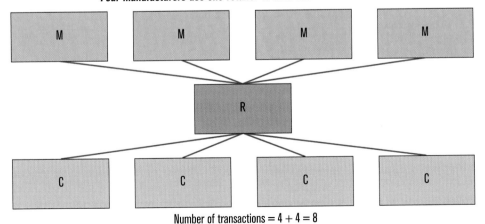

Four manufacturers deal with four consumers directly

Number of transactions = 4 × 4 = 16

Four manufacturers use one retailer to deal with four consumers

Number of transactions = 4 + 4 = 8

half as a result of the introduction of the retailer into the channel structure. Given that the costs of transactions can be very high, especially if personal face-to-face meetings are necessary to consummate transactions, the reduction in contacts through the use of intermediaries in the channel structure is in many cases absolutely vital for economical distribution.

Management's Desire for Control of Distribution

Even though the economics of the performance of distribution tasks may seem to call for a particular type of marketing channel structure, a firm's desire for control of the marketing channel may outweigh the economic considerations.[14] In general, the shorter the channel structure, the higher the degree of control, and vice versa. Further, the lower the intensity of distribution, the higher the degree of control, and vice versa. For example, suppose an economic analysis, based on specialization/division of labor and transaction efficiencies, calls for a long marketing channel structure with a fairly high degree of intensity at the various levels. However, management in the manufacturing firm feels a need to protect the image of the product and also believes it is necessary to provide high levels of customer service. To do so, the manufacturer is convinced that it needs a high degree of control, and so it may opt for only one level of intermediary, with a very high degree of selectivity in appointing them as channel members, based on their willingness to take direction from the manufacturer. This is exactly the situation Gucci, the Italian maker of world-famous luxury goods, found itself in. Focusing mainly on gaining distribution efficiency, Gucci ended up selling its products through several thousand retailers. This proliferation of retailers—many of whom were not of the highest stature—although providing economies of scale in the distribution of Gucci products, adversely affected the exclusive image of Gucci. Realizing the problem, Gucci restructured its marketing channels by drastically reducing the number of retailers selling its products to less than 500 worldwide. Moreover, all of these retailers were of the highest quality, and were willing to take close direction from Gucci to project a world-class quality image vital to the long-term success of Gucci.

FLOWS IN MARKETING CHANNELS

When a marketing channel is developed, a series of ***channel flows*** emerge. These flows provide the links that tie channel members and other agencies together in the distribution of goods and services. The most important of these flows are the:

1. Product flow.

2. Negotiation flow.

3. Ownership flow.

4. Information flow.

5. Promotion flow.

These flows are illustrated for Coors beer in Figure 10.4.

The ***product flow*** refers to the actual physical movement of the product from the manufacturer (Coors) through all of the parties who take physical possession of the product, from its point of production to consumers. In the case of Coors beer, the product comes from breweries and packaging plants in Colorado, Tennessee, and Virginia by way of company trucks or common carriers (transportation companies) to beer distributors (wholesalers), who in turn ship the product (usually in their own trucks) to liquor stores, supermarkets, convenience stores, restaurants, and bars (retailers), where it is finally purchased by consumers.

Figure 10.4   Flows in the Marketing Channels for Coors Beer

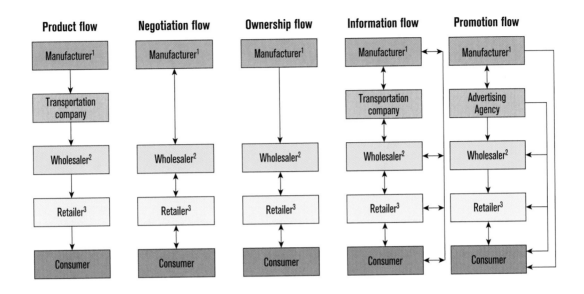

[1]Brewers and packaging plants
[2]Beer distributors
[3]Liquor stores, supermarkets, convenience stores, restaurants, bars

The *negotiation flow* represents the interplay of the buying and selling tasks associated with the transfer of title to Coors products. Notice in the figure that the transportation firm is not included in this flow because it does not participate in the negotiation tasks of buying, selling, and transferring title. Notice also that the arrows flow in *both* directions, indicating that negotiations involve a mutual exchange between buyers and sellers at all levels of the channel.

The *ownership flow* shows the movement of the title to the product as it is passed along from the manufacturer to final consumers. Here again, the transportation firm is not involved because it does not take title to the product, nor is it actively involved in facilitating its transfer. It is only engaged in the transportation of the physical product itself.

Turning now to the *information flow,* we see that the transportation firm has reappeared, since all parties participate in the exchange of information. We also see that all of the arrows showing the flow from the manufacturer to consumers are two-directional, as the flow of information can be either up or down. For example, Coors may obtain information from the transportation company about its shipping schedule and rates, and the transportation company may in turn seek information from Coors about when and in what quantities it plans to ship the product. The flow of information sometimes bypasses the transportation firm, as shown by the arrow leading from the manufacturer (at the right-hand side of the box) directly to the wholesalers, retailers, and consumers. This route of information flow occurs when the information sought does not concern the transportation company, such as details associated with the buying, selling, or promotion of Coors products.[15] For example, if the manufacturer makes available to beer distributors a special reduced price on particular beer varieties, such as Coors Zima Clear Brew or Coors Extra Gold beer, this information would be passed directly to the beer distributors, and would not be of concern to the transportation firm.

Finally, the *promotion flow* refers to the flow of persuasive communication in the form of advertising, personal selling, sales promotion, and public relations. Here, a new

Movement of products through channels is big business. Federal Express provides customers and businesses with fast, reliable, and time-definite transportation of more than 3 million items to 211 countries each working day. Fedex employs more than 145,000 employees, has 624 aircraft, and 42,800 vehicles in its integrated global network.

party, the advertising agency, is included in the flow because the advertising agency is actively involved in providing and maintaining the promotion flow, especially the advertising component of promotion. The two-directional arrow connected by a broken line between the manufacturer and advertising agency is meant to show that the manufacturer and advertising agency work together closely to develop promotional strategies. All other arrows are one-directional from the advertising agency, or directly from the manufacturer to the other parties in the marketing channel.

The concept of channel flows provides a useful framework for understanding the scope and complexity of marketing channels. By thinking in terms of the five flows, it becomes obvious that marketing channels involve much more than just the physical flow of the product through the channel. The other flows (negotiation, ownership, information, and promotion) must also be coordinated to make products conveniently available to customers. Moreover, the concept of flows in marketing channels captures the dynamic nature of marketing channels. The word *flow* suggests movement or a fluid state, and in fact this is the nature of marketing channels. New forms of distribution emerge, different types of intermediaries appear in the channel while others drop out, unusual competitive structures close off some avenues of distribution and open up others. Changing patterns of buyer behavior and new forms of technology such as the Internet add yet another dimension of change. Channel flows need to be adapted and managed to meet such changes.

MARKETING CHANNELS AS SOCIAL SYSTEMS

Once viewed only as economic systems, marketing channels are now seen as *social systems* as well, because they involve people interacting with each other in different organizations and institutions. Consequently, the rules that govern channel relationships are not only a matter of economics. In the broader social systems perspective, marketing channels are subject to the same behavioral processes associated with all social systems.[16] The behavioral processes of most significance in marketing channels are power and conflict.

Power in Marketing Channels

Marketing channel power refers to the capacity of one channel member to influence the behavior of another channel member. McDonald's, for example, as the franchiser of the world's largest chain of fast-food restaurants has been able to exercise tremendous power over its franchisees. Indeed, it is probably no exaggeration to say that no king or queen ever had any more power over their subjects than McDonald's enjoys over its franchisees. McDonald's operates what is known as a *business format franchise.* Under this arrangement, not only the products the franchisees sell, but also virtually all aspects of their operations from the design of the restaurants to the smallest details of operating procedures, such as how long french fries should be cooked, are controlled by McDonald's. All of these provisions are included in minute detail in a franchise contract which, once signed by the franchisees, means that they are legally bound to abide by all of the provisions spelled out in the contract. Thus, the social system in which McDonald's and its thousands of affiliated franchisees operate is probably closer to being a dictatorship than a democracy because McDonald's has most of the power.

For decades, most McDonald's franchisees were delighted with this unequal power relationship because a major source of McDonald's power came from its ability to reward the franchisees in the form of fat profits that turned thousands of them into millionaires. So, as long as most of the franchisees were making plenty of money, they were not very vocal about McDonald's dictatorial tactics. Recently though, fierce competition as well as blunders by McDonald's, such as the McLean and the Arch Deluxe burgers, have made franchisees less compliant.[17] Now quite a few franchisees are no longer content to let McDonald's rule the roost. These franchisees are especially concerned about McDonald's opening too many restaurants that takes sales away from existing franchisees. Some franchisees have even initiated lawsuits in the hope of using the legal system to gain countervailing power to offset McDonald's power over them.

Conflict in Marketing Channels

Marketing channel conflict in marketing channels is usually defined as *goal impeding behavior* by one or more channel members. In other words, when one channel member takes actions that another channel member perceives as reducing its ability to achieve its goals, conflict can be the result. In the McDonald's case discussed above, for example, McDonald's behavior in the form of opening so many new restaurants near existing ones was seen as goal impeding behavior by franchisees who owned the established restaurants in the same territories. They believed that McDonald's attempt to enhance its own bottom line by setting up so many new restaurants was hurting the franchisees' ability to reach *their* profit goals. As mentioned earlier, some of these conflicts have become so intense that lawsuits have been initiated by the franchisees.

Conflicts, whether over territorial encroachment, as in the case of McDonald's, or any of hundreds of other issues, are common in marketing channels. Although most of these conflicts will not involve lawsuits, they nevertheless can be intense and sometimes bitter. In general, such conflict is viewed as a negative force in marketing channels, because it diverts attention, effort, and resources from the main job of providing effective and efficient distribution of products to customers.[18]

MARKETING CHANNEL MANAGEMENT

Marketing channel management, frequently shortened to the term ***channel management,*** refers to the analysis, planning, organizing, and controlling of a firm's marketing channels.[19] Channel management can be a challenging and complex process, not only because

Interorganizational content refers to channel management that extends beyond a firm's own organization into other independent businesses.

many aspects are involved, but also because of the difficulties arising from the **interorganizational context** of the channel structure. That is, marketing channels are made up of independent business organizations such as manufacturers, wholesalers, and retailers as well as agents and brokers who, although linked together in a relationship to form a marketing channel, are still independent businesses. As such, these firms have their own objectives, policies, strategies, and operating procedures, which may or may not be congruent with those of the other members of the channel. Indeed, as mentioned earlier in this chapter, sometimes they come into outright conflict. Moreover, in marketing channels, usually there are no clear superior/subordinate relationships, or lines of authority, so typical of management in single-firm intraorganizational settings. Hence, managing marketing channels is frequently more challenging than managing within the intraorganizational setting of a single firm.

PERSPECTIVES FOR CHANNEL MANAGEMENT

Channel management can be viewed from two basic vantage points:

1. From that of the producer or manufacturer looking "down the channel" towards the market.

2. From that of the retailer (or other final reseller) looking "up the channel" back to the producer or manufacturer.

Although either of these perspectives is a valid one for examining the subject of channel management, the first one (the producer or manufacturer looking down the channel towards the market) is by far the most commonly used perspective. Indeed, virtually all modern analysis and research on the subject is from this vantage point. This is probably because channel management is regarded as a part of the larger field of marketing management, which has almost universally been treated from the perspective of the producer or manufacturer. Consequently, our discussion of channel management will be from the producer/manufacturer perspective.

DECISION AREAS OF CHANNEL MANAGEMENT

Channel management viewed from the perspective of the producer or manufacturer looking down the channel towards the market can be divided into six basic decision areas:

1. Formulating channel strategy.

2. Designing the channel structure.

3. Selecting the channel members.

4. Motivating the channel members.

5. Coordinating channel strategy with the marketing mix.

6. Evaluating channel member performance.

Figure 10.5 provides an overview of these decision areas. The rest of this chapter is organized around a discussion of each of these areas of channel management.

Formulating Channel Strategy

Channel strategy refers to the broad set of principles by which a firm seeks to achieve its distribution objectives to satisfy its customers. The Saturn Division of General Motors,

Figure 10.5 Major Decision Areas of Channel Management

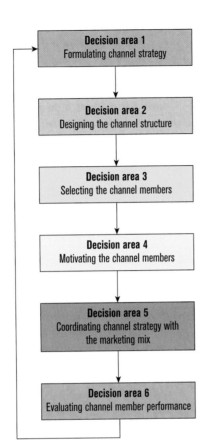

for example, developed an innovative channel strategy to meet the needs of a large segment of customers who were dissatisfied with the car buying experience available through existing automobile marketing channels. These customers did not want the high-pressure, sales gimmicks, and price haggling so common in traditional auto dealerships. Thus, Saturn's channel strategy provided a revolutionary way of selling cars through dealerships that would not pressure customers to buy, that would provide them with detailed product information, charge one price, and offer a 30-day return policy.[20]

This channel strategy involved a huge investment and commitment by Saturn, because the new General Motors division had to plan and organize for the selection and training of dealers to create an entirely new marketing channel structure and culture for selling cars, which previously had not existed in automobile marketing channels. Saturn felt that such an effort was worthwhile because the firm hoped to achieve a **sustainable competitive advantage** through its innovative marketing channel strategy. Ford and Chrysler would find it much more difficult and time consuming to develop their own new marketing channels comparable to Saturn's than it would be to imitate a new product feature, price incentive, or advertising campaign that Saturn might offer.

In recent years, more firms are discovering the value of innovative channel strategy for creating a sustainable competitive advantage.[21] These firms realize that of the *four Ps of the marketing mix* (product, pricing, promotion, place), only "place" (marketing channels) provides shelter from quick imitation from competitors. Why? Simply because rapid technology transfer has made it very difficult if not impossible to hold on to a competitive

www.saturn.com

Sustainable competitive advantage

is a competitive edge that cannot be easily or quickly copied by competitors in the short run.

Careers in Marketing

Using Her Degree in Direct Relation to the Fourth "P"

During her time at Texas A&M University, it was not difficult for Eleanor Shaw to decide on a major. She knew all along that she wanted to study business; but the difficulty came upon graduation when she was clueless as to what she actually wanted to do with this degree.

I would stroll the halls of the career fair and nothing seemed to spark my interest. Fortunately, I was forced to make a quick decision and accepted the position as a marketing analyst for Chef America, Inc., the makers of HOT POCKETS® Brand stuffed sandwiches.

As a marketing analyst for Chef America, I am exposed to many aspects of the marketing mix. I was lucky to find an entry-level marketing position that incorporates many aspects of the business, so that while learning and "paying my dues" I do not go mad staring at a computer screen all day. As the club analyst, I focus primarily on the warehouse club business for Sam's Clubs and Price Costco. HOT POCKETS® Brand stuffed sandwiches reach final consumers through many different channels: traditional retail, institutional food service, and warehouse clubs. Selling the product through the clubs requires a different combination of the marketing mix compared to more traditional retailers, because of the differences in the structure of the channels and the unique buying patterns of the customers.

Although the product sold in clubs is essentially the same as that sold in grocery stores, the other Ps of the marketing mix are quite different. Promotion is very limited in the clubs. I am responsible for coordinating graphic changes to packaging. The packaging must be enough

to entice the consumer to purchase the product, because little else is used for promotional purposes. Of course the price usually adds value, but the club consumer must be willing to buy in bulk.

The biggest difference between selling in clubs and traditional retailers is *place*. By selling to the clubs, we are reaching a different consumer than that found in the grocery store. Understanding this unique channel can determine the success of our products reaching consumers through the clubs. Coordination and timing are crucial to the introduction of a new item, and the channel structure can greatly affect the timing. Even within an individual club chain there are different types of structures to be considered. For example, Sam's Clubs use both cross-docking and traditional warehousing. Club buyers typically have more power than grocery store chains and are able to influence which items are sold. This makes it more important to exchange information to ensure that customers receive the products they desire and distribution objectives are met. Wal-Mart/Sam's provides a unique and extremely helpful information system to its vendors called Retail Link. I am always gathering sales and inventory information from this system to feed back through the channel. By understanding this information, we are better able to control this aspect of the marketing mix. We might be able to create a great product, but it must reach the consumer to be a successful product.

Retail and trade marketing analysts at Chef America focus on other aspects of the marketing mix that more strongly influence the success of HOT POCKETS® Brand stuffed sandwiches in other areas. For example, some analysts direct much attention to the success and failure of specific promotions. But, as the club analyst, much of my time is devoted to understanding the unique channel structure in which the warehouse clubs work.

---

advantage based on the "P" of superior products; competitors, domestic or foreign, can quickly match virtually any product innovation. Holding on to the "P" of a pricing advantage is even more difficult, because global competition assures that a competitor somewhere in the world will match or beat the price. The other "P," promotion, also does not provide for much sustainability, because there is simply too much advertising from literally thousands of promotional messages knocking each other out of the box in short order.

So channel strategy has moved to the center stage of marketing strategy as firms seek to gain a leg up on the competition that they can hold onto for awhile.[22] The range of firms using this approach cuts across many products and industries: WD-40, for example, the lubricating product that is present in 75 percent of U.S. homes, has used channel strategy to beat back such giants as 3M, DuPont, and GE who for years have tried to replace WD-40 with competing products. By paying extraordinary attention to keeping retailers happy with high-profit deals and special merchandise campaigns, WD-40 created a kind of big happy family between itself and tens of thousands of retailers. The Coca-Cola company has run circles around PepsiCo all over the world through superior channel strategy, not only by focusing on giant distributors and retailers, but by paying attention to the little

Internet

www.wd40.com
www.3M.com
www.dupont.com
www.ge.com

channel members as well.[23] In Japan, for example, Coke publishes trade magazines and holds special seminars for owners of *sakayas* (mom-and-pop stores) on how to operate more efficiently and compete with more modern outlets. In Paris, Coke uses five-foot inflatable Coca-Cola cans to help hundreds of tiny street corner shops. Heavy earth-moving equipment manufacturer Caterpillar has emphasized channel strategy to gain a sustainable competitive advantage by building a superior dealer organization that guarantees critical parts delivery anywhere in the world within 48 hours. This emphasis came in handy not very long ago when fierce product competition from Japanese competitors threatened Caterpillar's very existence. And of course, Amazon.com turned the book industry on its head with its strategy of using Internet-based marketing channels to sell books. Barnes & Noble, Borders, and other competitors are scratching their heads trying to copy Amazon.com's channel strategy but so far without much success.[24]

www.caterpillar.com

Designing the Channel Structure

Having considered the overall strategic role of channel strategy in the firm, management needs to turn its attention to the job of designing the firm's marketing channels. ***Channel design*** is the process of developing new channels where none had existed before, or making significant modifications to existing channels. The process of channel design can be broken down into four basic phases:

1. Setting distribution objectives.

2. Specifying the distribution tasks that need to be performed by the channel.

3. Considering alternative channel structures.

4. Choosing an optimal channel structure.

These phases are depicted in Figure 10.6.

Figure 10.6   Phases of the Channel Design Process

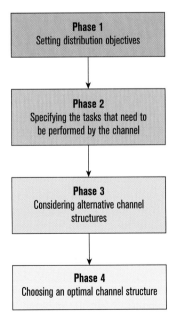

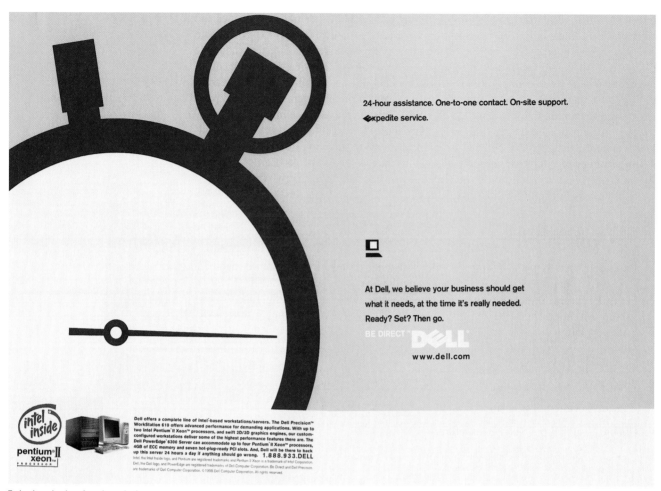

24-hour assistance. One-to-one contact. On-site support.

Expedite service.

At Dell, we believe your business should get
what it needs, at the time it's really needed.
Ready? Set? Then go.
BE DIRECT **DELL**
www.dell.com

Dell offers a complete line of Intel-based workstations/servers. The Dell Precision™
WorkStation 610 offers advanced performance for demanding applications. With up to
two Intel Pentium II Xeon™ processors, and swift 2D/3D graphics engines, our custom-
configured workstations deliver some of the highest performance features there are. The
Dell PowerEdge 6300 Server can accommodate up to four Pentium II Xeon™ processors,
4GB of ECC memory and seven hot-plug-ready PCI slots. And, Dell will be there to back
up this server 24 hours a day if anything should go wrong. **1.888.933.DELL**
Intel, the Intel Inside logo, and Pentium are registered trademarks and Pentium II Xeon is a trademark of Intel Corporation.
Dell, the Dell logo, and PowerEdge are registered trademarks of Dell Computer Corporation. Be Direct and Dell Precision
are trademarks of Dell Computer Corporation. ©1998 Dell Computer Corporation. All rights reserved.

Technology is changing channels. As seen here, Dell's "Be Direct" campaign illustrates the one-to-one contact of this simplest channel (from manufacturer to customer) by offering 24-hour assistance via a 1-800 number or their Web site.

Setting Distribution Objectives

As alluded to in the previous section on channel strategy, ***distribution objectives*** refer to what the firm would like its channel strategy to accomplish in terms of meeting the needs of its customers. At this stage of channel design then, distribution objectives need to be stated from the point of view of the *customer.* This is sometimes referred to as the *bottom up* or *backwards* approach to channel design because the starting point for designing the channel is also the end point of the channel—the customer. This is precisely the approach taken by the Saturn division of General Motors discussed earlier. The new auto company asked the question: "What do our customers want when they go out to buy automobiles?" Saturn's distribution objectives were then formulated in terms of developing auto dealerships that could provide the friendly, helpful, no-haggle environment sought by customers.

Dell Computers provides another example of setting distribution objectives from the bottom up, so as to design marketing channels that meet the needs of customers better than the competition. Michael Dell founded the company after experiencing frustration when trying to buy computers from dealers who knew less about computers than he did. This frustration is what led Dell to develop a direct channel using the telephone. When customers called, they were able to get information and advice of much better quality than they had received from computer stores, because the people manning the phones were knowledgeable computer salespeople rather than minimum-wage store clerks. The person-to-person interaction available in this channel enabled Dell to provide customized high-performance computers, technical support, and other value-added services to a segment of sophisticated personal computer users who wanted more than what was available from existing retail computer channels. Dell's innovative channel design of direct sales to customers via telephone (and later the Internet) has proved to be spectacularly successful, making Michael Dell a billionaire in the process!

Specifying the Distribution Tasks

Making products available to final consumers—how, when, and where they want them—calls for the performance of many distribution tasks. Such tasks can range from providing simple transportation for products, all the way to the development of sophisticated *electronic data interchange (EDI)* systems for linking the manufacturer's and channel members' computers together for instantaneous information transmittal.

But in specifying distribution tasks, firms often make the mistake of underestimating the level of detail and subtlety involved in particular industries. Consider, for example, what happened to the Snapple Beverage Corp. soon after it was purchased by Quaker Oats Company. By tying Snapple in with its highly successful Gatorade, Quaker hoped to gain tremendous synergy for the two drinks. So, Quaker designed a channel for Snapple that paralleled the channel for Gatorade, which was from factory to retailers' warehouses, from which individual stores then ordered what they needed to keep their shelves stocked. Quaker knew this pattern well and was comfortable with it. But Quaker failed to realize, that unlike Gatorade, which was treated in the channel as a consumer packaged product such as cereal, Snapple had to compete in the *soft-drink market.*[25] The channel for soft drinks places a much heavier burden on the producer and/or distributors, because individual stores do not usually place orders for soft drinks on an as-needed basis and then stock their own shelves. Instead, they rely on bottlers and distributors to perform these distribution tasks for them. Quaker had not made arrangements with these intermediaries to perform these tasks for retailers, and hence Quaker was totally out of step with industry practice. Quaker's failure to understand this distribution task performance requirement deprived Snapple of the retail shelf space it needed to compete in the intensely competitive soft-drink market. Within a couple of years, Quaker gave up and sold Snapple at a huge loss.

www.snapple.com

Considering Alternative Channel Structures

As discussed earlier in this chapter, the form or shape the channel takes to perform the distribution tasks is referred to as the channel structure. Also recall that the channel structure has three dimensions: (1) length, (2) intensity, and (3) the types of intermediaries used.

In terms of length, the number of alternatives available to the firm is usually limited to three or four at a maximum. These may range from using a direct structure from manufacturer to final customer as in the case of Dell Computer; one level of intermediaries as used by Saturn (auto retailers); two levels as used by Coors beer (wholesalers and retailers); or three levels of intermediaries, where an agent or broker may appear in the channel structure, which is common for many imported products.

The number of alternatives in the intensity dimension is even more limited, because intensity is so closely related to the nature of the product in question. Thus, the only realistic alternative for products intended for mass markets, such as Gillette razor blades, is intensive distribution in order to provide adequate market coverage. At the other end of the spectrum, expensive or prestigious products, such as BMW automobiles, require highly selective or even exclusive distribution to help maintain the aura and quality image of the product.

www.bmw.com
www.schnucks.com

Management's range of alternatives for the third dimension of channel structure, the types of intermediaries to use, is usually broader than for the first two. Within reason, management is limited only by its imagination in deciding what kinds of distributors it wants to include in its channel structure.[26] Supermarkets, for example, now sell all kinds of products besides groceries. Schnucks Markets Inc. of St. Louis sells furniture, ab-toning equipment, bed linens, TVs, and VCRs. HyVee, a supermarket chain based in Des Moines, has gone a step further with upscale merchandise such as $200 clocks, $250 tea sets, and $270 humidors.[27] So-called drug stores now sell almost every kind of product except drugs, or so it seems! And it is now possible to buy virtually anything from all types of mail-order companies or from firms operating on the Internet.[28]

Choosing an Optimal Structure

In practice it is not possible to choose an optimal channel structure in the strictest sense of that term. However, it is possible to choose an effective and efficient channel structure that can meet the firm's distribution objectives.

Many different approaches have been suggested over the years for choosing such a channel structure. Formal management science approaches, financial capital budgeting methods, and distribution cost analysis techniques have all been offered as a means for choosing channel structure. For the most part, these methods have not found much use in the real world. Much more common are approaches that rely on managerial judgment accompanied by some data on distribution costs and profit potentials. Judgment approaches can be made more formal through explicit identification of criteria to be used in choosing the channel structure. The most basic of these are:

▼ **Market variables:** The location of final customers, the numbers of customers and their density, together with their patterns of buying behavior are the key market variables to consider.

▼ **Product variables:** Such factors as bulk and weight, unit value, newness, technical vs. nontechnical, and perishability are product variables that are frequently important.

▼ **Company variables:** The financial capacity of the firm, its size, expertise, and desire for managerial control are some of the most important company variables.

▼ **Intermediary variables:** Cost, availability, and services provided are indicative of intermediary variables that management needs to consider.

▼ **Behavioral variables:** Factors such as the potential of particular channel structures to reduce conflict, while maximizing power, are key behavioral variables for management to consider.

▼ **External environmental variables:** Finally, variables such as economic conditions, sociocultural changes, competitive structure, technology, and government regulations can all be important environmental variables to consider when choosing channel structure.

Selecting the Channel Members

The selection of channel members, the last phase of channel design, consists of four steps:

1. Developing selection criteria.

2. Finding prospective channel members.

3. Evaluating prospective channel members against certain criteria.

4. Converting prospective members into actual members.

Developing Selection Criteria

Although general lists of channel member selection criteria, such as those shown in Figure 10.7, can provide a framework, each firm needs to develop criteria for selecting channel members that are consistent with its own distribution objectives and strategies. Thus, the list of criteria for a firm practicing highly selective distribution, such as Polo by Ralph Lauren, might include such factors as the prospective channel member's reputation and the competing product lines it carries. A firm using very intensive distribution, such as Bic pens, might use little more than one criterion consisting of the ability of the prospective channel members to pay the manufacturer for the products it ships to them.

Figure 10.7   General Criteria for Selecting Channel Members

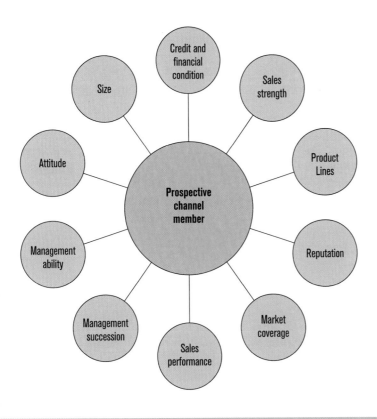

Finding Prospective Channel Members

The search for prospective channel members can utilize a number of sources. If the manufacturer has its own outside field sales force, this is generally regarded as the best prospect source because of the sales personnel's knowledge of prospective channel members in their territories. Other useful sources include customers, advertising, trade shows, and the Internet. Usually, a combination of several of these sources is used to find prospective channel members at both the wholesale and retail levels.[29]

Evaluating Prospective Channel Members

Once the prospective channel members have been identified, they need to be assessed against certain criteria to determine those who will actually be selected. This can be done by an individual manager (such as the sales manager) or by a committee. Depending upon the importance of the selection decision, such a committee might well include top management, even up to and including the chairman of the board if the selection decision is of great strategic importance. For example, when Goodyear Tire and Rubber Company selected Sears Roebuck and Company to sell its tires, Goodyear's CEO was involved in the decision because it would have long-term strategic implications for Goodyear.

Converting Prospective Members into Actual Members

We should not forget that the selection process is a two-way street. Not only do producers and manufacturers select retailers, wholesalers, or various agents and brokers, and franchisers select franchisees, but these intermediaries also select the manufacturers and franchisers.

Indeed, quite often it is the intermediaries, especially large and powerful retailers and wholesalers, who are in the driver's seat when it comes to selection. Wal-Mart for example can pick and choose virtually any manufacturers it wants. Consequently, the manufacturers or franchisers seeking to secure the services of quality channel members have to make a convincing case that selling their products will be profitable for the channel members.

Motivating Channel Members

Motivation of channel members refers to the actions taken by manufacturers (or franchisers) to get channel members to implement their channel strategy. Because efforts to motivate channel members take place in the interorganizational setting of the marketing channel, the process is usually more difficult than motivation in the intraorganizational setting of a single firm.

Motivation in the marketing channel can be viewed as a sequence of three steps:

1. Learning about the needs and problems of channel members.

2. Offering support to channel members to help meet their needs and solve their problems.

3. Providing ongoing leadership.

Although the stages in the motivation process are sequential, the process repeats itself because of the continuous feedback from steps two and three. This is illustrated in Figure 10.8.

Learning about Channel Members' Needs and Problems

If manufacturers or franchisers expect strong cooperation from channel members, their channel strategies should meet channel members' needs and help solve their problems. But this is easier said than done, because it is all too easy for manufacturers or franchisers to project their own views onto channel members rather than investigate the channel members' views. McDonald's fell into this trap when it tried to gain franchisee support for its

Figure 10.8   The Motivation Process in Marketing Channels

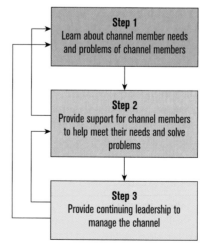

Step 1
Learn about channel member needs and problems of channel members

Step 2
Provide support for channel members to help meet their needs and solve problems

Step 3
Provide continuing leadership to manage the channel

ill-fated "Campaign 55" strategy. Campaign 55 was introduced by McDonald's in early 1997 and then hastily withdrawn after dismal customer response and even worse reactions by most McDonald's franchisees. The Campaign 55 promotion consisted of a special price deal on the famous Big Mac, which would sell for 55 cents during the promotion in honor of the founding of McDonald's in 1955. But to get the 55-cent price, consumers would have to buy a drink and fries with the purchase of the Big Mac. Consumers balked at the strings-attached promotion, while competitors like Burger King and Wendy's jumped on McDonald's in their advertisements by offering special deals with no strings. The franchisees were furious with McDonald's because they were not consulted and hence felt that the program was rammed down their throats. Had the franchisees been asked, most would have rejected the Campaign 55 promotion because they believed it was a big money loser for them. But what was most troubling was that many franchisees viewed this strategy as akin to using a "Bandaid to cure cancer." Campaign 55 was seen as a superficial, quick-fix gimmick that ignored more fundamental underlying needs and problems that franchisees were experiencing including lack of exciting new products to sell, pricing pressures, and franchisee proliferation.

McDonald's could have foreseen the problem if they had done a better job of learning about the real needs and problems of channel members. They should have avoided the tendency to project their own views and biases onto their channel members by taking a proactive approach to learning about channel member needs and problems.[30] This could have been accomplished through such approaches as: (1) researching channel members via in-house research teams, (2) investigating channel members using outside researchers, and (3) using channel member advisory committees.

In-house research consists of taking the same research methods used to gather information about final customers, and applying them to channel members in order to learn about their needs and problems.

Outside research can be used by firms who do not have an in-house research capability, or by those firms that want to avoid the possibility of bias that can creep into in-house research.

A *channel member advisory committee* consists of representatives from channel members and key executives from the manufacturer or franchiser who meet on a regular basis in some neutral location. This type of close interaction can foster the kind of candid dialogue needed to uncover channel member needs and problems, which may not emerge in the normal course of business.

Offering Support for Channel Members

Providing support for channel members can be done in a variety of ways, from an informal hit or miss approach to carefully planned strategic alliances.[31]

Informal support approaches are the most common in traditional channels. Advertising dollars, promotional support, incentives, contests, and increasingly in recent years *slotting fees* (cash payments to channel members to gain shelf space) are frequently offered by manufacturers to jump start the channel members' efforts to push the manufacturer's products. But these are often no more than cases of throwing money at a particular need or problem without thinking too deeply about it.[32]

Strategic alliances or *channel partnerships,* however, represent a more substantial and continuous commitment between the manufacturer and channel members. Support provided by the manufacturer is based on extensive knowledge of the needs and problems of the channel members and is carried out on a long-term basis. There are often specific performance expectations that have been worked out by the manufacturer in conjunction with the channel members. Procter & Gamble and Wal-Mart, for example, have built one of the strongest strategic alliances in the consumer packaged-goods industry. This partnership emphasizes close working relationships, including the stationing of P&G executives permanently on-site at Wal-Mart's headquarters to stay in close touch with Wal-Mart's top management. A sophisticated EDI system also provides a super efficient means for assuring availability of P&G products in all 2,500 Wal-Mart stores.

Producers (in this case, Coca-Cola) often motivate supermarkets by providing in-store display materials.

Providing Continuing Leadership

Even well-conceived motivation programs, based on a thorough attempt to understand the channel members' needs and problems together with a carefully targeted support program, still require leadership on a continuing basis to achieve effective motivation of channel members.[33] In other words, someone has to be in charge. Ethan Allen Interiors, Inc., provides a good example of a firm that takes a leadership role in motivating its 300 domestic and foreign independent retailers. Not only does this furniture maker provide continuing direction and advice on all aspects of the business from inventory control to store design, it also sends all of the retailers' salespeople to the company's training school, called Ethan Allen College, where they learn not only about home decorating techniques, but more importantly about the Ethan Allen way of doing things. The curriculum is designed to build teamwork and inspire confidence in the retailers to look to Ethan Allen for leadership in helping them to compete successfully in the fiercely competitive home furnishing business.

Coordinating Channel Strategy in the Marketing Mix

Channel strategy is not formulated in a vacuum. The other three Ps of the marketing mix—product, price, and promotion—must all be considered as well. What is especially important is to recognize the interrelationships among these marketing mix components, and to try to achieve synergy rather than conflict among the four Ps. Thus, channel strategy should enhance rather than detract from the firm's product, price, and promotion strategies.[34]

Product Strategy and Channel Strategy

Product strategy is often dependent on channel strategy because some key product strategies interface with channel strategy in ways that can mean the difference between success or failure. ***Product positioning strategy,*** which seeks to present products to customers in a way that gives them a certain image relative to competitive products, illustrates the relationship between product strategy and channel strategy. Consider, for example, a product such as Gargoyles Performance Eye Wear, which makes numerous high-end sunglasses ranging in price from $85–$200. The sunglasses are aimed at skiers, bikers, water-sports

www.gargoyles.com

enthusiasts, basketball players, and other sports aficionados. The large range of target customers and the relatively high prices reflect a product positioning strategy aimed at transforming sunglasses from a utilitarian product to an important fashion item associated with upscale, sports-oriented, glamorous lifestyles. Retailers play a crucial role in establishing the positioning strategy of these products. To position sunglasses as such an exciting and glamorous product with the high prices to match, retailers must create the kind of atmosphere that supports that image.[35] If retailers simply piled up these pricey sunglasses in a bin or stuck them on pegboard, the special aura associated with these products would be drastically undermined. So store atmosphere, display fixturing, and attentive personal selling at the retail level are crucial to the success of this product positioning strategy.

Pricing Strategy and Channel Strategy

Pricing strategy is closely related to channel management, because pricing decisions need to take into account channel issues if the manufacturer expects strong cooperation from the channel members. Clearly, such factors as the profit margins available to channel members, the different prices charged to various classes of channel members, prices of competitive products carried, special pricing deals, changing pricing policies, and the use of price incentives are all factors of major concern to many channel members. Thus, the manufacturer needs to make sure that it knows something about the expectations of channel members for these and other relevant pricing issues before embarking on any pricing strategy. A channel pricing miscue experienced by the Chrysler Corporation provides a case in point of why it is necessary to take into account channel members' views on pricing strategies. The Neon subcompact car introduced in the mid-1990s was touted as an automobile that could compete successfully in the under $10,000 market. With a base price advertised at just $8,975, Plymouth and Dodge dealers thought the Neons would move off their lots by the truckload. But a large gap occurred between the price that was advertised and what actually was available to consumers in dealer showrooms. Customers coming into the showroom asking to "see the new $9,000 car" were quickly turned off when they found out that a decently equipped Neon cost several thousand more. So, instead of a $9,000 car, the customer was looking at a $12,000–$14,000 car. At these prices, Neons piled up on dealers' lots.[36] As it had done over a decade earlier with the introduction of the K-car, Chrysler had erred in formulating its pricing for the Neon. The low advertised price was essentially used as a gimmick to build showroom traffic. It was then up to the dealers to convince customers to actually purchase the higher-priced and more profitable versions of the car, which in most cases were the only models available. But this pricing strategy had not worked for the K-car and was not working for the Neon. Dealers found it too difficult to undo the low-price expectations of customers. Needless to say, numerous dealers were seething at Chrysler for not asking for their input about this pricing strategy.

www.chrysler.com

Promotion Strategy and Channel Strategy

Promotion interfaces extensively with channel strategy, because many promotions undertaken by the manufacturer require strong channel member support and follow-through to work successfully. For example, major advertising campaigns frequently require point-of-purchase displays in the store, special deals and merchandising campaigns require channel members to stock up on extra inventory, and contests and incentives call for participation from retailers and wholesalers. When Apple Computer Inc. launched the iMac Computer in August of 1998, it spent over $100 million on the advertising campaign for the new computer. This was the largest advertising expenditure for a product launch in Apple's history. But in order for this massive advertising expenditure to be successful, retailers had to be willing to inventory tens of thousands of iMacs well in advance of the release date, provide space for extensive point-of-purchase displays, and participate in special promotional events such as contests and T-shirt giveaways. Retailers also had to prep their salespeople so that they could show off the new iMac to its best advantage and respond to sales objections, such as the lack of disk drives on the iMac.[37]

www.imac.com

Evaluating Channel Member Performance

The evaluation of channel member performance is necessary to assess how successful the channel members have been in implementing the manufacturers' channel strategies and achieving distribution objectives. Evaluations require the manufacturer to gather information on the channel members. But the manufacturer's ability to do this will be affected by its degree of control of channel members. Usually, the higher the degree of control, the more information the manufacturer (or franchiser) can gather, and vice versa.

Southland Corporation, the franchiser of 7-Eleven stores in the United States, is an organization that does enjoy substantial control of its franchisees. It has therefore been able to develop and implement a very sophisticated channel member evaluation system that enables Southland to monitor the performance of each of its 5,500 stores down to the smallest detail. By using a point-of-sale (POS) computer linked to headquarters, the home office can track the sales of thousands of individual products in each store. But what especially sets this channel member performance evaluation system apart from other similar POS performance monitoring systems is the monitoring it enables Southland to maintain on the actions of individual store managers. Headquarters can keep track of how much time each store manager spends using the analytical tools contained in the system, which store managers are expected to use to analyze sales data, demographic trends, and even local weather conditions in order to maximize sales opportunities and minimize inventory costs.[38]

www.7-eleven.com

LOGISTICS IN MARKETING CHANNELS

Logistics, also often referred to as *physical distribution (PD),* is commonly defined as "planning, implementing, and controlling the physical flows of materials and final goods from points of origin to points of use to meet customers' needs at a profit."[39] In more recent years, the term *supply chain management* has been used to describe logistical systems that emphasize close cooperation and comprehensive interorganizational management to integrate the logistical operations of the different firms in the channel.[40] Although a detailed discussion of the differences between what might be referred to as the "traditional" approach to logistics and the supply chain management approach is beyond the scope of this chapter. Table 10.1 provides an overview of the key distinctions. In any case, whether one chooses to use the term physical distribution, logistics, or supply chain management, the underlying principle is the building of strong cooperation among channel members through effective interorganizational management.[41]

The Role of Logistics

Even the most carefully designed and managed marketing channel must rely on logistics to actually make products available to customers. The creation of time and place utilities, essential for customer satisfaction, is therefore dependent upon logistics. The movement of the right amount of the right products to the right place at the right time is a commonly heard description of what logistics is supposed to do. But achieving this goal is no simple job. On the contrary, mass markets, with their great diversity of customer segments spread over vast geographic areas, can make the task of logistics complex and expensive. Thus, logistics has become a gigantic industry that pervades virtually all firms, from the largest to the smallest.[42]

Logistics Systems, Costs, and Components

For many years, logistics was equated mainly with transportation. Hence the field was narrowly defined in terms of the activities involved in shipping and receiving products

	Approach	
Element	**Traditional**	**Supply Chain**
Inventory management approach	Independent efforts	Joint reduction in channel inventories
Total cost approach	Minimize firm costs	Channel-wide cost efficiencies
Time horizon	Short-term	Long-term
Amount of information sharing and monitoring	Limited to needs of current transaction	As required for planning and monitoring processes
Amount of coordination of multiple levels in the channel	Single contact for the transaction between channel pairs	Multiple contacts between levels in firms and levels in channels
Joint planning	Transaction-based	Ongoing
Compatibility of corporate philosophies	Not relevant	Compatible at least for key relationships
Breadth of supplier base	Large to increase competition and spread risk	Small to increase coordination
Channel leadership	Not needed	Needed for coordination focus
Amount of sharing risks and rewards	Each on its own	Risks and rewards shared over the long term
Speed of operations, information, and inventory flows	"Warehouse" orientation (storage, safety stock) interrupted by barriers to flows; localized to channel pairs	"Distribution Center" orientation (inventory velocity) interconnecting flows, JIT Quick Response

Table 10.1 Comparison of Traditional and Supply Chain Approaches to the Management of Logistics

and was given relatively little management attention. But in recent decades, a broader perspective referred to as the **systems concept** has emerged for dealing with logistical problems. Rather than being thought of as separate and distinct from one another, factors as diverse as transportation, materials handling, inventory control, warehousing, and packaging of goods are now seen as interrelated components of a system. Decisions or actions affecting one component could have implications for other components of the logistical system. For example, a faster mode of transportation for moving a quantity of iMacs from California to New York could result in a lower level of inventory needed in New York, which in

System concept of logistics
entails viewing all components of a logistical system together and understanding the relationships among them.

Efficient order processing involves both materials handling and transportation.

turn could result in a smaller warehouse being required. Or conversely, a slower mode of transport for shipping the iMacs from California to New York might well mean that a larger inventory and a larger warehouse would be needed at New York because of the slower rate of resupply.

The concept of logistics as a system has served as the foundation of modern logistics management. In essence, those in charge of managing logistics seek to find the optimum combination of logistics components (transportation, materials handling, order processing, inventory control, warehousing, and packaging) to meet customer service demands.

The logistics manager also attempts to achieve the desired level of customer service at the lowest cost by applying the ***total cost approach.*** This concept is a logical extension of the systems concept, because it addresses all of the costs of logistics taken together, rather than the cost of individual components taken separately, and seeks to minimize the total cost. Consequently, when designing a logistics system, a company must examine the cost of each component and how it affects other components. For instance, a faster mode of transport used to ship the iMacs mentioned above might increase transportation costs. Since the inventory levels and warehouse needed in New York would be smaller (because the faster transportation mode allows for quicker resupply), the inventory carrying costs and warehouse costs will be lower. These savings in costs may be more than enough to offset the higher transportation costs. So, from the standpoint of the total cost of the logistics system, the increase in transportation costs for the faster mode of transport may well result in a lower total cost for logistics.

The use of the systems concept and the total cost approach to manage logistics is shown in Figure 10.9. This figure suggests not only that all the basic components of a system are related, but also that the systems concept and the total cost approach provide the guiding principles for blending the components. This blending allows delivery of the types

Figure 10.9   View of Logistics Management Based on the Systems Concept and the Total Cost Approach

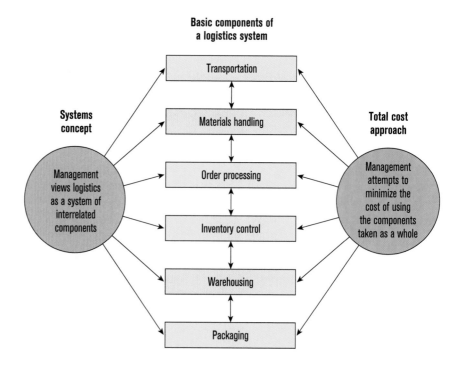

and levels of services desired by customers at the lowest total cost for the logistics system as a whole.

The basic components of a logistics system are transportation, materials handling, order processing, inventory control, warehousing, and packaging. Each of these components will now be briefly considered.

Transportation

Transportation is the most obviously necessary component of any logistics system, because in virtually all cases products must be physically moved from one location to another if a transaction is to be completed. Transportation is also often the component accounting for the highest percentage of the total cost of logistics.

From a logistics management standpoint, the overriding issue facing the firm is choosing the optimum mode of transportation to meet customer service demands. This can be a complex task because there are so many considerations. A few of these are: Should the firm use its own carriers or common carriers? What are the different rates available? What specific transportation services are offered? How reliable are various common carriers? What modes of transport are competitors using? Moreover, if the systems concept and total cost approach are applied, the logistics manager must think in terms of how the transportation component interacts with and affects the total cost of logistics. Such decisions require specialized knowledge and expertise—not only of logistics systems, but also of the specialized needs of the industry involved and of the latest technologies available.[43]

Materials Handling

Materials handling encompasses the range of activities and equipment involved in the placement and movement of products in storage areas. Questions that must be addressed when designing materials handling systems include:

▼ How should we minimize the distances products are moved within the warehouse during the course of receiving, storage, and shipping?

▼ What kinds of mechanical equipment (such as conveyor belts, cranes, and forklifts) should be used?

▼ How can we make the best use of the labor involved in receiving, handling, and shipping products?

For example, the growing use of ***cross-docking*** (sometimes referred to as ***flow-through distribution***) has significantly enhanced materials handling efficiency.[44] In cross-docking, products from an arriving truck are not stored in a warehouse and then resorted later to fill orders. Rather, the merchandise is simply moved across the receiving dock to other trucks for immediate delivery to stores. This eliminates the need to pick stored products at a later time. In short, products are moved straight from shipping to receiving.

Order Processing

The importance of order processing in logistics lies in its relationships with ***order cycle time,*** which is the time between when an order is placed and when it is received by the customer. If order processing is cumbersome and inefficient, it can slow down the order cycle time considerably. It may even increase transportation costs if a faster mode of transportation must be used to make up for the slow order processing time.

Order processing may often appear to be routine but may actually be the result of a great deal of planning, capital investment, and training of people. When many thousands of orders are received on a daily basis, filling the orders quickly and accurately can be a challenging task. Indeed, in the hospital supply industry where medical and surgical supplies account for some 750,000 different products, developing a modern order processing system is a nightmarish challenge, because there is no standard nomenclature for all these different products. Hence, confusion and costly mixups have caused large numbers of errors and hundreds of thousands of returns for credit. The industry is just now beginning to grapple with the order processing problems, but it will take years to attain the level of efficiency found in consumer product industries.[45]

Inventory Control

Inventory control refers to the firm's attempt to hold the lowest level of inventory that will still enable it to meet customer demand. This is a never-ending battle that all firms face. It is a critically important one as well. Inventory carrying costs—including the costs of financing; insurance; storage; and lost, damaged, and stolen goods—on average can amount to approximately 25 percent of the value of the inventory per year. For some types of merchandise, such as perishable goods or fashion merchandise, carrying costs can be considerably higher. Yet without inventory to meet customer demand on a regular and timely basis, a firm could not stay in business for very long.

Ideally, the firm would always want to be in the position of keeping inventory at the lowest possible level while at the same time placing orders for goods in large quantities, because holding the number of its own orders to the fewest possible enables the firm to minimize ordering costs. Unfortunately, there is a conflict between these two objectives. Average inventory carrying costs rise in direct proportion to the level of the inventory, while average ordering costs decrease in rough proportion to the size of the order. Thus, a trade-off must be made between these two costs to find the optimum levels for both. This point, usually referred to as the ***economic order quantity (EOQ),*** occurs at the point at which total costs (inventory carrying cost plus ordering costs) are lowest, as illustrated in Figure 10.10. As the figure shows, the logistics manager strives to achieve the lowest total cost by balancing inventory carrying and ordering costs.

One firm that has done a good job of controlling its inventory is Corning Consumer Products Co., a unit of Corning Inc. Having the right quantities of each Corelle dinnerware design pattern had become a huge problem, because it is so difficult to predict consumer buying patterns, especially around Christmas. To solve the problem, Corning developed a sophisticated inventory control system. A key feature of the system is the requirement that Corning keep a major portion of its Corelle dinnerware undecorated until it gets up-to-the-minute sales data from retailers. Soon after the system had been installed, it saved the company from a disastrous mistake. A week after a giant retail chain launched

www.corning.com

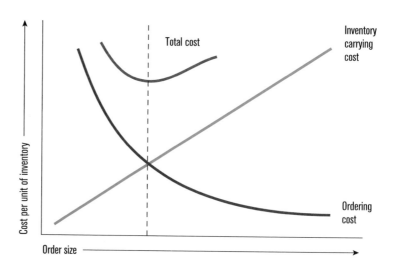

Figure 10.10 Economic Order Quantity (EOQ) Model

a special on 12-piece dinnerware sets, the computer-based forecasting model (a critical part of the inventory control system) predicted that the promotion would be a flop. Corning quickly warned another retailer to cancel its own order for 160,000 of these sets and replace it with an order for a more popular design. The unfinished dishes were completed with the newly-selected design and shipped out in less than two weeks.[46]

Warehousing

The warehousing or storage component of a logistics system is concerned with the holding of products until they are ready to be sold. Warehousing can actually be one of the more complex components of a logistics system. Quite often, when considering options for warehousing, the firm faces several key decisions, each of which can be difficult and complex. These decisions might include (1) the location of warehouse facilities, (2) the number of warehousing units, (3) the size of the units, (4) the design of the units including layout and internal systems, and (5) the question of ownership. Successful decisions in each of the areas require careful planning and may require input from experts in such fields as location analysis, real estate, operations research, and industrial engineering, in addition to logistics management.

Warehousing is closely linked to the ability of firms to provide high levels of customer service. For example, with the growth of the Internet as a mode of consumer shopping, far more shipments of *eaches*—single items as opposed to product lots—will create massive numbers of *onesie transactions* in which only a single item is purchased.[47] Moreover, consumers will expect these single items to be delivered very quickly. Experts in the warehousing industry believe such demands by Internet shoppers will increase rather than decrease the need for warehousing, because most Internet retailers will be storefronts with no inventory on hand. They will instead rely on numerous, well-located, and efficient warehouses—either their own or third party—to provide the level of product availability demanded by Internet shoppers.[48]

Packaging

Packaging and the costs associated with the packaging of products are relevant as a component of the logistics system because packaging can affect the other components of the system, and vice versa. For example, the type of transport used can affect packaging and packaging costs; in the case of air freight, for instance, packaging costs are generally reduced because risks of damage are generally lower than if rail or truck transportation were used. Materials handling and order processing procedures and costs can also be affected by packaging because well-designed packaging can help to increase efficiencies in these components of the logistics system. Effective packaging can also help control inventory carrying costs by reducing product damage. Further, warehouse space, and thus costs, can be saved if packaging is designed to be space efficient. Therefore, packaging is far more than just a promotional device for fostering product differentiation and attracting consumer attention. Packaging has an important logistical dimension that can make a significant difference in the effectiveness and efficiency of the logistics system. Indeed, a product in distinctive and attractive packaging will have even more appeal if it is also easy to handle, conveniently stackable, and shelf-space efficient.

THE OUTPUT OF THE LOGISTICS SYSTEM: CUSTOMER SERVICE

Good customer service is the desired end result of virtually all business activities, and logistics is a very important part of these efforts. This is particularly true for those aspects of customer service that are a direct function of the logistics system, including:

1. Time from order receipt to order shipment.

2. Order size and assortment constraints.

3. Percentage of items out of stock.

4. Percentage of orders filled accurately.

5. Percentage of orders filled within a given number of days from receipt of the order.

6. Percentage of orders filled.

7. Percentage of customer orders that arrive in good condition.

8. Order cycle time (time from order placement to order delivery).

9. Ease and flexibility of order placement.

These nine logistics services and many others (see Table 10.2) are often quantified and utilized as *logisitical service standards,* against which the manufacturer's actual performance is then measured.[49] For example, the first standard shown in the list above—time from order receipt to order shipment—might be set at 24 hours for 90 percent of all orders received. So, for every 100 orders received, the manufacturer must have 90 of the orders processed and shipped within 24 hours to meet the standard. The second service standard in the list—order size and assortment constraints—might be set in terms of some minimum quantity of products, and certain restrictions might be placed on mixing the various products unless specified minimum quantities of each item are ordered. A steel producer, for example, might set the minimum order for various gauges of sheet metal at two tons, and the inclusion of several gauges in a single order might require a certain combined minimum tonnage. The third standard—percentage of items out of stock, or *stockouts*—is almost always set in terms of a percentage of the items ordered during a given period that cannot be filled from inventory. Thus, if a manufacturer wants to fill 95 percent of the items ordered, its stockout percentage can be no higher than 5 percent to meet the standard. The other six service standards in the list can be quantified and used in a similar fashion.

In general, the higher the service standards offered, the higher the costs will be. While well-designed logistics systems and modern technology can keep these costs under control, it is usually not possible to completely escape the trade-off of higher costs for higher service standards.

A manufacturer must cover these costs either indirectly in the price it charges for products, or by passing them along to channel members in the form of service charges. In either case, there is little point in offering logistics services that channel members do not want, or higher levels of service than they desire. Types or levels of logistics service that go beyond real channel member demands simply increase costs for channel members without providing them with any desired benefits. Thus the key issue in defining logistics

Table 10.2	**Inventory of Logistical Aspects of Customer Service**
1. Order processing time	14. Claims response
2. Order assembly time	15. Billing procedures
3. Delivery time	16. Average order cycle time
4. Inventory reliability	17. Order cycle time variability
5. Order size constraints	18. Rush service
6. Consolidation allowed	19. Availability
7. Consistency	20. Competent technical representatives
8. Frequency of sales visits	21. Equipment demonstrations
9. Ordering convenience	22. Availability of published material
10. Order progress information	23. Accuracy in filling orders
11. Inventory backup during promotions	24. Terms of sale
12. Invoice format	25. Protective packaging
13. Physical condition of goods	26. Cooperation

service standards is to determine precisely the types and levels of logistics service desired by the channel members.

Chapter Summary

To satisfy the demands of hundreds of millions of customers, a myriad of goods and services from all over the world must be made available when, where, and how the customer wants these goods and services on a regular and continuing basis. It is through marketing channels, the networks of organizations that create time, place, and possession utilities, that this monumental task is accomplished. As one of the four "Ps" of the marketing mix, *place* (as created by marketing channels) plays a crucial role in marketing strategy as businesses attempt to compete in the marketplace.

The form or shape that a marketing channel takes is referred to as *channel structure,* which consists of the three dimensions of length, intensity, and types of intermediaries included in the channel. Channel structure is determined by three major forces: (1) the distribution tasks to be performed, (2) the economics of performing distributions tasks, and (3) management's desire for control of the channels of distribution.

When marketing channels are developed, five flows emerge: (1) product flow, (2) negotiation flow, (3) ownership flow, (4) information flow, and (5) promotion flow. All of these flows must be managed and coordinated to achieve effective and efficient marketing channels.

Marketing channels are not only economic systems but social systems as well. As such, power and conflict, inherent in all social systems, play an important role in channels of distribution.

Marketing channel management is the analysis, planning, organizing, and controlling of the firm's marketing channels. This process consists of six basic areas: (1) formulating channel strategy, (2) designing the channel structure, (3) selecting channel members, (4) motivating channel members, (5) coordinating channel strategy with the marketing mix, and (6) evaluating channel member performance. All of the components of channel management contribute to a firm's attempt to gain a sustainable competitive advantage.

Logistics, also referred to as *physical distribution* or *PD,* is the planning, implementing, and controlling of the physical flows of materials and final goods from points of origin to points of use in order to meet customers' needs at a profit. In recent years, the term *supply chain management* has also been used to describe this process. A logistics system consists of six major components: (1) transportation, (2) materials handling, (3) order processing, (4) inventory control, (5) warehousing, and (6) packaging. The logistics manager needs to use the *systems concept* in dealing with these logistical components to understand the relationships among them as well as the *total cost approach* to determine the costs associated with logistics. The service standards developed by the logistics manager should be based on customer needs rather than on the capabilities of the logistical system.

Key Terms

Time, place, and possession utilities are conditions that enable consumers and business users to have products available for use when and where they want them.

Channel structure consists of all of the businesses and institutions (including producers or manufacturers and final customers) who are involved in performing the functions of buying, selling, and transferring title.

Channel length is the number of levels in a marketing channel.

Channel intensity refers to the number of intermediaries at each level of the marketing channel.

Economies of scale and economies of scope are obtained by spreading the costs of distribution over a large quantity of products (scale) or over a wide variety of products (scope).

Interorganizational content refers to channel management that extends beyond a firm's own organization into other independent businesses.

Sustainable competitive advantage is a competitive edge that cannot be easily or quickly copied by competitors in the short run.

System concept of logistics entails viewing all components of a logistical system together and understanding the relationships among them.

Additional Key Terms and Concepts

marketing channel, distribution channel, or channel of distribution

facilitating channel

intensive distribution

exclusive distribution

distribution tasks, marketing functions, or channel functions

specialization or division of labor

channel flows

negotiation flow

information flow

marketing channel power

channel management

four Ps of the marketing mix

distribution objectives

motivation of channel members

informal support approaches

product positioning strategy

supply chain management

cross-docking or flow-through distribution

economic order quantity (EOQ)

onesie transactions

stockouts

form utility

sales channel

facilitating agencies

selective distribution

scrambled merchandising

concentration, equalization, and dispersion

accumulating, sorting and assorting

transaction efficiency

product flow

ownership flow

promotion flow

marketing channel conflict

channel strategy

channel design

electronic data interchange (EDI)

channel member advisory committee

strategic alliances or channel partnerships

logistics or physical distribution (PD)

total cost approach

order cycle time

eaches

logisitical service standards

Questions for Discussion

1. The opening of this chapter talks about the need for billions of customers around the globe to somehow be matched up with millions of products. How do marketing channels fit into this matching up process? Explain?

2. Explain the concepts of time, place, and possession utilities in terms of several products that you use on a daily basis.

3. Is the marketing channel always the most important component of the marketing mix or does it depend on the particular set of circumstance involved? Discuss.

4. What are the determinants of channel structure? Explain.

5. Why do distribution tasks need to be performed? Explain in terms of the various discrepancies.

6. How does specialization/division of labor as well as transaction efficiency relate to the economics of distribution task performance?

7. Identify and describe the five flows in marketing channels. What is the significance of the channel flows concept for understanding marketing channels?

8. Why is it important to view marketing channels as social systems as well as economic systems?

9. Define *marketing channel management* and what is meant by the *interorganizational context* of channel management.

10. Discuss the relationship between channel strategy and creating a sustainable competitive advantage. Is channel strategy the only way to gain a sustainable competitive advantage? Explain.

11. What are the four steps involved in the selection of channel members? How does channel member selection relate to channel strategy and channel design?

12. Successful motivation of channel members is dependent upon a process that involves several steps. What are these steps and why is it important to follow them when attempting to motivate channel members?

13. The text states that "channel strategy should enhance rather than detract from the firm's product, price, and promotion strategies." What does this have to do with coordinating channel strategy in the marketing mix? Discuss.

14. Define *logistics* or *physical distribution*. In the age of electronic commerce via the Internet, is this concept still valid? Discuss.

15. What is meant by the *systems concept* and *total cost approach?*

Internet Questions

Internet Exercise #1

Electronic commerce or e-commerce, where goods and services are bought or sold via the Internet, may well revolutionize marketing channels as we move into the next millennium. In 1998 an estimated 10 billion of sales took place over the Internet, a tripling of the dollar volume of 1997. Internet sales are expected to grow even more spectacularly in the future so that within a few years into the new millennium, hundreds of billions in sales may occur and account for as much as 10 percent of total retail sales by 2003. Of course, no one knows for sure that this will happen, but if growth continues at its present pace of tripling annually, electronic marketing channels will eventually be a gigantic force in the distribution of goods and services.

> Question: What is it about Internet shopping that makes it so appealing to so many consumers?

Provide your answer to this question by doing the following:

1. Go online and visit the Web sites of five different Internet sellers.

2. Make sure that you vary the product categories of the five sellers. (Do not, for example, pick five booksellers or five CD sellers.)

3. Click through each Web site and rate each on the 10-point scales below that compare the Internet channel with conventional channels.
   a. How would you rate the **convenience** provided by the Internet channel compared with a conventional one? (circle your answers)

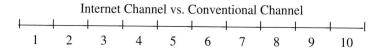

Internet Channel vs. Conventional Channel

1   2   3   4   5   6   7   8   9   10

   b. How would you rate the **selection** provided by the Internet channel compared with a conventional one? (circle your answers)

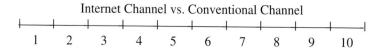

Internet Channel vs. Conventional Channel

1   2   3   4   5   6   7   8   9   10

   c. How would you rate the Internet channel vs. the conventional channel in offering **low prices?** (circle your answers)

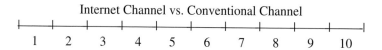

Internet Channel vs. Conventional Channel

1   2   3   4   5   6   7   8   9   10

   d. How would you rate the **fun** provided of shopping on the Internet channel compared with the conventional channel? (circle your answers)

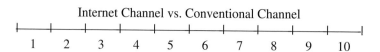

Internet Channel vs. Conventional Channel

1   2   3   4   5   6   7   8   9   10

   e. How **secure** do you feel if you were to use your credit card to make a purchase on the Internet channel vs. the conventional channel? (circle your answers)

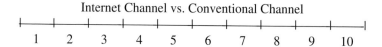

Internet Channel vs. Conventional Channel

1   2   3   4   5   6   7   8   9   10

4. Now, for each Web site that you visited, add up the scores for the five questions comparing Internet channels to conventional channels.

5. What is your reaction to the scores?

Internet Exercise #2

1. Pick out one of your favorite conventional retailers. This can be a small or large retailer in any product category, a department store, or a mass merchandiser. Visit the store in your normal fashion but be sure to do the following:
   a. Write down the time you spent getting to and from the store and the total distance traveled.
   b. Make note of any parking problems or, if public transportation was used, any hassles that stand out.
   c. After you entered the store, make note of how hard or easy it was to navigate the aisles and pick out the product(s) you were looking for.

    d. Jot down your thoughts on availability and helpfulness of salespeople.

    e. Record how long it took you to get through the check-out line.

2. Go online to the Web site of the same store you just shopped at. Or if no Web site for that store exists, find the Web site for another retailer that is comparable to the retailer you visited. Then do the following:

    a. Write down the time it took you to boot-up your computer and locate the Web site.

    b. Navigate (click) through the site and make notes of any problems you experience.

    c. If you are actually going to buy a product(s), jot down your thoughts on the ease or difficulty of doing so. If you are just shopping, write down your thoughts on the ease or difficulty of the selection process up to the point before actual purchase.

    d. Record how long the online shopping process took from the time you booted-up the computer until shut down.

    e. If you made a purchase online, record how long it takes before you actually receive the product.

3. Compare your two sets of notes on conventional shopping and Internet shopping and answer the following questions:

    a. What do you see as the **advantages** (if any) of shopping via the Internet vs. conventional shopping?

    b. What do you see as the **disadvantages** (if any) of shopping on the Internet vs. conventional shopping?

    c. Do you see yourself doing more shopping online in the future? Why or why not?

Internet Exercise #3

Check ads from newspapers, magazines, or TV and pick out any five firms that ask you to visit their Web sites and who provide their Web addresses in the ads. Now, visit those Web sites and answer the following questions:

1. Are you impressed with the Web site? Why or why not?

2. What information has been provided by the Web sites that was not offered in the ads?

3. Do you think that visiting these Web sites after seeing the advertisements was worth the extra time and effort involved? Why or why not?

4. If you were in the market for the products or services in question, would the material provided by your online visit make it easier for you to make a purchase? Explain.

Endnotes

[1]Mike France, "Are Corporate Predators on the Loose?" *Business Week* (February 23, 1998): pp. 124–126.

[2]Christine B. Bucklin, Stephen P. DeFalco, John R. DeVincentis and John P. Lewis III, "Are You Tough Enough to Manage Your Channels?" *The McKinsey Quarterly* (November 1, 1996): pp. 104–114.

[3]Robert D. Hof, "The Net Is Open for Business—Big Time," *Business Week* (August 31, 1998): pp. 108–109.

[4]Stephan A. Butscher, "Loyalty Programs Can Work for B-to-B Customers Too," *Marketing News* (June 22, 1998): p. 6.

[5]Bert Rosenbloom, *Marketing Channels: A Management View* 6th ed. (Fort Worth: The Dryden Press, 1999), pp. 4–6.

[6]Paul Beckett, "Visa Touts Ease of Shopping on Internet," *The Wall Street Journal* (October 30, 1998): p. B12.

[7]Rosenbloom, *Marketing Channels,* pp. 7–10.

[8]Bob Ortega, "How Big Brewers Are Sidling into Retail," *The Wall Street Journal* (May 18, 1998): pp. B1, B6.

[9]Gary L. Frazier and Kersi D. Antia, "Exchange Relationships and Interfirm Power in Channels of Distribution," *Journal of the Academy of Marketing Science* (Fall 1995): pp. 321–326.

[10]Bert Rosenbloom and Trina Larsen, "A Functional Approach to International Channel Structure and the Role of Independent Wholesalers," *Journal of Marketing Channels* (Summer 1993): pp. 65–82.

[11]Wroe Alderson, *Marketing Behavior and Executive Action* (Homewood, IL: Richard D. Irwin, 1957).

[12]John W. Cebrowski, "Global Success Tied to Key Management Considerations," *Marketing News* (July 20, 1998): pp. 14–16.

[13]Rosenbloom, *Marketing Channels,* pp. 19–22.

[14]Donald V. Fites, "Make Your Dealers Your Partners," *Harvard Business Review* (March–April 1996): pp. 84–95.

[15]Rekha Balu, "Big Brewers Find Price War Seems to Have No End," *The Wall Street Journal* (July 2, 1998): p. B6.

[16]Louis W. Stern and Jay W. Brown, "Distribution Channels: A Social Systems Approach" in *Distribution Channels: Behavioral Dimensions,* ed. Louis W. Stern, (New York: Houghton Mifflin, 1969): pp. 6–19.

[17]Shelley Branch, "McDonald's Strikes Out with Grownups," *Fortune* (November 11, 1996): pp. 157–58.

[18]Bert Rosenbloom, "Conflict and Channel Efficiency: Some Conceptual Models for the Decision Maker," *Journal of Marketing* (July 1973): pp. 26–30.

[19]Bert Rosenbloom, "Channel Management," in *Encyclopedia of Marketing,* ed. Michael J. Baker, (London: Routledge, 1995), pp. 551–570.

[20]Douglas Lavin and Krystal Miller, "Goodbye to Haggling: Savvy Consumers Are Buying Their Cars Like Refrigerators," *The Wall Street Journal* (August 20, 1993): pp. B1, B3.

[21]Donald V. Fites, "Make Your Dealers Your Partners," *Harvard Business Review* (March–April 1996): pp. 85–87.

[22]Angelo B. Henderson, "Ford Explores Idea of Joining Dealers," *The Wall Street Journal* (May 12, 1997): p. A2.

[23]Nikhil Deogun, "PepsiCo Chief's Stand on Exclusive Pacts Adds to Cola Wars Charged Atmosphere," *The Wall Street Journal* (May 15, 1998): p. A4.

[24]Robert D. Hof and Ellen Neuborne, "Amazon.com, the Wild World of E-Commerce," *Business Week* (December 14, 1998): pp. 106–112.

[25]Richard Gibson and Laurie M. Grossman, "Snapple Lowering of Profit Projection Underscores Continuation of Problems," *The Wall Street Journal* (November 7, 1994): p. A4.

[26]Michael Krantz, "Virtual Shopping Is Better Than the Real Thing," *Time* (July 20, 1998): pp. 36–41.

[27]Calmetta Y. Coleman, "Selling Jewelry, Dolls, and TVs Next to Corn Flakes," *The Wall Street Journal* (November 19, 1997): pp. B1, B2.

[28] "Click 'Til You Drop," *U.S. News and World Report* (December 7, 1998): pp. 42–45.

[29]Angelo B. Henderson, "GM's Saturn Division Plans to Add 125 Dealerships," *The Wall Street Journal* (February 20, 1998): p. B9.

[30]Richard C. Munn, "Marketers Must Align Themselves with Sales," *Marketing News* (November 9, 1998): p. 12.

[31]Kathleen Kerwin, "GM Brings Its Dealers Up to Speed," *Business World* (February 23, 1998): pp. 82–84.

[32]Jeffrey Tannenbaum, "To Pacify Irate Franchisees, Franchisers Extend Services," *The Wall Street Journal* (February 24, 1995): pp. B1, B2.

[33]Nirmalya Kumar, "The Power of Trust in Manufacturer–Retailer Relationships," *Harvard Business Review* (November–December 1996): pp. 92–106.

[34]Kenneth Leung, "Beyond Web Pages: Integrating the Internet," *Marketing News* (June 22, 1998): p. 9.

[35]Stephanie N. Mehta, "For Everything Under the Sun, Specialized Sunglasses," *The Wall Street Journal* (February 5, 1996): p. B1.

[36]Neal Templin, "As Neon Sales Sag, Chrysler Considers Producing More Lower-Priced Versions," *The Wall Street Journal* (January 13, 1995): p. A4.

[37]Jim Carlton, "From Apple, A New Marketing Blitz," *The Wall Street Journal* (August 14, 1998): pp. B1, B4.

[38]Norihiko Shirouzu and John Bigness, "7-Eleven Operators Resist System to Monitor Managers," *The Wall Street Journal* (June 16, 1997): pp. B1, B3.

[39]Philip Kotler, *Marketing Management, Analysis, Planning, Implementation, and Control* 9th edition (Upper Saddle River, N.J.: Prentice-Hall, 1997).

[40]Donald J. Bowersox and David J. Closs, *Logistics Management: An Integrated Supply Chain Process* (New York: McGraw-Hill, 1996).

[41]Tom Davis, "Effective Supply Chain Management," *Sloan Management Review* (1993): pp. 35–46.

[42]Neil Gross, "Leapfrogging a Few Links," *Business Week* (June 22, 1998): pp. 140–142.

[43]"Transportation Upgrade Boosts Productivity," *Grocery Distribution* (September/October 1997): pp. 28–32.

[44]Carol Casper, "Flow-Through: Mirage or Reality?" *Food Logistics* (October/November 1997): pp. 44–58.

[45]Rhonda L. Rundle, "Hospital Cost Cutters Push Use of Scanners to Track Inventories," *The Wall Street Journal* (June 10, 1997): pp. A1, A8.

[46]Michael M. Phillips, "Retailers Rely on High-Tech Distribution," *The Wall Street Journal* (December 19, 1996): pp. A2, A6.

[47]James Aaron Cooke, "The Retail Revolution Is Coming!" *Logistics Management* (April 1996): pp. 48–51.

[48]Steven E. Salkin, "Debunking the Myths of the Internet," *Warehousing Management* (October 1997): pp. 29–32.

[49]Carol C. Bienstock, John T. Mentzer, and Monroe Murphy Bird, "Measuring Physical Distribution Service Quality," *Journal of the Academy of Marketing Science* (Winter 1997): pp. 31–44.

Dell Computer Corporation: Will Internet Channels Keep Growth Going?

History

In 1983, during his first year in college, Michael Dell took his interest in tinkering with computers to a new level. During his first semester, as the now legendary story goes, Dell began to purchase outmoded IBM PCs from local retailers, upgrade them, and resell them not just to other students but to local law firms and small businesses. Dell's sales method was simple—door-to-door direct sales, bypassing the dealers and retail outlets through which virtually all computers were sold. The idea was so successful that during the summer after his first year of college, Dell sold $180,00 worth of PCs in only his first month! Shortly after his initial success, Dell modified his business. Instead of continuing to purchase older machines and upgrade them, Dell recognized that he could purchase new computer components, assemble them himself, and sell them directly to customers. This strategy enabled him to bypass the traditional channels of distribution adhered to by the established computer makers and offer PCs to his customers at a 15 percent discount. Dell's direct contact with customers allowed him to build products to order instead of maintaining an inventory. Dell's innovative concept of custom design and direct sales took off right from the start, and demand was overwhelming, so much so, that Michael Dell never returned to college.

Dell continued to grow throughout the 1980s at an astounding rate, enabling Michael Dell to fund growth internally. Dell's sales grew to a level that enabled him to secure bank financing using only his receivables as collateral, avoiding the need for venture capital.

It was not until 1987 that Dell offered stock, and the company did not go public until 1988. $30 million was raised in its initial public offering, netting Michael Dell $18 million.

By 1991, with Michael Dell just 23 years old, sales reached $800 million and then more than doubled to $2 billion in 1992. This high rate of growth, however, was too rapid for Dell to handle. Flaws in the design of Dell's notebook computers began to emerge, and managers were too young and inexperienced to handle many of the new problems often associated with companies attempting the transition from entrepreneurial start-up to large public company. In 1992, despite its enormous sales increases, Dell reported a $36 million loss for the year. Many industry experts felt that Dell had made its run and could not return to profitability.

Michael Dell was not listening to the skeptics and instead bulked up his management team by bringing in experienced managers to add much-needed maturity and knowledge. Dell recruited Mort Topfer from Motorola to handle the day-to-day operations. Topfer, an experienced executive, understood the purchasing and manufacturing of high-tech components and helped Dell set up a manufacturing facility in Asia. In addition to Topfer, Dell also recruited several key Apple Computer executives, who were working on the Apple

PowerBook laptop computer, to fix Dell's notebook computer problems. The results were astonishing. Within 12 months, many of the problems were worked out, and the following year Dell saw its profits hit $149 million. Despite the turnaround, skeptics abounded, consistently underestimating customer demand for direct sale computers. Many still had questions as to whether the growth could continue at such an exceedingly high rate, and whether Michael Dell had the skills to guide his company's growth in this highly competitive business.

Dell's Attempt at Traditional Retailing

Not everything Michael Dell did turned to gold. In fact there were some serious mistakes, such as an attempt in 1993 to sell computers via traditional retail channels. By selling computers via this channel, Dell faced new problems that the company had never before encountered. The competitive advantage that Dell had gained by selling computers direct to customers evaporated when placed in traditional retail distribution channels. Dell could no longer adjust its supply to fit customers' specialized demands, but instead had to create an inventory for resellers to stock. Further, since most of Dell's sales were to businesses, its computers faced a brand recognition problem when placed in retail stores, and invariably fierce price competition became a factor for Dell. Since retailers were now selling the computers, Dell could no longer avoid the increased costs associated with this traditional channel structure. So, the experiment at selling computers via retail channels was short-lived and unsuccessful. Dell discontinued this practice within the year and has since sold computers only via direct channels.

Dell's Order Processing System

While retaining the direct selling concept that Michael Dell utilized from the start, today's Dell computer has come a long way in the level of sophistication it uses to meet its customers' needs. Dell now sells about 4 million personal computers, notebook computers, servers, and workstations per year and generates a sales volume of $12.3 billion annually. Approximately 95 percent of Dell's sales are to businesses, and 5 percent to consumers. Orders can be placed by customers via a 1-800 number, a dedicated internal company sales rep, or through Dell's Web site. Each PC is still made to order, eliminating inventory buildup and excessive lag times. The whole process from initial order to loading for delivery takes only 36 hours. Large customers of Dell can even get their computers shipped via Dell's quick-ship program within twelve hours after manufacture.

Customer orders are immediately relayed to one of Dell's three plants in Austin, Texas, Penang, Malaysia, or Limerick, Ireland. Next, suppliers are notified. Dell's Austin plant manager says that all the suppliers know that components must be delivered to the plant within an hour of a request. Once the components arrive, they are taken from the trucks and placed on the assembly lines, so there is no component inventory or finished goods inventory in Dell's system.

Virtual Integration—The Next Step

The direct sales model that Dell continues to use provides other benefits besides customization. As founder, Michael Dell stated in a recent interview, the direct sales model allows Dell to build relationships with its customers. The relationship generates valuable information which in turn allows Dell to leverage its relationships with both suppliers and customers. When you add the advancements in data sharing, just-in-time-manufacturing, and the Internet to the mix, the traditional functions of each member of the supply chain become blurred, thus creating "Virtual Integration." Operating under this model, Dell could maintain a tightly coordinated supply chain, yet still concentrate on customization and specialization found in virtual corporations.

Technology is the key to Michael Dell's vision for virtual integration, enabling real time data exchange to track everything from product orders to service calls. The consistent real time exchange of information enables suppliers, component manufacturers, customers, and others to become an integral part of Dell's business, almost as if they worked inside the company. Although virtual integration exists in theory, it remains to be seen whether Dell can implement it successfully. And, if it does implement virtual integration, whether it will fuel further growth and profitability.

The Internet

Dell has been using the Internet as one of its channels for selling computers direct to customers. However, unlike other channels, the Internet provides an instantaneous global sales network. Michael Dell refers to it as the "ultimate direct model." Through its Web site, customers may place orders for Dell products, ask questions via e-mail, and even obtain customized computer systems and technical solutions. Instead of calling the company on the phone, customers may now simply log onto the Web site. As a result, Dell has had to hire fewer employees to take orders and provide technical support, saving the company money. The sales numbers for Dell's Web site are staggering. As of March 1997 Dell was selling $1 million per day via the Web site, and as of January 1999, this number has grown spectacularly to $10 million in sales per day. With much of the Internet market untapped, this number has the potential to grow even more.

Dell's corporate strategy is geared to increasing the use of the company's Web site. In fact, Dell envisions virtually all of its customers conducting virtually all of their business through the company Web site. Currently Dell's large corporate customers, which account for 35 percent of the company's revenues, and its Asian and European customers, do not use the Internet for their transactions.

Dell is not alone, however, in its use of the Internet. Several other companies are using the Internet successfully as extensions of their channels. Companies using the Internet successfully include networking giant Cisco Systems, and computer manufacturers Micron Technology and Gateway 2000. Both Micron and Gateway operate under business models similar to Dell's by taking orders from customers before building the machines. IBM has also implemented a build-to-order manufacturing system of its own, which is also available via the Internet. Given these other competitors, Dell faces new challenges that it has not encountered before. Indeed, for much of the 15 years of Dell's existence, it was the only computer manufacturer that could produce built-to-order computers at competitive prices. With increasing competition, falling component prices, and shrinking margins in build-to-order computers, Dell faces new challenges. The Internet is the means by which other competitors could potentially chip away at Dell's dominance by attracting large customers as well as the Asian and European customers that Dell has not yet integrated into its Internet services. By using the Internet, other computer manufacturers also avoid the increased costs associated with traditional channels of distribution, allowing them to lower prices and thereby eliminating Dell's price advantage. How Dell will adapt to these developments remains to be seen.

Discussion Questions

1. Is the Internet channel the ideal means for sustaining Dell's strategy of made-to-order computers and direct sales to customers?

2. Will the availability of the Internet as a marketing channel for competitors quickly erode Dell's competitive advantage?

Chapter 11

Retailing and Wholesaling

Patrick Dunne,
Texas Tech University

Associate Professor, Texas Tech University
Professor Dunne earned his Ph.D. in marketing from Michigan State University and his undergraduate degree from Xavier University. Dr. Dunne was the first academic to receive the American Marketing Association's Wayne A. Lemburg Award for "conspicuous individual accomplishments." He is the former vice president of the Publications Division of the American Marketing Association, and the former vice president of the Association Developmental Division of the AMA.

In his three decades of university teaching, Dr. Dunne has taught a wide range of marketing and distribution courses at both the undergraduate and graduate levels. He has won two teaching awards, has authored 10 books, and is a former member of several editorial review boards.

Sam Walton forever changed the face of retailing by remembering a lesson he learned from another great retailer—James Cash Penney. In 1940, after graduating from the University of Missouri, Walton became a trainee at the JC Penney's store in Des Moines, Iowa.

One day, Mr. Penney visited the store and watched young Sam sell a customer a pair of work pants and a shirt, which Walton proceeded to wrap in brown paper and tie with twine. After the customer left, Penney came over to the trainee and explained that the store didn't make money on the merchandise it sold, but on the paper and twine it saved. He then proceeded to neatly wrap and tie a package of identical merchandise with very little paper or twine. Sam Walton never forgot that lesson and from that moment on realized that a key to success in retailing was managing costs.

Returning from World War II, Sam Walton took over the Ben Franklin variety store in Newport, Arkansas. Over the next 15 years, Sam with his brother, Bud, opened several of these stores in Arkansas and Missouri. Over this period, Sam realized that the discount store concept was the "future" in retailing. He found that if he purchased an item for 80 cents, he could sell three to four times more of it by pricing it at 99 cents than he could if he priced it at the standard price of $1.19. While he made only half the profit per unit, his overall profit was greater because he was selling so many more units. Sam Walton had grasped the essence of **discounting:** by offering consumers a lower price, retailers can boost the number of sales to a point where they will earn more money than by selling fewer units at a higher price. Thus, Sam approached Butler Brothers, a regional wholesaler and the franchiser of Ben Franklin stores, and explained his idea. If they cut his price, he would open discount stores and buy his merchandise from them. Butler turned down his proposal and Sam Walton went into the discount business on his own. Soon, however, he was prying the lowest prices out of his new vendors and selling more merchandise than anyone expected.

Folks who knew Sam Walton claim that his greatest asset was his ability to learn from others, so as not to duplicate their mistakes, and gain from their successes. After all, when Sam opened his first Wal-Mart in 1962, there were already over 60 discount chains in operation, including Kmart and Target, which opened earlier that year. Years later, Walton observed that other retailers were using computers in their business, but only to check prices. Computers weren't used to gather sales and inventory data as they do today. Walton, however, saw these new uses of the computer as a means to further cut costs and lower prices even more.

Today Wal-Mart's advanced computer system enables it to not only scan sales but also make certain that inbound shipments coming in one side of a distribution center are transferred to the correct dock on the other side of the center for shipment to the over 2,000 stores. The computers not only manage product movement within the distribution centers, but connect the stores, distribution centers, and the vendors to Wal-Mart's

(Continued)

Robert F. Lusch,
Helen Robson Walton Chair in Marketing and the George Lynn Cross Research Professor, University of Oklahoma
Professor Lusch earned his Ph.D. from the University of Wisconsin and his undergraduate degree from the University of Arizona. He is the chairperson elect of the American Marketing Association. Dr. Lusch received the 1997 Distinguished Marketing Educator award from the Academy of Marketing Science and the 1997 Harold Maynard Award from the American Marketing Association. He is the former editor of the Southwestern Marketing Association, former vice president of education of the AMA, former vice president of finance of the AMA, and a former trustee of the AMA Foundation. He serves as editor of the *Journal of Marketing*.

Dr. Lusch's area of expertise is marketing strategy and distribution systems. He has authored 16 books and more than 150 articles.

Learning Objectives

After you have completed this chapter, you should be able to:

1. Understand the role of retailing in the U.S. economy.

2. Describe the major types of retail institutional formats.

3. Explain the differences in the various methods used to classify retailers.

4. Illustrate why atmospherics is so important in designing a retail store.

5. Discuss the evolution of competition in retailing.

6. Understand category management and what guides the category manager's decisions.

7. Identify the different types of wholesalers and their duties.

8. Explain how to select and work with wholesalers.

9. Evaluate the strategic renewal taking place among wholesalers.

headquarters in Arkansas via satellite using EDI (electronic data interchange). As a result of the introduction of the computer to retail management, Wal-Mart's selling, general, and administrative costs as a percentage of sales are currently less than 15 percent, while all of its competitors' operating expenses are over 20 percent and sometimes over 30 percent. For instance, Kmart, selling essentially the same type of merchandise as Wal-Mart, has operating expenses in the mid-to-low 20 percent range. ▪

Managers of retail stores must develop marketing strategies, as our opening profile of Sam Walton illustrates. Walton was aware that retailing's three most basic tasks are:

1. Getting consumers from your trading area into your store, and

2. Converting these consumers into loyal customers, while

3. Operating in the most efficient manner, so as to reduce costs and thereby having lower prices.

Walton, while still paying attention to the first two tasks, was one of the first retailers to emphasize the third task. By working with manufacturers and wholesalers, Wal-Mart has become the world's largest retailer and the largest employer in the United States. In the remainder of this chapter, we present some concepts and principles of retail marketing—the type of marketing you observe most frequently in your daily activities. We discuss the most popular types of retailing in the United States, and how retailers make decisions regarding the number of outlets, margins, turnover, and location. Following a discussion of the role of atmospherics in a store, we look at the evolution of retail competition by reviewing two different theories. We then explain how the intensified level of competition has driven retailers to become more concerned with category management in order to improve their financial performance. In addition, this chapter looks at wholesale marketing. We will describe the structure of wholesaling in our economy, discuss how manufacturers can market their products more effectively through wholesalers, and consider the ramifications of the strategic renewal now occurring in wholesaling.

THE ROLE OF RETAILING IN THE U.S. ECONOMY

Retailing consists of the final activity and steps needed to place merchandise made elsewhere in the hands of the consumer or to provide services to the consumer. Quite simply, any firm that sells merchandise or provides services to the ultimate consumer for personal or household consumption is performing the retailing function. Regardless of whether the firm sells to the ultimate consumer in a store, through the mail, over the telephone, through a television infomercial, over the Internet, door to door, or through a vending machine, it is involved in retailing. Some experts point out the importance of retailing by noting that retailers are "gatekeepers" since they are the final foot, or twelve inches, in a channel of distribution that may stretch thousands of miles.[1] After all, if consumers don't buy the retailer's offering, there isn't a need for a manufacturer to have a channel of distribution. *Wholesalers* are those persons or establishments that sell to retailers and/or other organizational buyers for industrial, institutional, and commercial use, but do not sell in significant amounts to ultimate consumers. For example, a Price-Costco Warehouse Club, even though it sells to consumers, would be considered a wholesaler since the majority of its sales are to small business operators. As a result, the government classifies all such sales as wholesale transactions.

Retailers, in conjunction with their channel partners (manufacturers and wholesalers), have made a significant contribution to the economic prosperity that Americans enjoy so much. In fact, the nations that have enjoyed the greatest economic and social progress have been those with a strong retail sector. Retailers have become valued and necessary members of society. While some may argue that we have too many retailers with too many stores operating today, we must not forget the social benefits that "overstoring" provides an economy. Some of the benefits that a vibrant retailing sector provides are: easier access to products, not having to settle on a second or third choice when shopping for a particular product, greater customer satisfaction, and higher levels of customer service.[2]

We can assess the magnitude of retailing by referring to the most recently published Census of Retail Trade, which is taken and published every five years (in years ending in 2 and 7), or by accessing data from the Survey of Buying Power published by *Sales and Marketing Management*. Currently there are approximately 2.4 million retail establishments in the United States with annual total sales of nearly $2.4 trillion. There are 24 retail establishments for every thousand households, with average annual sales of over $1 million. Most retailers, however, are smaller, and many have annual sales of less than $500,000 annually.[3]

These figures don't adequately reflect the changes that have occurred recently as a result of the number of new retail formats that have been developed over the last two decades. Most of these new businesses have actually been new institutional forms, such as retailing on the Internet, warehouse club retailing, supercenters, and home-delivery fast-food businesses. Change is truly the major cause of growth in retailing today. Remember, retailers are not obliged to conform to traditional ways of selling to consumers. Retailers and would-be-retailers are free to forge new retailing approaches that capitalize on emerging market opportunities. This is all the more evident when we consider the fact that fashion trends, which in the past would have lasted for years, now may last only a few months.

MAJOR TYPES OF RETAIL INSTITUTIONAL FORMATS

When most people think of retailing, they think of the various types of fixed-based physical stores. After all, the overwhelming majority of retail sales occurs in these stores. However, today retailing is much broader than simply thinking in terms of a physical store.

www.dell.com
www.avon.com
www.tupperware.com

Retailers are finding alternatives to requiring the customer traveling to a fixed-based store to purchase goods and services. For example, Dell Computer sells its computers and peripherals to households via the Internet, mail, or phone, and delivers them within two days. Saks Fifth Avenue sells merchandise not only in its stores, but also over television shopping networks. And Avon, Tupperware, and other direct sellers, while selling most of their goods via in-home parties, are selling over the Internet. Therefore, it is important to remember that when discussing the various types of retailers, one must first consider if they are selling from a fixed physical location or not.

Store-Based Retailers

As shown in Figure 11.1, there are six basic types of retailers using the store-based format: department stores, specialty stores, supermarkets, supercenters, category killers, and convenience stores. No one type is inherently better than the others. There are many examples of retailers operating successfully in more than one type of store-based format by using different marketing strategies, each making use of a unique blend of product, price, promotion, and place.

Department Stores

Department stores
are large-scale operations offering a broad product mix consisting of many different product lines with above-average depth, or variety, in each of their product lines.

Department stores were first introduced in the mid-1800s, about the time of the Civil War. May Company, Marshall Field, Federated Stores, and Dillard's are examples of well-known department stores. These stores generally have 120,000 to 300,000 square feet of selling space. The various related product lines carried in the store's product mix are merchandised in separate departments (including menswear, womenswear, toys, sporting goods, home furnishings, and furniture). Department stores offer many customer services, such as knowledgeable and helpful sales clerks, delivery and wrapping services, liberal return policies, and store credit cards.

Discount department stores, which were introduced in the mid-1940s just after World War II, feature low prices. Like conventional department stores, discounters carry a variety of product lines and use departmental merchandising techniques. However, they do so at lower prices than conventional department stores. Their lower prices are the result of offering fewer customer services, having less up-scale facilities, and using self-service to

www.maycompany.com
www.dhc.com
www.federated-fds.com
www.dillards.com

Figure 11.1   Six Basic Types of Store-Based Retailers

Department stores are large-scale operations containing a broad product mix consisting of many different product lines with above-average depth in each of them.

Specialty stores are relatively small-scale stores offering a great deal of depth in a narrow range of product lines.

Supermarkets are retailers that sell groceries and some general merchandise products through large-scale physical facilities with self-service and self-selection displays that enable the retailer to shift the performance of some marketing functions to the consumer.

Supercenters are cavernous, one-stop combinations of supermarkets and discount department stores, which range in size from 120,000 to 160,000 square feet, and carry between 80,000 to 100,000 products ranging from televisions to peanut butter to fax machines.

Category killers get their name from their marketing strategy of carrying such a large amount of merchandise in a single category at such good prices that they make it impossible for the customer to walk out without purchasing what they need, thus "killing" the competition.

Convenience stores stock frequently purchased products such as gasoline, bread, tobacco, and milk that tend to be consumed within 30 minutes of purchase, as well as offering services such as ATMs and car washes.

reduce operating expenses. Examples include Target, Wal-Mart, and Kmart, and are usually 40,000 to 100,000 square feet. Most communities with a population over 10,000 have either a conventional department store or a discount department store.

Specialty Stores

Specialty stores are common in womenswear, menswear, jewelry, footwear, electronics, furniture, sporting goods, painting supplies, flowers, liquor, pets, bridal wear, and fabrics. Most specialty stores range from 3,000 to 7,500 square feet, although some are much smaller, and others, such as furniture stores that may have over 100,000 square feet, are much larger. Some popular specialty stores are The Gap (leisure wear), Hickory Farms (specialty cheeses and snacks), and Athlete's Foot (jogging and athletic shoes).

Most successful specialty stores pursue a strong store-positioning strategy, in which all elements of the store's marketing mix are aimed at a well-defined target market, which is segmented from the total market based on some specific demographic or lifestyle variable. The Limited, which recently spun off both the 1,700 store Intimate Brands unit, composed of Victoria's Secret and Bath & Body Works stores, as well as Abercrombie & Fitch, is America's specialty store leader in total sales with 13 remaining operations including Limited stores, Express, Structure, Cacique, Galyan's Trading Post, and Lane Bryant.

Supermarkets

The *supermarket* (see Figure 11.1) concept of retailing was first developed in the 1930s, when the economic depression forced grocers to replace their small, inefficient, traditional, mom-and-pop corner stores in order to offer consumers lower prices. Selling groceries and some general merchandise products through large-scale physical facilities with self-service and self-selection displays enabled the supermarket retailer to shift the performance of some distribution functions to consumers. Today, most grocery retailing is still done through supermarkets such as Safeway, Albertsons, and Kroger, although supercenters are rapidly gaining market share.

The supermarket concept involves five basic principles directed at improving retail productivity and reducing the cost of distribution:

1. Self-service and self-selection displays.

2. Centralization of customer services at the checkout counter/desk.

3. Large-scale, low-cost physical facilities.

4. A strong price emphasis.

5. A broad assortment of merchandise to facilitate multiple-item purchases.

Recently, the supermarket retailing concept has been used in developing two new types of nonfood retailing, which are discussed later: the supercenter and the category killer. In addition to expanding the supermarket concept to include new types of stores, the traditional food supermarket's product mix is being expanded to include prepared, or ready-to-eat, foods. For example, many supermarkets now offer HMRs (home-meal-replacements) to compete with fast-food operators, as well as nonfood items such as clothing, small appliances, automotive supplies, nonprescription drugs, cosmetics, and fragrances. This phenomenon is referred to as scrambled merchandising. This results in unrelated lines of merchandise being carried by a single retailer. For example, convenience stores sell gasoline, bread, milk, beer, cigarettes, magazines, and fast food. The effects of scrambled merchandising can be easily seen in Figure 11.2, which shows the various locations where consumers can purchase different products.

Supercenters

One of the newest competitive retail types within the store-based format is the *supercenter* (see Figure 11.1). These cavernous, one-stop combination supermarkets and discount department stores, which range in size from 120,000 to 160,000 square feet, carry between

Specialty stores
are relatively small-scale stores offering a great deal of depth in a narrow range of product lines.

www.target.com
www.wal-mart.com
www.kmart.com
www.gap.com
www.hickoryfarms.com
www.theathletesfoot.com
www.limited.com
www.intimatebrands.com
www.safeway.com
www.albertsons.com
www.kroger.com

Scrambled merchandising
is the handling of merchandise lines based solely on the profitability criterion and without regard to the consistency of a particular product line with other products in the retailer's product mix.

Figure 11.2 The Effects of Scrambled Merchandising

Store	Loaf Bread	Hamburger	Dog Food	Candy	Paper Towels	Ice Cream	Motor Oil
Fast Food Outlet		●		●		●	
Supermarket	●	●	●	●	●	●	●
Convenience Store	●	●	●	●	●	●	●
Supercenter	●	●	●	●	●	●	●
Club Store	●	●	●	●	●	●	●
Pet Food Store			●				
Drug Store	●			●	●	●	●
Home Improvement		●		●	●		●

80,000 to 100,000 products ranging from televisions to peanut butter to fax machines. Supercenters offer the customer one-stop shopping, and as a result are capable of drawing customers from up to a 30–50 mile radius in some rural areas. They lower the customer's total cost of purchasing in terms of time and stores visited, without sacrificing service and variety.

However, while Wal-Mart, Kmart, and Target are banking their future on this new format, some retail analysts have questions about the viability of this new format. They wonder if older consumers can get around in these stores, if the younger ones will take the time to shop these mammoth stores, or if folks will buy tires, apparel, and tomatoes on the same shopping trip. However, since this country's major retailers are using supercenters as their major vehicle for growth over the next five years, it is difficult to predict failure. By 2002, the total number of stores of this format is expected to be more than double the 700 that existed in 1997. Nevertheless, it is doubtful that the supermarket operators, who have always operated with paper-thin net profit margins, will give up market share willingly.

Category Killers

Essentially the ultimate in specialty stores, the *category killer* (see Figure 11.1) got its name from its marketing strategy: carry such a large amount of merchandise in a single category at such good prices that it makes it impossible for the customer to walk out without purchasing what they need, thus "killing" the competition.

Toys 'R' Us, which began operations in the 1950s, has the distinction of being the first category killer. Today, Toys 'R' Us operates over 600 toy stores in the United States and over 300 toy stores in more than 20 countries around the globe. The company also operates over 200 Kids 'R' Us children's clothing stores in the United States. Beginning in the 1980s, the category killer retail format began to grow explosively. Some other well-known category killers include: Best Buy, Home Depot, Blockbuster Video, Circuit City, Just for Feet, Office Depot, PETsMART, Bed Bath & Beyond, AutoZone, Barnes & Noble Bookstores, and Sports Authority. Many category killers are also diverting business away from traditional wholesale supply houses. For example, Home Depot appeals to the professional contractor who traditionally traded with hardware wholesalers, and Office Depot caters to the business owner who traditionally purchased supplies from office supply and equipment wholesalers.[4]

Today, the category killer concept has even branched out into the automobile market. Glitzy, computerized auto category killer chains, such as AutoNation, Driver's Mart

www.toysrus.com
www.homedepot.com
www.officedepot.com

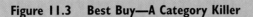

Figure 11.3   Best Buy—A Category Killer

Best Buy, a category killer, is able to obtain a significant market share by concentrating its inventory in the computer and electronic merchandise category.

Worldwide, and CarMax Auto Superstores, are giving nightmares to the nation's 22,000 traditional car dealers.

Convenience Stores

Convenience stores are generally small (2,000 to 4,000 square feet) and serve a neighborhood within 1.5 miles of the store. Because these stores offer greater time, place, and possession utility to the consumer, while operating with a lower turnover rate than do larger grocery stores, convenience stores often charge higher prices on comparable items. 7-Eleven, the originator of the convenience store concept, is still this country's largest convenience store chain. Today, however, the chain started by Dallas's Southland Corporation is owned by Japan's Ito-Yokado Corporation. The quickest growth in convenience stores is coming from the major oil companies, such as Texaco and Conoco, who have been rapidly converting gasoline stations into modern convenience stores.

Nonstore-Based Retailers

Today, there is a great diversity and variety in the types of nonstore-based retailers, and several industry analysts contend that changes here will lead to the next revolution in retailing. The mechanics for such a revolution are already in place, as a variety of established selling techniques permit consumers to purchase goods and services without having to leave home. With accelerated communications technology and changing consumer lifestyles, the growth potential for nonstore retailing is explosive. The five types of nonstore

Convenience stores
stock frequently purchased products such as gasoline, bread, tobacco, and milk that tend to be consumed within 30 minutes of purchase, as well as offering services such as ATMs and car washes.

www.7-eleven.com
www.texaco.com
www.conoco.com

retailing include street peddling, direct selling, mail order, automatic merchandising machines, and electronic shopping.

In addition, some innovative store-based retailers are using dual retail formats, both store-based and nonstore-based, with multiple techniques within each format, to reach their target markets. For example, JC Penney's not only continues to build traditional stores but also has an extensive mail-order catalog operation, where different catalogs are developed to target different customer segments. In addition, they are continuing to develop and enhance their Web site for retail shopping. In fact, most traditional store-based retailers have developed additional formats to reach their target market(s). Starbucks Coffee, for example, in addition to its traditional stores, has kiosks in airports and an Internet Web site that sells coffee direct to the customer. In addition, they are the coffee provider for United Airlines.

Street Peddling

Perhaps the oldest nonstore format is the ***street peddler.*** These retailers peddle their merchandise from a push-cart or temporary stall set up on a street. Street peddling is still common in many parts of the world.[5] Street peddlers are often seen in major U.S. metropolitan cities where they sell inexpensive items, such as T-shirts, watches, books, magazines, tobacco, candy, and hot-dogs, on street corners. Some cities, due to pressure from store-based retailers who pay higher taxes, are considering a ban on this retail format.[6]

Direct Selling

Direct sellers are primarily engaged in the retail sale of merchandise on a personal basis, through party plans (Tupperware Home Parties) or one-on-one contact in the home or workplace (Avon Products), away from a fixed place of business. Today, in the United States sales from direct selling total about $16 billion annually and are made by over 4 million individuals, who are not employed by the organization they represent, but rather are independent contractors. Worldwide direct selling sales are $50 billion, with Japan being the largest direct selling country. Major products sold in the United States include personal care items (Mary Kay Cosmetics), decorative home products (Princess House, Home Interiors and Gifts), cookware (West Bend, CUTCO), and encyclopedias (World Book, Encyclopedia Britannica). Today, with women increasingly out of the home, little "cold canvassing" is done, instead many companies use "cold calling" over the telephone to make appointments to show the merchandise. In addition, traditional direct selling techniques are being merged with newer marketing channels, such as mail order and catalogs; and merchandise is being shown and sold anywhere people gather, such as at state fairs, in shopping malls, and at airports. Although the time and place of direct selling have changed, the major attributes of direct selling remain the same: support from the parent organization for the independent contractor, knowledge and demonstration of the product by the salesperson, excellent warranties and guarantees, and the person-to-person component.

Mail Order

Mail-order houses, which send out nearly 14 billion catalogs a year,[7] are primarily engaged in the retail sale of products by catalog and mail order. Catalog sales continue to be a $60 billion industry. Included are mail order clubs (for books, CDs, and tapes), jewelry firms, novelty merchandise firms, and specialty merchandisers: such as sporting goods (L.L. Bean), children's apparel retailers (Right Start), and kitchenware (Williams-Sonoma).

Automatic Merchandising Machines

The operators of ***automatic merchandising machines*** are primarily engaged in the retail sale of products by means of vending machines. This industry does *not* include coin-operated service machines, such as amusement and game machines. Surprisingly, vending machines have been with us since about 215 B.C., when Egyptians devised a coin-operated holy water dispenser for places of worship.[8]

Electronic Shopping

The general belief among retail experts is that *electronic shopping* will take off in the next few years, as it increasingly becomes an interactive, immersive, at-home experience. Every major player in the retail industry, computer industry, telecommunications industry, and transaction processing industry is committed to this growth. No one is denying that there are still issues to be worked out, but nonstore retail leaders are already working on methods to provide true colors and standardized sizes, as well as an easy procedure for handling returns. The only prerequisite needed for Internet retailing's success is having enough homes with PCs or Web TVs to enable customers to access this format. Already 18 percent of the population is taking up Web surfing for more than five hours a week, and estimates are that retail revenues on the Internet will reach over $20 billion by 2005. And if the price of computers and online services continues to drop, then the numbers can only grow geometrically.[9]

Still, what is happening today is only the beginning of the explosion that is about to occur.[10] As the Internet grows to allow faster access to text and graphics that brings us information packaged in two-dimensional real time and fully immersive three-dimensional video, a whole new shopping experience will be created. The shoppers of the next decade may well opt for the convenience and heightened experience of virtual shopping, as browsing will be even easier and the choices more extensive. An individual's primary social activity outside the home won't be shopping, but rather enjoying real entertainment (attending a ball game or concert) or spending quality time with friends and family. Plus, the Internet may well allow us to share a common shopping experience with family and friends, even if they live half the world away.

However, before this Internet explosion can occur, several roadblocks must be overcome:

1. **Cost of being online:** Currently most consumers must pay a fee to a commercial provider for access to the Internet. What mall could exist if an admission fee was required before a customer could come in to make a purchase or even to browse?

2. **Payment fraud:** Even though the risk of credit card fraud is no higher for online customers than for traditional retailing, many consumers are reluctant to shop and pay online.

3. **Too many men, too few women:** Over two-thirds of current Internet users are males, who are not the predominate shoppers in this country. This is perceived by many to be a major obstacle since women "want to touch, feel, and smell the products they purchase."[11] Improved software interfaces may be the answer. One Internet grocery retailer, Massachusetts-based Streamline, provides software which supports "'real-time picture-based shopping,' which allows customers to examine labels and run side-by-side comparisons of products. . . . [the] window also includes a place to specify the size of eggplant or cucumber a customer prefers, or how much green he wants to see in a banana. . . ."[12]

4. **Loss of a cultural tradition:** For many consumers, shopping in stores remains a form of entertainment and social interaction. While online services provide some of this with chat rooms, just plain "people-watching" and meeting for coffee are not possible online.

5. **Inadequate delivery services:** Current delivery service companies may be incapable of handling the forecasted volume. Even if this is overcome, with the growing number of two-wage households, who will be home to accept delivery?

6. **Slow transmission rates and poor graphics:** Without expensive high-speed modems, long waiting periods are required to download high-end graphic presentations. Yet, when retail Web sites try to focus on speed, the quality of their image content often suffers.

7. **Possible channel conflicts:** Will manufacturers open their own online shopping stores to compete with their existing traditional retailers?

CLASSIFYING RETAILERS

LEARNING OBJECTIVE LO3

As noted above, retailing is a diverse business activity taking on many different forms. Retailers can be classified in terms of number of outlets, margin versus turnover, and location. By reviewing these methods of classifying retailers, we can better appreciate the diversity in retailing and the reason why retailers behave as they do.

Number of Outlets

As a rule, the more outlets a retailer has, the stronger the competitive edge the retailer can create. This is because the retailer can spread many fixed costs (such as advertising and top management salaries) over a larger volume of sales, thus achieving economies of scale. Yet, single-unit retailers do have some advantages. Since they are generally owner- or family-operated, they therefore tend to have harder working, more motivated employees. In addition, they can focus all their efforts on one trade area and tailor their goods or services to that area.

Besides, having a large number of outlets is not always enough to achieve market advantage. Sears, for example, operated 129 freestanding Home Life furniture stores across the country before selling them in late 1998. In spite of the numbers, Sears never had enough stores in any particular **trade area** to gain sufficient market share to realize economies of scale savings. As a result, smaller regional competitors, such as Rooms To Go with half the number of stores as Sears, were able to achieve greater total sales and lower operating expenses as a percentage of sales.

The U.S. Census Bureau classifies chain stores into two size categories: 2 to 10 stores and 11 or more. Retailers generally use the "11 or more units" definition when using the term *chain stores.* Figure 11.4 shows sales by chain stores as a percentage of total U.S. sales for 10 different merchandise lines. The statistics reveal that in 1995 chain stores accounted for nearly 40 percent of all retail sales (including 96 percent of all department store sales and 63 percent of all grocery store sales). Though large chain operations represented over 57 percent of nondurable goods sales, they only included 16 percent of durable goods sales. Figure 11.5 lists some of this country's major chain stores and their corporate parents.

Trade area
is the geographic area where the majority of a store's customers reside.

www.sears.com

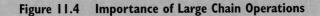

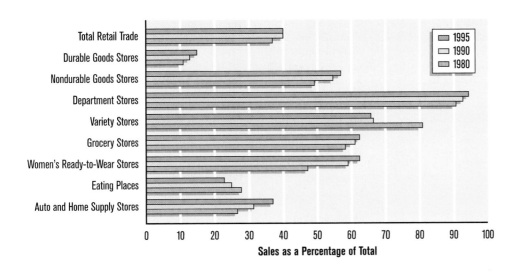

Figure 11.4   Importance of Large Chain Operations

Source: U.S. Bureau of the Census, Statistical Abstract of the United States: 1996 (116th edition), Washington, D.C., 1996. Table No. 1259. Retail Trade Sales of Multiunit Organizations, by Kind of Business: 1980–1995, p. 766.

Margins versus Turnover

Retailers can be classified in regard to their gross margins and rate of inventory turnover as shown in Figure 11.6. The **gross margin percentage** shows how much gross margin the retailer makes as a percentage of sales; this is also referred to as the **gross margin** return on sales. A 40 percent gross margin indicates that on each dollar of sales the retailer generates 40 cents over and above the retailer's cost of goods sold. This gross margin will be used to pay the retailer's **operating expenses**. **Inventory turnover** refers to the number of times per year, on average, that a retailer sells its inventory. Thus, an inventory turnover of four times indicates that, on average, the retailer turns over or sells its average inventory every three months. Likewise, an average inventory of $40,000 (retail) and annual sales of $240,000 means the retailer has turned over its inventory six times in one year ($240,000 divided by $40,000) or every two months.

Typically a retailer with a low profit margin and low inventory turnover will not be able to generate sufficient profits to remain competitive and survive. When you notice a retailer in your community who has gone out of business, this is usually the reason. On the other hand, retailers with low margins and high turnovers, such as discount department stores and supermarkets, can be quite profitable. Likewise, high-margin, low-turnover retailers, such as furniture stores, TV and appliance stores, and jewelry stores are quite common and successful in the United States. Finally, some retailers, such as the convenience stores we discussed earlier, are able to operate profitably on both high margins and high turnover for the limited amount of products offered in the store.

Location

Location can be a key element in a retailer's success. In fact, one retailing axiom is that "the three major decisions in retailing are location, location, and location." After all, all retail stores attract customers from a limited geographic area. For example, a convenience

Operating expenses
are the expenses the retailer incurs in running the business other than the cost of the merchandise, e.g., rent, wages, utilities, depreciation, insurance, etc.

Figure 11.5 America's Leading Retailers and Their Subsidiaries (Number of Stores)

Wal-Mart Stores, Inc. **Bentonville, AR**	Sam's Club (482) Wal-Mart (2,421) Wal-Mart Supercenter (502)	**The Gap, Inc.** **San Francisco, CA**	Banana Republic (265) The Gap (1,040) GapKids (586)[4] Old Navy Clothing (305)

Sears
Chicago, IL
	Sears [multiline stores] (850)
	Sears dealer stores (598)
	Sears paint and hardware
	  stores (200)
	Sears Parts Group (1,516)
	Sears Tire Group (1,087)
		The Great Atlantic &
		Pacific Tea Co.
		Montvale, NJ
			A&P/Super Fresh/Waldbaums
			  Food Mart (670)
			Dominion (85)
			Farmer Jack (100)
			Food Basics (50)
			Food Emporium (34)

Kmart Corp. **Troy, MI**	Kmart (2,019) Super Kmart Center (99)		Kohl's (51)

JCPenney Co., Inc.
Dallas, TX
	JCPenney (1,230)
	JCPenney catalog merchants/
	  sale centers (550)
	JCPenney Home Store (17)
	Eckerd Drug Stores (3,850)
		Venator Group
		New York, NY
			Athletic Group (3,588)
			  Champs Sports
			  Foot Locker
			  Going to the Game!
			  Kids Foot Locker
			  Lady Foot Locker
			  World Foot Locker

Dayton Hudson Corp.
Minneapolis, MN
	Dayton's (20)
	Hudson's (21)
	Marshall Field's (24)
	Mervyn's (269)
	SuperTarget (14)
	Target (807)
	Target Greatland (76)
			International General
			  Merchandise (526)
			  The Bargain Shop
			  Woolworth
			Northern Group (827)
			  Northern Elements
			  Northern Getaway
			  Northern Reflections
			  Northern Traditions

The Home Depot **Atlanta, GA**	Expo Design (6) The Home Depot (650)		Other Specialty (1,275) After Thoughts

American Stores Co.
Salt Lake City, UT
	Acme Markets (179)
	Jewel Food Stores (184)[1]
	Lucky Stores (442)
	Osco Drug (596)[2]
	Sav-On (350)
			The Best of Times
			  The San Francisco Music
			    Box Company
			Specialty Footwear (1,021)
			  Kinney
			  Various other chains

Federated Department **Stores, Inc.** **Cincinnati, OH**	Aeropostale (119) Bloomingdale's (28) The Bon Marche (42) Burdines (49) Charter Club (48) Goldsmith's (6) Lazarus (47) Macy's East (87) Macy's West (101)[3] Rich's (20) Stern's (25)	**The May Department** **Stores Co.** **St. Louis, MO**	Famous Barr (30) Filene's (41) Foley's (55) Hecht's (70) Kaufmann's (47) Lord & Taylor (64) Meier & Frank (8) Robinsons-May (55)
The Limited, Inc. **Columbus, OH**	Abercrombie & Fitch (186) Abercrombie & Fitch Kids (13) Bath & Body Works (1,101) Express (712) Galyan's (15) Henri Bendel (1) Lane Bryant (760) Lerner New York (668) The Limited (570) Limited Too (317) Structure (545) Victoria's Secret (874)	**The TJX Cos.** **Framingham, MA** **Toys 'R' Us** **Paramus, NJ**	HomeGoods (23) Marshalls (461) T.J. Maxx (58) T.K. Maxx (31) Winners Apparel Ltd. (76) Babies 'R' Us (98) Kids 'R' Us (215) Kids World (2) Toys 'R' Us (1,141)

1, 2 Includes 154 combo stores which are counted in the Jewel Food and Osco Drug totals.

3 Includes former Broadway/Emporium/Weinstock's units.

4 Some locations include Baby Gap departments.

Based on information supplied by John Konarski, Vice President of Research, International Council of Shopping Centers, July 1998.

Figure 11.6 Retailers Listed by Margin and Turnover

High Margin

| Low Turnover | High-Margin/Low-Turnover Retailers | High-Margin/High-Turnover Retailers | High Turnover |
| | Low-Margin/Low-Turnover Retailers | Low-Margin/High-Turnover Retailers | |

Low Margin

store attracts most customers from within a 1.5-mile radius, a drug store from within a 3-mile radius, and a discount department store from within a 10-mile radius. Service retailers must also pay particular attention to location. For example, a movie theater, dry cleaner, or barber shop will attract most of its customers from within a 3-mile area. As shown in Figure 11.7, there are four basic types of locations from which a store-based retailer can select: business districts, shopping centers/malls, freestanding units, and nontraditional locations.

As a rule, retailers selling convenience goods or services will have a smaller trade area than retailers of shopping or specialty goods and services. A physician specializing in cardiovascular diseases can attract patients from beyond the local community, but a general practitioner will only attract patients from his/her local community.

Business Districts

Historically, most retailers were located in the **central business district (CBD).** Many of the traditional department stores were first located here, along with a selection of specialty

Central business district (CBD)
is usually an unplanned shopping area that evolved around the geographic point in the city at which all public transportation systems converge.

Figure 11.7 Types of Store-Based Retail Locations

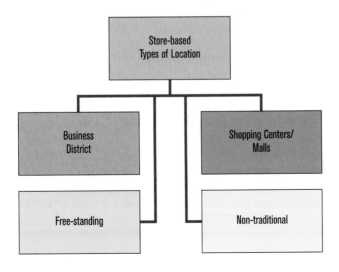

Store-based Types of Location

Business District

Shopping Centers/ Malls

Free-standing

Non-traditional

stores. They drew their clientele from the entire metropolitan area and from nonresidents visiting the city.

The CBD has several strengths and weaknesses to consider. Among its strengths are easy access to public transportation, wide product assortment, variety (in images, prices, and services), and proximity to commercial and cultural activities. Some weaknesses to consider are inadequate (and usually expensive) parking, older stores, high rents and taxes, traffic and delivery congestion, potentially high crime rate, and the general decaying conditions of many inner cities. However, despite these disadvantages, Kmart recently deviated from its historical suburban location policy to open two discount department stores in New York City (Manhattan). Despite the high costs and other disadvantages of such a location, the chain felt the high traffic and the expectation of more than $50 million in annual sales was an irresistible incentive.[13]

In most larger cities, secondary business districts and neighborhood business districts have developed. A *secondary business district (SBD)* is a shopping area that is smaller than the CBD and that revolves around at least one department or variety store at the intersection of two major streets. A *neighborhood business district (NBD)* is a shopping area that evolves to satisfy the convenience-oriented shopping needs of a neighborhood and generally contains several small stores, with the major retailer being either a supermarket or a variety store.

Shopping Centers/Malls

A *shopping center,* or *mall,* is a centrally owned and/or managed shopping district that is planned to have a **balanced tenancy**, and is surrounded by parking facilities. A shopping center has one or more **anchor stores** and a variety of smaller stores. Figure 11.8 lists the advantages and disadvantages of locating in a shopping center/mall.

According to the International Council of Shopping Centers, there are eight different types of shopping centers.[14] Here is a brief description of each:

1. A *neighborhood center,* which is the smallest in size, provides for the sale of convenience goods and personal services for the day-to-day living needs of the immediate neighborhood. It has a primary trade area of three miles.

Balanced tenancy

is a feature of a shopping center or mall where the stores are selected to complement each other in merchandise offerings.

Anchor stores

are the dominant large-scale stores that are expected to draw customers to a shopping center.

Figure 11.8   Advantages and Disadvantages of Locating in a Shopping Center/Mall

Advantages
1. Heavy traffic resulting from the wide range of product offerings
2. Nearness to the population
3. Cooperative planning and sharing of common costs
4. Access to highway and availability of parking
5. Lower crime rate
6. Clean, neat environment
7. More than adequate parking space

Disadvantages
1. Inflexible store hours (the retailer must stay open the hours of the center and can't be open at other times)
2. High rents
3. Restrictions as to the merchandise that the retailer may sell
4. Inflexible operations and required membership in the center's merchant organization
5. Possibility of too much competition and the fact that much of the traffic is not interested in a particular product offering
6. Dominance of the smaller stores by the anchor tenant

2. The *community shopping center* is next in size. In addition to the convenience goods and personal services of the neighborhood center, community centers provide a wider range of facilities for the sale of soft good lines (clothing) and hard good lines (hardware, furniture, and appliances). They are usually built around either a small department store, a variety store, a category killer, or discount department store. A community center has a trade area of 3–6 miles.

3. The *regional center* provides for a wide range of goods and services. It is built around one or more major department stores. The regional center is the second-largest type of shopping center and has a trade area of 5–15 miles.

4. The *super-regional center* provides for an extensive variety of merchandise as well as a variety of services and recreational facilities. It is built around at least three major department stores and has a trade area of 5–25 miles.

5. *Fashion/specialty centers* are comprised primarily of upscale apparel stores, boutiques, and craft shops carrying high quality fashion oriented merchandise at high price levels. They can also have restaurants and entertainment and has a trade area of 5–15 miles.

6. *Power centers* are dominated by several anchors, such as category killers, warehouse clubs, off-price stores, and discount department stores. They have a trade area of 5–10 miles.

7. *Theme centers* are shopping centers located in places of historical interest and where a lot of tourist traffic is generated, such as Faneuil Hall Marketplace in Boston.

Figure 11.9   The Mall of America

The Mall of America in Bloomington, Minnesota, with over 4 million square feet of space is the largest mall in the United States.

8. *Outlet centers* specialize in manufacturer's outlets that dispose of over-production of current merchandise lines, factory seconds (which are clearly marked), and leftovers from last season.

Freestanding Retailer

As the name implies, a *freestanding retailer* is not physically connected to other retailers, but instead has an individual building and parking area, generally located along a major traffic artery. Most cities have strips of freestanding retailers along their major traffic routes; Haverty's Furniture Stores are usually freestanding stores, as are many Wal-Mart Supercenters. However, many other retailers soon locate next to these previously freestanding outlets in order to benefit from the traffic they draw.

Nontraditional Locations

Increasingly retailers are identifying nontraditional locations for their stores which offer more place utility or locational convenience. Perhaps one of the oldest and best known operators of facilities in nontraditional retail locations is the Army and Air Force Exchange Services (AAFES), which operates over 10,000 stores in the United States and around the world on U.S. military bases. Stores in airports are increasing and now include not only cafeterias and restaurants but also apparel, giftware, jewelry, luggage, and bookstores. Local school boards[15] are now allowing fast-food outlets, such as Subway, Taco Bell, and Domino's, on their campuses; truck and travel stops along interstate highways are also incorporating food courts; and some franchisees such as Taco Bell and Dunkin' Donuts are putting small food service units in convenience stores. Hospitals are building emergency care clinics near where people live in the suburbs, and Wells Fargo is now putting drugstores and Starbucks in its branches.[16]

ATMOSPHERICS IN RETAILING

Like all marketers, retailers must identify their target market and make marketing decisions to satisfy the needs of that market. When doing this, retailers must realize that the store itself is a major part of their offering. After all, the store must aid the retailer to perform the first two tasks discussed at the beginning of the chapter: (1) attract consumers inside and (2) turn these consumers into loyal customers by enticing them to make a purchase. The retailer does this by creating a positive **store image** for the store, which is dependent on the **retail mix** offered by the store. Retailers need to be concerned with how customers perceive the in-store environment, and whether they are comfortable in it. Customers are more likely to make larger and more frequent purchases if the store's total environment is comfortable and welcoming, and encourages browsing. Factors that influence customers' perceptions include the merchandise, level of service offered by employees, fixtures, floor layout, sound, and odor.

The quality and style of the merchandise lines carried by a store affect the store's status in the eyes of the consumer. Furniture retailers that want to project a high-status image will carry Heritage, Henredon, and other upscale furniture lines. Austrian crystal and Irish linen are not likely to be found in the same housewares department as plastic glasses and oilcloth table coverings. Customers select where to shop for particular items according to their overall perception of the available stores; mothers might well go first to Target or Wal-Mart for children's playwear, but would probably skip over them in favor of JCPenney's or a specialty store when shopping for a prom gown.

Retailers seeking to be successful must also remember that they can differentiate themselves from the competition not only by having the right merchandise, but also by encouraging their employees to do a better job of satisfying the needs of their customers. There is general agreement that one of the most basic retailing strategies for creating competitive advantage is the delivery of high quality service.[17] Good service must meet or exceed the customer's expectations. Today, retailers have come to realize that offering good customer service is a primary requirement. Instead of frustrating the customer by not hav-

www.havertys.com
www.army.mil
www.af.mil
www.subway.com
www.tacobell.com
www.dunkindonuts.com
www.wellsfargo.com

LEARNING OBJECTIVE LO4

Store image
is the overall feeling or mood projected by a store through its aesthetic appeal to human senses.

Retail mix
is a store's combination of merchandise, prices, advertising, location, customer services, selling, floor layout, and building design.

Figure 11.10   Books Plus Food

By incorporating a cafe as an integral part of Barnes and Noble bookstores, a very relaxing and casual atmosphere is created.

ing the necessary stock on hand or the proper sales support on the floor, successful retailers realize that customer service is a major demand-generator for their merchandise. Retailers must remember that not having a properly trained employee to aid a customer will lower the customer's satisfaction with the retailer, often irreparably.

Even the store fixtures must be consistent with the overall image that the retailer wishes to project. Suits crowded together on plastic coat hangers do not reflect the image of quality that similar suits project when hung on wooden hangers with ample space on the rack to facilitate customer browsing. If a retailer wants the store to project a quality image, the display units themselves must be adequately spaced and accessible. The aisles must be uncongested and well laid out, and related products should be placed close enough to promote ancillary purchases (a handbag to complement a newly-purchased pair of shoes, blank videotapes to go with a new VCR, or the latest CDs near where you selected your new Discman).

Effective store design must appeal to the human senses of sight, sound, smell, and touch. Obviously, the majority of design activity in a retail store is focused on affecting sight, but research has shown that the other senses can be very important, too. Since smell is believed to be the most closely linked of all the senses for memory and emotions, retailers hope that its use as a key in-store marketing tool will put consumers in the "mood." Victoria's Secret, for example, places potpourri cachets throughout its store to create the ambiance of a lingerie closet.

Retailers have piped music, e.g., Muzak, into their stores for generations, believing that a musical backdrop will create a more relaxing environment and encourage customers to stay longer. Increasingly, music is being seen as a valuable marketing tool, since the right music can create an environment that is both soothing and reflective of the merchandise being offered. For example, a jeans retailer might play hip-hop over baggies and classic rock over the Dockers. Music also affects how long shoppers stay in a store, as well as how much consumers purchase.[18] For instance, while classical music is soothing and has been shown to encourage customers to shop longer[19] and select more expensive merchandise,[20] it may be inconsistent with the desired ambiance of a trendy fashion store catering to college-age women. Today, some retailers are experimenting with placing promotional announcements in with the background music. Other retailers have found a different use for "canned" music. 7-Eleven has installed speakers to play elevator music outside stores in Canada, California, Maryland, and Florida to repel teenagers and vagrants.[21]

EVOLUTION OF RETAIL COMPETITION

Since it is relatively easier to open a retail store, as opposed to a manufacturing plant, in terms of entry barriers (skill, expertise, and expense), new retail institutions appear continuously. Scholars studying retailing have developed several theories to explain and describe the evolution of competition in retailing. We will review two of them briefly.

Wheel of Retailing

The *wheel of retailing,* illustrated in Figure 11.11, is one of the oldest descriptions of one of the patterns of competitive evolution in retailing.[22] This theory states that new types of retailers enter the market as low-status, low-margin, low-price operators. This is the entry phase and allows these retailers to compete effectively and take market share away from the more traditional retailers. However, as they meet with success, these new retailers gradually acquire more sophisticated and elaborate facilities, thereby becoming less efficient, in a trading-up phase. This creates both a higher investment and a subsequent rise in operating costs. Predictably, these retailers will enter the vulnerability phase and must raise prices and margins, becoming vulnerable to new low-margin retail competitors who progress through the same pattern. This appears to be the case today with outlet malls. Once bare-bones warehouses for manufacturers' imperfect or excess merchandise, outlet

Figure 11.11   The Wheel of Retailing

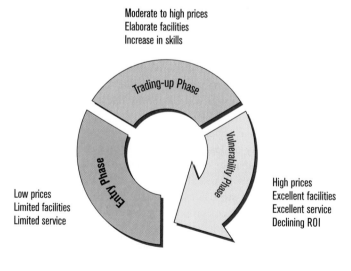

Moderate to high prices
Elaborate facilities
Increase in skills

Trading-up Phase

Vulnerability Phase

Entry Phase

Low prices
Limited facilities
Limited service

High prices
Excellent facilities
Excellent service
Declining ROI

malls have quickly evolved into fancy, almost up-scale malls where retailers try to outdo each other's accent lighting, private dressing rooms, and generous return policies. As a result, and with the cost of operating at such locations increasing and with the regular department stores becoming more competitive, there is now little difference between the outlet's prices and the department store's sale prices. This theory of competition can also be seen in the evolution of fast-food hamburger outlets.

Retail Life Cycle

Much like the product life cycle discussed in Chapter 8, the **retail life cycle** assumes that retail institutions pass through an identifiable cycle. This cycle includes four distinct stages that: (1) starts with an *introduction,* (2) proceeds to *growth,* (3) continues into *maturity,* and (4) ends with *decline.* Each stage will be briefly discussed in this chapter. Figure 11.12 illustrates the various stages of the retail life cycle for many of our current retail institutions.

Introduction
The process begins with an entrepreneur who is willing and able to develop a new cost savings approach to the retailing of certain products, and allows at least a portion of these cost savings to be passed on to the customer. In other words, a new type of retail institution is developed at this stage. During the introduction stage, profits are low, despite the increasing sales level, due to amortizing development costs.

Growth
During the growth stage, sales and usually profits explode. Many others begin to copy the company's ideas. Toward the end of this period, cost pressures that arise from the need for

Figure 11.12   The Retail Life Cycle

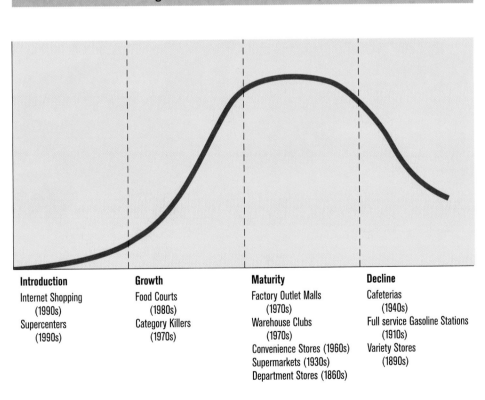

Introduction	Growth	Maturity	Decline
Internet Shopping (1990s)	Food Courts (1980s)	Factory Outlet Malls (1970s)	Cafeterias (1940s)
Supercenters (1990s)	Category Killers (1970s)	Warehouse Clubs (1970s)	Full service Gasoline Stations (1910s)
		Convenience Stores (1960s)	Variety Stores (1890s)
		Supermarkets (1930s)	
		Department Stores (1860s)	

Figure 11.13   McDonald's Has Grown and Changed

McDonald's has increased the cost of store operations over the last 40 years by adding indoor seating and indoor playgrounds and thus has fallen victim to the wheel of retailing.

a larger staff, more complex internal systems, increased management controls, and other requirements of operating large, multi-unit organizations overtake some of the favorable results. Consequently, late in this stage both market share and profitability tend to approach their maximum levels.

Maturity

In the maturity stage, market share stabilizes and severe profit declines are experienced for several reasons. First, managers have become accustomed to managing a high-growth firm that was simple and small, but now they must manage a large, complex firm in a non-growing market. Second, the industry has typically overexpanded. Third, competitive assaults will be made on these firms by new retailing formats (a bold entrepreneur developing a new cost savings approach, thus beginning a retail life cycle for yet another type of retail institution).

Decline

Although all types of retail institutions will inevitably reach the decline stage, retail managers will try to postpone it by changing their offerings. These attempts can postpone the decline stage, but a return to earlier, attractive levels of operating performance is not likely. Sooner or later a major loss of market share will occur, profits will fall, and the once promising idea is no longer needed in the marketplace.

Implications of the Retail Life Cycle

Three primary implications can be derived from the discussion of the retail life cycle:

1. Retailers should remain flexible so that they are able to adapt their strategies to various stages in the life cycle.

2. Since profits vary by stage in the retail life cycle, retailers need to carefully analyze the risks and profits of entering the various life cycle stages or expanding their outlets at various stages in the life cycle.

3. Retailers need to extend the maturity stage. Since they will have substantial investments in a particular form of retailing by the time the maturity stage arrives, they will have a strong interest in trying to work that investment for as long as possible.

The importance of these three points is reinforced by the fact that the retail life cycle is accelerating today. New concepts now move more quickly from introduction to maturity. The leading operators have aggressive growth goals and their investors demand a quick return on investment. For example, the downtown department store took 80 years to reach maturity; the variety store, 45 years; the supermarket, 35 years; the discount department store, 20 years; and most recently, the factory outlet malls have reached maturity within a span of less than 10 years. Many entrepreneurs with new ideas will be acquired by larger retailers with capital and expertise in concept roll-out.[23]

CATEGORY MANAGEMENT

Due to the shortening of retail life cycles, the more rapid turning of the wheel of retailing, and the rapid growth of hyper-competitive retailers (especially category killers, supercenters, and Internet-based competitors), retailers have begun to pay more attention to category management. *Category management* is a process of managing and planning all SKU's within a product cateogry as a distinct business. A *SKU* is a *stock keeping unit* and refers to a distinct merchandise item in the retailer's merchandise assortment. When all SKU's in a category are managed as a business unit, then the end result will be an increased ability to get consumers from the retailer's trading area into their store. It will also be easier to

Careers in Marketing

Jeff Thompson: The Evolution of a Full-Service Merchant Wholesaler

Jeff Thompson didn't start his business career in wholesaling. In 1981 when he was 10 years old, he began carrying newspapers for his hometown paper, the *Ada* (Oklahoma) *Evening News.* He increased the route from 50 to 150 papers per day, and in 1988, he was awarded the Oklahoma Press Association Newspaper Carrier of the Year award.

In 1986, when he was 14, Jeff started Peripheral Enhancements Corporation (then called Peripheral Outlet). Using $2,500 saved from his newspaper route, he began the business in his home basement by buying and selling used computers. This began his career in wholesaling. However, he essentially operated a cash and carry wholesale business, and thus his services were limited.

By the time he completed high school, Jeff evolved his company into computer memory sales due mainly to the fact that the smaller memory products required less space in his home for shipping and inventory. This change of direction into computer memory sales set into action explosive growth, and in 1989, worldwide sales totaled $500,000.

In 1989, Robert F. Lusch, then Dean of the College of Business at the University of Oklahoma, noticed an article on Jeff Thompson in the Sunday business section of the Oklahoma City newspaper. After reading this highly inspiring article, he got on the phone and tracked down Jeff. The next evening Jeff Thompson and Dean Lusch had dinner, and Dean Lusch convinced Jeff to attend the University of Oklahoma.

Working from his dorm room, Jeff continued to operate his company while attending college. In March 1990, sales exceeded $1 million in a single month, more than twice the sales of the entire previous year. By 1991, the company had 12 employees and its own building. At this point many more services began to be offered. From 1991–1996, Peripheral experienced a growth rate of 641 percent, earning it a spot on the 1996 *Inc. 500* list of the fastest growing American companies.

In 1996, the company changed its name to Peripheral Enhancements Corporation to reflect its expanding product lines, services, and markets. In 1997, Peripheral opened a new 10,000 square foot facility to begin assembling its own computer memory modules. Assembly operations are a function that is increasingly being performed by merchant wholesalers. Thus, the company had transformed itself from a limited service wholesaler to a full function wholesaler performing major assembly operations.

Today, at age 28, Jeff serves as president of Peripheral Enhancements Corporation, one of the largest worldwide wholesalers of computer memory components. Still based in his hometown of Ada, Oklahoma, the company also has a sales and marketing office in Dallas, Texas and major distribution points throughout most of the world.

In the summer of 1998, Jeff announced that his company would expand its presence in the market by acquiring the Kansas-based computer memory company, NewerRAM, as well as introducing a full line of digital film products marketed under the name, Peripheral SnapzTM.

Source: Press releases from Peripheral Enhancements Corporation and author's personal knowledge of Jeff Thompson.

---

convert these consumers into paying customers, while operating in the most efficient manner, so as to reduce operating costs.

Since retailers handle thousands of SKU's they have found category management very effective as a marketing tool. For example, a grocery store, which may stock up to 30,000 SKU's, may decide to have a category manager for bath tissue. This category manager would need to first define this category. It could be defined as soft, absorbent tissue paper used primarily for cleaning, wiping and drying after toilet use and would include dry and moist wipes used for this purpose. It would then be important to determine where customers purchased bath tissue. Although in the past consumers may have primarily purchased bath tissue at grocery stores, the category manager would now find that bath tissue is also frequently purchased at discount department stores, supercenters, and warehouse clubs. Some consumers are even purchasing bath tissue from Internet-based retailers such as NetGrocer and Peapod. The category manager would also be interested in the major brands and their share of market. It would also be helpful to know if these brands have different penetration levels in different marketing channels. Each of the brands would also have certain attributes that influence purchases; attributes such as price, softness, moistened, roll life, odor-free or scented, brand image, and so on. With this information and a thorough knowledge of the target market of the retail store and its competition, the category manager would attempt to develop a coordinated retail mix for the bath tissue category. This would include which brands to stock and what price points and price lines to establish. Decisions would also need to be made regarding in-store display and shelf space allocation, advertising expenditures, and promotion activities such as couponing.

But how does a category manager make these marketing decisions? The major goal of the category manager is to achieve a certain level of profit per square foot of space (allocated to the product category) and profit per unit of inventory investment (in the product category). These two measures of financial performance will guide all marketing decisions. The category manager quickly realizes that he or she can't infinitely increase the number of SKU's to better serve customers. This would require more inventory and space resources that are very valuable and constrained. In the bath tissue category, there are approximately 240 SKU's and by stocking all SKU's the retailer would increase the likelihood of serving its customers. However, it may not be very profitable. Therefore, the category manager may determine that 40 to 50 SKU's will serve 80–90 percent of its customer base or target market. The determination of the retailer's target market, which will be of a certain income level and social class, will help to determine the most popular bath tissue SKU's that should be stocked and promoted.

A key advantage of category management is that it allows the retailer to concentrate its purchases with a limited number of suppliers. This will provide the retailer with more channel power. For example, it may determine by stocking only Charmin and Northern bath tissue that it can gain promotional and price concessions from these manufacturers. These concessions can be used to support its marketing efforts and help it to better serve customers.

Category managers have also fully embraced information technology to help them better manage their categories. Each SKU has a distinct product identification code that is recorded at the cash register when a product is sold. This data when combined with other purchasing information can provide very valuable insights into how to better merchandise the category. For example, it may be found that bath tissue is most likely to be purchased with laundry detergent or other cleaning fluids. This can lead to ideas for cross merchandising or cross-promotions between product categories.

DIFFERENT TYPES OF WHOLESALERS

As noted at the beginning of this chapter, **wholesaling** is a larger sector of the U.S. economy than retailing. Total wholesale sales are almost $4 trillion compared to retailing's $2.4 trillion. Why are wholesale sales greater than retail sales? The answer lies in the fact that wholesalers sell not only to retailers, but also to manufacturers and other wholesalers. In fact, wholesalers can and do operate differently in the various types of distribution channels discussed in the previous chapter. Some will provide a wide ranges of services or handle broad lines of goods, others may specialize in selling only to other wholesalers or manufacturers, and others may take neither title or possession to merchandise they are selling. As shown in Figure 11.14, wholesalers can be grouped into three broad categories: manufacturer's sales branches, merchant wholesalers, and agent/brokers.

Like retailing, the wholesale sector, as shown in Figure 11.15, is constantly undergoing change. Three major trends are apparent in this figure: (1) manufacturer sales branches have the highest sales per establishment, (2) merchant wholesalers now account for over 80 percent of sales, and (3) while agents and brokers have held steady as a percentage of sales, they have had a major reduction in number of establishments, meaning they have the largest percentage increase in sales per establishment.

Wholesaling
involves the activities of those persons or establishments that sell to retailers and/or other organizational buyers for industrial, institutional, and commercial use, but do not sell in significant amounts to final consumers.

Manufacturer's Sales Branches

Manufacturer's sales branches actually include both sales outlets (which carry full inventory) and sales outlets (which don't carry inventory) that are owned by the manufacturer. These are usually located in areas of high demand and serve as a base of operation

Figure 11.14   Types of Wholesalers

Manufacturer's sales branches actually include both sales outlets (which carry inventory) and sales outlets (which don't carry inventory) that are owned by the manufacturer.

Merchant's wholesalers are independent firms that purchase a product from the manufacturer and resell it to other manufacturers, wholesalers, or retailers, but not to the final consumer. Merchant wholesalers can be categorized as full-service or limited-service wholesalers.

Full-service merchant wholesaler provides a wide range of services for retailers and business purchasers.

Limited-service merchant wholesalers perform only a few services for manufacturers or their customers or perform all of them on a more restricted basis than do full-service wholesalers.

Agents/brokers never take title to the merchandise. Their key function is to help bring potential buyers and sellers together.

Figure 11.15   Percent of Sales and Establishments by Type of Wholesaler 1929–1992

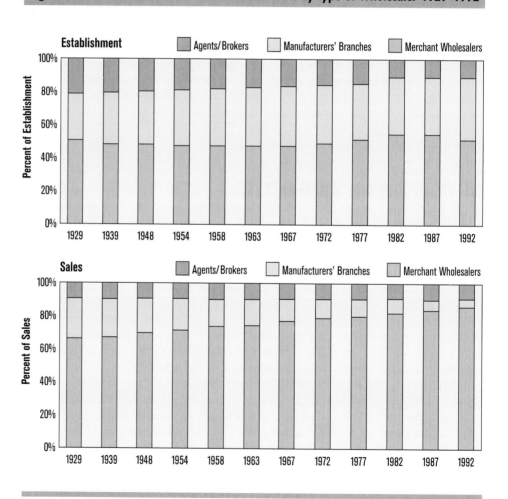

for the manufacturer's sales staff when calling on customers. The reasons why a manufacturer may choose to distribute its goods directly through company-owned facilities are: (1) some perishable goods need rigid control of distribution to avoid spoilage; (2) the

Figure 11.16 The Buying Function

Buying is a critical marketing function that retailers perform. Here we see Jody Spiera of Peter Luger's Steakhouse with Gachot & Gachot Wholesale meat market supervisor, John Buono of New York City.

goods have a high value per unit causing other middlemen not to want to handle the line; (3) the goods require complex installation or servicing; or (4) the goods need aggressive promotion. When inventory is carried at these outlets, the manufacturer is essentially performing most, if not all, of the wholesaling function. Predictably, the operating expenses of these manufacturer's outlets increase as the value of the inventory carried in stock increases. An example of a manufacturer using its own sales branches is Caterpillar.

Merchant Wholesalers

Most often manufacturers have found that it is more profitable not to use their own outlets to sell directly to retailers or other business firms, but rather to use **merchant wholesalers.** This channel is used when it is not economical for the manufacturer's salespeople to call directly on its users or to send them separate shipments. Thus, the merchant wholesaler provides economies of scale to the manufacturer. For example, if each wholesaler had 200 accounts, then by selling to only 10 wholesalers, the manufacturer could reach 2,000 customers, thereby reducing selling and distribution costs. An example of a manufacturer using wholesalers to sell its products to retailers is Kraft Foods. Merchant wholesalers can be categorized as full-service or limited-service wholesalers.

A *full-service merchant wholesaler* provides a wide range of services for retailers and business purchasers. Such a wholesaler may store merchandise in a convenient location, allowing its customers to make purchases on short notice thus minimizing their inventory costs. The full-service wholesaler typically maintains a sales force to call on retailers, make deliveries, and extend credit to qualified buyers. Full-service wholesalers are

Merchant wholesalers are independent firms that purchase a product and take title to that product from the manufacturer and resell it to other manufacturers, wholesalers, or retailers, but not to the final consumer.

www.fleming.com

common in the drug, grocery, and hardware industries. In the industrial-goods market, full-function merchant wholesalers (often called *industrial distributors*) market machinery, inexpensive accessory equipment, and supplies.

An example of a full-service merchant wholesaler is the Fleming Companies. Fleming, the nation's largest grocery wholesaler, helps independent grocery stores remain competitive with large chain store grocery stores such as Food Giant and Safeway by selling independent grocers merchandise at competitive prices while providing them with services such as store design, merchandise display, advertising layout, credit, and delivery.

Limited-service merchant wholesalers perform only a few services for manufacturers or their customers or perform all of them on a more restricted basis than does a full-service wholesaler. They may avoid some of the marketing functions by eliminating them entirely or passing them on to another marketing channel member or to the customer. Clearly, the less services performed by the wholesaler, the lower will be the markup it can charge on the merchandise it sells. Some of the more popular types of limited-service wholesalers are described in Figure 11.17.

Agents/Brokers

The key difference between agents/brokers and merchant wholesalers is that *agents/brokers* never take title to the merchandise. Their key function is to help bring potential buyers and sellers together. Like merchant wholesalers, they may or may not take possession of the merchandise they handle or provide all the services a full-service wholesaler performs. As was shown in Figure 11.15, agents and brokers today account for about 10 percent of wholesale sales.

A *manufacturer's agent* is an independent middleman that handles a manufacturer's marketing functions by selling part or all of a manufacturer's product line in an assigned geographic area. They are paid on commission but have little or no control over prices and terms of sale and may work for a number of firms that produce related, noncompeting products. Agents can earn between 3 and 20 percent on sales, depending on industry norms and how costly it is for them to perform the selling function. Manufacturer's agents are most likely to be used by manufacturers desiring to enter a new geographic market area, those with a limited product line, those with insufficient resources to develop their own sales force, and those seeking to enter a new market with a product unrelated to their existing product line.

Brokers are independent middlemen that bring buyers and sellers together and provide market information to one or the other parties. While most brokers work for the seller,

---

Figure 11.17   Types of Limited-Service Wholesalers

1. **Drop-Shipper (Desk Jobber).** Passes on customer orders with instructions to the manufacturer to ship directly to a location specified by the customer. Maintains no warehouse or inventory; *does not come in physical possession* of the goods. Usually contacts customer by telephone, so sales force may not be necessary and may be much less active in generating promotion. Particularly useful in bulky goods and where merchandise typically moves in carlot quantities. Sometimes called a "carlot wholesaler."

2. **Cash and Carry Wholesaler.** Does not provide customers with credit or delivery. The customers must pick up the merchandise from the wholesaler and pay for it with cash or check. This type of wholesaler typically does not have an outside sales force. Customers are usually small retailers or small industrial accounts.

3. **Truck Jobber (Wagon Jobber).** Their warehouse is their truck. Usually self-employed with little capital and generally does not extend credit to customers. May own their own goods, but usually gets merchandise on consignment from a larger full-service wholesaler. Travels to customers and sells directly from the back of the truck.

4. **Rack Jobber.** Maintains racks stocked with merchandise at the retailer's location. Heavy assumption of risk since the jobber holds title and the retailer is billed only for goods sold from the rack. Retailer's only investment is in the space allotted to the rack.

some do work for buyers. Brokers, who normally earn less than 5 percent of sales, simply negotiate a sale and are paid a fee only if the transaction is completed. Most brokers today operate in the food industry, however, they are also common in the industrial equipment industry.

SELECTING AND WORKING WITH WHOLESALERS

A major decision in designing any channel is selecting the right wholesaler(s) for the tasks to be performed and determining how to manage the wholesaler(s) chosen.

Selecting Wholesalers

To select the best wholesalers, manufacturers need a screening device to help assess the quality of potential wholesalers on at least five broad dimensions: (1) management skills, (2) financial characteristics, (3) physical facilities, (4) objectives and policies, and (5) marketing skills/strengths.

To help assess management skills needed to effectively and efficiently manage the resources at their disposal and the manufacturer's products, wholesalers need to be screened on such points as their record and reputation, the planning and management systems and procedures used, cooperation and helpfulness, and receptiveness to constructive management suggestions.

The wholesaler's financial strength, integrity, history, and future prospects must also be considered. For example, wholesalers in a poor financial position may not be able to perform the necessary marketing functions and services. Therefore, it is important to assess financial characteristics such as whether the wholesaler is making a profit, if it is sufficiently capitalized, if credit is adequate, and whether it can afford to keep adequate stocks on hand.

The wholesaler's equipment and facilities should be assessed carefully, as considerable variation exists among wholesalers on this dimension. Here, it is necessary to know if the wholesaler has the needed facilities and equipment to handle your product(s), the age and condition of the facilities and equipment, the maintenance schedule, the wholesaler's reputation regarding service standards, and whether the office set up is adequate to handle your business.

Another important dimension for screening wholesalers is the extent to which their objectives and policies are compatible with the manufacturer's marketing channel. In evaluating this dimension, the wholesaler's managerial objectives and policies must be assessed in respect to growth, the stability and reliability of the organization, and the possibility of conflicts.

Wholesalers need to have the marketing expertise and stamina to successfully market and distribute the manufacturer's product line. Therefore, the wholesaler's marketing know-how and the size, reputation, credibility, and attitude of the sales force must be assessed.

By carefully assessing wholesalers on these five dimensions, the manufacturer should be able to maximize the chances of selecting the best wholesalers. Unfortunately, the best available wholesalers may not always be willing to handle the manufacturer's product line. Consequently, it is important for the manufacturer to know how to properly manage wholesalers in order to obtain their commitment to the manufacturer's products.

Managing the Wholesalers

As pointed out earlier, manufacturers who operate through wholesalers typically do so because they find it less expensive and less capital intensive than performing the wholesaling activities themselves. However, manufacturers can only use wholesalers successfully if they get the wholesaler's cooperation in marketing their products. To accomplish this, manufacturers must obtain some degree of control over wholesalers.

Planned gross margin

is the difference between the price the manufacturer plans to sell the product to wholesalers and the price at which wholesalers can resell.

If manufacturers want the cooperation and commitment of wholesalers, they must offer them financial, promotional, training, and general management aids. Depending on the line of trade, some or all of these may be offered. The most important financial assistance that manufacturers can offer wholesalers is the **planned gross margin**, which must be large enough so that wholesalers can achieve an adequate profit after performing all the activities desired by the manufacturers. Other important forms of financial assistance might include inventory financing through liberal purchase terms, rebates, bonuses if quotas are achieved, seasonal dating to get wholesalers to stock up early in the season, and extra discounts for performing special services such as product recall or warranty services.

Frequently offered forms of promotional assistance include national or regional advertising with the wholesaler's name mentioned; advertising allowances for local advertising; brochures, pamphlets, and other sales material to be distributed to potential customers; suggested advertising layouts or content for local advertising (i.e., prepared advertising mats); and salespeople employed by manufacturers to generate new accounts for the wholesaler.

If the wholesaler has neither the human nor financial resources to properly train salespeople, the manufacturer may offer a sales training program. A good training program will help the wholesaler to service the manufacturer's merchandise line by informing sales representatives about the strengths and weaknesses of the manufacturer's products and those of competing products, and by teaching them how to make effective sales presentations. Training of service personnel may also be advantageous, especially if the manufacturer's product line is technically complex and needs pre-installation or post-installation service.

Wholesalers are becoming more concerned about internal operating problems, including problems of credit and collection, inventory control, finance, planning, and personnel. Consequently, some manufacturers are designing executive development programs to help wholesalers solve their operating problems. By offering such programs, manufacturers are recognizing the fact that their marketing efforts can only be successful if the wholesaler survives and prospers.

Finally, all of the wholesale distributors should be given a sales goal based on the market potential and competitive intensity in the geographic territory the wholesaler serves. The manufacturer and wholesaler must discuss this goal and arrive at some agreement on its reasonableness. Once the wholesale distributors are selected and offered the proper mix of assistance, they should be expected to meet their targeted goals. To assess their performance, an objective annual evaluation needs to be conducted.

STRATEGIC RENEWAL IN WHOLESALING[24]

Wholesalers have been threatened by larger manufacturers and large chain retailers. Many of these large manufacturers and retailers have attempted to design marketing channels that bypass the wholesaler. In turn, many wholesalers have sought a strategic renewal to make themselves more vital and important to their channel partners. This strategic renewal has primarily revolved around three areas: adoption of technology, commitment to TQM, and adoption of a marketing support philosophy.

Adoption of Technology

Technology—a diverse, complex, and rapidly-changing challenge confronting all companies—encompasses everything from bar coding and scanning devices to fully-automated warehouses, from electronic data interchange links to communications satellites and video text equipment. Technology can cut costs, increase productivity, enhance information management, and improve customer service and marketing. However, in the past wholesalers

Figure 11.18   A Channel Leader

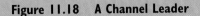

Ace Hardware stores, although independently operated, are part of a vertical marketing system where Ace Hardware wholesale buying cooperative is the channel leader.

who operate on thin profit margins avoided investing heavily in technology. This is beginning to change as an increasing number of wholesalers are adopting leading-edge technologies. Drug wholesalers and electronics distributors were among the pioneers in harnessing technology to improve their operations and communications. For example, Bergen Brunswig, a drug wholesaler, currently receives 99 percent of its orders through electronic order entry systems and sends 95 percent of purchase requests to suppliers electronically. Avnet, an electronics distributor, has an **EDI (Electronic Data Interchange)** system connecting it to suppliers and customers. Avnet's EDI system provides information such as supplier lead times, inventory levels, and order status for sophisticated inventory analysis. It can forecast inventory needs and send purchase orders to suppliers; later, it sends point-of-sale and inventory data back to suppliers along with electronic invoices.

Electronic Data Interchange (EDI)
is a set of protocols for computer-to-computer communication between businesses.

Commitment to TQM

Many wholesalers have begun exploring the advantages of *total quality management (TQM)* programs. Historically, wholesalers have measured tangible outcomes—such as sales, cases sold, tons handled, or profits generated—to assess company operations. At the same time, they measured productivity by comparing outcomes achieved to the resources required, such as sales to inventory or sales per employee. By focusing attention solely on how well tasks were being performed, companies often neglected to evaluate exactly what the tasks were or why they were being performed at all. TQM is a move toward managing processes to improve outcomes as perceived by customers, and many wholesalers are making strong commitments to such programs.

VWR, a distributor of laboratory equipment and suppliers, defines total quality performance as "understanding who the customer is, what their requirements are, and meeting those requirements, error-free, on time, every time." Furthermore, company goals are to exceed those requirements. As wholesalers continue to realize the benefits of zero-defect customer service, quality management programs will play an increasingly important role in providing competitive advantages in the marketplace. In turn, manufacturers and retailers who develop partnerships with these wholesalers will find it easier to achieve their own customer satisfaction objectives.

Marketing Support Philosophy

Traditionally wholesalers have viewed themselves as extensions of either their suppliers or their customers. Today many wholesalers define their companies as being in the "marketing support business." These wholesalers view themselves as marketing *with* their suppliers and customers, not distributing *from* and *to* them. They recognize their primary purpose is to help both suppliers and customers develop effective marketing programs. The marketing support-oriented wholesaler is willing to perform any task, activity, or function for either suppliers or customers that will result in more effective and efficient marketing for the entire channel. In the Hardware industry, TRU*SERV, a wholesaler that serves nearly 10,000 independent hardware retailers and Genuine Auto Parts that serves thousands of NAPA auto parts retailers, have fully embraced the marketing support philosophy.

Chapter Summary

The primary purpose of this chapter was to acquaint the reader with the major types of retailing and wholesaling institutions. Retailing, which has made a significant contribution to the economic prosperity that Americans enjoy so much, has three basic tasks:

1. Getting consumers from your trading area into your store,

2. Converting these consumers into loyal customers, while

3. Operating in the most efficient manner, so as to reduce costs and thereby having lower prices.

The chapter pointed out that when discussing the various types of retailers, the reader must first determine if the retailer is selling from a fixed physical location or not. The six basic types of store-based retailers, department stores, specialty stores, supermarkets, supercenters, category killers, and convenience stores, were then discussed, as well as a discussion of the five types of nonstore retailing, street peddling, direct selling, mail order, automatic merchandising machines, and electronic shopping. Many believe that nonstore retailing is where the next revolution in retailing will occur.

Because retailing is such a diverse business activity, the third section of this chapter reviewed several ways of categorizing retailers on a variety of dimensions, so that the reader can better appreciate the reasons why retailers behave as they do. These dimensions were number of outlets, margin versus turnover, and location. In our discussion of location, we looked at the four basic types of store-based locations from which a retailer can select: business districts, shopping centers/malls, freestanding units, and nontraditional locations.

Like all marketers, retailers must identify their target market and make marketing decisions to satisfy the needs of that market. When doing this retailers must realize that the store and the image it projects is a major part of their offering. A positive store image (the overall feeling or mood projected by a store through its aesthetic appeal to human senses) is dependent on the retail mix offered by the store: that combination of merchandise, prices, advertising, location, customer services, selling, and store layout and design.

Since it is relatively easy to open a retail store, new retail institutions appear continuously. Scholars studying retailing have developed several theories to explain and describe the evolution of competition in retailing. One of the most popular theories is the wheel of retailing, which states that new types of retailers enter the market as low-status, low-margin, low-price operators. Over time, these retailers upgrade their facilities, thereby becoming less efficient, and making them vulnerable to new types of low-margin retail competitors who progress through the same pattern.

Another explanation is the retail life cycle that assumes retail institutions pass through four identifiable stages: (1) introduction, (2) proceeds to growth, (3) then maturity, and (4) ends with decline. The competitive intensity and management activities differ over these four stages.

Due to the intensified retail competition, retailers have been increasingly employing category management. This is where all of the SKU's in a merchandise category are managed as a distinct business. Category managers are guided by the twin goals of increasing space and inventory productivity since space and inventory resources are constrained in retailing. Often the net result of category management is for the retailer to deal with fewer suppliers, which in turn can provide the retailer with more channel power.

Next the chapter discussed wholesaling, which involves the activities of those persons or establishments that sell to retailers and/or other organizational buyers for industrial, institutional, and commercial use, but do not sell in significant amounts to final consumers. Wholesalers can be grouped into three broad categories: manufacturer's sales branches, merchant wholesalers, and agent/brokers.

Manufacturer's sales branches are sales outlets owned by the manufacturer and are usually located in areas of high demand and serve as a base of operation for the manufacturer's sales staff when calling on customers. Merchant wholesalers are independent firms that purchase a product from the manufacturer and resell it to other manufacturers, wholesalers, or retailers, but not to the final consumer. These wholesalers, which can be full-service or limited-service, are used when it is not economical for the manufacturer's salespeople to call directly on its users or to send them separate shipments. Agents/brokers never take title to the merchandise. Like merchant wholesalers, they may or may not take possession of the merchandise they handle or provide all the services a full-service wholesaler performs.

For a manufacturer to operate successfully through wholesalers, they must be able to select and work with the chosen wholesalers. To select the best wholesalers, manufacturers need a screening device that assesses the quality of potential wholesalers on at least five broad dimensions: management skills, financial characteristics, physical facilities, objectives and policies, and marketing skills/strengths.

Once the wholesalers have been selected, if the manufacturers want their cooperation and commitment of wholesalers, manufacturers must offer them financial, promotional, training, and general management aids. Once the wholesale distributors are selected and offered the proper mix of assistance, they should be expected to meet their targeted goals. To assess their performance, an objective annual evaluation needs to be conducted.

Finally, the chapter concluded with a discussion of the strategic renewal undertaken by wholesalers to make themselves more vital and important to their channel partners. This renewal is the direct result of attempts by large manufacturers and retailers to design marketing channels that bypass the wholesaler. This strategic renewal has primarily revolved around three areas: adoption of technology, commitment to TQM, and adoption of a marketing support philosophy.

Key Terms

Department stores are large-scale operations offering a broad product mix consisting of many different product lines with above-average depth, or variety, in each of their product lines.

Specialty stores are relatively small-scale stores offering a great deal of depth in a narrow range of product lines.

Scrambled merchandising is the handling of merchandise lines based solely on the profitability criterion and without regard to the consistency of a particular product line with other products in the retailer's product mix.

Convenience stores stock frequently purchased products such as gasoline, bread, tobacco, and milk that tend to be consumed within 30 minutes of purchase, as well as offering services such as ATMs and car washes.

Trade area is the geographic area where the majority of a store's customers reside.

Operating expenses are the expenses the retailer incurs in running the business other than the cost of the merchandise, e.g., rent, wages, utilities, depreciation, insurance, etc.

Central business district (CBD) is usually an unplanned shopping area that evolved around the geographic point in the city at which all public transportation systems converge.

Balanced tenancy is a feature of a shopping center or mall where the stores are selected to complement each other in merchandise offerings.

Anchor stores are the dominant large-scale stores that are expected to draw customers to a shopping center.

Store image is the overall feeling or mood projected by a store through its aesthetic appeal to human senses.

Retail mix is a store's combination of merchandise, prices, advertising, location, customer services, selling, floor layout, and building design.

Wholesaling involves the activities of those persons or establishments that sell to retailers and/or other organizational buyers for industrial, institutional, and commercial use, but do not sell in significant amounts to final consumers.

Merchant wholesalers are independent firms that purchase a product and take title to that product from the manufacturer and resell it to other manufacturers, wholesalers, or retailers, but not to the final consumer.

Planned gross margin is the difference between the price the manufacturer sells the product to wholesalers and the price at which wholesalers can resell.

Electronic Data Interchange (EDI) is a set of protocols for computer-to-computer communication between businesses.

Additional Key Terms and Concepts

Discounting
Wholesalers
Supermarket
Category killer
Direct sellers
Automatic merchandising machines or vending machines
Chain stores
Inventory turnover
Neighborhood business district (NBD)
Neighborhood center
Regional center
Fashion/specialty centers
Theme centers
Freestanding retailer
Retail life cycle
Stock keeping unit or SKU
Full-service merchant wholesaler
Limited-service merchant wholesalers
Manufacturer's agent
Total quality management (TQM)

Retailing
Discount department stores
Supercenter
Street peddler
Mail-order houses
Electronic shopping
Gross margin percentage
Gross margin
Secondary business district (SBD)
Shopping center or mall
Community shopping center
Super-regional center
Power centers
Outlet centers
Wheel of retailing
Category management
Manufacturer's sales branches
Industrial distributors
Agents/brokers
Brokers

Questions for Discussion

1. Agree or disagree with the following statements: "Scrambled merchandising is really a very inefficient way of retailing. Retailers should specialize in the line(s) of merchandise they carry. Therefore, the use of scrambled merchandising should be decreasing over the remainder of this decade." Support your position.

2. Agree or disagree with the following statement: "Internet retailing is the most efficient form of retailing because it is open 24 hours a day, 365 days a year, and doesn't need wholesalers or retailers." Support your position.

3. Can the small independent retailer survive against the large chains like Target, Kroger, Dillard's, and Wal-Mart? What can they do to strengthen their competitive position?

4. Why is location so important in retailing today? What considerations must a retailer take into account when selecting a location for a specialty store? How would this be different from his thought process if he were opening a supercenter?

5. How does a store's atmospherics impact its image and its ultimate success or failure? Are there similar considerations for nonstore-based retailers? If so, what are they?

6. Describe the wheel of retailing theory. According to its premises, what new type(s) of retail operation might be seen in the future?

7. Why has category management become more important in retailing? What major goals does the category manager focus on in developing a retail mix for a category? Why?

8. Under what circumstances would it be advantageous for a manufacturer to use its own sales branches instead of going through a wholesaler?

9. What criteria should manufacturers use to select wholesalers to distribute their products? How might a manufacturer obtain the information he needs to make a good selection?

10. What types of assistance should manufacturers offer wholesalers to gain their cooperation and support? Why is this assistance advantageous to the manufacturer?

Internet Questions

1. Go to the home page for National Home Center News at www.homecenternews.com. On this home page you will find a link to the NHCN Top 500 Home Centers and the HNCN Top 350 Pro Dealers. The Top 500 Home Centers primarily sell to households, whereas the Top 350 Pro Dealers primarily sell to other businesses, such as building contractors and repair shops. Identify a home center and pro dealer in your area to visit. During your visit find out information about services provided, prices, store layout, and merchandise assortment. If the businesses you select have Web sites, make sure to visit them as well. Write a report describing the differences between the home center and pro dealer.

2. Go to the home page for the United States Census Bureau at www.census.gov. On this page you will find a link to the Census of Retailing. Access this site and locate the

summary retail statistics (sales and number of stores) for your state. Identify the line of retail trade in your state that has had the most rapid sales growth over the most recent five years of available data, and the one that has had the slowest growth. Why do you believe the fastest growing line of retail trade grew faster than the slowest line of retail trade. Try to develop several hypotheses or explanations.

3. Go to the home page for the United States Census Bureau at <u>www.census.gov.</u> On this page you will find a link to the Census of Wholesaling. Access this site and locate the summary retail statistics (sales and number of outlets) for your state. Identify the line of wholesale trade in your state that has had the most rapid sales growth over the most recent five years of available data, and the one that has had the slowest growth. Why do you believe the fastest growing line of wholesale trade grew faster than the slowest line of wholesale trade. Try to develop several hypotheses or explanations.

Endnotes

[1] Based on a personal conversation with Robert Kahn, July 1998.

[2] David Reibstein and Paul Farris, "Do Marketing Expenditures to Gain Distribution Cost the Customer?" *European Management Journal,* March 1995: pp. 31–38.

[3] U.S. Bureau of the Census, *Statistical Abstract of the United States: 1997* (117th edition) Washington, D.C., 1997, Table #1277, "Retail Sales by Type of Store and State: 1994 and 1995."

[4] Robert F. Lusch and Deborah Zizzo, *Competing for Customers: How Wholesaler/ Distributors Can Meet the Power Retailer Challenge,* Washington, D.C.: Distribution Research and Education Foundation 1995.

[5] "How India Offers the Feeding Without the Frenzy," *New York Times,* June 30, 1998: p. A 24.

[6] "Giuliani Gives Sidewalk Vendors a Reprieve as He Reconsiders a Ban," *New York Times,* June 18, 1998: p. A29.

[7] "Paddling Harder at L. L. Bean," *Business Week,* December 7, 1998: p. 72.

[8] Fact Sheet from the National Automated Merchandising Association, Chicago.

[9] "Click 'Til You Drop," *U.S. News & World Report,* December 7, 1998: pp. 42–45.

[10] The following is based on Michael Rollens, "Shopping in the Virtual World," Arthur Andersen Retailing Issues Letter, January 1996.

[11]"Please Don't Squeeze the Tomatoes Online," *U.S. News & World Report,* November 9, 1998: p. 51.

[12]Ibid.

[13]"A Special K," *Discount Merchandiser,* November 1996: pp. 24–27.

[14]Based on information supplied by John Konarski, Vice President of Research, International Council of Shopping Centers, July 1998.

[15]"School Cafeterias Are Enrolling Fast-Food Franchisees," *The Wall Street Journal,* July 28, 1998: p. B2.

[16]"Wells Fargo Plans to Put Drugstores in Banks," *The Wall Street Journal,* July 8, 1996: p. C19 and "'Marketplaces' Open in Old Bank Branches," *New York Times,* May 31, 1998: p. NE31.

[17]Pratibha A. Dabholkar, Dayle I. Thorpe, and Joseph O. Rentz, "A Measure of Service Quality for Retail Stores: Scale Development and Validation," *Journal of the Academy of Marketing Science,* Winter 1996: pp. 3–16.

[18]Gordon C. Bruner II, "Music, Mood, and Marketing," *Journal of Marketing,* October 1990: pp. 94–104.

[19]Ronald E. Milliman, "Using Background Music to Affect Behavior of Supermarket Shoppers," *Journal of Marketing,* Summer 1982: pp. 86–91.

[20]Charles Areni and David Kim, "The Influence of Background Music on Shopping Behavior: Classical Versus Top-Forty Music in a Wine Store," *Advances in Consumer Research,* 1993: pp. 336–340.

[21]"Muzak Once Again Calls the Tune in Retailers' War on the Unwanted," *Wall Street Journal,* December 14, 1992: p. B1.

[22]Malcolm P. McNair, "Significant Trends and Developments in the Postwar Period," in A.B. Smith (ed.), *Competitive Distribution in a Free High-Level Economy and Its Implications for the University* (Pittsburgh, PA: University of Pittsburgh Press, 1958).

[23]*Retailing 2000* (Columbus, OH: Management Horizons, 1995, p. 4).

[24]This section is based on Robert F. Lusch, Deborah Zizzo, and James M. Kenderdine, "Strategic Renewal in Distribution," *Marketing Management* (No. 2, 1993): pp. 20–29.

The Outlet Mall

Over the past decade Robin Montoya had watched with interest the development of factory-outlet malls. As a store manager of a national department store chain operating in the regional mall in Tulsa, Oklahoma, she knew that she would some day have to compete not only with the discount department store chains (such as Target), but also with the manufacturers who were supplying her store, as well as with the outlets associated with most of the leading national chains. After all, Saks Fifth Avenue now has Saks Off Fifth stores, Nordstrom has the Rack, and even Neiman Marcus has their Last Call outlet stores to get rid of their excess and unwanted merchandise. However, what surprised her was the rapid development of the outlet malls in recent years.

Prior to the Civil War, manufacturers began to sell at retail by either operating directly from their plants or by introducing small outlet stores near their plants. Still it was over a hundred years before manufacturers banded together and opened the first outlet shopping center near Reading, Pennsylvania, in 1972. For the next decade, only two or three outlets were added each year.

Given this slow growth pattern, these outlet centers didn't upset the retailers selling the manufacturers' products. Besides the early outlet centers generally sold only "seconds," or imperfect or flawed goods, as well as overproduced merchandise. However, the economic slowdown caused manufacturers to begin opening dozens of outlets each year to the point where almost 400 outlet centers have opened since the mid-1980s. And today's outlet malls no longer are satisfied to only sell seconds and overproduced merchandise. Now they are selling flawless products, deep in sizes and selections.

The outlet mall offers manufacturers who open stores in these malls three major advantages. First, it allows them to reach customers who normally wouldn't purchase their brand name products. Second, it is more profitable for a manufacturer to sell at a reduced "retail price" to the general public than it is to sell at wholesale to stores like Ms. Montoya's. Finally, with their plants operating at less than full capacity, the manufacturers could use outlet sales to increase their production and reduce average costs.

Today, Robin Montoya got the bad news. While attending a planning luncheon for the upcoming United Way campaign, Joyce Moore, a banker, told Robin that her bank was involved in underwriting a major loan for a land developer. This developer wants to build an outlet mall featuring over 80 manufacturers 60 miles northwest of Tulsa on an interstate highway near a major resort area. Included in the loan application was a list of just some of the manufacturers planning on opening stores in the new mall: Nike, London Fog, Liz Claiborne, Esprit, Van Heusen, Reebok, Levi's, Jordache, Fieldcrest Cannon, Chaus, and Eddie Bauer.

That night Montoya decided that early the next morning she would drive up the interstate to visit the site of the new mall. Just as she was getting out of her car at the new mall site, the land developer, Richard Reel, drove up and parked beside her. Robin went over and introduced herself to Reel. After some pleasantries, Reel stated that he assumed the reason behind Ms. Montoya's trip was that she was worried about the competition the new mall was going to provide. Robin admitted that she was indeed worried. Reel then invited Montoya into his office for coffee and a chat about his plans.

The developer began by saying "First, you have to understand, Robin, that we are not really going after the same target market. You are targeting the population of Tulsa. We are targeting an entirely different market. For one thing, our customers will have a higher income than your market. We fully expect that by locating in this resort area, over a third of our customers will have incomes higher than $75,000. In addition, most of our customers will spend one or two full days at our mall. That's why we have triple the parking spaces of a regional mall, so that RVs and charter buses can park. In fact, our market will draw from a radius of 300 miles."

Montoya noted that this was fine and good, but she was still worried about getting into a "price war" with her suppliers. Once again, Reel tried to reassure her. "Our prices here will not be as low as you think. In fact, the 'wheel of retailing' is taking place in all of today's new outlet malls. No longer are our stores 'bare-bones' operators. They have added services to match that of any department store. This in turn has caused prices on this season's merchandise to rise to a point somewhere lower than your prices but above the discounters' price that you are already competing against. What our stores will offer is selection, even if some of the merchandise is last season's, and the 'thrill of the hunt.' Also, your customers will have to consider travel time and costs when comparing your prices to ours. That's why our primary emphasis will be on the resort-area vacationer with a secondary emphasis on the interstate highway traveler." With that Mr. Reel stated that he was late for a meeting and had to leave.

Driving back to Tulsa, Robin was somewhat relieved at what she found out on her trip. She also felt confident that her store could compete with the outlet center. However, on arriving back at her office, she found a note stating that there would be a "special meeting" of all the regional mall's store managers tomorrow morning. It seems that the a manager of one the other three anchor stores wanted everyone in the mall to ban together and "reduce, if not totally eliminate, purchases from any manufacturer who was going to open a store in the new outlet mall." This manager was particularly concerned since he managed a regional chain that, unlike the national department store chains, got the majority of sales from the famous brand names that would be featured in the outlet mall. This manager emphasized in his request for the special meeting that even though he depended on national brands for over 80 percent of his sales, Robin still got 30 percent of her sales from national brands, and the other two anchors generated over 40 percent of their sales from national brands. Thus, the situation was important to all four managers.

Discussion Questions

1. Should Ms. Montoya attend this meeting? Why?

2. Should she contact her vendors? Why?

3. Do you believe that this outlet mall will impact her sales? Why?

Part 5

Integrated Marketing Communications

Chapter 12

Integrated Marketing Communications: Advertising, Promotions, and Other Tools

Terence A. Shimp,

Professor of Marketing and Distinguished Foundation Fellow, University of South Carolina

Professor Shimp earned his DBA from the University of Maryland, his MBA from the University of Kentucky, and his BA from West Liberty State College. He is the recipient of the best article award from the Association for Consumer Research and the Amoco outstanding teacher award from the University of South Carolina. Dr. Shimp serves on the editorial review boards for the *Journal of Consumer Research, Journal of Consumer Psychology, Journal of Marketing, Marketing Letters,* and the *Journal of Public Policy and Marketing.* He is past president of the Association for Consumer Research and president of the *Journal of Consumer Research* policy board.

After serving on the faculty at Kent State University for four years, Dr.

Gardenburger, Inc.—a small company located in Portland, Oregon with 1997 sales of approximately $57 million and sales during the first six months of 1998 of $38.8 million—makes vegetable patties and markets them to supermarkets, restaurants, and other outlets under the Gardenburger® brand name. In 1998 this company made a bold move to increase its brand equity vis-à-vis competitive brands of vegetable patties. The product category of vegetable patties is small but growing. Executives at Gardenburger believed that their brand could be substantially enhanced if more consumers knew about the brand. Toward this end, the decision was made to advertise Gardenburger patties in magazines and on television, including a placement on the concluding episode of *Seinfeld,* which was aired in May 1998. A single 30-second ad on the *Seinfeld*

finale cost in excess of $1.2 million and consumed approximately 10 percent of Gardenburger's annual advertising budget.

Was the investment worth it? According to company press releases, the *Seinfeld* placement along with ads aired on lesser-known television programs and in magazines, resulted in huge gains. Gardenburger's sales during the second quarter 1998 (April through June), when the major advertising effort took place, were over 90 percent higher—$25.7 million compared to sales of $13.5 million during the comparable period in 1997. Gardenburger's advertising was very successful in creating consumer brand awareness and encouraging trial purchase of the Gardenburger brand. The company's chief executive officer commented that "our capture of over 70 percent of the veggie patty category growth in the grocery channel indicates that consumers are buying the brand they saw on TV. Our advertising is also aiding our sales in all other channels." The huge gain in sales and market share was no doubt due in large part to the fact that Gardenburger's commercial placement during the final episode of *Seinfeld,* which reached an audience estimated at 106 million, was the second highest recalled and third most liked of the 28 commercials that ran on that program.[1]

Learning Objectives

After you have completed this chapter, you should be able to:

1. Appreciate the variety of marketing communications tools, and how they work together to accomplish communication objectives.

2. Understand the nature, importance, and features of integrated marketing communications.

3. Describe the concept of brand-equity enhancement and the role of marketing communications in facilitating this objective.

4. Comprehend the factors that determine how different marketing communications elements are effectively combined.

5. Discuss the five primary decision spheres involved in managing the marketing communications process.

6. Know the five major activities involved in formulating advertising strategy.

7. Recognize the role of sales promotion, appreciate the reasons why this form of marketing communications has experienced rapid growth, and know the tasks that it can and cannot accomplish.

8. Evaluate the nature and role of public relations.

9. Appreciate the role of sponsorship marketing and the practices of event marketing and cause-related marketing.

10. Understand the role, importance, and growth of point-of-purchase communications.

Shimp has been a faculty member at the University of South Carolina for 22 years as professor of marketing, program director of the marketing department, and the W.W. Johnson Distinguished Foundation Fellow.

Dr. Shimp's primary areas of research are the study of consumer learning, persuasion, and response to marketing and advertising communications. He has won nine teaching awards and is the author of *Advertising, Promotion, and Supplemental Aspects of Integrated Marketing Communications 5e,* from the Dryden Press.

Out of the thousands of brands on store shelves today, what is the chance that a consumer will *see* any one particular item, much less buy it? In today's society, consumers are rushed for time. They do not have the time to leisurely walk up and down every aisle, perusing all of the wares. A brand may be of high quality and fairly valued, but nonetheless it will fail to achieve sales and profit objectives if potential customers are unaware of it or do not perceive it favorably. Effective advertising and other forms of marketing communications are absolutely crucial to creating brand awareness, establishing positive brand identities, and moving products from distributors' warehouses and off store shelves. The Gardenburger success story in the opening vignette illustrates the power of advertising.

www.gardenburger.com

Marketing communications also are critical to the success of business-to-business marketers in their efforts to achieve market share and profit objectives. Many, if not most, business-to-business products share similarities from one supplier to the next. Product quality generally is not that different among competitors, and prices often are near equal. The real distinctions among business-to-business competitors frequently amount to created differences achieved through effective advertising and, more importantly, via superior service and personal selling attention.

Regardless of the nature of the product category or type of business, marketing communications are key to a company's overall marketing mission and represent a major determinant of its success; indeed, it has been claimed that marketing and marketing communications are inseparable: "[M]arketing . . . is communication and communication is marketing."[2]

This chapter first overviews the tools of marketing communications. A second major section discusses the nature of integrated marketing communications and the challenge of enhancing brand equity. Section three describes the objectives marketing communications accomplish and the factors that influence the choice of which marketing communications tools are most appropriate for a particular brand-marketing situation. Managing the marketing communications process is the focus of the fourth section. The sections thereafter are devoted, in turn, to the major marketing communications tools: advertising, sales promotion, public relations, sponsorship marketing, and point-of-purchase communications.

THE TOOLS OF MARKETING COMMUNICATIONS

This section provides an overview of each of the marketing communications elements. First, however, it will be useful to draw an analogy between getting the most out of the players on a basketball team and the challenge of mixing the marketing communications elements to achieve maximum success.

In brief (and simplistically), a basketball team includes 10–12 players, of whom five play as a unit at any time. The players differ in the roles expected of them and the strengths they offer. One player, the point guard, has primary responsibility for dribbling, controlling the tempo of the offense, and setting up plays. Another guard, the shooting guard, has a greater scoring responsibility. Yet, both guards also play defense as well as offense. The center, who typically is the tallest player on the team, has major responsibility for both "inside" scoring (i.e., close to the basket), rebounding, and defending against the opposing center. Two other players, the forwards, score from intermediate range and also have responsibility for rebounding and defending. The quality of a basketball team depends on all players working together and playing as a unit. Offense is important, but so is defense. Players who can score points quickly and in spurts are important, but so are those who are steady and dependable rather than erratic. A basketball team would not be a very good team it if consisted only of five Shaquille O'Neals, or five Michael Jordans, or five Larry Birds, or five of any single type of player. An outstanding team requires players representing contrasting dimensions—different height, weight, speed, quickness, shooting skill, rebounding savvy, shot-blocking ability, and so on.

So it is with the marketing communications mix and the various elements that comprise the mix. Personal selling, in a sense, is like a basketball team's point guard. It sets the tempo for all other marketing communications elements. Advertising is more flamboyant—the Michael Jordan of marketing communications. Public relations is a great adjunct to advertising, working together, assisting, and augmenting advertising to accomplish mutual goals. PR also is great when the need for defense is especially important—such as when a firm or one of its brands is surrounded with negative publicity. Sales promotion is like the player who scores a lot of points quickly; it can achieve sales results in a shorter period than can other marketing communications elements.

There is no need to strain the analogy further. The point should be clear: The marketing communications mix is like a team consisting of players who bring different abilities to the team, and perform different, but mutually reinforcing roles. Now we will briefly describe each tool and reserve detailed discussion for later sections.

www.perrier.com
www.dennysrestaurants.com

Personal Selling

Business-to-business marketers rely especially heavily on **personal selling.** In the consumer market, products such as insurance, automobiles, and real estate are sold mainly through personal selling efforts. Historically, personal selling involved face-to-face interactions between salesperson and prospect, but telephone sales and other forms of electronic communications are increasingly being used. Chapter 13 focuses exclusively on personal selling and sales management, so the present chapter will emphasize the other marketing communications elements.

Personal selling
is *person-to-person* communication in which a seller informs and educates prospective customers and attempts to influence their purchase choices.

Advertising

The purpose of **advertising** is to inform the customer about the advertiser's products and brand benefits and ultimately to influence brand choice. Advertising is paid for by an identified sponsor, the advertiser, but is considered to be *nonpersonal* because the sponsoring firm is simultaneously communicating with multiple receivers, perhaps millions, rather than talking with a specific person or small group. Advertising attempts to keep both the brand's name and image in the customer's mind over a long period of time.

Advertising
is *nonpersonal* communication that is paid for by an identified sponsor, and involves either *mass communication* via newspapers, magazines, radio, television, and other media (e.g., billboards, bus stop signage) or *direct-to-consumer communication* via direct mail.

Publicity

Publicity usually comes in the form of news items or editorial comments about a company's products. These items or comments receive free print space or broadcast time because media representatives consider the information pertinent and newsworthy for their reading or listening audiences. It is the job of a firm's public relations personnel to garner positive publicity for the company and its brands. These personnel also face the challenge of overcoming negative publicity when a company is faced with a product disaster (e.g., Perrier bottled water contaminated with benzene) or confronted with claims of unfavorable business practices (e.g., Denny's restaurants accused of racial discrimination).

Publicity
like advertising, is *nonpersonal* communication to a mass audience, but unlike advertising, publicity is not directly paid for by the company that enjoys the publicity.

Sales Promotion

Sales promotion is directed both at the trade (i.e., wholesalers and retailers) and at consumers. It is intended to create immediacy (a need to acquire the product right now), while advertising and publicity, by comparison, are designed more to favorably influence customer expectations and attitudes over the long-term. ***Trade-oriented sales promotions***

Sales promotion
consists of all marketing activities that attempt to stimulate quick buyer action, or, in other words, attempt to promote immediate sales of a product (thereby yielding the name *sales promotion*).

include the use of various types of allowances and merchandise assistance that activate wholesaler and retailer response. ***Consumer-oriented sales promotions*** include coupons, premiums, free samples, contests/sweepstakes, rebates, and other devices.

Sponsorship Marketing

Sponsorship marketing
is the practice of promoting the interests of a company and its brands by associating the company with a specific *event* (e.g., a golf tournament) or a charitable *cause* (e.g., the Leukemia Society).

In general, **sponsorship marketing** represents an opportunity for a company and its brands to directly target communications toward narrow, but highly desirable, audiences. The use of sponsorship marketing generally is not expected to substitute for more traditional forms of marketing communications such as advertising, but rather to complement these activities.

Point-of-Purchase Communications

Point-of-purchase communications
include all signage—displays, posters, signs, shelf cards, and a variety of other visual materials—that are designed to influence buying decisions at the point of sale.

Point-of-purchase communications are a final effort by the manufacturer to motivate consumers and encourage purchase of the manufacturer's brands. Research has shown that perhaps as many as three out of four buying decisions are made at the point of purchase.[3]

KEY PARTICIPANTS IN MARKETING COMMUNICATIONS

A general marketing manager—perhaps with the title, VP of Marketing—has overall responsibility for all aspects of a firm's marketing programs. However, most day-to-day, or tactical, marketing decisions occur at the product- or brand-management levels. A product manager for a business-to-business company, or a brand manager for a consumer-goods company, has profit-and-loss responsibility for the particular product or brand that she or he manages. The product or brand manager also is responsible for long-term (***strategic***) and short-term (***tactical***) decisions relating to the product or brand s(he) manages.

However, the various marketing communications decisions are not the sole responsibility of the product/brand manager. Instead, in most corporations there are managers of departments who are responsible for the planning and implementation of individual elements. Sales management, for example, is responsible for the personal selling function. (More on this in the following chapter.) Advertising managers have authority over the entire advertising function, much of which is "farmed out" to independent advertising agencies. These agencies create advertising copy, schedule media, and assess advertising effectiveness. Public relations managers provide news media with positive messages about the company and its activities. As with advertising, in many instances public relations are delegated to independent PR agencies. Likewise, sales promotion managers carry out various trade- and consumer-oriented promotions. Again, outside vendors that specialize in specific forms of promotions (e.g., premium offers, sweepstakes, and contests) oftentimes are contracted to perform these specialized services.

Regardless of the number of managers or independent agencies involved in the marketing communications process, product and brand managers must oversee the entire program and monitor its progress. One individual needs to have the "big picture" of the program at all times in order to ensure success of the program, as well as the brand itself. Advocates of integrated marketing communications, which is described in the following section, recommend that corporations reorganize by setting up an organizational unit headed by someone with a title such as Marketing Communications Director.[4] This MAR-COM "czar" would assure that all aspects of marketing communications are indeed integrated. Most companies have not gone to this extreme, but some outside vendors have integrated their services to form full-service marketing communication operations. Many agencies that historically just provided advertising services have expanded their operations to include direct-marketing services, public relations, and sales-promotion services.

Careers in Marketing

Lifelong Learning Is Important for Career Success

Tim Bennett graduated in 1992 with a BA in history from the University of North Carolina at Chapel Hill. His career plan at this point was to take some time off for traveling and then to pursue a Ph.D. in American History, leading to a career as a university professor. But as with many students, Tim had accumulated educational expenses and needed to pay some bills prior to commencing Ph.D. studies.

He took a job bartending at a restaurant in Durham, NC—the home of Duke University. The restaurant was in the throes of declining sales, and to reverse this trend a position was created for a manager of marketing and promotional efforts. Tim was hired into this position, and for the next three years he designed and implemented the restaurant's marketing programs. Though not formally trained in business, Tim realized that he really liked marketing and had a flair for it.

While the job offered a lot in terms of experience, the remuneration was woeful. Realizing that he either would have to seek alternative employment or pursue a graduate degree, Tim opted for the latter. But rather than entering a Ph.D. program in American History, as originally planned, he decided to enroll in the MBA program at the University of South Carolina in Columbia. While the undergraduate degree in History had provided Tim with well-honed reading and writing skills, he lacked the quantitative and analytical skills that a business manager requires. An MBA provided the opportunity for him to combine his liberal arts education and practical marketing experience with a total business management education.

In the second year of his MBA program, Tim joined an organization called the MBA Enterprise Corps. Through this organization he subsequently was offered a position in Moscow with a Russian company that was franchising American restaurant concepts. This seemed a perfect fit considering Tim's past restaurant experience and MBA preparation. Unfortunately, the economic turmoil that consumed Russia in 1998 cost him the job before he ever started. Two weeks before graduation, he was without a job or any job prospects.

It took four months of search, but he landed the type of job that justified the two-year investment in an MBA degree. As a person trained in marketing, Tim wisely targeted his job search, rather than engaging in a blind fishing expedition. In particular, he focused on companies in the field of food marketing. He sought a position that would allow him to work as a brand manager in the food industry—a field where Tim had accumulated a solid experiential base, and for which he had a passion, in view of his love for cooking. He began employment in September 1998 as an associate brand manager for Sara Lee Premium Deli Meats, working in Sara Lee Corporation's Bil Mar Foods Division.

It is an exciting time at Bil Mar because the focus is on building the Sara Lee name into a cross-category mega brand. The premise is that Sara Lee is a brand with very strong equity that has been underutilized. Tim's job is to help design and implement marketing programs for the deli category and to leverage Sara Lee's brand equity to that category. As most new managers, he has encountered difficulty in keeping the overall objective paramount while dealing with daily job pressures.

Although the MBA prepared Tim well for understanding the overall direction that has been established for the Sara Lee Premium Deli Meats brand, he realizes how little he really knew coming straight out of an MBA program. Perhaps this is the real value of an education. A business degree, whether at the undergraduate or graduate level, does not provide all the answers. What it accomplishes, however, is to provide the conceptual and analytical foundations that are necessary for lifelong learning. Like professionals in all fields, successful businesspeople must continually learn from their on- and off-the-job experiences. All life experiences must be considered for their potential application to one's job situation. Learning never ceases, it simply becomes less formal. Tim is well on his way to becoming a very successful marketing executive, because he is excited about the challenge of continuing to learn on the job.

Product and brand managers turn to these agencies and engage in "one-stop shopping," in much the same way that consumers do when shopping at department stores and other full-service retail outlets.

INTEGRATED MARKETING COMMUNICATIONS AND THE CHALLENGE OF ENHANCING BRAND EQUITY

Integrated marketing communications (IMC) is a system of management and integration of marketing communication elements—advertising, publicity, sales promotion, sponsorship marketing, and point-of-purchase communications—with the result that all elements adhere to the same message.

Companies in the past often treated the marketing communications elements as virtually separate activities, whereas current marketing philosophy holds that integration of all elements is absolutely imperative for success. One of the significant marketing trends of recent years is a move toward fully integrating all business practices that communicate something about a company's brands to present or prospective customers. This development is known as **integrated marketing communications (IMC).**

Key Aspects of Integrated Marketing Communications

Companies traditionally have resisted integration because managers of individual elements (advertising, sales promotions, etc.) have feared that change might lead to reduced budgets, authority, and power. The process becomes easier to understand and less intimidating when its premises receive closer inspection.

Start with the Customer

The IMC process requires careful study of customers' communication usage patterns and information needs, and only then does it determine the best way to communicate with customers. No effort is made to use the same advertising media or other communication tools to reach every target group. Instead, the target group's specialized media consumption patterns are studied, and communication decisions are made accordingly. Hence, for example, the back page of a comic magazine may represent the most effective and efficient medium for contacting a difficult-to-reach target group of teenage boys, whereas television advertising on Saturday morning often is unparalleled in effectiveness when attempting to reach preteens. The point is that the choice of communication media, or **contact points,** is dictated by the customer's needs and behavior, and not by the communicator's preferences or past successes. IMC involves an outside-in approach to decision making (i.e., from market to company) rather than imposing an inside-out solution on the market.

Achieve Synergy

Another key aspect of IMC is the need for *synergy.* All of the communication elements (advertising, sponsorships, etc.) must speak with a single voice; coordination is absolutely critical to achieving a strong and unified brand image.[5] The key theme, or selling point, in a brand's advertising campaign should be stressed by salespeople, focused on in sales promotions, featured on the brand's package, emphasized in sponsorships, and made prominent at the point of purchase. In short, all communication elements should convey the same, unified message. Consumers will be confused if disparate messages are delivered by different marketing communications elements.

Build Relationships

Another fundamental characteristic of IMC is the belief that successful marketing communication requires building a relationship between the brand and the customer. It can be argued, in fact, that relationship building is the key to modern marketing and that IMC is the key to relationship building.[6] A relationship is an enduring linkage between a brand and consumers; it entails repeat purchase and perhaps even loyalty. Companies have learned that it is more profitable to build and maintain relationships than it is to continuously search for new customers. This explains the growth in frequent-flyer programs used by airlines and the many "frequency" programs that other companies use to encourage customers to repeatedly purchase their products. For example, BP (British Petroleum) service stations provide customers with coffee cards. After five refills—each signified with stickers attached to the card—the customer receives the sixth refill for free.

www.bp.com

Key Changes Resulting From Integrated Marketing Communications

The adoption of an IMC mind-set necessitates some fundamental changes in the way marketing communications have traditionally been practiced. The following changes are particularly prominent:[7]

1. **Reduced Faith in Mass-Media Advertising.** Many marketing communicators now realize that communication methods other than mass-media advertising often better

serve the needs of their brands. Media advertising is not always the most effective or financially efficient medium for contacting customers and prospects.

2. **Increased Reliance on Highly Targeted Communication Methods.** Direct mail, specialty interest magazines, cable TV, sponsorship of events, and alternative media (such as videocassettes, CD-ROM, and messages via the Internet) are just some of the contact methods that enable pinpointed communications. The use of database marketing is a key aspect of this second feature. Today many business-to-business and consumer-oriented companies maintain large, up-to-date databases of present and prospective customers.

3. **Expanded Efforts to Assess Communications' Return on Investment.** A final key feature of IMC is its insistence on systematic efforts to determine whether marketing communications yield a reasonable return on investment. All managers, and marketing communicators are no exception, must be held financially responsible for their actions.[8]

Enhancing Brand Equity

A *brand* comes into existence when a product, retail outlet, or service receives its own name, term, sign, symbol, design, or any particular combination of these elements. Coca-Cola, Levi's, Lexus, Sony, Adidas, the New York Yankees, and *The Wall Street Journal* exemplify well-known and respected brand names. Gardenburger, which was introduced in the opening vignette, is a relatively unknown brand. All organizations and their products can be considered brands. Some brands, however, have greater equity than others. Looked at from the consumer's perspective, a brand possesses equity to the extent that consumers are familiar with the brand and have stored in memory favorable, strong, and unique brand associations.[9] That is, ***brand equity*** from the consumer's perspective consists of two forms of knowledge: ***brand awareness*** and ***brand image***. Figure 12.1 graphically portrays these two dimensions of brand knowledge, and subsequent discussion will fill in the details.[10]

Consider, for example, the Adidas brand of athletic shoes, which substantially increased its advertising budget in 1998 by a whopping 25 percent over the previous year's ad budget. Adidas' director of sales and marketing explained that the purpose of this increase was to (1) raise consumer awareness of the Adidas name and (2) pound home the message that Adidas is an authentic and high-performance athletic shoe.[11] You will note that he does not refer to brand equity per se, but this is precisely what he's talking about in reference to raising awareness and conveying a desired performance image for the Adidas brand.

Brand Awareness

Brand awareness is an issue of whether a brand name comes to mind when consumers think about a particular product category and the ease with which the name is evoked. It is the basic dimension of brand equity, in that from the vantage point of an individual consumer, a brand has no equity unless the consumer is at least aware of the brand. Thus, achieving brand awareness is the initial challenge for new brands, and maintaining high levels of brand awareness is the task faced continuously by all established brands. Marketing communications is instrumental in confronting both these challenges.

Brand Image

The second dimension of consumer-based brand knowledge is a brand's image. Brand image can be thought of in terms of the types of associations that come to the consumer's mind when contemplating a particular brand. A ***brand association*** is simply the particular thoughts or images that a consumer has about a brand. As shown in Figure 12.1, these associations can be conceptualized in terms of their (1) type (attributes, benefits, and overall attitude toward the brand), (2) favorability, (3) strength, and (4) uniqueness. The marketing

www.adidas.com

Figure 12.1   A Model of Brand Equity

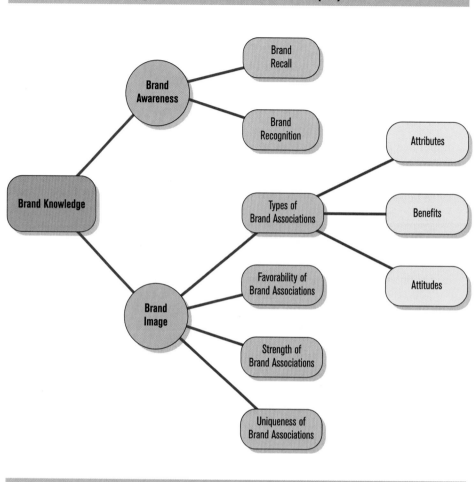

communications imperative is to effectively convey a brand's merits, such that consumers have mental associations about the brand that are favorable, strong, and perhaps unique (vis-à-vis competitive brands).

Efforts to enhance a brand's equity are initially accomplished through the careful choice of positive brand identity (that is, the selection of a good brand name or logo). But they must be reinforced by marketing and marketing communication programs that forge favorable, strong, and unique associations in the consumer's mind between a brand and its attributes/benefits. It is impossible to overstate the importance of efforts to enhance a brand's equity. Products that are high in quality and represent a good value potentially possess high brand equity. But effective and consistent marketing communication efforts are needed to build upon and maintain brand equity. A favorable brand image does not happen automatically. Sustained marketing communications are generally required. For example, it could be claimed that one of the world's greatest brands, Coca-Cola, is little more than colored sugar water. This brand nevertheless possesses immense brand equity because its managers are ever mindful of the need for continuous advertising executions that sustain the Coca-Cola story and build the image around the world. In the United States alone, the Coca-Cola Co. commanded approximately 44 percent of the nearly $55 billion carbonated soft-drink market in 1998.[12] Consumers don't buy this "colored sugar water" merely for its taste; they instead purchase a lifestyle and an image when selecting Coca-Cola over other available brands. It is effective advertising, exciting sales promotions, creative spon-

www.coke.com

Marketing Technologies

Integrated Marketing Communications, Brand Equity, and the Internet

The biggest brands on the Internet are those that built their equity on the Internet (e.g. AOL.com, Netscape.com, Yahoo.com). The traffic on these branded sites is currently many times greater than even the busiest consumer product sites (e.g. Kodak.com, Kraftfoods.com, Budweiser.com). Where Kodak.com, a leading consumer product Web site, averages less than 200,000 visitors per month, AOL.com averages over 19 million visitors! The reason is simple—content. Internet brands (AOL.com, etc.) offer services that are useful for "surfing" the Net itself and for satisfying consumers' informational, educational, and commercial needs. Simply put, Internet brands understand the marketing concept.

However, many of today's popular brands built their equity well before the rapid expansion of the Internet. The men and women who manage these brands spend many of their working hours, as well as off-hours, contemplating how to tap the potential of the Internet. Two questions are paramount: (1) What unique branding opportunities exist on the Internet? (2) What branding opportunities are better served by the Internet vis-à-vis other media options? Awaiting answers to these absorbing questions, most managers in the meantime are allocating a conservative portion of their budgets toward maintaining some sort of presence (e.g., banner ads and brand Web sites) on the Internet until something revolutionary happens. However, the sad reality is that only the truly motivated consumer is interested in voluntarily exposing him- or herself to a relatively boring and uninvolving banner ad or Web site.

One emerging answer to the Internet challenge is what Jupiter Communications, a top Net consultant, calls "rational branding." Rational branding involves marrying traditional brand marketing with concrete services only available online. The advertiser essentially rewards the consumer with some service as compensation for tolerating a brand message. This tactic is working well for brands that can offer time or money savings online. For example, MasterCard used to simply hype its credit cards online, but it now issues the "Shop Smart" seal of approval to E-commerce sites that use advanced credit-card security systems, thereby assuaging consumers' concerns about online credit-card theft. This service allows MasterCard to plaster its widely recognized logo all over a number of hot new Web sites. In the language of integrative marketing communications (IMC), each of these sites constitutes an additional contact point for MasterCard.

The challenge is greater for consumer packaged goods, though. The Internet's limited video and sound capabilities minimize the emotion-based brand marketing that typifies much packaged-goods advertising, especially on TV. Internet efforts have to be more clever and interactive to capture and hold consumers' attention. Consider the efforts of Ragu spaghetti sauce (www.ragu.com). Ragu offers online cookbooks, vacation guides, soap opera digests, sweepstakes, promotional giveaways, online stories written by consumers, licensed merchandise (e.g. videos), and additional content. These interactive "incentives" are in the best tradition of the IMC philosophy of building relationships between a brand and its consumers, and likely serve to enhance the equity of the Ragu brand for all consumers who visit this particular site. In reality, however, most consumers rarely if ever visit the Web sites of packaged goods.

Another answer to the Internet branding question is what Forrester Research, Inc. calls "experiential marketing." Experiential marketing allows consumers to enjoy virtual "free samples" or to make a virtual self-customized product. For example, Saturn (www.saturn.com) and Saab (www.saab.com) both offer interactive design shops where consumers can select colors, options, and performance packages while simultaneously viewing the results online. Saturn has supported its site with a humorous commercial featuring a college student using the Internet to order a Saturn from his dorm room, as easily as one might order a pizza from Domino's. Bristol-Myers Squibb Co.'s Clairol site allows consumers to scan in a personal photograph and experiment with different hair colors.

E-commerce will only accelerate its already phenomenal growth as more and more consumers come online and place faith in the security of online transactions. With increases in the numbers of consumers shopping online comes a more urgent need to understand the nature of Internet brand equity building and maintenance.

Questions

Using the discussion of brand equity in this chapter and Figure 12.1 as a guide, consider the following questions:

1. Select a favorite brand and discuss how it could implement "rational branding" to enhance or maintain its brand equity.

2. How might rational branding endanger brand equity?

3. Select a brand whose equity you think would be improved by "experiential marketing." Support your case with specific suggestions.

Source: Adapted from Ellen Neuborne and Robert D. Hof, "Branding on the Net," *Business Week,* November 9, 1998, 76–86.

sorships, and other forms of marketing communications that are responsible for Coca-Cola's positive image and massive market share.

Research has shown that when firms communicate unique and positive messages via advertising, personal selling, sales promotion, and other means, they are able to effectively differentiate their brands from competitive offerings and insulate themselves from future price competition.[13] Marketing communications play an essential role in creating positive brand equity and building strong brand loyalty.

Determining an Appropriate Mix of IMC Tools

LEARNING OBJECTIVE LO4

In determining an appropriate mix of marketing communications elements for a specific brand in a particular product category, a product or brand manager must weigh a variety of factors related to the category, the brand, and the market. The marketing manager typically has considerable discretion in determining which elements to use and how much relative emphasis each should receive. Should the entire budget go towards supporting the sales force, or should some be allocated to a network television advertising schedule? Will point-of-purchase materials be needed at retail? Will coupons or bonus packs help move more product? There is no right formula a manager can use to determine an optimum blend of elements. The manager must thoroughly analyze the product, the competition, the brand's strengths and weaknesses, and the target market to determine the brand's marketing communications needs and opportunities. The decision is guided by addressing each of the following issues:

▼ Who is the intended market?

▼ What are the objectives that the communicator hopes to accomplish?

▼ What is the nature of the product?

▼ What is the product life-cycle stage?

▼ What are competitors doing?

▼ What is the available budget for marketing communications?

▼ Will a push or pull strategy be more effective?

Who Is the Intended Market?

A marketer's approach will differ considerably depending on the character of the intended market. An earlier chapter established that in the business-to-business market the number of organizational buyers are fewer, decisions are often made in groups, and buyers are more geographically concentrated. The marketing budget would be more effectively used in personal selling to reach this target market. However, to reach buyers in the consumer market—where individual buyers number in the millions, where decisions are made by each consumer individually, and where consumers are widely dispersed throughout the country and perhaps, world—the marketing budget would be more effectively spent on advertising, sales promotion, and other communication devices. A clear understanding of the product's target market is vital in determining how best to allocate the promotional budget.

What Are the Objectives?

Figure 12.2 presents a framework, called the ***hierarchy of effects,*** that provides a useful way of thinking about the objectives that marketing communications is designed to accomplish. The hierarchy framework illustrates the idea that marketing communications progress the consumer from an initial stage of brand awareness, to interest in the brand, to desire, and finally, to action.

The different stages in the hierarchy are best understood by examining an actual communications situation. Consider again the magazine advertisement that was presented in the opening vignette (Gardenburger's Equity-Enhancing Effort). It will be helpful to peruse the advertisement before proceeding with your reading of the text. When Gardenburger veggie patties were introduced to the market, consumers were unaware of both the brand name and the particular set of advantages offered by this brand. Hence, the objective of Gardenburger's initial advertising efforts was to create ***consumer awareness*** of the Gardenburger brand name. However, creating awareness alone would not necessarily motivate consumers to choose this brand over alternative brands. Advertising had to persuade consumers that Gardenburger veggie patties taste like real meat, which for many consumers (especially those who really enjoy a hamburger) is a key consideration in trying Garden-

Figure 12.2   The Hierarchy of Effects

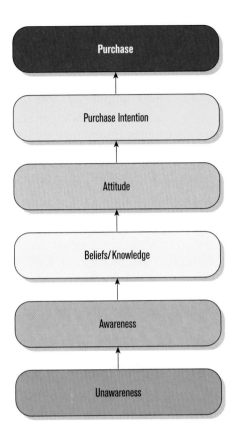

burger or any other brand in the vegetable burger category. The ad for Gardenburger at the opening of this chapter attempts to accomplish this by presenting a simple little story about Lucy the lion tamer wanting to eat a meaty burger, but not wanting lions to smell meat on her breath. This clever fictive device is designed to influence consumers' beliefs/knowledge that Gardenburger veggie patties actually taste like real meat, and to encourage the formation of positive attitudes and purchase intentions toward this brand. Gardenburger hopes that readers of the magazine ad will seriously consider purchasing the brand the next time they are in restaurants or supermarkets where vegetable patties are sold.

What Is the Nature of the Product?

The nature of the product itself will dictate the proper mixture of marketing communications elements. For example, an industrial machine that is marketed to a small segment of business-to-business customers will utilize different elements than will a brand of toothpaste, deodorant, snack food, or other convenience good. Although some advertising or sales promotions might be used by the industrial machine marketer, personal selling efforts must be emphasized to make sales. In this case, the marketer's budget may be divided as follows: personal selling—70 percent; trade-oriented media advertising—20 percent; and telemarketing and direct-mail advertising—10 percent.

In promoting consumer goods, especially convenience items, other forms of marketing communications take on added importance. In this case, the marketer's budget may be divided as follows: personal selling to the trade—20 percent; trade-oriented sales promotions—30 percent; advertising to consumers—25 percent; consumer-oriented sales promotions—20 percent; and point-of-purchase materials—5 percent. In these scenarios, no one element within the mix will be omitted completely from the budget. The focus on each element will change, though, depending on the product.

What Is the Product Life-Cycle Stage?

Is the brand well-established and in the maturity stage of the product life cycle, or is it a new product in the introduction stage? In the introduction stage, advertising is especially critical to create awareness and to inform consumers about the brand and its benefits. Trade-oriented sales promotions are essential for gaining wholesaler and retailer support, and consumer sales promotions (such as coupons and cents-off deals) are also important for purposes of creating consumer trial, especially when marketing consumer packaged goods. Later on as the product reaches the maturity stage, advertising and sales promotions both remain crucial, but both undergo qualitative changes. Advertising now is needed to maintain a positive brand image and differentiate the brand from competitive offerings, while sales promotions are used to encourage repeat purchase behavior.

What Are Competitors Doing?

Competitive action generally dictates what can or must be done. For example, in the deodorant category, if Soft 'n Dri offers a trade allowance that reduces the retail price to $1.99, and then offers a 75¢ coupon, consumers are able to buy this brand for only $1.24. Ban, Lady Speed Stick, and Secret cannot ignore this activity or they may see an erosion of their market shares, even if it's only on a temporary basis. These companies may be forced to take action to offset Soft 'n Dri's competitive push.

What Is the Available Budget?

The marketer's budget will determine what promotion mix can be emphasized. In the business-to-business market, a marketer may emphasize personal selling and forgo advertising if the total promotional budget is limited due to a poor performance the previous year or because the economic forecast for the coming year is unattractive. The sales force is a relatively fixed expense, whereas advertising can be increased or decreased depending on the situation and financial circumstances. In the consumer market, on the other hand, a nationally distributed brand is forced by the competition to devote some funds to advertising and sales promotions. The actual amount varies depending on the product category and the economic situation, but most brands invest anywhere from 2 to 10 percent of sales volume on advertising and an equal or greater amount to trade- and consumer-oriented sales promotions, collectively.

Will a Push or Pull Strategy Be More Effective?

The terms **push strategy** and **pull strategy** are metaphors that characterize the promotional activities marketers undertake to encourage channel members to handle products. Both the push and pull strategies utilize personal selling, advertising, sales promotion, and so on. Each strategy, though, requires a different emphasis on the individual marketing communications elements. Personal selling is much more important in the push strategy, whereas advertising is much more important in the pull strategy. It is important to recognize, however, that most manufacturers use a combination of push and pull techniques. These techniques complement one another rather than representing perfect substitutes.

Push strategy
involves aggressive trade allowances and personal selling efforts to obtain distribution for a new brand through wholesalers and retailers. The brand is "pushed" through the channel system in the sense that there is a *forward* thrust from the manufacturer to the trade.

Pull strategy
involves a relatively heavy emphasis on consumer-oriented advertising to encourage consumer demand for a new brand and thereby obtain retail distribution. The brand is "pulled" through the channel system in the sense that there is a *backward* tug from the consumer to the retailer.

MANAGING THE MARKETING COMMUNICATIONS PROCESS

As the previous sections illustrate, many factors must be considered in creating an effective mixture of marketing communications elements. Marketing communications—like any other business process—must be managed. The management of marketing communications involves five primary areas where strategies and tactics must be formulated: selecting target markets, establishing objectives, setting budgets, formulating and implementing message and media strategies, and evaluating program effectiveness.

Selecting Target Markets

Selection of target markets is the critical first step toward effective and efficient marketing communications. Targeting allows marketing communicators to pinpoint the product's potential audience and to more precisely deliver messages to this group. Targeting attempts to avoid wasting valuable promotional dollars on those consumers outside the target market. As discussed in Chapter 7, companies identify potential target markets in terms of a combination of characteristics—demographics, lifestyles, product usage patterns, geographical location—that will cause these consumers to act in a similar fashion. For example, the target market for Gardenburger veggie patties probably consists predominantly of younger women, say in the age range of 18–49, who are above-average in educational achievement, are health conscious, and who are disproportionately more likely to reside in urban centers.

Establishing Objectives

As discussed earlier in the chapter, it is important for marketing communicators to establish clear and achievable objectives as a prelude to designing messages and executing communication programs. Marketing communication objectives must fit within the company's overall corporate and marketing objectives. The objectives must also be realistic and stated in quantitative terms with the amount of projected change and the time duration specified. For example, the objective "to increase brand awareness" is too general to be of much value. A much better objective would be "to increase brand awareness by 20 percent within the next six months."

Setting the Budget

An organization's financial resources are budgeted to specific marketing communications elements in order to accomplish the sales and profit objectives established for its various brands. The amount of resources allocated to specific promotion elements is typically the result, in most sophisticated corporations, of an involved process. Companies use different budgeting processes in allocating funds to promotion managers. At one extreme is ***top-down budgeting (TD),*** in which senior management decides how much each subunit receives. At the other extreme is ***bottom-up budgeting (BU),*** in which managers of subunits (such as brand managers) determine how much is needed to achieve their objectives; these amounts are then combined to establish the total marketing budget.

Most budgeting practices involve a combination of top-down and bottom-up budgeting. For example, in the bottom-up/top-down process (BUTD), subunit managers submit budget requests to a chief marketing officer (say, a vice president of marketing), who coordinates the various requests and then submits an overall budget to top management for approval. The top-down/bottom-up process (TDBU) reverses the flow of influence by having top managers first establish the total size of the budget and then divide it among the various subunits. Research has shown that combination budgeting methods (BUTD and TDBU) are used more often than the extreme methods (TD or BU). The BUTD process is by far the most frequently used, especially in more sophisticated firms where marketing-department influence is high compared to finance-department influence.[14]

Formulating and Implementing Message and Media Strategies

Decisions must be made regarding the message to be communicated and the media within which the message will be sent. The message is a critical component of marketing communication effectiveness. Marketers must decide how best to present their ideas to achieve the established objectives. In creating a message, a marketer may choose from a variety of message alternatives including what image to create, how to position the brand, and what types of appeals to employ such as humor, nostalgia, and so on.

A variety of media strategies must also be considered by the marketer. *Media* typically connotes a mode of advertising such as via television, radio, or magazines. But the term *media* can be applied to any marketing communications element. Point-of-purchase materials, for example, can be a simple cardboard shelf talker, a take-one pad, or a sophisticated display. A sales promotion can range from a simple coupon distributed via freestanding insert to a more involved sweepstakes offer. Each of these alternatives is a different medium that has a unique rate of effectiveness as well as cost. The marketer must determine which message and media will be most effective—from both a communications as well as cost standpoint—in delivering the desired message.

Evaluating Program Effectiveness

Once a marketing communications program is in place and being implemented, the program must be evaluated for its effectiveness. Only through evaluation can one learn what works, what does not work, and why. This information will be critical in creating future programs and taking corrective action when necessary.

A program is evaluated by measuring the results of the program against the objectives established in the planning stage. For some elements it is relatively simple to assess effectiveness, because the results generated are easily attributable to just that element. Consider a direct-mail campaign where the measure of effectiveness is the *actual response rate,* or the number of orders received as a percentage of the number of mailings, say, a 2 percent response rate. Effectiveness is evaluated by comparing the actual response rate with the objective established in the form of a *projected response rate.* For a premium offer, the total number of consumers sending in proofs-of-purchase can be compared against the number of submissions contained in the original objective. In either event, corrective action is called for if the actual response rate falls significantly below that which was projected.

Other promotional elements such as advertising are more difficult to evaluate inasmuch as objective outcomes—such as the amount of sales generated in a period—are not directly or exclusively attributable to the ads per se. In other words, sales are the result of all marketing mix variables, not just advertising. Moreover, current sales are due to past marketing efforts, and are not solely attributable to current advertising; that is, the advertising and sales relation is typically *lagged,* with advertising in the current period influencing sales at later times, as well as in the current period. Due to these complications, advertisers typically assess advertising effectiveness in terms of so-called *communication outcomes* such as changes in consumers' awareness of the advertised brand, knowledge of copy points, or attitudes toward the brand. All of these factors, if measured and known before an advertising campaign begins, can be measured again at the end of the campaign and compared to objectives to determine effectiveness.

Now that we have introduced the nature and management of marketing communications, subsequent sections—starting with advertising and ending with point-of-purchase communications—will examine each marketing communications element in some detail.

ADVERTISING

There are three basic ways by which companies can add value to their offerings: by innovating, by improving quality, or by altering consumer perceptions. These three value-added components are completely interdependent:

> Innovation without quality is mere novelty. Consumer perception without quality and/or innovation is mere puffery. And, both innovation and quality, if

not translated into consumer perceptions, are like the sound of the proverbial tree falling in the empty forest.[15]

Advertising adds value to brands by influencing consumers' perceptions. Effective advertising causes brands to be viewed as more elegant, more stylish, more prestigious, perhaps superior to competitive offerings, and, in general, of higher perceived quality and/or value. When advertising is done effectively, brands are perceived as higher quality or of better value, which in turn can lead to increased market share and greater profitability. It is little wonder that Procter & Gamble, perhaps the leading consumer-goods firm in the world, fully appreciates advertising's value-adding role. Indeed, a P&G vice president of worldwide advertising has characterized strong advertising as "a deposit in the brand equity bank."[16]

Advertising also can be considered an economic investment, an investment regarded very favorably by numerous businesses throughout the United States and the world. In recognition of advertising's invaluable role, companies in the U.S. invested approximately $200 billion on advertising in 1998.[17] This amounts to over $700 in advertising for each of the nearly 270 million men, women, and children in the United States as of 1998. Advertising spending is also considerable in other major industrialized countries, but not nearly to the same magnitude as in the U.S. The biggest advertising spenders following the United States are Japan, Germany, the United Kingdom, France, and Canada. However, advertising expenditures in these countries are small compared to those in the United States, amounting in all countries except Japan to less than 12 percent of the amount spent on advertising in the United States. Even advertisers in Japan spend less than half as much per capita as do U.S. advertisers.[18]

Some American companies invest over $1 billion a year on domestic advertising. In a recent year, for example, Procter & Gamble spent $2.6 billion; General Motors, $2.4 billion; Philip Morris, $2.3 billion; Time Warner, $1.4 billion; and Sears, Roebuck & Co., $1.3 billion.[19] Even the U.S. government advertises to the tune of over $670 million.[20] The government's advertising goes to efforts such as military recruiting, the Postal Service, Amtrak rail services, the U.S. Mint (e.g., commemorative coins), and AIDS awareness.

Formulating Advertising Strategy

Advertising strategy entails five major activities: objective setting, budgeting, planning message strategy, developing media strategy, and assessing advertising effectiveness. The first two, *objective setting* and *budgeting,* were described earlier in context of the overall marketing communications process and are discussed only briefly in the present advertising context. Suffice it to say that the objective-setting and budgeting processes are fundamentally the same regardless of which marketing communications element is involved.

Setting Advertising Objectives
Advertising objectives provide the foundation for all remaining advertising decisions. There are three major reasons for setting advertising objectives:

1. The process of setting objectives literally forces top marketing and advertising management to agree upon the course advertising is to take for the following planning period, as well as the tasks it is to accomplish for a brand.

2. Objective setting guides the budgeting, message creation, and media selection aspects of advertising strategy.

3. Advertising objectives provide standards against which results can be measured.[21]

Advertising may be designed to accomplish goals such as the following: (1) to make the target market aware of a new brand, (2) to facilitate consumer understanding of a brand's

www.pg.com

www.gm.com
www.philipmorris.com
www.pathfinder.com/corp
www.sears.com
www.usps.gov

LEARNING
OBJECTIVE
LO6

attributes, (3) to create expectations about a brand's benefits, (4) to enhance attitudes toward the brand, (5) to influence purchase intentions, and (6) to encourage product trial.

Budgeting for Advertising

The advertising budgeting decision is, in many respects, the most important decision advertisers make. If too little money is spent on advertising, sales volume will not be as high as it could be, and profits will be lost. If too much money is spent, expenses will be higher than they need to be, and profits will be reduced.

Budgeting is also one of the most difficult advertising decisions. This difficulty arises because it is hard to determine precisely how effective advertising has been or might be in the future. The sales response to advertising is influenced by a multitude of factors (quality of advertising execution, intensity of competitive advertising efforts, customer taste, and other considerations), thereby making it difficult if not impossible to know with any certainty what amount of sales a particular advertising effort will generate.

Companies ordinarily set budgets by using judgment, applying experience with analogous situations, and using simple rules-of-thumb, or *heuristics*.[22] Although criticized because they do not provide a basis for advertising budget setting that is directly related to the profitability of the advertised brand, these heuristics continue to be widely used.[23] The two most pervasive heuristics, in use by both industrial and consumer-goods advertisers, are the percentage-of-sales and objective-and-task methods.[24] The ***percentage-of-sales method*** involves allocating a fixed percentage of past or anticipated sales revenue to advertising. For example, a company may allocate 5 percent of the next fiscal period's anticipated sales to advertising. If sales are estimated to be $100 million for the upcoming year, the promotional budget will be $5 million. The ***objective-and-task method*** involves the following three-step procedure: (1) specifying the objectives that a particular advertisement or entire ad campaign is intended to accomplish; (2) identifying the specific tasks that must be accomplished in order to reach those objectives; and (3) accumulating anticipated costs to achieve the specified tasks. The outcome of this systematic, three-step process is an advertising budget that should be sufficient to achieve critical objectives.

Creating Advertising Messages

Advertisers use a vast array of techniques to present their brands in the most favorable light and persuade customers to contemplate purchasing these brands. Frequently employed techniques include:

▼ Informational ads (such as automobile ads in the classified pages of a newspaper).

▼ Humorous executions (e.g., Little Caesar pizza ads).

▼ Sex appeals (e.g., Calvin Klein ads, see Figure 12.3).

▼ Celebrity endorsements (e.g., using ex-athletes such as Michael Jordan and entertainers like Bill Cosby).

▼ Various emotional appeals (nostalgia, romance, excitement, etc.).

www.littlecaesars.com

The techniques to persuasively advertise products are limited only by advertisers' creativity and ingenuity. It is beyond the scope of this text to go into detail concerning these and other advertising techniques. Rather, we pose a more straightforward question: What makes an advertisement good or effective? Although it is impractical to provide a singular, all-purpose definition of what constitutes effective advertising, it is meaningful to talk about general characteristics.[25] At a minimum, good or effective advertising satisfies the following considerations:

1. **It extends from sound marketing strategy.** Advertising can be effective only if it is compatible with other elements of an integrated and well-orchestrated marketing communications strategy.

Figure 12.3   An Illustration of Sex Appeal in Advertising

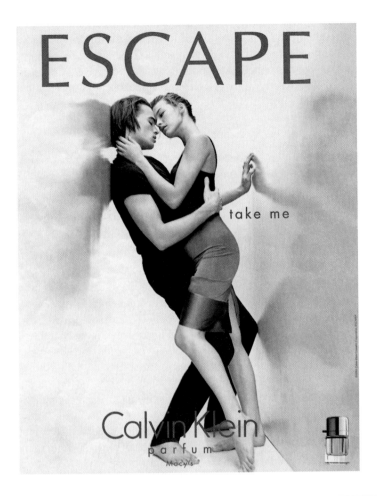

2. **It takes the consumer's view.** Consumers buy product benefits, not attributes. Therefore, advertising must be stated in a way that relates to the consumer's needs, wants, and values and not strictly in terms of the marketer's needs and wants.

3. **It is persuasive.** Persuasion usually occurs when there is a benefit for the consumer, and not just for the marketer.

4. **It finds a unique way to break through competitive clutter.** Advertisers continuously compete with competitors for the consumer's attention. This is no small task considering the massive number of print advertisements, broadcast commercials, and other sources of information available daily to consumers. Indeed, the situation in television advertising has been characterized as "audio-visual wallpaper," which implies sarcastically that consumers pay just about as much attention to commercials as they do to the detail in their own wallpaper after it has been on the walls for awhile.[26]

5. **It never promises more than it can deliver.** This point speaks for itself, both in terms of ethics and in terms of smart business sense. Consumers learn quickly when they have been deceived and resent it.

6. **It prevents the creative idea from overwhelming the strategy.** The purpose of advertising is to persuade and influence; the purpose is not to be cute for cute's sake

or humorous for humor's sake. The ineffective use of humor, for example, results in people remembering the humor but forgetting the selling message.

Effective advertising is usually *creative*. That is, it differentiates itself from the mass of mediocre advertisements; it is somehow different and out-of-the-ordinary. Advertising that is the same as most other advertising is unable to break through the competitive clutter and fails to grab the consumer's attention. It is easier to give examples of creative advertising than to define exactly what it is. Here are three examples of what many advertising practitioners would consider effective, creative advertising:

▼ The long-standing pink bunny campaign for Energizer batteries.

▼ Absolut vodka's continuing magazine campaign that focuses on this brand's "hip" image by portraying the brand's unique bottle shape in trendy situations. (For examples, see the collage in Figure 12.4.)

▼ The milk-mustache campaign that associates drinking milk with a wide variety of interesting and respected celebrities. (For examples, see the collage in Figure 12.5.)

www.energizer.com
www.gotmilk.com

Media strategy

consists of four sets of interrelated activities: (1) selecting the target audience, (2) specifying media objectives, (3) selecting media categories and vehicles, and (4) buying media.

Selecting Advertising Media

Outstanding message execution is to no avail unless the messages are delivered to the right customers at the right time, and with sufficient frequency. In other words, advertising messages stand a chance of being effective only if the **media strategy** itself is effective. Good messages and good media go hand in hand; they are inseparable—a true marriage. Improper media selection can doom an otherwise promising advertising campaign.

Creative advertisements are more effective when placed in media whose characteristics enhance the value of the advertising message and reach the advertiser's targeted customers at the right time. A variety of decisions must be made when choosing media. In addition to determining which media to use (television, radio, magazines, etc.), the media planner must also pick *vehicles* within each medium (e.g., specific magazines or TV programs), and decide how to allocate the available budget among the various media and vehicle alternatives. Additional decisions involve determining when to advertise, choosing specific geographical locations, and deciding how to distribute the budget over time and across geographic locations.

Successful media strategy requires, first, that the ***target audience*** be clearly pinpointed. Failure to precisely define the audience results in wasted exposures; that is, some non-purchase candidates are exposed to advertisements while some prime candidates are missed. Target audiences are usually selected based on geographic factors (e.g., ads are aimed at people residing in urban centers), demographic considerations (e.g., ads are directed to women aged 18–49), product-usage concerns (e.g., ads are focused on heavy product users), and lifestyle/psychographic characteristics (e.g., ads are directed to people with active, outdoor lifestyles).

A second aspect of media strategy is establishing specific *objectives*. Four objectives are fundamental to media planning: reach, frequency, continuity, and cost. Media planners seek answers to the following types of questions:

1. What portion of the target audience do we want to see (or read, or hear) the advertising message? (a ***reach*** issue)

2. How often should the target audience be exposed to the advertisement? (a ***frequency*** issue)

3. When are the best times to reach the target audience? (a ***continuity*** issue)

4. What is the least expensive way to accomplish the other objectives? (a ***cost*** issue)

Advertisers work with statistics such as ratings, gross rating points (GRPs), and cost per thousand, to compare different vehicles within the same medium and to make intelligent

Figure 12.4   Absolut-ly Hip

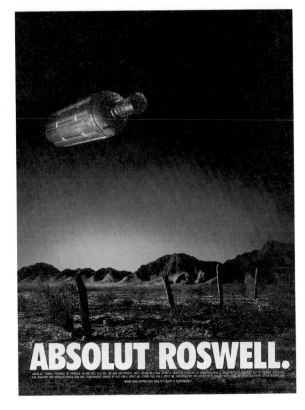

Figure 12.5   Milk Gains Appeal by Appealing to Celebrities

selections. For example, an advertiser might consider advertising its brand on *Friends,* a TV program that appeals to a wide audience and produces a *rating* of about 18 points at a cost of approximately $300,000 per 30-second commercial. The 18-rating means that of the approximately 98 million households in the United States, on average, 18%, or 17.6 million, are tuned in to this program. Theoretically, then, the advertiser would reach 17.6 million households every time it places a commercial on the *Friends* program. If, say, during a four-week period the advertiser placed a total of 8 commercials on *Friends* (i.e., 2 ads each episode), it would accumulate a total of 144 **gross rating points (GRPs).**

Cost per thousand (CPM) (where the *M* is the Roman numeral for 1,000) is a useful statistic for comparing the cost efficiency of vehicles in the same medium. For example, in 1998 a single 4-color full-page advertisement placed in *Sports Illustrated* cost the advertiser about $170,000 and reached approximately 25.6 million readers of this magazine. Therefore, the CPM = cost of ad placement ($170,000) / size of audience expressed in thousands (25,600) = $6.64.

The advertiser would compare this value with the CPM to advertise in alternative vehicles. For example, in 1998 a full-page 4-color ad placed in *Sport* magazine cost approximately $37,000 and reached approximately 5 million readers. Its CPM is $7.40 (i.e., $37,000 / 5,000). *Sports Illustrated* is a less expensive vehicle on a per-thousand basis than *Sport.* However, the choice of which magazine to select is based on considerations other than mere cost comparisons. Also crucial in the decision are considerations such as how closely a vehicle's readers/viewers match the brand's target audience and the fit between the image of the vehicle and the brand's desired image.

Advertisers have four major mass media from which to choose: television, radio, magazines, and newspapers. Each medium possesses various strengths and weaknesses. Some of the most prominent of these are summarized in Figure 12.6.

One additional advertising medium deserving brief mention is the Internet, or what is variously called the *information superhighway, cyberspace,* or the *World Wide Web.* Many advertisers are turning to the Internet as a supplemental and experimental advertising medium. Literally thousands of companies have created home pages containing information about their products. Zima (a unique beer from Coors brewing) was the first consumer brand to open a home page. Since then thousands of brands have developed their own home pages as millions of new users have gone on-line.

Internet advertising offers exciting prospects for advertisers. First, and most important, the Internet is an *interactive medium* where consumers seek out information and devote their time to a particular home page only if it offers informational, educational, or recreational value. In a sense, the Internet is the modern version of the *Yellow Pages—* "Let your mouse do the walking" so to speak. Both media are successful only to the extent that they are easy to access and provide useful and/or interesting information. Creative advertisements on the Net are potentially capable of drawing and holding consumers' attention and serving to build relations between consumers and advertised brands. Second, Internet advertising provides advertisers with a medium to reach audiences (predominantly relatively well-educated and young people) who are difficult to access via other media. Third, it is estimated that in a few years the Internet will offer video quality as good as TV and voice quality as good as telephone. This prospect will greatly expand the advertising value of this medium. Finally, the cost of advertising on the Net is extremely low compared to established media. On the downside, there are not as yet (as of 1998) any syndicated services that are comparable in stature to Nielsen (of TV ratings fame) that measure the effectiveness of advertising on the Internet. Needless to say, various companies are currently developing methods for this purpose.

Assessing Advertising Effectiveness

Assessing advertising effectiveness is a final critical aspect of advertising strategy, inasmuch as only by evaluating results is it possible to determine whether objectives are being accomplished. This often requires that baseline measures be taken before an advertising campaign begins (to determine, for example, what percentage of the target audience is

Gross rating points (GRPs) are the accumulation of rating points including all vehicles in a media purchase over the span of a particular campaign.

Cost per thousand (CPM) is calculated by dividing the cost of an ad placed in a particular ad vehicle (e.g., certain magazine) by the number of people (expressed in thousands) who are exposed to that vehicle.

Figure 12.6	Comparative Strengths and Weaknesses of Major Advertising Media

Medium	Strengths	Weaknesses
Television	▼ Dramatic presentation and demonstration ability ▼ High reach potential ▼ Attain rapid awareness ▼ Relatively efficient ▼ Intrusive and impactual ▼ Ability to integrate messages with other media such as radio	▼ Relatively downscale audience profile ▼ Network audience erosion ▼ Growing commercial clutter ▼ High out-of-pocket cost ▼ High production costs ▼ Long lead-time to purchase network time ▼ Volatile cost structure
Radio	▼ Target selectivity ▼ High frequency ▼ Efficient ▼ Able to transfer image from TV ▼ Portable, personal medium ▼ Low production cost ▼ Use of local personalities ▼ Ability to integrate messages with other media such as TV	▼ Commercial clutter ▼ Some station formats relatively uninvolving for listeners ▼ Relatively small audiences ▼ High out-of-pocket cost to attain significant reach ▼ Audience fractionalization
Magazines	▼ Efficient reach of selective audiences ▼ Ability to match advertising with compatible editorial content ▼ High quality graphics ▼ Reach light TV viewers ▼ Opportunity to repeat ad exposure ▼ Flexibility in target market coverage ▼ Can deliver complex copy ▼ Readership is not seasonal	▼ Not intrusive; reader controls ad exposure ▼ Slow audience accumulation ▼ Significant slippage from reader audience to ad-exposure audience ▼ Clutter can be high ▼ Long lead times to purchase magazine space ▼ Somewhat limited geographic options ▼ Uneven market-by-market circulation patterns
Newspapers	▼ Rapid audience accumulation ▼ Timeliness ▼ High single day reach attainable ▼ Short lead times to purchase newspaper space ▼ Excellent geographic flexibility ▼ Can convey detailed copy ▼ Strong retail trade support ▼ Good for merchandising and promotion ▼ Low production cost ▼ Excellent local market penetration	▼ Limited target selectivity ▼ High out-of-pocket costs for national buys ▼ Significant differential between national and local rates ▼ Not intrusive ▼ Cluttered ad environment ▼ Generally mediocre reproduction quality

aware of the brand name), and then afterwards to determine whether the objective was achieved. Because, as was noted at the beginning of this chapter, billions of dollars are invested on advertising, advertisers go to great lengths to measure the effectiveness of their advertisements. There literally is an entire industry of companies that are in business to measure advertising effectiveness. Companies have developed services to measure magazine readership—Simmons Market Research Bureau (SMRB) and Mediamark Research, Inc. (MRI). Other companies measure television audience size, most notably Nielsen and Arbitron. Then there are services to assess consumer recognition and recall of magazine ads (Starch Readership Service) and of television commercials (Burke Day-After Recall), and measures of the persuasive and emotional impact of TV commercials.

Perhaps the most notable development in advertising-effectiveness measurement is the advent of so-called **single-source systems.** Single-source systems have become possible with the advent of two electronic-monitoring tools: television meters and optical laser scanning of universal product codes (UPC symbols). Single-source systems gather retail purchase data from panels of households using optical scanning equipment and merge it

Single-source systems
are a measurement of the effectiveness of advertising (whether it leads to increased sales activity). They are unique in that all the relevant data is collected by a single source, processed, and then made available in a readily usable format to retailers and manufacturers.

with household demographic characteristics. Most importantly, it is then combined with information about other marketing variables that influence household purchases (e.g., television commercials, coupons, in-store displays, trade promotions, etc.).

Information Resource Inc. (IRI) pioneered single source data collection in 1979 with its **BehaviorScan** system. BehaviorScan operates panel households in select markets around the United States with approximately 2,500 panel members in each market. Ten thousand BehaviorScan households are installed with electronic television meters.[27] Panel members provide IRI with information about the size of their families, their income, number of televisions owned, the types of newspapers and magazines they read, and who in the household does most of the shopping.[28] IRI then combines all of these data into a single source, and thereby determines which households purchase what products/brands and how responsive they are to advertising and other purchase-causing variables.

Direct Advertising

In contrast to mass-media advertising, which is aimed at thousands or even millions of prospective customers, direct advertising typically is targeted to a single business or individual consumer. The growth of direct advertising and its growing sophistication has been due in large part to the advent of **database marketing.** Typical databases include purchase data and other types of relevant customer information, such as demographic details and geographic information. The information is used to profile customers and to develop effective and efficient marketing programs by communicating with individual customers and by establishing long-term communication relationships.[29]

Major advances in computer technology and database management have made it possible for companies to maintain huge databases containing millions of prospects/customers. **Niche marketing** can be fully realized by targeting promotional efforts to a company's best prospects (based on past product-category purchasing behavior), and who can be identified in terms of specific geographic, demographic, and psychographic characteristics. Growing numbers of marketers are making heavy investments in database marketing.[30] For example, in an interesting use of its database, Saab mailed all past owners an invitation to a sneak preview of its totally redesigned Saab 900. Thousands of people attended this unique promotion in twenty-one cities throughout the United States. Saab also uses its database to maintain relations with its customers by publishing a magazine called *Saab Soundings.*[31]

Database marketing offers companies four distinct "abilities":[32]

▼ **Addressability**—being able to identify every customer and reach each one on an individual basis. This could also be referred to as targetability.

▼ **Measurability**—knowing whether or not each customer purchased; exactly what he or she purchased; and how, where, and when he or she purchased along with his or her purchase history.

▼ **Flexibility**—having the opportunity to appeal to different customers in different ways at different times.

▼ **Accountability**—having precise figures on the gross profitability of any marketing event, and qualitative data showing the type of customers who participated in each particular event.

All types of marketers use direct mail as a strategically important advertising medium. *Business Week* magazine claims, albeit with some hyperbole, that marketers of all types of consumer goods "are turning from the TV box to the mailbox."[33] Some automobile manufacturers, for example, are budgeting as much as 10 percent of their advertising expenditures to direct mail.

Database marketing
involves collecting and electronically storing (in a database) information about present, past, and prospective customers.

www.saab.com

At least four factors account for this increasing use of direct mail by all types of marketers. First, the rising expense of television advertising, along with increased audience fragmentation, has led many advertisers to reduce investments in television advertising. Second, direct mail enables unparalleled targeting of messages to desired prospects—according to one expert, it is "a lot better to talk to 20,000 prospects than 2 million suspects."[34] Third, there is increased emphasis on measurable advertising results, and direct mail is the advertising medium that best lends itself to a clear identification of how many prospects have purchased the advertised product. Finally, targeted customers are responsive—surveys indicate that Americans like mail advertisements.

SALES PROMOTION

Incentives
are bonuses or rewards (sweepstakes, coupons, premiums, display allowances, etc.) for purchasing one brand rather than another.

Sales promotion can be defined as the use of any incentive by a manufacturer to induce the trade (wholesalers and retailers), and/or consumers, to buy a brand and to encourage the sales force to aggressively sell it. The incentive is *in addition to the basic benefits* provided by the brand and *temporarily changes its perceived price or value.*[35] The italicized features require comment. First, by definition, sales promotions involve **incentives,** that are additions to, not substitutes for, the basic benefits a purchaser typically acquires when buying a particular good or service. For example, getting 50 cents off the price of a new brand of shampoo would be little consolation if the shampoo failed to work properly. Second, the target of the incentive is the trade, final consumers, the sales force, or all three parties. Finally, the incentive changes a brand's perceived price/value, but only temporarily. This is to say that a sales-promotion incentive for a particular brand applies to a single purchase or perhaps several purchases during a period, but not to every purchase a consumer would make over an extended period.

The Shift from Advertising to Sales Promotion

Historically, at least through the mid-1970s, the promotional emphasis in many consumer-goods firms was on creating promotional pull. Manufacturers advertised heavily, especially on network television, and literally forced retailers to handle their products by virtue of the fact that consumers demanded heavily advertised brands. However, over the past two decades, pull-oriented marketing has become less effective. Along with this reduced effectiveness has come an increase in the use of push-oriented sales promotion practices.[36]

The result of these developments is that advertising expenditures in mass media (television, radio, magazines, etc.)—have declined in most firms as a percentage of their total promotional expenditures. On the other hand, expenditures on sales promotions, direct marketing, sponsorships, and point-of-purchase items have steadily increased. In fact, annual studies have shown that media advertising expenditures as a proportion of companies' total marketing communications spending have declined steadily for over a decade. Whereas media advertising averaged over 40 percent of companies' promotional budgets in the 1970s, by the early 1990s media advertising's portion of the total budget had fallen to just over 25 percent. Comparatively, consumer promotions (coupons, bonus packs, premiums, etc.) represented approximately 28 percent of the total promotional budget, and trade promotions constituted the remaining 47 percent.[37] These statistics make it clear that the biggest shift in promotional expenditures has been away from media advertising, toward expenditures to support the trade. The major form of trade promotions are deals, or discounts (called ***trade allowances***), that encourage wholesalers and retailers to purchase larger quantities of promoted brands during the period when the manufacturer places them on promotion.

Increased investment in sales promotions, especially trade-oriented promotions, has gone hand-in-hand with the trend toward greater push-oriented marketing. A variety of factors listed below account for the shift in the allocation of promotion budgets away

> **Figure 12.7   Factors Giving Rise to the Growth of Sales Promotions**
>
> **1.** Balance of power transfer.
> **2.** Increased brand parity and price sensitivity.
> **3.** Reduced brand loyalty.
> **4.** Splintering of the mass market and reduced media effectiveness.
> **5.** Short-term orientation and corporate reward structures.
> **6.** Trade and consumer responsiveness.

from advertising toward sales promotion and other forms of marketing communications. These are summarized in Figure 12.7.

1. **Balance of Power Transfer.** Until recently, national manufacturers of consumer goods generally were more powerful and influential than the supermarkets, drug stores, and mass merchandisers that carried the manufacturers' brands. However, the balance of power began shifting when network television dipped in effectiveness as an advertising medium and, especially, with the advent of optical scanning equipment, which allowed retailers to attain as much "informational market power" as previously had been possessed only by manufacturers. The consequence for manufacturers is that for every promotional dollar used to support retailers' advertising or merchandising programs, one less dollar is available for the manufacturer's own advertising.

2. **Increased Brand Parity and Price Sensitivity.** In earlier years when truly new products were being offered to the marketplace, manufacturers could effectively advertise unique advantages over competitive offerings. As product categories have matured, however, most new offerings represent slight changes from existing products, resulting in more similarities between competitive brands than differences. With fewer distinct product differences, consumers have grown more reliant on price and price incentives (coupons, cents-off deals, refunds, etc.) as a way of differentiating alternative parity brands. Because real, concrete advantages are often difficult to obtain, firms have turned increasingly to sales promotion as a means of achieving at least temporary advantages over competitors.

3. **Reduced Brand Loyalty.** Consumers have become less brand loyal than they once were. This is partly due to the fact that brands have grown increasingly similar, thereby making it easier for consumers to switch among brands. Also, marketers have effectively trained consumers to expect that at least one brand in a product category will always be on deal with a coupon, cents-off offer, or refund; hence, many consumers rarely purchase brands other than those on deal. The upshot of all of this dealing activity is that marketers' extensive use of sales promotions has reduced brand loyalty and increased switching behavior, thereby requiring evermore dealing activity to feed consumers' insatiable desire for deals.

4. **Splintering of the Mass Market and Reduced Media Effectiveness.** Advertising efficiency is directly related to the degree of homogeneity in consumers' consumption needs and media habits. The more homogeneous are these needs and habits, the less costly it is for mass advertising to reach target audiences. However, as consumer lifestyles have become more diverse and advertising media have become more narrow in their appeal, mass-media advertising is no longer as efficient as it once was. On top of this, advertising effectiveness has declined with simultaneous increases in ad clutter and escalating media costs. These combined forces have influenced many brand managers to devote proportionately larger budgets to sales promotions.

5. **Short-Term Orientation and Corporate Reward Structures.** The brand-management system and sales promotion are perfect partners. The reward structure in firms organized along brand-manager lines emphasizes short-term sales response rather than slow, long-term growth, and sales promotion is incomparable when it comes to generating quick sales response. In fact, for many brands of packaged goods, the majority of their sales are associated with some kind of promotional deal.[38]

6. **Trade and Consumer Responsiveness.** A final force that explains the shift toward sales promotion at the expense of advertising is that retailers/wholesalers (the trade) and consumers respond favorably to money-saving opportunities. Businesspeople and people in everyday life like deals, and this is what sales promotion is all about— "Buy my brand and save $x."

Sales Promotion: Roles and Objectives

Sales promotion is well suited for accomplishing the following ten tasks, which are summarized in Figure 12.8.[39]

1. **Facilitating the Introduction of New Products to the Trade.** Sales promotions to wholesalers and retailers are often necessary to encourage the trade to handle new products. In fact, many retailers refuse to carry new products unless they receive extra compensation in the form of trade allowances, display allowances, and other forms of allowances.

2. **Obtaining Trial Purchases from Consumers.** Marketers depend on free samples, coupons, and other sales promotions to encourage trial purchases of new products. Many consumers would never try new products without these promotional inducements.

3. **Stimulating Sales Force Enthusiasm for New, Improved, or Mature Brands.** Exciting sales promotions give salespeople extra ammunition to use when interacting with buyers; they revive enthusiasm and make the salesperson's job easier and more enjoyable.

4. **Invigorating Sales of a Mature Brand.** Sales promotion can invigorate sales of a mature brand that requires a shot in the arm.

5. **Increasing On- and Off-Shelf Merchandising Space.** Trade-oriented sales promotions enable a manufacturer to obtain extra shelf space for a temporary period.

Figure 12.8   Sales Promotion's Capabilities

1. Facilitate the introduction of new products to the trade.
2. Obtain trial purchases from consumers.
3. Stimulate sales force enthusiasm.
4. Invigorate sales of mature brands.
5. Increase merchandise space.
6. Neutralize competitive advertising and sales promotions.
7. Hold current users by encouraging repeat purchasing.
8. Increase product usage by loading consumers.
9. Preempt competition by loading consumers.
10. Reinforce advertising.

This space may be in the form of extra *facing* (i.e., rows of shelf space) or off-shelf space in a gondola or end-aisle display.

6. **Neutralizing Competitive Advertising and Sales Promotion.** Sales promotions can be used to offset competitors' advertising and sales-promotion efforts. For example, one company's 50 cents-off coupon loses much of its appeal when a competitor simultaneously comes out with a $1 coupon.

7. **Holding Current Users by Encouraging Repeat Purchases.** Brand switching is a fact of life faced by all brand managers. The strategic use of certain forms of sales promotion can encourage at least short-run repetitive purchasing. Premium programs, refunds, and various other devices are used to encourage repeat purchasing.

8. **Increasing Brand Usage by Loading Consumers.** Consumers tend to use more of certain products (e.g., snack foods and soft drinks) when they have more of them available in their homes. Thus, sales-promotion efforts that load consumers generate temporary increases in brand usage. Bonus packs and two-for-the-price-of-one deals are particularly effective loading devices.

9. **Preempting Competition by Loading Consumers.** When consumers are loaded with one company's brand, they are temporarily out of the marketplace for competitive brands. Hence, one brand's sales promotion serves to preempt sales of competitive brands.

10. **Reinforcing Advertising.** A final can-do capability of sales promotion is to reinforce advertising. An advertising campaign can be strengthened greatly by a well-coordinated sales promotion effort.

Sales promotions clearly are capable of performing important tasks. There are, however, distinct limitations that are beyond the capability of sales promotion. In particular, sales promotions cannot (1) compensate for a poorly trained sales force, (2) give the trade or consumers any compelling long-term reason to continue purchasing a brand, or (3) permanently stop an established brand's declining sales trend, or change the basic nonacceptance of an undesired brand.

Trade Promotions: Role and Objectives

As earlier noted, manufacturers use some combination of push and pull strategies to accomplish both retail distribution and consumer purchasing. Trade promotions, which are directed at wholesalers, retailers, and other marketing intermediaries, represent the first step in any promotional effort. Consumer promotions are likely to fail unless trade-promotion efforts have succeeded in getting wholesalers to distribute the product, and retailers to stock adequate quantities. The special incentives offered by manufacturers to their distribution channel members are then expected to be passed through to consumers in the form of price discounts offered by retailers and often stimulated by advertising support and special displays.[40] As we will see later, this does not always occur.

A manufacturer has various objectives for using trade-oriented sales promotions: (1) to introduce new or revised products, (2) to increase distribution of new packages or sizes, (3) to build retail inventories, (4) to maintain or increase the manufacturer's share of shelf space, (5) to obtain displays outside normal shelf locations, (6) to reduce excess inventories and increase turnover, (7) to achieve product features in retailers' advertisements, (8) to counter competitive activity, and, ultimately, (9) to sell as much as possible to final consumers.[41]

Manufacturers employ a variety of trade-oriented promotional inducements, most of which are some form of **trade allowance.**[42] These allowances/deals are needed to encourage retailers to stock the manufacturer's brand, discount the brand's price to consumers, feature it in advertising, or provide special display or other point-of-purchase support.[43]

Trade allowances
or trade deals, come in a variety of forms and are offered to retailers simply for purchasing the manufacturer's brand or for performing activities in support of the manufacturer's brand.

Off-invoice allowance

are deals offered periodically to the trade that allow wholesalers and retailers to simply deduct a fixed amount, say 15 percent, from the full price at the time the order is placed.

Bill-back allowance

is not simply deducted directly from the invoice at the time of ordering, but rather must be earned by the retailer by performing designated advertising or display services.

Slotting allowance

(*stocking allowance* or *street money*) is the fee a manufacturer is charged by a supermarket chain or other retailer to get that retailer to handle the manufacturer's new product.

Forward buying or bridge buying

is when retailers purchase enough product during a manufacturer's off-invoice allowance period to carry the retailers over until the manufacturer's next regularly scheduled deal.

Diverting

occurs when a manufacturer restricts an off-invoice allowance to a limited geographical area, resulting in some wholesalers and retailers buying abnormally large quantities at the deal price and then transshipping the excess quantities to other geographical areas.

Everyday low pricing (EDLP)

is a form of pricing whereby a manufacturer charges the same price for a particular brand day in and day out.

The most frequently used allowance is an **off-invoice allowance.** By using off-invoice allowances, manufacturers hope to increase retailers' purchasing of the manufacturer's brand and increase consumers' purchasing from retailers. This latter objective is based on the expectation that retailers will in fact pass along to consumers the discounts they receive from manufacturers, which unfortunately, does not always happen.

Another form of allowance is the **bill-back allowance.** Retailers receive allowances for featuring the manufacturer's brand in advertisements (***bill-back ad allowances***) or for providing special displays (***bill-back display allowances***). The retailer effectively bills (i.e., charges) the manufacturer for the services rendered, and the manufacturer pays an allowance to the retailer for the services received on behalf of the manufacturer's brand(s).

A final form of trade allowance, which applies specifically to new products, is a **slotting allowance.** The allowance is called *slotting* in reference to the slot, or location, that the retailer must make available in its distribution center to accommodate the manufacturer's product. The retailer who demands slotting allowances denies the manufacturer shelf space unless the manufacturer is willing to pay the up-front fee. Manufacturers tolerate slotting allowances because they are confronted with a classic dilemma: Either they pay the fee and eventually recoup the cost through increased sales volume, or they refuse to pay the fee and in so doing accept a fate of not being able to successfully introduce new products.

Off-invoice trade allowances create notable problems for the manufacturers that use them. A particularly major problem is that off-invoice allowances often induce the trade to stockpile products in order to take advantage of the temporary price reduction. This merely shifts business from the future to the present. Two prevalent practices are **forward buying** and **diverting,** both of which represent efforts on the part of wholesalers and retailers to earn money from *buying* on deal rather than from selling merchandise at a profit.[44]

Manufacturers' off-invoice allowances typically are available every four weeks of each business quarter (which translates to about 30 percent of the year), and a number of manufacturers sell upward of 80 to 90 percent of their volume at less than full price. When a manufacturer marks down a product's price by, say, 10 percent, wholesalers and retailers commonly stock up with a 10 to 12 week supply. Wholesalers and retailers are rationale businesspeople: they take advantage of deals!

A related buying practice, diverting, where the practice of transshipping allows wholesalers and retailers to circumvent a manufacturer's intent to limit the effect of a discount to a limited geographical area. It is estimated that the volume of merchandise involved in diverting amounts to at least $5 billion a year.[45]

Manufacturers lose billions of dollars every year due to inefficient and ineffective trade deals stemming from the trade's practice of forward buying and diverting. It is for this reason that the powerful Procter & Gamble Corporation (P&G) under the leadership of CEO Edwin Artzt undertook a bold move in the early 1990s to bust the practice of forward buying and diverting. P&G introduced a new form of pricing called **everyday low pricing,** or **EDLP.** Because no deal is offered, wholesalers and retailers have no reason to engage in forward buying or diverting. Hence, their profit is made via selling merchandise rather than by buying it. Today over 80 percent of P&G's brands are sold via EDLP pricing and the amount of forward buying and diverting have declined.

Consumer Sales Promotions: Roles and Objectives

A variety of sales promotion methods are used to encourage consumers to purchase one brand over another, to purchase a particular brand more often, and to purchase in larger quantities. Such activities as sampling, couponing, refunding, rebating, and offering premiums, sweepstakes, and contests, are all part of the promotions landscape.

Consumers would not be responsive to sales promotions unless there was something in it for them—and, in fact, there is. All sales-promotion techniques provide consumers with incentives or inducements that encourage certain forms of behavior desired by mar-

Figure 12.9 Major Consumer-Oriented Forms of Sales Promotions

Consumer Reward	Marketer's Objective		
	Trial Impact	Customer Holding/Loading	Image Reinforcement
Immediate	(1)	(3)	(5)
	▼ Sampling	▼ Price-offs	
	▼ Instant coupons	▼ Bonus packs	
	▼ Shelf-delivered coupons	▼ In-, on-, and near-pack premiums	
Delayed	(2)	(4)	(6)
	▼ Media- and mail-delivered coupons	▼ In- and on-pack coupons	▼ Self-liquidating premiums
	▼ Free-in-the-mail premiums	▼ Refunds and rebates	▼ Contests and sweepstakes
	▼ Scanner-delivered coupons	▼ Phone cards	

keters. Rewards are typically in the form of cash savings or free gifts. Sometimes rewards are immediate, while other times they are delayed. An ***immediate reward*** is one that delivers the savings or gift as soon as the consumer performs a marketer-specified behavior. For example, you receive cash savings at the time you redeem a coupon; pleasure is obtained immediately when you try, say, a free product while shopping in a grocery store. ***Delayed rewards*** are those that follow the behavior by a period of days, weeks, or even longer. For example, you may have to wait weeks before a free-in-the-mail premium object can be enjoyed. Generally speaking, consumers are more responsive to immediate rather than delayed rewards. Of course, this is in line with the natural human tendency to seek immediate rather than delayed gratification.

Manufacturers use sales promotions to accomplish three general categories of objectives: **trial impact, franchise holding/loading,** and **image reinforcement.** Figure 12.9 classifies a variety of sales promotion techniques by the specific objective each is primarily responsible for accomplishing, and by the type of reward, either immediate or delayed, provided consumers.[46] It is important to recognize that most forms of sales promotions perform more than a single objective. For example, refunds and rebates are classified as franchise holding/loading techniques but on some occasions they may also encourage trial purchasing. Note also that two techniques, coupons and premiums, have multiple entries. This is because these techniques achieve different objectives depending on the specific form of delivery vehicle. The choice of which sales promotion tool to use depends on the specific objectives that must be accomplished for a brand at a particular point in time, and an evaluation of the relative expense of using different tools. Coupons, for example, are especially widely used because different forms of couponing are capable of achieving different objectives, and the cost typically is not prohibitive.

PUBLIC RELATIONS

Public relations, or ***PR,*** is that aspect of promotion management uniquely suited to fostering ***goodwill*** between a company and its various publics. When effectively integrated with advertising, personal selling, and sales promotion, public relations is capable of accomplishing objectives other than goodwill. It can also increase brand awareness, build favorable attitudes toward a company and its products, and encourage purchase behavior.

Trial impact

refers to inducing nonusers to try a brand for the first time, or encouraging retrial by consumers who have not purchased the brand for an extended period.

Franchise holding/loading

includes manufacturers' efforts to hold on to their franchise of current users by rewarding them for continuing to purchase the promoted brand, or to load them so they have no need to switch to another brand.

Image reinforcement

involves the careful selection of the right premium object, or appropriate sweepstakes prize, to reinforce a brand's desired image.

PR is similar to advertising because both are forms of mass communications; the difference is that the publicity generated by PR receives free news space or air time in comparison to the paid-for space and time in the case of advertising. The public-relations department serves as the prime source of an organization's contact with the news media.

PR efforts are aimed at various publics, primarily the following: consumers, employees, suppliers, stockholders, governments, the general public, labor groups, and citizen action groups. Our concern, however, is only with the more narrow aspect of public relations involving an organization's interactions with customers. This marketing-oriented aspect of public relations is called ***Marketing PR,*** or ***MPR*** for short. Marketing PR can be further delineated as involving either proactive or reactive public relations.[47]

Proactive MPR

Proactive marketing public relations (Proactive MPR) is offensively rather than defensively oriented, and opportunity-seeking rather than problem-solving. The major role of proactive MPR is in the area of product introductions or product revisions.

Proactive MPR is another tool in addition to advertising, sales promotion, and personal selling for promoting a company's products. It is integrated with other promotional devices to give a product additional exposure, newsworthiness, and credibility. This last factor, *credibility,* largely accounts for the effectiveness of proactive MPR. Whereas advertising and personal selling claims are sometimes suspect—because we question salespeople's and advertisers' motives, knowing they have a personal stake in persuading us—product announcements by a newspaper editor or television broadcaster are notably more believable. Customers are less likely to question the motivation underlying an editorial-type endorsement.

Publicity is the major tool of proactive MPR. Like advertising and personal selling, the fundamental purposes of marketing-oriented publicity are to engender brand awareness, enhance attitudes toward a company and its brands, and possibly influence purchase behavior. Companies obtain publicity using various forms of news releases, press conferences, and other types of information dissemination. ***News releases*** concerning new products, modifications in old products, and other newsworthy topics are delivered to editors of newspapers and magazines, to station managers of television and radio, and are disseminated en masse to Internet Web sites such as *Yahoo! Finance.* ***Press conferences*** announce major news events of interest to the public. Photographs, tapes, and films are useful for illustrating product improvements, new products, advanced production techniques, and so forth. Of course, all forms of publicity are subject to the control and whims of the media. However, by disseminating a large volume of publicity materials and by preparing materials that fit the media's needs, a company increases its chances of obtaining beneficial publicity.

www.foodlion.com

www.pepsi.com

www.intel.com

Reactive MPR

Reactive MPR is a form of defensively oriented public relations that deals with developments (such as product defects or flaws) having negative consequences for the organization. Reactive MPR attempts to repair a company's reputation, prevent market erosion, and regain lost sales.

Reactive MPR is undertaken as a result of external pressures and challenges brought by competitive actions, changes in consumer attitudes, changes in government policy, or other external influences. Product defects and failures are the most dramatic factors underlying the need for reactive MPR. A number of negative-publicity cases have received widespread media attention in recent years. For example, Audi of America experienced an irreversible loss in sales after news reports were disseminated claiming that the Audi 5000-S sometimes lunged out of control when shifted into drive or reverse gears. Sales plummeted from approximately 74,000 units in 1985 to sales of approximately only 12,000 in 1991.[48] Food Lion, a regional supermarket chain, suffered grave losses and was forced to close some stores after news reports charged that Food Lion stores are unsanitary and that they sell out-of-date meat, fish, and poultry products. Cans of Pepsi Cola were rumored to be contaminated with hypodermic needles, but skillfully conceived public relations quickly dispelled this hoax.[49] Finally, Intel, the huge computer-chip manufacturer, was embarrassed by reports that its new Pentium chip failed to correctly perform some mathematical calculations. Although corrective technical alterations were made, Intel was slow in reacting to this negative publicity and suffered a temporary loss of credibility.[50]

SPONSORSHIP MARKETING

One of the fastest growing aspects of marketing and marketing communications is the practice of **corporate sponsorships.** In 1998, corporate expenditures on sponsorships amounted to approximately $5.9 billion and are increasing at an annual double-digit rate.[51] Sponsorships range from supporting athletic events (golf and tennis tournaments, college football bowl games, etc.), to underwriting rock concerts, to throwing corporate weight behind worthy causes such as efforts to generate funds for cancer research.

At least four factors account for the growth in sponsorships.[52] First, by attaching their names to special events and causes, companies are able to *avoid the clutter* inherent in advertising media. Second, sponsorships help companies *respond to consumers' changing media habits.* For example, with the decline in network television viewing, sponsorships offer a potentially effective and cost-efficient way to reach customers. Third, sponsorships help companies *gain the approval of various constituencies,* including stockholders, employees, and society at large. Finally, the sponsorship of special events and causes enables marketers to *target their communication and promotional efforts* to specific geographic regions and/or to specific lifestyle groups. For example, the marketers of Fleischmann's margarine aligned that brand with health-conscious aging Baby Boomers by sponsoring a 22-city Beach Boys concert tour.[53] Philip Morris reached 800,000 bowlers, many of whom smoke, by sponsoring the Merit brand bowling competition.[54]

Corporate sponsorships involve investments in *events* or *causes* for the purpose of achieving various corporate objectives, such as increasing sales volume, enhancing a company's reputation or a brand's image, and increasing brand awareness.

Event Marketing

Thousands of companies invest in some form of **event-related marketing (ERM)** sponsorship. Event marketing is separate from advertising, sales promotion, point-of-purchase merchandising, or public relations, but it generally incorporates elements from all of these promotional tools. It is growing rapidly because these sponsorships provide companies with alternatives to the cluttered mass media, an ability to segment on a local or regional basis, and opportunities for reaching narrow lifestyle groups whose consumption behavior can be linked with the local event. Events are effective because they reach people when they are in a relaxed atmosphere and receptive to marketing messages.[55]

As with every other marketing and promotion-management decision, the starting point for effective event sponsorship is to clearly specify the objectives that an event is designed to accomplish. Event marketing has no value unless it accomplishes these objectives. For example, to create a fun and exciting image for Cool Mint Listerine mouthwash, Warner-Lambert literally pitched tents at ski resorts. Product samples and Cool Mint headbands were distributed from the tents. The event was further tied in to retail displays that offered lift-ticket discounts to consumers who appeared at ski resorts with a Cool Mint proof-of-purchase.[56]

Event-related marketing (ERM) is a form of brand promotion that ties a brand to a meaningful cultural, social, athletic, or other type of high-interest public activity.

www.listerine.com
www.warner-lambert.com

Cause-Related Marketing

Cause-related marketing (CRM) is a relatively narrow aspect of overall sponsorship. It involves an amalgam of public relations, sales promotion, and corporate philanthropy; however, the distinctive feature of CRM is that a company's contribution to a designated cause is linked to customers engaging in *revenue-producing exchanges* with the firm.[57] The contribution is contingent on the customer performing a behavior (such as buying a product or redeeming a coupon) that benefits the firm.

Cause-related marketing (CRM) is a form of corporate philanthropy that links a company's contributions (usually monetary) to a pre-designated *worthy* cause with the purchasing behavior of consumers.

**Figure 12.10   A Truly Integrated Cause-Related Marketing Effort
by Stride Rite Shoes**

The following examples illustrate how cause-related marketing operates. For each Heinz baby-food label mailed in by consumers, H. J. Heinz Company contributed six cents to a hospital near the consumer's home. Nabisco Brands donated one dollar to the Juvenile Diabetes Foundation for each one dollar donation certificate that was redeemed with a Ritz brand proof of purchase. Hersheys donated 25 cents to local hospitals for children for each Hershey coupon redeemed. Dutch Boy paint contributed 25 cents to Healthy Families America for each gallon of paint it sold during a designated period. Figure 12.10 presents a cause-oriented ad for Stride Rite shoes for children. The ad informs consumers that Stride Rite will make a donation to Save the Children in the amount of 3–4 percent of the retail price of each pair of specially designed footwear sold.

POINT-OF-PURCHASE COMMUNICATIONS

Marketers use a variety of items at the point-of-purchase to draw attention to their brands and activate consumer purchases. These include various types of signs, mobiles, plaques, banners, shelf tapes, mechanical mannequins, lights, mirrors, plastic product reproductions, checkout units, full-line merchandisers, wall posters, motion displays, and other materials. Many of these materials are temporary items, with useful life spans of only weeks or months. Others are relatively permanent fixtures that can be used for years. Whereas temporary signs and displays are particularly effective for promoting impulse purchasing, permanent P-O-P units compartmentalize and departmentalize a store area to achieve high product visibility, facilitate customer self-service, prevent stock-outs, and help control inventory.

Companies invest heavily in point-of-purchase materials, over $13 billion in 1997, which was an increase of 5 percent above 1996.[58] This impressive growth is due to the fact that point-of-purchase materials provide a useful service for all participants in the marketing process.

▼ **Consumers** are served by point-of-purchase units that deliver useful information and simplify the shopping process by setting products apart from similar items.

▼ P-O-P serves **retailers** by attracting the consumer's attention, increasing his or her interest in shopping, and extending the amount of time spent in the store—all of which mean increased sales. P-O-P helps retailers utilize available space to the best advantage by displaying several manufacturers' products in the same unit (e.g., many varieties of vitamins and other medicinal items all in one well-organized unit). It enables retailers to better organize shelf space and to improve inventory control, volume, stock turnover, and profitability.

▼ For **manufacturers,** who are the marketers of branded products, P-O-P keeps the company's name and the brand name before the consumer and both reactivates and reinforces brand information the consumer has previously received through advertising. P-O-P calls attention to special offers such as sales promotions and helps stimulate impulse purchasing. P-O-P serves to complement the job already performed by advertising before the consumer enters a store.[59] Indeed, it represents the capstone for an integrated marketing communications program.

Because many product- and brand-choice decisions are made while the consumer is in the store rather than before he or she arrives at the store, point-of-purchase materials play a role, perhaps the major role, in influencing unplanned purchasing. Indeed, the Point-of-Purchase Advertising Institute performed a major study based on a national sample of supermarkets and mass merchandise outlets (e.g., Wal-Mart) and determined that 70–74 percent of purchase decisions for items carried in these types of retail outlets are made by shoppers while in the store.[60]

Chapter Summary

A brand and its attributes/benefits must be communicated to customers through marketing communications. In today's highly competitive and dynamic marketing world, effective communications are critical to a company's success. Marketing managers have considerable discretion in determining which marketing communications elements to use and how much relative emphasis each should receive. Various factors such as the target market, product life-cycle stage, objectives, competitive activity, budget, and nature of the product all affect the appropriate mix of marketing communications elements.

Where historically many marketing communication decisions were treated as rather disparate and managed by independent departments that failed to carefully coordinate their activities, there has been a trend toward integrated marketing communications, or IMC. Some key elements of IMC are that all marketing communication decisions start with the customer, which reflects the adoption of an outside-in mentality versus an inside-out position that historically has dominated this field. Another fundamental feature is that all communication elements must achieve synergy, or speak with a single voice. The belief that successful marketing communications must build a relationship between the brand and the customer is another key IMC feature.

Advertising is a critical component of marketing communications, especially in the United States, where annual expenditures in 1998 alone were approximately $200 billion. The process of developing advertising strategy consists of five major activities: setting objectives, formulating a budget, developing a message strategy, designing a media strategy, and assessing advertising effectiveness.

Sales promotion—the use of any incentive by a manufacturer to induce the trade (wholesalers and retailers) and/or final consumers to buy a brand and to encourage the sales force to aggressively sell it—is another key marketing communications element. Consumer promotions (such as coupons, cents-off deals, premiums, and sweepstakes) and trade-oriented promotions (primarily off-invoice allowances to wholesalers and retailers) constitute, on average, approximately three-fourths of businesses' marketing communications budgets. Sales promotions are particularly useful for purposes of introducing new or revised products to the trade, obtaining trial purchases from consumers, and enhancing repeat purchasing. However, sales promotions cannot compensate for inadequate personal selling or advertising, give the trade or consumers any long-term reason for buying a brand, or permanently stop an established brand's declining sales trend.

Public relations, or PR, is that aspect of promotion management uniquely suited to fostering goodwill between a company and its various publics. Public relations involves interactions with multiple publics (government, stockholders, etc.), but emphasis in this chapter is limited to the more narrow aspect of public relations involving an organization's interactions with customers. This marketing-oriented aspect of public relations is called marketing PR, or MPR for short. Marketing PR can be further delineated as involving either proactive or reactive public relations. Proactive MPR is another tool in addition to advertising and sales promotion for promoting a company's brands. Its major role is for disseminating information about brand introductions or revisions. Reactive MPR is undertaken as a result of external pressures and challenges brought by competitive actions, changes in consumer attitudes, changes in government policy, or other external influences. Reactive MPR typically deals with changes that have negative consequences for the organization, such as instances of product defects or failures.

One of the fastest growing aspects of marketing and marketing communications is the practice of corporate sponsorships. Sponsorships take two forms: event sponsorships (such as athletic and entertainment events) and cause-oriented sponsorships. Event marketing is growing rapidly because it provides companies alternatives to the cluttered mass media, an ability to segment on a local or regional basis, and opportunities for reaching narrow lifestyle groups whose consumption behavior can be linked with the local event. Cause-related marketing, a form of corporate philanthropy with benefits accruing to the sponsoring company, is based on the idea that a company will contribute to a cause every time the customer undertakes some action. In addition to helping worthy causes, corporations satisfy their own tactical and strategic objectives when undertaking cause-related efforts. By supporting a deserving cause, a company can enhance its corporate or brand image, generate incremental sales, increase brand awareness, broaden its customer base, and reach new market segments.

Communications at the point of purchase is another major growth area in marketing. This is due to the fact that point-of-purchase materials provide a useful service for all participants in the marketing process. P-O-P communications also serve as the capstone for an integrated marketing communications program.

Key Terms

Personal selling is *person-to-person* communication in which a seller informs and
educates prospective customers and attempts to influence their purchase choices.

Advertising is *nonpersonal* communication that is paid for by an identified sponsor, and involves either *mass communication* via newspapers, magazines, radio, television, and other media (e.g., billboards, bus stop signage) or *direct-to-consumer communication* via direct mail.

Publicity, like advertising, is *nonpersonal* communication to a mass audience, but unlike advertising, publicity is not directly paid for by the company that enjoys the publicity.

Sales promotion consists of all marketing activities that attempt to stimulate quick buyer action, or, in other words, attempt to promote immediate sales of a product (thereby yielding the name *sales promotion*).

Sponsorship marketing is the practice of promoting the interests of a company and its brands by associating the company with a specific *event* (e.g., a golf tournament) or a charitable *cause* (e.g., the Leukemia Society).

Point-of-purchase communications include all signage—displays, posters, signs, shelf cards, and a variety of other visual materials—that are designed to influence buying decisions at the point of sale.

Integrated marketing communications (IMC) is a system of management and integration of marketing communication elements —advertising, publicity, sales promotion, sponsorship marketing, and point-of-purchase communications— with the result that all elements adhere to the same message.

Push strategy involves aggressive trade allowances and personal selling efforts to obtain distribution for a new brand through wholesalers and retailers. The brand is "pushed" through the channel system in the sense that there is a *forward* thrust from the manufacturer to the trade.

Pull strategy involves a relatively heavy emphasis on consumer-oriented advertising to encourage consumer demand for a new brand and thereby obtain retail distribution. The brand is "pulled" through the channel system in the sense that there is a *backward* tug from the consumer to the retailer.

Media strategy consists of four sets of interrelated activities: (1) selecting the target audience, (2) specifying media objectives, (3) selecting media categories and vehicles, and (4) buying media.

Gross rating points (GRPs) are the accumulation of rating points including all vehicles in a media purchase over the span of a particular campaign.

Cost per thousand (CPM) is calculated by dividing the cost of an ad placed in a particular ad vehicle (e.g., certain magazine) by the number of people (expressed in thousands) who are exposed to that vehicle.

Single-source systems are a measurement of the effectiveness of advertising (whether it leads to increased sales activity). They are unique in that all the relevant data is collected by a single source, processed, and then made available in a readily usable format to retailers and manufacturers.

Database marketing involves collecting and electronically storing (in a database) information about present, past, and prospective customers.

Incentives are bonuses or rewards (sweepstakes, coupons, premiums, display allowances, etc.) for purchasing one brand rather than another.

Trade allowances, or trade deals, come in a variety of forms and are offered to retailers simply for purchasing the manufacturer's brand or for performing activities in support of the manufacturer's brand.

Off-invoice allowance are deals offered periodically to the trade that allow wholesalers and retailers to simply deduct a fixed amount, say 15 percent, from the full price at the time the order is placed.

Bill-back allowance is not simply deducted directly from the invoice at the time of ordering, but rather must be earned by the retailer by performing designated advertising or display services.

Slotting allowance (*stocking allowance* or *street money*) is the fee a manufacturer is charged by a supermarket chain or other retailer to get that retailer to handle the manufacturer's new product.

Forward buying or bridge buying is when retailers purchase enough product during a manufacturer's off-invoice allowance period to carry the retailers over until the manufacturer's next regularly scheduled deal.

Diverting occurs when a manufacturer restricts an off-invoice allowance to a limited geographical area, resulting in some wholesalers and retailers buying abnormally large quantities at the deal price and then transshipping the excess quantities to other geographical areas.

Everyday low pricing (EDLP) is a form of pricing whereby a manufacturer charges the same price for a particular brand day in and day out.

Trial impact refers to inducing nonusers to try a brand for the first time, or encouraging retrial by consumers who have not purchased the brand for an extended period.

Franchise holding/loading includes manufacturers' efforts to hold on to their franchise of current users by rewarding them for continuing to purchase the promoted brand, or to load them so they have no need to switch to another brand.

Image reinforcement involves the careful selection of the right premium object, or appropriate sweepstakes prize, to reinforce a brand's desired image.

Proactive marketing public relations (Proactive MPR) is offensively rather than defensively oriented, and opportunity-seeking rather than problem-solving. The major role of proactive MPR is in the area of product introductions or product revisions.

Reactive MPR is a form of defensively oriented public relations that deals with developments (such as product defects or flaws) having negative consequences for the organization. Reactive MPR attempts to repair a company's reputation, prevent market erosion, and regain lost sales.

Corporate sponsorships involve investments in *events* or *causes* for the purpose of achieving various corporate objectives, such as increasing sales volume, enhancing a company's reputation or a brand's image, and increasing brand awareness.

Event-related marketing (ERM) is a form of brand promotion that ties a brand to a meaningful cultural, social, athletic, or other type of high-interest public activity.

Cause-related marketing (CRM) is a form of corporate philanthropy that links a company's contributions (usually monetary) to a pre-designated worthy cause with the purchasing behavior of consumers.

Additional Key Terms and Concepts

Nonpersonal	Trade-oriented sales promotions
Consumer-oriented sales promotions	Strategic
Tactical	Contact points
Synergy	Brand
Brand equity	Brand awareness
Brand image	Brand association
Hierarchy of effects	Consumer awareness
Top-down budgeting (TD)	Bottom-up budgeting (BU)
Media	Actual response rate
Projected response rate	Communication outcomes
Advertising strategy	Heuristics
Percentage-of-sales method	Objective-and-task method
Vehicles	Target audience
Reach	Frequency
Continuity	Cost
BehaviorScan	Niche marketing
Trade allowances	Bill-back ad allowances
Bill-back display allowances	Immediate reward
Delayed rewards	Public relations, or PR
Goodwill	Marketing PR, or MPR
News releases	Press conferences

Questions for Discussion

1. When discussing integrated marketing communications (IMC), one key feature of this philosophy was that the IMC process should start with the customer. Compare this perspective with "the marketing concept," which you studied in Chapter 1.

2. Assume that you are head of marketing communications for a sorority, fraternity, or other campus organization. Your responsibility is to recruit 25 percent more members than you presently have. Explain how "starting with the customer" would apply to your choice of ways to recruit new members.

3. List your associations for each of the following "brands" and be prepared to share them in class: (1) Dennis Rodman, (2) Doc Martin boots, (3) Healthy Choice food items, (4) Wow! potato chips, (5) Harvard University, and (6) the People's Republic of China.

4. Compare and contrast the brand-equity model (Figure 12.1) with the hierarchy-of-effects framework (Figure 12.2). What specifically are the similarities and differences between these models?

5. Explain the meaning of "push" and "pull" efforts in marketing communications. Comment on the following statement: "A brand manager chooses between either pushing or pulling a brand through a distributing channel."

6. Locate two magazine advertisements that you consider good ads, and explain precisely why you regard each to be a good advertisement.

7. **a.** A one-page, four-color advertisement in *Ebony* magazine cost $49,975 in 1998. A syndicated service that measures magazine readership estimated that *Ebony*'s total readership that year was approximately 13 million adults. What was *Ebony*'s CPM in 1998?
   b. Advertisements for a particular brand are run on each of four television programs on a Thursday evening. Designating these programs as P1, P2, P3, P4, let us assume that the ratings for each program are: P1=13.5, P2=15.3, P3=17.4, and P4=19.8. How many gross rating points (GRPs) would this advertiser accumulate on this one evening of advertising?

8. Sales promotion is good at accomplishing increased brand usage by loading consumers. Can you recall any personal situations where you were "loaded" (not as in inebriated) and your brand usage increased?

9. Several examples of negative publicity were listed in the Reactive MPR section of the chapter. Are you familiar with any other examples of companies that have suffered such negative press? Discuss the effectiveness of the companies' "reactive MPR."

10. What factors would account for the fact that as many as three out of four purchase decisions made in supermarkets and mass merchandise stores are decisions made while shoppers are in the store?

Internet Questions

1. In context of the discussion of brand equity, brand image was conceptualized in terms of the types of associations that come to mind when thinking about a particular brand. If you already are familiar with the Gardenburger brand that was introduced in the

opening vignette, list the specific associations that come to your mind when thinking about this brand. If you are not familiar with this brand, locate its home page on the Web; then after reviewing this site, list the associations that you now possess, albeit only tentatively, for this brand.

2. Go online and locate the home pages for Domino's Pizza and Pizza Hut. Which has the better home page? Why? (Be specific!)

3. Go online and locate the home pages for Simmons Market Research Bureau (SMRB) and Mediamark Research (MRI). Write a brief report on the services that these two companies provide.

Endnotes

[1]"Gardenburger's Ad on Last Episode of Seinfeld Pays Off Big!" *Yahoo! Finance PR Newswire* June 3, 1998; "Gardenburger Reports 91% Rise in Net Sales during Second Quarter to $25.7 Million," *Yahoo! Finance PR Newswire,* July 20, 1998. The Web site for *Yahoo! Finance* is biz.yahoo.com.

[2]Don E. Schultz, Stanley I. Tannenbaum, Robert F. Lauterborn, *Integrated Marketing Communications* (Lincolnwood, IL: NTC Publishing Group, 1993), p. 46.

[3]*Measuring the In-Store Decision Making of Supermarket and Mass Merchandise Store Shoppers* (Englewood, NJ: Point-of-Purchase Advertising Institute, 1995).

[4]Schultz et al., *Integrated Marketing Communications.*

[5]This "one-voice perspective" is widely shared by various writers on the topic of IMC. See Schultz et al., *Integrated Marketing Communications;* Tom Duncan, "Integrated Marketing? It's Synergy," *Advertising Age,* March 8, 1993, p. 22; and Glen J. Nowak and Joseph Phelps, "Conceptualizing the Integrated Marketing Communications' Phenomenon: An Examination of Its Impact on Advertising Practices and Its Implications for Advertising Research," *Journal of Current Issues and Research in Advertising,* 16 (Spring 1994), pp. 49–66.

[6]See Schultz et al., *Integrated Marketing Communications,* pp. 52–53.

[7]Nowak and Phelps, "Conceptualizing the Integrated Marketing Communications' Phenomenon."

[8]Don E. Schultz, "Trying to Determine ROI for IMC," *Marketing News,* January 3, 1994, p. 18; Don E. Schultz, "Spreadsheet Approach to Measuring ROI for IMC," *Marketing News,* February 28, 1994, p. 12.

[9]The following discussion borrows liberally from Kevin Lane Keller, *Strategic Brand Management* (Upper Saddle River, NJ: Prentice Hall, 1998, chapter 2) and Kevin Lane Keller, "Conceptualizing, Measuring, and Managing Customer-Based Brand Equity," *Journal of Marketing* 57 (January 1993), pp. 1–22.

[10]This figure is from "Conceptualizing, Measuring, and Managing Customer-Based Brand Equity," p. 7.

[11]Terry Lefton, "Adidas Goes to Image Pitch with '98 $$ Boost," *Brandweek,* January 26, 1998, p. 37.

[12]"Coke's Market Share Rises to 43.9% As PepsiCo Slips," *The Wall Street Journal Interactive Edition,* February 13, 1998 (interactive.wsj.com).

[13]William Boulding, Eunkyu Lee, and Richard Staelin, "Mastering the Mix: Do Advertising, Promotion, and Sales Force Activities Lead to Differentiation?" *Journal of Marketing Research* 31 (May 1994), pp. 159–172.

[14]Nigel F. Piercy, "The Marketing Budgeting Process: Marketing Management Implications," *Journal of Marketing,* 51 (October 1987), pp. 45–59.

[15]*The Value Side of Productivity: A Key to Competitive Survival in the 1990s* (New York: American Association of Advertising Agencies, 1989), p. 12.

[16]John Sinisi, "Love: EDLP Equals Ad Investment," *Brandweek,* November 16, 1992.

[17]Robert J. Coen, "Ad Revenue Growth Hits 7% in 1997 to Surpass Forecasts," *Advertising Age,* May 18, 1998, p. 50.

[18]Todd Pruzan, "Spending '94: Europe Mired But Asia Grows," *Advertising Age,* February 20, 1995, pp. 1–9.

[19]"100 Leaders by U.S. Advertising Spending," *Advertising Age,* September 29, 1997, p. 4.

[20]Ibid.

[21]Charles H. Patti and Charles F. Frazer, *Advertising: A Decision-Making Approach* (Hinsdale, IL: The Dryden Press, 1988), p. 236.

[22]Gary L. Lilien, Alvin J. Silk, Jean-Marie Choffray, and Murlidhar Rao, "Industrial Advertising Effects and Budgeting Practices," *Journal of Marketing,* 40 (January 1976), p. 21.

[23]Fred S. Zufryden, "How Much Should Be Spent for Advertising a Brand?" *Journal of Advertising Research,* April/May 1989, pp. 24–34.

[24]Lilien et al, "Industrial Advertising Effects and Budgeting Practices," and Kent M. Lancaster and Judith A. Stern, "Computer-Based Advertising Budgeting Practices of Leading U.S. Consumer Advertisers," *Journal of Advertising,* 12, 4 (1983), p. 6.

[25]Adapted from A. Jerome Jewler, *Creative Strategy in Advertising* (Belmont, CA: Wadsworth Publishing Company, 1985), 7–8, and Don E. Schultz and Stanley I. Tannenbaum, *Essentials of Advertising Strategy* (Lincolnwood, IL: NTC Business Books, 1988), pp. 9–10.

[26]Stan Freberg, "Irtnog Revisited," *Advertising Age,* August 1, 1988, p. 32.

[27]Joe Schwartz, "Back to the Source," *American Demographics* (January 1989), pp. 22–26.

[28]"What the Scanner Knows about You," *Fortune,* December 3, 1990, pp. 51–52.

[29]Description adapted from Don E. Schultz, "The Direct/Database Marketing Challenge to Fixed-Location Retailers," in Robert A. Peterson (ed.), *The Future of U.S. Retailing: An Agenda for the 21st Century* (New York: Quorum Books, 1992), pp. 165–184.

[30]Jonathan Berry et al., "A Potent New Tool for Selling: Database Marketing," *Business Week,* September 5, 1994, 56–62; Glenn Heitsmith, "Database Promotions: Marketers Move Carefully, But Some Are Still Faking It," *Promo,* October 1994, pp. 37–50.

[31]"Car Maker Uses Direct to Drive Loyalty," *Promo,* January 1994, p. 21.

[32]Terry G. Vavra, *Aftermarketing* (Homewood, IL: Business One Irwin, 1992), p. 32.

[33]"What Happened to Advertising," *Business Week,* September 23, 1991, p. 69.

[34]Don Schultz as quoted in Gary Levin, "Going Direct Route," *Advertising Age,* November 18, 1991, p. 37.

[35]Terence A. Shimp, *Advertising, Promotion, and Supplemental Aspects of Integrated Marketing Communications, 4th. ed.* (Fort Worth, TX: The Dryden Press, 1997).

[36]Alvin A. Achenbaum and F. Kent Mitchel, "Pulling Away from Push Marketing," *Harvard Business Review,* 65, May–June 1987, pp. 38–40; Robert J. Kopp and Stephen A. Greyser, "Packaged Goods Marketing—'Pull' Companies Look to Improved 'Push'," *The Journal of Consumer Marketing,* 4 (Spring 1987), pp. 13–22.

[37]*The 16th Annual Survey of Promotional Practices* (Donnelley Marketing Inc., 1994).

[38]Robert C. Blattberg and Scott A. Neslin, "Sales Promotion: The Long and the Short of It," *Marketing Letters,* 1, 1 (1989), pp. 81–97.

[39]This discussion is guided by Charles Fredericks, Jr., "What Ogilvy & Mather Has Learned About Sales Promotion," *The Tools of Promotion* (New York: Association of National Advertisers, 1975), and Don E. Schultz and William A. Robinson, *Sales Promotion Management* (Lincolnwood, IL: NTC Business Books, 1986), chap. 3.

[40]Robert C. Blattberg and Alan Levin, "Modelling the Effectiveness and Profitablilty of Trade Promotions," *Marketing Science,* 6 (Spring 1987), p. 125.

[41]See Chakravarthi Narasimhan, "Managerial Perspectives on Trade and Consumer Promotions," *Marketing Letters,* 1, 3 (1989), pp. 239–251.

[42]*Fourth Annual Survey of Manufacturer Trade Promotion Practices* (Nielsen Marketing Reseach), December, 1992, p. 10.

[43]Rajiv Lal, "Manufacturer Trade Deals and Retail Price Promotions," *Journal of Marketing Research,* 27 (November 1990), pp. 428–444; Ronald C. Curhan and Robert J. Kopp, "Obtaining Retailer Support for Trade Deals: Key Success Factors," *Journal of Advertising Research,* 27 (December 1987/January 1988), pp. 51–60.

[44]Howard Schlossberg, "Exposed: Retailing's Dirty Little Secret," *Promo,* April 1994, pp. 50–55, and Patricia Sellers, "The Dumbest Marketing Ploy," *Fortune,* October 5, 1992, pp. 88–94.

[45]Ibid.

[46]For further discussion, see Shimp, *Advertisisng, Promotion, and Supplemental Aspects of Integrated Marketing Communications,* pp. 486–522.

[47]Jordan Goldman, *Public Relations in the Marketing Mix* (Lincolnwood, IL: NTC Business Books, 1984).

[48]David Kiley, "After Peugeot and Sterling, Who's Next?" *Adweek's Marketing Week,* August 19, 1991, p. 9.

[49]Marcy Magiera, "Pepsi Weathers Tampering Hoax," *Advertising Age,* June 21, 1993, pp. 1, 46; Marcy Magiera, "The Pepsi Crisis: What Went Right," *Advertising Age,* July 19, 1993, pp. 14–15.

[50]Alex Stanton, "Pentium Brouhaha a Marketing Lesson," *Advertising Age,* February 20, 1995, p. 18.

[51]"The 1998 Annual Report of the Promotion Industry," *Promo,* July 1998, pp. S16–S17.

[52]Meryl Paula Gardner and Phillip Joel Shuman, "Sponsorship: An Important Component of the Promotions Mix," *Journal of Advertising,* 16, 1 (1987), pp. 11–17.

[53]Kerry J. Smith, "Nabisco Sets Sail with Beach Boys," *Promo,* May 1994, p. 69.

[54]Howard Schlossberg, "Weighing in with Events," *Promo,* May 1994, pp. 66–67.

[55]Heitsmith, "Event Promotions: Get Them by Their Hearts and Minds," p. 32.

[56]Ibid., p. 103.

[57]P. Rajan Varadarajan and Anil Menon, "Cause-Related Marketing: A Coalignment of Marketing Strategy and Corporate Philanthropy," *Journal of Marketing,* 52 (July 1988), pp. 58–74.

[58]"The 1998 Annual Report of the Promotion Industry," p. S9.

[59]Kevin Lane Keller, "Cue Compatibility and Framing in Advertising," *Journal of Marketing Research,* 28 (February 1991), pp. 42–57.

[60]*Measuring the In-Store Decision Making of Supermarket and Mass Merchandise Store Shoppers.*

[61]Adapted from Bradley Johnson, "$100 Mil iMac Blitz Is Tops in Home Computer History," *Advertising Age,* August 17, 1998, 43; Jim Carlton, "Corporate Focus: From Apple, a New Marketing Blitz," *The Wall Street Journal,* August 14, 1998, B1; "iMac's Success Spawns Imitators of Translucent Product Casing," *The Wall Street Journal Interactive Edition,* January 4, 1999; Walter S. Mossberg, "Jobs Makes a Leap in Design of PCs and Advances an Inch," *The Wall Street Journal Interactive Edition,* January 14, 1999. Also, **cgi.fathfinder.com/time/digital/yir/1998/apple.html;** and **cnet.com/Content/Reports/Special/Awards98/ss01.html.**

CHAPTER CASE

An Integrated Marketing Communications Campaign for Apple's iMac

The iMac is the name of an exciting new computer introduced by Apple Computer Inc. in late 1998.[61] Although too early to tell at the time of this writing, the iMac may represent the salvation of a company whose fortunes were in doubt prior to iMac's introduction. The iMac was virtually an instant success when introduced in August 1998, selling about a quarter million units in the first six weeks after launch and representing one of the hottest products during that year's holiday season. Although a very good PC, the iMac's retail price at $1,299 was, if anything, at a premium level compared to functionally competitive PCs. Indeed, specification-wise the original iMac was nothing exceptional with only 32MB of RAM, a 4GB hard drive, and a 233-MHz processing chip.

However, the iMac's design *was* special. With bluish-green translucent case (the initial version), one-piece unit, rounded (versus angular) shape, and preinstalled software, the iMac was unlike any other personal computer that consumers had seen. After only five months on the market, Apple introduced five new translucent iMac cases in shades of raspberry, strawberry, tangerine, lime, and grape. Beyond its unique design, the iMac was exceptionally user-friendly, requiring virtually no set up time. This perhaps explains why nearly one third of the iMac buyers were first-time computer owners. However, the iMac was not without flaws, the most notable being the absence of a floppy drive and little ability to add any peripherals.

What role did marketing communications play in achieving a successful product launch? The creative communications program started with the choice of a clever brand name: iMac is a conjunction of "i" for internet and "Mac," which is an abbreviated version of Macintosh, the name of the famous computer introduced under Jobs' initial reign at Apple in 1984. This brand name thus unites the tradition of the famous Macintosh name, which has a cult-like following among its loyal users, with the excitement and dynamic character of the rapidly evolving Internet.

Beyond the choice of an appealing brand name, Apple invested heavily in an introductory advertising campaign. Approximately $100 million was spent in 1998 to introduce the iMac through television, radio, magazines, newspapers, and billboards. The magnitude of investment was greater than Apple or any other PC maker had ever committed to advertising. Advertisements carried the catchy slogan, "I think, therefore iMac," a slogan borne from the creative genius of Steve Jobs, the original founder of Apple and the current top person in the company.

Point-of-purchase materials also were used to attract consumer attention. Many retailers offered free software and T-shirts. In an introductory blitz, computer retailers held midnight madness sales, with 20-foot-high inflatable iMacs hovering over stores. Sales promotions played a role as well. Steve Jobs personally signed five "golden tickets" and had them placed in iMac shipping boxes. Radio advertisements informed listeners that iMac purchasers lucky enough to open a box with one of the five golden tickets would receive free iMacs each year for the next five years.

Discussion Questions

1. A good brand name generally must satisfy several criteria. These include (1) distinguishing the brand from competitive offerings, (2) describing the brand and its attributes/benefits, (3) providing compatibility with the brand's desired image and with its product design, and (4) achieving memorability and being easy to pronounce. With these considerations in mind, evaluate the iMac name.

2. Using Figure 12.1 as a guiding framework, evaluate iMac's brand equity. That is, based on what you personally think about the iMac and from what you have heard others say, what types of associations do people have for the iMac and how favorable, strong, and unique are these associations?

3. When discussing integrated marketing communications, the chapter identified three key features, the last of which was the need to build relationships with customers. If you were the iMac brand manager, what actions would you undertake to build relations with purchasers and increase the odds that these purchasers would again buy an iMac (or another Apple product) the next time they are in the market for a new computer?

Chapter 13

Personal Selling and Sales Management

Judy A. Siguaw,
Associate Professor of Marketing, School of Hotel Administration, Cornell University
Dr. Siguaw earned her master's and doctorate degrees from Louisiana Tech University and her bacherlor's degree from Lamar University. She has earned the Chancellor's Excellence in Teaching Award from the University of North Carolina at Wilmington, a research award from the Marketing Science Institute, and the Jane Fenyo Award from the Academy of Marketing Science. She serves as the faculty advisor for the Cornell student chapter of the Hotel Sales and Marketing Association International and also as a trustee of the Hospitality Sales & Marketing International Foundation Board. Most recently, she was part of the four-member research team that was awarded a major grant from Ameri-

Ecolab Inc. is the world's leading supplier of detergents and sanitizing products for many industries including hotels, restaurants, supermarkets, water systems, commercial laundries, food and beverage, health care, education, and farming. To implement its "Circle the Customer—Circle the Globe" strategy, Ecolab now operates in the United States, Canada, Asia Pacific, Africa, and Latin America, and in Europe through a joint venture with Henkel-Ecolab. During its 75 years of business, Ecolab has experienced continued diversification and growth, partially fueled by its corporate culture of "spirit, pride, determination, commitment, passion, and integrity."

Ecolab's innovative, value-added products provide a competitive advantage that differentiates it in the industry. However, Ecolab's biggest asset is the superior, customer-oriented service provided by its sales force of over 8,600 associates. These professional salespeople develop, service, and manage their assigned territories using consultative selling practices to recommend the best products, systems, and practices for customers to achieve optimized cleaning and sanitizing results.

National and global corporate accounts—largely composed of food and beverage companies, and multi-unit chain corporations in the hospitality industries—comprise the largest part of Ecolab's business. The Ecolab sales force responsible for these accounts clearly demonstrates Ecolab's commitment to the customer: "Ecolab takes total responsibility for customer results, and multi-unit accounts can rest assured that their customers will see the same high standards of cleanliness no matter which location they visit." Further, Ecolab works with each corporate account's headquarters to identify general customer needs and to develop programs that satisfy those needs. The newly developed programs are then coordinated for implementation by the local sales managers who are responsible for the customers' individual business units, and who help solve local issues the individual units may encounter. As a result, Ecolab can claim many major companies as their customers.

For recruitment into its worldwide sales force, Ecolab typically seeks college graduates who have majored in business, hospitality management, education or liberal arts. Ecolab also recruits candidates from the food service industry, such as food distributors or food and beverage managers at restaurants. Potential sales force candidates are evaluated on their selling and consultative skills, as well as their mechanical aptitude. Once hired, these new sales representatives spend approximately a year in training. They first receive two to five weeks of sales training and product instruction at the corporate headquarters in St. Paul, Minnesota, then spend the remaining training period working closely with more experienced sales associates.

The typical Ecolab sales associate spends the day calling on prospective customers, and visiting and following-up with current customers. While on the road, the sales associate stays in touch with customers by accessing ECOlink, Ecolab's 24-hour national customer service center. The sales associate checks this resource several times a day to be apprised of needs for immediate service, product orders, or other customer requirements. In addition, sales associates carry alpha-numeric pagers so they can be immediately

(Continued)

can Express and the American Hotel Foundation for a study on best practices in the U.S. lodging industry.

Dr. Siguaw's research interests include personal selling, sales management, and channels of distribution. She has published and reviewed for *Journal of Marketing, Journal of Marketing Research, Journal of the Academy of Marketing Science, Journal of Strategic Marketing,* and others. She is a co-author of *American Lodging Excellence: The Key to Best Practices in the Lodging Industy,* available from the American Hotel Foundation.

Prior to entering academia, Dr. Siguaw spent 10 years in the corporate environment, including a sales position with General Foods Corp., a subsidiary of Philip Morris. Today, Dr. Siguaw frequently serves as a sales consultant.

Learning Objectives

After you have completed this chapter, you should be able to:

1. Identify and understand the factors that make personal selling such a critical component of promotion.

2. Discuss how selling has evolved.

3. Evaluate the advantages and disadvantages of sales as a profession.

4. Describe the selling environments and types of personal selling.

5. Understand and explain the sales process.

6. Appreciate the tasks and functions of the sales manager.

7. Recognize the legal and ethical issues confronting the salesperson and the sales organization.

contacted by ECOlink in the event of a customer emergency. Sales associates also utilize e-mail to stay in touch with each other and their sales managers, and many associates use laptop computers to generate service reports for customers.

Diverse career tracks are available for successful sales associates. Of course, they may choose to remain in a sales position, but management options abound. For example, Allan Schuman, president and chief executive officer of Ecolab, started his career in sales.

Regardless of the part of the world in which they operate, the Ecolab sales force adheres to its customer-oriented hallmark: "a focus on problem-solving and performance-based solutions for customers." This philosophy will continue to aid Ecolab's exceptional growth in future years.[1] ■

Everyone sells. If you have ever interviewed for a job, you were "selling" yourself by trying to persuade the interviewer that you would be the best person for the job. If you have ever tried to persuade a friend to do some activity that you wanted to do, you were "selling" your idea. When you were younger, you were "selling" every time you tried to persuade Mom or Dad to buy you something you wanted, and you were probably quite persistent in order to obtain what you desired. As an adult, you will find that you must "sell" regardless of what your job title is—whether it is selling your ideas to your boss, convincing your supervisor that you deserve a raise or promotion, or persuading customers to purchase your products. Not only do salespeople sell, so do accountants, engineers, financial analysts, insurance agents, stockbrokers, computer programmers, scientists, and nearly all other professions.

In the everyday selling situations mentioned previously, you have probably been successful in achieving your goals sometimes, but at other times have not been as successful. How can you improve your success rate? By learning to excel in sales through the acquisition of good selling skills. The material in this chapter provides you with a good start in that direction. First, we define personal selling and explain its importance in the promotion mix. Next, we discuss the evolution of personal selling and the pros and cons of the selling profession. We then present the various types of personal selling and selling environments, and the sales process. An explanation of the growing professionalism of selling through certification follows. We then discuss the sales management function, including the characteristics and duties of a good sales manager. We conclude by discussing sales force technology, and legal and ethical issues.

IMPORTANCE OF PERSONAL SELLING

Personal selling is one of the most important elements of the promotional mix and a critical activity of marketing management; it is also the most expensive form of promotion that a firm can undertake. Recent figures indicate that the average sales call costs the organization $113.96,[2] and typically only one sales call in three is successful. Why then would a firm choose to utilize personal selling and incur the associated costs?

There are three primary reasons why personal selling is such an important component of a promotional strategy. First, because personal selling involves direct communication between a sales representative and a prospective customer, it is the only form of promotion that allows the firm to immediately respond to the needs of the prospect. That is, as the salesperson makes his or her presentation, the salesperson can continuously adapt the presentation to the needs of the prospect. The ability to constantly adapt to the prospective customer, in turn, results in a greater number of sales. Second, personal selling allows for immediate customer feedback, so a firm has timely information regarding customer satisfaction with its offerings. Other forms of promotion, such as advertising, are company-sponsored communications directed toward the target market, but direct, *immediate* feedback from customers is not usually possible. Finally, personal selling results in an actual sale—the salesperson can leave a customer's office with an order in hand. Thus, personal selling is one of the few forms of promotion that can be *directly* traced to the sale of a specific product. Consequently, good companies truly value their sales forces.

Due to the costs associated with personal selling, this form of promotion is not used as often for consumer markets where there are many, geographically dispersed buyers whose individual purchases will not support the average cost of a sales call. Personal selling, however, is often a must in the business-to-business market, and may be used in consumer markets where buyers tend to be fewer in number, more geographically concentrated, and more inclined to purchase in larger quantities and dollar amounts. Additionally, personal selling is usually a necessity for complex products, high-involvement buying situations, and transactions involving trade-ins.

EVOLUTION OF PERSONAL SELLING

At one time, sales companies believed customers had to be forced into making a purchase. Salespeople utilizing the **hard sell** sought to make the immediate sale without being concerned about meeting the needs of the customer; this type of selling attitude resulted in singular transactional exchanges. That is, when customers purchased from these "hard sell" representatives and learned that the products truly did not meet the customers' needs, they recognized that the salespersons were not working to satisfy their customers. Consequently, these customers would not purchase from those salespersons again, so these representatives gained only a one-time transaction. Additionally, the hard sell sometimes bordered on the unethical or even illegal.

Today, many businesses are embracing approaches other than the hard sell; thus, personal selling has begun to stress the important concept of **relationship selling.** That is, the salesperson focuses on meeting customer needs, not just selling his or her product. When the salesperson clearly identifies customer needs and seeks to provide the best product to meet those needs, the salesperson is able to develop a long-term relationship with the customer.

Personal selling
is direct oral communication designed to explain how an individual's or firm's goods, services, or ideas fit the needs of one or more prospective customers.

Hard sell
involves trying every means to get the prospective customer to buy, regardless of whether it is in the prospect's best interest.

Relationship selling
requires the development of a trusting partnership in which the salesperson seeks to provide long-term customer satisfaction.

| Figure 13.1 | Where Will Your Customer Be Tomorrow? |

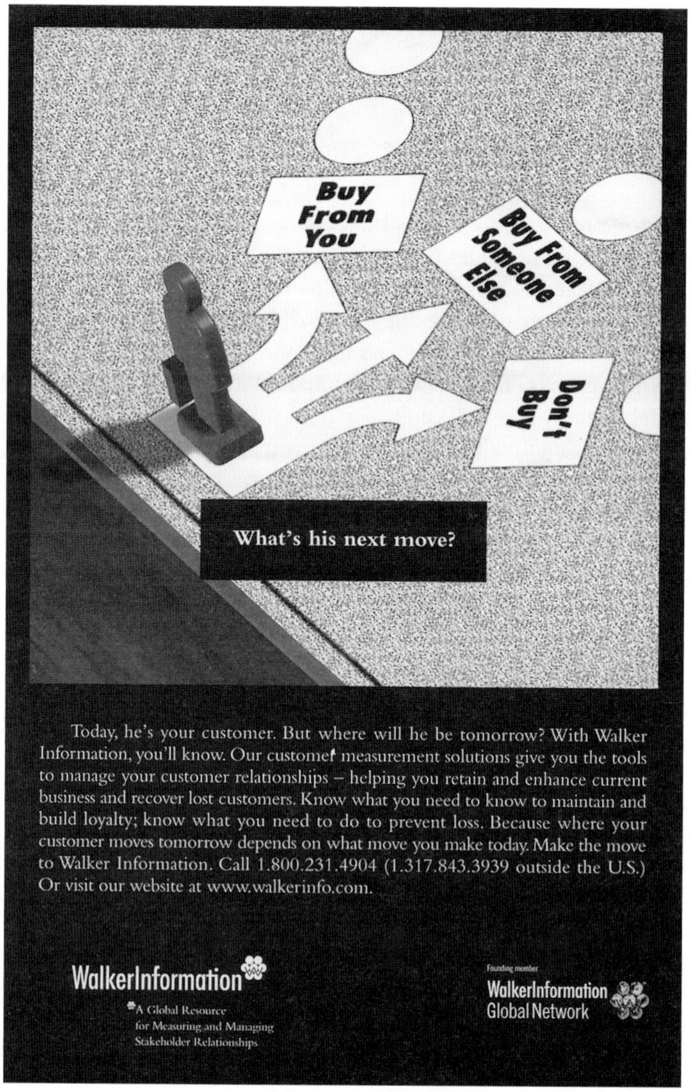

The importance of relationship selling emphasized.

Not only does the customer benefit from this relationship, but the salesperson benefits by way of the many future sales that are yielded from this relationship over time. In today's environment, the goal is to develop long-term relationships with customers.

WHY CHOOSE THE SALES PROFESSION?

LEARNING OBJECTIVE LO3

Several studies suggest college students are not interested in pursuing a career in the sales profession.[3] Unfortunately, the all too frequent portrayal of salespeople as fast-talking, glad-handing, slick characters with highly questionable ethics has tainted the sales profession, so that many people think of selling as an undesirable profession. They fail to realize how highly dependent large and small companies are on the revenues that salespeople generate.

Figure 13.2   Leading-Edge Technology

IT CHARMS ITS PREY, STRIKES QUICKLY AND DISAPPEARS.

IT'S YOUR TYPICAL BUSINESS SOFTWARE COMPANY.

(*SMOOTHUS TALKUS REPTILIUS*)

Don't make any sudden moves. Keep your ears open. And trust your instincts. That's the best advice we can give to someone looking for a new business management system. At Lawson Software, we encourage you to take your time. Talk to the current customers of every software provider you're considering. Find out whether those features you saw in the demo are actually up and running elsewhere. Ask about service and support. And, of course, ask about the products. Are they fully integrated? Process oriented? Web accessible?

fig. 1

fig. 2

The answers may surprise you. Lawson Software's enterprise financials, human resources, procurement and supply chain process suites lead the industry in providing innovative ways to gather, process and access vital information. We were the first to utilize web technology, enabling our customers to share information more freely and cost-effectively. Our Self-Evident Applications™ practically eliminate training costs. And our people are known for their accessibility and straightforwardness. In other words, we don't bite. Visit Lawson Software at www.lawson.com/guide or call 1-800-477-1357.

LEADING EDGE TECHNOLOGY WITHOUT THE ATTITUDE™

©1998 Lawson Software

LAWSON Software™

Contrasting the image of slick salespeople with truly professional salespeople.

If you do not think this is true, try staying in business without selling something! Further, salespeople provide the expertise in the field for customers seeking product information. Salespeople also spot and report potential competitive and market trends, so their companies can respond appropriately.[4] Consequently, salespeople are truly vital to the business world.

The outlook for employment in the sales profession looks great! Employment in sales occupations continues to grow. By the year 2005, the United States Department of Labor expects the number of people employed in sales positions to increase by 24 percent, placing sales as a growth profession 4 percent higher than any other profession.[5] Thus, in the next decade, the profession of selling probably offers more employment opportunities than any other career choice.

Sales positions also offer many advantages that are summarized in Figure 13.4. There is great flexibility in sales activities, so no two workdays are alike.[6] There are intrinsic rewards gained in meeting the needs of customers, and feeling that you have helped someone else. There are also extrinsic rewards. First, the potential compensation is quite high.

Figure 13.3   Classified Ads

Job opportunities in sales abound.

Figure 13.4   Benefits of Sales Occupations

- Flexibility in day-to-day activities
- Intrinsic reward from helping customers
- Good compensation
- Travel opportunities
- Limited supervision
- Increasing responsibilities
- High-visibility career track

The salary for a sales trainee averages $23,290, plus the costs of travel and entertainment create a total compensation package of $33,790 for the beginning sale representative.[7] Frequently, the compensation includes a company car, laptop computer, and cellular telephone to make the total compensation package even more valuable. For experienced sales

Figure 13.5   Desirable Salesperson Traits

executives, salaries range from $50,000 to over $200,000 per year.[8] Further, sales positions frequently offer travel opportunities, increasing responsibility, and limited supervision. Finally, it is also a great career track because of its high visibility. For example, a survey of 50 presidents and chief operating officers of privately-owned apparel companies noted that 57 percent of these top executives had started their careers in sales.[9] Moreover, the average yearly sales growth for companies whose Chief Executives Officers (CEOs) have sales backgrounds are higher, at 18.70 percent, than the average sales growth for all other companies.[10]

Sales, like all professions, also has its downside. The hours can be long, and it is not unusual for salespeople to experience **role conflict** (e.g., the firm may demand that the salesperson obtain a high price for the firm's product, while the customer may demand a low price), **role ambiguity** (e.g., many organizational departments—billing, shipping, production, marketing, public relations—may influence the salesperson's activities and create uncertainty about what is expected of the salesperson), and **job anxiety** (e.g., the salesperson must perform, often simultaneously, many tasks: meeting sales objectives, servicing old accounts and producing new accounts, developing and conducting effective sales presentations, developing product and competitor knowledge, submitting timely reports to the company, and controlling sales expenses).[11] Good salespeople must be self-motivated, organized, enthusiastic, adaptive, competitive, goal-oriented, empathetic, and most importantly, **customer-oriented,** as shown in Figure 13.5. This latter trait has been found to be the biggest differentiating factor between successful and mediocre salespeople.

Role conflict
is the anxiety caused by conflicting job demands.

Role ambiguity
is anxiety caused by inadequate information about job responsibilities and performance-related goals.

Job anxiety
is tension caused by the pressures of the job.

Customer-oriented
means the salesperson seeks to elicit customer needs/problems and then take the necessary steps to meet those needs or solve the problem in a manner that is in the best interest of the customer.

SELLING ENVIRONMENTS AND TYPES OF SELLING

Personal selling occurs in different environments, and each environment determines which types of selling are utilized. The three environments in which personal selling may occur are over-the-counter selling, field selling, and telemarketing.

Over-the-Counter Selling

Order taker
is a salesperson who only processes the purchase that the customer has already selected.

Suggestion selling
occurs when the salesperson points out available complementary items in line with the selected item(s), in order to encourage an additional purchase.

Order getter
is a salesperson who seeks to actively provide information to prospects, persuade prospective customers, and close sales.

Field selling
involves calling on prospective customers in either their business or home locations.

Professional salespeople
help prospective customers to define their needs and then suggest the best means of meeting those needs, even if that requires suggesting that the prospects use a competitive product.

Over-the-counter selling is usually conducted in retail outlets. As a consumer, you choose to enter a store where you may be greeted by a retail salesperson. If the store you have selected is heavily oriented toward self-service, your only interaction with a salesperson may be when you have to track one down to obtain an answer to a specific question you have regarding the merchandise. In this type of store, the over-the-counter salesperson will usually act only as an **order taker,** merely ringing up and appropriately packaging what you wish to purchase without imparting any product specific knowledge. On the other hand, if the store is oriented toward personal service, the salesperson is likely to try to identify what it is you are seeking and to help you with merchandise selection. The salesperson may even practice **suggestion selling.** For example, if you go into a store with the intention of purchasing a business suit, the salesperson may make suggestions regarding styles and colors. After your selection is made, the salesperson may suggest a tie or blouse that will match the suit. In these situations, the salesperson is acting as an **order getter.**

Field Selling

As in over-the-counter selling environments, salespeople involved in **field selling** may act as order takers, such as in the food industry, or as order getters, such as in the encyclopedia business. Many salespersons found in the field selling environment, however, are categorized as professional salespeople, national account managers, missionary salespeople, or support salespeople.

Professional Salespeople
Professional salespeople may be found in all industries, but especially in industries where products may be adapted to individual customer needs, such as high-tech computers. The companies for which they work may assign these professional salespeople a variety of job titles, including account executive, sales consultant, or sales representative.

National Account Managers
National account managers are highly skilled salespersons who call on key customers' headquarters sites, develop strategic plans for the accounts, make formal presentations to top-level executives, and assist with all the product decisions at that level.[12] Consequently, important customers associate one key person—the national account manager—with the

Figure 13.6   Selling Environments and Types of Selling

Selling Environments	Selling Types
Over-the-Counter	Order Taker
	Order Getter
Field Selling	Professional Salespeople
	National Account Managers
	Missionary Salespeople
	Support Salespeople
Telemarketing	Outbound
	Inbound

Careers in Marketing

Yellow Fever: A Career in Advertising Sales

In 1995, during her senior year at the University of North Carolina at Wilmington, Jennifer Ledford took a course in personal selling as one of the Marketing electives in her major. Her stellar performance in the course gave her confidence that she might excel in sales as a profession.

As her December graduation neared, she began interviewing for sales positions with various companies, and received several offers. However, while casually scouting out the Career Fair at the university, she struck up a conversation with representatives from Bell South. She learned that they were looking for account executives to call on and persuade businesses to place Yellow Pages ads in the company's telephone directories; she left her résumé with them. The next day Jennifer began Bell South's interview process, which stretched out over a three-day period. During this time, Jennifer was personally interviewed and successfully completed four different rounds of sales tests. A week later, Jennifer was offered the job.

In January 1996, Jennifer was sent to Atlanta for six weeks of training. During the day, Jennifer attended sales training classes with several other Bell South representatives, and at night she studied the course materials and did "homework." After the classroom training, the new trainees were split into teams and sent to very small, nearby Georgia towns where they had to begin selling their training "book," meaning they had to sell Yellow Pages ads for the telephone directory for each small town. Jennifer outsold all the other trainees on the training book!

After completing sales training, Jennifer was assigned to a territory in North Carolina. She and her sales team, which consists of a number of other account executives, travel to all the towns/cities within the territory. Depending on the size of market, the team may spend from one week to months in a town. Their objective is to call on every business in each community to persuade them to purchase Yellow Pages ad space. If the customer already has a current ad running, the account executive may encourage the customer to upgrade the ad—increase the size, add color or pictures—in the next directory.

Since her start with Bell South, Jennifer has outsold her team members on six of the eight books in which she has been involved. Jennifer attributes much of her success to her desire to excel. Although Bell South sets quotas for her, Jennifer creates her own personal goals. Her goal-directed efforts have paid off. In her first year with Bell South, her commission-based salary exceeded $35,000; she doubled this figure in her second year. In addition, she won three sales awards her first year, and four in her second year. She has also received an appointment to the President's Club each year. As a result, she has won all-expense paid trips to New Orleans and Cancun.

Jennifer loves her job and feels that it offers good compensation and opportunities for advancement. In fact, although she is currently the youngest Bell South Yellow Pages employee, she was recently asked to accept a management position. She is very excited to be a part of such a dynamic profession, and encourages other college graduates to enter the sales profession.

Source: Interview with Jennifer Ledford, June 1998.

---

vendor company, and the vendor company does not need to have its other salespeople call on all the local branches of a large, diverse customer. For example, the Procter & Gamble national account manager for Wal-Mart conducts sales presentations at the Arkansas headquarters site, and any decisions made pertaining to Procter & Gamble products at the headquarters level will then be passed down to all of Wal-Mart's retail outlets. Procter & Gamble does not have to have individual salespeople calling on every Wal-Mart store and trying to influence decision makers at that level. National account managers are expected to know their customers' businesses intimately; consequently, national account managers call on very few accounts. Indeed, it is not unusual for a national account manager to be responsible for just one customer, if the customer is a very large one. Customers who are assigned national account managers have very large sales potential and more complex buying behaviors, due to their multiple locations and various operating units. The national account manager's job is to provide these special accounts with greater attention and service to ensure that a partnership develops between the two organizations.

www.bellsouth.com
www.pg.com
www.wal-mart.com

Missionary Salespeople

Missionary salespeople differ from that of professional salespeople in that they do not seek to obtain a direct order from their customers. Although they are charged with providing product information to customers, their primary goal is to persuade customers to place orders with distributors or wholesalers. For example, the goal of Kraft Foods salespeople is to convince the managers of grocery stores to place orders with food wholesalers for

www.kraft.com

Kraft products. Pharmaceutical representatives are also missionary salespeople. Their job is to provide detailed information to physicians, so that the physicians will prescribe the drug to patients. These patients, in turn, will purchase the prescription from one of the pharmaceutical firm's resellers, such as a drug store.

Support Salespeople

Support salespeople do not actually perform all the steps in the sales process; instead, their job is to support the sales force in a number of ways. Technical support salespeople serve as technical advisors to the sales force and prospective customers on complex products such as data networking systems. They are often teamed with a sales representative to assist with the technical aspects of sales presentations. Other support salespeople, sometimes known as merchandisers, may set up product displays in the customer's business after the sales representative has obtained the customer's permission to do so. Still other types of support salespeople complete and follow up on order processing, and do other related administrative tasks in order to free the salesperson to spend more time with customers.

Telemarketing

The third selling environment is *telemarketing,* or utilizing the telephone for prospecting, selling, and/or following up with customers. Telemarketing may be *outbound,* in which case the salesperson uses the telephone to call customers. *Inbound* telemarketing, on the other hand, refers to those firms that have customers calling the vendor company to place orders; these firms often employ toll-free phone numbers as a convenience for their customers.

THE SALES PROCESS

LEARNING OBJECTIVE LO5

There are eight basic steps in the sales process: prospecting, the pre-approach, the approach, need identification, presentation, handling objections, gaining commitment, and follow-up. In the *traditional selling method,* little time is spent on the early stages of the process—especially the approach and need identification. Consequently, the prospective buyer is not usually convinced that they really need the product, so gaining commitment from the buyer is difficult, tedious, and time-consuming. In the *professional selling method,* a great deal of time is spent in the early stages—prospecting, pre-approach, approach, and need identification phases—so that commitment is gained as a very natural, or logical, next step. Essentially, customers are convinced that the product will solve their problem, or meet their need, because care has been taken to establish that need and link it to the benefits of the product early in the sales process. In the following sections, each of the eight steps in the sales process is discussed.

Prospecting

Qualified sales leads are potential customers that have a need for the salesperson's product, and are able to buy; that is, they have the financial means to purchase the product and the authority to make the buying decision.

Referrals are usually obtained by the salesperson asking current customers if they know of someone else, or another company, who might have a need for the salesperson's product.

Prospecting involves finding **qualified sales leads.** There are many ways to find sales leads: cold-calling, working trade shows, networking through industry associations or social organizations, and reading trade journals and newspaper business pages. One of the better means of finding leads, though, is through **referrals.** Generating just one referral is as effective as making 12 cold calls.[13] Prior to asking for referrals, the salesperson should ensure that the current customer is satisfied. But once a strong relationship has been established, the salesperson should not hesitate to ask for a referral. Referred leads usually mean faster closings, shorter sales cycles, and larger initial transactions.[14] Unfortunately, few salespeople ask for referrals, although over 80 percent of customers report they would gladly provide them.[15]

Figure 13.7   The Sales Process

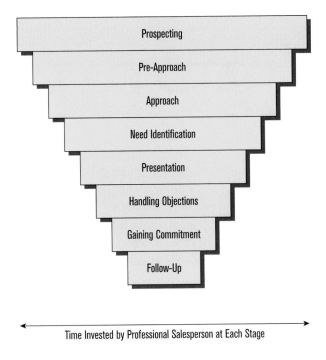

Prospecting

Pre-Approach

Approach

Need Identification

Presentation

Handling Objections

Gaining Commitment

Follow-Up

Time Invested by Professional Salesperson at Each Stage

Although most salespeople dislike making cold calls, nearly all salespeople must conduct some **cold-calling** at some point in their careers. Some cold-calling is done by the telephone. When utilizing the telephone for cold calls, most salespeople attempt only to secure a definite appointment with the prospect, although other salespeople will attempt to complete the sale over the phone. Cold-calling may also involve stopping by the customer's business or home location without a pre-arranged appointment. While this face-to-face interaction can be quite effective, some customers may have very strict rules concerning when salespeople will be allowed to see their employees for solicitation purposes. Salespeople should familiarize themselves with the company policies of prospective customers before dropping in to visit.

Many salespeople have a fear of cold-calling because they fear rejection. On average, a salesperson has to make three to five sales calls for every one sale; however, for some industries, this ratio may be 1 in 10 or 1 in 25 calls. Consequently, the salesperson should not become discouraged. The representative can remain motivated by remembering that sales is a numbers game—the sales representative will likely hear many "no's" before he will hear a "yes." Tom Hopkins, author of *How to Master the Art of Selling,* suggests recognizing that if each sale provides you with $100 in commission, and you average 5 calls per sale, then each "no" you hear is worth $20.[16]

Cold-calling
means contacting prospective customers without a prior appointment.

Pre-Approach

The pre-approach is the collection of information about the potential customer and the customer's company prior to the initial visit. In very much the same way that a job candidate should research a firm with whom he is going to interview, the salesperson should also research any prospective client and the client's company.[17] The salesperson should seek to find the answers to questions such as the following: Who will be the decision maker? What are that person's interests? What is that person's job title? What does the

Figure 13.8   Resealable Packaging

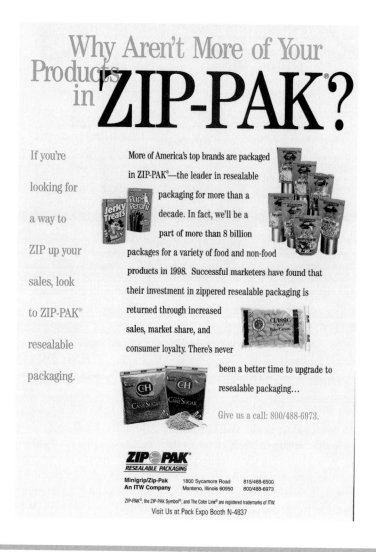

Prospecting through advertising.

company do? Who are their primary competitors? Which of the salesperson's direct competitors are currently doing business with the customer? What are the rules the prospective customer may have regarding salespeople? In other words, the sales representative should want to obtain as much information as possible about the prospect and their company. One quick source for this information may be the local library or the Internet. Many firms have Internet Web sites that provide useful company information. Researching the prospect and the prospect's company will indicate that the salesperson is serious about earning the prospect's business. This information also assists the salesperson in planning the initial presentation to the prospective customer.

The Approach

The approach is the development of rapport with the customer. Using the information the salesperson has already gathered, the salesperson begins developing a relationship with the customer. The salesperson wants to illustrate that he is working to understand and

Figure 13.9   Deloitte & Touche Ad

Using referrals to increase sales.

assist in meeting the prospective customer's needs. In this stage, it is important that the salesperson adapt to the potential customer's social style.

There are four basic social style categories, which are depicted in Figure 13.10.[18]

1. The **driver** is action- and goal-oriented, and makes quick decisions. To adapt to this social style, the salesperson should provide the bottom-line information first, and then work backward to fill-in essential details. The driver will want only the basic facts and will not want to socialize a great deal.

2. The **analytical** is very fact- and detail-oriented. This individual will require time to make decisions, while all the facts are carefully weighed. To adapt to this social style, the salesperson should inundate the analytical with facts and figures that can be supported with documentation. Like the driver, the analytical is not very interested in developing a personal relationship with the salesperson.

3. The **expressive** loves to socialize and will frequently base the purchase decision on the relationship with the salesperson. To adapt to this social style, the salesperson should

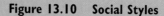

Figure 13.10   Social Styles

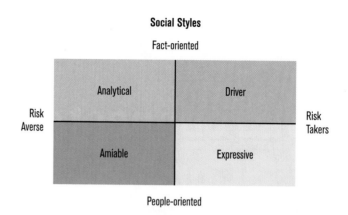

be prepared to establish a personal relationship with the expressive by telling anecdotal stories, by socializing outside the office, and by relating personal information.

4. The *amiable* tends to be a visionary with big ideas for the future, but is not a detail-oriented individual. The amiable is hesitant to make quick decisions and will seek consensus from others before reaching a purchase decision. The amiable also seeks to have a personal relationship with the salesperson, as this relationship helps reduce some of the anxiety that is felt about making a decision. To adapt to this social style, the salesperson should establish a personal relationship and should provide assurances that will reduce the amiable's feeling of risk. Further, the sales representative should present the product based on what it will do for the customer in the "big picture," and avoid getting into discussions of minute details.

Other factors must be considered in the approach stage. This is the salesperson's chance to make a good first impression. Consequently, the salesperson should dress neatly and professionally. Prospects should be greeted with a firm handshake and direct eye contact. Throughout the sales interview, the salesperson should maintain an open body posture to indicate interest and openness to the customer; that is, the salesperson should keep feet flat on the floor, body leaning slightly forward, direct eye contact, arms open (uncrossed), and hands open, palms slightly upward. The salesperson should also let the customer know that he is actively listening, by rephrasing or summarizing important points the customer has made.

Need Identification

Success at the need-identification stage of the sales process requires asking probing questions of the prospective customer to determine needs. These needs may be organizational and/or personal needs. Organizational needs may involve finance, image, or performance issues, whereas personal needs may involve the ego or personal image. To obtain information about the prospect's needs, the salesperson should ask open-ended questions. Such questions are designed to elicit a true expression of the prospect's opinions and feelings, regardless of whether these opinions are favorable or unfavorable to the salesperson's point of view. The salesperson should use open-ended, or probing, questions frequently throughout the sales presentation to ensure that the customer's needs and potential concerns are addressed. The key here is to learn what prospective customers want, not just try to sell whatever the salesperson has to offer.[19] After needs have been identified, the salesperson should gain the prospect's permission to begin the presentation.

Presentation

Customers buy products not because of the features they offer, but because of the needs these features satisfy. Therefore, the focus of the sales presentation is the salesperson's explanation of how the features of the product provide "benefits" that specifically address the prospect's needs or problems that have been previously identified. These benefits should answer the buyer's often unvocalized question, "What's in it for me?" For example, rather than simply telling buyers that a shampoo contains special conditioners (feature), the marketer must tell the buyers that their hair will be softer and shinier (benefit) because of these special conditioners. Or, as Marriott has learned: "The guest end-benefit is a successful trip; the hotel's role is to enable this success."[20]

www.marriott.com

Figure 13.11   Keeping the Customer Happy

Marriott: Emphasizing customer benefits, not just product features.

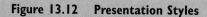

Figure 13.12 Presentation Styles

Flexible Presentations
- Identify customer needs
- Customize presentation

Memorized Presentations
- Does not address specific needs of customer
- Script features key benefits and selling points

Presentations may be flexible or memorized. ***Flexible presentations*** allow the salesperson to identify the customer's needs and customize the presentation specifically for the individual customer. This type of presentation is sometimes called a *need-satisfaction presentation,* and is the preferred method for professional salespeople. ***Memorized presentations*** require that the salesperson commit a scripted presentation to memory. This type of presentation, sometimes called a *canned presentation,* does not address the specific needs of each customer; however, the script has been built around the best key benefits and selling points of the company and the product. Salespeople who sell to consumers in their homes may employ this method of presentation. For example, book companies that sell door-to-door often have their sales representatives use memorized presentations with successful results.

During the presentation, the salesperson should be prepared to provide documentation for any statements of fact that are made. This documentation can come from a variety of sources, including letters of testimony from satisfied customers, independent reports, newspaper or magazine articles, company brochures or other literature, and product demonstrations. For example, a hotel sales manager might explain to a potential client that numerous companies have used the hotel's facilities to hold their annual meetings and have been quite satisfied. The salesperson should then produce letters of testimony from various companies that support the claim of satisfied corporate clientele.

To improve the effectiveness of their sales presentations, many salespeople now incorporate the latest technology via laptop computers. Thus, sales representatives may employ computer graphics and/or Web sites in their sales presentations to generate greater attention and interest from prospective customers.

Handling Objections

Prospective buyers frequently raise objections as to why they should buy a particular product. These objections may not mean that the prospect really is not interested in the product. Instead, objections likely indicate the salesperson has failed to provide adequate information to the buyer, or has not demonstrated how the product meets the needs of the prospect. Consequently, the prospective customer is afraid that they may be making a mistake in purchasing the product.[21] Thus, when faced with objections, the salesperson should approach the objection as a sign of interest on the part of the prospect, and provide information that will ensure the prospect's confidence in making the purchase. As a salesperson becomes more experienced, he will recognize that certain objections occur on a regular basis. After discerning what these common objections are, the salesperson should work to provide information early in the presentation that will counter these objections. For example, if the salesperson routinely hears prospective buyers say, "The price is too high," the salesperson should strive to emphasize the higher quality or special attributes offered by the product. Consequently, the prospect will recognize that added features/higher quality compensate for the higher price; thus, good value is still offered. Further, the salesperson should provide evidence of the higher quality of the product through brochures, independent consumer reports, product demonstrations, or other documentation.

Gaining Commitment

Commitment is gained when the prospect agrees to take the action sought by the salesperson. Usually, this means the buyer purchases the product, or at least signs a purchase agreement. However, prospects will not usually come right out and say they want to buy the salesperson's offering; the salesperson must ask for commitment. In other words, the salesperson must ask for the order, just as the interviewee should ask for the job.[22] Failure to ask for the order is frequently the cause of a salesperson's unsuccessful presentation. Indeed, salespeople do not ask customers to buy in approximately 70 percent of all sales calls! Yet, the sales profession recognizes the importance of this stage of the sales process, as evidenced by the numerous books written on gaining commitment.[23]

Follow-Up

The last step in the sales process, follow-up, requires that the salesperson complete any agreed-upon actions. Unfortunately, while salespeople may work very hard to get a customer, they frequently fail to follow through on their promises, so they cannot keep these customers. As you have learned in previous chapters, it is much more expensive to obtain a new customer than it is to keep an old one; consequently, it is imperative that the salesperson keep any promises he has made to the customer.

Additionally, the salesperson should stay in touch after the sale by writing thank-you notes, clipping and mailing newspaper articles of interest to the prospect, and calling on the customer on occasion just to ensure that the customer is still happy with his or her purchase decision.

SALES CERTIFICATION

As selling evolves into the development of strategic partnerships with customers, salespeople are heralding a new level of professionalism through sales certification. Several organizations now offer certification programs that are designed to increase the professionalism and expertise of the salespeople. Applicants for sales certification must meet a specified point criterion based on a combination of education and sales experience; pass a challenging written exam; provide professional references; and agree to adhere to a code of ethics.[24] They are also encouraged to participate in continuing education programs to maintain certification. Three organizations that offer salesperson certification programs are the Hospitality Sales and Marketing Association International (HSMAI), the National Association of Sales Professionals (NASP), and the Sales and Marketing Executives International (SMEI).[25] These certification programs are designed to increase the credibility and professionalism of the salesperson, and earn the public's respect for the sales profession.

www.hsmai.org

www.nasp.org

www.smei.org

SALES MANAGEMENT

Selling is the revenue stream of the corporation. Managing this vital function requires strong skills so that the sales force will continue to generate the money to fund the rest of the organization. Sales management, then, is the process of planning, directing, controlling, and implementing the personal selling function of the organization.

Sales managers must be good leaders who can recruit, train, motivate, and evaluate their sales representatives; manage territories; and develop sales plans and sales forecasts, while accomplishing the goals of the organization (see Figure 13.13).[26] They also need to be able to identify business opportunities and to create appropriate strategies. They must constantly encourage the sales team to exceed customer expectations, develop long-term relationships, and create added-value for the customer.[27]

Recruiting

Sales managers must recruit the right individuals for any open sales positions. A sales force composed of the right people makes a big difference in how large a company can grow. The individuals the sales manager hires should possess the attributes previously discussed: empathy, competitiveness, goal-orientation, customer-orientation, enthusiasm, organization, and self-motivation. In addition, the sales manager should recruit those individuals whose values and goals match those of the firm. This congruency will facilitate greater job satisfaction for the new recruit.

To hire the best salespeople, the sales manager should not rely solely on a résumé, but should pay close attention to how the candidate conducts him- or herself throughout the interview process. For example, if the first contact is by telephone, the candidate should ask for an appointment. If he does not, then likely this candidate will not ask for orders from prospective customers. The candidate should also demonstrate persistence by staying in touch with the sales manager, and not just waiting for the sales manager to call back. Additionally, the candidate should be a good listener. If the candidate is talking more than 50 percent of the time, then the candidate may not be effective at listening to prospects and customers. Finally, the candidate should ask for the job. If the candidate does not, the candidate will likely be too timid to ask for commitment from prospective customers.[28]

Many sales organizations have resorted to objective tests to assist them in selecting the best sales candidates. You may recall, from the Careers in Marketing box in this chapter *(Yellow Fever: A Career in Advertising Sales),* that Jennifer was required to pass several objective tests before being considered a prime candidate for the sales job. Some companies have determined that certain personality types perform better in their industries; therefore, after passing initial screening interviews, candidates are subjected to personality tests. Only those candidates that fit a certain personality profile move on to the next level in the selection process. Other companies test for certain sales skills such as adaptability or intellect. Again, those candidates not obtaining an adequate score are dropped from the pool of eligible candidates. Still other organizations subject their sales candidates to role playing early in the selection process. Those candidates who perform well in the role play progress to the next step. These somewhat more objective methods for selecting sales recruits are designed to reduce some of the difficulty firms have in finding the best candidates for their sales forces.

Figure 13.13   Sales Manager's Tasks

- Recruiting
- Training
- Motivating

- Compensating
- Evaluating
- Territory Organization

Sales Force Training

After hiring the best candidates, the sales manager must orient the recruits to the company culture. Additionally, the sales manager must train the new sales representatives on product and customer knowledge and selling skills. Although sales training is expensive—many companies invest between $22,500 to more than $100,000 to train a new sales representative—the payoff is worth it.[29] Indeed, experts suggest the return on investment for sales training is as high as $273 for every dollar spent.[30] Further, training is essential to the success of the sales force. Consequently, all sales representatives, regardless of how long they have been selling, should periodically receive training to keep up-to-date and to keep their skills honed.

The focus of training should be on product knowledge and sales skills. Good product knowledge is essential for making presentations and handling objections; whereas, the acquisition of good sales skills is necessary for moving effectively through the sales process. Sales representatives should be taught to identify the social styles of customers and alter their presentations for each customer type. In other words, sales representatives should know and practice adaptive selling. In addition, the sales force should learn to develop attention-getting openings and good listening skills, focus on customer needs, handle objections, and be able to close the sale. More advanced salespeople should be trained in strategic account management and the development of long-term customer relationships. They should understand the importance of identifying the organizational structure, key decision makers, and decision influencers in their customers' organizations. They must learn more about their customers' businesses and how they can help customers be more profitable. Finally, all salespeople should be trained in how to utilize the latest technology to improve their ability to serve customers.

Frequently, sales training requires travel to a distant location and overnight stays in a hotel. For companies with large sales forces, the cost of such training can run into millions of dollars, which precludes conducting frequent training. In today's high-tech world, though, many companies are training their sales forces with online or Internet-based learning. The salespeople involved are able to use their own computers and link into a training

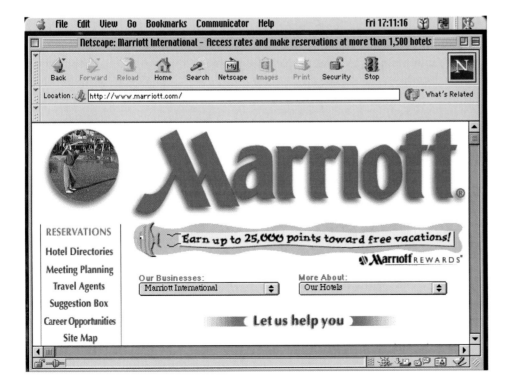

Marketing Technologies

Marriott Sales Force Surfs the Web

Similar to the Web site of many lodging chains, Marriott's home page on the Internet (www.marriott.com) allows the consumer to make hotel reservations at any of Marriott International's 1,900 properties, which include Marriott Hotels, Resorts and Suites; The Ritz-Carlton Hotel Company; Renaissance Hotels; New World; Marriott Executive Residences; Courtyard by Marriott; Residence Inn by Marriott; TownePlace Suites by Marriott; Ramada International; Fairfield Inn by Marriott; Springhill Suites by Marriott; and Marriott Conference Centers brands. But the Marriott Web site also serves as a critical tool for the Marriott sales force.

In recent years, the Marriott sales force has embraced a more consultative selling approach; consequently, Marriott is moving into a situation where the salespeople will no longer be responsible for selling just one property, but selling all properties to a specific market. Thus, the sales force members have become account managers serving multiple properties, a capability that would not be possible without Internet technology.

Richard D. Hanks, Executive Vice President of Sales for Marriott, explains that the Marriott Web site "allows each salesperson to search and configure any number of properties for a customer." For example, a large multinational firm, facing the possibility of a strike at 30 of its business facilities, wanted to have managers from other locations on hand to step in for striking workers. The firm telephoned Marriott with the locations of each of the firm's business facilities and inquired of Marriott's ability to lodge 40 to 50 people in each of the 30 cities. The firm also wanted to know exactly how far it would be from each of the firm's facilities to the closest Marriott property. Traditionally, the salesperson

handling this request would have had to call various properties in each of the 30 cities to find out which property was actually closest and to determine room availability. Many hours would have been consumed before the Marriott salesperson would have been able to provide all of the requested information to the client. In this case, however, the salesperson was able to turn to the Web site, which actually includes a mapping function of 16 million locations, and provide the client with the necessary data in less than an hour.

Overall, the Internet has allowed the Marriott sales force to better handle complex requests and develop a customized product for proposal development. Mr. Hanks envisions a much greater usage of the Internet as a Marriott sales tool in the coming years.

Questions

1. Visit the Marriott Web site at www.marriott.com and try out their mapping feature by typing in a destination city you might want to visit in the future. Then input any specific requirements you may have for the hotel.

2. What advantages does this feature offer the customer?

3. How could you use best use this Web site if you were part of the Marriott sales force?

4. Are there other features that you think this Web site should include to improve its usefulness to either the customer or the sales force?

Source: Richard Hanks, Executive Vice President of Sales, Marriott International.

session from their homes or from their hotel rooms, if they are on the road visiting clients. This technology allows the salespeople to come together in a virtual classroom where they can interact with classmates and the instructor.[31] Consequently, firms are now able to offer their salespeople more frequent training, without requiring that the representatives leave their sales territories and their customers.

Motivating the Sales Force

Sales representatives are individuals, and what motivates one, may not motivate the other.[32] Sales managers have to employ a variety of methods for keeping all of these diverse individuals motivated, or incited, to put forth maximum effort. After all, the sales profession can be a high-pressure job that involves frequent rejection. For some salespeople, working to beat the set quota and winning sales contests is a great motivator. Winning builds confidence and reinforces the notion that the salesperson is a great sales representative. Other sales representatives are motivated by extra training sessions that challenge them and groom them for upper management positions. Sales managers may also find some top-performing representatives are motivated by acting as a mentor to newer sales representatives, or by being sought for their advice and wisdom. Finally, some salespeople are most motivated when their strong customer service efforts are recognized throughout the company, such as printing a letter from a grateful client in the company newsletter.[33] The

Figure 13.14   Selling Technological Advances

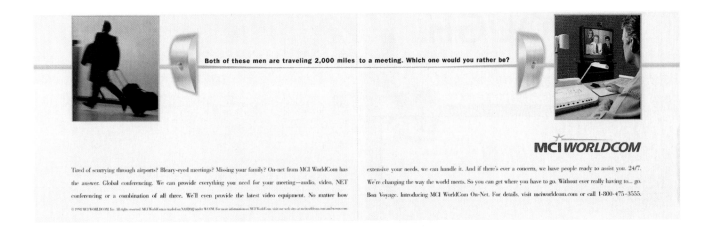

Sales managers can constantly motivate and evaluate even geographically dispersed sales teams using the latest communications technology.

sales manager must identify what best motivates each of his sales representatives and then strive to reward them in that manner.

Sales Force Quotas

Sales force quotas are used throughout the sales industry to provide further motivation to salespeople and to encourage salespeople to focus on the priorities of the company. Basically, the sales manager provides each sales representative with a reward when the sales representative, or in some cases, the sales team, reaches a prespecified performance level called the *quota*.[34] The quota should be high enough to encourage the sales force to put forth greater effort, yet low enough to appear obtainable. Otherwise, the quotas that the sales manager sets may serve to only discourage rather than motivate the sales force. Similarly, the reward offered for meeting or exceeding the quota should be of sufficient value. If it is too low, the sales force may deem that it is not worth their extra effort.

Sales Coaching

Coaching involves regular praising of salespeople to let them know their efforts are appreciated. It also involves rapport-building, open communication, and modeling behavior. The goal of the sales coach is to develop mutual trust and respect between himself and the sales force, which in turn encourages the sales force to listen to and follow directives from the sales manager. Good sales management feedback has also been found to reduce the role conflict and role ambiguity often associated with the sales profession. Finally, the sales manager serves as a model to the sales force so they know what behavior and actions to emulate. Sales manager coaching has consistently been found to motivate salespeople to improve their performance.[35]

Sales Force Compensation

Sales managers may also be responsible for determining how the sales force will be compensated for their efforts. Of course, the sales manager may choose to pay the sales force a *straight salary,* in which pay is based on units of time (year, month, week, or hour). This form of compensation allows the sales force to have greater security, but may reduce the desire for any one sales representative to put forth extra efforts, since a direct reward for

Figure 13.15 Map of Compensation by Region

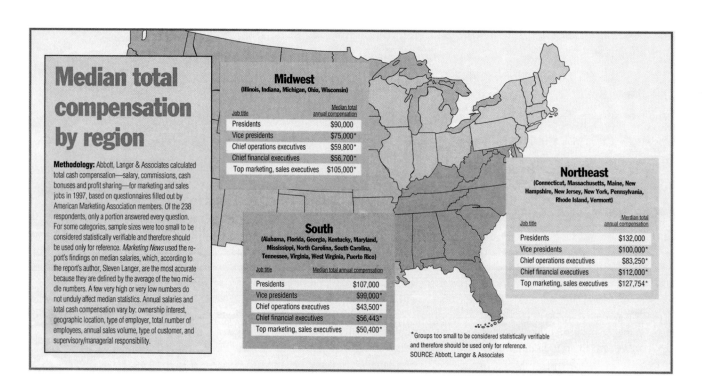

Median total compensation by region

Methodology: Abbott, Langer & Associates calculated total cash compensation—salary, commissions, cash bonuses and profit sharing—for marketing and sales jobs in 1997, based on questionnaires filled out by American Marketing Association members. Of the 238 respondents, only a portion answered every question. For some categories, sample sizes were too small to be considered statistically verifiable and therefore should be used only for reference. *Marketing News* used the report's findings on median salaries, which, according to the report's author, Steven Langer, are the most accurate because they are defined by the average of the two middle numbers. A few very high or very low numbers do not unduly affect median statistics. Annual salaries and total cash compensation vary by: ownership interest, geographic location, type of employer, total number of employees, annual sales volume, type of customer, and supervisory/managerial responsibility.

Midwest
(Illinois, Indiana, Michigan, Ohio, Wisconsin)

Job title	Median total annual compensation
Presidents	$90,000
Vice presidents	$75,000*
Chief operations executives	$59,800*
Chief financial executives	$56,700*
Top marketing, sales executives	$105,000*

South
(Alabama, Florida, Georgia, Kentucky, Maryland, Mississippi, North Carolina, South Carolina, Tennessee, Virginia, West Virginia, Puerto Rico)

Job title	Median total annual compensation
Presidents	$107,000
Vice presidents	$99,000*
Chief operations executives	$43,500*
Chief financial executives	$56,443*
Top marketing, sales executives	$50,400*

Northeast
(Connecticut, Massachusetts, Maine, New Hampshire, New Jersey, New York, Pennsylvania, Rhode Island, Vermont)

Job title	Merdian total annual compensation
Presidents	$132,000
Vice presidents	$100,000*
Chief operations executives	$83,250*
Chief financial executives	$112,000*
Top marketing, sales executives	$127,754*

*Groups too small to be considered statistically verifiable and therefore should be used only for reference.
SOURCE: Abbott, Langer & Associates

The salaries of marketing and sales executives compare favorably to other top corporate executives.

this effort will not result. The sales manager may choose to compensate the sales force on the basis of *straight commission,* in which pay is based on units of results. In which case, the sales representatives' pay is based on only how much they sell. For many companies, this has been the traditional means of rewarding the sales force. Straight commission, however, can create a great deal of insecurity in the sales representatives since some factors not in their control, like an economic recession, may cause a downturn in their sales and, hence, a downturn in their salaries. The third method by which the sales manager may compensate the sales force is through a combination *(salary plus commission)* of the previous two. Accordingly, the sales manager pays the sales force a sufficient base salary that provides just enough money for a very basic standard of living, but also pays a commission on sales that is high enough to serve as an incentive for extra sales efforts. This base salary plus high commission can allow a motivated salesperson to earn a six-figure income.

In today's environment where the focus is on long-term relationships, many companies are finding it necessary to adapt their method of compensating the sales force. The use of compensation plans incorporating high commissions on sales units only encourages the sales force to make quick sales without regard to actual customer needs, and does not encourage the sales force to take the time to establish relationships with their customers. Consequently, some companies have set up different types of compensation plans in which a portion of commission money may be tied to customer satisfaction, customer retention rates, share of customer's business, or other nonrevenue objectives, and only a small portion is linked directly to sales dollars.[36] Such a compensation plan facilitates long-term relationships between the salesperson and the customer, and in the long run, will better benefit the company.

Evaluation of Performance

Another task of the sales manager is the evaluation of the sales force's performance. Evaluation of the sales force should not be performed only once a year. In conjunction with sales coaching guidelines, sales managers should provide continual guidance and feedback.

The sales manager may choose to evaluate, or assess, the sales force on a combination of quantitative or qualitative factors. However, past studies have found that sales managers weigh subjective, qualitative factors more heavily than quantitative variables when assessing salesperson performance. The most popular qualitative factors used for evaluation are communication skills, product knowledge, attitude, selling skills, initiative/aggressiveness, appearance/manner, and knowledge of the competition. The most commonly used quantitative factors are sales volume in dollars, sales volume to previous year's sales, number of new accounts, net dollar profits, and sales volume by dollar quota. Although qualitative measures of employee appraisals have their value, experts suggest that sales managers should use more quantitative methods of evaluation to reduce bias in the evaluation process.[37]

Territory Organization and Management

Sales managers have a number of options when it comes to organizing the sales territories of their salespeople. Sales territories may be organized by product line or by geographical area; these methods have been the more traditional means of organizing sales forces in the past. Under geographical and product-line territory organization, the salesperson is often required to sell to *all* customers within a geographic area, although his/her product line may be somewhat limited. In either case, though, he calls on customers that represent dozens of different industries.

Today, however, more and more sales managers are organizing sales territories around customers.[38] In this case, the salesperson is asked to call on customers in one or two specific industries, regardless of where the customer is located geographically. This allows the salesperson to become an expert in the particular industry to which he is assigned. Consequently, the salesperson can develop a better understanding of the customer's problems, which facilitates the development of a close, long-term relationship between the sales representative and the customer.

Territory Allocation
After deciding by which method to organize the territories, the sales manager must then decide how to divide up the territories among the company's salespeople. There are two criteria that should guide territory allocation: (1) each salesperson should feel her territory offers as much potential as each colleagues' territory, and (2) each salesperson should feel the territory division does not require that she work any harder than any other salesperson. To achieve these goals, the sales manager must determine the *revenue potential* of each account (regardless of whether the account is a current or potential customer), and how much of the sales representative's time is required to service each account.[39] Then, individual sales territories can be allocated to the sales representatives in an equitable manner.

Territory Potential
The sales manager should also help the sales force maximize their territories' potential. The sales manager can accomplish this by encouraging sales representatives to devote their time and efforts to profitable accounts, and not waste efforts on accounts that are not potentially profitable to the company. Sales managers need to ensure that sales representatives are getting the maximum potential from all their accounts, and not meeting their quotas because of the large purchases of one key buyer. Finally, sales managers need to

utilize market research to ensure no potential accounts are being overlooked in any given territory.[40]

Once territories are established, the sales manager should review them on a quarterly basis. This will not only assist the sales manager with the sales budget, but may indicate where realignment of territories needs to occur. Key areas to check are those territories where the salesperson consistently exceeds, or fails to make, his quota. When the salesperson regularly exceeds the set quota, the sales manager should ensure that this occurrence is not due to the territory potential being so large that the sales representative has to make virtually no effort to reach quota. If this is the case, the quota should be raised, or if the territory potential warrants it, a new representative should be added to the area. In the case of the salesperson who never makes quota, the sales manager must determine if this is a function of a poor salesperson or of a territory with truly poor potential. In the latter situation, the representative's territory should be expanded to include new accounts.[41]

SALES FORCE TECHNOLOGY

The use of technology among sales forces is growing. Today's sales force and sales managers must be computer literate. Many sales organizations are now equipped with notebook computers that they use to electronically communicate with their offices several times a day. Indeed, sales data are now routinely processed electronically for faster service to the customer. Computers are also used to prepare customer presentations, and as

www.palm.com
www.oracle.com

Rapid advancements in technology means sales representatives have the convenience and flexibility of sharing and managing information while traveling. Hand-held devices, like 3Com's PalmPilot, can store thousands of addresses, years of appointments, and hundreds of to-do items, memos, and e-mail messages. Software enhancements, such as Oracle's Mobile OSM, allow sales representatives to stay connected with managers and customers, and access and transfer remote sales data.

noted earlier, may be a vehicle for sales training. Additionally, sales managers and the sales force are likely to have cellular phones and portable fax machines.

Sales representatives must be knowledgeable regarding spreadsheet software, and other sophisticated software applications that may be specific to their industry. Also, the sales manager wants to ensure that her representatives have a competitive edge by using a database that maintains customer information and tracks customer purchase behaviors.[42] Finally, some sales managers are suggesting their sales forces use a software program that allows a sales representative to enter her geographical location, and the program immediately provides a listing and location of all current and potential accounts in the area. Such a program allows the sales representative to use her time more efficiently.

LEGAL AND ETHICAL ISSUES IN SELLING AND SALES MANAGEMENT

Legal Responsibilities

A sales representative has certain legal obligations to their employer.

1. The salesperson is required to obey the instructions of the company.

2. The salesperson must act with "due diligence."

3. The salesperson is responsible and accountable for the company's property.

4. The salesperson is expected to exhibit loyalty.

5. The salesperson must relay information to the company that is relevant.[43]

Failure to meet these duties subjects the salesperson to termination, forfeiture of compensation, and liability for damages to the company.

At the same time, the company has legal responsibilities to the salesperson.

1. The company must comply with any agreement made between the company and the salesperson.

2. The company must act in good faith.

3. The company must reimburse the salesperson for reasonable expenses incurred while carrying out the business of the company.

4. The company is required to warn the salesperson of any risks associated with carrying out the company's business.

5. The company must protect the salesperson against legal liability for any damage, loss, or injury that occurs in the course of business.[44]

Unethical/Illegal Behaviors

Selling, like many other professions, offers many opportunities for unethical and illegal behaviors, and unfortunately, ethical issues are often closely tied to the type of relationships that sales representatives have with their customers and sales managers.[45] Some common unethical, and sometimes illegal, practices found in the sales arena include price discrimination and unfair pricing; gifts, gratuities, and bribes; misleading advertising; unfair competitive practices; defrauding customers; unfair credit practices; and price collusion with competitive firms.[46]

Salespersons must be especially prudent in claims made to customers regarding the performance, capabilities, or qualities of the salespersons' products. That is, sales representatives need to guard against overzealousness in their efforts to "make the sale." They must ensure that their presentations do not contain any false or misleading statements or promises about the products under consideration. Sales misrepresentation, which has recently come under heavy scrutiny from the courts, can result in large fines for the salesperson's company, and the salesperson's expulsion from professional organizations.[47]

Sales management can reduce unethical or illegal behaviors and the ethical conflicts often experienced by sales representatives, by communicating clear, unambiguous messages concerning appropriate behaviors in various situations likely to be encountered by salespeople. These messages should be strongly supported by company codes of conduct. Sales managers can further reduce unethical behavior by appropriately reprimanding sales representatives that choose to conduct themselves improperly.[48]

Sexual Harassment

An issue of special concern for salespeople and sales managers is sexual harassment. Because salespeople serve as boundary spanners between their own company and the companies of their customers, they can be especially vulnerable targets for sexual harassment by people outside of their own organizations (e.g., customers). That is, the relationships and social interaction necessary for the sales profession may make sales representatives especially susceptible to sexual harassment. Furthermore, sexual harassment affects both males and females.[49]

Sexual harassment may take the form of sexual favors, unwanted sexual advances, or other behaviors of a sexual nature, when submission to these behaviors becomes a condition of employment, affects employment decisions such as promotions, and substantially interferes with an individual's work performance, or creates a hostile work environment.[50] Sexual harassment results in reduced job performance and physiological and emotional health problems for the person who is harassed, which in turn affects the bottom line of the company. Consequently, sales managers should provide training on the nature and outcome of sexual harassment, to prevent sexual harassment from occurring within the company.[51]

Sales managers must take timely action if they are aware of occurrences of sexual harassment; otherwise the sales organization can be held legally responsible.[52] If the alleged harasser is a customer, the sales manager must protect the salesperson, even if such an action requires losing the customer's business.[53] Such protection may necessitate reassigning the salesperson, or providing supervision for the salesperson when he calls on that customer. In any event, the sales manager should not make it appear the salesperson is being punished for reporting sexual harassment.[54]

Chapter Summary

Personal selling is one of the most important elements of the promotion mix and a critical element of marketing. It is also, on a per contact basis, the most expensive form of promotion a firm can undertake—the average sales call costs $113.96. Personal selling involves direct communication between the sales representative and the customer. In comparison to other forms of promotion, salespersons can adapt their presentations to suit the needs of individual customers; immediate feedback from the customer can be responded to during sales presentations, and the effectiveness of personal selling can be more easily measured.

Personal selling provides exciting and challenging career opportunities. Salespeople are in a position to spot and report potential competitive and market trends, so their companies can respond appropriately. Salespeople often cite the intrinsic reward of helping customers achieve their goals as one of the primary benefits of a sales career. Moreover, selling is extrinsically rewarding. The total compensation package for sales trainees exceeds $33,000, and veteran salespeople can potentially earn $50,000 to over $200,000 depending on the industry. Further, sales positions frequently offer travel opportunities, responsibility, limited supervision, and high visibility. The CEOs of many firms started their careers in sales.

Personal selling occurs in different environments, and each environment determines which types of selling are utilized. The three environments in which personal selling may occur are over-the-counter selling, field selling, and telemarketing. Over-the-counter selling typically includes the sales jobs of order getter, order taker, and suggestion selling. Field selling includes professional salespeople, national account managers, missionary salespeople, and support salespeople. Telemarketing can be outbound or inbound.

Although sales occurs in many environments and many types of selling are available to job seekers, in general, sales offers an exciting, rewarding profession that now emphasizes relationship selling, and the development of partnerships based upon the long-term satisfaction of customers' needs. As sales has increasingly focused on relationship selling, sales organizations have sought to further the professionalism of sales representatives by offering certification programs.

The eight-step sales process was also presented. The sales process is composed of prospecting, the pre-approach, the approach, need identification, the presentation, handling of objections, gaining commitment, and follow-up. This process is designed to assist the development of long-term relationships because it necessitates the identification of customer needs and assists the salesperson in explaining how the salesperson's product can benefit the customer.

Because selling is instrumental in generating revenue for an organization, sales management requires the skills of planning, directing, controlling, and implementing the personal selling function. Sales managers are responsible for many tasks including recruiting, training, motivating, compensating, and evaluating the sales force. They are also responsible for sales territory organization and management, and the technological automation of the sales force. Finally, sales managers must be aware of potential ethical issues with which the sales force may struggle, and set appropriate guidelines to prevent and control these issues.

Key Terms

Personal selling is direct oral communication designed to explain how an individual's or firm's goods, services, or ideas fit the needs of one or more prospective customers.

Hard sell involves trying every means to get the prospective customer to buy, regardless of whether it is in the prospect's best interest.

Relationship selling requires the development of a trusting partnership in which the salesperson seeks to provide long-term customer satisfaction.

Role conflict is the anxiety caused by conflicting job demands.

Role ambiguity is anxiety caused by inadequate information about job responsibilities and performance-related goals.

Job anxiety is tension caused by the pressures of the job.

Customer-oriented means the salesperson seeks to elicit customer needs/problems and then take the necessary steps to meet those needs or solve the problem in a manner that is in the best interest of the customer.

Order taker is a salesperson who only processes the purchase that the customer has already selected.

Suggestion selling occurs when the salesperson points out available complementary items in line with the selected item(s), in order to encourage an additional purchase.

Order getter is a salesperson who seeks to actively provide information to prospects, persuade prospective customers, and close sales.

Field selling involves calling on prospective customers in either their business or home locations.

Professional salespeople help prospective customers to define their needs and then suggest the best means of meeting those needs, even if that requires recommending that the prospects use a competitive product.

Qualified sales leads are potential customers that have a need for the salesperson's product, and are able to buy; that is, they have the financial means to purchase the product and the authority to make the buying decision.

Referrals are usually obtained by the salesperson asking current customers if they know of someone else, or another company, who might have a need for the salesperson's product.

Cold-calling means contacting prospective customers without a prior appointment.

Additional Key Terms and Concepts

National account managers
Support salespeople
Outbound
Driver
Expressive
Flexible presentations
Revenue potential

Missionary salespeople
Telemarketing
Inbound
Analytical
Amiable
Memorized presentations

Questions for Discussion

1. In your day-to-day routine, identify situations in which you have had to persuade someone to accept your ideas or suggestions. What did you do? Were you successful or unsuccessful? Can you identify other ways that may have worked better?

2. As a regional sales manager for a large consumer goods company, you are interested in attracting college graduates to your sales force. Develop a marketing plan to do so. Determine why students are often not interested in sales as a profession and then develop the benefits of the sales position that will overcome these objections. What steps should be taken by your company to encourage more students to seek jobs in sales?

3. Think about the best salesperson you have ever met. What did you like about this individual? What traits did he possess? What made this salesperson better than others you have met? Describe the worst salesperson you have ever met. What did this individual do that you disliked? What made him the worst?

4. There are many methods of prospecting, that is, finding qualified individuals who may become customers. A few methods are listed in this chapter; however, do a little brainstorming and see how many more methods you can identify.

5. Pretend you want to convince a friend to join a school organization with which you are affiliated. What might you say? Using the steps in the sales process, outline your presentation to your friend. Next, role play against a classmate and see if you can present a valid argument based on the classmate's needs.

6. Assume the president of your company, a life insurance company, still believes in pushing his agents to use the hard sell. As the sales manager, how could you convince him that relationship selling is a better way of doing business? Compare the two methods of selling and write convincing arguments to support the use of relationship selling.

7. As Vice President of Sales and Marketing for a large hotel chain, you are reviewing the current compensation plan for the national sales force. Sales representatives are presently hired in at a low base pay of $18,000. After three months of training, these representatives are eligible for 20 percent commission on their sales, but their base pay disappears. Quotas are also set for each representative; those who fail to achieve at least 80 percent of their quota objective for three of four quarters are terminated. What do you think of this plan? Should you support it or should you develop a new one? If you choose to create a new compensation plan, what arguments will you make to the president of your hotel chain to persuade her to accept it?

8. As a good salesperson, you should prepare responses to objections that you expect will be forthcoming from potential customers. Two of the most common objections heard in sales are "Your price is too high," and "I need to think about it." Assume you sell cellular telephones; prepare a brief list of responses for each objection that will assist you in moving the customer toward commitment.

9. Automation and the Internet are rapidly changing the way selling is conducted. As this trend continues, do you think salespeople will be phased out of business? Why or why not?

10. A female sales representative, Carol, has been working for you less than six months. During this time, as part of an overall training program, you have placed her in the field for one-month stints with different, experienced sales representatives. Last night Carol called your home and requested an immediate meeting with you. You agreed to meet with her first thing in the morning. At the meeting, she informs you that one of the sales representatives you had assigned her to work with has made sexually explicit suggestions to her. You are surprised as this particular representative, Jim, has always been one of your top salespeople, and has a reputation for being a solid family man. He is also at least 20 years older than Carol. What should you do now?

Internet Questions

1. Visit the award-winning *Sales Doctors Magazine* at www.salesdoctors.com. (Be sure to include the "s" at the end of salesdoctors, otherwise you will not arrive at the correct Web site.) Discuss the sales tips submitted by readers to learn effective sales techniques that have worked for others. What was most interesting to you? Also, check out these other top sales sites:

   Sales Biz at www.salesbiz.com/salesbiz/

   The Selling Arena at www.psahome.com

   Guerilla Marketing Online at www.gmarketing.com

2. Visit www.monster.com, which contains 50,000 job listings for the United States and several other countries. Select sales entry jobs that may be of interest to you. What type of salesperson is needed? What qualifications are being sought in job candidates? What do you need to do to prepare yourself for these employment positions?

3. Just for fun, go to the LifeSavers Candystand Web site at www.candystand.com. The site, which attracts more than 300,000 visitors a month, is loaded with interactive games designed for children and teenagers, yet it also serves to convey product information. Further, LifeSavers obtains valuable verbatim comments and suggestions directly from its customers through the site's "What Do You Think?" feature. How might a Web site for an organization use a similar feature to increase its sales?

Endnotes

[1] Ecolab Web site (www.ecolab.com); Ecolab Fact Book; Mike Monahan and Pat Caldie of Ecolab, St. Paul, Minnesota.

[2] Michelle Marchetti, "Hey Buddy, Can You Spare $113.25?" *Sales & Marketing Management* (August 1997): pp. 69–77.

[3] Charles Butler, "Why the Bad Rap?" *Sales & Marketing Management* (June 1996): pp. 58–66; Andy Cohen, "Leading Edge: Sales Strikes Out on Campus," *Sales & Marketing Management* (November 1997): p. 13.

[4] Charles Butler, "Why the Bad Rap?" *Sales & Marketing Management* (June 1996): pp. 58–66.

[5] Caryne Brown, "Have I Got a Career for You," *Black Enterprise* 23 (February 1993): pp. 145–152.

[6] Ibid.

[7] Marchetti, "Hey Buddy, Can You Spare $113.25?"

[8] Michelle Wirth Fellman, "We're in the Money," *Marketing News* 32: 1 (March 16, 1998): p. 12; Abbott, Langer & Associates, *Compensation in Marketing/Sales Management and Support Jobs, 1998 Edition* (Chicago: American Marketing Association, 1998).

[9] Bill Seitchik, "Hired Hands: The Big Payoff," *Bobbin* 33 (June 1992): pp. 86–89.

[10] From April 1998 study by Sales & Marketing Executives International with results compiled by the Alexander Group. Study results are available through Sales & Marketing Executives International or at www.smei.org.

[11] Many articles and books have been published regarding the effects of role conflict, role ambiguity, and job anxiety. See, for example, Douglas N. Behrman and William D. Perreault, Jr., "A Role Stress Model of the Performance and Satisfaction of Industrial Salespersons," *Journal of Marketing* 48 (Fall 1984): pp. 9–21; Gilbert A. Churchill, Neil M. Ford, and Orville C. Walker, *Sales Force Management* (Homewood, IL: Richard D. Irwin, 1990); Eli Jones, Donna Massey Kantak, Charles M. Futrell, and Mark W. Johnston, "Leader Behavior, Work Attitudes, and Turnover of Salespeople: An Integrative Study," *The Journal of Personal Selling & Sales Management* (Spring 1996): pp. 13–23.

[12] Thomas R. Wotruba and Stephen B. Castleberry, "Job Analysis and Hiring Practices for National Account Marketing Positions," *The Journal of Personal Selling & Sales Management* 13 (Summer 1993): pp. 49–65.

[13] Sarah Lorge, "Selling 101: The Best Way to Prospect," *Sales & Marketing Management* (January 1998): p. 80.

[14] Ibid.

[15] Ibid.

[16]Tom Hopkins, *How to Master the Art of Selling* (New York: Warner Books, 1994).

[17]Brian Tracy, *Advanced Selling Strategies* (New York: Simon & Schuster, 1995).

[18]David Merrill and Roger Reid, *Personal Styles and Effective Performance* (Radnor, PA: Chilton, 1981).

[19]Richard Hanks, Vice President, Marriott Corporation, from presentation made at the Hospitality Sales and Marketing Association International Summit Conference (April 3, 1998), Anaheim, CA.

[20]Ibid.

[21]Dan Sherman, *You Can Be a Peak Performer* (Million Dollar Press, 1996).

[22]Sarah Lorge, "How to Close the Deal," *Sales & Marketing Management* 150 (April 1998): p. 84.

[23]For example, see Thomas J. Stanley (1997), *Selling to the Affluent: The Professional's Guide to Closing the Sales That Count* (New York: McGraw-Hill, 1997).

[24]For more information on sales certification programs, see Rolph E. Anderson, "Personal Selling and Sales Management in the New Millennium," *The Journal of Personal Selling & Sales Management* 16 (Fall 1996): pp. 17–32; Earl D. Honeycutt Jr., Ashraf M. Attia, and Angela R. D'Auria, "Sales Certification Programs," *The Journal of Personal Selling & Sales Management* 16 (Summer 1996): pp. 59–65.

[25]These organizations may be contacted at the following: Hospitality Sales & Marketing Association International, 1300 L Street, NW, Suite 1020, Washington, D.C. 20005, 202-789-0089; National Association of Sales Professionals, 8300 N. Hayden Rd., Scottsdale, AZ 85288-2458, 602-951-4311; Sales & Marketing Executives International, 5500 Interstate North Parkway #545, Atlanta, GA 30328.

[26]Rolph Anderson, Rajiv Mehta, and James Strong, "An Empirical Investigation of Sales Management Training Programs for Sales Managers," *The Journal of Personal Selling & Sales Management* 17 (Summer 1997): pp. 53–66.

[27]Rolph Anderson, "Personal Selling and Sales Management in the New Millennium," *The Journal of Personal Selling & Sales Management* 16 (Fall 1996): pp. 17–32.

[28]*Entrepreneur* Magazine's Small Business Square (1998), "*Entrepreneur*'s Special Report: Super Sales Tips," online at **www.entrepreneurmag.com/specialreport/saletip.**

[29]"Average Costs of Sales Training per Salesperson," *Sales & Marketing Management* 142 (February 26, 1990): p. 23; Gilbert A. Churchill, Neil M. Ford, and Orville C. Walker, *Sales Force Management* (Homewood, IL: Richard D. Irwin, 1990).

[30]R. R. Donnelley & Sons study cited by Anthony R. Montebello and Maureen Haga, "To Justify Training, Test, Test, Again," *Personnel Journal* (January 1994): pp. 83–87.

[31]Melanie Berger, "Technology Update: On-the-Job Training," *Sales & Marketing Management* (February 1998): pp. 122–125.

[32]Vincent Alonzo, "Motivating Matters: The Case for Trophies," *Sales & Marketing Management* (February 1998): pp. 34–35.

[33]Chad Kaydo, "Motivating Call Center Reps," *Sales & Marketing Management* 150 (April 1998): 82; Chad Kaydo, "How to Motivate Sales Stars," *Sales & Marketing Management* (May 1994): pp. 89–92.

[34]For a detailed discussion of sales quotas, see Rene Y. Darmon, "Selecting Appropriate Sales Quota Plan Structures and Quota-Setting Procedures," *The Journal of Personal Selling & Sales Management* 17 (Winter 1997): pp. 1–16; Charles M. Futrell, John E. Swan, and John T. Todd, "Job Performance Related to Management Control Systems for Pharmaceutical Salesmen," *Journal of Marketing Research* 13 (February 1976), pp. 25–33; Leon Winer, "The Effect of Product Sales Quota on Sales Force Productivity," *Journal of Marketing Research* 10 (May 1973): pp. 180–83; Thomas R. Wotruba, "The Effect of Goal Setting on the Performance of Independent Sales Agents in Direct Selling," *The Journal of Personal Selling & Sales Management* 9 (Spring 1989): pp. 22–29.

[35]For a review of sales coaching, see Gregory A. Rich, "The Constructs of Sales Coaching: Supervisory Feedback, Role Modeling and Trust," *The Journal of Personal Selling & Sales Management* 18 (Winter 1998): pp. 53–63.

[36]Geoffrey Brewer, "Brain Power," *Sales & Marketing Management* (May 1997): 38–48; Don Peppers and Martha Rogers, "The Money Trap," *Sales & Marketing Management* (May 1997): pp. 58–60.

[37]For a review of evaluation factors, see Donald W. Jackson, John L. Schlacter, and William G. Wolfe, "Examining the Bases Utilized for Evaluating Salespeoples' Performance," *The Journal of Personal Selling & Sales Management* 15 (Fall 1995): pp. 57–65.

[38]Geoffrey Brewer, "Brain Power," *Sales & Marketing Management* (May 1997): pp. 39–42, 46–48.

[39]Michelle Marchetti, "Covering Your Turf," *Sales & Marketing Management* (May 1997): pp. 51–57.

[40]Ibid.

[41]Erika Rasmusson, "Protecting Your Turf," *Sales & Marketing Management* (March 1998): p. 90.

[42]Don Peppers and Martha Rogers, "The Money Trap," *Sales & Marketing Management* (May 1997): pp. 58–60.

[43]Leslie M. Fine and Janice R. Franke, "Legal Aspects of Salesperson Commission Payments: Implications for the Implementation of Commission Sales Programs," *The Journal of Personal Selling and Sales Management* 15 (Winter 1995): pp. 53–68.

[44]Ibid.

[45]Edmund L. Pincoffs, *Quandaries and Virtues: Against Reductivism in Ethics* (Lawrence, KS: University of Kansas Press, 1986).

[46]Lawrence B. Chonko, John F. Tanner Jr., William A. Weeks, "Ethics in Salesperson Decision Making: A Synthesis of Research Approaches and an Extension of the Scenario Method," *The Journal of Personal Selling and Sales Management* 16 (Winter 1996): pp. 35–52.

[47]"Misrepresentation," *Supply Management* 3 (January 15, 1998): p. 44; Amy S. Friedman, "Chubb Among Latest to be Served with Sales Lawsuit," *National Underwriter* 100 (September 2, 1996): pp. 3, 65.

[48]Lawrence B. Chonko, John F. Tanner Jr., William A. Weeks, "Ethics in Salesperson Decision Making: A Synthesis of Research Approaches and an Extension of the Scenario Method," *The Journal of Personal Selling and Sales Management* 16 (Winter 1996): pp. 35–52.

[49]Cathy Owens Swift and Russell L. Kent, "Selling and Sales Management in Action— Sexual Harassment: Ramifications for Sales Managers," *The Journal of Personal Selling & Sales Management* 14 (Winter 1994): pp. 77–87.

[50]Leslie M. Fine, C. David Shepherd, and Susan L. Josephs, "Sexual Harassment in the Sales Force: The Customer Is NOT Always Right," *The Journal of Personal Selling & Sales Management* 14 (Fall 1994): pp. 15–30; Cathy Owens Swift and Russell L. Kent, "Selling and Sales Management in Action—Sexual Harassment: Ramifications for Sales Managers," *The Journal of Personal Selling & Sales Management* 14 (Winter 1994): pp. 77–87.

[51]Swift and Kent, "Selling and Sales Management in Action—Sexual Harassment: Ramifications for Sales Managers."

[52]Barbara Lindemann and David Kadue, *Sexual Harrasment in Employment Law* (Washington, D.C.: The Bureau of National Affairs, 1992).

[53]Fine, Shepherd, and Josephs, "Sexual Harassment in the Sales Force: The Customer Is NOT Always Right"; Swift and Kent, "Selling and Sales Management in Action—Sexual Harassment: Ramifications for Sales Managers."

[54]Swift and Kent, "Selling and Sales Management in Action—Sexual Harassment: Ramifications for Sales Managers."

Out on a Ledge: A Sales Case

Jessica is a new sales representative for Miermot Roofing. Her job is to call on various distributors, like building supply companies, and convince them to carry her company's products. She is also to seek out new housing developments, and attempt to persuade the developer to use her company's roofing tiles. She has recently learned that a local contractor, Stephen Owens, is developing 352 acres in the northwest part of the city for an upscale housing subdivision. In total, 175 executive-style homes (over 3,000 square feet) will be constructed. In addition, a recreation area with a large swimming pool and tennis courts will be situated in the center of the development. Near this, the centerpiece of the development, will be a large multipurpose building. One area of it will hold an exclusive, members-only restaurant, while the other half of the upper floor will offer private conference rooms and banquet rooms. The lower level will house a state-of-the-art spa, including saunas, a jacuzzi, a lap pool, an aerobics room, and a weight room.

Jessica has also learned that Kevin Jones, another contractor, is building a new nursing home facility across town. It will house the elderly who are no longer able to care for themselves; many may be bedridden. It will also serve as a residence for younger people with severe mental retardation. The facility will be quite large, as it will serve a heavily populated regional area that is not currently served by such an institution.

Jessica has scheduled upcoming appointments with both Mr. Owens and Mr. Jones. From the information she has gathered, Jessica believes her line of Casa ceramic roof tiles would be perfect for the new Owens' housing development and the Jones' nursing home facility. Although Stephen Owens has always used regular composition roofing in his previous subdivisions, Jessica is hoping she can convince him the Casa tiles would convey a special level of elegance and affluence that regular roofing just cannot do. The Casa tiles come in many styles, colors, and finishes, and they are guaranteed to last a lifetime, unlike regular roofing which must be replaced every 15–20 years. The Casa roofing tiles are also fireproof and can withstand even the worst weather conditions—even hurricane-force winds. Additionally, due to Casa's unique system, the tiles require less time to install than composition roofs.

Jessica knows Mr. Owens will be concerned about the price of the Casa ceramic tiles because they are twice the price of regular roofing materials. And while Mr. Owens wants the homes to look customized, he must also avoid using only the best materials in each one, as to do so would cause his homes to be priced above the market. She is also aware that Mr. Owens wants to avoid a cookie-cutter look in the subdivision; that is, he wants each house to have unique characteristics. At the same time, he wants the houses to have some congruency so that they don't appear to architecturally clash.

Jessica also believes using Casa tiles on the nursing home would provide Mr. Jones with a better, safer product than composition roofing shingles. Jessica knows Mr. Jones will also be concerned about pricing and appearance. He wants the facility to look welcoming to its residents and their families, but he must keep costs in line. One of Mr. Jones' biggest concerns, though, is safety. Many of the facility's residents are infirm and will be unable to remove themselves from any danger that might present itself. Consequently, every room in the nursing facility will be equipped with monitoring devices, smoke detectors, and fire alarms.

Jessica's sales manager, Michael Lyon, has asked Jessica to outline her sales presentation to Mr. Owens and Mr. Jones. He is especially interested in how Jessica will explain the benefits the tiles provide. He instructs Jessica to be prepared to tell these prospects how each will benefit from purchasing Casa tiles instead of using composition roofing. He also wants Jessica to prepare a list of possible objections that she may hear from Mr. Owens and Mr. Jones, and for each objection, she is to prepare a suitable response. Finally, Michael asks Jessica to write out several ways to ask for commitment from Mr. Owens and Mr. Jones. Michael knows from experience that actually closing the sale is often the hardest thing for new sales representatives to do. This preparation will help ensure Jessica is well-prepared for her meeting with these prospects.

Discussion Questions

1. Are Mr. Owens and Mr. Jones good prospects? Do they have a need for Casa tiles? If so, what are the needs that make them good candidates for these roofing tiles?

2. Prepare at least three statements that tie together a feature of the tile and the specific benefit it provides to Mr. Owens. Prepare three additional statements for Mr. Jones.

3. From the information given, what are some possible objections Jessica may hear from Mr. Owens and from Mr. Jones? How should Jessica respond to these objections?

4. How should Jessica ask for Mr. Owens' business? For Mr. Jones' business? Provide at least two statements Jessica could use to ask for commitment from each one.

Part 6

Pricing

Chapter 14
Pricing Strategies and Determination

Chapter 14

Pricing Strategies and Determination

Joel E. Urbany,

Professor of Marketing, University of Notre Dame

Dr. Urbany earned his Ph.D. from the Ohio State University. In 1998 he was awarded *Business Week's* Most Popular Professor Rating for the MBA program at the University of Notre Dame. In 1993 he received the Outstanding Second Year Professor award for an MBA program from the University of South Carolina, and in 1988 he won the Alfred G. Smith Award for Teaching Excellence from the University of South Carolina. Dr. Urbany is a member of the editorial review boards of the *Journal of Consumer Research, Marketing Letters* and serves as an invited reviewer for several publications including *Marketing Science, Journal of Marketing, Jour-*

In 1996, Post Cereal, a division of consumer products giant Philip Morris, faced a dire situation. Losing ground to industry leaders Kellogg's and General Mills, Post had seen its market share drop from 16.8 percent to 15.6 percent in a year's time (a very large decline in this market). In addition, private label brands—the unique brands that bear retailers' names—were sneaking up on the national brands. With improvements in quality over the years, along with maintaining a significant price advantage (often one-third less than name brands), store brands' market share had grown from 3 percent in 1987 to 10 percent in 1996. Consumers had started to grumble about the prices of national cereal brands and had also begun to vote with their dollars for other products. No food category had had more price increases than breakfast cereal since World War II, and consumers were outraged at having to pay over $4 a box for some brands. According to *The Wall Street Journal,* consumers had also begun to turn to "products like bagels, toaster pastries, and ready-to-heat microwave food." Volume shipments of cereal had actually shrunk by 1 percent in the year ending June 1995, reversing an average 3 percent growth rate for the previous 40 years.

Added to this pressure was the fact that consumer organizations had begun to put the heat on the cereal industry. Specifically, U.S. Rep. Sam Gejdenson (D–CT) and his House counterpart U.S. Rep. Charles Schumer (D–NY) released a report in March of 1995 entitled *Consumers in a Box: A Consumer Report on Cereal.* This report found that breakfast cereal prices had increased by 90 percent between 1983 and 1994, substantially more than other product categories. Their second report, issued in March of 1996 *(Consumers Still in a Box: The High Price of Breakfast Cereal),* continued to criticize the industry's pricing and advertising practices.

This led Post to act. On April 15, roughly a month after the publication of Gejdesnson and Schumer's 1996 report, Philip Morris announced price cuts of about 20 percent on its Post and Nabisco ready-to-eat cereals. Although Post held the third-place share in the market, its price reductions cut into Kellogg's market share significantly. On June 10, Kellogg's followed suit, announcing an average 19 percent price cut on selected cereals, including Frosted Flakes, Raisin Brand, and Fruit Loops. It did not take long for General Mills to go down the same path. On June 20, General Mills initiated an 11 percent price reduction on such name brands as Cocoa Puffs, Trix, and Lucky Charms.

Gejdenson and Schumer released a third report in 1997, which concluded that the 1996 price cuts had ranged between 11 and 20 percent (averaging 16 percent per box), netting consumers an estimated $238 million. However, Gejdenson continued to hammer on the industry, noting that some of the companies had cut prices only selectively (i.e., only on some brands). Shortly after the 1997 report was issued, Gejdenson was quoted as saying that "not only did the cereal companies cut their overall prices by less than consumers were led to believe, but just three weeks ago General Mills celebrated the one year anniversary of industry price cuts by increasing its prices roughly a dime a box." Further, the report was now critical of the industry's substantial reduction in couponing.

The outcomes? The overall cereal market has shrunk to $7.2 billion in 1998 from $8.0 billion just four years ago (the market declined 1.7 percent in the year ending

(Continued)

Learning Objectives

After you have completed this chapter, you should be able to:

1. Define price and explain the factors that determine a firm's prices.

2. Explain how cost-based pricing methods work and what their primary drawbacks are.

3. Determine a short-term, profit-maximizing price, and explain a firm's possible objectives that may make the price inappropriate.

4. Identify the strategic concerns in pricing decisions.

5. Evaluate reasons why base prices change over time in both business and consumer markets.

6. Have an up-to-date understanding of the implications of new technology for pricing behavior in the market, particularly price "customization."

nal of Marketing Research, and *Journal of Retailing.*

Dr. Urbany's research focuses on information economics, managerial decision making, and buyer behavior. He has consulted with and conducted executive education programs for a wide variety of companies including Bayer, Flagstar, Inc., Donnelly Corp., Milliken, Marsh Supermarkets, and Ambac International.

March 22, 1998 to 2.48 billion boxes). Kellogg's market share has dropped to 32 percent from 35 percent in 1993, representing a decline of approximately $500 million in revenue! General Mills is similarly struggling—its flagship brand Wheaties lost 12 percent of its market share in 1997, and the company has prices 17 percent above the industry average (57 percent above private label brands). The price cuts have not staved off competition from more convenient morning foods, and private labels have now achieved an 18 percent share of the market. Interestingly, though, prices have more recently been back on the rise. Quaker Oats raised its prices on several cold cereals 3.8 percent, following a 2.6 percent price increase by General Mills in the summer of 1997. Even with this price increase, Quaker Oats officials indicated that prices are still 6 percent below where they were in November 1995! Trends in healthy eating seem to be resuscitating sales for some cereal categories, and product innovation (e.g., reclosable bags) may be paving the way for further price increases.[1] ▨

Of the traditional marketing mix variables, the development of effective pricing strategies remains perhaps the most elusive. Consider the following sample of expressed opinions regarding pricing practices over the last 50 years:

> ". . . pricing policy is the last stronghold of medievalism in modern management . . . [Pricing] is still largely intuitive and even mystical in the sense that the intuition is often the province of the big boss."[2]

> ". . . for marketers of industrial goods and construction companies, pricing is the single judgement that translates potential business into reality. Yet pricing is the least rational of all decisions made in this specialized field."[3]

> ". . . pricing is approached in Britain like Russian roulette—to be indulged in mainly by those contemplating suicide."[4]

"Perhaps it is reasonable that marketers have only recently begun to focus seriously on effective pricing. Only after managers have mastered the techniques
of creating value do the techniques of capturing value become important."[5]

Pricing decisions are complex, not solely driven by cost, or demand, or public out-
rage. What factors influenced Post's initial decision to cut prices? They include the entry
of new competitors (private labels, bagels), pressure from an increasingly powerful consumer confronted with many new choices, rivalrous relationships within the industry, and
the added pressure from the political environment. As the industry declines, we then see at
least two competitors seeking to extract more profit by raising prices. In this chapter, we
explore the complex array of factors that influence pricing decisions and consider the role
of price in a company's marketing mix. The first portion of the chapter examines the basics behind setting base prices, the usual approaches that firms take, and how those approaches can be improved. The other half focuses on the factors that determine why base
prices change over time. We begin, though, with a definition of price.

WHAT IS PRICE?

So what is **price**? It is not just the number on the price tag in the store (although that is
clearly what most customers think of). In general terms, any exchange involves a price,
and it is not always monetary. As such, price can be or incorporate rent, tuition, wages,
salary, fees, fare, lease payment, interest rate, or time donated. In short, price is an exchange rate—it defines the sacrifice that one party pays another to receive something in exchange.[6] Our specific focus will be on *price as a monetary value charged by an organization for the sales of its products.* In this chapter, we will distinguish between two general
categories of pricing decisions: (1) setting a base price for a product and (2) making adjustments to that product's price over time (see Figure 14.1).

Price
is some unit of value given up by one
party in return for something from
another party.

DETERMINANTS OF BASE PRICE

Cost-Plus Pricing: The Natural (But Sometimes Wrong) Way to Set Base Prices

There are many factors that influence pricing decisions, but the one that businesspeople most
naturally think about is cost. Research conducted on pricing in large corporations concluded:

. . . the easiest way to think about a price is first to think like an accoun-
tant: price equals costs plus overhead plus a fair profit. *Cost-plus pricing,*

Figure 14.1   Basic Pricing Decisions and Primary Driver: Cost

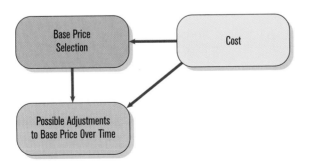

furthermore, is a useful ritual, with great public-relations advantages . . . a smart, prudent businessman) . . . admits only to wanting a "fair" return.[7]

It is no surprise that costs come into play quite significantly in setting **base prices.** Managers are generally (although not always) aware of their costs of doing business. As a result, the practice of setting prices based upon costs has become firmly established in the American marketplace. Both early and fairly recent studies of managerial pricing have found cost to be a dominant consideration in pricing decisions.[8] Below, we illustrate cost-plus pricing and evaluate its advantages and drawbacks. We then use the following example as a springboard to discuss other pricing methods and factors that influence pricing.

The Symphony

Let's say you're a manager for a symphony orchestra.[9] The symphony season is just starting in this town, and you've been hired as marketing director. One of your early assignments is to figure out a ticket price for a new concert series in the coming months. You have information about demand in the past (for several programs in the past, the symphony sold about 950 of its 1,100 seats). In addition, the following costs have been identified:

Fixed overhead	$1,500
Rehearsal costs	$4,500
Performance costs	$2,000
Variable costs per patron (programs, tickets)	$1 per patron

Note that some of these costs are fixed and some are variable. **Fixed costs** are costs that have no relationship to volume. They are, by definition, fixed. They do not change if more customers come to the show. The first three cost categories in our example (fixed overhead, rehearsal costs, and performance costs), totaling $8,000, are all fixed. **Variable costs,** on the other hand, are costs that are incurred for each customer. In this case, they are fairly small—only $1 per customer for tickets and programs.

To determine a price per patron using a cost-plus rule, you need to evenly spread all costs over each patron. Again, past history suggests an average attendance of 950 people. **Average total cost** can be calculated simply by adding an "average" fixed cost figure to variable cost.

$$\text{Average total cost} = \text{Variable cost} + \frac{\text{Fixed cost}}{\text{Unit sales}}$$

In the current case, average total cost would be:

$$\$1 + \frac{(\$1,500 + 4,500 + 2,000)}{950} = \$9.42$$

So, for every "unit" you sell (in this case, each of the 950 seats), the orchestra incurs a cost of $9.42, accounting for both fixed and variable costs.

Cost-Based Pricing Approaches

There are two common approaches to setting prices based upon cost. One is to use a standard rule-of-thumb mark-up. The second is to build up the price by adding together both cost per unit and desired profit.

Standard Mark-Up Let's say that the orchestra has always used a rule-of-thumb in the past: mark-up costs by 20 percent. This is effectively saying that, "for every unit we sell, we want 20 percent of the selling price to represent profit—an extra incremental profit over and above costs." The price can be easily calculated as follows:

$$\text{Selling price} = \frac{\text{Unit cost}}{(1 - \text{Markup \%})} = \frac{\$9.42}{(1 - .20)} = 11.775$$

So, you might charge a price of $11.75 (rounded off to the nearest quarter).

Target Return Pricing   Another similar approach would be for the orchestra to add a target profit to the unit cost figure (to cover both cost and profit):

$$\text{Selling price} = \text{Unit cost} + \text{Desired profit per unit}$$

The desired profit figure could come from a couple of places. First, there may be a rule-of-thumb that "we'd like to earn $2 a head coming in" (which would make the price $9.42 + $2.00 = $11.42). Alternatively, the desired profit per unit may be determined based upon the company's desired return on investment.[10]

So, let's say you apply the standard mark-up (as many retailers do, for example), and you set your price at $11.75. Have you done a good job? Well, yes and no.

▼ You have been smart in accounting for your costs, both fixed and variable.

▼ The pricing method is fair—it is steeped in tradition and is a widely accepted business practice.

For these reasons, no one could argue with your approach. However, there are some drawbacks:

▼ The fundamental flaw of this approach to pricing is that *it ignores demand.* This approach assumes a certain demand level as a given, independent of price. This, as we shall see, is at odds with one of the most fundamental relationships in all of business: quantity sold is a function of price. Generally speaking, as price goes up, demand goes down (and vice versa). Yet, you're assuming that 950 seats will be sold no matter what the price! Note what happens if different demand levels are assumed. The average unit cost would be much higher if we assumed sales of only 850 tickets (in fact, in this case, average unit cost would be $1 + [$8,000/850] = $10.41 rather than $9.42). This means that the $11.75 price would not be high enough to produce the 20 percent profit mark-up you desired. Alternatively, if ticket sales were 1,050, your unit cost would actually end up being lower ($1 + [$8,000/1,050] = $8.62), and your price could be lower than $11.75 and still produce the desired mark-up return on sales. In the marketplace, because price influences customer perception of value, demand is a function of price. In other words, price determines demand, not the other way around.

▼ In addition, a cost-plus pricing rule *fails to account for competition.* Competitors' prices have a significant impact on sales and profit outcomes as well, since consumers make choices from competitive sets of alternatives rather than a single one. So, for example, if a new symphony was started in a nearby city, it might well compete for the dollars that patrons might normally spend on our symphony. As such, this might have implications for how high we set our price relative to competing alternatives. In fact, failing to consider these issues can have devastating consequences. Wang Laboratory developed and introduced the world's first word-processing software in 1976. The product was a great success and Wang came to dominate the market. The company's pricing, though, was cost-driven. Competition eventually increased and growth slowed, yet the company did not bring down prices to maintain the value position of their software. The reason? Their pricing was basically cost-driven. Wang managers constantly recalculated unit costs and prices to capture increasing overhead cost allocations. Prices remained high and customers made their way to less expensive alternatives.[11]

As you can see, cost-plus pricing takes into account neither price sensitivity nor competition, both of which are essential considerations in setting prices effectively. Further, as noted earlier, cost-plus pricing generally involves allocating fixed costs on a per-unit basis—that is, treating them as variable costs—even though fixed costs do not change with the number of units sold.

The next sections provide some detail on the factors that can and should be considered in pricing. They review additional techniques and considerations for setting an initial base price for a product. We discuss next the most fundamental of all pricing concepts.

Demand

Elasticity of demand
is the relationship between the change in price and the quantity sold.

Our price of $11.75 is designed to cover average total costs for the projected 950 seats sold, and produce a 20 percent profit mark-up on costs. Yet, as discussed above, in setting price this way you have failed to consider one of the fundamental principles of economics: that price causes demand (not the other way around!). If your price is lower, demand usually is higher, and vice versa. Economists have made this concrete for us by articulating a simple concept called **elasticity of demand,** which helps us better understand the *relationship* between price and sales.

As will soon be discussed, elasticity of demand may be difficult to estimate. However, even the first few steps of thinking in terms of market response are very important and always helpful, even without precise knowledge of it. In fact, let's start with the assumption that you know very little about how much demand you'll get at different prices. Even under these circumstances, there is one brief analysis you can and should do before anything else, since it will help you frame good questions about potential demand. This is break-even analysis.

Break-even Analysis

Break-even analysis (BEA) is a standard analysis technique that should be performed for nearly every business decision, particularly those for new products. BEA doesn't tell you what your demand will be at a given price point, but it does tell the very important tale of what sales level you need for a particular price to be profitable. The key question in this analysis is "at a price of $11.75, how many units (seats) do we need to sell to break even?"

Break-even point
literally means "to have zero profit." It is that point at which total cost and total revenue are equal.

The calculation for the **break-even point** is straightforward:

$$\text{Break-even sales} = \frac{\text{Fixed Costs}}{\text{Selling price} - \text{Variable costs}}$$

In the BEA, we treat fixed and variable costs separately (as we generally should). The numerator of the equation includes all fixed costs, which we have to pay regardless of how many seats we fill. In the denominator, we have our *contribution margin.* For each seat, we make $11.75 – $1.00 = $10.75, which captures the contribution of each ticket sold to covering fixed costs and producing a profit. At the $11.75 price, our break-even sales are:

$$\text{Break-even sales} = \frac{\$8,000}{\$11.75 - \$1.00} = 744.2 \text{ tickets}$$

A Price	B Variable Cost	C Contribution Margin	D Fixed Costs	E Units Needed to Break Even	F Fixed Costs plus $2,000 Profit Goal	G Units Needed to Cover FC and Profit Goal
			Table 14.1	Break-even Analysis for the Symphony		
8	1	7	8,000	1,143	10,000	1,429
9	1	8	8,000	1,000	10,000	1,250
10	1	9	8,000	889	10,000	1,111
11	1	10	8,000	800	10,000	1,000
12	1	11	8,000	727	10,000	909
13	1	12	8,000	667	10,000	833
14	1	13	8,000	615	10,000	769
15	1	14	8,000	571	10,000	714

If we sell 745 tickets at a price of $11.75, we will just break even—that is, our total costs will equal our total revenue. Note that we can vary price and see how BE sales change. In Table 14.1, the break-even sales figures at various prices appear in column E. If we go with the highest price under consideration ($15), we need to sell 571 seats at a minimum—just to have zero profit at the end. At $8 per ticket, you would have to sell more seats than the auditorium's capacity (which is 1,100) just to break even. You may have anticipated the next step. Since we clearly do not want to just break even, how can we account for profit in this analysis? Let's say the symphony board views this series as the group's big money maker and would like to bring in a profit of $2,000 per show. How many tickets do you have to sell at each price to cover fixed costs and produce a $2,000 profit? To determine this, you simply add the $2,000 profit figure to the fixed costs and again divide by the contribution margin. So, at a price of $10, you would need to have "standing room only" (sales of 1,111 seats) to cover fixed cost and meet the profit goal, while at a price of $11.00, you would need to sell 1,000 seats.

Some very important information emerges from the figures in column G of the table. Again, since the auditorium has only 1,100 seats, it is clear that a price of $10 or less is not feasible. The price of $11.75 determined earlier could cover fixed costs and produce the desired total profit if 930 tickets can be sold ($10,000/[$11.75 – $1.00]). At a $15 price, we would need to sell 714 tickets to meet the profit objective.

At this point, we simply know what sales will be required at each price to cover costs and meet the profit objective. But the analysis also forces us to face an extremely important question: For a given price, *can we sell the requisite number of tickets*? (Can we sell at least 933 tickets at a price of $11.75?) In other words, what will demand be at each price point? To consider this question in more detail, let's take a short side-road here and introduce the concepts of the demand schedule and elasticity of demand.

The Demand Schedule and Elasticity of Demand

Generally, we know that as price goes up, fewer people will buy a product. As price goes down, the opposite usually happens. Tables 14.2, 14.3, and 14.4 present hypothetical **demand schedules** for wheat, automobiles (back in the Model T era), and movies.[12] The first three columns of each of these tables show what quantity (B) is projected to be sold at each price (A), and then the resulting total revenue (C = A * B). Consider the demand schedule for wheat (Table 14.2). If wheat is priced at $5, 9 million bushels per month will be demanded by customers. If the price drops to $4, demand jumps up, but only to 10 million bushels and total revenue actually drops. Total revenue drops for every lower price point in this table.

Demand schedules

provide a systematic look at the relationship between price and quantity sold.

		Table 14.2	**Demand Schedule for Wheat**		
A Price per Bushel	**B** Quantity Demanded (million bu. per month)	**C** Total Revenue (mil. $) (A * B)	**D** Percentage Change in Price	**E** Percentage Change in Quantity	**F** Elasticity (E)
$1	20	$20	−50.0%	25.0%	−0.5
$2	15	$30	−33.3%	20.0%	−0.6
$3	12	$36	−25.0%	16.7%	−0.7
$4	10	$40	−20.0%	10.0%	−0.5
$5	9	$45	0	0	0

Note: In calculating the percentage changes, we use the bigger number of the pair as the "base." Alternatively, the base could be the average of the two Ps or the two Qs being compared. This produces similar results.

In contrast, Table 14.3 illustrates Henry Ford's belief that consumers would be very responsive to the lowering of automobile prices. Dropping price from $2,500 to $2,000 increases sales by a factor of six (10,000 cars demanded jumps to 60,000). For nearly every price point reduction, the total revenue in column C increases.

Finally, Table 14.4 indicates that the demand for movies changes at the exact same rate as does price. When this happens, total revenue is the same regardless of the price charged.

		Table 14.3	**Demand Schedule for Model T Automobiles**		
A Price per Auto	**B** Quantity Demanded (thousands per year)	**C** Total Revenue (A * B)	**D** Percentage Change in Price	**E** Percentage Change in Quantity	**F** Elasticity (E)
$500	300	$150,000	−50.0%	33.3%	−0.7
$1,000	200	$200,000	−33.3%	40.0%	−1.2
$1,500	120	$180,000	−25.0%	50.0%	−2.0
$2,000	60	$120,000	−20.0%	83.3%	−4.2
$2,500	10	$25,000	0	0	0

		Table 14.4	**Demand Schedule for Movies**		
A Price per Ticket	**B** Quantity Demanded per day	**C** Total Revenue per day (A * B)	**D** Percentage Change in Price	**E** Percentage Change in Quantity	**F** Elasticity (E)
$1	1,200	$1,200	−50.0%	50.0%	−1.0
$2	600	$1,200	−33.3%	33.3%	−1.0
$3	400	$1,200	−25.0%	25.0%	−1.0
$4	300	$1,200	−20.0%	20.0%	−1.0
$5	240	$1,200	0	0	0

Economists quantify the relationship between price and quantity sold using a concept called *elasticity*. The **elasticity coefficient** is simply the absolute value of the percentage change in quantity divided by the percentage change in price.

$$\text{Elasticity coefficient } E = \frac{\text{Percentage change in } Q}{\text{Percentage change in } P}$$

Inelastic demand is reflected by an elasticity coefficient of less than 1. Take a look again at Table 14.2. Columns D, E, and F calculate these percentage changes (using the higher price point as the base for the calculations[13]) as well as the elasticity. The demand for wheat is inelastic; that is, the absolute values of the elasticity coefficients are less than 1.0. If the price of wheat were to drop, total revenue would drop. Note that the other side of this is that if price increases from a market price of $1, for example, then total revenue *increases*. If you're looking only at total revenue, then *higher prices are favored when demand is inelastic.*

Elastic demand is reflected by an elasticity coefficient of greater than 1. Demand is elastic in the automobile example for price changes, except the change from $1,000 to $500 (Table 14.3). Generally speaking, *when demand is elastic, lower prices are favored* (again, when considering total revenue). An excellent current day illustration of highly elastic demand is seen in the number of new customers entering the computer market with the advent of sub-$1,000 personal computers. By year end 1997, sub-$1,000 PCs accounted for 30 percent of all U.S. computer sales, and one-third of those sales were to consumers who had never purchased a PC before.[14]

Unitary elasticity means that the coefficient is exactly equal to 1. Table 14.4 shows that movies have unitary elasticity. In these cases, quantity demanded changes at the same rate as does price.

Profit-Maximization

Given the information contained in a demand curve, the firm can determine the **profit-maximizing price** by simply calculating the profit at each price point and determining which price produces the highest profit. To illustrate, see Table 14.5, which extends the Model T example from Table 14.2 by factoring in a variable cost per car of $350. With this additional information, the price that produces the maximum profit can be easily determined by identifying which price produces the largest **total contribution** (which equals [column C] Total Revenue minus [column D] Total Variable Cost). Given this demand schedule, the company would maximize profit for the car by pricing it at $1,500, which produces a total contribution of $138,000.[15] You can verify this by looking at **marginal revenue** and **marginal cost** (columns F and G in Table 14.5). These reflect the *changes* in total revenue and total cost from price to price. Lowering price from $2,500 to $2,000 is good: revenue jumps $95,000 while costs jump only $17,500 (marginal revenue exceeds marginal cost). The same goes for dropping price from $2,000 to $1,500 (MR = $60,000, MC = $21,000). But, when you drop to a price of $1,000, the marginal revenue generated is just $20,000, and is exceeded by marginal cost ($28,000), indicating that this would not be a profitable move.

If calculating maximum profit is this easy, why don't more companies set prices this way? In reality, other pricing goals—like meeting competition or achieving market share goals (discussed below)—tend to be used more frequently than profit maximization. This is partly because demand curves are difficult to estimate. While managers are likely to apply their own intuitive sense of market price response into their pricing, it is rare that they will have the nice, neat information about demand provided in Table 14.2. There are so many variables that affect sales in a given market that isolating the effect of price is quite difficult. However, it can be done several ways:

1. **Analytic Modeling.** The most sophisticated approach is to develop a statistical model that predicts sales based upon historical observations of sales, and such variables as the firm's price, advertising, and sales force levels, competitive tactics, and other

LEARNING OBJECTIVE LO3

Marginal revenue
is the change in a firm's total revenue per unit change in its sales level.

Marginal cost
is the change in a firm's total costs per unit change in its output level.

	Table 14.5		Calculating Maximum Profits for the Model T			
A Price per Auto	**B** Quantity Demanded (thousands per year)	**C** Total Revenue (A * B)	**D** Total Variable Cost (B * $350)	**E** Total Contribution	**F** Marginal Revenue	**G** Marginal Cost
$500	300	$150,000	$105,000	$45,000	($50,000)	$35,000
$1,000	200	$200,000	$70,000	$130,000	$20,000	$28,000
$1,500	120	$180,000	$42,000	$138,000	$60,000	$21,000
$2,000	60	$120,000	$21,000	$99,000	$95,000	$17,500
$2,500	10	$25,000	$3,500	$21,500	0	0

Variable cost: $350

variables that may influence demand (e.g., variables capturing economic conditions). This approach allows one to isolate the effect of price on demand.

2. **Experiments.** Firms might run experiments where they change prices in certain markets but not in others, allowing them to see more precisely how such price changes influence sales.

3. **Customer Surveys.** Another approach to identifying a demand curve is to survey customers or present them with purchase scenarios in which they evaluate the product and indicate their intention to purchase at various prices. One has to be careful about interpreting these results, as customers may overstate intentions. However, such an approach can be helpful in estimating price response.[16]

4. **Managerial Judgment.** Often, managers have good insight into sales response in a market. Although there may be some error in assessment, obtaining consensus estimates of demand across several managers who are familiar with a market can provide a useful picture of the demand curve.

At long last, let's return to our symphony pricing problem. Assume that you ask a convenience sample of target symphony customers to evaluate the likelihood that they would go to the symphony at different prices. You present the symphony as an alternative against other activities (e.g., baseball games, going out to eat, going to the art museum, going to a movie). Projecting your results to the larger population, you are able to estimate demand at each price point (see Table 14.6, columns A and B).

	Table 14.6	Elasticity and Total Revenue: Symphony Problem			
A Price	**B** Estimated Demand	**C** Percent Change in Price*	**D** Percent Change in Quantity	**E** Elasticity	**F** Total Revenue (A * B)
$11	1,129	−8.3%	2.6%	−0.31	$12,419
$12	1,100	−7.7%	3.2%	−0.41	$13,200
$13	1,065	−7.1%	5.0%	−0.70	$13,845
$14	1,012	−6.7%	3.9%	−0.58	$14,168
$15	973	0	0	0	$14,595

*Uses the higher price numbers as base for calculating percentage changes.

Note that we have dropped the prices under $11 from consideration since the break-even analysis showed them to be infeasible. You ask a few local experts in the industry to look your estimates over, and everyone concurs that they are reasonable. The elasticities calculated between price points (columns C–E in Table 14.6) clearly indicate that demand is inelastic (i.e., since the absolute value of all of the elasticity coefficients are less than 1). As in the wheat example earlier, this suggests that customers are not highly responsive to price. Demand does not drop off significantly when price is raised, nor does it increase substantially when price is cut. Note that total revenue only drops as you go from higher to lower prices.

However, we are not seeking to maximize total revenue. Instead we are seeking to maximize profit. As you know, variable cost is $1.00 and fixed costs are $8,000. What price produces the maximum profit? (Don't read ahead or look at Table 14.7 until you figure this out.)

The answer, perhaps not surprisingly, is the highest price ($15), which produces a total contribution of $13,622 compared to the next highest, $13,156, when price is $14 (see column E of Table 14.7). The table also provides fixed costs in column F and a total profit calculation in column G to confirm that the same price point ($15) is selected as profit-maximizing whether fixed costs are included or not. Incorporating fixed costs here is equivalent to subtracting a constant, which illustrates why fixed costs are not relevant to determining the profit-maximizing price in this example.

So, the profit-maximizing approach would have you setting price at $15,[17] selling approximately 975 tickets, and earning substantially more than the $2,000 profit goal.

How do you like the $15 price? A little further consideration illustrates why pricing is a little bit science and a little bit art. There actually are other considerations to be taken into account, which suggest that the short-term profit-maximizing price would not be the "right" price. In this case, the issue is auditorium capacity. The symphony board may be willing to give up some profit (as long as we've reached the $2,000 goal) in order to fill up the auditorium. Filling up the auditorium would be a public relations victory, allowing us to promote the fact that the performances are "sold out" and improving the symphony's outcomes in the longer term. Hence, other strategic considerations or objectives come into play. Figure 14.2 displays a larger set of factors, which may influence the selection of a base price. We examine these factors next.

Strategic Concerns

Important strategic factors that will play a role in setting a base price are positioning strategy, objectives, specific new product pricing strategies, and price-quality inferences.

Table 14.7	Total Contribution and Total Profit: Symphony Problem					
A **Price**	**B** **Estimated** **Demand**	**C** **Total Revenue** **(A * B)**	**D** **Total Variable** **Cost (B * $1)**	**E** **Total** **Contribution**	**F** **Fixed** **Costs**	**G** **Total** **Profit**
$11	1,129	$12,419	$1,129	$11,290	$8,000	$3,290
$12	1,100	$13,200	$1,100	$12,100	$8,000	$4,100
$13	1,065	$13,845	$1,065	$12,780	$8,000	$4,780
$14	1,012	$14,168	$1,012	$13,156	$8,000	$5,156
$15	973	$14,595	$973	$13,622	$8,000	$5,622

Variable Cost: $1.00

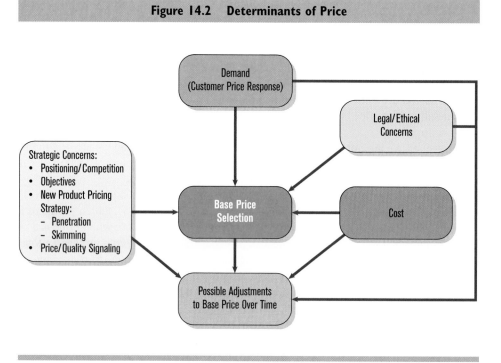

Figure 14.2   Determinants of Price

Positioning Strategy/Competition

Envision two different home furnishing stores in Atchison, Kansas (population 11,000). One store has reasonably inexpensive household goods (e.g., dishes, glasses, towels, bedding, and decorating items) and small pieces of furniture, many from national manufacturers. The store is neat and clean. It has something of a "warehouse" feel to it, with wire shelving and wide aisles and bright lighting. Employees make a little above minimum wage, and management makes every effort to keep costs low to maintain low prices to consumers. In contrast, consider another local store called Neil Hill's, which is set in a turn-of-the-century bank building in the downtown area and is run by an entrepreneur named Mary Carol Garrity. Inside, the store looks like a home, with high walls and many different rooms with carpeted floors. It doesn't have shelves. Instead, it has merchandise hanging from walls and ceilings, ranging from $2 candle holders to $7,000 French antiques. It sells the same kinds of products as the first store (home furnishings), but the merchandise is all very unique. Products come from large city markets and are hand-selected by the owner, who has the unusual knack of being able to identify and buy merchandise that will become popular before it becomes trendy. She changes the merchandise frequently, and regularly redecorates the store, often repainting the walls and changing the look of every room. The owner greets many of her customers by name, and works closely with them (many times after hours) on decorating ideas. Incredibly, 95 percent of this store's sales are made to people who live more than 50 miles away, primarily in Kansas City.

The two stores represent opposite ends of a ***competitive strategy positioning continuum*** anchored by "low cost leadership" on one end and "differentiation" on the other.[18] The first store might be any local, regional, or national competitor that competes by maintaining very low costs of purchasing and operation. Neil Hill's, however, seeks to create an absolutely unique (if not peculiar) shopping experience for customers. As a result, the two stores have very different pricing policies. The first store would likely attempt to maintain everyday low prices and have frequent sales. Neil Hill's, on the other hand, would have much higher prices, in part, because the cost of its unique merchandise is higher, but also because customers are *far less sensitive* to price than they would be at the more mundane price-oriented store.[19] One can find this strategic distinction between brands in

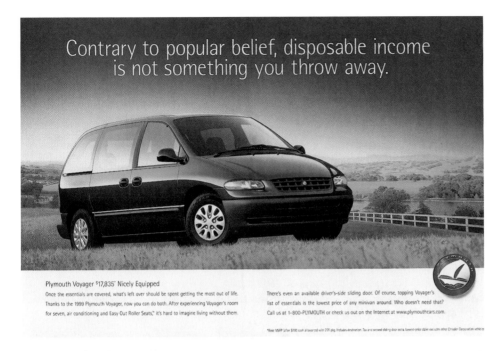

Two Chrysler van products positioned at different price points. Voyager = "lowest price of any minivan around." Town and Country = "Penthouse."

almost any product category (e.g., Timex versus Rolex, Honda versus Harley Davidson, private label cookies versus Pepperidge Farms). With uniqueness comes a price premium.

Returning to our symphony example, it is not likely, given the nature of the product category and the audience, that a cost leadership strategy would generally be effective. Differentiation, though, might involve positioning the symphony experience as distinct and prestigious; making it fun and unique—perhaps offering dinner and wine with performances, an opportunity to meet with members of the orchestra or special guest stars, or rotating concert locations between very unique, attractive locations. Such efforts would merit higher prices in part because costs would be higher, but also because of the higher value being returned to patrons.

A concrete illustration of how these different strategies capture value is provided in Table 14.8, which contrasts estimated income statements for Suave and Vidal Sassoon.

Table 14.8 Contrasting Prices, Volumes, and Margins: Suave (Low Cost Leader) vs. Vidal Sassoon (Differentiator), 1984		
Price, Cost, Volume	**Suave**	**Vidal Sassoon**
Unit price (to retailers, per ounce)	.063	.266
Unit Cost	.036	.072 (est.)
Volume (million ounces)	1,161	133
Income Statement (all $ figures in millions)		
Total revenue	$73.1	$35.4
Total variable cost	$ 2.8	$ 9.6
Total contrib. to fixed costs	$31.3	$25.8
Advertising	$ 6.0	$13.5
Promotion	$17.9	$ 5.8 (est.)
Operating profit	$10.7	$ 6.5
Return on sales	14.6%	18.4%

www.vidalsassoon.com

ROI
stands for Return on Investment.

Suave's high volume compensates for its very low price and margin. Vidal Sassoon, in contrast, offers a more distinctive and higher quality shampoo (along with a more intensive advertising campaign to support it), and as such charges retailers a price per ounce more than *four times* that of Suave's. Interestingly, Sassoon has only one-tenth the volume that Suave does, yet is estimated to be more profitable (as measured by return on sales) because of its substantially higher prices and margin. Each brand is profitable, but they travel different routes to profitability: one through volume and one through margin. Clearly, competitive positioning strategy is an important determinant of base price level.

Objectives

We saw in our symphony example that $15 was the profit-maximizing price. Yet, management may have another goal in mind: fill up the auditorium (i.e., maximize sales). *Goal-setting* (or *objective-setting*) is an important part of a firm's strategic planning process. Plans occur at both the corporate and business levels, and the objectives for a particular brand or business (like Suave) are in part a function of the corporation's objectives (Helene-Curtis). In a classic work on pricing in large corporations conducted by the Brookings Institute, four predominant objectives in pricing were identified: to achieve a target **ROI,** to create stabilization of price and margin, to reach a market share target, and to meet or prevent competition. We address each of those individually and then consider two other commonly-discussed objectives (profit maximization and survival).

Theory of dual entitlement
holds that consumers believe there are terms in a transaction to which both consumers and sellers are "entitled" over time. Cost-driven price increases are believed to be fair because they allow the seller to maintain her/his profit entitlement. Demand-driven price increases are not believed to be fair, however, since they allow a seller to increase per-unit profit.

Pricing to Achieve a Target ROI This was found to be the most common approach to pricing in the Brookings' study. Assuming a standard volume, firms add a particular margin to standard cost, which is expected to produce a target profit rate on investment. Across 20 firms, the target return figure averaged 14 percent, ranging between 8 and 20 percent.

Pricing to Create Stabilization of Price and Margin Generally, this approach reflects the goal of avoiding the fluctuations in prices that are characteristic of a commodity market. Managers in the Brookings' study reflected a desire to "refrain from upping the price as high as the traffic will bear in prosperity." This motive raises questions about the fairness of frequent price changes (particularly increases), a point which has been raised more recently in an economic theory labeled dual entitlement.[20] The **theory of dual entitlement,** in fact, argues similarly that concerns about fairness may constrain price increases.

Pricing to Reach a Market Share Target Particularly when there is no patent protection on a product, firms may pursue a market share target. In most cases, firms will seek a significant share upon entry into the market. For example, 3M's Scotch Brite Never Rust soap pad was priced aggressively enough to gain a 15.4 percent market share upon introduction, taking significant share from SOS and Brillo.

Pricing to Meet or Prevent Competition The logic behind meeting competitors' prices is straightforward. Meeting price cuts will eliminate a competitive disadvantage, while meeting price increases (although less likely) can fatten margins. This reflects a classic tit-for-tat strategy, which has been found to be effective in promoting higher profits for all players.[21] An additional benefit is that a consistent pattern of matching competitors' price moves sends rivals the signal that "undercutting price is not a good idea because we will simply match you." In the 1980s, following a horrific price war in a regional soft drink market, Brian Dyson of Coca-Cola Enterprises (a major Coke bottler in Atlanta) made it clear in an interview in *Beverage World* that CCE would not tolerate further aggressive pricing from rivals, noting that ". . . if somebody attempts to lowball the price on us, we will meet that. We insist on a level playing field."

Pricing for Profit Maximization As noted, the pursuit of this objective requires substantial cost and demand information. It has rarely been articulated as a goal by executives being interviewed about their pricing.

Pricing for Survival A company experiencing trouble may seek to produce an acceptable cash flow, to cover marginal costs, and simply survive. This may result when competition is especially intense, when consumer needs are changing, and/or when there exists substantial excess capacity. Chip-Maker Advanced Micro Devices reported a loss of $64.6 million in the second quarter 1998 in the face of price-cutting by rival Intel, a slowdown in demand for personal computers, and downturns in its other semiconductor businesses. In order to hang on in the face of competing with Intel's value, the company dropped average microprocessor prices from $105 to $86 in the second quarter, significantly cutting into margins.[22]

New Product Pricing

Two classic pricing strategies are commonly discussed for new products: skimming vs. penetration.

Price Skimming The strategy of **market (price) skimming** requires that a large enough segment of the customer market (innovators, see Chapter 8) is willing to pay the high price for the unique value that the product provides, and that competitors cannot quickly enter with similar products at lower prices. For example, VCRs were initially priced as high as $800–$900, but have gradually come down to around $200. Other products that followed similar price patterns are compact disc players, cellular phones, and multi-media computers. Intel is also well-known for this strategy, pricing its microprocessors for up to $1,000 per chip, but then dropping that price as new superior chips are developed. Skimming is a strategy that would obviously be more likely followed by a firm pursuing a clear differentiation strategy.

Price Penetration By pursuing a **penetration strategy** in the face of a retail book marketplace dominated by large chains such as Borders and Barnes & Noble (together having 13 superstores in Atlanta alone), a small bookseller called *Chapter 11* thrives with price-cutting.[23] The store's slogan is "Prices So Low, You'd Think We Were Going Bankrupt" and it prices aggressively, discounting best sellers 30 percent and all books at least 11 percent. Its new stores are small, in low cost locations, and designed for quick shopping, all tactics quite different from the larger competitors. Such a "penetration" strategy is the

Market (price) skimming
is a strategy of pricing the new product at a relatively high level and then gradually reducing it over time.

Penetration strategy
requires that the firm enter the market at a relatively low price in an attempt to obtain market share and expand demand for its product.

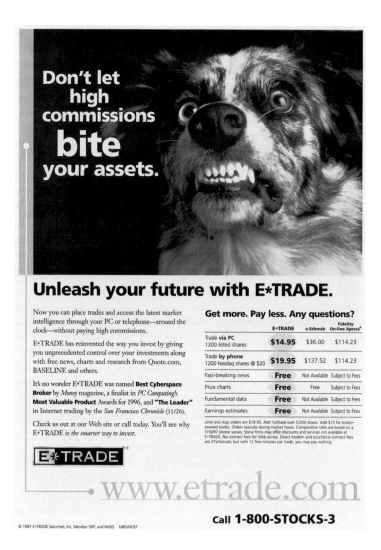

The Internet has opened up other avenues for companies to implement price penetration strategies. Shown here, E*Trade focuses on low price stock trading.

www.iflyswa.com
www.dell.com

opposite of a skimming strategy. Firms following such a strategy sometimes even enter a market at a loss, hoping to make up initial losses with longer-term repeat purchases. This strategy makes sense when competitive imitation will occur quickly, costs are likely to drop a good deal with increases in volume, and target consumers are relatively price sensitive. Southwest airlines has been able to obtain 75 percent of Florida's intrastate air traffic, while simultaneously increasing the size of the market through its low pricing.[24] Dell provides another good example of a price penetrator. With its customization process and Web-based order system, its costs are 9 percent below the industry average.[25] Penetration pricing is the standard strategy followed by low cost leaders.

Price–Quality Judgments

One of the downsides of penetration pricing is that customers may infer low quality from low price. This is most likely to happen under the following circumstances:

1. **When customers are uncertain about brand quality prior to purchase.** The quality of some products is difficult to judge because of their complexity (e.g., computers and cameras), while other products are difficult to assess simply because one cannot "try them out" prior to buying them (e.g., many consumer package goods like food products). For example a new household cleaner called Pathmark Premium was introduced at a price of $0.89. Pathmark had the same cleaning formula as market leader Fantastik, which was priced at $1.79. Despite aggressive in-store promotion of the new product,

it failed because its price could not convince consumers (who would have to buy it to truly assess its quality) that it would be effective.[26] Similarly, Omega destroyed a brand name, more prestigious than Rolex in the 1970s, by pursuing a penetration pricing strategy with a series of lower-priced products.[27] The latter case is a particularly frightening scenario in that the negative perceptions created by the low price overpowered a great brand name.

2. **When the risk to customers of a bad decision is high.** When the risk of a bad choice is high, customers will often rely on price to suggest quality. Risk may vary across product categories (e.g., in general, the perceived risk associated with service purchases is higher than that for goods), perceived variance among products within the category (e.g., risk is low if all refrigerators are perceived to provide roughly the same performance), and consumption situations (e.g., a disposable camera used to take pictures at a wedding or on the first day of first grade).

Although there continues to be a debate about how frequently (and when) customers use price as a signal of quality, it is fairly safe to assume that customer uncertainty about quality for a new brand is often very high, so that price–quality inference is a concern. It is also clear that firms pursuing differentiation strategies should maintain relatively high prices, for an additional reason beyond those discussed earlier: to credibly communicate their high quality to customers who may have uncertain quality assessments.

Legal Concerns

The laws of the land represent an additional set of considerations that influence the setting of base price. Prudent marketers must be attentive to legal and ethical concerns in pricing. As proof, consider a case involving John Taylor,[28] who in 1983 was an honest, hard-working division manager at Allegheny Pepsi, a large bottling company that controlled numerous Pepsi franchises. In late spring of that year, Taylor traveled to Norfolk, Virginia at the request of his boss, George Goodwin, to meet with Bob Miller, the regional division manager for their competitor, Mid-Atlantic Coke. Taylor listened at the meeting as George Goodwin described the significant price-cutting that had been taking place in the market and how it was hurting both firms' profit. Goodwin suggested ". . . let's forget all the problems we've had up to this point . . . let's just agree not to have it continue on." He then pulled out a notepad and wrote down prices for each size soda package, and these prices were agreed upon by both competitors.

Such **price-fixing** was fairly common in the soft-drink industry at this time. Yet, price-fixing is illegal because it restricts competition and leads to higher prices for customers. John Taylor did not design the price-fixing scheme, but he did help to implement it. On occasion, he would make sure his sales reps did not give customers any deals that would break the implicit agreement with Coke. When a disgruntled customer learned about the agreement, he contacted the police and the FBI. In the legal proceedings that followed, Taylor declined offers of immunity. Ironically, his boss George Goodwin—architect of the price-fixing plan—took an immunity offer and became a star witness in the federal government's case *against* John Taylor. In spite of recognizing Mr. Taylor's good character and the awkward situation in which the price-fixer received immunity, the judge was compelled to sentence Taylor to three years in jail and a $15,000 fine. Several others went to jail over this incident.[29]

This case illustrates the dramatic personal and professional consequences that can result from illegal pricing behavior. Ironically, Mr. Taylor did not benefit financially from the price-fixing arrangement, as he was just doing his job. Certain illicit practices can become commonplace in an industry and seem legitimate because "this is the way we've always done it." That's a slippery slope to walk, however. An understanding of the law will help in providing input into pricing decisions. Several types of pricing behavior are illegal in the United States. We review some of them next.[30]

Price-fixing
is a conspiracy to fix competitive prices.

Sherman Antitrust Act
prohibits any contract, combination, or conspiracy that restrains trade. It was passed by Congress in 1890 in an effort to prevent companies from controlling (monopolizing) an industry.

Cartel
is an organization of firms in an industry where the central organization makes certain management decisions and functions (often regarding pricing, outputs, sales, advertising, and distribution) that would otherwise be performed within the individual firms.

Price discrimination
occurs when a seller offers a lower price to some buyers than to other buyers.

Price Fixing

Price fixing is a violation of the Sherman Antitrust Act which prohibits any contract, combination, or conspiracy that restrains trade. It is one of the key reasons that cartels exist. Recently, Archer Daniels Midland pleaded guilty in 1996 to criminal charges of price fixing in the distribution of lysine (an amino acid that speeds livestock growth). ADM paid $100 million in penalties.[31] In their individual trials, the executives were found guilty in mid-September 1998 and prosecutors are seeking the maximum three-year sentence for their violating the Sherman Antitrust Act.[32]

Price Discrimination

Price discrimination is *not* illegal when the buyers are consumers (who do not compete with one another). But, if a manufacturer offers different retailers different prices without economic justification, this behavior violates the Robinson–Patman Act (1936), which amended the earlier Clayton Act (1914). Price discrimination is legal when:

1. **It is cost-justified.** For example, there may be cost differences in selling to two different customers. Wal-Mart, for example, obtains more favorable prices than smaller retailers because of its sheer size, and the economies that manufacturers obtain in selling in such high volumes. Alternatively, if the manufacturer's costs go up, one customer may be charged a higher price than another customer who bought before the price increase.

2. **The seller is attempting to match a competitor's lower prices.** The Robinson–Patman Act has a "good-faith clause" that allows a seller to charge a lower price to Store X than to Store Y, if a competitor is already charging Store X a lower price.

3. **There is no apparent harm to competition.**

Resale Price Maintenance

If I'm a manufacturer and you're a retailer selling my product, we are in violation of the law if we get together and *agree upon* some minimum price to be charged to consumers at retail. I can, however, suggest retail price levels to you. Further, I can stop dealing with you if you do not follow my recommendation.[33] The primary concern regarding *resale price maintenance* is that retail price competition not be eliminated by manufacturers and retailers agreeing upon specific minimum prices.

Predatory pricing
is a practice where one firm attempts to drive out rivals (usually smaller ones) by pricing at such a low level that the rival cannot make money.

Predatory Pricing

Predatory pricing has been alleged recently in the airline market. Spirit Airlines abandoned its Detroit–Philadelphia service when Northwest cut its one-way fares to $49 on all seats and added 30 percent more seats. Following Spirit's departure from the route in September of 1996, Northwest's one-way fare climbed to over $230 and the number of seats available dropped.[34] This is the classic pattern of predatory pricing in which an incumbent firm apparently attempts to drive out newer, smaller rivals with aggressive pricing. The practice of aggressive pricing and capacity expansion has come under intense scrutiny recently in the airline industry[35]—although no convictions have been made. It is quite difficult to prove predatory behavior, as federal law requires demonstrating that the alleged predator priced below an appropriate measure of its average cost and that it had a reasonable expectation that it would recoup its losses.[36] Northwest has argued that it is competing "fairly but aggressively"[37] and that smaller airlines often survive in spite of these aggressive tactics.[38] Predatory pricing continues to be "rarely tried and even more rarely successful."[39]

www.spiritair.com
www.nwa.com

Exaggerated Comparative Price Advertising

A very common price advertising tactic is to compare an advertised sale price to a former price; for example: Was $49.99, Now $29.99. Adding a comparison price has been found to significantly improve consumers' perception of savings and value in an advertised offer.[40] If such a comparative price is bona fide and "was offered to the public on a regular basis for a reasonably substantial period of time," it is perfectly legal.[41] Yet, many retailers appear to stretch this guideline, using comparison prices of questionable validity.

While such charges have been considered by many state attorneys-general, few cases have gone to trial. An exception was a case against May D&F, which resulted in a judgment against the retailer. May D&F had institutionalized a policy in which a profitable "intermediate mark-up" price was set for a product (e.g., $79.99 for a Krups coffee maker), but a much higher "promotional mark-up" price was also set ($119.99), which would be charged for as few as 10 days at the beginning of the six-month selling season. After the initial 10 days, the store would promote the item as "originally $119.99, now $79.99" for much of the remaining season. May D&F was found to be in violation of FTC standards for comparative price advertising.

www.krups.com

Ethical Concerns

There are many questions raised by customers and public policy groups about pricing practices, primarily concerning what often appears to be exorbitant prices charged by firms. As we noted at the beginning of this chapter, the cereal industry has been the target of such criticism, as has the pharmaceuticals industry and the banking industry (for excessive ATM fees). Consider these additional pricing scenarios:

▼ A hardware store raises its price for snow shovels on the morning after a big snow storm.

▼ A supermarket chain charges higher prices in its inner-city stores than its stores in the suburbs.

▼ A microchip manufacturer charges initially very-high prices for its new generation chip and then sharply reduce prices after the less price-sensitive buyers have purchased.

▼ A retailer prices dresses at 400 percent above cost.

▼ A consultant prices her services at $5,000 per day.

▼ A bank charges a $1.50 fee for ATM usage to customers who do not have an account with the bank.

Are these all ethical pricing practices? Are they all unethical? People from different backgrounds are likely to apply very different frameworks and standards in making their judgments. Further, we might judge them differently depending upon whether we are buyers or sellers! All of the above behaviors can be justified from a business perspective in one of two ways: (1) demand exceeds supply, so equating the two (specifically, rationing demand) requires high prices, and/or (2) the value or return that the buyer receives from each transaction merits these higher prices. These are powerful arguments, yet it should be noted that customers do not always buy into them. Higher prices—even those justified on the basis of supply and demand—may be viewed as unfair by customers and may create resentment, which will affect long-term business. For example, a majority of consumers surveyed felt that the hardware store owner in the first example behaved unfairly.[42] Two-thirds of consumers surveyed about recent ATM fees said they changed their usage in response to the fees, with 11 percent saying they stopped using ATMs altogether.[43] And we saw earlier in the chapter how the cereal industry's pricing has come down in response to public resentment.

Regarding ethical standards, the law defines minimally acceptable behavior. In some states, there are **gouging laws,** which attempt to prevent substantial price increases in response to special circumstances.[44] Business common sense defines another standard: one does not want to alienate customers and lose them. There are also personal standards of ethics, which each of us needs to think about and develop:

Firms can facilitate ethical marketing behavior from their employees by suggesting that employees apply each of the following tests when faced with an ethical predicament: (1) act in a way that you would want others to act toward you (the Golden Rule), (2) take only actions which would be viewed as proper by an objective panel of your professional colleagues (the professional ethic), and (3) always ask, would I feel comfortable explaining this action on TV to the general public? (the TV test).[45]

All of the factors discussed thus far—costs, demand, strategic, legal, and ethical considerations—have an impact on setting base prices *and* adjustments to base prices. The next section examines the specific reasons why marketers make changes in base prices over time.

EXPLAINING ADJUSTMENTS TO BASE PRICE OVER TIME

Most of the pricing decisions that are made for a product in its lifetime are *price change decisions*. Base price may change as a natural function of different objectives over the product life cycle, in response to specific **competitive price moves**, or as a function of special pricing tactics that may create a "schedule" of prices or even unique prices for different customers. In addition, prices may change for short periods of time as a result of the ever-popular practice of price promotion. Figure 14.3 summarizes each of these factors. We examine them in turn.

Figure 14.3   Determinants of Price Adjustments Over Time

Demand
(Customer Price Response)

Legal/Ethical
Concerns

Strategic Concerns:
• Positioning/Competition
• Objectives
• New Product Pricing
  Strategy:
  – Penetration
  – Skimming
• Price/Quality Signaling

Base Price
Selection

Cost

Product Life
Cycle Stage

Possible Adjustments
to Base Price Over Time

Competitive
Price Moves

Price Flexing:
Consumers
• Price Promotion
• Couponing
• Segmented Pricing
• Customization

Price Flexing:
Business Customers
• Price Shading
• Cash/Payment Discounts
• Volume Discounting
• Geographic Pricing
• Sales Promotion Allow.
• Creative Alternatives
• Customization

Source: Adapted from Peter R. Dickson, *Marketing Managmeent* (Fort Worth: The Dryden Press, 1996).

Variation in Objectives over the Product Life Cycle

As discussed in Chapter 8, the firm's objectives in pricing and other elements of the marketing mix will vary over the product life cycle. DuPont's classic strategy is described as follows:

> DuPont's strategy for the best part of 50 years was to develop "proprietary" products and to charge all it could get for them as long as the getting was good. So were the giants in data processing, pharmaceuticals, machine tools, and other high technologies. But these proprietary profits inevitably fire up competition, which invades the market with innovations of its own. Thus, the story of Western industrial progress is the story of the progressive liquidation of proprietary positions.[46]

In the introductory phase, paying attention to costs is important, and the firm may choose to pursue a skimming or penetration strategy (see earlier sections). In the growth phase, the firm is faced with the opposing forces of growing demand, yet increasing competition. This necessitates aggressive pricing if the firm cannot hold on to a unique product advantage. Maturity is likely to bring either stable, competitive prices or price wars if some rival attempts to get aggressive (again, this assumes no unique advantage of any rival). The firm should do its best to maintain stable prices and not rock the boat in maturity. Alternatively, some firms will attempt to innovate to break out of the commodity trap. In decline, the firm should try to keep prices up if the decision has been made to harvest the brand. The DuPont example above illustrates that there is likely to be a declining trend in prices over time, as an industry matures. Predicting when and how much to cut prices is an important task.

Competitive Price Moves

Very often, one firm's price change prompts a reaction from another. This is particularly true today as markets move quickly into maturity and face commodity status. Even brands as strong as Rubbermaid are affected by such competitive forces. Once a Wall Street darling and able to charge a price premium for its innovative new products, Rubbermaid has more recently had to lower prices in the face of growing competition and increasing retailer pressure to discount.[47] Similarly, Nucor Corporation has been faced with record steel imports coming from Russia and Japan (among others). Nucor recently announced a 20 percent price cut for its most important steel products.[48] When competitors enter and improve products as an industry moves into the growth phase of its life cycle, the incumbent almost always has to respond with price and/or innovation. This is dramatically illustrated in the case of Johnson & Johnson who, after seven years of R&D, completed a workable stent. A stent is a unique device that cardiologists use to keep arteries propped open following an angioplasty procedure. Incredibly, in just 37 months following introduction, J&J had 1996 sales of $1 billion and a 91 percent share of this market that it created. Yet, J&J's pricing remained quite high, and it was initially reluctant to give hospitals—even those accounting for a substantial volume of stents—breaks on price. As competitors (Guidant and Arterial Vascular Engineering) entered the market with equivalent or superior products, J&J did not respond quickly enough with product innovation or pricing, and its market share went into a free fall. Analysts projected it would be *8 percent* by year end 1998.[49]

It has been found that of all the marketing mix decisions, price is the one most likely to motivate a response from competitors.[50] Companies tend to keep a sharp eye on competitors' prices, especially in mature markets where overall demand is price inelastic. More recently, it has been found that management's decision to follow a competitor's price

www.nucor.com

change is affected by the decision-maker's perception of product price elasticity, as well as the behavior of other competitors.[51]

Price Flexing: Different Prices for Different Buyers

A naive look at pricing would lead to the assumption that once price is set, it then remains constant and is the same for all buyers. We have seen above that prices are not static—they may change in response to changes in the firm's objectives over the product life cycle and in response to competitive price moves. Yet, even more variation in prices is introduced by both established promotion and discount practices, and innovative pricing practices related primarily to new information technology. We discuss each of these in turn.

Price Flexing to Business Customers

Although the Robinson–Patman Act places constraints on manufacturers' ability to charge business customers different prices, there is a tremendous amount of price flexing that takes place in the form of a wide variety of discounts and allowances. For example, *Computerworld* reported recently that instead of using fixed pricing, "IBM will negotiate software charges on a case-by-case basis in emerging application areas such as electronic commerce and enterprise resource planning."[52] To IBM, this policy may have some appeal because potential customers view it as an opportunity to save money and as an incentive to try new applications. The cost to IBM, though, is the hassle of negotiating every deal and then managing nonstandard bid licenses. There are many other ways that a supplier may end up selling to different buyers for different prices. Traditional approaches that result in flexible prices include the following:

Price Shading This occurs when, during a negotiation, a salesperson reduces the base price of a product. This may occur for a variety of reasons, but is most likely due to the attractiveness of obtaining the business of the particular customer under discussion (e.g., a large customer or one who promises a potentially profitable long-term relationship). It may be common for some haggling to take place and may, in fact, be a badge of honor among purchasing agents to achieve some discount off-list price. For companies attempting to pursue a strategy of differentiation, though, price shading is not desirable. Booklet Binding, Inc. is a company who, through sales training, reinvented their sales culture to get the salesforce (and customers!) focused more on value-added products and services and less on price shading.[53]

Cash or Payment Discounts These are discounts the buyer receives for either paying in cash or paying promptly. A standard payment term is "two-ten, net thirty," meaning that the buyer gets a 2 percent discount for paying in less than 30 days (otherwise, they pay the total net cost). This practice effectively price discriminates between slow- and fast-paying customers.

Volume Discounting Customers who buy in larger volumes are often given more favorable terms. In fact, this is one of the key justifications for price discrimination in the eyes of the Robinson–Patman Act: total handling, shipping, and clerical expenses are lower (per unit) for larger volumes sold. Providing such discounts also encourages customers to purchase in large volumes, which has the added benefit of reducing the customer's probability of doing business with competitive firms.

Geographic Pricing It is common for business customers in different regions to receive different prices since transportation costs may be accounted for in pricing. Sellers deal with freight charges in different ways. **Free on board (FOB) pricing** requires the customer to pay for all costs of transportation. This simplifies things for the seller, but also creates a disadvantage in that her products become increasingly expensive to buyers who

Free on board (FOB) pricing leaves the cost and responsibility of transportation to the customer.

are geographically further away. An alternative to FOB pricing is **uniform delivered pricing,** where, in effect, the seller averages the costs of transportation across all customers. A good example of this is postage stamp pricing—it costs 32 cents to send a letter anywhere in the United States.

Uniform delivered pricing means that the seller charges all customers the same transportation cost regardless of their location.

Sales Promotion Allowances These are discounts that business customers (like retailers) receive for putting the manufacturer's product on sale to consumers for a particular period of time. As discussed in Chapter 12, such allowances have become a staple in business today, particularly in consumer package goods.

Creative Alternatives to Discounting[54] Consider the following recent scenario:

> Peregrine Inc., a Southfield (Mich.) auto-parts maker, is about to close a big contract with a paint supplier. In the old days, it would be pushing for an up-front price discount. But today, the company is getting very different concessions: a multiyear contract with guaranteed on-time deliveries, low reject rates, and no down-the-road price hikes.[55]

Suppliers are getting very creative today with their price-flexing, such that list price appears to stay fairly constant, but other tactics provide the flex. A few examples:

1. Some manufacturers provide generous financing for buyers. For example, Lucent Technologies, Inc. will sell equipment to startups in return for some negotiated share of the startup's (sometimes shaky) revenue.

2. Some customers are requiring long-term contracts with suppliers that guarantee no price increases for the life of the deal.

3. Suppliers may provide services (e.g., repairs) at no cost.

4. An increasing number of customers are demanding promises of quality improvement over the course of a contract at the same or lower price.

Similarly, economist Alan Blinder found in a series of interviews with executives in the 1980s that the most plausible explanation of why list prices often don't change very much is that, instead of changing prices, sellers adjust delivery lags or service.[56]

Price Customization While price-shading, discounting, and the creative approaches to price flexing discussed above clearly reflect some degree of "customizing" price for customers, new technology may make it possible for prices to be literally customized on a transaction-by-transaction basis, depending upon the conditions of supply and demand at the moment. In the free market, prices are determined by the interplay of supply and demand. Prices will be higher when demand exceeds supply and they will drop as more suppliers (or more supply) enter the market. Traditionally, supply and demand adjustments have taken days, weeks, or months to occur, as information about current supply and demand slowly found its way to buyers and sellers. However, new technology has made the sharing of supply and demand information nearly instantaneous, as "the Internet, corporate networks, and wireless setups are linking people, machines, and companies around the globe—and connecting sellers and buyers as never before."[57] Consider the following examples:[58]

▼ In some cases, this new, more customized pricing comes in the form of **online auctions.** For example, Grant Crowley, president of Crowley's Yacht Yard, Inc. in Chicago, recently purchased several PCs for his company via Onsale, Inc., a Net auction site, at a 40 percent savings over what he would have paid at the store.

▼ Using Energy Marketplace, businesses save money by shopping around for the best prices for energy (gas). The Web site introduces great efficiency into the system, as

www.onsale.com
www.energymarket.com

Onsale.com advertises "Your computer is here. At cost."

small and midsize gas providers can list their daily prices on the exchange and get access to a large market, and customers receive a wide variety of choices.

www.arbinet.com

▼ Arbitrage Networks has developed the technology—currently available in carrier-to-carrier exchanges—that will allow every long distance call to be instantaneously placed on the carrier that has the lowest price. This is accomplished by having carriers supply moment-to-moment information about their network availability and price, and then accessing computers and switching networks powerful enough to match incoming calls with lowest-cost carriers at any given time.

In short, new technology presents the capability to bring supply and demand together in real time, producing highly efficient markets and, potentially placing significant downward pressure on price. Such customization has become increasingly available in consumer markets as well.

Price Flexing to Consumers

While there are some circumstances in which consumers negotiate pricing (e.g., new or used automobiles), you may think that retailers use a "one-price" approach almost exclusively. With a few exceptions—particularly smaller local shops, antiques, and used goods—sellers do appear to charge fixed prices for products. Even the automobile industry is seeing a trend toward *single-pricing,* both with Saturn's innovative sales approach and the online car vendors (e.g., Auto-By-Tel, AutoVantage, or Microsoft's CarPoint), who each sell products at no-haggle prices.[59]

Interestingly, though, there is more price-flexing taking place in consumer markets than meets the eye. It takes the form of price promotion, couponing, segmented pricing, and, as we saw earlier with the business market, an increasing trend toward customization. We review each of these below.

Price Promotion Price promotion is a ubiquitous and effective practice in many situations, particularly early in a product's life, where the objective would be to encourage trial and to allow the seller to maintain a higher list price. The dangers of price promotion in more mature markets can be illustrated with a simple example.

Let's say that you and your competitor sell widgets to the consumer market, and you each have a reasonable market share and comfortable profit of $20 million per period. Your competitor, though, decides to try a 10 percent temporary price reduction and boosts his profit to $27 million for the period. This is fine for your rival, but you lost market share and your profit dropped to $13 million for that same period, since the competitor stole some of your market share. So, what do you do? You retaliate with a price promotion of your own! You and your competitor go back and forth like this a few times, and you find that you're both promoting at 10 percent off most of the time and that you're now each making $18 million each period, instead of the $20 million that you were making before the price promotions were initiated!

This is a version of the famous *prisoner's dilemma* from game theory, which poses the paradox of a joint decision-making situation in which the players do best by cooperating (not promoting), but each player has an individual incentive to "defect" (in our case, to do a price promotion). If both players defect, both are worse off. Once promotions get started, it may become clear to the firms that their profitability is lower, but they have a hard time raising prices back up again. Why is this so?

The reason is that consumers respond well to promotions, which encourages manufacturers to do more of them. As consumers grow accustomed to such price specials, any firm who does not price promote is likely to lose sales. So, promotions tend to increase over time, leading consumers to be more sensitive to price.[60] As this happens, retailers adapt to promotions by forward-buying or diverting product. All in all, everyone's attention goes to price, when price is highlighted through increasing promotion. As a response to this vicious cycle of competitive promotions—and its related inefficiency—Procter & Gamble instituted Every Day Low Pricing (EDLP) in the early 1990s (also known as *value pricing*). This pricing initiative was led by Edwin Artzt, a Procter & Gamble leader who is profiled in the Careers in Marketing box.

Couponing *Couponing* provides another means of price discrimination in that it gives some consumers—those who wish to take the time and effort to clip coupons—the capability of paying lower prices. Most coupons come from *free-standing inserts (FSIs)* in the weekend newspaper but, increasingly, coupons are available at point-of-purchase and printed on grocery register tapes. Into the early 1990s, manufacturers were following a trend of continuously increasing the number of coupons distributed per year. A significant change has occurred more recently in that consumer package goods firms, led again by Procter & Gamble, are looking into cutting back many incentives, including coupons.[61] *Advertising Age* reports that coupon distribution declined 10 percent to 276 billion coupons in 1997, attributing the change to a shifting of funds into frequent-shopper cards and electronic discounts. Note that coupon redemption fell 18 percent to 4.8 billion in 1997, reflecting an overall paltry 1.7 percent redemption rate. Signifying marketers' efforts to increase coupon effectiveness, coupon face value increased slightly, from 60 cents in 1996 to 61 cents in 1997.[62]

Price promotions
are short-term price reductions designed to create an incentive for consumers to buy now rather than later and/or stock up on the specialled product.

Everyday Low Pricing (EDLP)
refers to the pricing strategy in which a firm charges the same low price every day.

www.adage.com

Careers in Marketing

Edwin L. Artzt and the EDLP Solution

Edwin Artzt is a tough manager. His ability to carry out tough decisions brought about big changes at Procter & Gamble. One big change occurred in the early 1990s, a time when—like many consumer product manufacturers—Procter had gotten "hooked" on price promotions.

The Problem

Consider a situation in which a manufacturer gives a retailer a reduced price every so often, which allows the retailer to sell that product on special to its customers. In response to such promotions, retailers and end consumers show their appreciation by making purchases in large quantities. Competitors notice the success of price promotions and begin to offer them as well. Once all manufacturers begin offering price promotions, the deals begin to look the same to consumers. As such, some firms get more aggressive by having more frequent (or deeper) promotions.

Such aggressiveness (reinforced by retailers' and consumers' positive reactions) led in the 1970s and 1980s to an increasing reliance on price promotion. While Procter & Gamble had internal rules which limited promotional money to 5 percent of the sales of any business, this soon gave way to a new promotional reality. As Ed Artzt explained in the trade press:

> Somewhere along the line, and I don't know where, we argued that 5 percent was impractical, so let's raise it to 10 percent. Sooner or later the policy goes away . . . you've lost control. And you don't even know what it's costing you.

Amazingly, the company found at one time that 17 percent of product sales were made on deal, including some categories in which deals accounted for *100 percent* of sales!

The costs, P&G discovered, were substantial. Production schedules often swung wildly when a promotion was run. Factories would run overtime at the end of the quarter (when promotions were used to help managers meet their quarterly goals), but then would be underutilized for weeks. The volume of paperwork on promotional deals exploded and retailers disputed more invoices as billing became less accurate. At one point, P&G was making *55 daily price changes* on 80 different brands. On top of this, retailers began to develop warehouse and logistics capacity to enable them to load up on, (i.e., forward-buy) products offered by manufacturers at discounted prices. Alternatively, retailers might sell the extra product they purchased on promotion to retailers in other regions who did not have access to the manufacturer's deal (diverting).

The EDLP Solution

Procter & Gamble was the first company to have the courage to cut back on promotions in an effort to improve the efficiency of promotional spending. In 1991, the company adopted a "value pricing" or Every Day Low Price (EDLP) strategy to lower list prices and slash discounts across most of its U.S. product line to try to stem some of the above problems. For example, rather than charge a regular price of $4.65 per jar and occasionally a promotional price of $3.90, the EDLP or value price for the coffee might be $4.39. In 1992 and 1993, for example, the prices of Tide and Cheer were cut twice, the second time by 15 percent. In that span, the price of Pampers diapers was reduced three times, 17 percent in all. This reduced the price gap between Pampers and store brands (private labels) from 40 percent to 25 percent.

With the new policy, these "everyday" prices would be available all the time, allowing both P&G and its retailers to plan future sales with more accuracy and to avoid the dramatic up and down swings in sales attributable to price promotions. A growing number of big-volume retailers who themselves used EDLP policies (like Wal-Mart) warmed to P&G's policy very quickly. At the same time, there were many road blocks. For example, many conventional grocery retailers who had gotten accustomed to profiting from the ups and downs of promotional pricing were not happy, and some dropped Procter & Gamble products. In addition, the company soon came to the realization that Every Day Low Pricing would work only when a firm has "every day low costs."

Mr. Artzt pushed company management to identify major sources of cost reduction. Eleven teams were assigned to evaluate every inch of the company. One team assigned to benchmark the costs of the sales organization found in their analysis of 41 work processes that Procter had the highest overhead in the industry. The teams developed many cost reduction strategies, including methods that better coordinated orders across salespeople and a continuous replenishment system with retailers, whereby information at a given retailer's checkout was immediately transferred to P&G's computers, which allowed orders for product replenishment to be generated automatically.

Through Ed Artzt's leadership and persistence, P&G stuck to its guns and, as of 1993, the strategy was paying off. The company's measure of factory efficiency had increased from 55 percent to over 80 percent. The number of price changes dropped to almost zero and inventories in North American markets were down significantly. Although profits were down 31 percent in the year ending March 1994 as a result of charges due to plant closings and layoffs, P&G has since grown its profitability substantially, with year-ending profits of $3.4 and $3.8 billion in 1997 and 1998, respectively.

Sources: Jack W. Lindgren and Terence A. Shimp, *Marketing* (Fort Worth: The Dryden Press, 1996), 20-22; Dan Moreau and Joan Goldwasser, "New and Improved P&G Cleans Up," *Kiplinger's Personal Finance Magazine* 47 (September, 1993): 26; Silvia Sansoni and Zachary Schiller, "Is that Ed Artzt Pushing Pasta?" *Business Week* (April 15, 1996): 102; Bill Saporito and Ani Hadjian, "Behind the Tumult at P&G," *Fortune* 129 (March 7, 1994): 74+;

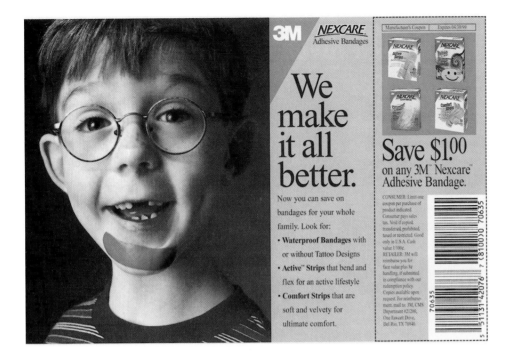

A free-standing insert.

www.Quicken.Com

Pricing for Different Segments Marketers very often have different marketing programs for different consumer segments.

1. *Geographic Segments.* It is possible that price sensitivity varies across geographic regions. For example, some grocery retailers have different price zones and prices are likely to vary across those zones. Competition and consumer profiles may differ between geographic segments. To generate interest among potential patrons in outlying areas, the symphony (discussed earlier) might plan smaller, fun ensemble concerts at performance halls or public places in other locales priced at or below variable cost.

2. *Usage Segments.* It is common for marketers to recognize high volume users and reward them with different prices. For example, regular customers at a particular grocery store who carry the stores' frequent shopper card will receive discounts at checkout that other shoppers will not receive. Where capacity is an issue for the manufacturer or service provider, the heaviest users may actually pay more. IBM has applied the strategy for its Internet service, whereby accounts exceeding a threshold level of usage are charged an hourly fee in addition to the based monthly rate. In contrast, symphonies and theatres will often have packages whereby patrons who commit to coming to a certain number of events receive a reduced price.

3. *Demographic Segments.* A symphony might provide special prices for students or children to encourage attendance, or may give discounts to senior citizens. This is a common strategy used by museums, athletic events, and amusement parks.

4. *Time Segments.* There are many examples of how "time" provides a relevant basis for segmenting markets for pricing. Resort hotels have on- and off-season rates, reflecting differences in demand for those seasons. Similarly, plumbers have regular and overtime, or weekend rates, capturing the same concept. A bakery might lower prices at the end of the day to move leftover merchandise. A symphony might have a Saturday morning or afternoon concert to reach new markets, accompanied by lower pricing.

Customization As discussed above for business markets, new technology may have a significant effect on the prices consumers pay for products and may lead to significant

Marketing Technologies

Price Shopping Dream

Imagine a marketplace where you can find exactly what you want and pay exactly what you can afford. Sound too good to be true? Well, you're right—for now anyway. But with the vast capabilities of the Internet, many Web sites are making strides toward just such a reality. Companies around the globe have seized the opportunity to provide instant information and feedback to consumers who never even have to leave their homes.

One such site is Priceline.com (www.priceline.com), which began as a service offering consumers the chance to name their own price for airline tickets. From the consumer's end, Priceline's process is relatively simple. Enter the Web site address in a Web browser, click an icon, and in only a few moments, you can be filling out the online form, specifying the dates of your flight, the cities traveling between, and a host of other specifics regarding the potential flight. Having submitted a bid, the consumer can expect to have e-mail confirmation of their bid almost instantaneously and hear back an acceptance or refusal in less than an hour.

Priceline utilizes a reverse auction model: given the consumer's bid, the company seeks out the best offer from vendors who have excess capacity. If the consumer's bid price is acceptable to a particular vendor, the consumer's credit card is charged and they are committed to the purchase. Priceline's auction model was deemed unique enough to be granted U.S. Patent number 5,794,207 in August 1998.

For all of Priceline's advantages, much still has to be worked out before this can be an efficient enough system to replace the conventional method of making travel arrangements. At present, Priceline.com does not allow one to specify flight times and provides only the capability of arranging for a two-leg round trip. In addition, the required submission of a credit-card number to be automatically charged if the bid is accepted makes some consumers uneasy.

Yet, the potential for growth is enormous, particularly as another trend continues to emerge among Internet shopping sites: the linking together of complementary (and not so complementary) products for purposes of cross-selling. In addition to the airline tickets, at Priceline one can also bid on hotel rooms, new cars, mortgages, and home equity loans. In the future, Priceline is planning to expand into the realms of insurance, rental cars, and cruises, among others. Expect competition to be fierce, however, as it is far less constrained by geographic boundaries. There are dozens of Web sites at which consumers can now shop for home mortgage rates (e.g., [www.interest.com, www.banxquote.com](www.interest.com)) and established services exist that create a real Internet marketplace for new and used automobiles (e.g., [www.carpoint.msn.com, www.autobytel.com](www.carpoint.msn.com)). In addition, many search engines (e.g., [www.yahoo.com, www.excite.com](www.yahoo.com)) have their own price search capabilities that can seek the lowest prices on the Internet for specified items (see the Internet questions at the end of the chapter).

In all, it has never been a better time to be a price shopper.

Sources: Paul Davidson, "Web Site Lets You Set Price," *USA Today* (September 16, 1998); Alex Grove, "Priceline.com Sparks a Patent Controversy," *Red Herring* (December 1998); Rudy Maxa, "Make a Bid for Your Bed," MSNBC Web Page (December 17, 1998).

---

variation in the prices that consumers pay for the same item. Consumers can participate in the Internet auctions described earlier. Further, Arbinet's services (linking callers to the lowest cost long-distance provider) may be available for consumers in two years. In fact, some envision a "smart" phone that automatically seeks the lowest cost carrier each time a long-distance call is placed. Beyond this, the Internet is affecting consumers' ability to search for and access low prices. For example, airlines today often send out e-mail alerts of last-minute fare specials to fill up unfilled seats. Only consumers on the airline's e-mail list receive notice of these fares. Yet, another service called Priceline allows consumers to specify their travel plans, and then name their price for the flight(s). Priceline acts as a go-between for participating airlines and consumers, forwarding bids to the airlines and relaying acceptances or refusals to consumers. The Priceline Web site received more than 1 million visits in the week after it was launched, and within two months had sold 100,000 tickets.[63]

www.priceline.com

Chapter Summary

This chapter has provided an overview of pricing behavior in firms, with a focus on factors that influence the setting of base prices, and the key reasons underlying why base prices are adjusted over time. We started by discussing how the natural starting point for pricing decisions is cost, and how cost-based methods of pricing seem to predominate in the marketplace. Yet, we pointed out the difficulties with such approaches, particularly when demand is uncertain. Pricing decisions must, then, take into account the relationship between price and demand. The transition from a cost-based approach to a more market-driven approach begins with a break-even analysis, which motivates the question "can we sell the number of units needed at this price to make the desired profit?" From here, estimates of a demand schedule provide important input into pricing decisions, as do consideration of the firm's strategic position, competitive prices, and legal and ethical considerations.

It is also significant to remember that there are many reasons why firms change base prices over time. Prices change both because objectives change over the product life cycle, and because competitors likely change prices. Further, we discovered reasons for price flexing for both business users and consumers. Some of these reasons for flexible pricing are due to traditional discounting and price promotional practices. But we also discussed the impact of new technology and the Internet. They are providing the possibility of aligning conditions of supply and demand almost instantaneously, leading to near-customized, or at least very efficient pricing.

Key Terms

Price is some unit of value given up by one party in return for something from another party.

Elasticity of demand is the relationship between changes in price and quantity sold.

Break-even point literally means "to have zero profit." It is that point at which total cost and total revenue are equal.

Demand schedules provide a systematic look at the relationship between price and quantity sold.

Marginal revenues are the change in a firm's total revenue per-unit change in its sales level.

Marginal costs are the change in a firm's total costs per-unit change in its output level.

ROI stands for Return on Investment.

Theory of dual entitlement holds that consumers believe there are terms in a transaction to which both consumers and sellers are "entitled" to over time. Cost-driven price increases are believed to be fair because they allow the seller to maintain her/his profit entitlement. Demand-driven price increases are not believed to be fair, however, since they allow a seller to increase per-unit profit, while the buyer receives nothing in return.

Market (price) skimming is a strategy of pricing the new product at a relatively high level and then gradually reducing it over time.

Penetration strategy requires that the firm enter the market at a relatively low price in an attempt to obtain market share and expand demand for its product.

Price-fixing is a conspiracy to fix competitive prices.

Sherman Antitrust Act prohibits any contract, combination, or conspiracy that restrains trade. It was passed by Congress in 1890 in an effort to prevent companies from controlling (monopolizing) an industry.

Cartel is an organization of firms in an industry where the central organization makes certain management decisions and functions (often regarding pricing, outputs, sales, advertising, and distribution) that would otherwise be performed within the individual firms.

Price discrimination occurs when a seller offers a lower price to some buyers than to other buyers.

Predatory pricing is a practice where one firm attempts to drive out rivals (usually smaller ones) by pricing at such a low level that the rival cannot make money.

Free on board (FOB) pricing leaves the cost and responsibility of transportation to the customer.

Uniform delivered pricing means that the seller charges all customers the same transportation cost regardless of their location.

Price promotions are short-term price reductions designed to create an incentive for consumers to buy now rather than later and/or stock up on the specialled product.

Everyday Low Pricing (EDLP) refers to the pricing strategy in which a firm charges the same low price every day.

Additional Key Terms and Concepts

Cost-plus pricing

Fixed costs

Average total cost

Contribution margin

Inelastic demand

Unitary elasticity

Total contribution

Goal-setting or objective-setting

Gouging laws

Online auctions

Prisoner's dilemma

Free-standing inserts (FSIs)

Usage segments

Time segments

Base prices

Variable costs

Break-even analysis (BEA)

Elasticity coefficient

Elastic demand

Profit-maximizing price

Competitive strategy positioning continuum

Resale price maintenance

Competitive price moves

Single-pricing

Couponing

Geographic segments

Demographic segments

Questions for Discussion

1. A manufacturer of golf equipment has developed a new driver call the Big Bomber. The company has $80 million invested in operating capital. The unit cost of producing this driver is $100 and the projected volume of product and sales is 1.5 million units. In the text, we discussed how an orchestra could set price by incorporating a desired figure for profit into its pricing calculation (we added $1 per customer to the price). In the case of the Big Bomber, we are looking to determine a per-unit cost for the product by accounting for a particular dollar amount that the company is seeking to earn on its investment. If the company's objective is to earn a 30 percent return on investment with this driver, what should the price be? How would you determine it?

2. If cost-plus pricing is used as a means to coordinate among oligopolistic rivals and is used consistently over time with adjustments made in mark-up levels as sales figures are studied, could it lead to profit-maximizing prices?

3. Answer the following questions, explaining the relationships among changes in price, demand (units sold), and profit. Explain whether demand appears to be elastic or inelastic in each case.
   a. Hewlett-Packard dropped prices on personal computers during 1997 by offering customers discounts of up to 50 percent. Unit sales shot up 70 percent during this period. Yet, the personal computer division *lost $50 million.* What would explain this odd combination of performance outcomes? (Note: There were no especially large accounting write-offs for the PC business during this period.)
   b. Heublein, Inc. raised prices 8 percent on its Popov brand of vodka to an average of $4.10 a fifth of vodka. Popov lost 1 percent of its market share. What would determine whether or not Popov actually lost money?
   c. Scott Mt. Joy is co-founder of Nieto Computer Services, a three-year old Houston computer and network-services company. In 1995, the company charged $35 to $50 an hour for its contract work. By 1998, those rates were $75 to $150. "We

raised hourly rates (two years in a row) and lost one or two clients out of 130," says Mr. Mt. Joy. What would explain this inelastic demand?

4. Given the data below, at what price does this manufacturer of barbecue grills maximize profit?

A Price	B Estimated Quantity Sales	C Variable Cost
125	100,000	70
130	95,000	70
135	85,000	70
140	75,000	70

5. As noted in the opening vignette of this chapter, Quaker Oats recently raised prices on several cold cereals by 3.6 percent. Quaker could defend the practice one of two ways:
   a. It could argue that it is only trying to regain some of its profitability lost as a result of the 1996 price war.
   b. It could argue that its price increases are meant to offset the rising cost of doing business. Labor and advertising costs are increasing, and the company also has higher costs due to product innovation (e.g., zip-pak closes on bagged cereals).
   Which approach do you think would be perceived as more fair by consumers? Why?

6. Diamonds are a luxury. Water is an essential requirement for human life. Why are diamonds so much more expensive than water?

7. Consider your answer to question 6, then answer the following two questions:
   a. *Business Week,* March 29, 1998: "Step into a Kmart or Wal-Mart store these days and you can pick up a diamond bracelet for $29.99—about the same price as a toaster . . . prices of smaller diamonds are plunging." Why do you think this is happening?
   b. In contrast, water is more expensive (bottled water). What makes consumers willing to pay $1.09 for a 16-ounce bottle of water?

Internet Questions

1. Identify two services that sell automobiles via the Internet. How do they communicate price information? Why? What impact do you think these services will have on the cost of purchasing automobiles in the future?

2. Go to **netgrocer.com.** Sign-up for the service (you don't need to give them a credit-card number) and then go shopping for breakfast. How much would it cost you if you ordered a box of Wheaties, a box of Nutrigrain bars, and Orange Tang in the 31.70 ounce container? Compare this to the local grocery store and explain the differences in pricing.

3. Go shopping for a video copy of the following movies: *It's a Wonderful Life, Gone with the Wind, Good Will Hunting,* and the Beatles' *Yellow Submarine.* (Hint: **Yahoo.com, Excite.com, Junglee.com**) What are your best prices for each of these items? What are the implications of this search capability for the pricing of products and services in the future?

Endnotes

[1] John Greenwald, "Cereal Showdown," *Time* 147(18) April 29, 1996. Press release from the office of U.S. Rep. Sam Gejdenson. July 24, 1997. (**www.house.gov/gejdenson/**

CERREP3.htm); Sam Gejdenson and Charles Schumer, "Snap, Crackle, Drop: Cereal Price Cuts Provide Partial Relief for American Families," (July 24, 1997); Carleen Hawn, "General Mills Tests the Limits," *Forbes* (April 6, 1998); James P. Miller, "Kellogg to Study Salaried Workers, Setting Stage for Possible Cutbacks," *The Wall Street Journal,* September 8, 1998; Tim Carvel, "Cereal Wars: A Tale of Bran, Oats, and Air," *Fortune* (May 13, 1996), p. 30; Richard Gibson and E. S. Browning, "Investors Have to Wait to Milk Cereal Stocks," *The Wall Street Journal* (June 11, 1996): pp. C1–C2; "Quaker May Make Splash in Cereal Fight," *USA Today* (June 18, 1996): p. 4B; Bloomberg Business News, "For Prices of Cereal: General Mills Plans Reductions of 11 percent," *New York Times* (June 20, 1996): p. C2; Richard Turcsik, "Sales Are Gaining Crisply, Powered by More Vitamins, More Fiber, and Heartfelt Ad Campaigns," *Supermarket News* (May 18, 1998): 51; "Quaker Oats Raises Cereal Prices; Brand Loyalty May Give a Lift to Profit, Analysts Say," *Food and Drink Weekly,* June 8, 1998.

[2]J. Dean, "Research Approach to Pricing," in *Planning the Price Structure,* Marketing Series No. 67 (1947) American Management Association, New York, p. 4.

[3]A. W. Walker, "How to Price Industrial Products," *Harvard Business Review* 45: pp. 8–45.

[4]"Finding the Right Price Is No Easy Game to Play," *Chief Executive* (September 1981): pp. 16–18.

[5]Thomas T. Nagle and Reed K. Holden, *The Strategy and Tactics of Pricing,* 2nd ed. (Englewood Cliffs, NJ: Prentice Hall, 1995), p. 15.

[6]John H. Lindgren, Jr. and Terence A. Shimp, *Marketing: An Interactive Learning System* (Fort Worth: The Dryden Press, 1996), p. 378.

[7]Gilbert Burck, "The Myths and Realities of Corporate Pricing," *Fortune* (April 1972): pp. 85+. See also, Richard Thaler, "Mental Accounting and Consumer Choice," *Marketing Science* (Summer 1985): pp. 199–214.

[8]R. Hall and C. Hitch, "Price Theory and Business Behavior," *Oxford Economic Papers,* 1939; and Thomas V. Bonoma, Victoria L. Crittenden, and Robert J. Dolan, "Can We Have Rigor and Relevance in Pricing Research?" in T. DeVinney (ed.), *Issues in Pricing: Theory and Research* (Lexington, MA: Lexington Books, 1988).

[9]This example is adapted from Thomas T. Nagle and Reed K. Holden, *The Strategy and Tactics of Pricing* (2nd ed.) (Englewood Cliffs, NJ: Prentice-Hall, 1995), pp. 19–22.

[10]For target ROI pricing, the desired profit per unit is calculated as follows:

$$\text{Desired profit per unit} = \frac{(\text{Target Return} * \text{Investment})}{\text{Projected Unit Sales}}$$

[11]Thomas T. Nagle and Reed K. Holden, *The Strategy and Tactics of Pricing* (Englewood Cliffs, NJ: Prentice-Hall, 1987), p. 3.

[12]Tables 14.2, 14.3, and 14.4 are taken from Paul A. Samuelson, *Economics: An Introductory Analysis 4th ed.* (New York: McGraw-Hill, 1958), pp. 370–374.

[13]For example, the percentage price change going from $5 to $4 in Table 14.2 is ($4 – $5)/ $5 = 20 percent. The percentage change in quantity sold is (10 – 9)/10 = 10 percent.

[14]*Business Week,* "Cheap PCs," (March 23, 1998): p. 28.

[15]Note that there are no fixed costs included in Table 14.3, which may seem a bit odd. It is important to recognize that fixed costs do not help in determining the profit-maximizing price for one simple reason: they are the same no matter what price we charge. As such, the only fixed costs that would be relevant would be those that change as a function of pricing. For example, going with a very low price for a product may require extra investment in production capacity to make sure enough product is available. The fixed costs associated with additional production would then be relevant and should be accounted for.

[16]Simulated purchase tasks have been found to provide reasonably accurate assessments of consumer response to price. See John R. Nevin, "Laboratory Experiments for Estimating Consumer Demand: A Validation Study," *Journal of Marketing Research* (August 1974): pp. 261–268, and Raymond R. Burke, Bari A. Harlam, Barbara E. Kahn, and Leonard M. Lodish, "Comparing Dynamic Consumer Choice in Real and Computer-Simulated Environments," *Journal of Consumer Research* (June 1992): pp. 71–82.

[17]One could argue that the symphony consider an even higher price as profits show a continual upward trend as price gets higher.

[18]Michael Porter, *Competitive Strategy* (New York: Free Press, 1980).

[19]We should note that, although Neil Hill's prices are likely to be equal to or lower than a similar store in Kansas City because of the lower costs of doing business in Atchison, driving from Kansas City is part of the price of shopping Neil Hill's. The combination of an absolutely unique shopping experience and fair prices (relative to Kansas City alternatives) is likely a strong draw. See Kevin Helliker, "Word of Mouth Makes Kansas Store a Star," *The Wall Street Journal* (November 7, 1997): p. B1.

[20]See Daniel Kahneman, Jack L. Knetsch, and Richard H. Thaler, "Fairness as a Constraint on Profit Seeking: Entitlements in the Market," *American Economic Review* 70 (September 1986): pp. 728–741.

[21]Robert Axelrod, *The Evolution of Cooperation* (New York: Basic Books, 1984).

[22]Dean Takahashi, "AMD Posts Loss Amid Price War, Sluggish Demand," *The Wall Street Journal* (July 9, 1998): p. B3.

[23]Jeffrey Tannebaum, "Small Bookseller Beats the Giants at their Own Game," *The Wall Street Journal* (November 4, 1997): p. B1.

[24]Scott McCartney, "Southwest Airlines Lands Plenty of Florida Passengers," *The Wall Street Journal* (November 11, 1997): p. B4.

[25]See Peter Burrow, Gary McWilliams, and Robert D. Hof, "Cheap PCs," *Business Week* (March 23, 1998): pp. 28–32; Don Peppers and Martha Rogers, "Lessons from the Front," *Marketing Tools* (January/February 1998): pp. 39–42; and Lisa Chadderdon, "How Dell Sells on the Web," *Fast Company* (September 1998): pp. 58–59.

[26]Peter R. Dickson, *Marketing Management* (Fort Worth: The Dryden Press, 1996), p. 618.

[27]Reed K. Holden and Thomas T. Nagle, "Kamikaze Pricing," *Marketing Management* 7(2) (1998): pp. 30–40.

[28]These individuals' names have been changed.

[29]Andrew Galvin, "The Price of Fixing Prices," *Journal of Pricing Management* (Summer 1990): pp. 46–51.

[30]See the Federal Trade Commission's publication, "Promoting Competition, Protecting Consumers: A Plain English Guide to Antitrust Laws," at the FTC's Web site: **www.ftc. gov/bc/compguide/index.htm**

[31]Scott Kilman, "In Archer-Daniels Saga, Now the Executives Face Trial," *The Wall Street Journal* (July 9, 1998): p. B10.

[32]Scott Kilman, "Federal Jury Convicts Ex-Executives in Archer-Daniels-Midland Lawsuit," *The Wall Street Journal* (September 18, 1998).

[33]See, for example, Ben Elfman & Son, Inc., et al. v. Criterion Mills, Inc., et al., CCH 69,611 (DC MA, October 1991); BNA ATRR No. 1538 (October 24, 1991), 507, summarized in the *Journal of Marketing* (July 1992): p. 100.

[34]Wendy Zellner, "How Northwest Gives Competition a Bad Name," *Business Week* (March 16, 1998): p. 34.

[35]In fact, the Department of Transportation has recently instituted a policy that defines "unfair exclusionary tactics" and penalizes any airline engaging in such tactics. See *Airline Financial News,* "Department of Transportation to Major Airlines: Forewarned Is Fair Warned," April 13, 1998.

[36]Joseph P. Guiltinan and Gregory T. Gundlach, "Aggressive and Predatory Pricing: A Framework for Analysis," *Journal of Marketing* (July 1996): p. 88.

[37]Zellner, "How Northwest Gives Competition a Bad Name."

[38]"Majors Fault DOT for Ignoring Law, History, Real-World Economics," *Aviation Daily* (July 30, 1998): p. 180.

[39]Ibid.

[40]Joel E. Urbany, William O. Bearden, and Dan C. Weilbaker, "The Effect of Plausible and Exaggerated Reference Prices on Consumer Perceptions and Price Search," *Journal of Consumer Research* (June 1988): pp. 95–110; Kent B. Monroe, *Pricing: Making Profitable Decisions,* 2nd ed. (New York: McGraw-Hill, 1990).

[41]These are the Federal Trade Commission Guides, as cited in *The State of Colorado* vs. *The May Department Stores Company,* Case No. 89 CV 9274, District Court, City and County of Denver, Colorado, 1990.

[42]See Daniel Kahneman, Jack L. Knetsch, and Richard H. Thaler, "Fairness as a Constraint on Profit Seeking: Entitlements in the Market," *American Economic Review* 70 (September 1986): pp. 728–741.

[43]Christine Dugas, "Consumers Walking Away from ATM Charges," *USA Today* (August 16, 1996): p. 1B.

[44]For example, the Georgia Legislature passed a price-gouging law in 1994 to prevent hotels and wholesalers from taking advantage of visitors to the Olympics in Atlanta in 1996. It is unclear how successful the law was, as many hotels were still observed to

double or triple room rates. See Donna Rosato, "Some Room Rates have Done a Triple Jump," *USA Today* (July 15, 1996): p. 1B.

[45]John H. Lindgren, Jr. and Terence A. Shimp, *Marketing: An Interactive Learning System* (Fort Worth: The Dryden Press, 1996): p. 403.

[46]Gilbert Burck, "The Myths and Realities of Corporate Pricing," *Fortune* (April 1972): p. 87.

[47]Timothy Aeppel, "Rubbermaid Is on a Tear, Sweeping Away the Cobwebs," *The Wall Street Journal* (September 8, 1998): p. B4.

[48]Chris Adams, "Nucor Cuts Steel Prices Amid Rush of Imports," *The Wall Street Journal* (September 11, 1998): p. A2.

[49]Ron Winslow, "How a Breakthrough Quickly Broke Down for Johnson & Johnson," *The Wall Street Journal* (September 18, 1998): p. A1.

[50]Venkataraman, Chen, and MacMillan, in a study of the airline industry, find that price moves produce a competitive reaction with 75 percent probability. The probability that a competitor would match a nonprice move was 17 percent. S. Venkataraman, Ming-Jer Chen, and Ian C. MacMillan, "Anticipating Reactions: Factors that Shape Competitor Responses," in George S. Day and David J. Reibstein (eds.), *Wharton on Dynamic Competitive Strategy* (New York: John Wiley and Sons, 1997).

[51]Peter R. Dickson and Joel E. Urbany, "Retailer Reactions to a Competitor's Price Change," *Journal of Retailing* 70 (Spring 1994): pp. 1–22; Joel E. Urbany and Peter R. Dickson, "Competitive Price-Cutting Momentum and Pricing Reactions," *Marketing Letters* 2(4) (1991): pp. 393–402.

[52]Jaikumar Vijayan, "IBM Proposes Flexible Software Pricing," *Computerworld* (April 6, 1998): p. 57.

[53]Joshua Hyatt, "Hot Commodity," *Inc.* (February 1996): pp. 50–60.

[54]This short section is based on the article by Howard Gleckman and Gary McWilliams, "Ask and It Shall Be Discounted," *Business Week* (October 6, 1997): pp. 116–120.

[55]Ibid.

[56]Alan S. Blinder, "Why Are Prices Sticky? Preliminary Results from an Interview Study," *American Economic Association Papers and Proceedings,* May 1991, pp. 89–96.

[57] Amy Cortese and Marcia Stepanek, "Good-Bye to Fixed Pricing?" *Business Week* (May 4, 1998): p. 71.

[58]Ibid., 72.

[59]Jim O'Brien, "Hot Off the Wire," *Computer Shopper* (August, 1998): p. 474; and Mary Connelly, "Philosophy of Car Pricing Is Clear: Cut Out Games," *Advertising Age* (March 28, 1994): pp. S28–34.

[60]Carl F. Mela, Sunil Gupta, and Donald R. Lehmann, "The Long-Term Impact of Promotion and Advertising on Consumer Brand Choice," *Journal of Marketing Research* (May 1997): pp. 248–61.

[61]Kenneth Hein and Vincent Alonzo, "P&G Scales Back Promotions," *Incentive* (April 1997): p. 15.

[62]"Distribution of Coupons Falls 10% to 276 Billion," *Advertising Age* (March 23, 1998): p. 32.

[63]David Leonhardt, "Make a Bid, but Don't Pack Your Bags," *Business Week* (June 1, 1998): p. 164.

Additional References

Backman, J. 1953. *Price Practices and Price Policies.* Ronald Press, New York.

Chief Executive 1981. "Finding the Right Price Is No Easy Game to Play." *Chief Executive* (September): 16-18.

Dean, J. 1947. "Research Approach to Pricing." In *Planning the Price Structure.* Marketing Series No. 67. American Management Association, New York.

Marhall, A. 1979. *More Profitable Pricing.* McGraw-Hill, London.

Nagle, Thomas T. and Reed K. Holden. 1995. *The Strategy and Tactics of Pricing.* Englewood Cliffs, NJ: Prentice Hall.

Walker, A.W. 1967. "How to Price Industrial Products." *Harvard Business Review* 45:38-45.

Grocery Pricing: The Ourstore Company Case

T his case study was designed to be a realistic representation of a retail grocery market. It is based upon the author's experience and does not present specific retailer or city names. Case facts are presented briefly to keep the presentation simple and to make the important facts clear.

Tom Evans is the marketing area vice-president of the Ourstore Company, a retail grocery chain. He is currently faced with the company's pricing and advertising decisions for the coming week (the week of June 29, 1999) in the Anytown market (population 800,000). Ourstore's retail stores in Anytown are primarily superstore format, averaging 35,000 square feet. Tom must decide how to respond to the following changes in the competitive environment.

Ourstore's major competitor in Anytown is the Leader Company. Leader is a large national chain and has traditionally been the market share leader in the Anytown market. Both Ourstore and Leader stores are full-service operations. Two other full-service chains in the market are the Feisty Company and the Opponent Company. The latest market share figures (obtained from a research report dated March 19, 1999) are as follows:

Chain	Number of Stores	Share of the Anytown Market (based on total $ volume)
Leader	25	40%
Ourstore	16	23%
Opponent	16	22%
Feisty	6	10%
All others	—	5%

The New Competitive Environment

On June 8, 1999, the Feisty chain (with 6 stores and a 10 percent market share in Anytown) began an everyday low-price (EDLP) promotional blitz. Feisty now promotes "rock-bottom" everyday low prices in all its print advertising and has cut prices dramatically on many of its products. There is no information yet available on overall market share changes that have occurred since Feisty began its EDLP campaign.

Price Surveys

The following table contains excerpts from prices surveys taken by a local market research firm in Anytown on April 20, 1999 (two months *before* Feisty's EDLP campaign began) and on June 22, 1999 (two week's *after* Feisty's EDLP campaign began). The price

Price Survey—Anytown Market (Selected Products Carried by Major Competitors)							
	April 20, 1999 Store Prices			June 22, 1999 Store Prices			
Product	Ourstore	Leader	Opponent	Ourstore	Leader	Opponent	Feisty
Bananas (branded 1 lb.)	0.49	0.49	0.49	0.49	0.49	0.49	0.39
Kellogg's Corn Flakes (24 oz.)	1.89	1.89	1.87	1.89	1.89	1.87	1.67
Oscar Meyer Sliced Bologna (8 oz.)	1.39	1.39	1.39	1.39	1.39	1.39	1.09
Whole Milk (1 gal.)	2.49	2.39	2.49	2.39	2.39	2.39	1.97
Minute Maid Orange Juice (frozen 1 oz.)	0.89	0.83	0.85	0.89	0.89	0.85	0.69
Hellman's Mayonnaise (1 qt.)	1.99	1.99	1.99	1.99	1.99	1.99	1.59
Coke (2 litre)	1.79	1.79	1.79	1.79	1.79	1.79	1.19
Maxwell House Coffee (1 lb. regular grind)	3.19	3.09	2.99	3.09	3.09	2.99	2.67

surveys show that Leader did not lower its prices to meet Feisty's new prices last week. The Opponent Company (16 stores, 22 percent market share) also did not lower its prices in response to Feisty's EDLP campaign.

Consumer Behavior in Anytown

Several recent research studies, coming from a major university and an industry organization (both located in Anytown) indicate that Anytown consumers do not comparison shop extensively. More specifically, the research indicates that:

1. Only 25 percent of Anytown consumers actively compare competitive stores' prices (by shopping around and reading advertising).

2. Most Anytown consumers shop one grocery store all the time.

These results have been consistent over several recent research studies.

What Should Tom Do?

Tom has to set prices for the week of June 29, determining whether or not to respond to Feisty's low-price challenge. To date, he has not changed pricing strategy. Tom is under no pressure from the home office either to follow or not follow the new price competition. The decision has to be based upon his evaluation of the current consumer and competitive situation. What prices would you recommend for the following items? Why?

Item	Ourstore's Wholesale Cost	Recommended Retail Price
Bananas (branded 1 lb.)	$0.25	
Kellogg's Corn Flakes (24 oz.)	$1.70	
Oscar Meyer Sliced Bologna (8 oz.)	$0.93	
Whole Milk (1 gal.)	$1.45	
Minute Maid Orange Juice (frozen 16 oz.)	$0.85	
Hellman's Mayonnaise (1 qt.)	$1.65	
Coke (2 litre)	$0.93	
Maxwell House Coffee (1 lb. regular grind)	$2.75	

The Future
of Marketing

Chapter 15

Marketing on the Internet

John H. Lindgren, Jr.,
Consumer Bankers Association Professor, Area Coordinator of the Marketing Group, and Director of the Price-Waterhouse Coopers Center for Innovation in Business Learning, McIntire School of Commerce, University of Virginia

Dr. Lindgren received his D.B.A. from Kent State University. An active consultant, he has developed an expertise in multimedia learning and Web design. Dr. Lindgren has designed Web sites for institutions and has served as a consultant to the University of Virginia, U.S. Department of Commerce, Touche Ross and Company, Berman Technologies, International Auto, Star (Texaco) Enterprise, Crestar Bank, Jefferson National Bank, First Pennsylvania Bank, Hamilton Bank, and the Federal Reserve Banks for Atlanta and Chicago.

He has served on the faculty of banking programs throughout the

L et us assume that your professor asks you to write a paper titled, "Marketing at IBM: Its Past and Present Successes." What would you do first? If you were like millions of other students nationwide, the first step would be to go to the Web. You probably would first go to your best guess at IBM's Web address. That is, you would probably type in http://www.ibm.com. If you did type this address, you would get to IBM's home page.

You would probably be pleased to find a link on the first page to the history of IBM and "The Story of IBM: The Early Years." After clicking that link, you would see that the history is presented as a timeline with sound and video files for your multimedia pleasure. A written narrative is also presented with graphics to support the history. Alternatively, if you did not want to read or listen to all of this, you could just get the highlights.

You notice that you can gather information on many aspects of IBM. There is a button to take you to recent "News about IBM." Another button describes the "Products/Services" that are offered. One section describes the "Support" IBM offers for software and hardware. You can also gather information on collaborating or "Partnering" with IBM either as a hardware or software reseller. The last area you find is a gold mine of data for your paper. It is "About IBM" and you find financial information, research, and a link back to the history section.

Next, you would probably surf the electronic magazines to find other articles written on IBM. You might do this through the search engines such as Yahoo! or by using the site searches at each of the electronic magazines.

Interestingly, all this information would be gathered before you even thought to go to the library. A mere 10 years ago, you would have been in the periodicals room or stacks of your library digging out this information. While it might only take you a few minutes to do all this on the Web, you could easily spend many long hours in the library gathering the same material.

Learning Objectives

After you have completed this chapter, you should be able to:

1. Understand the history of the Internet.

2. Describe electronic commerce.

3. Identify the types of consumers using the Internet.

4. Illustrate the ways that electronic commerce can improve business practices.

5. Recognize and understand the uses of the different types of Internet sites.

6. Discover the benefits of Internet marketing.

7. Evaluate the drawbacks of Internet marketing.

8. Discuss marketing insights on the Internet.

United States, including the Graduate School of Retail Bank Management, The Savings Institutions, Advanced Marketing School, The Virginia Bankers School of Bank Management, The Inter-American School of Savings and Loans, and The National Banking School. He is the recipient of eight teaching awards.

In the past, Professor Lindgren served as the director of the Center for Financial Services Studies, academic director of the Ph.D. Institute, and program director of the Society of Marketing Professional Services Institute. In addition, he is a former vice president of the American Marketing Association and a former board member of the AMA.

Dr. Lindgren has co-authored six books and monographs in the field of marketing and serves on the editorial boards of several marketing publications. He is also the author of *Marketing: An Integrated Learning System*, published by The Dryden Press.

Internet
is a worldwide network of interconnected computer networks that carry data and make information exchange possible.

World Wide Web (WWW or Web)
is a subset of the Internet comprised of a collection of hyperlinked documents (not computers) that use a common protocol.

The **Internet** includes a number of data networks set-up by companies and organizations, the **World Wide Web** and e-mail, plus a multitude of proprietary networks that are gravitating to the Web.[1] The World Wide Web is the fastest growing of the Internet components for two reasons. First, the development of user-friendly interfaces, such as Netscape's Navigator/Communicator and Microsoft's Explorer. These interfaces allow both businesses and consumers to use the Web with ease. The second reason the World Wide Web is growing so fast is that these interfaces allow business-to-business users and consumers to readily combine data, graphics, sound, and video over a medium that is increasingly accessible to wider audiences.

HISTORY OF THE INTERNET

"New sites on the World Wide Web have been cropping up at the rate of one per minute."[2] Given this phenomenal rate of growth, let us take a look at how and where it started. The beginnings of the Internet can be traced back to World War II. Franklin D. Roosevelt appointed Vannevar Bush to the wartime Office of Scientific Research and Development. At that time, Vannevar Bush, an electrical engineer, was the vice president of MIT. The Office of Scientific Research and Development was charged with bringing together thousands of scientists to discover ways of applying science to modern warfare. At the end of the war, Vannevar Bush turned his attention to ways that the scientific community could share information worldwide. While he did not have the computer power to implement his visions, he did inspire others to follow his ideas. In 1965 Ted Nelson took Bush's ideas and tried to develop a software system called Xanadu. This system consisted of the theoretical underpinnings of **hypertext.** Nelson's Xanadu could never be implemented, but it laid the groundwork for the work of Tim Bernes-Lee at the European Particle Physics Laboratory (French acronym CERN).

Hypertext
is any text that contains links to other documents.

HTML (HyperText Markup Language)
is the coding language used for creating hypertext documents and formatting pages for use on the Web.

URL (Uniform Resource Locator)
is the Internet address for a Web document or other file.

HTTP (HyperText Transport Protocol)
is the protocol for moving hypertext across the Internet. It allows for the transfer of images, sound, video, and other files between computers.

In 1969 the U.S. Department of Defense established a program called ARPANET (Advanced Research Projects Agency Network). The purpose of this network was to provide secure communications between organizations engaged in defense-related research. This network used the TCP/IP (Transmission Control Protocol/Internet Protocol) communications protocol. Shortly after the establishment of the ARPANET, the National Science Foundation created a similar network, NSFNet. NSFNet was established to enable researchers and academics in nondefense fields to make use of the network. The NSFNet became the backbone of the Internet.

In 1989, Tim Bernes-Lee of CERN invented the three things that have allowed the World Wide Web to explode in terms of growth on the Internet. His inventions include three elements that have become part of our language today. Those elements are: **HTML (HyperText Markup Language), URL (Uniform Resource Locator), and HTTP (HyperText Transport Protocol).**

WHERE WE ARE TODAY

Intranets
connect the computers within a business together.

Extranets
connect computers outside the firm with the intranet at the firm.

The growth of the Internet required three separate developments in order for it to become an efficient marketing tool. First, businesses had to develop their electronic commerce **intranets** and **extranets** that connect to the Internet. Second, network server growth had to achieve the levels necessary to allow the fast connections required for effective communications. Finally, a sufficient number of consumers (either at work or at home) must have access to the Internet either through a PC or some kind of Web TV device. Let us look at growth in all three of these areas.

Electronic Commerce

Electronic commerce includes all the activities of a firm that use the Internet to aid in the exchange of products. The term includes business activities between manufacturers, intermediaries, and ultimate consumers. Electronic commerce actually started over twenty years ago with the development of EDI (Electronic Data Interchange) and EFT (Electronic Funds Transfer) systems in the late 1970s and early 1980s. Other forms of electronic commerce include credit cards, ATMs (Automated Teller Machines), and telephone banking activities.[3] These developments along with the expansion of the Internet have offered new opportunities to firms both large and small.

The business-to-business market is the largest segment of the overall electronic commerce market. According to the Simba Information Inc., business-to-business commerce totaled approximately $19 billion in 1998.[4] This represents over two-thirds of the total activity on the Internet. The electronic commerce marketplace is forecast to grow at more than 30 percent a year for the next five years. At this rate, this market will reach $102 billion by the year 2002. Business-to-business commerce is expected to continue to make up the majority of this total. Many business analysts believe that these numbers are probably very conservative. Given the explosive growth of this medium, they may be understated by two- or threefold.

Today over 97 percent of large businesses report that they have Internet sites, while only 10 percent of small businesses report a Web site.[5] Of those businesses that utilized Web sites, 53 percent report that their site is used for sales activities while only 30 percent presently report that their site is profitable.

Internet Hosts

The second development that has allowed the Internet to become an efficient marketing tool was the expansion of high-speed connections to the Internet, which are called ***Internet hosts*** or ***Internet Service Providers (ISPs)***. These hosts are the interface with the Internet for hundreds, if not thousands, of businesses and individuals. In 1990, there were only 1,000 Internet hosts; however, by January 1999 this number had exploded to over 90 million. This growth curve shows no sign of leveling off at the present time.[6]

Consumers Using the Internet

While the growth of Internet usage by consumers does not equal that by business-to-business users, there is still significant growth in this area. Use of the Internet has been doubling every 18 months and is expected to continue at that rate for the near future. By the end of 1998, there were over 87 million Internet users, either connected at work or at home, in North America.[7] North America represents the largest segment of the world market, which is estimated at 153 million users.

According to the third quarter results of the 1998 Worldwide Internet/Online Tracking Service (WWITS™) by IntelliQuest, growth of Internet usage by consumers in the U.S. alone has reached almost 73 million adults with over 40 million expected to go online in 1999 alone.[8] The Internet users in the United States have begun to more closely resemble the average American in the future. The 1998 Tracking Service found that 51 percent of those planning to get Internet access during 1999 are over the age of 35. Almost half (49 percent) have a high school education or less, and more than half of those planning to go online (58 percent) make less than $50,000 a year.

The Pew Research Center[9] found similar results for 1998 with its telephone survey of over 3,000 adults. The profile of Internet users from the past year demonstrates the changing demographics on the Internet. Results showed the following:

The New Internet Users			
	Started Using Net	In Past Year	More Than a Year Ago
	Percent of all Net users	46	53
Percent of users who are:	Male	48	55
	Female	52	45
Age:	18–29	25	30
	30–49	52	50
	50–64	16	15
	65+	4	4
Income:	$50,000+	35	45
	$30,000–49,000	23	22
	Under $30,000	23	16
Education:	College graduate	29	46
	Some college	32	30
	High school graduate	33	19
	Less than high school	6	3
Use Net for:	Work	24	30
	Pleasure	52	39
	Mix	22	31

Source: Pew Research Center, 1998 telephone survey, www.people-press.org/tech98sum.htm

Internet consumers use the Internet for e-mail and news. However, shopping and banking are fast growing trends. Figure 15.2 summarizes the reasons that consumers use the Internet.

Almost 17 million Americans have purchased at least one product online during the 1998 calendar year.[10] By year-end 1999, this number is expected to double to 36.1 million. The same study forecast that by the year 2002, the United States would have 63.7

Figure 15.1   Growth in Internet Usage (North America)

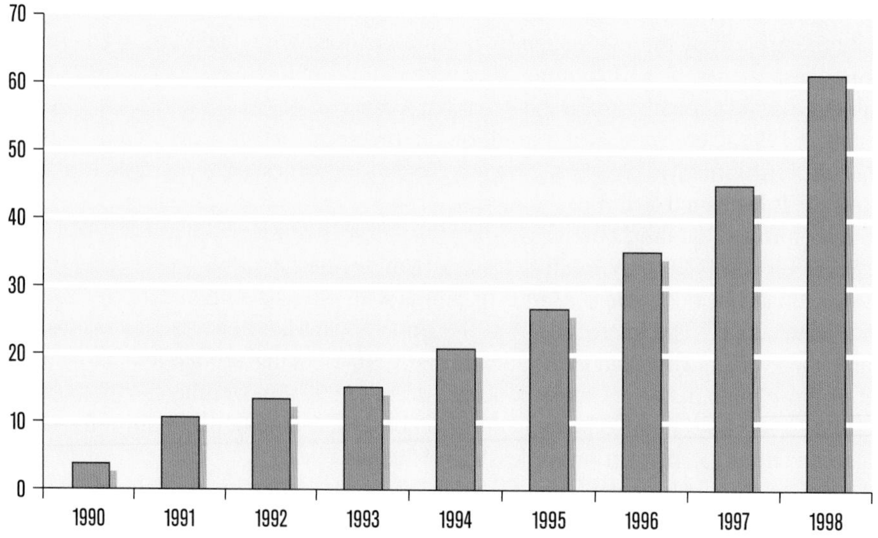

Source: Nua, Ltd. Web site. www.nua.ie/surveys/

million online buyers, representing nearly one-third of all Americans 14 and older. Interestingly, while almost 17 million people purchased online during 1998, nearly *double* that figure, 33 million people, used the Web to research and compare products. (See Figure 15.3.)

Figure 15.2   Reasons for Using the Internet

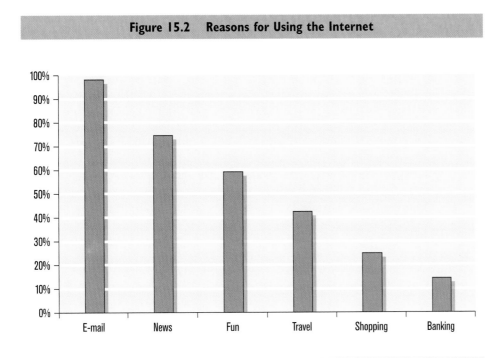

Source: Internet World Web site: www.iw.com/daily/stats/1998/04/1001-home.html

Figure 15.3   Purchase Behavior versus Information-Seeking Behavior on the Web

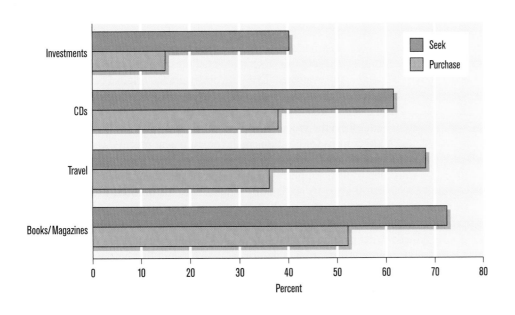

Source: Georgia Tech College of Computing Web site. www.cc.gatech.edu/gvu/user_surveys/survey-1998-04/graphs/shopping/q3.htm

CyberDialogue forecast that some 9 million shoppers would purchase products offline during the 1998 holiday season after first gathering information online.[11]

IMPROVING BUSINESS PRACTICES USING THE INTERNET

Electronic Data Interchange (EDI)

is a computer-to-computer communications protocol that allows basic information on purchases and invoices to be exchanged.

Initial uses of the computer in business focused on the performance of accounting tasks, payroll processing, and production planning. In the 1980s, businesses began to develop private networks that allowed firms within distribution channels to interchange purchase orders, shipping instructions, and reorder forms. These private networks used the **EDI (Electronic Data Interchange)** protocol. In addition to these EDI networks, firms began to develop internal networks to pass information from department to department at locations throughout the world. These networks are extremely expensive to maintain, and thus only the largest firms could afford to build and maintain this kind of private network.[12]

The Internet brought electronic commerce to all firms: small, medium or large. Since the Internet only requires a server to be connected, even the smallest firms can use the Internet for internal communications, as well as a connection for business-to-business relationships. A firm's private networks can also be connected to the Internet. These networks are typically accessed via some kind of password system.

Electronic commerce has expanded on the Internet primarily because of e-commerce's potential impact on four major areas of business practices.[13] These areas include reduced costs, inventory reduction, improved customer service, and market/product development opportunities. Each of these benefits is discussed below.

Reduced Costs

Cost reduction is one of the major benefits of using the Internet. Many firms have justified their investment in a Web site based on cost savings. Firms such as Federal Express and Cisco have saved millions of dollars through the implementation of a Web strategy. FedEx dramatically reduced their customer service costs with a minimal investment, while Cisco uses the Web to provide their customers with the most up-to-date information on their products.

Other firms such as GE have reduced costs through the analysis of the supply chain. The identification and evaluation of suppliers for component parts and other materials can be an expensive and time-consuming process. A typical firm's buying center evaluates hundreds of suppliers, and selects products that will be used to produce other goods. Product specifications, availability, delivery times, service schedules, pricing, and a multitude of other items must be continually evaluated. EDI networks were the original conduits for the exchange of this information along established distribution channels. But with the advent of the Internet, a firm can research suppliers and products beyond its normal distribution channel that might better meet the procurement specifications. Small firms can potentially compete with much larger firms for positions in the procurement process. Using the Internet, supply centers will be able to select from a broader range of sources and build close relationships with each of their suppliers. In addition, the Internet has the potential to reduce overall procurement costs by automating manual systems of reorder and invoicing.

A major area for cost reduction results from the use of online data versus printed information. Obvious savings include printing and mailing costs, but less obvious savings occur when you consider volume and flexibility. The size of an e-catalog is virtually limitless, and changes to the information (sale prices, new product line entries, etc.) are far easier to implement and publish online. This area of cost reduction is particularly important for direct marketers who have traditionally used printed color catalogues.

If a firm pursues a market expansion strategy through direct contact with its customers, it must either increase the number of salespeople or the number of customer contact personnel to service the increased customer base. This type of expansion can increase costs dramatically. A market expansion strategy on the Internet, where customer self-service is the norm, allows a firm to add new customers at little or no additional cost.

Inventory Reduction

If a firm holds inventories, there are costs associated with the holding of that inventory. These costs include **storage costs** (costs associated with storing inventory), **handling costs** (costs associated with transferring inventory to the customer), and **obsolescence costs** (costs associated with holding inventory that is not selling due to a loss in demand for the product). The result of better management of inventory is not only lower inventory, but also a better matching of that inventory to specific customer needs through the use of **just-in-time systems.**

Amazon.com is an example of a firm that has been able to expand because of an efficient just-in-time delivery system. Amazon.com has differentiated itself by offering 4.7 million[14] books, music, and other titles online, versus the typical bookstore that houses 175,000[15] books at one time. The typical bookstore's reliance on bricks, mortar, and people limits both their customer base and offerings.

Just-in-time systems
fully integrate the production or sales process and timelines, allowing a firm to reduce its dependence on inventory.

Improved Customer Service

Customer service can be improved greatly on the Internet, as firms automate the process to allow for customer-self service. Firms such Federal Express and Wells Fargo[16] have shown excellent savings and improved customer service by moving away from labor-intensive phone contact to customer-controlled information systems. As discussed later in the chapter, FedEx now sends over 3.1 million packages a day with a 99 percent on time rating, and the tracking of those packages is now totally automated and accessible by a customer self-service system.[17]

Bricks and mortar limit traditional bookstore expansion.

Figure 15.4   Global Contact with Customers

Frontline employees
are those individuals within the organization who experience direct interaction with customers.

Many firms like Cisco use the Internet as a communication device to keep their **frontline employees,** and their customers up-to-date on product changes. In addition, the potential of the Internet as a delivery system for training programs is being explored, which potentially can result in substantial savings. Rather than take people off the job for training and incur the expenses for travel and facilities to bring together trainers and trainees, many companies today have developed virtual universities, delivered over the Internet, to keep their employees up-to-date. The benefits of this kind of just-in-time training can improve overall customer satisfaction by providing better-trained and informed employees and/or customers.

Market/Product Development Opportunities

Companies using the Internet can be open 24 hours a day, not only in the United States, but also around the world. (See Figure 15.4.) To maintain a customer contact with service customers in all countries of the world, without an automated system on the Internet, could be very costly.

The Internet allows a firm to market its products throughout the world and avoid the significant costs associated with face-to-face selling to customers. Even the smallest company can sell its products globally with little more than a Web Page, and the use of a delivery company such as FedEx or UPS, which will handle all of the export papers, as well as the shipping of the product.[18]

TYPES OF INTERNET SITES

As fast as the Internet is expanding, the number and variety of Internet sites is exploding. Sites can be classified into four major categories: company/brand sites, service sites, selling sites, and information sites. These categories are obviously not mutually exclusive and collectively exhaustive, but this typology is presented to allow the reader to begin to see how companies are using the Internet for either cost savings or profit. Table 15.1 contains a few example sites for each of these categories. As you visit each site, think about how each company has positioned itself to maximize the benefits of its site.

Company/Brand Sites

A number of companies that do not presently expect to sell products online have developed Internet sites. The purpose of the sites is to provide users of the Internet with information about their company and brands. Visitors to these sites will find information about the company history, mission, financial statements, public relations, press releases about the company, and even up-to-the-minute stock quotes. Additionally, ***company/brand sites*** are packed with information on how to use their product, how it is made, and how it can be used with other products.

The Coca-Cola Web site now includes 12 sections, and new items are added regularly. As of today, the sections include:

www.coke.com

▼ "The Coca-Cola Company" (the corporate side of the site).

▼ "Speak Your Mind" (a feedback and site visitor interactive section).

▼ "Trading Post" (section for collectors, traders, and visitors to purchase or trade coke paraphernalia).

Table 15.1	Four Categories of Internet Web Sites	
Types of Sites	**Company**	**URL**
Company/brand sites	Coke	www.coke.com
	Tide	www.tide.com
	Sunkist	www.sunkist.com
Service sites	Wells Fargo	www.wellsfargo.com
	Federal Express	www.fedex.com
Selling sites	Amazon.com	www.amazon.com
	Chrysler	www.daimlerchrysler.com
	L. L. Bean	www.llbean.com
Information sites	CNN/Sports Illustrated	www.cnnsi.com
	Wall Street Journal	www.wsj.com
	Yahoo!	www.yahoo.com

Figure 15.5

▼ "It's a Mystery" (launching point to random interesting Web links).

▼ "The World of Coca-Cola Pavilion" (history and fun about the company).

▼ "Sports and Entertainment" (a collection of sports links).

▼ "Digital Workout" (a game section).

▼ "Try Our Little Brain Twister" (puzzles and word games).

▼ "Hit The Wall" (animated extravaganza and links to similar sites).

▼ 3 International sites from Belgium, Japan, and France.

www.tide.com
www.sunkist.com

The Tide homepage contains similar information to that included on the Coca-Cola home page. The purpose of this site is not to sell Tide products direct from the manufacturer, but to enhance the brand equity of the product line. Due to competitive reasons (P&G does not want to compete with regular retailers), consumers visiting the site cannot purchase Tide products directly from Procter & Gamble. While they do have a "Shop Here" section, visitors are directed to either online retailers or stores located in their geographic area. The site does sell products that are not available in retail stores, such as Ricky Rudd (Tide-sponsored race driver) collectibles.

Some companies also have Internet connections for their suppliers. Sunkist includes a hyperlink on their site that is available to Sunkist growers. These growers can access newsletters, citriculture tips, and related resources. Nongrower visitors to the site are given access to information about the company, citrus products, news stories about Sunkist, recipes, and engineering breakthroughs; however, the site does not sell Sunkist products.

Service Sites

Customer *service sites* have developed rapidly on the Web because of the self-service nature of the Internet. The purpose of service sites is to provide a customer service interface for the company, without the need for a live person.

Before the introduction of Automatic Teller Machines (ATMs) in the banking industry, this industry was plagued by limited hours and a reliance on human contact. Banks built additional branches to get closer and closer to their ultimate customers. They also extended their hours and provided telephone services to extend their market. The introduction of ATMs allowed banks to extend banking hours to 24 hours a day without the need for 24-hour personnel. Additionally, the inclusion of ATMs in grocery stores and other retail establishments allowed banks to expand geographically without the necessity of building additional branches. The cost savings in bricks and mortar, as well as the personnel savings, have had significant impact on the profitability of banks in the past decade.

Many companies have been able to decrease customer service costs, while at the same time increasing overall customer satisfaction by using online Internet services. Wells Fargo first offered online services in 1989, and in 1995 introduced retail banking over the Internet. In 1995, Wells Fargo was taking 60 million calls per year, and 80 percent of those calls were from customers who just wanted balance information.[19] The savings in telephone charges and personnel alone allowed them to expand their Web offerings to include full banking services. Through the Wells Fargo Web site, customers can access their account balances, review their transaction history, transfer funds between accounts, pay their bills, buy and sell securities, apply for consumer accounts and lines of credit, receive real-time decisions on applications for home equity loans/lines of credit, and order specialized checks or foreign currency.

www.wellsfargo.com

Figure 15.6

www.fedex.com

Webmaster

is the title given to the individual who is responsible for maintaining and updating a Web site.

Perhaps the most dramatic savings, which can be realized through a firm's service site, are exemplified by the achievements of Federal Express. FedEx built its own private network to track the millions of packages they ship each day. This private network and the Internet have combined to allow them to accomplish a 99 percent on-time delivery rate, while shipping over 3.1 million packages daily.[20] In 1994, FedEx was spending millions of dollars on telephone charges and customer-support personnel to answer customer questions about the whereabouts of their packages. The development of the FedEx Web site, which helps customers interactively track their packages, has created tremendous savings for the company. How *much* money does it save? Nancy Raileanu, FedEx's **Webmaster,** says that an average of 500,000 packages per month were tracked on the site over the first six months. She figures that half of those were "curiosity" tracks by people just checking out the feature for the fun of it. But the other half would have called the company's 800 number. Such telephone calls average two minutes each. At an independently estimated cost to FedEx of about $0.50 per call, including personnel costs, that works out to about $125,000 in savings per month. Railienu says that the company spent only $50,000 on initial development of the site and $50,000 promoting it.[21]

Selling Sites

Selling sites are virtual stores that allow consumers to purchase products over the Internet. They typically represent a new channel of distribution for the seller. Most of the companies who now have selling sites probably utilized direct marketing (direct mail or catalogues) in the past. But a few, such as Amazon.com, have emerged as new ventures using the Internet as their entry into the direct selling media. (See Figure 15.7.)

www.amazon.com

Amazon.com started on the Web in July 1995, with the mission to educate, inform, and inspire. Today they offer 4.7 million books, CDs, audiobooks, DVDs, computer games, and related products. Since their inception, Amazon.com has sold to over 6.2 million people from more than 160 countries around the world.[22]

At the Amazon.com site, visitors can search for books or CDs by author, artist, title, subject, or keyword. There are browsing rooms that allow visitors to gather information about titles, sections to get recommendations for further reading, and links to allow one to read reviews written by the media or by other regular readers. Other Web-site owners can join the Associates Program that allows them to incorporate a link that recommends books, music, and other products (available at Amazon.com) in return for referral fees. Since its inception in July 1996, the Associates Program has signed up over 100,000 members.[23]

While the purpose of the Amazon.com site is to sell directly to the ultimate consumer, some sites are designed as sales promotional tools to aid the consumer in the decision making process. This kind of site allows visitors to screen themselves to see how they match with the company's products. One might consider this a logical extension of market segmentation. Consumers provide information about themselves, and the site attempts to match their individual needs and wants with the product offerings of the company.

www.daimlerchrysler.com

One site that accomplishes this process of moving the customer closer to the buying decision is the DaimlerChrysler site. The site offers many ways for consumers to collect information on their next vehicle. Each brand has its own page, so that a consumer could click to the Jeep Grand Cherokee page and receive information about that model. Another way to navigate is to look at all the cars at once and then click on those of interest. If the consumer wants specific attributes, they can navigate based on type of car, or even the type of incentive that is available.

After the visitor chooses the make and model, he can actually get a quote on the price of the car from dealers. This price quote is available only from Chrysler's Five Star dealers, but provides those dealers with excellent prospects. The information about prices, models, and options can aid the consumer in their choice of a vehicle. Additionally, the site has information about the history of the company with links to the parent company (Daimler-

Figure 15.7

Chrysler), the technology awards won by the company, innovations in the auto industry, and even a page for Chrysler owners to post pictures and stories about their Chrysler.

Many direct catalogue marketers have developed Web sites because of the lower cost of presenting the catalogue online versus the printing and mailing costs associated with direct mailing to consumers. While most direct catalogue marketers have not abandoned their printed catalogues, most are prepared for the next logical advance in direct marketing; that is, online selling. Online selling requires that the Web owners not only sell but also provide information related to the product lines. An excellent example of an online marketer is L.L. Bean. The site offers visitors the opportunity to receive any of their catalogues through the mail, or allows visitors to shop online. One special section of the L.L. Bean site is the section on outdoor activities. Visitors can receive information on Outdoor Discovery Schools, National Parks, or specific outdoor activities such as fly-fishing, camping, winter camping, backpacking, cycling, snowshoeing, and cross-country skiing. In addition, a complete history of the company and background material on its founder, Leon Leonwood Bean, is available on the site. While the company still does over 90 percent of its business via telephone, the Web site shows definite promise for cost savings and revenue generation in the future.[24]

www.llbean.com

Information Sites

Information sites generate revenue either through advertising or subscription rates charged to members. This type of site uses member loyalty and usage of the site to attract advertisers.

Figure 15.8

www.cnnsi.com

www.wsj.com

Members *subscribe* to these sites either through payment of a fee, or by providing membership profiles that can be used to sell advertising.

A number of printed publications have developed Web sites to reinforce their presence in the marketplace. CNNSI is a unique example of two firms (CNN and Sports Illustrated) that have joined together to provide sports lovers with volumes of information on every sports topic. (See Figure 15.8.) This *news media on the Internet* allows organizations that typically reported the news daily and weekly to now deliver news almost up-to-the-minute. Sports enthusiasts can get not only each week's *Sports Illustrated* magazine online, but can also access past issues. If that is not current enough, the sports fan can get information about games that are in progress, actually getting play-by-play information. Additionally, a visitor to the site can get statistics (both daily and season-to-date) about the teams as well as the players. Finally, sports fans can use the site to purchase the magazine and other sports-related products. This kind of site generates revenue through banner advertising and the sale of related products.

An example of a subscription-based site that generates revenue from member subscription fees and banner advertising is the *The Wall Street Journal* Interactive site. Similar to the CNNSI site, *The Wall Street Journal* Interactive Edition (WSJIE) provides up-to-the-minute financial information, while incorporating the daily feature articles from *The Wall Street Journal.* The links on this site allow subscribers to get historical information on financial products, track markets and investments, follow special industries such as technology, and even do research on topics of interest to the subscriber. In addition, the WSJIE site has an affiliate program that allows other businesses to integrate the WSJIE into their site. *The Wall Street Journal* Interactive Edition pays these businesses for any subscriptions that come from **click throughs.** While many publications have failed to gather subscribers on the Web, the WSJIE has found a formula that seems to be working. They were able to attract over 100,000 subscribers in their first year of operation.[25]

Another type of information site is represented by the ***search engines*** that people use to find information on the Internet. Since the Internet is so rich with information, surfers must have some mechanism to allow them to find the information they are seeking. Search engines such as Yahoo! generate revenue by selling banner advertising to businesses selling products. Yahoo! segments the advertised offerings based on the type of search the person is doing. For example, try typing in any computer-related word in a Yahoo! search, and you will probably see banner advertising for IBM. In addition, to the search feature on the Yahoo! site, visitors are able to get up-to-the-minute news from Reuters, purchase products at auction, or even build a virtual store online by clicking on the Yahoo! Store. Another feature of the Yahoo! site is the Yahoo! Clubs for visitors to join. These are virtual communities that share information between members.[26]

BENEFITS OF INTERNET MARKETING

The Internet can aid a company's overall marketing strategy in a number of ways. First, the Internet allows a company to increase its presence and brand equity in the marketplace. Company and brand sites give the marketer the opportunity to communicate the overall mission of the company/brand, provide information on the attributes and/or ratings of the company/brand, and can give information on the history of company/brand. In addition, firms can communicate information on the marketing mix offered.

Secondly, the Internet allows marketers to develop a prospective customer into a customer. Providing important information during the decision-making process can help the potential customer clarify the search. Information about a product's attributes and those of competitive products can aid in the decision-making process. In addition, the Web site can demonstrate products in actual use. This kind of information aids the consumer in building interest in the brand.

The Internet can move the customer closer to purchasing the product by allowing Web site visitors to match their needs with the offerings of the company. It is extremely important to remember that while traditional marketing techniques tend to be **push-oriented,** the Internet is a **pull-oriented** technique. This requires Internet Web site designers to think differently than traditional marketers about what should or should not be in the site offering.

Thirdly, the Internet can improve customer service by allowing customers to serve themselves when and where they choose. The self-service nature of Internet sites can be the cost savings that will ultimately pay for some sites. As more and more consumers begin to use the Internet, companies can serve these individuals without expensive distribution costs. The expansion of the number of customers served only requires that the organization have enough servers available.

The fourth benefit to marketers is that of information transfer. Traditionally, marketers gathered information via focus groups, mail surveys, telephone surveys, and personal interviews. These techniques can be very expensive to implement. The Web offers a mechanism for the company to collect similar information at a fraction of the cost. It is important to recognize the potential bias that might exist in such a sample. However, as the number and demographics of Internet users begin to represent a firm's target market, the collection of information on the Web might offer many benefits to the data collection process.

Not only can information be gathered from consumers, but information can also be shared with consumers. The Web can be used to provide expensive or specialized material to consumers that request such information from the company. Annual reports are now a typical part of every company's Web site. Rather than print millions and millions of copies that might be requested by consumers, the company now provides Web copies that consumers read on screen or print at their own expense. Other specialized material can also

Click through
is a process when a consumer clicks on a banner advertisement, and then "clicks through" to subscribe and/or purchase from the banner host.

www.yahoo.com

Push-oriented
means that the marketer decides what the consumer will see and where.

Pull-oriented
means the consumer chooses what to look for, when to look for it, and how much detail to gather.

Marketing Technologies

Information Technology and Marketing

"Ever since I typed out my first paper in WordPerfect 5.1 for DOS in one of the computer labs, I took a strong liking to the power of computing technologies to improve existing processes. This is of course in retrospect . . . I doubt that I was thinking along those lines when it happened. It was just a fun alternative to typewriters, and seemed to provide more opportunities for configuration (macros) and customization (programming)." Stuart Whitney Wong has come a long way from that first paper on the computer.

After receiving the International Baccalaureate high school diploma from the International School of Paris in 1986, Stuart was accepted with early admission to the University of Virginia. His adjustment to Virginia took a little getting used to. Having come from a graduating class of 30 or so students, it was quite a shock for Stuart to sit in on the 300+ student chemistry lectures! Luckily, he had placed out of most of the math, science, English, and foreign language requirements, which freed his schedule up to explore other disciplines. Stuart knew he wanted to double-major in French and something else.

Towards the end of the first two years, I had really enjoyed a computer programming class and was interested in the business applications of technology. I knew that I did not want to be a pure programmer.

After his first two years, he applied for and was accepted to the McIntire School of Commerce. For the next two years, Stuart studied Management Information Systems (MIS), Marketing, and French. He explains his choice,

The business grounding in accounting, finance, and the softer issues such as marketing and organizational management were all new to me. Not quite pure science, not quite social science . . . somewhere in between. I was much less comfortable with these subject matters than in pure sciences, but that was part of the challenge. I rooted myself in MIS and

French. Those were essentially my fallback subjects . . . both were subjects that I didn't really think twice about. Marketing was a different game . . . more comprehensive in strategic outlook with a strong reliance on creative skills as well as analytical skills. The business frameworks provided different lenses from which to critique business problems.

To increase his technical skills after his undergraduate degree program, Stuart stayed at Virginia to get an MS in MIS. In 1995, Stuart accepted a position with Booz-Allen & Hamilton, Inc. He worked as a multimedia programmer, network administrator, and lab manager for the next two years.

At Booz-Allen & Hamilton I refined my technical skills and received a good deal of exposure to teamwork, project and client management. However, once the lab evolved from four people to ten people, and the project pipeline was steady, it was time to move on. I was responsible for the running of the technical side of the lab and wanted greater exposure to the management side. I felt that I needed to develop those skills further, and decided to apply for an MBA program.

To further capitalize on his international background, Stuart attended the European Institute of Business Administration in Fontainebleau, France (INSEAD) for his MBA program. Graduating in December of 1998, Stuart just accepted a marketing IT (Information Technology) position with Hoffmann-La Roche in Basel, Switzerland. He is excited to be working in business-to-business marketing in their vitamins division, along with data warehouse and enterprise planning systems projects.

Source: E-mail interview with Stuart Whitney Wong, January 22, 1999, while he was traveling in South East Asia.

be provided for consumers to access as they choose. The fulfilling of information requests via the Web can offer substantial savings to the company.

But, the greatest potential for the future is probably in direct marketing where catalogues can be offered online. These catalogues can be changed with ease if prices and/or product offerings change. This could represent substantial savings for organizations that would normally print new catalogues and mail those catalogues to consumers.

DRAWBACKS OF INTERNET MARKETING

Although it is evident that there are numerous advantages for companies marketing via the Internet, there are two major drawbacks of Internet marketing, particularly at this time. These two drawbacks are a limited target audience and consumer resistance to change. Both of these are likely to change as the Internet diffuses throughout our society.

Limited Audience

For those of us that use the Internet daily for information, e-mail, and as a mechanism to purchase products, it seems that everyone is using it. However, a very large segment of our society has yet to embrace the Internet (presently 73 million users in the U.S.). As stated earlier in this chapter, a majority of Internet users fit a definite profile. Although this profile might match the target market of some companies, it does not match the target market profile of all companies.

As of 1998, statistics indicate that approximately 58 percent of the U.S. population has Internet access, either at home or at work. But, there are a number of under-represented segments on the Web.[27] The rural poor (earning less that $5,000 per year) have only a 7.9 percent rate of PC ownership, and less than 2.5 percent of these have Internet access. Both rural and central city minorities have lower penetration rates than the population as a whole. Female heads of households are also significantly behind the general population (25 percent). These numbers clearly indicate under-representation within certain segments of our society. Although Internet use is increasing and these numbers are changing at a very fast rate, until the demographics of Internet usage mirror our society as a whole, companies must use caution in over emphasizing the Internet in their overall marketing mix.

Resistance to Change

As we all know, people are resistant to change in general. This resistance was clearly demonstrated when people began to move from shopping at retail stores to purchasing goods via mail order catalogs. This same resistance is being demonstrated as people begin to purchase products over the Internet.

Today, many people would think nothing of giving their credit card number to someone whom they know nothing about during a mail-order telephone purchase. But, there is clear resistance to typing their credit card number into the computer and clicking a "send" button. How can the customer feel assured that the number is going to the right person? The media has fueled this uncertainty with stories of "computer piracy" and "hacker invasions." Someone educated in Internet security knows that decrypting a credit card number electronically is much more difficult than picking up a receipt with a number printed on it. But the average user may not realize the benefits of encryption, or even know how to tell if a Web site is secure. The problem returns again to the basic fear of the unknown.

The change in behavior that will be necessary for this new distribution technique to really take off requires that firms understand how to make consumers feel less overall risk when purchasing over the Internet. One simple answer is to educate consumers about the process, but that will take time. Warranties, security measures, and other ways to augment the purchase process and the overall product offering, in order to reduce the perceived risk to consumers, must be evaluated by companies who wish to overcome consumers' resistance to change.

MARKETING INSIGHTS ON THE INTERNET

Marketing on the Internet is unique in comparison to other types of marketing. Analysis of the various types of Internet sites yields a number of insights. These insights can be categorized into five guiding principles for Web sites:

▼ Selling on the Web is *interactive.*

▼ Promotion on the Internet is pull-oriented.

▼ Exchange of information is key.

▼ Sites must do more than just sell.

▼ Size and location are no longer obstacles to success.

Selling on the Web Is Interactive

When a company approaches customers through traditional media, the customers are usually passive in the communication process. The customers are typically not interacting with the company, they are simply reading an advertisement or viewing a commercial on television. The ads are *just there* as a part of an activity the potential customer has chosen to pursue. Magazines and newspapers feature their *articles* on the cover and in headlines, the ads are just part of the package. Television commercials *interrupt* the show you have chosen to watch, and unless you are watching a videotape, you can't fast-forward past them. The Internet is a far more active medium, where the individual can be much more selective about what is viewed. Customers must make an active choice (click) to see something, and they can view it as long or as briefly as they like.

Even in the personal selling process, where the customer traditionally becomes more active, there are differences when one markets on the Web. Table 15.2 illustrates the steps in the traditional personal selling process and suggests different techniques that can be used when marketing on the Web.

What we can see from the following table is that having the customer active rather than passive in the process affords the marketer the ability to not only save money but to provide a higher level of service. Web sites can be used to identify needs and wants, dis-

Table 15.2	Steps in the Personal Selling Process Adapted to the Web	
	Personal Selling	**Web Selling**
Prospecting	Gathering names from databases, referrals from past customers and trade shows, cold calling	All of those traditional methods, except cold calling*, plus: search engines, participation in listserv discussions, and links from other sites
Preapproach	Collecting information about the customer and their company prior to the initial visit	Data collection online, site searches, screening links
Approach	Developing a relationship with the customer (based on the four basic social style categories)	Selecting an appropriate URL, developing an effective opening Web screen
Need identification	Probing with open-ended questions to identify the customer's needs and wants	Creating clear navigation pathways that allow for an *individualized* experience of the Web site (tracking the selected pathways can give the company insights into the customer's thought process)
Presentation	Discussing the key benefits and selling points, often modifying the format to suit the needs identified earlier	Using graphics and screen design to allow the customer to explore the product's features
Handling objections	Listening and replying to objections	Ensuring that all potentially foreseen objections are addressed
Gaining commitment	Asking for the sale and closing the sale by filling out the paperwork	Making it easy for the customer to make the commitment (convenient "shopping carts" for taking the order online)
Follow-up	Complete any agreed upon actions and stay in touch with the customer to monitor and maintain the relationship (traditionally by telephone and/or mail)	The same actions but more frequently utilizing personal e-mail and individualized follow-up offers

*Cold calling in Web terms might be considered analogous to *spamming*, the sending of unsolicited e-mail sales letters, which is highly frowned upon in Internet society.

cover preferences, provide information and service, develop loyalty, and position the firm for future sales from the prospect.

Promotion on the Internet Is Pull-Oriented

Firms promote themselves in different ways using the medium of the Web. Negotiating hyperlinks with related products is a critical promotional tool on the Web, and ***banner advertising*** has become very popular in recent years as a way to hyperlink these sites together. Mass media typically pushes the messages to consumers, while consumers on the Web must actually pull the advertisements by clicking on links that pique their interest. Web sites must be designed in such a way that consumers can quickly see the value of spending time at the Web site. Table 15.3 summarizes a number of important issues to consider when designing Web sites.

Placing a company's brochures online is a sure way to chase consumers from your site. ***Electronic brochures,*** that is, digitizing your brochures and placing them on the Web, do not work! Consumers know this media is interactive and expect to interact.

Web marketing also changes the other promotional activities of the firm. All future advertisements must contain the Web address for the company if the firm expects to grow its equity in the Web site.

Exchange of Information Is Key

The Internet is an information-rich environment. When consumers visit a Web site, they are typically looking for in-depth, specialized information. If valuable information is not provided, it is unlikely that we can get the consumer to return to the site. Web site managers should look for ways to keep the material fresh and current. Features such as financial news or sports information, from organizations such as *The Wall Street Journal* Interactive Edition or CNN/Sports Illustrated, can be integrated into a site to enhance the richness of the experience of visiting the site.

Consumers are willing to provide information about themselves in exchange for the valuable information they are seeking. Many sites today request visitors to fill out brief questionnaires about the visitor and their likes/dislikes. This information can be extremely valuable in designing the marketing offering for a company. It may also be utilized to sell advertising on the company's site to other firms. The essential observation is that consumers are willing to exchange valuable information as long as they get valuable information and/or experiences in return.

Table 15.3 Keys to Web Design	
Things to Do	**Things to Avoid**
Provide description of the firm	Scrolling
Ensure fast load times	Large graphic files
Create consistent navigation pathways	Reliance on one browser
Make the site interactive	Broken links
Register with search engines	Excessive use of plug-ins
Register the domain name	Obscure URLs
Copyright the site	Copycatting other sites
Use trademarks appropriately	Plagerism of material
Market the site in other materials	Allowing the Web site to grow stale

Sites Must Do More Than Just Sell

Designers of Web sites need to be cognizant that their sites must do more than just sell. Web sites that offer other benefits to the customer, such as analysis of needs, assistance in product selection, information on usage with complimentary products, and meeting places for interested customers, can provide the reason for a customer to come back to the site over and over again. Sites such as Virtual Vineyards provide information on the use of wines in cooking, the types of wines, how they should be used, as well as an abundance of other information on wines and the wine industry. The success of this site comes from the fact that they do much more for customers than just recommend wine.

www.virtualvin.com

Size and Location Are No Longer Obstacles to Success

Small businesses can be big on the Web, and big businesses can be small on the Web. Today, even the smallest firm can compete globally by using the expertise of the transportation companies. These transportation companies (i.e., FedEx and UPS) make it easy to export products as well as deliver them worldwide. On the other hand, even the largest firm can enter specialized markets, if it can automate its systems sufficiently to make it cost-effective to service tiny market segments. In addition, larger firms can focus on individual needs by designing self-service systems on the Web that can deliver specialized information and perform many of the customer contact functions.

Chapter Summary

The use of the Web in business (e-commerce) has exploded in the last few years. Today over 97 percent of large businesses report that they have an Internet site, and the percentage of sites for small firms, although less, is growing. As a result, the integration of a firm's or brand's Web site into the overall marketing mix is no longer an option. Firms have been forced to gravitate to the Web because of customers and competition. Millions of customers are moving to the Web to collect information about companies, products, and brands. Multitudes of businesses, both large and small, are considering this new medium. More and more of these businesses have realized the benefits of building relationships with other businesses on the Web. As this diffusion takes place, the Web has become increasingly a daily part of our lives. Students use the Web before they go the library; customers have begun to use the Web to gather information on companies, products, and brands; and finally businesses have begun to use this tool as an integral component in their overall communications.

This chapter has discussed the origins of the Internet and the impact of the Internet on today's business activities. Electronic commerce has expanded on the Internet because of four major areas of improved business practices: reduced costs, inventory reduction, improved customer service, and market/product development opportunities. Typically, business use of the Internet to communicate with customers is accomplished through four main categories of sites: company/brand sites, service sites, selling sites, and information sites.

The Internet can potentially benefit a company's marketing strategy in a number of ways. First, the Internet facilitates the growth of a company's brand equity in the marketplace. Secondly, the Internet allows marketers to develop a prospective customer into an existing customer by providing important product information that aids the customer decision process. A third benefit is that the Internet can improve the firm's overall customer service by allowing customers to serve themselves when and where they choose. Finally, the Internet offers two-way communication that enables companies to interact with their customers.

Although there are many positives associated with the Internet, the system does have its limitations. The Internet is still in its infancy, and a very large segment of society has yet to embrace it. Those that do use the Internet on a regular basis are not a representative sample of the total population. There is also consumer reluctance to purchase products over the Internet. Far more customers use the Internet solely for informational purposes, rather than to make actual purchases.

Clearly, marketing on the Internet is different from other types of marketing. In comparison to traditional media, the Internet customer is much more active and "pulls" the company's message through by clicking. Consequently, active sites must be constructed that entice the customer to become interested and pursue additional product information. Hence, sites must do more than just sell. Web sites that offer other benefits (such as analyzing needs, assisting in product selection, offering information pertaining to complimentary products, and providing meeting places for interested customers) create additional incentives for customers to return to their Web sites. Finally, the Internet, from a marketing standpoint, is a great equalizer. Businesses of all sizes can effectively compete on the Web.

The Digital Revolution is here and will have effects similar to any social revolution. A mere ten years ago the Internet thrust itself upon our society. Consumers and businesses have struggled with this new media; however, browsers and Web editors have become easier and easier to use. Both groups have begun to see the benefits of this new medium. As this innovation diffuses throughout our society, it becomes increasingly important for businesses to make the Internet an integral component of their offerings in the marketplace.

Key Terms

Internet is a worldwide network of interconnected computer networks that carry data and make information exchange possible.

World Wide Web (**WWW** or **Web**) is a subset of the Internet comprised of a collection of hyperlinked documents (not computers) that use a common protocol.

Hypertext is any text that contains links to other documents.

HTML (HyperText Markup Language) is the coding language used for creating hypertext documents and formatting pages for use on the Web.

URL (Uniform Resource Locator) is the Internet address for a Web document or other file.

HTTP (HyperText Transport Protocol) is the protocol for moving hypertext across the Internet. It allows for the transfer of images, sound, video, and other files between computers.

Intranets connect the computers within a business together.

Extranets connect computers outside the firm with the intranet at the firm.

Electronic Data Interchange (EDI) is a computer-to-computer communications protocol that allows basic information on purchases and invoices to be exchanged.

Just-in-time systems fully integrate the production or sales process and timelines, allowing a firm to reduce its dependence on inventory.

Frontline employees are those individuals within the organization who experience direct interaction with customers.

Webmaster is the title given to the individual who is responsible for maintaining and updating a Web site.

Click through is a process when a consumer clicks on a banner advertisement, and then "clicks through" to subscribe and/or purchase from the banner host.

Push-oriented means that the marketer decides what the consumer will see and where.

Pull-oriented means the consumer chooses what to look for, when to look for it, and how much detail to gather.

Additional Key Terms and Concepts

Internet hosts or Internet Service
    Providers (ISPs)
Obsolescence costs
Banner advertising
Company/brand sites
Selling sites

Storage costs
Handling costs
Search engines
Electronic brochures
Service sites
Information sites

Questions for Discussion

1. Briefly discuss the history of the Internet. How did it get started? Who were the important people who brought it to life? What were the essential inventions that allowed the expansion of the Internet?

2. Thinking about the diffusion of computers throughout our society, what are some of the factors that will limit the expansion of the Internet?

3. Discuss the types of participants on the Internet. How many are there? What do they do on the Internet? Are they purchasing products on the Web?

4. Identify a product that is not presently using the Internet as a part of its marketing mix and discuss the advantages of including Internet marketing in its overall offering.

5. Discuss the size and potential for businesses on the Internet. How fast is this area growing? What are the largest segments of business on the Internet?

6. Discuss the areas of improvement to businesses that come about because of using the Web. What ways can the firm either reduce costs or expand offerings?

7. What are the four types of Internet sites? Discuss their distinguishing characteristics.

8. Discuss the four benefits of Internet marketing.

9. Discuss the two major drawbacks to Internet marketing.

10. Analyze the five guiding principles for Web sites.

Internet Questions

1. Visit the IntelliQuest Web site (**www.intelliquest.com**). How does IntelliQuest aid technology companies in improving their marketing?

2. The Graphic, Visualization, & Usability Center at Georgia Tech (**www.gvu.gatech. edu/user_surveys**) conducts periodic surveys on WWW Users. Obtain a basic demographic profile of Web users from the latest survey, and discuss the potential significance of the information to a marketing executive.

3. There are a number of discussion groups (Listservs) to aid the Internet marketer. Two of these groups are an Internet sales discussion group located at **www.audettemedia.com/i-sales/Internet-Sales Discussion List** and an Internet

advertising discussion group located at www.internetadvertising.org/subscribe.html. Join one of these groups and provide a brief report on the benefits of belonging to such a group.

Endnotes

[1] For the purposes of this chapter, the terms Internet and Web will be used interchangeably.

[2] Evan I. Schwartz, *Webonomics: Nine Essential Principles for Growing Your Business on the World Wide Web* (New York, NY: Broadway Books of Bantam Doubleday Dell Publishing Group, Inc., 1997), p. 1.

[3] Nabil R. Adams, Oktay Dogramaci, Aryya Gangopadhyay, and Yelena Yesha, *Electronic Commerce: Technical, Business, and Legal Issues* (New Jersey: Prentice Hall PTR, 1999), pp. 1–3.

[4] *Business-to-Business E-Commerce to Dominate Online Marketplace,* dateline August 13, 1998 published on the Sell It! Web site (www.sellitontheweb.com)

[5] Data available from Computer World Web site, www.computerworld.com/home/ Emmerce.nsf/All/stats/

[6] Data available from Internet Domain Survey conducted twice yearly by Network Wizards at www.nw.com

[7] Data available from Nua, Ltd. Web site, www.nua.ie/surveys/how_many_online/ n_america.html

[8] Data available from IntelliQuest Web site, www.intelliquest.com/

[9] Data available from Pew Research Center, www.people-press.org/tech98sum.htm

[10] *Online Buyers to Double by End of 1999,* dateline December 2, 1998 as published by CyberAtlas at cyberatlas.internet.com/market/retailing/emark.html

[11] Ibid.

[12] *The Emerging Digital Economy,* U.S. Department of Commerce, Washington, D.C., April, 1997. Also, available at www.ecommerce.gov/emerging.htm

[13] Ibid.

[14] Amazon.com Company Information published on their Web site at www.amazon.com/ exec/obidos/subst/misc/company-info.html/

[15] Schwartz, *Webonomics,* p. 98.

[16] Lisa M. Bowman, ZDNN, *Is Online Banking Ready to Take Off?* October 9, 1998 as published by Ziff-Davis on their Web site at www.zdnet.com/zdnn/stories/ zdnn_smgraph_display/0,4436,2147450,00.html

[17] Data available from FedEx at www.fedex.com/us/about/pressreleases/ pressrelease090998.html

[18]Federal Express information available at www.fedex.com/us/services/international/index.html and United Parcel Service information at www.ups.com/bussol/logistics/customs.html

[19]Schwartz, *Webonomics,* p. 128.

[20]Data published in *Who Is FedEx?* at www.fedex.com/us/about/facts.html

[21]Schwartz, *Webonomics,* p. 118.

[22]Data published in *Amazon.com Company Information* published at www.amazon.com/exec/obidos/subst/misc/company-info.html/

[23]Data published in *Amazon.com's Associates Program Is a Hit with Music Sites,* August 3, 1998 at www.amazon.com/exec/obidos/subst/misc/music-associates-press-release.html/

[24]L.L. Bean Web site, www.llbean.com/

[25]Schwartz, *Webonomics,* p. 35.

[26]John Hagel, III and Arthur G. Armstrong, *Net Gain: Expanding Markets through Virtual Communities* (Boston: Harvard Business School Press, 1997), exact data at www.cyberatlas.com/big-picture/demographics/least.html.

[27]Data available from CyberAtlas at www.cyberatlas.com

A Different Kind of Résumé

John Adams is just entering his final year at the state university. He has spent the past three years studying business and has decided to have a double major in management information systems and marketing. John enjoys management information systems because he has learned how to make the computer do what he wants it to do, especially through programming. He did not like, however, the systems-design aspects of MIS that kept him behind his desk and away from his computer.

Marketing is John's strongest major because he particularly enjoys its creative aspects, especially the promotional components. He is bored by topics like distribution, logistics, and pricing. He loves to use the Internet in school and wants very much to get a position with a firm that allows him to develop Web sites. John feels that this kind of position would allow him to bring together what he likes most about his two majors—programming and promotion.

The Office of Career Planning at the state university requires that all students create a résumé before using the university's interview services. John struggled with this task, because the résumé was limited to one page in length. He thought it would be impossible to sufficiently bring together both of his concentrations and include his education, experiences, and career aspirations. He was able to complete the résumé, but he was not satisfied that he had demonstrated his qualifications for a Web designer's job. He felt ill-prepared for the job-hunting process.

As he thought about the résumé writing task, he realized he had at his fingertips the ability to demonstrate his qualifications and not be limited to just one page. He would design his own Web site to demonstrate to potential employers his qualifications. As John thought about what should be included in his Web page, he realized the importance of developing specific objectives, designing the site for ease of navigation, utilizing graphics appropriately, and a host of other Web design issues. He wanted to rush to the computer and begin programming, but knew that the background preparation required for creating detailed storyboards would increase the overall value of his site.

Discussion Questions

1. What are the overall objectives of the site? Outline what the major sections might be.

2. What key elements should be included on the opening page of the site? What features could be included to enhance the impact and appeal of this page?

3. What might each of the major sections look like, and what should be included in each? How can he coordinate the sections into an integrated whole?

4. What kind of navigation might he use? What factors might influence his choices?

5. What sites exist on the Web that can help in the design?

6. What would the storyboards for the site look like?

Appendix I

Planning for Marketing Decisions[1]

THE NATURE AND IMPORTANCE OF PLANNING

Planning is the basis for sound decision making in any situation in life. Whether you are planning a wedding, a vacation, or a multimillion dollar sponsorship program, numerous efforts pertaining to the particular activity must be coordinated and planned well in advance. Without planning, the activity may have disastrous results.

Consider, for example, a wedding. John and Susan get engaged, and then announce in March that they wish to marry in June because they simply can't wait any longer. The bride, groom, and their parents meet to discuss the wedding. In making a list of things to do, the top priorities are to secure the church and reception site for the desired date. Once those details are set, invitations, flowers, bride's and bridesmaids' dresses, and tuxedos must be ordered. Next, the music, menus, cake, and invitation list must be decided on. And finally, table seating, the rehearsal dinner, and the honeymoon must be planned.

If any of these elements are overlooked or not followed up on, John and Susan's wedding day will be ruined in their eyes. For example, if the responsibility of ordering the flowers is not assigned to a particular person, there is a risk that no flowers will be displayed at the church or on tables at the reception. If the responsibility of ordering and mailing invitations is not assigned to someone, there is a risk that no guests will attend the wedding. John and Susan want everything perfect for that day, so tasks are assigned to the bride, groom, and parents, and the group decides to meet in two days to discuss their progress.

When they next meet, John and Susan are very upset. The church and the reception sites are both booked on their desired date. John and Susan learn that most engaged couples have secured these details many months in advance. Susan also discovers that the dress she wants will take six months to order. And Susan's parents find that the cost of the reception with the desired number of guests far exceeds their budget. The group is forced to rethink their original plan and make the necessary modifications, allowing for these environmental factors.

This example demonstrates several elements that are key to any planning activity:

▼ **Timing.** Planning must occur well in advance of the activity. Planning postponed until the last minute will only have negative results.

▼ **Tasks.** Every activity consists of a number of specific tasks. All details about each task must be planned in order for the entire activity to be successful.

▼ **Responsibility.** Every task needs a specific coordinator. If one person is not held accountable, the task may not get done.

▼ **Follow-up.** Even if responsibility for each task has been delegated, one individual must follow-up on and coordinate the progress of the overall activity. Even the most responsible person may slip up and forget something.

▼ **Budgeting.** Budgeting is essential in planning. Plans that are too expensive for an individual or organization can have serious financial consequences. Through planning, costs are estimated and deemed acceptable or unacceptable.

These elements are critical in business planning. However, business planning has more far-reaching consequences than a wedding. Thousands of jobs and millions of dollars rely on solid planning efforts by management.

There are several levels of planning in any organization. The most important level is *strategic planning,* or the organization's overall game plan. This plan typically encompasses the firm's long-range goals and dictates direction for all departments in the firm. The means of achieving the company goals and the resources needed are detailed in full. The plan establishes goals and strategies, delineates activities, and assigns responsibility for every facet of the organization.

Marketing planning is the game plan for a particular product or product line. The marketing plan is the detailed scheme of the marketing strategies and activities associated with each product's marketing mix. The strategic plan is the company's overall plan; the marketing plan details the marketing efforts and strategies as outlined in the strategic plan.

Tactical planning is another level of organizational planning. *Tactical planning* involves specifying details that pertain to the organization's activities for a certain period of time. For example, the scheduled dates for a radio or television campaign for the third quarter would be included in a tactical plan. So, too would the details regarding the fourth-quarter price deal offered to dealers. The production department's tactical plan may include the testing of a new quality control program on a packaging line. The tactical plan is a detailed account of the firm's short-term activities as outlined in the strategic plan.

Strategic planning is an effective means for an organization to coordinate efforts among various departments, analyze its competitive position within its environment, and allocate its resources. The strategic planning process causes all employees involved in the

Learning Objectives

After you have completed this appendix, you should be able to:

1. Explain the five key elements of planning.

2. Describe the levels of organizational planning.

3. Discuss the five fundamental elements of strategic planning.

4. Describe BCG's Product Portfolio-Analysis Model.

5. Describe GE's Attractiveness-Business Position Model.

6. Discuss the characteristics of a marketing plan.

7. Understand the components of a marketing plan.

process to thoroughly think through the strategies that will prove most effective in achieving company goals. We will now turn to a discussion of the fundamental elements involved in strategic planning.

FUNDAMENTALS OF STRATIGIC PLANNING

Strategic planning is comprised of five fundamental elements as shown in Figure A.1.

Organization Mission

An organization's mission is the most important element in strategic planning. As part of the mission statement the organization must define its business, or what makes it different from competition. The entire strategic plan is built around this element. By focusing on its mission, management can concentrate their energies on making sound decisions, allocating resources, and generating profits in the long run. A mission statement is a guideline for the organization's decision making for both the short and long run. The mission provides direction to the strategic planning and marketing planning processes as is illustrated in the following mission statement of the Coca-Cola Company:

> We exist to create value for our share owners on a long-term basis. . . . As the world's largest beverage company, we refresh that world. We do this by developing superior soft drinks, both carbonated and noncarbonated, and profitable nonalcoholic beverage systems that create value for our Company, our bottling partners, our customers, our share owners and the communities in which we do business.
>
> In creating value, we succeed or fail based on our ability to perform as worthy stewards of several key assets: (1) Coca-Cola, the world's most recognized trademark, and other highly valuable trademarks; (2) the world's most effective distribution system; (3) satisfied customers, who make a good profit selling our products; (4) our people, who are ultimately responsible for building this enterprise; (5) our abundant resources, which must be intelligently allocated; and (6) our strong global leadership in particular and in the business world in general.[2]

Coca-Cola's mission statement has three characteristics that are typical of corporate mission statements. First, the statement is a vision: the chairman of the board views the entire world as a potential target market with his company satisfying the needs of the entire target. Second, the statement is motivational both for employees and for stockholders. And third, the statement refers to certain philosophies or guidelines that will be followed: In the case of Coca-Cola, to refresh the world and to perform as stewards of the six noted key assets. Marketing plans can be developed supporting these elements.

Figure A.1 **Elements of Strategic Planning**

▼ Organization mission
▼ Strategic business units
▼ Objectives
▼ Strategic planning tools
▼ Marketing plans

Strategic Business Units

Large companies offering diverse product lines or operating in several countries create *strategic business units (SBUs),* or smaller divisions, to facilitate planning and general operations. Smaller companies also use SBUs as a means of organizing operations. An SBU can be one specific product, one product line, or a particular business. Each SBU establishes its own mission statement, objectives, and strategic and marketing plans independent of other SBUs in the organization. The SBU operates as a separate entity. Typically, the individual SBUs have their own management teams and operational goals, while maintaining common management and production facilities.

Digital Equipment Corporation (DEC), for example, recently restructured its business units, organizing them around product groups rather than on vertical markets. The corporation has five business units: client/server software unit; the OpenUMS client/server systems and software unit; the Unix and Microsoft Windows NT client/server software unit; the networking products unit; and the memory and peripheral upgrades unit. The presidents of the five units report to DEC's sales and marketing chief.[3]

Objectives

An organization's mission statement directs the organization's objectives. All strategic and marketing plans are based on these objectives. Every department and SBU can have its own objectives, but these objectives must be guided by the organization's overall objectives.

Any objective must be clear, concise, and realistic. Objectives are typically based on profit, market share, growth, or diversity. For example, an objective for the marketing department may be "to obtain a 15 percent market share and maintain a profit margin of 20 percent by the end of the fiscal year" for a specific product or product line. An objective for the production department may be to "reduce the level of rework from packaging from 5 percent to 3 percent by the end of the fiscal year." An important part of any objective is the time frame assigned for achievement. A time frame is necessary to determine whether or not the objective has been met by the department or SBU. Many organizations base management bonuses on the achievement of objectives.

Strategic Planning Tools

Tools are available to help managers in their strategic and marketing planning efforts. Careful planning efforts are acutely important to most large organizations that are structured into multiple SBUs with many product offerings. The fundamental issue is one of resource allocation and prioritization. Which products (SBUs) are most, and least, deserving of additional investments? The situation faced by business planners can be compared to that which confronts medical personnel in times of war and medical crises, when these personnel are faced with the wrenching task of determining which of many injured people should receive immediate aid. *Triage* is the medical practice that is used in times of medical crisis. Patients are prioritized in terms of how badly they require immediate medical care, and how likely it is that their lives can be saved. Those patients who badly need care and are likely to survive are the top priority for assistance, whereas those who either are unlikely to survive or are not in desperate condition are lower in the priority scheme.

The following sections examine two frameworks that are broadly analogous to the practice of triage. These models are the Boston Consulting Group's Product-Portfolio Analysis and General Electric's Market Attractiveness-Business Position Model.

BCG's Product-Portfolio Analysis

An organization's products can be viewed as a portfolio, with each having a different growth rate and market share. Product-portfolio analysis offers suggestions for appropriate marketing strategies to best utilize an organization's scarce cash and other limited resources.[4]

The BCG model (illustrated in Figure A.2) classifies products from the perspective of a single company and its particular products or SBUs. Classification is based on two dimensions. The horizontal axis represents the relative market share that a particular product realizes, vis-à-vis the dominant brand in the category. This axis delineates relative share into "high" and "low" categories.

Consider, for example, a product category with four brands and the following market shares: Brand A, the industry leader, enjoys a relative market share that is twice as large as its nearest rival, Brand B. Comparatively, Brands B, C, and D realize relative shares of 0.5 (i.e., 25/50), 0.4 (20/50), and 0.1 (5/50), respectively. If the point of division between the right and left quadrants of the matrix is at a relative share of 1.0, Brand A has a relatively high market share, whereas Brands B, C, and D are all relatively low.

The vertical axis in the BCG matrix is based on the product, market, or industry growth rate. Here, the dividing point between upper and lower quadrants is traditionally set, albeit arbitrarily, at 10 percent. Realizing that the population growth rate in the United States is around 2 percent per annum, many staple products (milk, bread, industrial commodities) generally grow at a rate commensurate with the population, and, as such, are considered relatively low on the scale. It is in the area of new technologies and fads that growth rates are high. Innovative new products experience growth rates of 50 percent or higher in early years, and then eventually decrease over time.

With these distinctions in mind, Figure A.2 categorizes four general types of products, and gives each a metaphoric name, suggesting implications that each holds for a firm's marketing strategy: cash cows (to be milked), stars (to sustain their ascendancy), problem children (to treat with caution), and dogs (to avoid).

▼ **Cash Cows:** Cash cows are products that enjoy high market share but show low levels of market growth. These are generally very profitable products that generate more cash than what is needed to maintain the market share. Strategically, corporate-wide efforts should be to manage cash cows by investing in improvements to

Figure A.2   The BCG Product-Portfolio Model

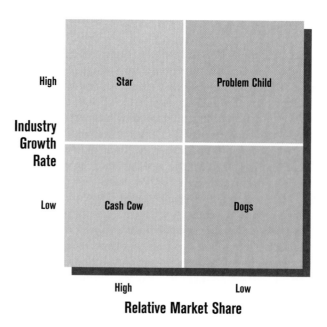

maintain superiority, attempting to maintain price leadership, and using excess cash to support development of new products and growth elsewhere in the SBU.

▼ **Stars:** Stars are products with high market growth rates and high market shares. Stars are market leaders with substantial profits. A large investment is required, though, to generate any growth. Strategically, effort must be made to protect existing share by obtaining a large share of new users and investing in product improvements, better market coverage, and perhaps price reductions.

▼ **Problem Children:** Problem children are products that enjoy rapid growth but low market shares and poor profit margins. Problem children have enormous demand for cash, and risk becoming dogs, since growth inevitably will slow if cash is not forthcoming. Strategically, marketers of a problem child must either invest heavily to earn a disproportionate share of new sales or buy existing shares via acquisition of a competitor.

▼ **Dogs:** Dogs are products with low market shares and low market growth rates. Dogs operate at a cost disadvantage and have few opportunities for growth inasmuch as the markets are not growing and there is little new business. Marketers of dog products can pursue several strategies: (1) focus on a particular segment of the market and attempt to outperform competitors in that segment; (2) harvest the product by cutting back to minimum levels all marketing support and other investments; (3) divest the product by selling the business to a competitor; or (4) eliminate the product from the product line.

Ideally, an organization should have a balance of products in its portfolio to be successful. Products that generate cash offset those products that require additional investment for growth. If a firm has too many cash cows or dogs, overall company growth is unlikely. Likewise, if it has disproportionate numbers of stars or problem children, the cash demands may be excessive to provide sufficient support for these products. The logic underlying product portfolios is similar to financial investment logic: Don't place all your eggs in one basket! Having only a single type of security in one's investment portfolio can lead to disaster if the market for that one offering experiences a sudden decline.

General Electric's Attractiveness/Strength Model

General Electric has provided another model useful for strategically evaluating how a company's or SBU's products are faring and what changes might be needed. The GE model (see Figure A.3), like the BCG matrix, is a two-dimensional matrix that portrays the position of a company's products or SBUs. Unlike the BCG, however, which classifies products on the basis of only two considerations (relative market share and industry growth rate), the GE model employs several measurements and observations to classify products. *Market,* or *industry, attractiveness* is measured on the vertical dimension of the model. An attractiveness index is constructed for each of an organization's products or SBUs based on such factors as market growth rate, market size, seasonality of demand, economies of scale in the production of a product, extent and likelihood of competition, and the overall cost. More attractive products enjoy larger growth rates, less seasonal demand, less competition, and so on. The vertical axis of the matrix delineates three levels of attractiveness: low, medium, and high.

A product's *business position,* depicted on the horizontal axis, refers to an organization's strength or ability to take advantage of market opportunities. As with attractiveness, a product's or SBU's strength is indexed based on such considerations as product quality, adequacy of distribution channels, the company's relative market share, price competitiveness, sales force quality, and so on. Business position is divided into three qualitative groupings: strong, medium, or weak.

Crossing the three attractiveness groupings with the three business-strength breakdowns results in a matrix with nine cells. Individual products or SBUs are shown as circles

LEARNING **OBJECTIVE** LO5

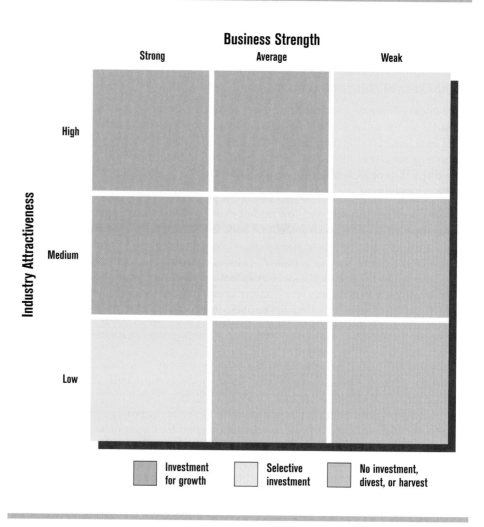

Figure A.3   GE's Attractiveness/Strength Matrix

in the matrix, with the circle's size representing a product's (or SBU's) dollar sales volume in relation to other product's (SBU's) in the matrix. The ideal situation is for an organization to have products with high market attractiveness and strong business positions (the upper-left portion of the matrix). The worst situation is a product with low market attractiveness and weak business position (the lower-right corner).

The intention is to use the model to chart the status of products of SBUs and determine which products are the best candidates for investment and growth, and which are possible candidates for elimination. Resource-allocation decisions, in other words, are based on comparing each product or SBU against other company offerings. Products or SBUs in the upper-left portion of the matrix require investment and management attention; those in the bottom right are candidates for harvesting or divesting.

Marketing Plans

LEARNING OBJECTIVE LO6

The final fundamental element of strategic planning is the marketing plan. As was outlined earlier, the marketing plan is the detailed scheme of the marketing strategies and activities associated with each product's marketing mix. The marketing plans emanate from and are inspired by the overall strategic plan. Marketing plays an instrumental role in determining the strategic plan, and in turn, marketing plans are influenced and directed by the strategic plan.

Marketing plans can take many forms depending on the size of the company and the number of products within its portfolio. A marketing plan can be developed for the entire family of products, for each product line, or for each individual product. Most marketing plans are short-term, covering a one-year period. Other marketing plans are much longer, encompassing a period of two to ten years. A combination of the two, that pairs a one-year operational plan with a section on long-range goals and plans, is the best of both worlds.

MARKETING PLANNING

Once the strategic plan is developed and approved, marketing planning takes place. Marketing plans can be created for the entire product category or for specific brands, depending on the size of each. For example, Procter & Gamble's marketing plan for Pringle's Potato Chips probably includes the entire line—sour cream and onion, original, rippled, barbecue, and so on. There is no need to develop a complete marketing plan for each of these products. On the other hand, even though it is a product within the line, Diet Coke probably has a marketing plan of its own, separate from Coca-Cola.

Marketing plans vary in length. Some companies require only an outline of the overall plan, with details provided on a quarterly basis in a tactical plan. Other companies require a complete product history with a detailed plan covering the upcoming year.

Marketing plans also vary in formality. Some companies do not require a formal marketing plan. A marketing budget is assigned for a product, and the product manager submits proposals as potential promotions arise. In this case, management is taking a Band-aid approach to marketing—competitive "fires" are put out with a quick-and-dirty promotional effort. These companies fail to realize, though, that many of these fires could be avoided if proper planning had taken place well in advance.

The most successful marketing efforts are driven by a formal marketing plan, which includes specific objectives, necessary resources, planned activities, and expected results. A detailed plan is critical in creating and coordinating effective marketing activities. Marketing plans take different forms and follow many formats. The seven major components of a typical marketing plan are listed in Figure A.4 and explored in the following sections.[5] In our discussion, a marketing plan will be simulated for the consumer product, Rold Gold Pretzels.[6] The discussion includes facts about the product line, but the planned activities are purely conjectural. They are simply included to illustrate the salient points. Also, keep in mind that the actual plan will be much more detailed and greater in length.

LEARNING
OBJECTIVE
LO7

Figure A.4   Components of a Marketing Plan

▼ Executive summary
▼ Analysis of the marketing situation
▼ Assessment of opportunities and threats
▼ Specification of marketing objectives
▼ Formulation of marketing strategies
▼ Preparation of action programs and budgets
▼ Development of control procedures

Executive Summary

The executive summary is a recapitulation of the entire marketing plan. Usually included in the summary are: a recap of the previous twelve months, the objectives of the plan, a list of planned activities, and the resources required to support the plan. The executive summary is useful for those in upper management who need to be aware of these facts and figures, but who are not intimately involved with the implementation of the details. In its barest essentials, an executive summary statement for Rold Gold Pretzels would look something like this:

> The Rold Gold Pretzel product line increased sales from $122 million in 1997 to $181 million in 1998, a jump of 48 percent over the prior year. The increase was achieved by the introduction of the brand's first national ad campaign, increased trade support, and line extensions. Sales for the next 12-month period are expected to be $208 million, an increase of 15 percent over the prior year. One trade promotion will be run in each quarter, supported by a coupon drop in freestanding inserts and a national ad campaign in two of the four quarters. The estimated budget to support these activities is $22 million, an increase of 12 percent over the prior year.

Analysis of the Marketing Situation

The analysis of the marketing situation is a breakdown of the brand's current status in the marketplace. The prior year's activities are reviewed and analyzed. Actual sales results are compared to the stated objectives in the prior year's plan. Competitive activities that affected the brand are also included. This section acts as the "state of the union" for the brand. An analysis of Rold Gold's situation would be along the following lines:

> Pretzels currently represent a $1 billion dollar industry. It is considered the salty snack industry's fastest growing category. The Rold Gold brand is the market leader with a market share of 18 percent. Sales increased 48 percent over the prior year. In 1997, the brand had no ad support. In 1998, a national ad campaign supported the brand with Jason Alexander, from TV's *Seinfeld,* as the spokesperson. Four trade promotions were run, one per quarter. Coupons were distributed twice during the year. All of these factors contributed to the huge increase in sales and the brand's market dominance. Eagle brand pretzels matched the Rold Gold deal levels to the trade, but ran no supporting media or promotional efforts.

Assessment of Opportunities and Threats

In this section, all opportunities regarding the brand are examined, as well as any threats. Threats may come in the form of production or quality control problems within the company, competitive activities that pose problems, or potential problems within the marketing environment. Opportunities may come in the form of increased distribution, new markets, additional line extensions, changes in consumer behavior that are conducive to a brand's success, and so on. Rold Gold's assessment, in simplified terms, may look something like the following:

> Rold Gold enjoys an 85 ACV (all-commodity volume) level of distribution according to the latest Nielsen figures.[7] The objective for this coming year is to achieve a 90 ACV distribution level. Sales efforts will focus on the South-

west, where distribution is the lowest. Also, efforts in the Northeast will focus on cracking a major wholesaler who controls $50 million in sales of salty snack foods. A pretzel nugget is being pursued by R & D. Samples of several types are available and being tested in focus groups. Sales and marketing efforts will also focus on a major chain in the Midwest that has threatened to discontinue the Rold Gold line. Additional support will be given in the form of in-ad coupons. Eagle brand is being highly promoted in the Northwest and taking some Rold Gold share away. The Eagle trade allowances will be met by Rold Gold and the situation will be reviewed on a monthly basis.

Inconsistent quality has been found in the pretzels produced at the XYZ site. Production and quality control are aware of the problems and new procedures have been established to prevent further inconsistencies. [This latter statement is hypothetical, not factual.]

Specifications of Marketing Objectives

This section details the objectives upon which the marketing plan is based. As was stated earlier, objectives must be clear, concise, and realistic. Objectives are typically based on profit, market share, growth, or diversity. An important part of any objective is the time frame assigned for achievement. A time frame is necessary to determine whether or not the objective has been met by the plan, department, or SBU.

The objective of the Rold Gold marketing plan in the upcoming 12 months is to:

▼ Increase sales of the line by 15 percent to $208 million.

▼ Increase market share from 18 percent to 21 percent.

▼ Achieve a 90 ACV for the line.

▼ Maintain a 19 percent profit margin on the line.

Formulation of Marketing Strategies

The formulation of the marketing strategies details how the marketing objectives will be accomplished. Target markets are outlined as are the marketing mixes that will be used to satisfy the needs of these target markets. All activities that are included in the plan and the budget are detailed in full. This section acts as the blueprint for the building process for the brand that will take place over the next 12 months. Rold Gold's strategy might appear in abbreviated form as follows:

The national ad campaign introduced in 1998 will continue. Ad flights will be scheduled twice a year, in June and December, the peak selling periods for salty snack foods. The ads will continue to use Jason Alexander as spokesperson, since he is hip and has great appeal. We will continue to stress that the products are low in fat because they are baked; they are a good value; and they appeal to all age groups.

Trade allowances at the current level of $1.20 per case will be continued once per quarter except in the Northwest where the Eagle's level of $1.80 per case will be met.

Additional new product slotting allowances will be offered to those accounts who do not currently carry the line, in an effort to increase distribution. Two new line extensions will be added in the second quarter. The introduction will be supported by trade allowances only.

Preparation of Action Programs and Budgets

This section of the marketing plan details any programs that are designed to result in some specific action, as well as the budget required to support the marketing activities created to achieve the company's objectives. This section is critical in that the entire year's budget is either approved, increased, or decreased based on the plan. If a mistake is made in the budgeting, the manager and the brand may have to live with the mistake for the entire year. All figures must be accurate and precise.

In total, Rold Gold's required budget for the upcoming 12 months is as follows:

	(in millions)
Ad campaign	$5.5
Trade allowances	13.0
Special slotting allowances	1.0
Introduction of line extensions	1.5
Regional in-ad coupon support	1.0
Total	$22.0

Special distribution programs as outlined above are scheduled for the first quarter. Heavier allowances in the Northwest are scheduled for the second quarter.

Development of Control Procedures

This final section details how results of the plan will be measured on an ongoing basis. Management may require a monthly or quarterly update of sales measured against projections. If sales are far from projections, action can be taken to alleviate the situation. Control procedures keep the marketing plan on course.

Sales of Rold Gold will be monitored on a monthly basis. Actual case sales for the month and cumulative year will be compared to the prior year same period and to objectives. Achievement of the market share and distribution figures will be reviewed semi-annually, when Nielsen figures are updated and available. Since Nielsen figures are a few months behind in reporting, final judgment as to the achievement of these goals will be delayed until the Nielsen figures for the entire year are released. Profit margin figures will be judged on the basis of total revenues less total costs for the brand.

Appendix Summary

Planning is the basis for sound decision making in any situation in life. Strategic planning and forecasting are key activities that influence and direct the development of specific marketing strategies.

The most important level of planning is strategic planning, or the organization's overall game plan. This plan typically encompasses the firm's long-range goals and dictates direction for all departments in the firm. Strategic planning differs from marketing planning, or the game plan, for a particular product or product line. The marketing plan is the detailed scheme of the marketing strategies and activities associated with each product's marketing mix—product, pricing, distribution, and promotional decisions. Tactical planning is another level of organizational planning that involves specifying details that pertain to the organization's activities during the current period.

Strategic planning is comprised of four fundamental elements: (1) organization missions (how an organization defines its business, or what makes it different from the competition); (2) strategic business units (smaller divisions created to facilitate planning and general operations); (3) objectives (clear, realistic goals based on measurable achievements such as sales or market share); and (4) strategic planning tools (tools designed to help managers in their strategic and marketing planning efforts).

Marketing plans emanate from and are inspired by the overall strategic plan. Marketing plans vary in length and formality. A marketing plan can cover a specific product or an entire product line or category. A typical marketing plan includes an executive summary, an analysis of the marketing situation, an assessment of opportunities and threats, specification of marketing objectives, a formulation of marketing strategies, the preparation of action programs and budgets, and the development of control procedures.

Endnotes

[1] This Appendix was adopted from Lindgren and Shimp, *Marketing: An Interactive Learning System* (Fort Worth: The Dryden Press, 1996).

[2] The Coca-Cola Company's 1997 Annual Report.

[3] Susan E. Fischer and Kimberly Patch, "DEC Reorganizes Amid Transition; Moving Back toward Product-Based Units," *PC Week,* January 31, 1994, p. 103.

[4] This discussion is adapted from George S. Day, "Diagnosing the Product Portfolio," *Journal of Marketing* 41 (April 1977), pp. 29–38.

[5] For further reading on marketing planning, see William A. Cohen, *The Marketing Plan* (New York: John Wiley & Sons, Inc., 1995), and Donald R. Lehmann and Russel S. Winer, *Analysis for Marketing Planning,* 2nd ed. (Homewood, IL: Irwin, 1991).

[6] Jennifer Lawrence, "The Marketing 100," *Advertising Age,* July 4, 1994, p. S8.

[7] *All-commodity volume (ACV)* is a term used by marketing and advertising practitioners to refer to total sales of a product. An 85 ACV level simply means that Rold Gold brand has obtained distribution in retail outlets that account for 85 percent of the total pretzel volume in the United States.

Appendix 2

Careers in Marketing

Like most college students, Howard University marketing major Anthony Mason began pursuing career opportunities at the start of his senior year. The 22-year-old New Yorker had been keeping abreast of news in the business world and, since he was particularly interested in working for Ford Motor Company, he had paid special attention to news affecting the automobile industry.

On the day of his campus interview with Ford recruiters, Mason chose to wear a plain-cut gray suit and white shirt with a conservative tie. He carried several extra résumés with him because, he says, "You really can never be too prepared." About 10 minutes before the actual interview began, Mason wondered nervously whether he had forgotten anything and had sufficiently prepared himself. He gained consolation from the knowledge that, regardless of how the interview turned out, he already had job offers in hand from International Paper and Citibank.

The interview with the two Ford recruiters lasted only 15 minutes, but was a grueling session of questions and answers for Mason. "Give me a situation in which you had to persuade someone to agree with you. How did you overcome that conflict? What was the result?" Mason took his time answering questions and carefully worded his responses. He recalls, "The questions took me a while to think about, but I felt really good coming out. They were up-front and told me what the deal was, the positive and the negative. That's what I look for in an interview—a taste for what the job will be like." Ford was obviously impressed—Mason was invited to Detroit for a final interview.[1]

INTRODUCTION

Each June, thousands of college graduates like Anthony Mason enter the job market, flooding prospective employers with résumés and cover letters requesting interviews. Of the many career paths chosen by business graduates, marketing is the single largest employment category in the U.S. labor force, and job growth in the field is expected to accelerate. The U.S. Bureau of Labor Statistics estimates that the number of jobs in marketing, advertising, and public relations management will grow much faster than the average for all occupations through 2005.

The dawning of the 21st century is witnessing an expansion of marketing activities far beyond the narrow boundaries of consumer packaged goods and business products. Every successful organization—profit-seeking or not-for-profit—recognizes the necessity of effective marketing to accomplish its goals of providing customer satisfaction by offering high-quality goods or services to specific markets. Art institutes, museums, religious and human-services organizations, festivals, college and professional sports teams, and charitable, cultural, and entertainment events employ most of the same marketing techniques typically associated with producers and retailers of consumer and business products. All of these organizations seek out highly motivated, professionally educated marketing specialists to design and implement these customer-driven programs.

This appendix, along with the videos and computer software that supplement the text, provides information to help you make educational and career decisions.

▼ Video Career Profiles are designed to give you insights into how marketers see themselves and their jobs. They are included in most of the end-of-chapter videos.

▼ Special career design software, *Discovering Your Marketing Career,* will help you to focus your goals more narrowly by identifying careers related to your interests and aptitudes.

These tools will help you to create an educational and employment plan to guide your marketing career in the right direction.

This appendix briefly describes many of the marketing positions you have read about throughout the text. Specifically, the descriptions focus on the following aspects of marketing careers:

▼ Electronic résumés.

▼ Specialized programs at various universities.

▼ Use of an internship to create a competitive advantage in the workplace.

▼ Types of positions available, job descriptions, career paths, and salaries.

▼ Marketing employment trends and opportunities.

▼ Employment prospects for women and minorities in marketing.

▼ Sources of additional information.

As you begin a career in marketing, you will have to apply many of the principles and concepts you have studied in this course, including how to target a market, capitalize on brand equity, position a product, and use market research techniques. Even in jobs that seem remote from the marketing discipline, this knowledge will help you to stay focused on the most important aspect of business: the customer. Looking for a job that will fulfill your career goals is much the same as marketing a product (your skills) to a customer (the company).

YOUR RÉSUMÉ

The résumé is probably the most important document that a job seeker can provide to a potential employer. The résumé's written record of credentials often provides the only information available to employers on which to base their evaluation and selection of a job candidate. For this reason, the résumé becomes a critical tool for obtaining an entry-level position.

A résumé is a comprehensive summary of academic, professional, and personal accomplishments that makes focused statements about a job candidate. There is no one best way to write a résumé; however, it should provide accurate information that is related to the type of job desired in a direct, concise manner. Many computer software packages are available that require little more than filling in the blanks. Your Career Services Center can assist you in résumé writing, as well.

Three basic formats are used in preparing a résumé:

1. **Chronological:** Arranged in reverse chronological order; emphasizes job titles and organizations with descriptions of responsibilities held and duties performed. This format highlights continuity and career growth.

2. **Functional:** Accents accomplishments and strengths, placing less emphasis on job titles and work history. This format reduces repetitive language in job descriptions.

3. **Combined:** Emphasizes skills first, followed by employment history. This format suits students who need to show their responsibility and potential, but have employment histories not directly related to their desired jobs.

Résumé Proofreader Wanted

Over the years, human resources recruiter Robert Half & Associates has collected a number of nuggets from résumés submitted by jobseekers, of which a select few follow:

▼ I operate computers like my father drove tractors—by the seat of his pants.

▼ It's best for employers that I not work with people.

▼ Enclosed is the ruff draft of my resume.

▼ Size of employer: Very tall, probably over 6'5".

▼ P.S.: If you hire me away from this nightmare, you'll also save me thousands in therapy.

▼ Left job to rum the family business.

▼ Am a perfectionist and rarely if if ever forget details.

Most résumés include full names, mail and e-mail addresses, and telephone and fax numbers. Statements of career objectives typically follow. Academic information is provided next, followed by experience and work history. Applicants with limited work histories and no internship experience typically focus on relevant personal activities and interests. Most résumés close with lists of references.

Applicants are stronger candidates for employment when they can cite academic, work, and internship experiences related to their career objectives. For this reason, it is critical that you include any and all pre-professional and extracurricular activities in your résumé.

The important thing to remember in writing an effective résumé is to present the most relevant information in a clear, concise manner that emphasizes your best attributes.

Cover Letter

Letters of transmission, or cover letters, serve several purposes. Primarily, however, they seek to motivate employers to read the enclosed résumé.

The cover letter must provide specifically targeted information, from addressing the letter to the appropriate person in the organization to mentioning when to expect a follow-up call. The following list offers several tips mentioned by career-services counselors:

▼ Always address the letter to a specific person.

▼ Follow the salutation with a colon, not a comma.

▼ State which position you are applying for, where you learned about it, and why you are interested in that position.

▼ List specific examples of skills and contributions you offer; set a confident but not arrogant tone.

▼ Avoid overuse of *I* and *me* in the cover letter. Do not use slang or cliché phrases.

▼ Make certain your cover letter is neat and attractive; print it on high-quality paper, and limit it to one page.

▼ Mention any follow-up action that you plan to take, such as a call, and state when you will call.

▼ Express appreciation for being considered for the position.

▼ Sign the letter in black or blue ink.

Again, the Career Services Center on campus is likely to offer assistance in preparing cover letters as part of its job search support services for students and alumni. Correct form and accuracy are important in a cover letter, since employers often use the cover letter to evaluate written communication skills.

After a reasonable time has passed—one to three weeks—it is appropriate to call to verify that the résumé arrived, and to inquire about any additional questions and/or possible dates for interviews.

Letters of Recommendation

Letters of recommendation serve as testimonials to your performance in academic and work settings. The best references provide information relative to the desired industry or marketing specialty, as well as opinions of your skills, abilities, and character. References may be obtained from former or current employers, supervisors from volunteer experiences, professors, and others who can attest to your academic and professional competencies.

An effective letter of recommendation typically contains the following elements:

1. Statement of the length and nature of the relationship between the writer and the job candidate.

2. Description of the candidate's academic and career growth and potential.

3. Review of important achievements.

4. Evaluation of personal character (what kind of colleague the candidate will make).

5. Summary of the candidate's outstanding strengths and abilities.

Career Facts

▼ Almost half of the major firms in North America look for employees through online recruiting sources. The most popular sources: the Internet (47 percent), electronic résumé banks (21 percent), and automated telephone listings (19 percent).

▼ While 20 million Japanese are currently enrolled in English-language classes, less than 50,000 U.S. students are learning to speak Japanese.

▼ Women comprise one-third of the world's workforce. More than half of all women between the ages of 18 and 64 work outside the home—59 percent in developed nations and 49 percent in developing regions.

Don't let failure get to you. Some of today's top business leaders who didn't give up include:

▼ **Jack Welch,** CEO of General Electric, who managed a plastics plant that blew up.

▼ **Ed Artzt,** CEO of Procter & Gamble, who had to deal with a warehouse full of a new detergent that crystallized just before he was to bring it to market.

▼ **Bernard Marcus,** who founded Home Depot after being fired from a regional hardware chain.

▼ Need additional examples? How about **Sam Walton,** whose first store failed, or **Walt Disney,** who was fired from an ad agency because he couldn't draw.

Because letters of recommendation take time and effort, allow ample time for your references to compose them—as long as a month is not unusual. When you ask someone to write a letter of recommendation, you should always provide a résumé and any other information relative to the recommendation, along with a stamped, pre-addressed (typed) envelope.

Supporting Documents

In addition to a cover letter, résumé, and letters of recommendation, candidates should include photocopies of transcripts, writing samples, or graphics products in their credentials packages. For example, if you are applying for a position in public relations, advertising, or sports marketing, you may want to include examples of professional writing, graphics, or audio/visual tapes to support written evidence of your credentials. Research and service projects that resulted in published or unpublished articles may also fill out the package.

Electronic Résumés

The electronic age has affected every aspect of the business world, including finding a job. Today, most of the *Fortune* 1,000 companies and many other large corporations use special computer software to receive, sort, store, and retrieve résumés from hopeful job applicants.

A computer system can scan data from thousands of résumés in a few seconds to find a dozen promising candidates for a job opening. For example, a company seeking an international marketing specialist may need a person with fluency in multiple languages and experience with international trade laws and practices. By searching for specific key words, the software retrieves the résumés that contain the desired information.

Gone are the days when a flashy résumé printed on expensive, colored paper was sufficient to catch the attention of most recruiters. Now a computer is likely to review these documents. That means your résumé must contain the key words associated with your skills, experience, achievements, interests, and personality. In fact, printing your résumé in a fancy font can often confuse the computer's scanning process, causing it to discard your unreadable résumé!

Dow Chemical keeps 20,000 résumés in its computer system and relies solely on its customized software to select the most suitable candidates for a position. Previously, the total cost involved in hiring a single Dow employee averaged $10,000. After installing the $100,000 computerized personnel-search system, the cost per hire fell to $7,500, and the firm recouped the money it spent for the installation after only 40 hires. Massachusetts-based Stratus Computers receives 15,000 résumés a year.

Job seekers also benefit from electronic recruiting. These systems have extended the life span of a résumé from less than a year to two or more. Traditionally, job candidates submitted résumés in response to advertisements for particular job openings. Recruiters reviewed the résumés at that time for that job. Now, however, they can review a stored résumé for any job that becomes available during a much longer time span, giving applicants more chances at all the jobs that become available.

Over 2 million Web sites currently carry job postings. The most comprehensive job banks list openings around the globe. The largest, Monster Board, contains 221,000 job listings. In second place with 175,000 listings is Headhunter.net. JobWeb's job bank currently contains listings from over 1,600 employer organizations. All three of these online employment exchanges update their job rosters daily.

Each of these sites is designed to make it easy for you to identify job opportunities that best match your interests. If, for example, you decide to limit your job search to a single city such as Boston, you would simply type BOSTON into Monster's QuickSearch screening system and almost immediately get over 2,600 listings. You could then narrow your scope to, say, *sales positions* and the list would shrink to 203 Boston listings.

www.monster.com
www.headhunter.net
www.jobweb.org

Experts predict rapid development of a nationwide or even a worldwide database of résumés, allowing companies to search among everyone in the world looking for work. Both Monster Board and JobWeb maintain online résumé banks that many employers and employment recruiters often peruse.[2]

SPECIALIZED GRADUATE EDUCATION

Not everyone will graduate with a bachelor's degree and enter the job market. Many marketing graduates choose to continue their studies by pursuing MBA degrees or entering master's programs specially suited to their career goals. A student who wishes to extend formal education in a specialized degree program should seek advice on specific programs from instructors who teach in these areas. For example, a market research professor is likely to have information on master's programs in that field at such institutions as the University of Georgia and Southern Illinois University at Edwardsville.

INTERNSHIPS CREATE COMPETITIVE ADVANTAGE

Internships have been described as a critical link in bridging the theory-practice educational gap. They serve as learning experiences for interns, providing a practical application of classroom theory as well as a means of gaining hands-on experience. Internships are becoming even more critical to networking and job hunting as students strive to reach ambitious career goals. They help to carry students between the academic present and the professional future.

An internship is a partnership between the student, the university, and the agency or internship site. All of these parties assume definite responsibilities, perform specific functions, and achieve benefits as a result of their involvement. Internships offer valuable culminating experiences for marketing students. They provide opportunities to apply the ideas and theories presented in the classroom to the experience in a work environment.

Through an internship, an individual makes the transition from student to professional and establishes a link between theory and practice. Interns gain valuable, practical work experiences under the supervision of both university faculty and on-site marketing practitioners.

The internship fills out a student's professional credentials and allows for exploration of career options while observing and interacting with professionals at work. In some instances, internships are precursors for specific employment opportunities, allowing students to demonstrate technical proficiency while providing cost-effective personnel training for the industry as a whole.

The effectiveness of an internship experience depends on the quality of involvement by the student, the agency or site, and the university coordinator. Students interested in completing internships should discuss the matter with their instructors. Instructors can explain university requirements and identify any on-campus specialists who recommend potential interns, help them complete applications, and arrange interviews with potential internship providers. An excellent source of information about the nation's outstanding internships can be found at your local bookstore: Mark Oldman and Samer Hamadeh, *America's Top 100 Internships* (New York: Villard Books, published annually).

MARKETING POSITIONS

The basic objective of any firm is to market its goods or services.[3] Marketing responsibilities vary among organizations and industries. In a small firm, the owner or president may assume marketing responsibilities. A large firm needs a staff of experienced marketing, advertising, and public-relations managers to coordinate these activities. Some typical marketing-management positions are described in the following sections. (Please remember, however, that specific titles of positions may vary among firms.)

Marketing, Advertising, and Public-Relations Managers

Marketing management spans a range of positions, including vice president of marketing, marketing manager, sales manager, advertising manager, promotion manager, and public-relations manager. The vice president directs the firm's overall marketing policy, and all other marketers report through channels to this person. Marketing managers work with product development and market-research managers to develop the firm's detailed marketing strategies. Sales managers direct the efforts of sales professionals by assigning territories, establishing goals, developing training programs, and supervising local sales managers and their personnel. Advertising managers oversee account services, creative services, and media services departments. Promotion managers direct promotional programs that combine advertising with purchase incentives in order to increase the sales of the firm's goods or services. Public-relations managers conduct publicity programs and supervise the specialists who implement them.

Job Description
Top marketing-management positions often involve long hours and extensive travel. Work under pressure is also commonplace. For sales managers, job transfers between headquarters and regional offices may disrupt family life. Approximately 460,000 marketing, advertising, and public-relations managers are currently employed in the United States in virtually every industry.

Career Path
For most marketing, sales, and promotion-management positions, employers prefer degrees in business administration, preferably with concentrations in marketing. In highly technical industries, such as chemicals and electronics, employers prefer bachelor's degrees in science or engineering combined with master's degrees in business administration. Liberal arts students can also find many opportunities, especially if they have business minors. Most managers are promoted from positions such as sales representatives, product or brand specialists, and advertising specialists within their organizations. Skills or traits that are most desirable for these jobs include maturity, creativity, high motivation, resistance to stress, flexibility, and the ability to communicate persuasively.

Salary
The median annual salary for marketing, advertising, and public-relations specialists ranges from $24,000 for a marketing assistant to $146,050 for a marketing vice president. The median incomes for specific positions in each field are shown in Table A.1.

Table A.1 Median Salaries for Marketing-Management Positions	
Marketing assistant	$24,000
Advertising manager	44,000
Sales promotion manager	45,000
Brand manager	61,000
Direct-marketing manager	66,000
Regional sales manager	69,000
VP for marketing	146,050

Sales Representatives

Millions of items are bought and sold every day. The people a firm hires to carry out this activity work under a variety of titles, such as sales representative, account manager, manufacturer's representative, sales engineer, sales agent, retail salesperson, wholesale sales representative, and service sales representative. Most companies require that all marketing professionals spend some time in the field to experience the market firsthand and understand the challenges faced by front-line marketing personnel.

Job Description

All salespeople must fully understand and competently discuss the products offered by the company. Salespeople usually develop prospective client lists, meet with current and prospective clients to describe the firm's products, and then follow up. In most cases, the salesperson must learn about each customer's business needs in order to identify products that best satisfy them. These professionals answer questions about the characteristics and costs of their offerings and try to persuade potential customers to purchase them. After the sale, many representatives revisit their customers to see that the products met their needs and to explore further business opportunities or referrals with them. Some sales of technical goods and services involve lengthy interactions. In these cases, a salesperson may work with several clients simultaneously over a large geographical area. Those responsible for large territories may spend most of their time traveling to make sales presentations. Retail or telephone salespeople may spend most of their work days on the phone or on the sales floor.

Work as a sales representative can be rewarding for those who enjoy interacting with people, like competition, and feel energized by the challenge of expanding sales in their territories. Successful sales professionals should be goal-oriented, persuasive, self-motivated, and independent people. In addition, patience and perseverance are important qualities for a sales representative.

Career Path

The background needed for a sales position varies according to the product line and market. A college degree is desirable, and many companies run their own formal training programs for sales representatives that can last up to two years. This training may take place in a classroom, in the field with a mentor, or—most often—a combination of both methods. Similarly, the career ladder in retail sales typically involves moving to positions of greater responsibility and higher earnings potential over a period of time.

Salary

Salary ranges for sales positions vary widely. In a recent year, annual earnings for middle-level sales representatives in service industries averaged $48,400; those selling technical services typically earn more than those selling nontechnical services. Annual earnings for manufacturers' and wholesale representatives averaged about $46,500. Sales trainees can expect to earn between $19,800 and $35,400, depending on the industry they join; producers of industrial goods pay the most and service providers pay the least for trainees. As Table A.2 indicates, salaries increase substantially at higher levels of management.

Advertising Specialists

Advertising is one of the ten hottest career fields in the United States today. In fact, for the second year in a row, the position of interactive advertising executive has made the list of high-demand career specialties with a starting salary of $25,000, a five-year median salary of $65,000, and a potential salary of more than $250,000. The position also carries a high "coolness" factor of 8 on a scale of 10 and a low burnout factor of 3. Within the next 10 years, employment in this category is expected to grow by 400 percent.[4]

Table A.2 Median Compensation in Sales Professions	
Senior sales representative	$68,300
Major account representative	71,200
National account representative	76,100
District sales manager	83,700
National account sales manager	85,600
Regional sales manager	92,300
Top sales executive	122,700

Many firms maintain small groups of advertising specialists who serve as liaisons between those companies and outside advertising agencies. The leader of this liaison function is sometimes called a *marketing communications manager.* Positions in an advertising agency include the categories of account services, creative services, and media services. Account services' functions are performed by account executives, who work directly with clients. An agency's creative services department develops the themes and presentations of the advertisements. This department is supervised by the creative director, who oversees the copy chief, art director, and their staff members. The media services department is managed by the media director, who oversees the planning group that selects media outlets for ads.

Job Description
Advertising can be one of the most glamorous and creative fields in marketing. Because the field combines the best of both worlds, that is, the tangible and scientific aspects of marketing along with creative artistry, advertising attracts people with a broad array of abilities.

Career Path
Most new hires begin as assistants or associates for the positions they hope to acquire, such as copywriters, art directors, and media buyers. Often, a newly hired employee must receive two to four promotions before becoming manager of these functions. College degrees in liberal arts, graphic arts, journalism, psychology, or sociology, in addition to marketing training, are preferred for entry-level positions in advertising.

Salary
In recent years, professionals in the advertising industry have enjoyed a considerable increase in average annual earnings. Table A.3 lists the average base salaries for various positions in advertising agencies in the United States.

Table A.3 Average Salaries for Positions in Advertising	
Advertising copywriter	$50,000
Art director	47,500
Account executive	62,500
Creative director	300,000

Public-Relations Specialists

Specialists in public relations serve as advocates for businesses and other organizations. They strive to build and maintain positive relationships with various publics. They may assist company executives in drafting speeches, arranging interviews, overseeing company archives, responding to information requests, and handling special events, such as sponsorships and trade shows, that provide promotional value to the firm.

Job Description

Public-relations specialists normally work a standard 40-hour week, but sometimes they need to rearrange their normal schedules to meet deadlines or prepare for major events. Occasionally they are required to be on the job or on call around the clock to respond to an emergency or crisis. Over 109,000 public-relations specialists are employed in the United States, two-thirds of them in service industries. Public-relations positions tend to be concentrated in large cities near press services and communications facilities. However, that centralization is changing with the increased popularity of new communications technologies such as the Internet and World Wide Web, which allow more freedom of movement. Many public-relations consulting firms are located in New York, Los Angeles, Chicago, and Washington, D.C.

Essential characteristics include creativity, initiative, good judgment, and the ability to express thoughts clearly and simply—both in writing and in spoken statements. An outgoing personality, self-confidence, and enthusiasm are also recommended traits of public-relations specialists.

Career Path

A college degree combined with public relations experience, usually gained through an internship, is considered excellent preparation for public relations. Many entry-level public-relations specialists hold degrees with a major in advertising, marketing, public relations, or communications. New employees in larger organizations are likely to participate in formal training programs; those who begin their careers at smaller firms typically work under the guidance of experienced staff members. Entry-level positions carry such titles as research assistant or account assistant. Potential career paths include promotion to account executive, account supervisor, vice president, and eventually senior vice president.

Salary

According to a recent salary survey, the median salary for all public-relations job titles was $46,204. Entry-level PR specialists in corporate settings typically earn higher salaries than their counterparts in not-for-profit organizations. By contrast, senior public-relations executives of not-for-profit organizations receive higher salaries, on average, than those in the business sector. The highest pay in PR goes to those involved in investor relations and international and environmental affairs. Entry-level salaries average $49,800 for a publicity agent and $55,400 for an in-house publicist.

Purchasing Agents and Managers

The two key marketing functions of buying and selling are performed by trained specialists. Just as every organization is involved in selling its output to meet the needs of customers, so too must all companies make purchases of goods and services required to operate their businesses and turn out items for sale.

Modern technology has transformed the role of the purchasing agent. The transfer of routine tasks to the computer now allows contract specialists, or procurement officers, to focus on products, suppliers, and contract negotiations. The main function of this position is to purchase the goods, materials, supplies, and services required by the organization. These agents ensure that suppliers deliver quality and quantity levels that suit the firm's needs; they also secure these inputs at reasonable prices and make them available when needed.

Purchasing agents must develop good working relationships both with colleagues in their own organizations and with suppliers. As the popularity of outsourcing has increased, the selection and management of suppliers have become critical functions of the purchasing department. In the government sector, this role is dominated by strict laws, statutes, and regulations that constantly change.

Job Description

Purchasing agents can expect a standard work week with some travel to suppliers' sites, seminars, and trade shows. Over 600,000 people work in purchasing jobs in the United States, most of them in manufacturing and government.

Career Path

Organizations prefer college-educated candidates for entry-level jobs in purchasing. Strong analytical and communication skills are required for any purchasing position. Often, new hires into the field enroll in extensive company training programs to learn procedures and operations; training may include a production planning assignment. In private and public industries, professional certification is becoming an essential criterion for advancement. A variety of associations serving the different categories of purchasing confer certifications on agents, including Certified Purchasing Manager, Professional Public Buyer, Certified Public Purchasing Officer, Certified Associate Contract Manager, and Certified Professional Contract Manager.

Salary

An entry-level purchasing agent can expect to earn $42,240 annually. The industry average is $52,800, and the typical salary for a firm's chief purchasing agent should approximate $63,360.

Wholesale and Retail Buyers and Merchandise Managers

Buyers working for wholesalers and retail businesses purchase products for resale. Their goal is to find the best possible merchandise at the lowest price. They also influence the distribution and marketing of this merchandise. Successful buyers must understand what appeals to customers and what their establishments can sell. Bar codes on products and point-of-purchase terminals have allowed organizations to accurately track products that are selling and those that are not; buyers frequently analyze this data to improve their understanding of customer demand. Buyers also check competitors' prices and sales activities and watch general economic conditions to anticipate customer buying patterns.

Job Description

Approximately 361,000 people are currently employed in the United States as wholesale and retail buyers and merchandise managers. These jobs often require substantial travel, as many orders are placed on buying trips to shows and exhibitions. Effective planning and decision-making skills are strong assets in this career. In addition, the job involves anticipating consumer preferences and ensuring that the firm keeps needed products in stock, so it requires resourcefulness, good judgment, and self-confidence.

Career Path

Most wholesale and retail buyers begin their careers as assistant buyers or trainees. Larger stores seek college-educated candidates, and extensive training includes job experience in a variety of positions. Advancement often comes when buyers move to departments with larger volumes or become merchandise managers to coordinate or oversee the work of several buyers.

Salary

Median annual earnings of wholesale and retail buyers average $25,100. However, income depends on the amount and type of product purchased as well as seniority. Buyers often receive cash bonuses based on their performance.

Market Research Analysts

Market research analysts provide information that helps marketers to identify and define opportunities; they generate, refine, and evaluate marketing actions and monitor marketing performance. Market research analysts devise methods and procedures for obtaining needed data. Once they compile data, analysts evaluate it and then make recommendations to management.

Job Description

Firms that specialize in market research and management consulting employ the majority of the nation's market research analysts. Positions are often concentrated in larger cities, such as New York, Washington, D.C., and Chicago. Those who pursue careers in market research need to work accurately with detail, display patience and persistence, work effectively both independently and with others, operate objectively and systematically, and be effective oral and written communicators in presenting their results. Creativity and intellectual curiosity are essential for success in this field.

Career Path

A bachelor's degree with emphasis in marketing provides sufficient qualifications for many beginning jobs in market research. Because of the importance of quantitative skills, this education should include courses in calculus, linear algebra, statistics, sampling theory and survey design, and computer science. Students should try to develop experience in conducting interviews or surveys while still in college. A master's degree in business administration or a related discipline is advised to improve opportunities for advancement.

Salary

As Table A.4 indicates, compensation in this field ranges from $36,740 for market research analysts to over $80,000 for a typical director of market research. Compensation levels throughout the industry have shown large percentage increases over the past ten years, and this trend will likely continue.

Logistics: Materials Receiving, Scheduling, Dispatching, and Distributing Occupations

Often overlooked by marketing students, the area of logistics offers a myriad of career positions. Titles under the heading of logistics include materials receiving, scheduling,

Table A.4 Mean Compensation for Market Research Positions	
Director	$80,860
Assistant director	67,560
Statistician	50,380
Senior analyst	45,770
Analyst	36,740

Table A.5 Mean Compensation for Logistics Positions	
Top logistics management executive	$135,100
Top supply-chain manager	176,000
Transportation manager	71,400
Top quality control executive	118,700
Outbound operations manager	47,100
Inbound operations manager	42,200
Inventory planning and control manager	76,700
Freight rate specialist	44,000
Dispatcher (transportation)	39,900

dispatching, materials management executive, distribution operations coordinator, distribution center manager, and transportation manager. The logistics function includes responsibility for production and inventory planning and control, distribution, and transportation.

Job Description

Approximately 3.8 million people are employed in logistics positions in the United States today, including materials receiving, scheduling, dispatching, and distribution. These positions demand good communication skills and ability to work well under pressure.

Career Path

Computer skills are highly valued in these jobs. Employers look for candidates with degrees in logistics and transportation. However, graduates in other business disciplines often succeed in the field.

Salary

Annual earnings for logistics management positions are reported in Table A.5.

TRENDS AND OPPORTUNITIES

Table A.6 reports projections from the Bureau of Labor Statistics of employment for selected marketing occupations through 2005. Some sales positions, such as those in

Table A.6 Employment Projections for Selected Marketing Positions through 2005		
Occupation	Recent Employment	Projected Growth through 2005
Insurance sales workers	418,000	14–24%
Manufacturers' and wholesale sales representatives	1,503,000	14–24
Marketing, advertising, and public relations managers	461,000	over 35
Purchasing agents and managers	621,000	14–24
Real estate agents, brokers, and appraisers	374,000	14–24
Retail sales workers	4,261 000	25–34
Securities and financial services sales representatives	246,000	over 35
Service sales representatives	612,000	over 35
Wholesale and retail buyers	621,000	14–24

the financial and services sectors, are forecasted to do particularly well over this time period.

DIVERSITY IN THE MARKETING PROFESSION

The job market has changed dramatically in the past 30 years. Ethnic minorities and women of all races have increased their presence, and they will continue to do so. While Table A.7 indicates that the battle for equality is not yet over, it does show considerable progress for women, African Americans, and Hispanic Americans.

According to the Small Business Administration, women are starting small firms at twice the rate of males. Women-owned businesses in the United States employ more people than all of the Fortune 500 companies. However, employment of African-Americans and Hispanics in marketing is not proportionate with their shares of the total population.

The wage gap between genders continues to generate serious concern. In 1979, women holding bachelor's degrees earned average annual wages of $30,161, while men brought in $54,391. Almost 20 years later, women had increased their earnings some $9,000 to $39,271, while men's salaries grew by about $7,000 to $61,008. Although the disparity seems to be narrowing, the problem remains an important one.[5] Table A.8 compares the salaries of men and women working in various advertising positions.

Table A.7   Female and Minority Employment in Selected Marketing Occupations

Occupation	Percentage of Total Employees		
	Female	African American	Hispanic
Purchasing managers	41.5%	6.6%	3.1%
Marketing, advertising, public relations managers	35.7	2.2	3.3
Sales occupations	49.5	7.8	6.9
Supervisors/proprietors	38.9	5.6	5.6
Sales representatives:			
Advertising sales	52.9	4.2	4.7
Insurance sales	37.1	5.8	4.6
Real estate sales	50.7	3.4	4.5
Retail/personal services	65.6	11.4	8.9
Securities/financial services	31.3	5.7	5.0

Table A.8   Median Base Salary by Gender and Advertising Position

Position	Male	Female
CEO	$130,000	$123,000
Creative director	95,000	74,000
Art director	55,000	48,000
Chief copywriter	58,000	53,000
Media director	72,000	52,000
Senior account executive	78,000	64,000
Account executive	47,000	42,000

ADDITIONAL INFORMATION SOURCES

General information about careers in marketing is available from the sources listed below. Information sources are grouped by the job categories described in the discussion of marketing positions.

General Marketing
American Marketing Association
250 South Wacker Dr. Suite 200
Chicago, IL 60606
http://www.ama.org/

Sales
Sales and Marketing Executives International
458 Statler Office Tower
Cleveland, OH 44115

Manufacturers' Agents National Association
23016 Mill Creek Road
P.O. Box 3467
Laguna Hills, CA 92654

National Retail Federation
100 West 31st Street
New York, NY 10001
http://www.nrf.com/

Securities Industry Association
120 Broadway
New York, NY 10271
http://www.sia.com/

Advertising and Promotion
American Association of Advertising Agencies
666 Third Ave., 13th Floor
New York, NY 10017

American Advertising Federation
Education Services Department
1400 K St. NW, Suite 1000
Washington, DC 20005

Council of Sales Promotion Agencies
750 Summer St.
Stamford, CT 06901

Promotion Marketing Association of America, Inc.
322 Eighth Ave., Suite 1201
New York, NY 10001

Public Relations
Public Relations Society of America, Inc.
33 Irving Place
New York, NY 10003–2376
http://www.prsa.org/

PR Reporter
P.O. Box 600
Exeter, NH 03833

Public Relations News
Service Department
127 East 80th St.
New York, NY 10021

Purchasing
National Association of Purchasing Management, Inc.
P.O. Box 22160
Tempe, AZ 85285
http://www.napm.org/

National Institute of Governmental Purchasing, Inc.
115 Hillwood Ave.
Falls Church, VA 22046

National Contract Management Association
1912 Woodford Rd.
Vienna, VA 22182

Federal Acquisition Institute
General Services Administration
18th and F Streets NW
Washington, DC 20405

Wholesale and Retail Buyers and Merchandise Managers
National Retail Federation
100 West 31st St.
New York, NY 10001
http://www.nrf.com/

Market Research
Marketing Research Association
2189 Silas Deane Hwy., Suite 5
Rocky Hill, CT 06067

DISCOVERING YOUR MARKETING CAREER—A SOFTWARE APPLICATION

If you purchased a new copy of *Contemporary Marketing,* Ninth Edition, you should have received a CD-ROM with software to help you plan your career along with your copy of the text. If your book contains a CD-ROM disk titled, *Discovering Your Marketing Career,* please continue reading.

Selecting a career ladder to climb is no easy task. In today's competitive job market, the most desirable and highest-paying jobs will go to the most qualified candidates. A degree in marketing will prepare you for a number of entry-level positions. However, job-hopping in order to determine the career that best suits you is likely to create a detrimental image for you. Successful applicants understand well their own interests and abilities, the general characteristics of the jobs they seek, and how their interests and abilities might fit an employer's needs. You should have noticed that these three criteria resemble closely the elements leading to customer satisfaction in all business transactions.

Discovering Your Marketing Career is a computer application that will help you to determine which marketing careers most closely match your skills, experience, and interests. The software invites your input to questionnaires for each major career track in marketing to help you determine how well each one suits you. After you complete the questionnaire, the software generates an in-depth report assessing your compatibility with that track. The report also prints out a detailed profile of the career itself, its long-term opportunities, and compensation levels. Once you have narrowed down your interests, you can begin engaging in the software's job search activities. The activities include guidelines for field research on careers, résumé preparation, letter writing, and preparation of telephone scripts. By matching your interests to the demands of a particular marketing career, you can decide which elective courses will strengthen your marketability as a job candidate.

Endnotes

[1]Melissa E. James, "Postcards from the Class of '95," *Sales & Marketing Management,* June 1995, pp. 73-77.

[2]Malcolm Fitch, "Cruise the Web to Land the Job of Your Dreams, " *Money,* May 1997, pp. 29-30. See also Del Jones, "Resume Advice: It's as Simple as Black and White," *USA Today,* January 24, 1996, p. 4B.

[3]A portion of the information in this section is adapted from the *Occupational Outlook Handbook* Washington, D.C.: U.S. Department of Labor, 1996.

[4]"Want a Job in One of the 10 Hottest Career Fields?" *Adweek,* April 8, 1996, p. 20.

[5]Beth Belton, "Degree-Based Earnings Gap Grows Quickly," *USA Today,* February 16, 1996, p. B1.

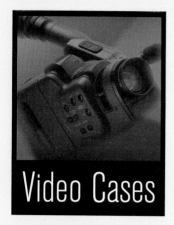

Video Cases

CASE 1
TOMMY HILFIGER

Designer Tommy Hilfiger is no novice when it comes to relationship marketing. In need of financing to expand his line of designer menswear, Hilfiger formed a partnership with Silas Chou, owner of Hong Kong's oldest textile and apparel firm. The relationship was an unusual one, since most designers simply license their names and designs to manufacturers. But the Chou–Hilfiger alliance made both men partners in design and production. The move turned out to be a brilliant one. Drawing on Chou's long experience in textiles and manufacturing, Hilfiger found that he could produce quality clothing for less than half the cost of competing designer lines such as Ralph Lauren's.

The partnership allowed Hilfiger to differentiate his brand. "I'm positioned in a unique way," he says. "There's a 12-lane highway between The Gap at the low end and Ralph Lauren at the higher end. And that's where I am, affordable, but the same quality as the best."

Chou also benefited from the partnership. His company needed a direct link with an internationally recognized clothing brand. His family business had made its fortune in private-label contracting, but that business was moving from Hong Kong to lower-wage regions in northern China and to India and Vietnam. As Chou points out, "I may be the last generation of the traditional manufacturing family in the Far East. The comparative advantage is gone. Hong Kong is too expensive. That's why I looked to brand names. This is a great business for my children and grandchildren."

In 1989, the first year of their partnership, Hilfiger and Chou generated sales of $25 million. By 1997, Tommy Hilfiger USA was generating over $400 million in sales. During this period, the Hilfiger clothing line expanded into jeans, underwear, athletic wear, golf clothing, women's wear, eyeglasses, wristwatches, and a fragrance.

To market his fragrance, Hilfiger again decided to practice relationship marketing, and once again through an unusual arrangement. He signed a licensing agreement with Aramis Inc., an Estée Lauder subsidiary. For the previous half century, Estée Lauder had avoided partnerships with outside designers, choosing instead to develop its own fragrance brands. But the Lauder family saw the alliance with Hilfiger as an ideal means of competing in the designer men's fragrance market. "The whole Lauder family is behind this," says Aramis Executive Creative Director Jeanne Chinard. "We were all waiting for him. He is the perfect match for us."

Aramis, which once controlled 50 percent of men's fragrance sales in department stores, had seen its market share drop to about 13 percent. Company executives were counting on Tommy to put Aramis back in the race with Calvin Klein and Ralph Lauren.

The first-year marketing plan for the new fragrance included plans to distribute 750,000 free samples at department stores, supported by magazine advertising, spot TV, and outdoor ads promoting the theme "a new American fragrance." Hilfiger planned to promote Tommy by tying the fragrance imagery into his clothing ads.

Realizing the importance of distribution to the success of a new fragrance, Aramis marketers preceded the launch of the product—dubbed Tommy: The New American Fragrance—by contacting a number of department store chains, including Hudson's Department Stores with which Aramis had enjoyed a long-standing supplier-customer partnership. Hudson's comprises more than 30 midwestern department stores operated, along with Marshall Field's and Dayton's, by Minneapolis-based Dayton Hudson Corp. Aramis saw Tommy as an opportunity to enhance its strategic alliance with Hudson's by co-marketing the new fragrance.

"The person we are appealing to is the person coming to the Hudson stores to purchase new fragrances," says Aramis Regional Marketing Director Daniel Basil. "We know they have a success going in how they marketed Tommy in the ready-to-wear area."

Hudson's marketers also saw benefits from the co-marketing plan with Aramis. "Fragrances are a very important merchandise category for department stores such as Hudson's for two reasons," says company President Dennis Toffolo. "It's very profitable. It generates huge sales. We do close to $200 million in our department store division today with men's and women's fragrances. The men's portion runs about 25 to 30 percent of the $200 million. The Tommy launch could produce about $600,000 to $700,000 for Hudson's."

The co-marketing agreement gave Hudson's exclusive rights to launch and stock the new Tommy fragrance in its geographic area. For its part, Hudson's developed a marketing plan for promoting Tommy in each market through TV ads and visuals within the stores. In-store display designs coordinated with the national Tommy advertising campaign.

Preparing and training Hudson's sales associates for the product launch was another key component in the marketing plan for Tommy. Aramis account executives worked closely with store salespeople to explain the store visuals and motivate them to sell the new product. Dayton Hudson and Aramis co-sponsored a Tommy launch party for each Hudson's store. Sales training followed, focusing on product knowledge, clientele building, advertising, and individual store selling goals. Each store designated a sales associate as the Tommy team captain to coordinate activities and to provide feedback to Aramis.

An important part of the training centered on teaching the sales associates how to apply database marketing. Because Hudson's customers were heavy purchasers of Tommy Hilfiger clothing, they were likely to be receptive to the new fragrance carrying the Tommy name and marketed using similar imagery. Sales associates learned how to use the Hudson's database to obtain lists of customers who had purchased Tommy Hilfiger clothing. These customers received invitations to receptions introducing the new fragrance, along with offers of a free gift and the opportunity to be among the first purchasers of the new product.

The co-marketing alliance between Hudson's and Aramis proved highly successful for both partners, and it strengthened their relationship. The retailer delivered on its promise to enthusiastically promote the new fragrance, and the fragrance maker honored its promise of exclusivity, not allowing any other retailer to carry Tommy during its initial launch period.

Questions
1. Some established brands, such as Tommy Hilfiger, are appealing to Generation Y while other established brands such as Levi's are struggling. According to the information provided in Chapter 1, what are the keys to marketing to Generation Y? Why do you think Tommy Hilfiger has been successful with Generation Y?
2. Based on the information provided in this case, describe Tommy Hilfiger's marketing mix.
3. The manner in which Tommy Hilfiger conducts business is most closely associated with what era: the production era, sales era, marketing era, or relationship marketing era? Please explain your answer.
4. Database marketing played an important role in Hudson's ability to market Tommy. Sharrow Davies Townsend is a San Francisco-based marketing consulting firm that provides database marketing counsel to businesses. Visit the company's Web site at:

www.sharrow.com

How does Sharrow define *database marketing?* What benefits does it claim for this type of marketing? What challenges does it identify?
5. Explain the role of database marketing in Hudson's relationships with its customers.

Sources: Telephone interview with Tommy Hilfiger Public Relations Department, May 15, 1997; Jonathan Van Meter, "Hip, Hot Hilfiger," *Vogue,* November 1996, pp. 306-309; Justin Doebele, "A Brand Is Born," *Forbes,* February 26, 1996, pp. 65-66; Matthew Tyrnauer, "It's Tommy's World," *Vanity Fair,* February 1996, pp. 108-113; and Elaine Underwood, "Tommy Hilfiger on Brand Hilfiger," *Brandweek,* February 5, 1996, pp. 23-27.

CASE 2
AT&T

Telecommunications firms are among the strongest proponents of development projects for the information superhighway—the huge and rapidly evolving pathway that links telecommunications and data resources to businesses, not-for-profit organizations, and individual households. To ensure America's long-term economic competitiveness, AT&T, along with many other U.S. firms, competes fiercely to design, build, manage, and service the various components that make up the information pipeline. As a global telecommunications leader, AT&T intends to maintain a conspicuous presence on the superhighway by turning technology into useful services that customers want and selling those services at reasonable prices.

To compete successfully in today's global market, AT&T CEO Robert Allen has restructured the firm into three separate global corporations:

▼ The new AT&T, a company focused on offering customers a full menu of communications and information services.

▼ Lucent Technologies, Inc., a company producing telecommunications equipment and systems, software, and products, with research activities conducted by Bell Laboratories.

▼ NCR, a company concentrating on transaction-intensive computer systems and services.

The company intended the restructuring to reduce the size and complexity of its operations. By operating not as one large company but as three smaller, more manageable companies, each can pursue its own business strategy and react quickly to marketplace changes. According to Allen, "Our decision to restructure was driven by seismic shifts in customer needs, technology, and public policy. Make no mistake about it, these are fundamental changes. They offer unprecedented new opportunities for us, but they also carry the threat of washing away any company that chooses to cling to the status quo and ignore the power of these changing conditions."

Customers clamor ever more loudly for information goods and services with global reach due to worldwide economic growth, technological advances, and the declining cost of information technology. Residential customers and businesses, from multinationals involved in global commerce to work-at-home entrepreneurs, are driving the expanding demand for new, customized services that combine voice, data, image, facsimile, and online transmissions.

Public policy changes continue to reshape the competitive landscape. For example, the Telecommunications Act of 1996 allows long-distance companies and local telephone service firms to enter each other's markets. Although still dominated by state-owned monopolies, the global phone industry is also changing as nations continue to privatize and deregulate their phone markets.

The pace of change in this already-competitive landscape is intensifying dramatically as new firms enter the telecommunications industry and existing competitors broaden their service offerings. For example, in the interactive multimedia business, the diverse list of suppliers includes phone companies such as AT&T, cable TV franchises, computer firms, wireless cellular service providers, and publishing and entertainment giants. Technology is evolving so rapidly that the lifespans of new technologies have decreased over the last 10 years from a 5-year average to less than 24 months. The Internet and its graphical interface, the World Wide Web, is changing the way businesses interact with customers.

The new AT&T wants to base its strategy on delivering a bundle of services to customers over the information superhighway. A market leader in some services and a new player in others, the company is focusing on five areas: long-distance calls, local calls, wireless communications, online (Internet) services, and access to home entertainment. Allen says, "Our future is a long distance from long distance. We're moving to a full menu of communications and information services."

The U.S. leader in residential long-distance phone service with a 65 percent market share, AT&T is strengthening its position by adding new features such as the AT&T One Rate plan, a simplified pricing structure that lets consumers make direct-dialed long-distance calls to anyone, any time, anywhere in the United States for 15 cents a minute. As a new competitor in the local market, AT&T has announced its intention to provide local phone service in all 50 states. It plans to offer local calling either by reselling network capacity purchased from local providers or by building its own infrastructure.

Already the largest U.S. wireless service provider, AT&T has acquired 23 licenses to offer personal communications services. This technology resembles wireless services, but it operates at another radio frequency to extend its reach to more than 80 percent of the U.S. population. Its WorldNet Service has enabled the company to begin competing as an Internet service provider. The company's home entertainment delivery system makes it the first national communications company to bring consumers programming choices from DIRECTV and U.S. Satellite Broadcasting. The AT&T Universal Card—a combination credit, ATM, and calling card—provides customers with a convenient payment option for many of its services.

Global markets offer major growth opportunities for AT&T. "What's important," says Allen, "is that we expand as quickly as possible around the world." AT&T is implementing this vision by forming partnerships, strategic alliances, and consortiums to market telecommunications services to businesses and consumers worldwide. A consortium led by AT&T and GTE owns 40 percent of CANTV, a phone company in Venezuela. AT&T formed a joint venture with Unisource, a consortium owned by Dutch KPN, Spanish Telefonica, Swedish Telia, and Swiss BTT. AT&T's WorldPartners alliance includes Kokusai Denshin Denwa (Japan's largest international carrier), Singapore Telecom, and other Asian carriers. According to Victor Pelson, head of global operations, AT&T's biggest competitor in the international arena is Concert, an alliance formed by MCI and British Telecommunications PLC.

AT&T is also designing easy-to-use services for international travelers. Its WorldConnect service allows customers to place calls to and from more than 75 countries over company-owned lines. WorldPlus service allows travelers to set up AT&T accounts to pay for local calls in more than 40 countries.

With its financial strength, global reach, strong brand name, and new freedom from regulation, AT&T is poised to be a big player on the information highway. "Our decision to restructure reflects our determination to shape and lead the dramatic changes that have already begun in the worldwide market for communications and information services—a market that promises to double in size before the turn of the new century," says Allen.

Questions

1. What forces in marketing's external environment influenced Allen's decision to restructure AT&T?
2. Which of the key points in monitoring competition discussed in Chapter 4 do AT&T marketers face? Give examples from the video.
3. Give examples of AT&T's actions to manage its new environment.
4. AT&T is developing and enhancing services in long-distance calling, local calling, wireless communications, Internet services, and home entertainment. Review the company's home page at:

<u>www.att.com</u>

Give a brief description of each service area. Find companies on the Web that offer competing services, and compare AT&T's products to those of its competitors. For each service area, which company would you choose? Why?

Sources: Telephone interview with AT&T Corporate Executive Office, May 13, 1997; *AT&T Quarterly Shareowners Report,* October 17, 1996; *AT&T Special Report to Shareowners,* September 1996; Andrew Kupfer, "What, Me Worry?" *Fortune,* September 30, 1996, pp. 121-124; "Intelligent Networking Will Rule the World," *Industry Week,* August 19, 1996; *Annual Report,* 1995, AT&T; and Julia Flynn, Catherine Arnst, and Gail Edmondson, "Who'll Be the First Global Phone Company?" *Business Week,* March 27, 1995, pp. 176-180.

CASE 3
WHIRLPOOL CORP.

Within a few months after becoming CEO of Whirlpool Corp. in 1987, David Whitwam met with his senior managers to plot a strategy for securing future company growth. At the time, Whirlpool was the market leader among U.S. appliance makers, but it generated only weak sales outside North America. Operating in a mature market, it faced the same low profit margins as major competitors like General Electric and Maytag.

Whitwam and his management team explored several growth options, including diversifying into other industries experiencing more rapid growth, such as furniture or garden products; restructuring the company financially; and expanding vertically and horizontally. The group sharpened its focus to consider opportunities for expanding the appliance business beyond North American markets. After all, the basics of managing the appliance business and the product technologies are similar in Europe, North America, Asia, and Latin America. As Whitwam put it, "We were very good at what we did. What we needed was to enter appliance markets in other parts of the world and learn how to satisfy different kinds of customers."

Whirlpool industry data predicted that, over time, appliance manufacturing would become a global industry. As Whitwam saw it, his company had three options: "We could ignore the inevitable—a decision that would have condemned Whirlpool to a slow death. We could wait for globalization to begin and then try to react, which would have put us in a catch-up mode, technologically and organizationally. Or we could control our own destiny and try to shape the very nature of globalization in our industry. In short, we could force our competitors to respond to us."

Whitwam and his team chose the third option and set out on a mission to make Whirlpool "one company worldwide." They aimed much higher than simply marketing products or operating around the globe. For decades, Whirlpool had sold some appliances in other countries to buyers who could afford them. Whitwam wanted to expand this reach by establishing a vision of a company that could leverage global resources to gain a long-term competitive advantage. In his words, this effort meant "having the best technologies and processes for designing, manufacturing, selling, and servicing your products at the lowest possible costs. Our vision at Whirlpool is to integrate our geographical businesses wherever possible, so that our most advanced expertise in any given area—whether it's refrigeration technology or distribution strategy—isn't confined to one location or one division. We want to be able to take the best capabilities we have and leverage them in all of our operations worldwide."

As its first step in transforming a largely domestic operation into a global powerhouse, Whirlpool purchased the European appliance business of Dutch consumer-goods giant, Philips Electronics. Philips had been losing market share for years, running its European operations as independent regional companies that made different appliances for individual markets. "When we bought this business," Whitwam recalls, "we had two automatic washer designs, one built in Italy and one built in Germany. If you as a consumer looked at them, they were basically the same machines. But there wasn't anything common about those two machines. There wasn't even a common screw."

The Whirlpool strategy called for reversing the decline in European market share and improving profitability by changing product designs and manufacturing processes and by switching to centralized purchasing. The change reorganized the national design and research staffs inherited from Philips into European product teams that worked closely with

Whirlpool's U.S. designers. Redesigned models shared more parts, and inventory costs fell when Whirlpool consolidated warehouses from 36 to 8. The transformation trimmed Philips's list of 1,600 suppliers by 50 percent, and it converted the national operations to regional companies.

Whitwam believed that the drive to become one company worldwide required making Whirlpool a global brand—a formidable task in Europe, where the name was not well-known. The company rebranded the Philips product lines, supported by a $135 million pan-European advertising campaign that initially presented both the Philips and Whirlpool names and eventually converted to Whirlpool alone.

Another important component of the Whirlpool global strategy—product innovation—sought to develop superior products based on consumer needs and wants. "We have to provide a compelling reason other than price for consumers to buy Whirlpool-built products," says Whitwam. "We can do that only by understanding the consumer better than anyone else does and then translating our understanding into clearly superior product designs, features, and after-sales support. Our goal is for consumers to prefer the Whirlpool brand because it offers greater overall value than competing products."

One successful product innovation led to the Whirlpool Crispwave microwave oven. Extensive research with European consumers revealed a desire for a microwave that could brown and crisp food. In response, Whirlpool engineers designed the VIP Crispwave, which can fry crispy bacon and cook a pizza with a crisp crust. The new microwave proved successful in Europe, and Whirlpool later introduced it in the United States.

Whirlpool's global strategy includes a goal to become the market leader in Asia, which will be the world's largest appliance market in the 21st century. In 1988, it began setting up sales and distribution systems in Asia to help it serve Asian markets and to make the firm more familiar with those markets and potential customers. The company established three regional offices: one in Singapore to serve Southeast Asia, a second in Hong Kong to handle the Chinese market, and a Tokyo office for Japan. Through careful analysis, Whirlpool marketers sought to match specific current products with Asian consumers. They studied existing and emerging trade channels and assessed the relative strengths and weaknesses of competitors in the Asian markets. The company set up joint ventures with five Asian manufacturers for four appliance lines with the highest market potential: refrigerators, washers, air conditioners, and microwave ovens. With a controlling interest in each of the joint ventures, the newly global company confidently expects to excel in the world's fastest-growing market.

Whirlpool has come a long way since embarking on its global strategy. Revenues have doubled to more than $8 billion. The company now reaches markets in more than 140 countries, leading the markets in both North America and Latin America. Whirlpool is number three in Europe and the largest Western appliance company in Asia. For building its integrated global network, "Whirlpool gets very high marks," says an industry analyst. "They are outpacing the industry dramatically."

Questions

1. Relate Whirlpool's global strategy to Chapter 3's discussions of international expansion.
2. Explain how changes in Whirlpool's economic, sociocultural, and political–legal environments might affect its marketing strategy.
3. Whirlpool offers different combinations of product lines to customers in different parts of the world. Visit the Whirlpool Web site at:

www.whirlpool.com

Review the list of countries where Whirlpool currently operates. Do its products carry the Whirlpool brand name in each country? How might the Internet help the company to increase global brand recognition of the Whirlpool name?

Source: Portions of this video case were researched from material downloaded April 16, 1997 from **http://www.whirlpool.com**

CASE 4
WALKER INFORMATION & GTE

In the wake of the Telecommunications Act of 1996, competition in the telecommunications industry is breaking out in full force. The Act changed federal law to allow long-distance and local telephone service providers to enter each other's markets. This development brings great news for consumers, who will benefit from exciting offerings at competitive prices. For the phone companies, however, the new era in telecommunications presents difficult challenges. Chuck Lee, chairman and CEO of GTE, says, "In the past, local service providers functioned as monopolies in controlled markets. Now the marketplace is going to set the pace. It will be a free-for-all. Darwinian economics. Survival of the fittest."

According to Jeff Bowden, a consultant who has worked with GTE, "Most telcos [telephone companies] are genetically designed to build things, not serve customer needs. Packaging goods and services cost-effectively redefines the whole nature of the telephone company. It's easier to move organizational boxes around, form a bunch of business units, bring in marketing people, and forget about the customer."

Market research helps GTE find out what customers want, need, and expect from their telephone company. With annual revenues topping $20 billion, GTE is one of the world's largest telecommunications firms, the largest U.S.-based local telephone company, and a leading cellular-service provider. The company began several years ago to prepare for today's open, competitive environment. It has downsized to cut costs, divested operations, and reorganized its divisions to remove layers of hierarchy. But several surveys have revealed that many GTE customers, given the choice, would switch their phone service. Organizational customers, too, have criticized the company as large, monopolistic, and slow to respond to customer needs.

Walker Information is helping GTE gain a competitive edge in the new marketplace by leading the company along the path of customer focus. Walker is a full-service market research firm with 11 offices worldwide and annual sales of $37 million. The Indianapolis-based firm's six divisions handle different areas of research. Walker's Customer Satisfaction Measurement (CSM) division helps organizations like GTE to identify what their customers want and determine the best ways to meet those needs.

Walker joins several other market research firms in working with GTE to measure its performance and develop new customer satisfaction strategies. This research has led to several new programs that enhance communication with customers and cost effectively meet their needs.

One initiative involves customers directly in development projects for new services. For instance, GTE engineers developed the ACCESSibility Database Service in response to requests from organizational customers that use its ACCESS Settlement and Exchange Service. Customers complained about the number of financial reports generated by the service and asked GTE to create an easy-to-use database that would provide the same information. GTE software engineers visited customer sites, conducted weekly conference calls, and shipped new versions of the database to customers every two to three weeks. This close cooperation gave customers a direct say about how the product would work. "The entire process has been extremely valuable," says Marlene Collman, manager of carrier relations for customer Ameritech Mobile Communications. "When GTE delivered the product, we received exactly what we wanted—not a version that didn't quite fit the bill." The process worked so well, in fact, that GTE plans to incorporate this strategy in all future product-development projects.

Another initiative includes extensive market research into what customers want from personal communication services (PCS). This new generation of wireless technology promises to improve the clarity of voice messages and provide added services such as paging, voice mail, and data transmission. GTE launched what may be the largest PCS trial ever, involving 3,000 Tampa residents. Participants chose among several wireless service categories, including the option of totally replacing their residential phone service for more than a year. "We need to answer questions as to how big the market is and what the demand is," explains John Dion, general manager of personal communications networks. "The 'field of dreams' [approach] doesn't work. We need to assess and serve public needs rather than try to get customers to adapt to technology."

A third program involves an extensive study of the company's business procedures by teams of outside consultants together with GTE employees from all levels. The teams conducted more than 1,000 field interviews, made over 10,000 on-the-job observations, and visited 80 top-performing companies to study their methods. One result is the creation of the Customer Call Center, a facility that allows repair service representatives to solve problems while GTE customers remain on the line. With this "One Touch" concept, almost one-third of all customers who report trouble to repair centers now find their problems solved before they hang up their phones. Just three years ago, the ratio was one out of 200. Responding quickly has helped to convince customers that GTE is a knowledgeable company that values their calls. Also, during one year alone, quick response eliminated the need for 3.5 million service order and repair dispatches.

"GTE," says vice president Mark Feighner, "is trying to establish a continuous response to changing customer and market requirements." The company has made progress in measuring customer satisfaction and developing new products such as Internet access through its GTE.NET service. It's learned that people want to deal with a single provider for all of their telecommunications services, including local, long-distance, and wireless calling and data transmission. Customers also want convenient features that make their lives easier. GTE has responded to these expectations by developing several new services. With Express dialtone, customers who move can obtain full phone service at their new address within two hours by plugging a phone into a wall jack. With SmartCall, customers can choose from an array of optional features, such as caller ID, call waiting, and three-way calling. With GlobalRoam, international travelers can place and receive wireless calls from numerous countries, with the calls automatically billed to their home cellular numbers. InContact allows a customer to connect home, business, and cellular phones; voice mail; and pagers with one number.

Questions

1. What environmental conditions have increased the need for GTE to measure customer satisfaction?
2. Which of the seven steps in the basic market research process does this case illustrate?
3. What types of data has GTE used to explore its customer satisfaction strategies?
4. The work of Walker Information helped GTE to develop GTE.NET, making it the first local telephone company to sign up Internet subscribers. Go to the company's Web site located at:

www.gte.net

Review the services it offers. Design a research study that Walker Information might develop to study the satisfaction of customers using GTE's Internet services.

www.walkernet.com

Include Walker Information's CSM (Customer Satisfaction Measurement) function in the design.

Sources: Telephone interview with Kathleen Briody, Public Affairs Coordinator for GTE, May 16, 1997; and "Top 100 Companies by U.S. Research Revenues," *Advertising Age*, May 20, 1996, p. 40.

CASE 5
ROGAINE (PHARMACIA & UPJOHN INC.)

How do you feel about baldness? Do you emphasize acceptance, based on a belief that a person's character determines what's important, not his outward appearance? Do you perceive bald people as somehow different from full-haired people? Does your attitude about baldness differ between men and women? What if you started losing *your* hair? Would your self-concept change?

Pharmacia & Upjohn Inc., a worldwide pharmaceuticals and health-products company, needed answers to questions like these as it designed a marketing strategy to introduce Rogaine, a prescription drug intended to restore hair growth. Originally developed as a treatment for hypertension, clinical tests revealed that Rogaine encouraged moderate hair growth on some balding male volunteers. Pharmacia & Upjohn applied to the U.S. Food and Drug Administration (FDA) for approval to market Rogaine as a hair-growth product in the United States. The company also began selling it as Regaine in Europe.

Consumer psychologist Dr. Gar Roper conducted research to uncover men's feelings and reactions about the prospect of hair loss and to learn what would motivate them to contact their doctors to obtain prescriptions for Rogaine. From in-depth personal interviews, Dr. Roper learned that hair loss gave men a general feeling of diminishing confidence and strength. He also learned that men deal with two signals concerning society's acceptance of male baldness.

On one hand, the research found a growing public acceptance of baldness. Bald-Headed Men of America had attracted 20,000 members, and the organization seemed likely to continue to grow. Says founder John Capps III, "Baldness is a matter of mind over matter—if you don't mind, it doesn't matter." On the other hand, society seems to pay close attention to a person's appearance. In a study analyzing consumers' reactions to the balding process, a social psychologist showed pictures of six men in various stages of hair loss to 204 male and female undergraduate students. Study results indicated a tendency among the average undergraduate female, age 21, to shy away from the balding men. The psychologist concluded that people form differing views of balding men.

Some of those men agree. Comments one, "I believe that a person looks better with a full head of hair." He wears a hairpiece that he glues onto his scalp with a special adhesive. Another hair loss sufferer spent $30,000 on eight hair transplant treatments. He says, "It was important for my own sense of well-being, as well as for professional reasons. I feel better about myself."

Rogaine's marketing team used such insights to guide development of advertising that would effectively reach the consumer while staying within the FDA's strict regulatory guidelines. Initial marketing efforts targeted at doctors, nurses, and pharmacists sought to introduce them to Rogaine. Advertising targeted at consumers followed, with the objective of informing consumers that those concerned about hair loss could contact a physician who could prescribe the drug. The ads also included a toll-free phone number. FDA restrictions prohibited Pharmacia & Upjohn from mentioning the name *Rogaine* in the ads. This soft-sell approach established good consumer awareness, but it produced disappointing results, perhaps because most men needed a stronger inducement to get them to a doctor's office.

Rogaine marketers decided to adopt a more aggressive marketing strategy, recognizing the need for a more direct appeal to consumers. With FDA approval, they included the Rogaine name in commercials and urged men to ask their physicians to prescribe it. They developed a video that featured doctors giving technical information; the video also showed men who tried Rogaine with varying degrees of success. Pharmacia & Upjohn created a Dermatology Division to focus on relationship marketing through coordinated ads and public relations messages. The company also became involved in event marketing to build its database, followed by direct marketing and telemarketing.

Pharmacia & Upjohn also experimented with rebates. A patient could choose between a certificate worth $10 toward a first bottle of Rogaine or $20 for sending in the box tops from the first four emptied bottles. Rogaine marketers began targeting hair stylists and barbers by offering "handling fees" to shops that displayed Rogaine. Through these programs, Rogaine's marketing team achieved impressive results in reaching male consumers.

Next, the team turned to a different consumer segment: women. An estimated 20 million American women suffer from hair loss, often due to chemotherapy treatments or to *alopecia areata,* an immune system disorder. In conducting personal interviews with women, Dr. Roper learned that they feel compelled to do something about baldness, because bald women simply cannot manage in society as men can. Women also wanted more information about hair loss than did men. Ads targeting women included a toll-free phone number and the offer of a free information kit. Pharmacia & Upjohn developed a 30-minute infomercial as an effective way to reach women. Jeff Palmer, a Pharmacia & Upjohn public relations specialist, says, "We could give them more information in this format than we could in a 60-second commercial."

Pharmacia & Upjohn has received FDA approval to sell Rogaine over the counter. This change will bring new challenges to Rogaine marketers as they work to apply consumer analysis and promote their innovative product.

Questions

1. What core values might motivate a consumer to try Rogaine?
2. How does self-concept relate to a consumer's decision to purchase Rogaine?
3. How did Rogaine marketers move consumers through the steps in the consumer decision-making process?
4. Visit the Rogaine Web page at:

www.rogaineonline.com

It offers information on the product's use by men and women. (The page features an interesting and very efficient site map.) Rogaine Online offers a "Users Only Area" as well as testimonials from Rogaine users. Why does Pharmacia & Upjohn offer this service? Who would be likely to use it? How does a consumer access this service? Does it help to attract new Rogaine users?

Sources: Telephone interview with Upjohn Consumer Affairs, May 16, 1997; Michael Wilke, "Pharmacia Prescribes Big Role for OTC Veteran," *Advertising Age,* October 7, 1996, p. 40; and "Rogaine Opens New Category for Infomercials: Pharmaceuticals," *Advertising Age,* March 11, 1996, p. 10A.

CASE 6
THE DELFIELD COMPANY

Business-to-business marketers seldom get the chance to showcase their firm's products in a blockbuster movie. The Delfield Company enjoyed just such an opportunity when the producer of *Jurassic Park* called on it to supply stainless steel equipment for one of the most famous kitchen scenes in movie history. Headquartered in Mount Pleasant, Michigan, Delfield is a leading supplier of commercial kitchen equipment to the food-service industry. The company designs and produces more than 200 products for restaurants, schools, hotels, grocery stores, and military installations. Products include refrigerators, freezers, counters, ventilation systems, cafeteria systems, and display cases.

As a supplier to major chains such as Taco Bell, Arby's, Burger King, Kmart, and KFC, Delfield sees close relationships as the key to success in the business-goods market. Kevin E. McCrone, president and CEO of Delfield, says, "We view the relationships as part of our core business strategy. We have to know what kinds of problems our customers deal with every day. We have to know what space limitations are required and what obstacles our customers meet and face everyday. If we don't, then we won't be able to design and adapt our products to meet their demands."

Delfield has established its strong market position through strategies that emphasize staying close to its customers, giving employees the skills and tools they need to produce quality products, and investing in resources that allow the company to provide excellent customer service. Delfield uses speed and flexibility as competitive weapons in order to quickly respond to changing customer needs.

The company fields 138 representatives who work daily with customers to learn about their needs. Menu changes often drive a kitchen's need for new equipment. Delfield's customers add new products, such as pizza or salads, to compete in new segments and to target different types of consumers. Some customers need help opening food outlets in non-traditional locations such as movie theaters, airports, stadiums, and gas stations; these innovative operations require specially designed equipment.

For example, Delfield formed a strategic alliance with its customer Kentucky Fried Chicken to develop and implement a new concept in fast food. KFC's management had detected two important characteristics in the fast-food market: Customers seemed to like the comfort of buying their food from a familiar restaurant, and competitors had already set up shop in many of the prime, store-front locations traditional for fast-food restaurants. KFC looked for alternative restaurant sites that would ensure convenience and accessibility for customers and decided to place new outlets in high-traffic areas such as stores, airports, and university student centers.

The strategy required a solution to one central problem: Limited space demanded much smaller fast-food restaurants in these settings than regular, stand-alone outlets could accommodate. KFC needed equipment compact enough to fit in a 100-square-foot outlet but capable of meeting all the needs of a regular-sized restaurant.

Delfield took the lead in developing these new compact kitchens, known as SIB ("Small Is Beautiful") units. For seven months, Delfield engineers worked with KFC personnel and other vendors in that firm's supply chain to determine specifications for cooking equipment, fryers, hoods, and ventilation systems. After assembling a prototype SIB unit, Delfield invited representatives from KFC and the other suppliers to a meeting to view the design, evaluate it, and modify it before launching full-scale production.

One participant, who had experience in the operations end of the business, suggested that the high positions of the ovens would cause problems by forcing restaurant employees to lift large pans of hot food over their heads. Because many fast-foot restaurants hire women and senior citizens, who might find this lifting difficult if not dangerous, designers lowered the unit by three inches. The meeting was a huge success, and KFC ordered eight SIB units from Delfield. Delfield continued to modify the design, based on suggestions from KFC, to make the units more efficient, for instance, by adding components, extra handles, and magnetic latches instead of mechanical ones.

KFC installed one SIB unit in a Wal-Mart store in New York state; it planned others for airports, shopping malls, and food courts. The restaurant chain even negotiated to place one in the staff cafeteria of a major corporation.

Delfield sees a very positive long-term outlook for these small units. According to Richard Zuehlke of Delfield's major account development division, "Building managers want to maximize sales per square foot, and they've found that food is one of the best ways to do this. Consumers like the idea because it's so convenient. They're at the store anyway, so why not pick up something to go from KFC?"

Working closely with customers to meet their needs has made Delfield a market leader, in the process earning the company industrywide recognition. It won an award for food-facilities design by designing versatile equipment to support three different types of restaurant service—servery, full service, and family style—at a Colorado resort.

Delfield buys many component parts and materials from its own team of suppliers. In selecting suppliers, Delfield considers a list of critical questions: Is the company large enough to meet its needs? Do its products and processes meet Delfield's high quality standards? Can the prospective supplier meet strict delivery schedules? Can it offer the technology and service that Delfield needs? Does it reliably maintain its prices?

Delfield builds relationships with its suppliers over long periods of time. For example, it worked with Washington Specialty Metals for many years before choosing the company as its sole source of stainless steel sheets. Delfield also forms strategic alliances with its suppliers. For example, one vendor, a maker of vacuum-formed, plastic trim collars for refrigerated cabinets, announced an 80 percent price hike due to its high scrap rate; in response, Delfield engineers helped to redesign the cabinets. "In vacuum forming, the sharper the radius, the more difficult the process becomes," says plant manager Ted Reed. "We'd never given any consideration to that in our designing. It was insignificant to us whether the corner had to be that sharp. So we gave the supplier the opportunity to go to a one-half-inch radius on at least eight parts. It had no effect upon us, but improved their operation significantly." The new design reduced the vendor's scrap rate, allowing the company to cancel the price increase.

Questions

1. Do Delfield's alliances with suppliers and customers give it a competitive edge? Support your answer.

2. Which of the three organizational buying situations discussed in Chapter 6 does the purchase of an SIB unit represent? Explain your answer.

3. The Delfield Company's strategic alliances with several companies have directly contributed to the company's success. To form these kinds of relationships, business people must make difficult choices between prospective partners and design complex arrangements to forge the best connections. Numerous companies—some profit-oriented, some not-for-profit—offer services that help clients to build strategic alliances. Find three of these companies on the Web. What services does each one provide? Search the Web and find specific examples of companies and products that have been successful as a result of a strategic alliance. Explain your findings.

Source: Telephone interview with Richard Zuehlke, major account development officer, the Delfield Company, April 18, 1997.

CASE 7
MARRIOTT INTERNATIONAL

Marriott International offers a broad spectrum of lodging products to meet the varying needs of travelers worldwide. Meeting the changing needs of its guests is Marriott's highest priority. CEO Bill Marriott visits as many as seven hotels a day to make sure that his managers and employees keep satisfying guests, so those valued customers will return for another stay. He chats with guests to find out what Marriott can do to improve their visits. Such customer focus helps Marriott to outperform competitors in occupancy and revenue per available room. With sales topping $8.9 billion, Marriott's occupancy rates typically run 10 percentage points above the U.S. industry average.

Marriott entered the hotel business in 1957. During the late 1970s and early 1980s, the constantly changing demands of lodging customers and signs of market saturation by full-service hotels led its managers to consider diversifying their hotel operations. They conducted customer research to identify new market segments and developed products for them: the Courtyard chain for the segment focused on moderate prices; Residence Inn for the long-term-stay market; and Fairfield Inn for the economy segment.

Marriott's success depended on aggressive marketing of its four hotel brands to specific market segments. Management chose to target the $95 billion company travel market, a huge and fast-growing segment of the overall U.S. market. Each of Marriott's four lodging brands offers services geared to the varying needs of specific groups of business travelers.

Marriott hotels, resorts, and suites attract key organization personnel by offering high-quality service and many amenities. Guests can conduct business in their rooms, assisted by technology such as modems, call waiting, and voice mail. These hotels, with between 250 and 1,000 rooms, provide ideal settings for large meetings and conventions. Recreational facilities include pools and health clubs. Room rates range from $90 to $245.

Each Courtyard property, a moderately-priced hotel chain, has on average 150 guest rooms and a full-service restaurant and lounge. Designed by business travelers for business travelers, the rooms have separate seating and sleeping areas, large desks, reach-anywhere telephones, and cable TV. The Courtyard concept was designed for customer convenience in room designs and quick check-in and check-out functions. Each hotel offers a small gym room, swimming pool, and conference room that accommodates up to 30 people. Rates range from $60 to $90.

Residence Inns are extended-stay hotels. About 115 rooms feature separate living and dining areas and fully equipped kitchens. Many rooms have fireplaces. Several properties have spacious penthouses. Housekeeping services are provided daily, including shopping, laundry, and dry cleaning. A complimentary continental breakfast and evening hospitality hour are provided to all guests. Room rates vary between $75 and $100.

Fairfield Inn is an economy hotel targeted at business travelers who are not interested in amenities such as on-premise restaurants and lounges. Each hotel has about 135 rooms with large, well-lit work desks and reach-anywhere phones. Most hotels have outdoor pools and meeting rooms for up to ten people. Services such as fax, photocopying, and same-day dry cleaning are available. Room rates range from $45 to $55.

In developing four different products to satisfy specific groups of business travelers, Marriott applied the principles of market segmentation. Its First Choice program targeted large companies to create customized travel programs that would meet the lodging needs of large firms such as Dow Chemical Company. William Rose, vice president of human resources at Dow, says that his company's annual travel expenses amount to about $100 million in North America. "When you're spending $100 million on something, if you want to manage that, and it's growing pretty rapidly, you've got to break it down into its components. A significant part of that is our lodging."

Marriott wants to build close, long-term relationships with companies like Dow, so its hotels become the first choice for these customers' lodging services. Working with these customers, Marriott conducts research to determine its needs and how its products meet them. Marriott marketers conduct focus groups with frequent travelers to learn what they want, when they travel, and what services are important to them. From such a qualitative survey with Dow's business travelers, Marriott discovered a preference for nonsmoking rooms, flexibility of early check-in and late check-out times to accommodate appointment schedules, and complimentary breakfast.

From credit card data supplied by potential customers, Marriott marketers analyze the company's lodging expenses. They also assess the firm's current hotel directory. This study shows divisions between segmented customer needs. Marriott then presents each customer with a research profile of its travel patterns and needs for quality, moderate, economy, and extended-stay lodging, in the process demonstrating how its hotels match the company's needs.

After evaluating Marriott's analysis of its lodging requirements, Dow decided to participate in the First Choice program because it offered significant benefits. In choosing a lodging supplier, Dow considers the following criteria: volume discounting, the ability to provide different lodging segments ranging from economy to quality, the ability to develop a long-term relationship with a reputable supplier, product quality and consistency, safety, and dollar savings.

As a First Choice customer, Dow's William Rose says, "I think that we have a very good match here. Basically, we are buying quality, and Marriott has long been recognized for their total quality management and so has Dow. We're not looking for the lowest price. We're looking for the best total value. And I think that's what they're selling and it's what we're looking for."

Marriott continues to study the market to identify new niches. Now it's turning its focus to international expansion, conducting research to determine how its segmentation strategy can satisfy business travelers in Mexico, Europe, and the Pacific Rim.

Questions

1. Describe how Marriott's segmented approach to lodging meets criteria for successful segmentation discussed in the Chapter 7.

2. Relate Marriott's marketing decisions to the steps in the target market selection process.

3. Which bases of segmentation described in Chapter 7 apply to Marriott's four lodging products?

4. In February 1997, Marriott introduced a new brand—Marriott Executive Residences. The company has also acquired a 49 percent share of the Ritz-Carlton Hotel Co. Go to Marriott's home page:

www.marriott.com

Identify the segment that Marriott is targeting with each of these two products. What is your assessment of these segmentation strategies? Should Marriott develop additional products for other segments?

Sources: Shelly Branch, "So Much Work, So Little Time," *Fortune,* February 3, 1997, p. 116; Allen E. Richardson, "Marriott Eyes Global Growth Options," *USA Today,* March 11, 1996, p. 5B.

CASE 8
CADILLAC

People crowded 12 deep to get a look when General Motors unveiled its new Cadillac Seville STS at the International Automobile Show in Detroit. The highly acclaimed new model generated the first excitement in many years for Cadillac.

For decades, the Cadillac name had symbolized prestige and success. But during the 1980s, the brand suffered as many consumers came to view the cars as gas-guzzling, boulevard cruisers. The nameplate remained popular with older consumers who remembered its glory days, but it struck out with younger people, who preferred foreign luxury cars from Lexus, BMW, Infiniti, and Mercedes. Cadillac marketers saw a need for sweeping changes.

Cadillac is the flagship, luxury brand of General Motors, the world's automaker with a 17 percent global market share. GM has positioned Cadillac as the blue-chip component of its product portfolio, which includes Saturn, Pontiac, Chevrolet, GMC trucks, Oldsmobile, and Buick. Cadillac models successfully maintained the division's status as America's leading luxury car maker until the mid-1980s. To restore the luster, GM management completely revamped Cadillac's product development.

In the past, Cadillac had produced new models through phased development, beginning when designers drafted new plans and passed them on to engineers, who developed the ideas into cars that they hoped consumers would buy and manufacturing engineers could build. Time-consuming changes slowed the process as manufacturing revealed problems with the original designs. In 1955, GM spent less than two years developing a new car model. By the early 1980s, product development took five years or longer.

Cadillac's new-product development process started with consumers, who provided input to guide later design and development. According to Jim Kornas, a GM marketing executive, Cadillac adopted a "simultaneous management approach" to product development. For the first time, Cadillac created a venture team to produce a product. The cross-functional team was responsible for the design, engineering, manufacturing, distribution, and marketing of the Seville STS. Consumers and suppliers participated on the vehicle development team from the very beginning of the project. Even Cadillac's advertising agency, D'Arcy, Masius, Benton, & Bowles Advertising, sat in as a team member.

In an important first step, the STS development team conducted focus groups to determine what the targeted younger car buyers wanted in a luxury car. The STS designers, engineers, and marketers learned that younger buyers thought that Cadillac lacked technology, good engineering, and handling performance. They said Cadillac models lacked any attributes that they wanted. A simple statement seemed to sum up their core belief: "Cadillac doesn't make a car for me." From focus groups, the STS team learned that important attributes for younger buyers included comfort, good handling and performance, and a sporty yet luxurious appearance.

Based on this information, designers prepared a variety of sketches for their new car's interior and exterior. They then returned with these designs to focus group members and asked for reactions. Special computer software helped the team to evaluate the alternative designs for ease of assembly, structural efficiency, and potential production costs. This step revealed the most feasible manufacturing process for the new vehicle before the designs had progressed beyond rough sketches.

Because design costs account for 70 percent to 90 percent of a product's overall cost, using the design for manufacturing (DFM) procedure lowered product costs. This offered the advantage of reducing the number of parts. Older models required 240 components in the bumper system; the new ones needed just 126 parts, saving GM $51 per car. Another benefit was higher quality, because the reduction in parts also reduced the chances for squeaks, rattles, and loose connections. "Problems disappear when parts disappear," said one designer.

During the screening stage, the STS team identified features worth including in the new design. For example, cost-conscious team members wanted to design the car's roof/C-pillar joint as a lap joint, less expensive to produce than a brazed joint but also less attractive. Other team members insisted on the better-looking alternative, despite the higher cost. The team finally decided to go with the brazed joint, believing that it would enhance the car's image as a high-quality vehicle. Team members knew that they had made the right decision when the Lexus LS400 appeared on the market with hand-brazed C-pillars.

During the development stage, STS designers crafted scale models of the car and tested them with consumers. Then they designed a prototype model and introduced it, after testing, as a prelaunch prototype to the media and consumers at the International Automobile Show in Detroit. The new design received rave reviews, and the event generated valuable publicity, as the STS was honored as "car of the year" by three major automobile magazines.

The STS team highlighted press reviews and focus group results in the advertising campaign that launched the new car. A television commercial announced, "The Cadillac Seville STS: The first automobile in history to win not one, not two, but all three major automotive magazine awards in the same year. There's never been a car so acclaimed. It could change the way you think about American cars."

Cadillac intended the advertising to bring young luxury car buyers into its showrooms. The product launch proved so successful that buyers had to wait months for ordered cars as consumer demand far exceeded forecasted sales. Despite this success, the STS team continued to work on innovations. A year later, Cadillac introduced the Northstar system, which set new standards in performance, engineering, and technology. The 4.6-liter Northstar V-8 engine produced more horsepower than the engines of competing luxury models such as the Lexus LS400, Infiniti Q45, and BMW 540i.

Cadillac offered OnStar, a multifaceted customer service system based on another technological innovation, as an option on the 1997 Seville model. OnStar combines the technologies of cellular phones, vehicle on-board computers, and the global positioning system (GPS) satellite navigation system. From voice-activated car phones built into the vehicle's console, drivers can communicate with the OnStar service center to gain access to many services. For example, it can unlock car doors by remote control, notify police and fire departments when a driver has an accident, call a tow truck for roadside service, and provide directions to chosen destinations.

Questions

1. Which of the product growth opportunity strategies discussed in Chapter 8 did Cadillac use in developing the Seville STS?
2. How did Cadillac organize the product development process? What benefits did it gain from this type of organization?

3. Which steps in the product development process described in Chapter 8 does this video case present?

4. As part of the new product's features, Cadillac has introduced the OnStar system. Visit the company's home page located at:

www.cadillac.com

What information do you find about the OnStar system? What services does OnStar provide beyond emergency assistance? Do buyers receive OnStar services as part of the actual product? Are these services necessary to the success of Seville STS?

Sources: Brian Bremner, Larry Armstrong, Kathleen Kerwin, and Keith Naughton, "Toyota's Crusade," *Business Week,* April 7, 1997, pp. 104-114; and Mike Allen, "Beyond the Car Phone," *Popular Mechanics,* August 1996.

CASE 9
ANDERSEN CONSULTING

Andersen Worldwide is a $9.5 billion company with two lines of business: accounting/auditing services and consulting services. The consulting business helps its organizational customers to devise strategies that will improve their global competitiveness. Consultants help organizations to improve their strategies, human resources, business processes, and technological systems. Notebook computers serve as virtual offices for consultants on assignment, allowing these experts to use and showcase the same technologies they recommend for their clients.

Customers purchase Andersen's consulting services because "fundamentally they don't have some of the specialist skills that we have internally and they don't have access to the pool of knowledge that we have bought from around the world," says William Stancer, Andersen's marketing director in Europe, the Middle East, Africa, and India. "And if we can take an experience that we've had with a client in Minneapolis and extrapolate that and provide that to a telecommunications company in Belgium, then that is adding real value to that company."

As specialists in managing change for others, staff members of Andersen's consulting unit recognized a need for changes in their own organization. "We weren't getting invited to a lot of very exciting opportunities even though in our view we were the best and biggest in doing this work," says Skip Battle, Andersen's former worldwide managing partner for market development. "We realized we had to develop a separate image for the consulting services marketplace or we wouldn't have the kind of growth we wanted." In 1989, the consulting business took a new name—Andersen Consulting. Continuing to operate as part of Andersen Worldwide, the new unit faced two marketing challenges: (1) it had to establish a new brand identity that would position it for success in the highly competitive global consulting marketplace; (2) it had to transform its decentralized marketing operations into an integrated global marketing effort.

Andersen Consulting lacked both a marketing function and a formal marketing structure. Consulting partners in different geographic areas hired local resources to perform marketing activities, leaving the company's marketing without a national connection and industry and global focus. "That doesn't work in the business we're in," says James Murphy, worldwide managing partner for marketing and communications, who signed on with Andersen Consulting to develop a coordinated marketing program.

Andersen Consulting conducted internal research to test the effectiveness of its marketing activities. The results showed poor focus and weak coordination. Then the company initiated a comprehensive global market research project to learn about customers' perceptions and expectations. The Global Buyer Value Study gathered input from customers in the United States, Canada, and five European countries, revealing performance gaps between customer expectations and Andersen's service delivery in four areas: on-time completion of projects, on-budget completion, industry-specific expertise, and leading-edge solutions.

The findings from this study led development of advertising to promote an image for Andersen Consulting among its target audience. The campaign set a goal of establishing an image of Andersen Consulting as an innovative and farsighted organization that would get things done and deliver results. The campaign targeted organizational "change navigators," representatives among the top four executives in large organizations who wanted to effect change in their companies, recognized the need to take risks to do so, and would look to Andersen Consulting to help guide the change process.

"In this business," says Murphy, "advertising can't close a sale. It can't even help you with the sales discussion. But it can create a personality for you. It can present an aura around your brand. It can connect with the mindset of your buyers. And that's what we decided early on was the role of advertising for Andersen Consulting." In a business that emphasized personal selling targeted at a very narrow audience, Andersen was the first management consulting firm to advertise.

To ensure effectiveness in the campaign, Andersen involved its clients in creating and implementing its image-development program. Senior functional and MIS executives reviewed storyboards for print and broadcast ads and reported whether they found the messages compelling, the visuals stimulating, and the concepts appropriate for production.

Advertising messages focused on positioning the firm to meet the expectations of the marketplace and on making connections on issues confronting large organizations. One ad showed a formally dressed quintet performing classical music when a basketball bounced onto the set and landed in the lap of a musician. The musicians left their instruments and started tossing the ball around as the voiceover explained, "If you'd like your organization to become more adept at handling change, Andersen Consulting can help you integrate all the parts because these days, the organization that performs together, transforms together."

Advertising helped Andersen Consulting to establish a brand identity, but the company still needed to coordinate its global marketing efforts. It accomplished this goal by organizing marketing activities based on the industries it served and by supporting the groups through an Integrated Marketing Model. The model's three components included image development, market development, and business development.

Image development relied on advertising, public relations, direct mail, and sponsorship of global special events such as the Andersen Consulting World Championship of Golf tournament. Market development efforts sought to identify market segments, conduct research to determine customer needs, and determine how Andersen Consulting could differentiate its services from those of competitors. For example, the company designed business integration centers for specific industries. At The Retail Place, retail clients encountered new technology that could improve their operating effectiveness. "We bring to life in these integration centers the practical applications of our thinking," says Murphy, "so our clients can come in and see exactly what it could mean to them in their environment."

The business development component of the firm's Integrated Marketing Model focused on building relationships with customers. Andersen Consulting formed business development teams country-by-country to focus on each client's unique business needs. The personalized attention helped to make clients feel special about their relationships with Andersen Consulting.

The company's Integrated Marketing Model helped it to project a consistent image throughout the world. Andersen Consulting has invested heavily in managing its brand, and the effort has paid off. When the company conducted a global awareness study in 1989, results were very low at 26 percent. The percentage today is in the mid-90s. With revenues of over $5 billion, Andersen Consulting has grown to become the world's largest management consulting firm.

Questions

1. What role did advertising play in helping Andersen Consulting establish a global brand identity?
2. Which of the four characteristics that distinguish services from goods affect the marketing program for Andersen Consulting's service?
3. What components can you identify in Andersen Consulting's program for marketing its services to customers?
4. Andersen Consulting's Web site promotes "A Universe of Ideas & Information." Go to their Web site at:

www.ac.com

What elements of this site are effective in continuing to provide clients with leading-edge services? Does this Web site provide a competitive advantage for Andersen Consulting while supplying information and ideas?

Sources: Some of the research material for this video case was downloaded April 18, 1997 from **http://www.andersenconsulting.com**; Elizabeth MacDonald, "Andersen Appears to Rule Out Breakup," *The Wall Street Journal,* December 23, 1996, p. A2; and "Andersen's Androids," *The Economist,* May 4, 1996, p. 72.

CASE 10
NEXT DOOR FOOD STORES

People today hurry a lot. They eat in a hurry. They go to work in a hurry. They want to buy things in a hurry. Convenience stores fill the need for quick and convenient shopping. Next Door Food Stores is a chain of 30 convenience stores in Michigan and Indiana offering rapid service 24 hours a day and stocking some 30,000 grocery and general merchandise items.

Glen Johnson started the company in 1926 as Johnson Oil, a supplier of oil to farmers, and through the years he expanded it into a full-service gasoline business. In the early 1980s, his grandson, David Johnson, took over the business and decided to refocus it by combining the gasoline stations with convenience food stores. This change in focus forced David Johnson to make an important channel strategy decision: Should Next Door perform its own wholesaling or should it form relationships with independent wholesaling intermediaries?

Because Next Door lacked enough sales volume to support its own distribution warehouse, Johnson decided to use several different independent wholesalers. Most products that Next Door sells require intensive distribution. Rack jobbers supply products such as magazines, newspapers, snack foods, and chips. They regularly visit the stores to replenish merchandise from supplies in their trucks. Full-function merchant wholesalers supply the retailer with hundreds of grocery items.

Fabiano Brothers, Inc., is a large beverage distributor that provides a complete assortment of services to Next Door. "Our role is to provide the maximum benefit to the retailer," says Jim Philips, Fabiano's wine division manager. "When we sell a product, we have to be absolutely assured that that product is going to sell for the retailer." Fabiano helps Next Door's managers to determine which products stores should stock based on product movement and the space requirements of each item.

Shelf space is very limited in convenience stores. On average, the square footage of convenience stores is between 3,000 and 3,500 square feet, compared to an average of 30,000 square feet in supermarkets. With space at a premium, Next Door needs to maximize its inventory turnover in order to make a profit. Fabiano supplies sales reports to store managers weekly or monthly, depending on store size, that include information such as inventory turns and product sales and profits. Next Door managers base shelf-space allocation decisions on this information.

Because storage space at convenience food stores is also very limited, Next Door needs products delivered frequently and in small quantities. "In a convenience store, we buy by the box," says James Salisbury, Next Door's vice president of operations. At its warehouses, Fabiano Brothers receives truckload shipments of beverages on large pallets from manufacturers, breaking them down into smaller packages for retailers like Next Door. Fabiano operates its own fleet of trucks to deliver the products just-in-time, helping Next Door to keep its inventory at a minimum and to control its carrying costs. The wholesaler also deploys its own sales force. Sales reps maintain sales history data and track current trends, such as beverage sales by flavor and size, to help merchandise each store based on local market needs.

Tracking current trends helped Fabiano Brothers to recognize the growing popularity of "new-age" beverages such as bottled and flavored water, sports drinks, and flavored tea drinks. Next Door was one of the first retailers in its operating area to allocate refrigerated display space to these new beverages. When Arizona Beverage Company entered the new-age drink category in 1993, it selected Fabiano Brothers as its wholesale distributor because that firm already served the convenience stores "where we want to be," says Sal Demilio, regional manager for Arizona Beverage. The company's flavored tea drinks fit well into Fabiano's product portfolio, and the wholesaler saw great sales potential in the new products introduced in unusually large 24-ounce cans with innovative package graphics.

To ensure effective operation of this channel strategy, Arizona Beverage and Fabiano work together to develop annual plans. With manufacturing plants throughout the country, Arizona Beverage expects Fabiano to provide extensive distribution and to meet its projected sales targets. "We're there every day where the manufacturer can't be," says Philips, providing service functions such as a sales force calling daily on customers and truck deliveries as often as retailers need them.

Beverages such as Coke and Pepsi are distributed directly to Next Door outlets by local bottling plants. When Coca-Cola representatives offered Next Door a substantial financial incentive for an exclusive distribution relationship, the retailer's management accepted the offer and removed all Pepsi products from its stores. "That was the worst thing we could have done," says Salisbury. "People complained and customers left and said 'we're never coming here because you took our Pepsi out.' We did not convert those Pepsi drinkers to Coke. That was just not going to happen." Next Door returned the financial incentive to Coca-Cola, thanked the company for the offer, and called the local Pepsi bottlers, asking them to bring back their products.

Although the exclusive distribution experiment didn't work out, another experiment—selling branded food within the convenience store setting—is producing much better results. Next Door Food has formed an alliance with fast-food competitor Subway Sandwich Shops, allocating a portion of each store's floor space to operate a franchised Subway outlet. Next Door employees operate the shop, following a standard set of procedures detailed in Subway's operations manual for franchisees. The retailing innovation benefits both Subway and Next Door. Subway and other fast-food brands realize that convenience stores control prime locations, and they want to tap into that strength as part of their expansion programs. The national recognition of fast-food brands draws customers into convenience stores. One Next Door manager said that the Subway shop has increased in-store sales by 10 percent. On-the-go consumers who want a fast and convenient shopping trip can now visit a Next Door Food Store to fill up their gas tanks, pick up a Subway sandwich, and buy a can of Arizona Iced Tea.

Questions

1. How has Next Door created value for its customers through its channel strategy?
2. Which wholesaling services do Fabiano Brothers provide for Next Door Food Stores?
3. The National Association of Convenience Stores, the industry trade association, maintains a Web site as an Internet resource for the convenience store industry. Visit the site at:

www.cstorecentral.com

Explain how the Web site could assist Next Door Food Stores in its marketing decisions.

Source: Telephone interview with Barry Chapman, director of human resources, Next Door Food Stores, May 1997.

CASE 11
KMART

The pioneer of discount retail mass merchandising, Kmart, opened its first store in 1962. The innovative concept succeeded brilliantly from the start because it fit the times. Vast columns of consumers migrating to the suburbs wanted convenient places to shop—places like Kmart stores with their wide assortments of affordably priced merchandise and plenty of parking space. The Troy, Michigan-based company opened hundreds of new stores during the 1960s and 1970s, emerging as the world's top discount retailer by 1980. "Wal-Mart we considered a small country store down in Bentonville, Arkansas," says William Parker, Kmart's vice president of merchandising. "We were doing $18 billion in 1980 and they were doing $7 or $8 billion. Today they do $67 billion, we do $42 billion."

During the 1980s, Kmart continued to add new stores, but not new customers, resulting in steadily declining sales per square foot. New discount retailers such as Toys 'R' Us, Phar-Mor, Target, Best Buy, and Wal-Mart were growing, each taking away a segment of Kmart's business. "Many competitors took what Kmart had done and out-Kmartized Kmart," says J. Patrick Kelly, Professor of Marketing at Wayne State University.

The stream of customers through Kmart's doors dwindled for other reasons, too. The company had lost its focus on servicing customers. "Our stores had become old and tired and outdated," says former Kmart CEO Joseph Antonini. "While customers like our value and our prices and our merchandise, they wanted a better shopping experience." Kmart's research indicated that 49 percent of Wal-Mart shoppers drove past Kmart stores on the way to those rival outlets.

Kmart initiated a companywide renewal strategy to adapt to evolving consumer tastes and competitive challenges. The renewal effort sought to refocus the company on marketing to consumers. To make Kmart a pleasant place to shop, the company started a store modernization program of redesigning and refurbishing existing stores, which included widening the aisles and improving the lighting systems. The initiative also replaced older stores with newer, more modern ones. One of the first and most distinct changes the company implemented involved the redesign of the familiar Kmart logo. The new logo—a large red *K* with the word *mart* in white type inside—signaled to consumers the presence of a new or remodeled store.

The renewal strategy also integrated advanced technology and a comprehensive program of marketing, advertising, company communications, and merchandising. "Everything we are doing," says Antonini, "from store modernization to sophisticated technology systems, is being driven by a single idea—that Kmart will only get a larger share of the market by better focusing on and more quickly satisfying the ever-changing needs of the consumer."

At the foundation of Kmart's renewal program, continuous analysis carefully tracks consumer needs. The company conducted focus groups throughout the country to learn what customers liked and disliked about shopping at Kmart and what the company could do to improve their experiences. For example, many shoppers complained that Kmart's dressing rooms were too small and didn't have enough mirrors. Customers also didn't like the curtained enclosures, preferring instead rooms with doors that would lock and give more privacy. Kmart responded by renovating its dressing rooms, making them larger, adding more mirrors, and replacing the curtains with solid doors.

Consumer research also indicated that today's customers want quality merchandise. Kmart responded by developing quality standards. Merchandise buyers now refer to product quality specifications in negotiations with vendors to ensure that the goods they buy meet Kmart's standards. The company also built a quality assurance and technical design facility to test merchandise and verify that it meets standards before it reaches store shelves.

To remedy shopper complaints about frequent stockouts, Kmart started to update its technology. Management placed a high priority on a program to establish state-of-the-art computer information systems and satellite communications. Kmart invested heavily in automated, supplier-managed inventory systems and electronic data interchange. The company installed point-of-sale scanning at all 50,000 registers and a satellite communication system linking registers to corporate headquarters. These new technologies enable management to track every purchase so they can learn what sells and what doesn't. Kmart buyers use this information in their merchandising decisions, and suppliers use it to manage inventory levels and replenish stock, preventing out-of-stock situations.

Through its own video broadcasting network, Kmart keeps in touch with store personnel three to four times a week. Kmart uses the network as a training tool to update employees about new goods and services and to communicate news about the company.

Another part of Kmart's renewal strategy is Super Kmart, a combination general discount store and supermarket under one roof designed to provide convenient, one-stop shopping. Kmart is also planning a "Dream Store of the Future" concept as a way to eclipse its competitors and increase customer loyalty. Kmart is the only retailer participating in a pilot project sponsored by the National Information Infrastructure Testbed, a consortium examining how emerging technologies such as the Internet, smart cards, and advanced telecommunications will transform retailing. Other project participants include 3M, Hughes Electronics, Hewlett-Packard, IBM, and NCR. Together with these companies, Kmart is using new technologies to develop systems that will offer services for the newest evolution in retailing such as eliminating checkout lines, automatic home delivery for out-of-stock items, and cart scanning rather than scanning individual items.

Kmart's current CEO, Floyd Hall, continues to push forward with the renewal strategy. He wants to increase Kmart's sales per square foot from $195 to $240 in three years. (Wal-Mart tops $300 in sales per square foot and Target tops $250.) To reach his goal, Hall has tied store managers' annual bonuses to customer satisfaction ratings they receive from mystery shoppers. To attract shoppers, Hall has started weekly promotions of high-volume merchandise. He is also allocating space at the front of stores to the Pantry, a redesign concept similar to a convenience store, where shoppers can quickly fill needs like snacks, cereal, and laundry soap. Hall's ideas are increasing store traffic. "I see a lot of improvement in their stores," says Robert Buchanan, a NatWest Securities Corp. retail analyst, who has issued a buy rating for Kmart stock for the first time in ten years.

Questions

1. What elements of Kmart's renewal strategy are intended to change consumers' perceptions of the company?
2. What role does technology play in Kmart's renewal strategy?
3. Which element of retailing strategy do you think adds the most important contribution to renewing Kmart?
4. Go to Kmart's Web site located at:

    www.kmart.com

    What is Kmart's mission statement? Does the company's renewal effort align well with the mission statement? Support your decision. What modifications would you suggest for the mission statement?

Source: Chris Woodyard, "Shoppers Get Kmart's Attention: Merchant Polishes Its Image with Cleaner Stores, Wider Aisles," *USA Today,* April 9, 1997, Section B.

CASE 12
W. B. DONER

What's a zoo to do when government funding dries up at about the same time that the community loses interest? Faced with the loss of state funding and an alarming decline in attendance, the Detroit Zoo turned to W. B. Doner for help. Doner is a full-service advertising agency co-headquartered in the Detroit suburb of Southfield, Michigan, and Baltimore, Maryland. The 60-year-old agency's annual billings of $550 million rank it as the 45th largest ad agency in the world. Its status as a full-service agency permits Doner to help clients meet their marketing objectives through such services as strategic planning and research, media, public relations, and creative.

"Great creativity can change the destiny of a company," was a favorite saying of agency founder W. B. "Brod" Doner. He spent decades instilling in his team a passion for creative efforts that would persuade and motivate buyers to act, thus producing results for the client. His philosophy emphasized creating advertising that would "charm, disarm, and deliver." The agency's success in these efforts clearly shone in Doner's creative work for the Detroit Zoo, work that would deliver results that exceeded zoo management's expectations.

Doner's creative team began their analysis of the zoo's problems by focusing on its ability to compete for entertainment dollars. Doner CEO Alan Kalter phrased the question this way: "What are we going to do to stimulate visits to the zoo?" The agency's creative staff decided to focus on ways to offer added value to zoo visitors. Their brainstorming sessions led to a new exhibit featuring giant models of dinosaurs moving around a natural setting. The zoo named the exhibit *Dinosauria,* and the specially-designed logo appeared on company letterheads and internal documents as well as on media kits assembled to publicize the new attraction.

The Dinosauria exhibit targeted several objectives. One was to increase zoo attendance by 20 percent. Another was to tighten the zoo's relationship with the community. As Zoo Director Ron Kagan put it, "The idea is not to have a blockbuster in order to bring people here one time. We really wanted to relate the community to the zoo and how wonderful it is."

Doner used the Dinosauria logo as the centerpiece of its advertising campaign for the new exhibit. Highlighting the Detroit Zoo's status as a not-for-profit organization, Doner's media staff solicited offers of free advertising and space from the media, eventually lining up radio, TV, and magazine partners to deliver the zoo's message to the public. Their efforts produced overwhelming success: Zoo attendance jumped 33 percent over the previous year. The increase in visitors stimulated an $800,000 spurt in revenue from admissions and sales of food and beverages and gift-shop goods. The added cash inflows replaced most of the loss in state funding.

Doner's work with the Detroit Zoo does not produce revenues for the firm: it is done on a *pro bono* (free) basis as part of the agency's contributions to the community. However, it is rewarded financially for its successful effort for profit-seeking. Doner's work in helping British Petroleum establish a worldwide brand identity is one example of a commercial project. BP had managed its global operations country by country, and the firm had also mounted different promotional campaigns in different countries. Increased competition from other global brands, however, forced BP marketers to realize the need to project a unified worldwide image. Advertising Director Roy Croft summed up the marketing problems caused by the company's individual country campaigns: "It gave us a very fragmented image, certainly among those of our customers who traveled between markets."

Market research uncovered a sturdy, old-fashioned image for BP among consumers, who regarded it as a second-level brand below such competitors as Exxon, Texaco, and Fina. Most travelers recognized the BP brand and associated it with BP gas stations, but they did not acknowledge the company's status as an international supplier of fuel for railroads, airplanes, ocean liners, trucks, and helicopters. This research led to the creation of Doner's mission campaign, with ads showing swarms of helicopters, trains, trucks, and a jet converging on a BP gas station. The campaign was translated into 19 languages and ran in 30 markets. Post-tests conducted in these markets showed improvement in both brand awareness and brand image, moving BP from third or fourth place in every market to either first place or tied for first place.

For the past 10 years, Doner has also created advertising and special promotions for the 2,800-outlet Arby's restaurant chain. "The agency is unique in its ability to create ad campaigns that build equity for the Arby's brand while also driving next-door sales," says Arby's Franchise Association CEO Lloyd Fritzmeier. Doner has helped to position Arby's as the quality and taste leader in fast-food restaurants. Fritzmeier views Doner "as one of our most important partners—not as a supplier or vendor. We are fortunate to have an agency that understands our customers, our industry, our brand, and our franchise system."

Another retailer that appreciates Doner's understanding of its industry and customers is Lowe's, the giant home improvement and building materials retail chain. Doner created the "Lowe's Knows" campaign to differentiate Lowe's from such competitors as Home Depot and Builder's Square. "The ultimate battleground and the end point of differentiation for companies like ours—big-box retailers—is service," says Lowe's Senior Vice President of Marketing Dale Pond. "And customers typically define service as salespeople who are knowledgeable about the retailer's products and about using them." Doner addressed that customer perception in creating the "Lowe's Knows" theme and such variations as "Lowe's Knows Plumbing" and "Lowe's Knows Landscaping." The campaign has worked so well that the theme has become part of all Lowe's communications, from recruitment brochures to store signage.

Questions

1. Based on the comments in this case made by clients, what characteristics differentiate W. B. Doner from other advertising agencies?
2. Do you agree with the statement made by Doner's founder that "Great creativity can change the destiny of a company"? Support your answer with examples from this case.
3. Give examples of how Doner helps clients to achieve the advertising objectives discussed in the chapter.
4. Successful marketing plans frequently rely on thorough customer research. Visit the Detroit Zoo Web site at:

<u>www.detroitzoo.org</u>

Does the zoo's home page solicit customer information? Write a brief proposal suggesting changes to this home page to improve its effectiveness as a research tool.

Sources: The following articles appeared in the March 3, 1997 issue of *Advertising Age:* John McDonough, "Shop's 'Vest Picket' Origins Lead to Billings of a Half-Billion Dollars," pp. C1-C2; John DeCerchio, "Ososis, Fiat Passed Doner Philosophy," p. C6; Dale Pond, "Service-Oriented Ads Succeed for Lowe's," p. C8; Lloyd Fritzmeir, "Building Equity While Driving Sales for Arby's," p. C8; and Bob Purvis, "BP Goes for TV Creative," p. C10.

CASE 13
VALASSIS COMMUNICATIONS

"We have always believed that our sales organization should have tremendous visibility, power, authority, and input in everything we do," asserts Valassis Communications CEO David Brandon. "We adopt the philosophy that everything starts with the sale and satisfying the customer. Virtually all the rest of the employees and the rest of the functions of the company are there to support the sales effort."

In 1971, Valassis introduced an innovative product in the coupon industry, the free-standing insert, or FSI. FSIs are glossy, multipage, color-coupon supplements placed in the middle of Sunday newspapers and often in daily papers. About 90 percent of all coupons in the United States are distributed through this method, including discount offers and promotional messages from America's top packaged-goods marketers. Each week more than 56 million coupon supplements, each averaging 28 pages, are distributed to some 400 newspapers nationwide.

FSIs are extremely popular with both consumers and marketers. Newspaper readership surveys consistently report that the Valassis coupon supplements rank second only to the front-page news in popularity. Consumer-goods marketers frequently incorporate FSIs in their marketing programs, lured by the advantages of high-quality color reproduction, targeted to reach specific regions and cities, and cost efficiency compared to other methods of coupon distribution.

The complex process of producing an FSI begins when a Valassis salesperson convinces a client to place a coupon promotion in a future edition of a newspaper. The salesperson communicates the order to the category management department, which records the physical size of the promotional purchase and the product category, such as cereal or baby food. A computerized-layout program supports design of the complete booklet. Customer orders are then processed and forwarded to the printing area where the ad layouts are finalized and the booklet is printed. The FSIs are then distributed to newspapers throughout North America.

Every Valassis employee who comes into contact with a customer is considered to be a member of the sales team. The company commits itself to teamwork among its employees and with customers with the goal of exceeding customer expectations. According to Executive Vice President Al Schultz, "If there's a problem with a printed product that we've produced, the head pressman can meet with the customer and feel a part of the process. I believe that teamwork goes well beyond just the people who are dealing with the customers every day to virtually everyone in our organization—from top executives to people who are pulling inserts off the back of a press."

The Valassis sales and service philosophy is based on individualized customer service. But the company didn't start out with that approach. "There was a time," Brandon recalls, "that I felt that if you just regimented everything and got very process oriented and very uniform and consistent that you would be rewarded. What we started finding was that as our customers started to move in their own directions, we were impeding their ability to get where they wanted to go because we were asking them to adapt to our system. And they're the customer!"

Valassis learned the hard way that "customers don't want to be lumped together with a bunch of other customers and be retrofitted into some kind of packaged, homogenized program that a company offers for service quality," says Brandon. Therefore, Valassis management developed a new sales and service approach that substantially increased the number of employees in customer service, sales assistance, and backup support roles. At one point, Valassis had three times the number of service-related employees as did its major competitors. Although many competitors viewed this as an advantage due to the added overhead costs incurred by Valassis, Brandon saw it quite differently. "What we really did was amass this very powerful weapon that allowed us to outperform them in the marketplace in a way that our customers see the most."

The Valassis sales force plays a major role in ensuring customer satisfaction. Salespeople are expected to work in the field building relationships with customers rather than in the office. As Brandon points out, "We pay them extremely well. We incent the living daylights out of them. We reward them for extraordinary performance. And we really put them out front to lead our organization."

Valassis sales managers take a flexible approach in evaluating their salespeople, measuring performance by sales volume, market share, and ability to generate sales at profitable prices. Since the firm believes in empowering its employees, salespeople exercise considerable discretion in how they perform sales tasks. However, every Valassis salesperson must maintain high ethical standards. "There's nothing so important in a salesperson as their ethics," says Schultz. "In this market today, if you don't have credibility and a high degree of ethics, you're not going to be successful long term."

Because Valassis uses a consultative selling approach, creativity and problem-solving skills are vital to each salesperson's success. Research and creative pre-call planning are keys to helping salespeople convince potential clients of the value of investing a significant portion of their advertising budget in FSIs. Valassis subscribes to the Lexis/Nexis online news service to assist its sales force in preparing sales presentations. Sales representatives review recent articles about their clients looking for information on market share, sales revenues, advertising expenditures, and current issues and problems. This knowledge helps a salesperson to understand a particular customer's needs and develop ways in which Valassis can help to satisfy them.

Many long-term customers depend on Valassis sales representatives to play major roles in planning their FSI promotions. When baby food maker Gerber, a frequent Valassis client, wanted a special coupon insert for a Baby Week promotion, the Valassis team developed a unique promotion. Gerber Consumer Service Director Mack Jenks was extremely impressed with the result. "Valassis showed that they were thinking progressively. They weren't taking the vehicle that had been the same thing the past 15 years. I was impressed that they were willing to think beyond that."

Creating new and different promotions keeps Valassis a leader in the industry. "I don't think you could find two customers that we do business with where we do anything the same," says Brandon. "We adapt to them. We give them what they want. They like it that way."

Questions

1. Review the three primary reasons why personal selling is such an important component of a promotional strategy. Does Valassis effectively demonstrate any of these? Explain why or why not.

2. Describe how Valassis implements the principles of relationship selling and team selling.

3. Over 25 years ago, Valassis introduced the innovation of the free-standing insert. Today, the Internet has created another channel for coupon distribution. Conduct an Internet search for online coupons before answering the following questions:

   a. What kinds of online coupons did you find?

   b. In your opinion, does the system you encountered offer an effective way to distribute coupons? Explain your answer.

   c. Compare online coupons with FSIs from a recent issue of your local newspaper. What are the pros and cons of each? Consider the interests of both businesses and shoppers in your answer.

Sources: Personal interviews with David Brandon and Al Schultz of Valassis Communications, Inc., and Mack Jenks of Gerber, March 1997.

CASE 14
SECOND CHANCE CORP.

How do you set the price for a product that could mean the difference between life and death for its customer? Richard Davis had to make that decision in determining the price for a bulletproof vest he designed. Davis is CEO of Second Chance Corp., a major supplier of body armor to police departments and law enforcement agencies throughout the world.

Most people don't realize the importance of body armor in the daily routine of today's law enforcement officers. Several trends threaten the safety of police officers and heighten the demand for protective armor, including the dramatic increase in violent crime, the proliferation of firearms, and the growing number of high-caliber semiautomatic and automatic weapons in the hands of criminals.

Davis started his company after falling victim to a violent crime while on duty as a police officer. As a reaction, he developed a new type of comfortable and concealable bullet-resistant vest designed to protect the vital organs of the torso. The new body armor was introduced with an unforgetable video demonstration of Davis wearing his Second Chance vest and shooting himself to demonstrate his confidence in the product's effectiveness.

Second Chance offers three lines of comfortable, custom fit vests. The basic vest, The ComfortLite brand, starts at around $200. The middle-of-the-line product, the SuperfeatherLite, is priced between $500 and $600. The Monarch, Second Chance's high-end line, carries a price tag of $800 to $1,000.

Low entry barriers attract many competitors to the body armor industry. Newcomers can begin operating with minimal capital investments, but weak experience, poor distribution networks, and inability to offer custom-designed, uniform-quality products doom most of them to go out of business in a few years. New entries soon follow and struggle with the same production and marketing handicaps. Second Chance executives consider three to four large, reputable firms as their major competitors, and they carefully monitor the marketing activities of these rivals to assess potential threats in their market.

A number of factors affect prices of Second Chance products: production costs, trade discounts for channel members, prices charged by competitors, and customer perceptions of product value. This pricing strategy differs from those of most competitors, who tend to set minimum profit margin goals and then pursue volume pricing strategies. Group vice president Thomas Bachner explains why Second Chance pursues a different strategy: "Our philosophy is to peg the value of the product and get as much high-volume business with that high value so we can maximize our profit margins."

The pricing of the Monarch brand is an excellent example of this strategy. This vest is thin, light, soft, flexible, and the only waterproof product in the marketplace. Although its production cost is only slightly higher than those of other Second Chance vests, company marketers deliberately set the price higher than that of any other vest in the market to support its perceived value.

The largest current target market for Second Chance products is the law enforcement community of North America. Department buyers consider a number of evaluative criteria to determine which vest to purchase for their officers. At the top of the list of criteria is the range of bullets the body armor needs to stop. Second, buyers check for certification by the National Institute of Justice. Then they consider price and comfort. Some buyers are highly price sensitive; others are not. Price-sensitive buyers typically include part-time officers or those who patrol economically depressed areas. Other buyers rank comfort as the main concern. When comfort-oriented buyers see Second Chance's Monarch ad showing two hands crushing the vest into a ball, they frequently call the company to ask where they can buy it without asking about price.

Most of Second Chance's sales volume is generated through police equipment distributors and dealers. The company publishes a recommended retail price list and offers trade discounts to channel members along a graduated scale that depends on purchase volume. Discounts range from 3 percent up to 57 percent for dealers that purchase at least $150,000 annually. To encourage quick payments, Second Chance pays all freight charges for prepaid shipments.

For very large orders, Second Chance participates in competitive bidding. Bachner has developed a breakeven analysis system to help him in preparing bids. The company recently won a lucrative bid to supply the City of Chicago with 12,000 vests. Even though Second Chance's price was fourth lowest of 15 bidders, it received the contract after the Chicago Police Department evaluated lowest bidders on three factors: ability to custom fit, company reputation, and ability to produce in volume and deliver at least 400 vests per week.

Second Chance currently exports body armor to the United Kingdom, Sweden, Italy, Venezuela, Mexico, and Canada. Exports account for 10 to 25 percent of total sales. In pricing exports, Second Chance marketers take into account a number of additional factors, including competition in local markets, rates of exchange, special tariffs, and value-added taxes. Distributors in each international market purchase the vests at specified prices that vary according to annual sales volume. Since these representatives bring knowledge about their own markets, Second Chance relies on them to set the retail prices for the different product lines.

In a little more than two decades, Second Chance has become the leader for the body armor industry in units sold and in the numbers of lives saved annually. It also enjoys strong brand preference in the law enforcement industry. Always paying primary attention to satisfying the needs of the end user, Second Chance is successful in marketing the right products at the right prices.

Questions

1. Which of the pricing objectives discussed in Chapter 14 apply to Second Chance?
2. Is demand for body armor price elastic or price inelastic? Explain.
3. In addition to its lines of concealable body armor, Second Chance has used its expertise to develop a number of other products. Visit the firm's Web site at:

www.secondchance.com

Identify the product extensions that Second Chance has added to its offerings. Should the firm apply the same pricing strategy for the new products that it uses for lines of concealable body armor? Explain.

Sources: Personal interview with Thomas Bachner, group vice president of Second Chance Corp., March 1997.

CASE 15
YAHOO!

Rare is the Net surfer who remains unacquainted with "Yet Another Hierarchical Officious Oracle," better known as Yahoo! With 170,000 new pages daily joining the 90 million pages already on the World Wide Web, search engines like Yahoo! have become indispensable tools to help Web travelers navigate through the Internet and find information. On a typical day, 2 million visitors will access the Yahoo! site.

Yahoo! creators Jerry Yang and David Filo trace the beginnings of their company to 1994 when, as Ph.D. students at Stanford, they started compiling lists of their favorite Web pages. This activity led to the creation of a free directory called *David's Guide to the World Wide Web*. The enthusiastically positive response from people who used the directory convinced Yang and Filo to turn their hobby into a business. They conducted market research by asking other Internet surfers for suggestions, and they developed customized software to locate, identify, and edit material stored on the Internet. Then they launched Yahoo! "My dad used to call us yahoos," says Filo, "which is fitting since the Internet is a wild frontier."

The explosive growth of the Internet coupled with corresponding increases in the number of users created a need for a search engine like Yahoo! "Somebody could create a great Web page about soccer," explains Filo, "but nobody would know it was there. What we did was organize the Web for people." When a user clicks on Yahoo!, the screen displays an alphabetized list of topics ranging from *entertainment* to *social sciences*. Clicking on a topic button such as entertainment calls up another list with subcategories like books, comics, and television. Keeping in mind their target market of young Internet users, most under 35, Yang and Filo decided to create a separate series of "cool links," as well. This feature, labeled "the coolest stuff on the Web," enabled Yahoo! users to quickly connect with exciting Web pages like the FBI's Ten Most Wanted list and NASA's space shuttle information.

Yang and Filo's marketing plan specified sources of revenues that would ensure profitability. To encourage use of the site, Yahoo! does not charge users for the service itself. Instead, the firm generates revenues from advertising and licensing fees paid by online services. A Yahoo! advertiser pays a fee for each *impression,* that is, every time a computer loads a Web page with its ad.

A major event in Yahoo's success occurred when Netscape chose to replace Netscape Destinations with Netscape Guide by Yahoo! This move made Yahoo! the default directory for the company's Netscape Communicator Web browser suite. When Navigator users click on the Guide button, they are automatically routed to Yahoo! and offered a choice of eight of the most popular information categories on the Web.

Even though they pioneered search engine technology, Yang and Filo realized that others could easily duplicate their service. They knew that their long-term success depended on adding customer value to what was otherwise a commodity-type product. Indeed, competitors such as Excite, Lycos, and Infoseek quickly entered the new industry. As Yang put it, "If we are a tools company, we are not going to survive. Microsoft will just take over our space. If we are a publication, like a *Fortune* or a *Time,* and we create brand loyalty, then we have a sustainable business."

Yang and Filo decided to create brand loyalty by moving Yahoo! toward becoming a media company. First, they formed an alliance with the Japanese media conglomerate Softbank and launched two brand extensions: a print and online magazine called *Yahoo! Internet Life* and a personal computer information center on the Web called *Yahoo! Computing.* In partnership with such publishers as Fodor's and the *Village Voice,* Yahoo! is also creating online city guides for New York, Chicago, Los Angeles, Boston, San Francisco, and Dallas/Fort Worth.

The goal of these targeted geographic metro guides and online magazines is to transform the Yahoo! Web site into a *destination* that tempts each visitor to browse several pages instead of just typing in a keyword on the first page. The metro guides are excellent advertising vehicles, since they match local advertisers with targeted audiences within specific regions.

Another Yahoo! alliance aimed at strengthening the company's drive to become a media company involves MTV Music Television. The two first recently launched a co-branded venture called *MTV Yahoo! Unfurled,* a combination of music-related editorials and an online guide to other music sites on the Web. "We're partnering with Yahoo! because it's the search engine that's really built a brand name for themselves," says MTV executive Matt Farber. "We both understand the importance of branding, and that's essential to our partnership." Because the MTV and Yahoo! target audiences share a number of demographic characteristics, the alliance is expected to attract new users for each company. "We're partnering to fill the gaps in each of our sites,"says Yahoo! Director of Production Tim Brady. "To retain music users, we need to offer more than just music lists."

Yahoo! has invested over $50 million in advertising designed to promote its brand. The firm recently launched its "Do You Yahoo?" campaign with ads in such magazines as *Wired, Red Herring,* and *Fortune* backed by local radio commercials. Sales offices in major U.S. cities also seek additional advertisers on the Yahoo! Web site.

The list of Yahoo! online services continues to grow. *Yahooligans* is an online directory for children, and *Beatrice's Web Guide* is targeted at women. The company has also moved into narrowcasting, an electronic delivery service for customized information, by launching *My Yahoo!* This service delivers content update from a user's favorite Web sites and news about new sites that relate to the user's personal interests.

With $8.6 million in annual revenues, Yahoo! continues to adapt to the Internet's ever-changing environment. By sponsoring and participating in a variety of community programs, Yang and Filo's company helps to promote the development of Internet education and programming. Yahoo! is connecting classrooms to the Internet, providing free educational seminars and offering promotional exposure for not-for-profit organizations on its Web sites.

Questions

1. Peter Drucker defined the purpose of business as creating a customer. How has Yahoo! created a customer as implied by Drucker's definition?
2. Relate the concepts (found in earlier chapters of your text) of the target market, marketing mix, and the marketing environment to this case.
3. The fourth era in marketing's history focuses on relationship marketing. Give examples that illustrate how Yahoo! is embracing this concept.
4. Yahoo! generates a sizable portion of its total revenues from advertising. Visit the Yahoo! home page at:

www.yahoo.com

Review the ads and the advertisers whose messages appear there. Evaluate the ads in comparison with traditional ads appearing in magazines and on billboards, radio, and television. What motivated these advertisers to select this medium for their messages?

Source: "Netscape and Yahoo! to Launch Netscape Guide by Yahoo!," March 19, 1997.

CASE 16
SLAZENGER USA

Golf has done a complete flip-flop. It used to be the game of the well-to-do. During the 1950s and early 1960s, 70 percent of all golf play took place at posh private country clubs, where members outfitted themselves with merchandise at the adjacent pro shops. By the mid-1970s, however, 70 percent of golfers were teeing off at public courses. "That change in the character of the player also changed the character of the business," says David Branon, president and CEO of Slazenger USA, a privately-held manufacturer headquartered in Greenville, South Carolina. "An industry that had been largely dominated by the on-course pro shop was suddenly a multiple outlet industry."

A host of retailers—mass merchandisers, discount retailers, and large sporting goods stores—were stocking their shelves with balls, gloves, bags, and clubs made by Callaway, Wilson, Titleist, Dunlop, and other golf equipment manufacturers to entice the growing number of public-course golfers into their stores. These changes in the golf industry negatively affected golf professionals who operated small, on-course pro shops at private clubs. "He got none of the deals, he got none of the best prices, he could bring no clout or volume to the negotiating table," says Branon.

In 1987, Branon started his company to serve the needs of private-club golf professionals and their customers. Research indicated that the golf pro's customers, private club members, had a high level of discretionary income, played more rounds of golf each year than the average player, and were likely to spend more for apparel and golf equipment than other golfers. In developing the marketing strategy for this segment, Branon made an important product positioning decision by obtaining a U.S. license to use the internationally known Slazenger brand name. "The Slazenger brand has been around since 1881," says Branon. "It has a lot of international panache and a lot of heritage to it and we basically imported the romance of the brand." To enhance the image of its brand, Slazenger has long associated its products with the most prestigious golf and tennis tournaments in the world. It has sponsored events such as the British Open and, since 1972, the Wimbledon lawn tennis championship.

The high visibility of the brand boosted Slazenger USA's early marketing efforts. "In the beginning, we played off of their success around the world," says Don Swarat, senior vice president of sales. "I know some of the earliest accounts I could open were military accounts because they had personnel who had been to Europe and that were familiar with the brand so they were willing to take a chance on that brand over here."

Branon believed the best way to capture the romance of the Slazenger brand would be by developing an upscale line of clothing marketed exclusively through on-course golf professionals so they could protect their prices and profits. Branon offered his menswear at the same price to all pros, whether they ordered 10 items or 10,000. The exclusive distribution of Slazenger USA apparel allowed golf pros to maintain high prices and healthy profit margins, because it freed them from competing with high-volume discount retailers. The exclusive arrangement also enabled the pros to put their private club names and logos on the clothing.

Branon decided to broaden his product offerings to include other golf products such as balls, gloves, and clubs. By offering a complete product mix to the golf pro, Slazenger USA could "increase our meaningfulness to him and increase the validity of our presentation to him as a pro-shop-only company," says Branon. One golf pro says, "They're the first company I've been approached by from a representative standpoint of coming in and making a commitment to the golf pro."

Slazenger USA backs up its commitment to the golf professional with a network of highly trained and skilled sales representatives who work to build strong customer relationships. Visiting customers monthly, sales reps travel in vans equipped as showrooms on wheels, from which they show golf pros their newest products. They also assist the pros in setting up product displays and offer marketing advice to increase product sales. In establishing the company's promotional strategy, "We said we would set out and drive the success of the brand from inside the shop, not outside with massive media campaigns," says Branon. With this approach, "the advocacy of the golf pro would control the marketing power of the brand."

Slazenger also promotes its brand by participating in trade shows. The company's elaborate display at the annual Professional Golf Association trade show in Orlando allows Slazenger marketers to meet with golf pros from around the country who come to see the newest equipment and apparel. The PGA show "gives us an opportunity to project our image . . . as a quality company and a service company," says Swarat. "It gives us an opportunity to listen, because every golf manufacturer is at the show and the buyer goes there to compare."

Developing unique products also helped Slazenger USA to strengthen its relationships with golf pros. The company wanted to enter the golf club market, but realized that mass marketing didn't fit its philosophy of offering exclusive products for pro shops. In response, the company developed the custom-built Crown Limited Club Fitting System. The system relies on the golf pro's expertise to properly fit golf clubs to match each golfer's unique characteristics.

The customized club-design process begins with 3,348 club head variations and incorporates information about the golfer's health, learning styles, playing and practice habits, swing tendencies, and flight patterns. The pro takes kinetic measurements to evaluate the golfer's upper body strength, flexibility, and range of motion, and analyzes the golfer's swing speed. The golf pro uses the results of these tests to specify the design of customized clubs that will help the golfer to perform at his or her best. The clubs are then assembled and sent to customers within 72 hours from the time the order is placed by phone or fax. One golf pro says that the custom-designed clubs "improve my credibility tremendously along with getting my customers a lot more satisfied and happy and enjoying the game."

Slazenger USA has successfully achieved specialty status for its premium-priced product lines. "The best way to protect the special nature of a product is to make the product special," says Branon. "You really have to pay attention to the product. We deal with probably the most discriminating element of both the trade and the consumer. The most dangerous animal in the world is the cynical consumer. We are monomaniacal about the quality of the product."

Questions

1. What types of consumer products does Slazenger USA sell? Describe characteristics of the products that support your classification.
2. Give examples of how Slazenger USA developed a marketing strategy for branding, promoting, pricing, and distributing its products.
3. What benefits did Slazenger USA gain by developing a complete product line?
4. The Internet has provided an additional channel for promoting and distributing a number of products. Considering its current market niche, could Slazenger USA effectively use the Web to enhance its current success? Review other Web sites for golf products, then outline a Web site plan for Slazenger. Include the following criteria in your proposal:
   a. Intended audience.
   b. Information content (explain the value of each element and how it will help Slazenger to achieve its objectives).
   c. Objectives of the site.
   d. Suggested methods of measuring the success or failure of the Web site.

Sources: Telephone interview with Carrie Webb, Slazenger USA Customer Relations Specialist, May 16, 1997; and Kerry Capell, "Tailored Clubs Could Trim Your Score," *Business Week,* February 19, 1996, p. 94.

CASE 17
KROPF FRUIT COMPANY

Fresh, firm, and juicy. That's what most people want in their apples. Americans have made apples one of their favorite fruits, consuming 10 billion pounds of them each year. Apples come in many varieties, and each person has definite ideas about which is best, whether the personal favorite is a Gala, Red Delicious, or even a Granny Smith.

Thanks to modern technology, fruit growing and packing companies like Kropf Fruit can supply fresh apples throughout the year. Christian Kropf started this family fruit business in Lowell, Michigan, over a century ago. Through the years, Kropf Fruit has prospered as a supplier to retail grocers throughout the year. Key ingredients in the firm's success were delivering quality apples and building long-term relationships with both area growers and retail customers.

As a medium-sized processor, Kropf entered the decade of the 1990s facing important marketing planning and strategy decisions that would redefine the very nature of the firm by 2000. Kropf executives had identified several important trends, including changes in consumer preferences, consolidation in the retail grocery industry, and increased competition. Supermarket consumers were abandoning such traditional apple favorites as Jonathan, Red Delicious, and Golden Delicious in favor of newly introduced varieties such as Gala and Fuji. In addition, large chain-store operations had continued to increase their domination of the industry, building giant superstores and acquiring independents and smaller chains that had long been Kropf's primary customers. To win over the large chains as customers, a fruit processor had to be capable of filling large-volume orders. Such orders would often supply 2,000 stores rather than 200 or fewer. Because each chain's business was so large, competition among suppliers for this business also intensified.

Kropf managers thought they saw a strategic window of opportunity in these trends that might allow them to position the company for the future. First, they had to decide whether Kropf should continue as a medium-sized grower or expand to serve the needs of large customers. They ultimately decided to pursue a growth strategy supported by a new marketing plan. CEO Roger Kropf explained the long-term commitment this way: "From the day you start a tree in the ground, it's going to take four to seven years before you see a money return on your investment."

The Kropf marketing planning process began by defining the firm's mission: To remain a family business while providing customers with high-quality fruit. It set an objective of growing to meet the growing needs of retailers by becoming a major packing and processing company.

In conducting a SWOT analysis, Kropf managers identified several company strengths:

▼ Willingness to adapt to changing markets.

▼ An open attitude and a willingness to try new marketing and merchandising ideas.

▼ A welcoming reception for suggestions from customers and input regarding what they liked.

▼ Loyal support from other growers who supplied Kropf with additional fruit.

The analysis also identified areas of weakness:

▼ The firm's current inability to supply the large quantities of fruit demanded by national retailers.

▼ Oversupply of apple varieties that were losing popularity with consumers.

▼ Inadequate equipment to grade, sort, and store new apple varieties.

Kropf executives saw opportunities in exporting to international markets, altering the firm's product mix by converting some orchards to grow new apple varieties, and expanding and upgrading its packing facilities. They saw competition from new types of exotic fruit as a major threat.

Based on this assessment, management devised a marketing strategy to achieve their objectives. The plan involved increasing orchard acreage by at least 50 percent to grow new apple varieties. In addition, the plan called for designing new processing facilities with capacity to handle 50 percent more fruit than Kropf currently needed. The installation of high-technology processing and refrigeration equipment would help Kropf to process fruit quickly and efficiently at the lowest possible cost.

Much of Kropf's short-term tactical planning centers around determining apple supply and demand. Apple producers can forecast sales to customers much more easily than they can predict production yields, which vary because of weather conditions. Kropf prepares annual sales forecasts based on past and projected world and U.S. production statistics published by the U.S. Department of Agriculture as a starting point. Kropf marketers adjust these data to the firm's geographic market and to its mix of apple varieties. If the forecast indicates inadequate expected yields from the firm's own orchards and grower-partners, Kropf contracts to purchase additional apples from other growers to meet anticipated customer needs.

Even though Kropf has only partially completed its 10-year growth plan, interim reviews of its execution suggest that the growth strategy was the right choice. The firm had already made significant progress in implementing the new plan by planting some 80,000 new trees and installing new processing equipment. CEO Roger Kropf also acknowledges that the strategic plan is opening marketing doors that the firm's sales representatives were never able to enter before, enabling them to negotiate with some of the largest retailers in the nation. "These retailers today will talk to us in the same way as they might talk to a Chiquita or a Dole or a very large conglomerate. They give us equal time today that prior to this we wouldn't have gotten."

Driven by its new strategic plan, Kropf has grown to become one of the largest regional fruit processors and distributors in the United States. It markets 18 apple varieties ranging from the well-established Golden Delicious to the newer Ginger Gold. It not only markets the yield from its own 1,500 acres, but also another 4,000 acres owned by more than 60 growers. As the grocery industry continues to consolidate, Kropf will continue to adopt appropriate growth strategies.

Questions

1. Relate the Kropf Fruit Company strategic planning process (found in Appendix 1, "Planning for Marketing Decisions") to the steps in the planning process discussed in Appendix 1.
2. How important is relationship marketing to Kropf in implementing its growth strategy? Recommend measures by which the firm can strengthen these relationships.
3. SWOT analysis played an important role in the development of the Kropf strategic plan. Visit the Mind Tools Web site at:

www.mindtools.com

Review the questions suggested there for SWOT analysis. Then find an actual SWOT analysis on the Web. Does the actual analysis of the firm you selected follow the guidelines suggested by Mind Tools? Evaluate the actual analysis. How could it be improved?

Source: "SWOT Analysis—Strengths, Weaknesses, Opportunities, Threats," downloaded April 1997 from **http://www. mindtools.com/swot.html**

CASE 18
CHERRY CAPITAL AIRPORT

Traverse City offers visitors a variety of attractions. Some visitors are lured to the northwestern Michigan city by such attractions as the National Cherry Festival, nearby ski slopes, or opportunities for leisurely vacations along the shores of Lake Michigan. Folks from big cities like Chicago and Detroit are relocating to Traverse City, lured by the twin benefits of its rapidly growing, diverse economy and a simpler lifestyle.

In fact, only one part of Traverse City's infrastructure seemed left out of the area's growth—the local air terminal, Cherry Capital Airport. Most people traveling into and out of the city chose to travel by car rather than to fly. In fact, one research study revealed that 70 percent of people traveling by air chose to drive two hours to Grand Rapids or, even worse, four hours to Detroit to catch planes there. Unless airport management could do something to convince people to use Cherry Capital Airport, they saw a bleak future for local air service.

They traced Cherry Capital's problems directly to the 1978 deregulation of the airline industry. Deregulation ushered in a new era in which airports had to compete for air service. "With deregulation, we suddenly had no jet flights to Detroit or Chicago," says Hal VanSumeren, executive director of the Traverse City Area Chamber of Commerce. "Service deteriorated to a point that our manufacturers were telling us that they were no longer going to expand in our area until air service was improved."

Cherry Capital's marketers decided to devise an integrated marketing communications strategy aimed at increasing passenger traffic and improving airline service. As Airport Director Steve Cassens put it, "Not only do we have to sell the customer who's coming to the airport, but we have to convince the airlines that they should be in this market."

Business travelers are important to the success of any airport since they book many flights on short notice and at relatively high fares. These revenues allow the airlines to offer discounted fares to other passengers. "You can't discount seats unless you have that core group that's using the airlines on a regular basis," says Cassens. The number of airlines serving an airport has a major impact on the level of service it offers to the flying public. Realizing this fact, Cherry Capital marketers knew they had to persuade airline decision makers that their airport could command a sufficiently large market to support profitable flights to and from Traverse City.

Cassens and his staff identified four target audiences: passengers, businesses, airlines, and travel agents. They began by conducting a market research study to learn about the travel patterns, preferences, and priorities of current and potential air travelers. At the top of the list of factors influencing customer satisfaction was frequency of flights. Second on the list was competitive fares, followed by the types of aircraft that service an airport's flights. These findings became the basis for Traverse City's new integrated marketing communications strategy.

One component of the new strategy was personal selling. Airport personnel made personal sales calls to area travel agents, informing them of the services provided by the local airport and the increased frequency of outbound and inbound flights. Sales people also supplied prospects with data showing the competitiveness of air fares for flights from the airport and encouraged them to recommend Cherry Capital to their clients.

Special events such as air shows added another promotional element to boost exposure for the airport among potential passengers and to promote good will in the community. These events permitted Cherry Capital to showcase its modern facilities to potential air travelers, and they encouraged visitors to become familiar with the roads leading to the airport. To generate publicity for the airport, Cherry Capital marketers nurtured relationships with media outlets and assisted them in preparing radio and TV stories and public-interest articles to appear in area newspapers.

Advertising was a major element in Cherry Capital's IMC strategy. The ad campaign theme was inspired by Cassens' experience while driving on a Michigan road. Narrowly avoiding a duck that was crossing the road on foot, Cassens wondered why a duck would walk when it could fly. Then the inspiration for the campaign hit him: Ads could ask the same question of Traverse City travelers who made long auto drives when they could have flown. Thus, the "Fly from Nearby" campaign was born. Television ads featured a goose choosing Cherry Capital's convenient service. The ads gave the goose a personality and put him in humanlike situations.

One ad, "Goose on Foot," showed the feathered star landing, crossing the road, and waddling into Cherry Capital's attractive terminal. Narration announced, "Starting your trip from Cherry Capital Airport is convenient and saves you time and money. So why take to the road when you can fly?" Another ad featured the goose making a dramatic U-turn in a car after getting a call on his cell phone with the urgent message to get to Chicago immediately because "your sister's having an egg!" An "Office Goose" ad targeted at business travelers portrayed the bird behind an executive-sized desk signing a contract with his floppy foot. When told to go to Boston right away, the business bird again took advantage of Cherry Capital Airport, described by the narrator as "your connection to the world."

The award-winning campaign captured public attention, and the "Fly from Nearby" theme was expanded from TV ads to radio, magazine, and newspaper messages. It also filled sales presentation materials and airport communications. To promote the airport on the Internet, Brauer designed an entertaining and informative Web site. Traverse City travelers can access the site to learn about flight schedules, local events, and weather conditions.

Cherry Capital's promotions have changed travelers' attitudes about the airport and its services, resulting in growth in passenger traffic from 180,000 in 1989 to over 300,000 today. The airport expects to double that number over the next ten years. The promotions have also succeeded in bringing in travelers from a larger geographic area. Increased traffic has resulted in increased jet service and more daily flights. Airlines now servicing Traverse City include major carriers such as Northwest and American, as well as regional carriers such as United Express and Great Lakes Airlines. Daily nonstop flights take travelers to and from Chicago and Detroit. Cherry Capital is now profitable and undergoing a major expansion program to accommodate expected future growth.

Questions

1. Explain how Cherry Capital applied integrated marketing communications in achieving its promotional objectives.
2. Does Cherry Capital's promotional strategy represent a pulling strategy, a pushing strategy, or both? Support your answer with examples.
3. Visit the Cherry Capital Web site at:

<u>www.tvcairport.com</u>

Do you feel that this Web site is an effective component of the airport's integrated marketing communications package? Suggest methods for improving the site as a component of the airport's overall promotional campaign.

Sources: Personal interviews with Steve Cassens, director, Cherry Capital Airport, March 1997, and Hal VanSumeren, executive director, Traverse City Area Chamber of Commerce.

CASE 19
DOW CHEMICAL COMPANY

With revenues of more than $20 billion, Dow Chemical Company is the fifth largest chemical producer in the world. Dow manufactures and supplies more than 2,500 product families, including chemicals, plastics, agricultural products, and environmental services. Most of Dow's products become raw material inputs by business customers.

Dow produces chemicals at 400 processing plants in more than 30 countries. The production process for chemicals involves pumping materials in gas or liquid form out of storage tanks along many pipelines into mixing tanks, where chemical reactions generate the desired products. After later distillation or purification in a tower, pumps move the finished products by pipeline to storage tanks.

Dow's logistics system links the processing plants to business customers worldwide. From its storage tanks, Dow delivers products to buyers via many transportation modes. Oceangoing vessels move products between continents, and barges transport them along rivers and seacoasts. On land, tanker trucks move small shipments short distances, while railroads move large shipments long distances in tanker and hopper cars.

Transporting hazardous chemicals is just one of many challenges Dow faces in continually improving its logistics system. "The real key to logistics is meeting all customers' needs by having the right product at the right place at the right time," says Bill Fillmore, supply chain project leader. In North America, Dow spends over $1 billion a year on logistics activities. Improving logistics provides critical help in maintaining Dow's ability to compete, because improvements enhance customer service, reduce costs, and increase company profits.

In the past, customers bought chemicals on price alone. Today, customers want just-in-time delivery service to reduce their inventory levels and their costs. Logistics efficiency is also a major source of cost reduction at Dow. "We're working to improve the materials management processes at Dow to improve the value of the company and to contribute to shareholder value," says Richard Gerardo, vice president of materials management, North America. A $2-billion-a-year improvement program seeks to increase sales by $1 billion and reduce costs by $1 billion, more than half of the savings coming from materials management improvement. Reducing logistics costs boosts Dow's profits. Gerardo explains, "If you increase sales by a dollar, about 10 percent goes to the bottom line. If you reduce costs by a dollar, a dollar goes to the bottom line."

Dow is using information technology, quality management techniques, and supply chain management to boost the efficiency and effectiveness of its logistics system. Computer systems at processing plants monitor and control movement and storage of products. An electronic data interchange system transmits customer orders from computers at headquarters in Midland, Michigan, to processing plants. Computerized systems track a customer's shipment from the time it leaves the processing plant until it arrives at its destination. Using laptop computers, account managers can instantly communicate shipment status information to customers via e-mail.

Dow and its channel partners practice quality management techniques such as employee empowerment and preventive maintenance to improve chemical logistics safety, quality, and reliability. Employees responsible for transporting hazardous materials in the field are empowered to make necessary decisions on the spot. Through preventive maintenance of logistics equipment, Dow works to ensure safety and reliable deliveries. For example, Dow uses detector cars equipped with ultrasonic devices plus twice weekly visual inspections to monitor rail carriers' tracks.

Dow provides extensive training to its employees as well as customer and supplier employees to keep them up to date on hazardous material transport regulations and safety procedures. In 1996, William Stavropoulos, Dow's president and CEO, announced a $1 billion investment in training, facilities, and research to meet new corporate environmental, safety, and health goals by 2005. One goal targets a global reduction of 90 percent in injury and illness rates, processing safety incidents, and leaks, breaks, and spills. Going beyond mere compliance with local and federal safety and health regulations, the company's proactive environmental strategy seeks to design logistics systems that have no adverse impacts on the natural environment.

Dow conducts phone surveys with customers, asking them to evaluate its product and service performance and compare this performance to that of Dow's best competitors. The program records customer responses to questions such as "How do you rate Dow on a scale of one to five for on-time delivery?" for later playback so employees literally hear the voice of the customer. According to Dick Sosville, vice president of sales and marketing for Dow North America, the customer satisfaction surveys move Dow toward the goal of becoming a more market-driven company. "Nearly 85 percent of our people never have direct contact with a customer, but all have a hand in serving the customer," says Sosville. "We use the tapes to think about the customer first."

Dow and its channel partners apply supply chain management techniques to improve logistics. For example, one cross-functional team assembled members from Dow, a rail carrier, and a customer to tackle the customer's problem with excess inventory. At any one time, the customer's plant stored 15 rail tank cars of a chemical produced at Dow's processing plant in Freeport, Texas, but it needed only 2 tank cars of the chemical to satisfy its daily production needs.

The team mapped the current logistics process and uncovered three big problems. First, shipping produced inconsistent transit times from Dow's plant to the customer's plant. The average transit time was eight days, but that varied by plus or minus four days. Second, the inconsistent transit time forced the customer to hold excess inventory as protection against running out of stock due to a delayed shipment. Third, the complex transportation routing system required close coordination between four carriers at three interchange points. The team pinpointed one particular interchange that caused the delay and inconsistency in transit time.

After studying the current process and discussing optional routes and interchange points, the team members mapped out a new logistics process and set a goal of keeping two tank cars at any one time at the customer's plant, giving the customer just-in-time deliveries to support its daily production needs. Implementation of the new logistics system has resulted in reductions in inventory, tank car usage, and rail interchanges, producing cost savings of more than $200,000 a year.

Questions

1. What role does logistics play in Dow Chemical's marketing strategy?
2. What value-added services does Dow's logistics system provide to customers?
3. What quality improvement initiatives help Dow to enhance the service it provides to customers?

4. Dow has demonstrated a strong commitment to an effective and efficient logistics function. To ensure success in this goal, it offers various career opportunities within logistics. Go to Dow's Web site at:

www.dow.com

Evaluate the logistics positions listed there, and identify ones that appeal to you. (*Note:* Exercises similar to this one appear in Appendix 2, "Careers in Marketing.")

Sources: Some of the research material for this case was downloaded April 18, 1997 from **http://www.dow.com**; William Miller, "Making Pollution Prevention Pay," *Industry Week,* May 20, 1996, p. 136-L; William Keenan Jr., "Plugging into Your Customer Needs," *Sales & Marketing Management,* January 1996, pp. 62-66.

CASE 20
ARCHWAY COOKIE CO.

Ah, the cookie aisle. Who can pass it without slipping a package or two into the grocery cart? People involved in the cookie industry view this aisle less benignly. The trade, from producers to wholesalers to retailers, refers to the cookie aisle as a combat zone. Cookie marketing competition is intense, with all participants fighting for more market share. That's because the cookie industry is mature, and the rate of growth averages a very slow 1 percent to 2 percent per year. In this industry, firms gain additional sales only by taking market share away from competitors.

The cookie industry displays an oligopolistic market structure. Nabisco is the market leader with about a 33 percent market share, followed by Keebler with 13 percent. Combined sales of dozens of private-label store brands account for another 13 percent of the market. The remaining 40 percent is divided among a number of brands, including Pepperidge Farm, Sunshine, and Archway.

The Archway Cookie Co. controls about 4 percent of the U.S. cookie market. Headquartered in Battle Creek, Michigan, Archway bakes and distributes about $400 million worth of cookies each year. Harold and Bruce Swanson founded Archway in 1936 as a small bake shop specializing in donuts, cakes, and cookies. When they decided to expand operations and begin selling their cookies in grocery stores, both the Swansons and their retailer partners were amazed at the positive customer response.

"What makes Archway particularly strong from a competitive standpoint is that we make a product that holds to the traditional values of Americans," says Senior Vice President Thomas Olin. Archway cookies are large, soft, have no preservative, and generally contain no artificial ingredients. Their unique home-baked taste comes from slow baking and cooling processes. Over 100 different varieties of Archway Home Style cookies are currently marketed in several different cookie categories. For example, Archway offers 15 varieties in the oatmeal category, such as apple-filled and date-filled flavors. Customers can see what they're buying because Archway presents its cookies in see-through packages.

A strict policy ensures the freshness of Archway cookies. Distributors who deliver Archway cookies to grocery stores also rotate the packages on the retailers' shelves. Moreover, they remove packages a month *before* the freshness date stamped on the labels, while competitors pull their products from retail shelves on the date marked on the package. Distributors carry handheld computers to provide retailers with timely billing data and to give Archway marketers accurate, up-to-date sales and inventory information.

Archway's product strategy, packaging, and distribution enable the company to pursue a value-oriented pricing strategy. "Essentially what we're trying to capture is a value relationship with the consumer," says Olin, "and [that value] is based on the freshness of the products, the varieties we offer, the taste, and the quality of raw materials, as well as the shape of the package."

Archway marketers practice value pricing to carve out a distinctive niche in the competitive cookie environment. The company pursues two major pricing objectives. "First, we try to establish ourselves in the middle of the road in the consumer marketplace," says company representative Eugene McKay III. "We don't want to be perceived as being a high-priced product. Our second pricing objective is to make sure that we have a fair rate of return internally, meaning that not only must the company make a reasonable profit, but our distributors and the retailers also have to make their fair share." Attractive profit margins within the distribution system provide important incentives for channel members to promote Archway cookies to their customers.

Archway sells its products to wholesale distributors, which resell them to grocery stores. Consider, for example, a package of cookies carrying a suggested retail price of $2.00. The Archway distributor typically purchases the cookies for $1.33 and resells them to the retail grocer for $1.60. Each marketing intermediary covers operating expenses and generates profits based on the margin between the purchase price and the price it receives upon selling the product.

Archway marketers consider a number of factors in setting suggested retail prices as well as the prices they charge their wholesale customers. Pricing variables include production and marketing costs, the prices of competing products, and typical markups in the industry. In addition, price lining differentiates product lines. For example, the Super Pak cookie line is a value-priced line. Each package contains 18 cookies and carries a higher price than the smaller packages, but it offers a better per-unit value to customers.

The fastest-growing segment of the cookie market is the fat-free cookie. With a 175 percent annual growth rate, fat-free cookies are a profitable venture to both manufacturers and retailers. Archway generally prices its fat-free products higher than conventional alternatives due to the high consumer demand. As McKay points out, "Consumers may be willing to spend more for certain types of products if there's a higher perceived value, or a need for that product. . . . If we establish it as a fat-free product, the consumer is willing to pay much more for it."

Archway runs price-off promotions periodically to increase sales volume and attract new customers. Its Cookies for Kids program combines a price-off promotion with cause marketing. For the promotion, Archway asks retailers to set up a special in-store display and reduce the prices of the cookies. Each package sold results in a donation to the Children's Miracle Network hospital in the local community. The promotion has proven highly successful, inducing shoppers to boost their cookie purchases at reduced prices for a worthy cause; at the same time, the promotion increases Archway's volume three to four times the sales that it would have generated without the promotion.

Questions

1. Which pricing strategy described in Chapter 14 best describes Archway's methods? How would the firm's pricing decision differ if it had selected the opposite strategy?

2. Describe Archway's value pricing policy for its fat-free line of cookies.

3. Visit the Archway Web site at:

   www.archwaycookies.com

   Does the online information available to customers support the firm's value-pricing strategy? Give examples to support your answer. Compare Archway's home page to those of such competitors as Nabisco, Keebler, and Pepperidge Farm. How do the sites reveal the companies' pricing strategies?

Sources: Interviews with Thomas Olin and Eugene McKay III, senior vice presidents, Archway Cookie Co., May 1997.

GLOSSARY

Advertising is *nonpersonal* communication that is paid for by an identified sponsor, and involves either *mass communication* via newspapers, magazines, radio, television, and other media (e.g., billboards, bus stop signage) or *direct-to-consumer communication* via direct mail.

Agent is a marketing intermediary who does not take title to the products but develops marketing strategy and establishes contacts abroad.

Anchor stores are the dominant large-scale stores that are expected to draw customers to a shopping center.

Antidumping laws are laws designed to help domestic industries that are injured by unfair competition from abroad due to imports being sold at less than fair value.

Attitudes are learned predispositions to respond to an object or class of objects in a consistently favorable or unfavorable way.

Balanced tenancy is a feature of a shopping center or mall where the stores are selected to complement each other in merchandise offerings.

Bill-back allowance is not simply deducted directly from the invoice at the time of ordering, but rather must be earned by the retailer by performing designated advertising or display services.

Biogenics is the study of the biological characteristics that people possess at birth, such as gender, race, and age.

Brand equity is the marketplace value of a brand based on reputation and goodwill.

Break-even point literally means "to have zero profit." It is that point at which total cost and total revenue are equal.

Built-in obsolescence is the design of a product with features that the company knows will soon be superceded, thus making the model obsolete.

Business market consists of all organizations that buy goods and services for use in the production of other products and services or for resale.

Cartel is an organization of firms in an industry where the central organization makes certain management decisions and functions (often regarding pricing, outputs, sales, advertising, and distribution) that would otherwise be performed within the individual firms.

Cause-related marketing (CRM) is a form of corporate philanthropy that links a company's contributions (usually monetary) to a pre-designated worthy cause with the purchasing behavior of consumers.

Census blocks are geographical areas made up of several city blocks or part of a rural county identified as such by the Census Bureau.

Central business district (CBD) is usually an unplanned shopping area that evolved around the geographic point in the city at which all public transportation systems converge.

Change agent is a person or institution that facilitates change in a firm or in a host country.

Channel intensity refers to the number of intermediaries at each level of the marketing channel.

Channel length is the number of levels in a marketing channel.

Channel structure consists of all of the businesses and institutions (including producers or manufacturers and final customers) who are involved in performing the functions of buying, selling, and transferring title.

Click through is a process when a consumer clicks on a banner advertisement, and then "clicks through" to subscribe and/or purchase from the banner host.

Cluster analysis is the geographic grouping and labeling of individuals based on their buying behavior, demographics, and lifestyles.

Code law is law based on a comprehensive set of written statutes.

Cold-calling means contacting prospective customers without a prior appointment.

Commercial enterprises are the sector of the business market represented by manufacturers, construction companies, service firms, transportation companies, professional groups, and resellers that purchase goods and services.

Common law is law based on tradition and depending less on written statutes and codes than on precedent and custom.

Competitively advantaged product is a product that solves a set of customer problems better than any competitors' product. This product is made possible due to this firm's unique technical, manufacturing, managerial, or marketing capabilities, which are not easily copied by others.

Complementary marketing is a contractual arrangement where participating parties carry out different but complementary activities.

Concentration strategy is the market development strategy that involves focusing on a smaller number of markets.

Concept is a written description or visual depiction of a new product idea. A concept includes the product's primary features and benefits.

Conquest marketing is the process of recruiting new customers as opposed to keeping existing customers.

Consumer behavior is the mental and physical activity undertaken by household and business consumers that result in decisions and actions to pay for, purchase, and use products.

Consumption satiation means that more consumption over time of one product leads to less interest in the consumption of another unit of the same product.

Context is the setting in which the information is received; this includes social, cultural, and organizational contexts

Contract manufacturing is using another firm for the manufacture of goods so that the marketer may concentrate on the research and development as well as marketing aspects of the operation.

Control sample is that part of a sample group that is left unchanged and receives no special treatment, and serves as a basis of comparison to allow analysis of the results of an experiment.

Convenience stores stock frequently purchased products such as gasoline, bread, tobacco, and milk that tend to be consumed within 30 minutes of purchase, as well as offering services such as ATMs and car washes.

Core Benefit Proposition (CBP) is the primary benefit or purpose for which a customer buys a product. The CBP may reside in the physical good or service performance, or it may come from augmented dimensions of the product.

Corporate sponsorships involve investments in *events* or *causes* for the purpose of achieving various corporate objectives, such as increasing sales volume, enhancing a company's reputation or a brand's image, and increasing brand awareness.

Cost per thousand (CPM) is calculated by dividing the cost of an ad placed in a particular ad vehicle (e.g., certain magazine) by the number of people (expressed in thousands) who are exposed to that vehicle.

Criteria for Successful Segmentation includes target markets that are heterogeneous, measurable, substantial, actionable, and accessible.

Customer-oriented means the salesperson seeks to elicit customer needs/problems and then take the necessary steps to meet those needs or solve the problem in a manner that is in the best interest of the customer.

Database marketing involves collecting and electronically storing (in a database) information about present, past, and prospective customers.

Degree of individualism is the extent to which individual interests prevail over group interests.

Demand schedules provide a systematic look at the relationship between price and quantity sold.

Demand-side market failure is the cumulative effect of the marketing practices of many thousands of advertising campaigns that has a residual negative impact on the values of buyers and the demand for various products (e.g., voting).

Demographics are measures such as age, gender, race, occupation, and income that are often used as a basis for selecting focus group members and market segments.

Department stores are large-scale operations offering a broad product mix consisting of many different product lines with above-average depth, or variety, in each of their product lines.

Differentiation is the process of creating and sustaining a strong, consistent, and unique image about one product in comparison to others.

Distributor is a marketing intermediary who purchases products from the domestic firm and assumes the trading risk.

Diversification strategy is the market development strategy that involves expansion to a relatively large number of markets.

Diverting occurs when a manufacturer restricts an off-invoice allowance to a limited geographical area, resulting in some wholesalers and retailers buying abnormally large quantities at the deal price and then transshipping the excess quantities to other geographical areas.

Economies of scale and economies of scope are obtained by spreading the costs of distribution over a large quantity of products (scale) or over a wide variety of products (scope).

Elasticity of demand is the relationship between changes in price and quantity sold.

Electronic Data Interchange (EDI) is a computer-to-computer communications protocol that allows basic information on purchases and invoices to be exchanged.

Electronic Data Interchange (EDI) is a set of protocols for computer-to-computer communication between businesses.

Electronic data interchange (EDI) is the computer-to-computer exchange of invoices, orders, and other business documents.

Ethical vigilance means paying constant attention to whether one's actions are "right" or "wrong," and if ethically "wrong" asking why you are behaving in that manner.

European Article Numbering (EAN) The European version of the Universal Product Code that is located on a product's package that provides information read by optical scanners.

Event-related marketing (ERM) is a form of brand promotion that ties a brand to a meaningful cultural, social, athletic, or other type of high-interest public activity.

Everyday low pricing (EDLP) is a form of pricing whereby a manufacturer charges the same price for a particular brand day in and day out.

Everyday Low Pricing (EDLP) refers to the pricing strategy in which a firm charges the same low price every day.

Exchange is an activity in which two or more parties give something of value to each other to satisfy perceived needs.

Expectancy disconfirmation approach is an approach that measures customer satisfaction by comparing expectations to perceptions.

Export Management Companies (EMCs) are firms that specialize in performing international services as commissioned representatives or as distributors.

Expropriation is a government takeover of a company's operations frequently at a level lower than the value of the assets.

Extended problem solving occurs when the search is extensive and deliberation prolonged.

External stimuli are informational cues from the marketplace that lead the consumer to identify a problem.

Extranets connect computers outside the firm with the intranet at the firm.

Features are the way that benefits are delivered to customers. Features provide the solution to customer problems.

Field selling involves calling on prospective customers in either their business or home locations.

Foreign direct investment is an international entry strategy that is achieved through the acquisition of foreign firms.

Form utility is achieved by the conversion of raw and component materials into finished products that are desired by the marketplace.

Forward buying or bridge buying is when retailers purchase enough product during a manufacturer's off-invoice allowance period to carry the retailers over until the manufacturer's next regularly scheduled deal.

Franchise holding/loading includes manufacturers' efforts to hold on to their franchise of current users by rewarding them for continuing to purchase the promoted brand, or to load them so they have no need to switch to another brand.

Franchising is a form of licensing that grants a wholesaler or a retailer exclusive rights to sell a product or a service in a specified area.

Free on board (FOB) pricing leaves the cost and responsibility of transportation to the customer.

Frontline employees are those individuals within the organization who experience direct interaction with customers.

Genetics is a branch of science that deals with the heredity and chemical/biological characteristics of organisms.

Geodemographic information allows identification of customer segments based on geographical location and demographic information.

Globalization approach is the approach to international marketing in which differences are incorporated into a regional or global strategy that will allow for differences in implementation.

Governmental units comprise the sector of the business market represented by federal, state, and local governmental units that purchase goods and services.

Gray marketing is the marketing of authentic, legally trademarked goods through unauthorized channels.

Gross rating points (GRPs) are the accumulation of rating points including all vehicles in a media purchase over the span of a particular campaign.

Hands-on consumer research is conducted by direct observation by managers of the way current customers use specific products and brands. The opposite is arm's-length research which is undertaken by external suppliers.

Hard sell involves trying every means to get the prospective customer to buy, regardless of whether it is in the prospect's best interest.

HTML (HyperText Markup Language) is the coding language used for creating hypertext documents and formatting pages for use on the Web.

HTTP (HyperText Transport Protocol) is the protocol for moving hypertext across the Internet. It allows for the transfer of images, sound, video, and other files between computers.

Hypertext is any text that contains links to other documents.

Image reinforcement involves the careful selection of the right premium object, or appropriate sweepstakes prize, to reinforce a brand's desired image.

Incentives are bonuses or rewards (sweepstakes, coupons, premiums, display allowances, etc.) for purchasing one brand rather than another.

Inefficient targeting results when advertising and distribution reaches too broad an audience, most of whom are not interested in the product.

Institutional context refers to the groups and organizations a person belongs to. The institutional context includes the workplace, religious and educational institutions, family and friends, and peer groups.

Institutional customers comprise the sector of the business market represented by health-care organizations, colleges and universities, libraries, foundations, art galleries, and clinics that purchase goods and services.

Instrumental values are the means or behavioral standards by which we pursue our goals.

Integrated marketing communications (IMC) is a system of management and integration of marketing communication elements—advertising, publicity, sales promotion, sponsorship marketing, and point-of-purchase communications—with the result that all elements adhere to the same message.

Intellectual property rights is the protection provided by patents, copyrights, and trademarks.

Internal stimuli are perceived states of discomfort—physical or psychological.

International intermediaries are marketing institutions that facilitate the movement of goods and services between the originator and customer.

International marketing is the process of planning and conducting transactions across national borders to create exchanges that satisfy the objectives of individuals and organizations.

Internet is a worldwide network of interconnected computer networks that carry data and make information exchange possible.

Interorganizational content refers to channel management that extends beyond a firm's own organization into other independent businesses.

Intranets connect the computers within a business together.

Invisible organization and systems are the service firm's infrastructure such as rules, regulations, and processes that impact the customer's service experience, but yet are unseen by the customer.

Involvement is the degree of personal relevance of a product to a consumer.

Job anxiety is tension caused by the pressures of the job.

Joint ventures result from the participation of two or more companies in an enterprise in which each party contributes assets, owns the new entity to some degree, and shares risk.

Just-in-time systems fully integrate the production or sales process and timelines, allowing a firm to reduce its dependence on inventory.

Key buying influentials are those individuals in the buying organization who have the power to influence the buying decision.

Labor specialization is the process of increasing and improving production process skills in a specific industry through specialization.

Learning is a change in the content of long-term memory. As humans, we learn because what we learn helps us respond better to our environment.

Learning curves track the decreasing cost of production and distribution of products or services over time as a result of learning by doing, innovation, and imitation.

Level of equality is the extent to which less powerful members accept that power is distributed unequally.

Licensing agreement is an arrangement in which one firm permits another to use its intellectual property in exchange for compensation, typically a royalty.

Limited problem solving occurs when the consumer invests some limited time and energy in search and evaluating alternative solutions.

Managerial commitment is the desire and drive on the part of management to act on an idea and support it in the long run.

Marginal costs are the change in a firm's total costs per-unit change in its output level.

Marginal revenues are the change in a firm's total revenue per-unit change in its sales level.

Marginal utility is the want-satisfying power of the next unit of the same product that is consumed.

Market potential is the level of sales that might be available to all marketers in an industry in a given market.

Market (price) skimming is a strategy of pricing the new product at a relatively high level and then gradually reducing it over time.

Market segment is a group of consumers that are alike based on some characteristic(s).

Marketing channels are the networks of organizations that move a product from the producer to its intended market.

Material achievement is the extent to which the dominant values in society are success, money, and things.

Media strategy consists of four sets of interrelated activities: (1) selecting the target audience, (2) specifying media objectives, (3) selecting media categories and vehicles, and (4) buying media.

Merchant wholesalers are independent firms that purchase a product and take title to that product from the manufacturer and resell it to other manufacturers, wholesalers, or retailers, but not to the final consumer.

Micromarkets are very small market segments, such as zip code areas or even neighborhoods.

Modified rebuy is a purchase where the buyers have experience in satisfying the need, but feel the situation warrants reevaluation of a limited set of alternatives before making a decision.

Motivation is the state of drive or arousal that impels behavior toward a goal-object.

Motivational research is a research method directed at discovering the conscious or subconscious reasons that motivate a person's behavior.

Multi-domestic approach is the approach to international marketing in which local conditions are adapted to in each and every target market.

Multinational corporations are companies that have production operations in at least one country in addition to their domestic base.

Needs are unsatisfactory conditions of the consumer that lead him or her to an action that will make the condition better.

New-task buying situation is a purchase situation that results in an extensive search for information and a lengthy decision process.

Niche marketing is the process of targeting a relatively small market segment with a specific, specialized marketing mix.

Off-invoice allowance are deals offered periodically to the trade that allow wholesalers and retailers to simply deduct a fixed amount, say 15 percent, from the full price at the time the order is placed.

Open-ended questions allow respondents to determine the direction of the answer without being led by the question. They also prevent "yes" or "no" answers.

Operating expenses are the expenses the retailer incurs in running the business other than the cost of the merchandise, e.g., rent, wages, utilities, depreciation, insurance, etc.

Order getter is a salesperson who seeks to actively provide information to prospects, persuade prospective customers, and close sales.

Order taker is a salesperson who only processes the purchase that the customer has already selected.

Outsourcing is using another firm for the manufacture of needed components or products or delivery of a service.

Penetration strategy requires that the firm enter the market at a relatively low price in an attempt to obtain market share and expand demand for its product.

Perception is the process by which an individual selects, organizes, and interprets the information received from the environment.

Perceptual mapping is a commonly used multidimensional scaling method of graphically depicting a product's performance on selected attributes or the "position" of a product against its competitors on selected product traits.

Personal selling is direct oral communication designed to explain how an individual's or firm's goods, services, or ideas fit the needs of one or more prospective customers.

Personal selling is *person-to-person* communication in which a seller informs and educates prospective customers and attempts to influence their purchase choices.

Personal worth refers to the financial resources available to a consumer. These comprise a person's income, assets, inheritance, and borrowing power.

Planned gross margin is the difference between the price the manufacturer sells the product to wholesalers and the price at which wholesalers can resell.

Point-of-purchase communications include all signage— displays, posters, signs, shelf cards, and a variety of other visual materials—that are designed to influence buying decisions at the point of sale.

Positioning is the image that customers have about a product, especially in relation to the product's competitors.

Positioning refers to how a product is perceived by customers in the marketplace relative to the competition.

Predatory pricing is a practice where one firm attempts to drive out rivals (usually smaller ones) by pricing at such a low level that the rival cannot make money.

Price is some unit of value given up by one party in return for something from another party.

Price discrimination occurs when a seller offers a lower price to some buyers than to other buyers.

Price promotions are short-term price reductions designed to create an incentive for consumers to buy now rather than later and/or stock up on the specialled product.

Price-fixing is a conspiracy to fix competitive prices.

Proactive marketing public relations (Proactive MPR) is offensively rather than defensively oriented, and opportunity-seeking rather than problem-solving. The major role of proactive MPR is in the area of product introductions or product revisions.

Problem recognition is a consumer's realization that he or she needs to buy something to get back to the normal state of comfort.

Process-related information is information that provides an understanding of how the product fits into the workflow of the company.

Product development process consists of a clearly defined set of tasks and steps that describes the normal means by which product development proceeds. The process outlines the order and sequence of the tasks and indicates who is responsible for each.

Product life cycle is the cycle of stages that a product goes through from birth to death: introduction, growth, maturity, and decline.

Products are the set of features, functions, and benefits that customers purchase. Products may consist primarily of tangible (physical) attributes or intangibles, such as those associated with services or some combination of tangible and intangible.

Professional salespeople help prospective customers to define their needs and then suggest the best means of meeting those needs, even if that requires recommending that the prospects use a competitive product.

Profit repatriation limitations are restrictions set up by host governments in terms of a company's ability to pay dividends from their operations back to their home base.

Prototype is a product concept in physical form. A prototype may be a full working model that has been produced by hand or a nonworking physical representation of the final product. It is used to gather customer reaction to the physical form (aesthetics and ergonomics) or to initial operating capability. It is also used in internal performance tests to assure that performance goals have been met.

Psychogenics refers to the study of individual states and traits induced by a person's brain functioning.

Psychographics are characteristics of individuals that describe them in terms of their psychological and behavioral makeup.

Publicity, like advertising, is *nonpersonal* communication to a mass audience, but unlike advertising, publicity is not directly paid for by the company that enjoys the publicity.

Pull strategy involves a relatively heavy emphasis on consumer-oriented advertising to encourage consumer demand for a new brand and thereby obtain retail distribution. The brand is "pulled" through the channel system in the sense that there is a *backward* tug from the consumer to the retailer.

Pull-oriented means the consumer chooses what to look for, when to look for it, and how much detail to gather.

Purchase-decision involvement is the degree of concern and caring that consumers bring to bear on the purchase decision.

Push strategy involves aggressive trade allowances and personal selling efforts to obtain distribution for a new brand through wholesalers and retailers. The brand is "pushed" through the channel system in the sense that there is a *forward* thrust from the manufacturer to the trade.

Push-oriented means that the marketer decides what the consumer will see and where.

Qualified sales leads are potential customers that have a need for the salesperson's product, and are able to buy; that is, they have the financial means to purchase the product and the authority to make the buying decision.

Reactive MPR is a form of defensively oriented public relations that deals with developments (such as product defects or flaws) having negative consequences for the organization. Reactive MPR attempts to repair a company's reputation, prevent market erosion, and regain lost sales.

Referrals are usually obtained by the salesperson asking current customers if they know of someone else, or another company, who might have a need for the salesperson's product.

Relationship selling requires the development of a trusting partnership in which the salesperson seeks to provide long-term customer satisfaction.

Reliability means the consistency of data. It is often tested by reexamining customer opinions using the same survey on a different occasion, or by another method of measurement.

Retail mix is a store's combination of merchandise, prices, advertising, location, customer services, selling, floor layout, and building design.

ROI stands for Return on Investment.

Role ambiguity is anxiety caused by inadequate information about job responsibilities and performance-related goals.

Role conflict is the anxiety caused by conflicting job demands.

Routine problem solving occurs when no new information is considered.

Royalty is the compensation paid by one firm to another under licensing and franchising agreements.

Sales potential is the share of the market potential that a particular marketer may hope to gain over the long term.

Sales promotion consists of all marketing activities that attempt to stimulate quick buyer action, or, in other words, attempt to promote immediate sales of a product (thereby yielding the name *sales promotion*).

Scrambled merchandising is the handling of merchandise lines based solely on the profitability criterion and without regard to the consistency of a particular product line with other products in the retailer's product mix.

Self-concept refers to a person's self-image.

Sherman Antitrust Act prohibits any contract, combination, or conspiracy that restrains trade. It was passed by Congress in 1890 in an effort to prevent companies from controlling (monopolizing) an industry.

Single-source systems are a measurement of the effectiveness of advertising (whether it leads to increased sales activity). They are unique in that all the relevant data is collected by a single source, processed, and then made available in a readily usable format to retailers and manufacturers.

Situational ethics is that societal condition where "right" and "wrong" are determined by the specific situation, rather than by universal moral principles.

Slotting allowance (*stocking allowance* or *street money*) is the fee a manufacturer is charged by a supermarket chain or other retailer to get that retailer to handle the manufacturer's new product.

Social responsiblity is the collection of marketing philosophies, policies, procedures, and actions intended primarily to enhance society's welfare.

Sogoshosha are the trading companies of Japan including firms such as Sumitomo, Mitsubishi, and Mitsui.

Specialty stores are relatively small-scale stores offering a great deal of depth in a narrow range of product lines.

Sponsorship marketing is the practice of promoting the interests of a company and its brands by associating the company with a specific *event* (e.g., a golf tournament) or a charitable *cause* (e.g., the Leukemia Society).

Stage-Gate process is a common new product development process that divides the repeatable portion of product development into a time-sequenced series of stages, each of which is separated by a management decision gate. In each stage, a team completes a set of tasks that span the functions involved in product development. At the end of each stage, management reviews the results obtained and, based on the team's ability to meet the objectives in that stage, provides the resources to continue to the next stage ("go"), requests additional work ("recycle"), or stops the project ("kill").

Standardized approach is the approach to international marketing in which products are marketed with little or no modification.

Store image is the overall feeling or mood projected by a store through its aesthetic appeal to human senses.

Straight rebuy is routine reordering from the same supplier of a product that has been purchased in the past.

Strategic alliances are informal or formal arrangements between two or more companies with a common business objective.

Suggestion selling occurs when the salesperson points out available complementary items in line with the selected item(s), in order to encourage an additional purchase.

Sugging refers to an illegal survey(s) conducted under the guise of research but with the intent of selling.

Supply-side market failure results when the individual activities of a supplier inadvertently lead to destructive effects on the overall supply.

Sustainable competitive advantage is a competitive edge that cannot be easily or quickly copied by competitors in the short run.

System concept of logistics entails viewing all components of a logistical system together and understanding the relationships among them.

Tacit information consists of things customers know, but which are difficult or nearly impossible to articulate. This intuitive information, while frequently critical to product success in the marketplace, is the most difficult to provide to the NPD team during product development.

Terminal values are the goals we seek in life.

Theory of dual entitlement holds that consumers believe there are terms in a transaction to which both consumers and sellers are "entitled" to over time. Cost-driven price increases are believed to be fair because they allow the seller to maintain her/his profit entitlement. Demand-driven price increases are not believed to be fair, however, since they allow a seller to increase per-unit profit, while the buyer receives nothing in return.

Time, place, and possession utilities are conditions that enable consumers and business users to have products available for use when and where they want them.

Trade allowances, or trade deals, come in a variety of forms and are offered to retailers simply for purchasing the manufacturer's brand or for performing activities in support of the manufacturer's brand.

Trade area is the geographic area where the majority of a store's customers reside.

Trading company is a marketing intermediary that undertakes exporting, importing, countertrading, investing, and manufacturing.

Tragedy of the commons is the name given to the process where individuals, pursuing their own self-interest, overuse a common good to such an extent that the common good is destroyed.

Transaction-Based Information System (TBIS) is a system that captures and analyzes all of the transactions between a firm and its customers.

Trial impact refers to inducing nonusers to try a brand for the first time, or encouraging retrial by consumers who have not purchased the brand for an extended period.

Uncertainty avoidance is the extent to which people feel threatened by ambiguous situations and have created beliefs and institutions to try to avoid these feelings.

Uniform delivered pricing means that the seller charges all customers the same transportation cost regardless of their location.

Universal Product Code (UPC) is a bar code on a product's package that provides information read by optical scanners.

URL (Uniform Resource Locator) is the Internet address for a Web document or other file.

Validity in customer survey results refers to their accuracy in measuring what they are intended to measure.

Value analysis is a method of weighing the comparative value of materials, components, and manufacturing processes from the standpoint of their purpose, relative merit, and cost in order to uncover ways of improving products, lowering costs, or both.

Value proposition is a program of goods, services, ideas, and solutions that a business marketer offers to advance the performance goals of the customer organization.

Values are end-states of life, the goals one lives for.

Voice of the Customer (VOC) is an in-depth, one-on-one interviewing process to understand a set of customer needs in great depth.

Voice of the customer is the expression of the preferences, opinions, and motivations of the customer that need to be listened to by managers.

Wants are desires to obtain more satisfaction than is absolutely necessary to improve an unsatisfactory conditions.

Webmaster is the title given to the individual who is responsible for maintaining and updating a Web site.

Wholesaling involves the activities of those persons or establishments that sell to retailers and/or other organizational buyers for industrial, institutional, and commercial use, but do not sell in significant amounts to final consumers.

World Trade Organization (WTO) is the institution that administers international trade and investment accords. It supplanted GATT in 1995.

World Wide Web (WWW or Web) is a subset of the Internet comprised of a collection of hyperlinked documents (not computers) that use a common protocol.

LITERARY CREDITS

Chapter 1 Opener from *Business Week,* February 15, 1999. Reprinted by permission of McGraw-Hill, Inc.

Figure 1.3 from Lindgren & Shimp, *Marketing: An Interactive Learning System,* 1/e, Copyright © 1996 by Harcourt Brace and Company. Reproduced by permission of the publisher.

Figure 2.1 from Lindgren & Shimp, *Marketing: An Interactive Learning System,* 1/e, Copyright © 1996 by Harcourt Brace and Company. Reproduced by permission of the publisher.

Figure 2.2 from *Fortune* Magazine, February 1, 1999. p. 40. Copyright © 1999 by Time, Inc. Reprinted with permission.

Figure 2.5 courtesy of The Conference Board, New York.

Figure 2.6 reprinted by permission of the American Marketing Association.

Figure 3.2 reprinted by permission of the publisher from *Entry Strategies for International Markets,* p. 56, by Franklin R. Root (Lexington, Mass: Lexington Books, D.C. Heath & Co. Copyright 1994), D.C. Heath & Co.

Figure 3.3-Sources: "The Puff, the Magic, The Dragon," *The Washington Post,* September 1, 1994. B1, B3: "Big Names Draw Fine Line on Logo Imagery," South China Morning Post, July 7, 1994, p. 3.

Figure 3.4 from Joel Bleeke and David Ernst, "Is Your Strategic Alliance Really a Sale?" *Harvard Business Review,* 73 (January-February 1995); and Melanie Wells, "Coca-Cola Proclaims Nestea Times for CAA," *Advertising Age,* January 30, 1995.

Figure 3.6 adapted from V. Yorio, *Adapting Products for Export* (New York: The Conference Board, 1983): 7.

Figure 4.1 adapted from *The Marketing Plan* by Howard Sutton (New York, The Conference Board), 1990.

Figure 4.3 from Peter R. Dickson, *Marketing Management,* ©1997 by Harcourt Brace and Company. Reproduced by permission of the publisher.

Table 4.2 from William Dillon, Thomas J. Madden, and Neil H. Firtle, *Marketing Research in a Marketing Environment* (Homewood, IL: Irwin, 1990), p. 201.

Figure 4.4 adapted from David R. Lehmann and Russel S. Winter, *Analysis for Marketing Planning* (Homewood, IL: Irwin, 1991), p. 22.

Table 4.6 from Howard Sutton, *Competitive Intelligence,* (New York: The Conference Board, 1988).

Figure 5.1 from Sheth & Mittal, *Customer Behavior,* 1/e, Copyright © 1999 by Harcourt Brace and Company. Reproduced by permission of the publisher.

Figure 5.5 from Sheth & Mittal, *Customer Behavior,* 1/e, Copyright © 1999 by Harcourt Brace and Company. Reproduced by permission of the publisher.

Table 6.1 adapted by permission of the publisher from Gene R. Laczniak, "An Empirical Study of Hospital Buying," *Industrial Marketing Management* 8 (January 1979), p. 61. Copyright © 1979 by Elsevier Science Publishing Co., Inc.

Figure 6.6 adapted from Patrick J. Robinson, Charles W. Faris, and Yoram Wind, *Industrial Buying and Creative Marketing* (Boston: Allyn and Bacon, Inc. 1967), p. 14.

Figure 7.3 Exhibit: Segmenting, Profiting and Responding to Bank Segments from "First Commerce Segments Customers by Behavior, enhancing Profitability," by Debora Connelly & Barbara Read, *Journal of Retail Banking Services,* Spring, 1997, pp. 23-28. Reprinted by permission.

Figure 7.6 from demographics.cacilcom/dfdoc/zipsearch.cfm onn 5/15/98.

Figure 7.7 from "Elvis Lives Again," by Brad Edmondson & Linda Jacobson from *American Demographics,* January, 1998, pp. 18-19. Copyright © 1998 by American Demographics, Inc.

Figure 7.8 from "Sticky Times for Customer Services, " by Michael Schrage in *Computerworld,* February 23, 1998, p. 35.

Figure 7.10 Sources: Susie Stephenson, "Tackling Teens," *Restaurants & Institutions,* February 15, 1997, pp. 57-60, and "More Than Just Lunch Money," *Marketing News,* May 11, 1998.

Figure 7.17 from "Today's Global Market: Who is the Elusive Global Consumer?" *Chain Store Executive with Shopping Center Age,* December 15, 1993, pp. 28-30.

Figure 8.1 from Lindgren & Shimp, *Marketing: An Interactive Learning System,* 1/e, Copyright © 1996 by Harcourt Brace and Company. Reproduced by permission of the publisher.

Figure 8.2 from Dickson, *Marketing Management,* 2/e, Copyright © 1996 by Harcourt Brace and Company. Reproduced by permission of the publisher.

Figure 8.6 from "PDMA Research on New Product Development Practices: Updating Trends and Benchmarking Best Practices," by Abbie Griffin, (1997) *Journal of Production Innovation Management,* 14: pp. 6, 429-458.

Figure 8.11 from Robert G. Cooper, *Winning at New Products* (Reading, MA: Addison Wesley, 1993), p. 140, Figure 6.2.

Figure 9.1 adapted from G. Lynn Shosback, "Breaking Free from Product Marketing," *The Journal of Marketing* (April, 1977), p. 77.

Table 9.4 from "The 100 Best Companies to Work For in America," *Fortune,* 137 (1) January 12, 1998, p. 88.

Figure 9.3 cover, *Fortune* Magazine, March 16, 1998, Vol. 1137, No. 5. Copyright © 1998 by Time, Inc. Reprinted with permission.

Table 9.5 adapted from Mary Jo Bitner, "Servicescapes: The Impact of Physical Surroundings on Customers and Employees," *Journal of Maarketing* 56 (2) April 1992, p. 60.

Figure 9.09 Cartoon: "The Far Side: The Theatre of the Gods" © 1988 Universal Press Syndicate. Reprinted by permission.

Table 9.6 from "Now Are You Satisfied?" *Fortune* 137 (3) February 16, 1998, pp. 162-164.

Figure 9.13 from "Is Customer Retention Worth the Time, Effort, and Expense," *Sales and Marketing Management,* 15 (Dec. 1991), pp. 21-22. Copyright © Bill Communications, Inc. Reprinted with permission.

Table 10.1 from Martha C. Cooper and Lisa M. Ellram, "Characteristics of Supply Chain Management and Implications for Purchasing and Logistics Strategy," *International Journal of Logistics Management* (4) No. 2 (1993), p. 16.

Table 10.2 excerpted from John T. Mentzer, Roger Gomes, and Robert E. Knapfel, Jr., "Physical Districution Service: A Fundamental Marketing Concept?" *Journal of the Academy of Marketing Science,* Winter 1988, p. 55.

Figure 11.2 Source: George Chister, "Solution Selling: the Key to Supermarket Survival," *International Trends in Retailing,* June, 1998, p. 36. Used by permission of the publisher, Arthur Anderson.

Figure 11.4 Source: U.S. Bureau of the Census Abstract of the United States, 1996, 116th editions, Washington, DC. 1996 Table No. 1259, Retail Trade Sales of Multiunit Organizations by Kind of Business, 1980-1995, p. 766.

Figure 11.15 Source: U.S. Bureau of the Census and Distribution Research Program, The University of Oklahoma.

Figure 12.1 adapted from Kevin Lane Keller, "Conceptualizing, Measuring, and Managing Customer-Based Brand Equity," *Journal of Marketing,* 57 (January, 1993), p. 7.

Figure 12.6 adapted from *Marketer's Guide to Media,* Fall/Winter 1994-1995, 17, 2, (New York, ADWEEK, 1994).

Figure 12.9 from Terence A. Shimp, *Advertising, Promotion, and Supplemental Aspects of Integrated Marketing Communications,* 4/e, Copyright © 1997 by Harcourt Brace and Company. Reproduced by permission of the publisher.

Figure 13.15 Source: Abbott, Langer & Associates.

Table 14.2 from Paul A. Samuelson, *Economics: An Introductory Analysis,* 4/e (New York: McGraw-Hill, 1958), pp. 370-374.

Table 14.3 from Paul A. Samuelson, *Economics: An Introductory Analysis,* 4/e (New York: McGraw-Hill, 1958), pp. 370-374.

Table 14.4 from Paul A. Samuelson, *Economics: An Introductory Analysis,* 4/e (New York: McGraw-Hill, 1958), pp. 370-374.

Table 14.8 adapted from Mark S. Albion & Edward J. Hoff, *Business Decision Making with 1-2-3* (Englewood Cliffs, NJ: Prentice-Hall, 1984).

Figure 15.2 © 1999 Parton Media. All rights reserved.

Figure 15.3 courtesy of the Georgia Institute of Technology, Atlanta, GA.

Figure AP.1 from Lindgren & Shimp, *Marketing: An Interactive Learning System,* 1/e, Copyright © 1996 by Harcourt Brace and Company. Reproduced by permission of the publisher.

Figure AP.2 from Lindgren & Shimp, *Marketing: An Interactive Learning System,* 1/e, Copyright © 1996 by Harcourt Brace and Company. Reproduced by permission of the publisher.

Figure AP.3 based on Derek F. Abell and John S. Hammond, *Strategic Market Planning: Problems and Analytical Approaches* (Englewood Cliffs, NJ): Prentice Hall, 1979), p. 213.

Figure AP.4 from Lindgren & Shimp, Marketing: *An Interactive Learning System,* 1/e, Copyright © 1996 by Harcourt Brace and Company. Reproduced by permission of the publisher.

PHOTO CREDITS

WEB PAGE & LOGO CREDITS

Chapter 1 Opener Lee Pipes © Lee Jeans Company.
Chapter 6 Opener © 1998 J.M. Smucker Company.
Figure 6.2 © 1996-1998 The Boeing Company, All rights reserved.
Figure 8.1 McDonald's logo used with permission of McDonald's Corporation.
Figure 8.1 Nike logo courtesy of Nike, Inc.
Figure 8.1 Prudential logo courtesy of Prudential Insurance Company of America.
Figure 8.4 © 1999 Toyota Motor Company.
Figure 13.1 © 1999 Marriott Hotels. Used with permission.
Chapter 5 Opener courtesy of IBM Corporation.
Figure 15.5 Courtesy of Coca-Cola, Inc.
Figure 15.6 Courtesy of Wells Fargo & Company.
Figure 15.7 Amazon.com is a registered trademark or trademark of Amazon.com, Inc. in the U.S. and/or other countries. Copyright © 1999 Amazon.com Inc. All rights reserved.
Figure 15.8 © 1999 CNN/SI. A Time Warner Company. All rights reserved.

NAME INDEX

COMPANY INDEX

A

A. C. Nielsen, 110–11, 123, 438
Absolut, *435*
Ace Hardware, *405*
Adidas, 215, 423
Advanced Micro Devices, 513
Albertsons, 381
Allegheny Pepsi, 515
Allstate, *52*
Amazon.com, 24, 35, 120, 281, 349, 386, 552, *553*
America Online (AOL), 133–35, 425
American Airlines, 310, *311*
American Broadcasting Corporation (ABC), 141–42
American Express, 86, 225
American Society for Quality Control, 310
Ameritech Mobile Communications, 602
Amtrak, 431
Andersen Consulting, 611–612
Andersen Worldwide, 611
Anheuser-Busch Co., 333–34
Apple Computer Inc., *4*, 119–20, 248–49, 281, 357, 458–59
Aramis Inc., 596–597
Arby's, 618
Archway Cookie Co.,632–633
Arizona Beverage Company, 614
Arm & Hammer, 282
Athlete's Foot, 381
AT&T, *67*, 225, *270*, 598–599
Audi of America, 446
Aurora Electronics, 39
Avon Products, 380, 384

B

Barnes & Noble, *393*, 513
Beech-Nut, 256
Bell Atlantic Corp., 174
Bell South, 469
Best Buy, *383*
Bic, 337, 352
Black & Decker, 180
BMW, 351
Boeing, *181*, 184
Booz-Allen & Hamilton, Inc., 556
Borders, 151, 513
BP. *See* British Petroleum (BP)
Bristol-Myers Squibb Company, 425
British Petroleum (BP), 422, 617–618
Burger King, 215
Burke Day-After Recall, 438
Butler Brothers, 377

C

Cadbury Schweppes, 85
CalComp, 270, *271*

Calvin Klein, 147, *433*
Camel cigarettes, 216
Campbell Soup, 62, *64*
Canon, 86
CASRO. *See* Council of American Survey Research Organizations (CASRO)
CERN. *See* European Article Physics Laboratory
Chef America, Inc., 348
Cherry Capital Airport, 628–629
Cheseborough-Ponds, 246
Chevron, *53*
Chrysler Corporation, 180, 200, *229*, 265, 269, 357, *511*, 552
Cisco, 546, 548
Clark Equipment Company, 198
CNN, 554
Coca-Cola Co., *12*, 18, *83*, *85*, 86, 147, 228, 255, *311*, 348–49, *356*, 424–25, 549–50, 568, 614
Colgate Palmolive, 90, 230, *311*
Color Pet, 17–18
Conoco, 383
Continental Airlines, *311*
Coors, 343, 351
Corning Inc., *83*, 362–63
Council of American Survey Research Organizations (CASRO), 113
CUTCO, 384
CyberDialogue, 545–46

D

Daewoo, 82
Daimler-Benz, *67*
Dayton Hudson Corporation, *388*, 596–597
DEC Vax, 30
Delfield Company, 605–607
Delia's, 3
Dell Computer Corporation, 159, 187, 335, 350–51, 351, 373–75, 380, 514
Deloitte & Touche, *473*
Denny's restaurants, 419
Detroit Zoo, 617
Digital Marketing Services (DMS), 133–35
Dillard's, 380
Dow Chemical Company, 582, 608, 630–631
Dr. Pepper, 11, 14
Dunkin' Donuts, *78*, 392
DuPont, 184, *303*, *304*
Duracell, 120
Dutch Boy, 448

E

Ecolab Inc., 460–62
Encyclopedia Britannica, 384
Energy Marketplace, 521–22
Ericsson, *83*
Estee, 213
Estée Lauder, 596–597
Ethan Allen Interiors, Inc., 356
eToys, 35

E*Trade, *16, 514*
European Article Physics Laboratory, 542
Exxon Chemical, *271*

F

Fabiano Brothers, Inc., 613–614
Federal Express, 36, 225, 335, 546, 547, 552
Federated Department Stores, Inc., 380, *388*
Fiat, *67*
Filene's Basement, 136–37
Fisher-Price, 108, 255
Food Line, 446
Foot Action, 234
Foot Joy, 213, 215
FootLocker, 234
Ford Motor Company, *43, 67,* 186, 258, 269
Forrester Research, Inc., 425
Fujitsu, 82

G

Gadzooks, 213
Gap, Inc., 334, 381, *388*
Garato, 72
Gardenburger, Inc., 416–18
Gargoyles, 356–57
Gateway Computer, *38*, 38–39, 375
GE. *See* General Electric
General Electric, *67*, 255, 292, 546, 571–72
General Foods, 253, 267
General Mills, 82, 254–55, 499–500
General Motors Corporation, 19, *67, 81, 82,* 178, 292, 431
   Cadillac division, 212, *311*, 609–610
   Saturn Division, 346–47, 350, 351, 425
General Public Utilities, 310
Genuine Auto Parts, 406
Gerber, 620
Gerland's Fruit Fair, Inc., *224*
Gillette, 337, 351
Goodyear Tire and Rubber Company, 353
Government Printing Office, 116
Great Atlantic & Pacific Tea Co., The, *388*
GTE, 602–603
Gucci, 342

H

H. J. Heinz Company, 255, *311*, 448
Hallmark, 337
Hampton Inn, 320–21
Harley-Davidson, 184, *196*
Hershey Foods, *311*
Hershey's Foods, 448
Hewlett-Packard, *83*
Hickory Farms, 381
Hoffmann-LaRoche, *89*
Home Depot, 40, 382, *388*
Home Interiors and Gifts, 384

645

SUBJECT INDEX

N

O

Marketing Publications Online

AdTalk	www.adtalk.com
Advertising Age	www.adage.com
Advertising Age International	www.adage.com/international
Advertising & Marketing Review	www.ad-mkt-review.com
AdweekAsia	www.asianad.com
AdweekOnline	www.adweek.com
American Demographics	www.demographics.com/publications/ad
Catalog Age Weekly	www.catalogmag.com
Direct	www.directmag.com
DMNews.com	www.dmnews.com
Elrick & Lavidge Marketing Today	elavidge.com/mtd
Forecast	www.demographics.com/publications/fc
INSIDE 1to1	www.1to1.com/articles/inside1to1.html
Journal of International Marketing	www.ama.org/pubs/jim
Journal of Marketing	www.ama.org/pubs/jm
Journal of Market Research	www.ama.org/pubs/jmr
Journal of Public Policy & Marketing	www.ama.org/pubs/jppm
Kid Screen	www.kidscreen.com
Marketing Competence	www.argo-navis.com/competence
Marketing Health Services	www.ama.org/pubs/mhs
Marketing Management	www.ama.org/pubs/mm
Marketing News	www.ama.org/pubs/mn
Marketing Online	www.marketingmag.ca
Marketing Research	www.ama.org/pubs/mr
Marketing Tools	www.demographics.com/publications/mt
Musings	www.marketware-tech.com/musings.htm
New Magazine	www.newmagazine.com
Pool	www.poolonline.com
Potentials	www.trainingsupersite.com
Promo	www.promomagazine.com
Quirk's Marketing Research Review	www.quirks.com
Response	www.responsemag.com
Reveries.com	www.reveries.com
Sales & Field Force Automation Online	www.sffaonline.com
Sales & Marketing Management	www.salesandmarketing.com
Sales Doctors	www.salesdoctors.com
Selling Power	www.sellingpower.com
Strategy	www.strategymag.com
Top Seller Ezine	www.prosales.com/ezine
The Weekly Guerilla	www.gmarketing.com/tactic/weekly.html